014540589 Liverpool Univ

KU-523-468

FUNDAMENTALS OF
MULTINATIONAL
FINANCE

Fifth Edition

Global Edition

University of Liverpool

Withdrawn from stock

The Pearson Series in Finance

Berk/DeMarzo
Corporate Finance*

Corporate Finance: The Core*

Berk/DeMarzo/Harford
Fundamentals of Corporate Finance*

Brooks
Financial Management: Core Concepts*

Copeland/Weston/Shastri
Financial Theory and Corporate Policy

Dorfman/Cather
Introduction to Risk Management and Insurance

Eakins/McNally
Corporate Finance Online*

Eiteman/Stonehill/Moffett
Multinational Business Finance

Fabozzi
Bond Markets: Analysis and Strategies

Fabozzi/Modigliani/Jones
Foundations of Financial Markets and Institutions

Finkler
Financial Management for Public, Health, and Not-for-Profit Organizations

Foerster
Financial Management: Concepts and Applications*

Frasca
Personal Finance

Gitman/Zutter
Principles of Managerial Finance*

Principles of Managerial Finance—Brief Edition*

Haugen
The Inefficient Stock Market: What Pays Off and Why

Modern Investment Theory

Holden
Excel Modeling in Corporate Finance

Excel Modeling in Investments

Hughes/MacDonald
International Banking: Text and Cases

Hull
Fundamentals of Futures and Options Markets

Options, Futures, and Other Derivatives

Keown
Personal Finance: Turning Money into Wealth*

Keown/Martin/Petty
Foundations of Finance: The Logic and Practice of Financial Management*

Kim/Nofsinger
Corporate Governance

Madura
Personal Finance*

Marthinsen
Risk Takers: Uses and Abuses of Financial Derivatives

McDonald
Derivatives Markets
Fundamentals of Derivatives Markets

Mishkin/Eakins
Financial Markets and Institutions

Moffett/Stonehill/Eiteman
Fundamentals of Multinational Finance

Nofsinger
Psychology of Investing

Pennacchi
Theory of Asset Pricing

Rejda/McNamara
Principles of Risk Management and Insurance

Smart/Gitman/Joehnk
Fundamentals of Investing*

Solnik/McLeavey
Global Investments

Titman/Keown/Martin
Financial Management: Principles and Applications*

Titman/Martin
Valuation: The Art and Science of Corporate Investment Decisions

Weston/Mitchell/Mulherin
Takeovers, Restructuring, and Corporate Governance

denotes MyFinanceLab titles   Visit **www.myfinancelab.com to learn more.*

FUNDAMENTALS OF

MULTINATIONAL FINANCE

Fifth Edition

Global Edition

MICHAEL H. MOFFETT
Thunderbird School of Global Management

ARTHUR I. STONEHILL
Oregon State University and University of Hawaii at Manoa

DAVID K. EITEMAN
University of California, Los Angeles

PEARSON

Boston   Columbus   Indianapolis   New York   San Francisco   Hoboken
Amsterdam   Cape Town   Dubai   London   Madrid   Milan   Munich   Paris   Montreal   Toronto
Delhi   Mexico City   Sao Paulo   Sydney   Hong Kong   Seoul   Singapore   Taipei   Tokyo

...agement: Donna Battista
... Ashley Santora
...te Fernandes
...McDonagh
...rgent
...Moylan
...tt Dustan
...ims
...kins
...DeShazo
...rin Gardner
...Jeff Holcomb
...edith Gertz
...bal Edition: Vrinda Malik
...tor, Global Edition: Daniel Luiz
...a Production, Global Edition: M. Vikram Kumar
...anufacturing Controller, Production, Global Edition: Trudy Kimber
...or Manufacturing Buyer: Carol Melville
Art Director/Cover Designer: Jonathan Boylan
Executive Media Producer: Melissa Honig
Rights and Permissions Project Manager: Jenell Forschler
Cover Image: ©xiao yu\Shutterstock
Full-Service Project Management, Composition, and Text Illustrations: Laserwords, Inc.
Text Design and Copyediting: Gillian Hall, The Aardvark Group
Proofreader: Holly McLean-Aldis
Indexer: Jack Lewis

Credits and acknowledgments borrowed from other sources and reproduced, with permission, in this textbook appear on the appropriate page within text and as follows: Photo on part and chapter opening pages by dell/Fotolia.

Pearson Education Limited
Edinburgh Gate
Harlow
Essex CM20 2JE
England

and Associated Companies throughout the world

Visit us on the World Wide Web at:
www.pearsonglobaleditions.com

© Pearson Education Limited 2016

The rights of Michael H. Moffett, Arthur I. Stonehill and David K. Eiteman to be identified as the authors of this work have been asserted by them in accordance with the Copyright, Designs and Patents Act 1988.

Authorized adaptation from the United States edition, entitled Fundamentals of Multinational Finance, 5th edition, ISBN 978-0-205-98975-1, by Michael H. Moffett, Arthur I. Stonehill and David K. Eiteman, published by Pearson Education © 2016.

All rights reserved. No part of this publication may be reproduced, stored in a retrieval system, or transmitted in any form or by any means, electronic, mechanical, photocopying, recording or otherwise, without either the prior written permission of the publisher or a license permitting restricted copying in the United Kingdom issued by the Copyright Licensing Agency Ltd, Saffron House, 6–10 Kirby Street, London EC1N 8TS.

All trademarks used herein are the property of their respective owners. The use of any trademark in this text does not vest in the author or publisher any trademark ownership rights in such trademarks, nor does the use of such trademarks imply any affiliation with or endorsement of this book by such owners.

ISBN 10: 1292076534
ISBN 13: 9781292076539

British Library Cataloguing-in-Publication Data
A catalogue record for this book is available from the British Library.

10 9 8 7 6 5 4 3 2 1
15

Typeset in 10/12 Times Ten by Laserwords, Inc.

Printed and bound by RR Donnelley Kendallville in the United States of America.

Preface

Fundamentals of Multinational Finance, Fifth Edition, reflects the multitude of changes sweeping over global business today. This edition has been revised to reflect a global marketplace that has moved five years beyond global financial crisis and into an era in which new country markets and players like that of China, India, and Turkey are altering the global financial landscape. The book has been focused on the challenges faced by the business leaders of tomorrow in multinational business—with three points of emphasis.

- **Organizations.** The term *multinational enterprise* (MNE) applies to organizations of all kinds—the publicly traded, the privately held, the state-run, the state-owned organizations—all forms that permeate global business today. Who owns and operates the organization alters its goals and therefore its management.

- **Markets.** Country markets like that of China and India are no longer the sources of low-cost labor for global manufacturers. They are increasingly the focus for sales and growth of all firms, manufacturing and services, for earnings and growth. Although they may still be categorized as "emerging," they are the economic drivers and primary challenges for global finance and global financial management.

- **Leadership.** Individuals in positions of leadership within these organizations and markets are faced with a changing global landscape in which emerging market finance is no longer on the outer edge of financial management, but moving to its core. These leaders of MNEs face numerous foreign exchange and political risks, which are actually more volatile, with global capital moving in and out of countries at an ever-increasing rate. These risks can be daunting but they also present opportunities for creating value if properly understood. In the end, the primary question is whether business leaders are able to navigate the strategic and financial challenges that business faces.

New in the Fifth Edition

The theme for this Fifth Edition could be described as the maturation of the emerging markets. The cast of characters dominating global finance is changing, with economies and currencies from Russia, China, India, Brazil, Turkey, to name a few, moving to the forefront of global business. All companies, from start-ups in Mumbai to mature multinationals in Montreux, are facing similar currency risks and cross-border business risks as more of global commerce has moved to a digital interface across a much greater number of countries.

The MNEs in this new world arise from all countries, industrialized and emerging alike, and are all in search of ever-cheaper labor, raw materials, and outsourced manufacturing, while all are competing for the same customers across all markets for sales, profits, and cash flow. These markets—whether they be labeled as BRICs (Brazil, Russia, India, China) or some other popular label—represent the majority of the earth's population and therefore its consumers. We have pursued this theme throughout the book.

5

The following is a short overview of the features in the Fifth Edition.

■ We have increased the detail on changing currency regimes, theory, and practice, as emerging market currencies become ever-greater contributors to global cash flow.

■ We have introduced the challenges faced by governments and central banks as cryptocurrencies like Bitcoin have shaken the very foundations of traditional definitions of "currency."

■ We have added new content throughout the book on the growing complexity of major emerging markets which are more open to capital movements, but also subject to sudden government or central bank intervention in pursuit of sovereign goals and objectives.

■ We increased our coverage of the multitude of different currency regimes and devices used by sovereigns over their currencies and markets, currencies like the Chinese yuan, the Russian ruble, the Indian rupee, the Turkish lira, and the South African rand.

■ We have introduced a number of new Mini-Cases with these currency complexity themes, while retaining a number of the most popular cases from previous editions.

■ We have supplemented each chapter with a number of insights into the subtle nuances of the conduct of financial management with new *Global Finance in Practice* boxes.

Fundamentals, Fifth Edition, has been restructured to be much shorter and tighter. The creation of a more intense exploration of global finance without sacrificing depth or detail was achieved through the integration of a number of concepts and topics.

■ Chapters on the international monetary system cover both the fundamental principles of defining a currency with the complexities of macroeconomic policy and digital exchange.

■ Chapters covering the creation and use of currency and interest rate derivatives for hedging and speculation have been selectively reorganized.

■ Chapters on raising equity capital and international portfolio theory have been integrated into one unified exploration of the global cost and availability of capital.

■ Chapters on the sources of capital and changing financial structures utilized by multinational firms have been reorganized for a more integrated presentation, combining theory and current practice.

International finance is a subject of sophistication, constant change, yet rich in history. We have tried to bridge the traditional business practices with digital practices with a mix of currency notations and symbols throughout the book, using both the common three-letter currency codes — USD, CNY, EUR — with the traditional currency symbols — $, ¥, £, € — which are seeing a resurgence as countries like Russia and Turkey have introduced new "currency identities" of their own.

Audience

Fundamentals of Multinational Finance, Fifth Edition, is aimed at university-level courses in international financial management, international business finance, international finance, and similar titles. It can be used at either the undergraduate or graduate level as well as in executive education and corporate learning courses.

A prerequisite course or experience in corporate finance or financial management would be ideal. However, we review the basic finance concepts before we extend them to the multinational case. We also review the basic concepts of international economics and international business.

We recognize the fact that a large number of our potential adopters live outside of the United States and Canada. Therefore, we use a significant number of non-U.S. examples, Mini-Cases, and *Global Finance in Practice* examples seen in the business and news press (anecdotes and illustrations).

Organization

Fundamentals of Multinational Finance, Fifth Edition, has been redesigned and restructured for tightness—critical elements of the field but in a much shorter delivery framework. This has been accomplished by integrating a number of previous topics along financial management threads. The book is in five parts unified by the common thread of the globalization process by which a firm moves from a domestic to a multinational business orientation.

- Part 1 introduces the global financial environment
- Part 2 explains foreign exchange theory and markets
- Part 3 explores foreign exchange rate exposure
- Part 4 details the financing of the global firm
- Part 5 analyzes international investment decisions

Pedagogical Tools

To make *Fundamentals of Multinational Finance*, Fifth Edition, as comprehensible as possible, we use a large number of proven pedagogical tools. Again, our efforts have been informed by the detailed reviews and suggestions of a panel of professors who are recognized individually for excellence in the field of international finance, particularly at the undergraduate level. Among these pedagogical tools are the following:

- A student-friendly writing style combined with a structured presentation of material, beginning with *learning objectives* for each chapter, and ending with a summary of how those learning objectives were realized.
- A wealth of *illustrations and exhibits* to provide a visual parallel to the concepts and content presented. The entire book uses a multicolor presentation, which we believe provides a visual attractiveness that contributes significantly to reader attention and retention.
- A running case on a hypothetical U.S.-based firm, *Trident Corporation*, provides a cohesive framework for the multifaceted globalization process, and is reinforced in several end-of-chapter problems.
- A *Mini-Case* at the end of each chapter illustrates the chapter content and extends it to the multinational finance business environment. And, as noted, six of the 17 are new to the Fifth Edition.
- *Global Finance in Practice* boxes in every chapter illuminate the theory with accounts of actual business practices. These applications extend the concepts without adding to the length of the text itself.
- Every chapter has a number of end-of-chapter Exercises requiring the use of the Internet, while a variety of Internet references are dispersed throughout the chapters in text and exhibits.

- A multitude of end-of-chapter Questions and Problems assess the students' understanding of the course material. All end-of-chapter Problems are solved using spreadsheet solutions. Selected end-of-chapter Problem answers, indicated by an asterisk (*), are now included at the back of the book.

A Rich Array of Support Materials

A robust package of materials for both instructor and student accompanies the text to facilitate learning and to support teaching and testing.

- **Online Instructor's Manual.**   The Online Instructor's Manual, prepared by William Chittenden of Texas State University, contains complete answers to all end-of-chapter Questions, Problems, and chapter Mini-Cases. All quantitative end-of-chapter Problems are solved using spreadsheets prepared by the authors, which are also available online.

- **Online Test Item File.**   The Online Test Item File, prepared by Borijan Borozanov of the Thunderbird School of Global Management, contains over 1,200 multiple-choice and short essay questions. The multiple-choice questions are labeled by topic and by category: recognition, conceptual, and analytical types.

- **Computerized Test Bank.**   The Test Item File is also available in Pearson Education's TestGen Software. Fully networkable, it is available for Windows and Macintosh. TestGen's graphical interface enables instructors to view, edit, and add questions; transfer questions to tests; and print different forms of tests. Search-and-sort features enable the instructor to locate questions quickly and arrange them in a preferred order. The TestGen plug-in automatically grades the exams and allows the instructor to view and print a variety of reports.

- **Online Mini-Case PowerPoint® Presentations.**   Each of the 17 Mini-Cases has a stand-alone PowerPoint presentation available online.

- **Online PowerPoint Presentation Slides.**   The extensive set of PowerPoint slides provides lecture outlines and selected graphics from the text for each chapter.

- **Web Site.**   A dedicated Web site at www.pearsonglobaleditions.com/moffett contains the Web exercises from the book with wired links, electronic flash cards of glossary terms, and selected solutions and spreadsheets for end-of-chapter problems.

    All of the teaching resources are available online for download at the Instructor Resource Center at www.pearsonglobaleditions.com/moffett.

International Editions

Fundamentals of Multinational Finance and *Multinational Business Finance* have been used throughout the world to teach students of international finance. Our books are published in a number of foreign languages including Chinese, French, Spanish, Indonesian, Portuguese, and Ukrainian.

Acknowledgments

We are very thankful for the many detailed reviews of previous editions and suggestions from a number of colleagues. The final version of *Fundamentals*, Fifth Edition, reflects most of the suggestions provided by these reviewers. The survey reviewers were anonymous, but the detailed reviewers were:

Dev Prasad, *University of Massachusetts Lowell*
Anand M. Vijh, *University of Iowa, Tippie College of Business*
Yoon S. Shin, *Loyola University Maryland*
Raymond M. Johnson, *Auburn University Montgomery*
Cheryl Riffe, *Columbus State Community College*

Additionally, we would like to thank Rodrigo Hernandez of Radford University who meticulously reviewed the Fifth Edition for accuracy.

We would also like to thank all those with Pearson Education who have worked so diligently on this edition: Katie Rowland, Kate Fernandes, Erin McDonagh, and Meredith Gertz. In addition, Gillian Hall, our outstanding project manager, deserves much gratitude.

Finally, we would like to dedicate this book to our parents, Bennie Ruth and the late Hoy Moffett, the late Harold and Norma Stonehill, and the late Wilford and Sylvia Eiteman, who gave us the motivation to become academics and authors. We thank our wives, Megan, Kari, and Keng-Fong, for their patience while we were preparing *Fundamentals of Multinational Finance*.

Glendale, Arizona   M.H.M.
Honolulu, Hawaii   A.I.S.
Pacific Palisades, California   D.K.E.

Pearson wishes to thank the following people for their work on the content of the Global Edition:

Contributors

Monal Abdel Elbaki, Durban University
Leon Chuen Hwa, Nanyang Techonological University

Reviewers

Shamel El Hamawy, Ain Shams University
Pauline Ho, Hong Kong Polytechnic University
Emmanouil Noikokyris, Kingston University
Martin Pereyra, University of Missouri - Columbia
Stefan Pink, Johannes Kepler University Linz
Ravindran Raman, Wawasan Open University
Gary Rangel, Monash University Malaysia

About the Authors

Michael H. Moffett Michael H. Moffett is Continental Grain Professor in Finance at the Thunderbird School of Global Management, where he has been since 1994. He has also held teaching or research appointments at Oregon State University (1985–1993); the University of Michigan, Ann Arbor (1991–1993); the Brookings Institution, Washington, D.C.; the University of Hawaii at Manoa; the Aarhus School of Business (Denmark); the Helsinki School of Economics and Business Administration (Finland); the International Centre for Public Enterprises (Yugoslavia); and the University of Colorado, Boulder.

Professor Moffett received a B.A. (Economics) from the University of Texas at Austin (1977); an M.S. (Resource Economics) from Colorado State University (1979); an M.A. (Economics) from the University of Colorado, Boulder (1983); and Ph.D. (Economics) from the University of Colorado, Boulder (1985).

He has authored, co-authored, or contributed to a number of books, articles, and other publications. He has co-authored two books with Art Stonehill and David Eiteman, *Multinational Business Finance*, and this book, *Fundamentals of Multinational Finance*. His articles have appeared in the *Journal of Financial and Quantitative Analysis*, *Journal of Applied Corporate Finance*, *Journal of International Money and Finance*, *Journal of International Financial Management and Accounting*, *Contemporary Policy Issues*, *Brookings Discussion Papers in International Economics*, and others. He has contributed to a number of collected works including the *Handbook of Modern Finance*, the *International Accounting and Finance Handbook*, and the *Encyclopedia of International Business*. He is also co-author of a number of books in multinational business with Michael Czinkota and Ilkka Ronkainen, *International Business* (Seventh Edition) and *Global Business* (Fourth Edition), and *The Global Oil and Gas Industry: Strategy, Finance, and Management*, with Andrew Inkpen.

Arthur I. Stonehill Arthur I. Stonehill is a Professor of Finance and International Business, Emeritus, at Oregon State University, where he taught for 24 years (1966–1990). During 1991–1997 he held a split appointment at the University of Hawaii at Manoa and Copenhagen Business School. From 1997 to 2001 he continued as a Visiting Professor at the University of Hawaii at Manoa. He has also held teaching or research appointments at the University of California, Berkeley; Cranfield School of Management (U.K.); and the North European Management Institute (Norway). He was a former president of the Academy of International Business, and was a western director of the Financial Management Association.

Professor Stonehill received a B.A. (History) from Yale University (1953); an M.B.A. from Harvard Business School (1957); and a Ph.D. in Business Administration from the University of California, Berkeley (1965). He was awarded honorary doctorates from the Aarhus School of Business (Denmark, 1989), the Copenhagen Business School (Denmark, 1992), and Lund University (Sweden, 1998).

He has authored or co-authored nine books and 25 other publications. His articles have appeared in *Financial Management*, *Journal of International Business Studies*, *California Management Review*, *Journal of Financial and Quantitative Analysis*, *Journal of International Financial Management and Accounting*, *International Business Review*, *European Management Journal*, *The Investment Analyst (U.K.)*, *Nationaløkonomisk Tidskrift (Denmark)*, *Sosialøkonomen (Norway)*, *Journal of Financial Education*, and others.

David K. Eiteman David K. Eiteman is Professor Emeritus of Finance at the John E. Anderson Graduate School of Management at UCLA. He has also held teaching or research appointments at the Hong Kong University of Science and Technology, Showa Academy of Music (Japan), the National University of Singapore, Dalian University (China), the Helsinki School of Economics and Business Administration (Finland), University of Hawaii at Manoa, University of Bradford (U.K.), Cranfield School of Management (U.K.), and IDEA (Argentina). He is a former president of the International Trade and Finance Association, Society for Economics and Management in China, and Western Finance Association.

Professor Eiteman received a B.B.A. (Business Administration) from the University of Michigan, Ann Arbor (1952); M.A. (Economics) from the University of California, Berkeley (1956); and a Ph.D. (Finance) from Northwestern University (1959).

He has authored or co-authored four books and 29 other publications. His articles have appeared in *The Journal of Finance*, *The International Trade Journal*, *Financial Analysts Journal*, *Journal of World Business*, *Management International*, *Business Horizons*, *MSU Business Topics*, *Public Utilities Fortnightly*, and others.

Brief Contents

Contents

Global Financial Environment

CHAPTER 1

Multinational Financial Management: Opportunities and Challenges

I define globalization as producing where it is most cost-effective, selling where it is most profitable, and sourcing capital where it is cheapest, without worrying about national boundaries.

—Narayana Murthy, Founder and Executive Chairman of the Board, Infosys.

LEARNING OBJECTIVES

- Examine the requirements for the creation of value

- Consider the basic theory, *comparative advantage*, and its requirements for the explanation and justification for international trade and commerce

- Discover what is different about international financial management

- Detail which market imperfections give rise to the multinational enterprise

- Consider how the globalization process moves a business from a purely domestic focus in its financial relationships and composition to one truly global in scope

- Examine possible causes of the limitations to globalization in finance

The subject of this book is the financial management of *multinational enterprises* (MNEs)—*multinational financial management*. MNEs are firms—both for-profit companies and not-for-profit organizations—that have operations in more than one country, and conduct their business through branches, foreign subsidiaries, or joint ventures with host country firms.

New MNEs are appearing all over the world today, while many of the older and established ones are struggling to survive. Businesses of all kinds are seeing a very different world than in the past. Today's MNEs depend not only on the emerging markets for cheaper labor, raw materials, and outsourced manufacturing, but also increasingly on those same emerging markets for sales and profits. These markets—whether they are emerging, less developed, or developing, or are BRIC (Brazil, Russia, India, and China), BIITS (Brazil, India, Indonesia, Turkey, South Africa, which are also termed the *Fragile Five*), or MINTs (Mexico, Indonesia, Nigeria, Turkey)—represent the majority of the earth's population and, therefore, potential customers. And adding market complexity to this changing global landscape is the risky and-challenging international macroeconomic environment, both from a long-term and short-term perspective. The global financial crisis of 2008–2009 is already well into the business past, and capital is flowing again—although in and out of economies—at an ever-increasing pace.

How to identify and navigate these risks is the focus of this book. These risks may all occur on the playing field of the global financial marketplace, but they are still a question of *management*—of navigating that complexity in pursuit of the goals of the firm.

Financial Globalization and Risk

Back in the halcyon pre-crisis days of the late 20th and early 21st centuries, it was taken as self evident that financial globalisation was a good thing. But the subprime crisis and eurozone dramas are shaking that belief. . . . what is the bigger risk now—particularly in the eurozone—is that financial globalisation has created a system that is interconnected in some dangerous ways.

—"Crisis Fears Fuel Debate on Capital Controls,"
Gillian Tett, *Financial Times*, December 15, 2011.

The theme dominating global financial markets today is the complexity of risks associated with financial globalization—far beyond whether it is simply good or bad, but how to lead and manage multinational firms in the rapidly moving marketplace.

■ The international monetary system, an eclectic mix of floating and managed fixed exchange rates, is under constant scrutiny. The rise of the Chinese renminbi is changing much of the world's outlook on currency exchange, reserve currencies, and the roles of the dollar and the euro (see Chapter 2).

■ Large fiscal deficits, including the current eurozone crisis, plague most of the major trading countries of the world, complicating fiscal and monetary policies, and ultimately, interest rates and exchange rates (see Chapter 3).

■ Many countries experience continuing balance of payments imbalances, and in some cases, dangerously large deficits and surpluses—whether it be the twin surpluses enjoyed by China, the current account surplus of Germany amidst a sea of eurozone deficits, or the continuing current account deficit of the United States, all will inevitably move exchange rates (see Chapter 3).

■ Ownership, control, and governance vary radically across the world. The publicly traded company is not the dominant global business organization—the privately held or family-owned business is the prevalent structure—and their goals and measures of performance vary dramatically (see Chapter 4).

■ Global capital markets that normally provide the means to lower a firm's cost of capital, and even more critically, increase the availability of capital, have in many ways shrunk in size and have become less open and accessible to many of the world's organizations (see Chapter 1).

■ Today's emerging markets are confronted with a new dilemma: the problem of first being the recipients of capital inflows, and then of experiencing rapid and massive capital outflows. Financial globalization has resulted in the ebb and flow of capital in and out of both industrial and emerging markets, greatly complicating financial management (Chapter 5 and 8).

These are but a sampling of the complexity of risks. This first chapter is meant only as an introduction and a taste. The Mini-Case at the end of this first chapter, *Bitcoin—Cryptocurrency or Commodity?*, is intended to push you in your thinking about how and why money moves across the globe today.

The Global Financial Marketplace

Business—domestic, international, global—involves the interaction of individuals and individual organizations for the exchange of products, services, and capital through markets. The global capital markets are critical for the conduct of this exchange. The global financial crisis of 2008–2009 served as an illustration and a warning of how tightly integrated and fragile this marketplace can be.

Assets, Institutions, and Linkages

Exhibit 1.1 provides a map of the global capital markets. One way to characterize the global financial marketplace is through its assets, institutions, and linkages.

Assets. The assets—financial assets—at the heart of the global capital markets are the debt securities issued by governments (e.g., U.S. Treasury Bonds). These low-risk or risk-free assets form the foundation for the creation, trading, and pricing of other financial assets like bank loans, corporate bonds, and equities (stock). In recent years, a number of additional securities have been created from existing securities—derivatives, whose value is based on market value changes of the underlying securities. The health and security of the global financial system relies on the quality of these assets.

EXHIBIT 1.1   **Global Capital Markets**

The global capital market is a collection of institutions (central banks, commercial banks, investment banks, not-for-profit financial institutions like the IMF and World Bank) and securities (bonds, mortgages, derivatives, loans, etc.), which are all linked via a global network—the *Interbank Market*. This interbank market, in which securities of all kinds are traded, is the critical pipeline system for the movement of capital.

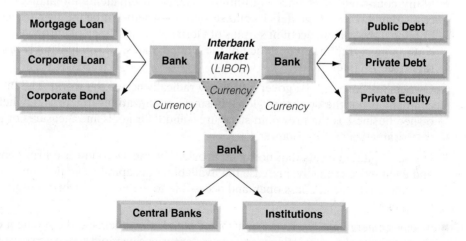

The exchange of securities—the movement of capital in the global financial system—must all take place through a vehicle—currency. The exchange of currencies is itself the largest of the financial markets. The interbank market, which must *pass-through* and exchange securities using currencies, bases all of its pricing through the single most widely quoted interest rate in the world—LIBOR (the London Interbank Offered Rate).

Institutions. The institutions of global finance are the central banks, which create and control each country's money supply; the commercial banks, which take deposits and extend loans to businesses, both local and global; and the multitude of other financial institutions created to trade securities and derivatives. These institutions take many shapes and are subject to many different regulatory frameworks. The health and security of the global financial system relies on the stability of these financial institutions.

Linkages. The links between the financial institutions, the actual fluid or medium for exchange, are the interbank networks using currency. The ready exchange of currencies in the global marketplace is the first and foremost necessary element for the conduct of financial trading, and the global currency markets are the largest markets in the world. The exchange of currencies, and the subsequent exchange of all other securities globally via currency, is the international interbank network. This network, whose primary price is the London Interbank Offered Rate (LIBOR), is the core component of the global financial system.

The movement of capital across currencies and continents for the conduct of business has existed in many different forms for thousands of years. Yet, it is only within the past 50 years that these capital movements have started to move at the pace of an electron in the digital marketplace. And it is only within the past 20 years that this market has been able to reach the most distant corners of the earth at any moment of the day. The result has been an explosion of innovative products and services—some for better, some for worse, and as described in *Global Finance in Practice 1.1*, not always without challenges.

GLOBAL FINANCE IN PRACTICE 1.1

The Trouble with LIBOR

"The idea that my word is my Libor is dead."

— Mervyn King, Bank of England Governor.

No single interest rate is more fundamental to the operation of the global financial markets than the *London Interbank Offered Rate* (LIBOR). LIBOR is used in loan agreements, financial derivatives, swap agreements, in different maturities and different currencies, every day—globally. But beginning as early as 2007, a number of participants in the interbank market on both sides of the Atlantic suspected that there was trouble with LIBOR.

LIBOR is published under the auspices of the British Bankers Association (BBA). Each day, a panel of 16 major multinational banks are requested to submit their *estimated borrowing rates* in the unsecured interbank market which are then collected, massaged, and published in three steps.

Step 1. The banks on the LIBOR panels must submit their estimated borrowing rates by 11:10 a.m. London time. The submissions are directly to Thomson Reuters, which executes the process on behalf of the BBA.

Step 2. Thomson Reuters discards the lowest 25% and highest 25% of interest rates submitted. It then calculates an average rate by maturity and currency using the remaining 50% of borrowing rate quotes.

Step 3. The BBA publishes the day's LIBOR rates 20 minutes later, by 11:30 a.m. London time.

This process is used to publish LIBOR for 10 different currencies across 15 different maturities. The three-month and six-month maturities are the most significant maturities due to their widespread use in various loan and derivative agreements, with the dollar and the euro being the most widely used currencies.

The Trouble

One problem with LIBOR is the origin of the rates submitted by banks. First, rates are not limited to those at which actual borrowing occurred, meaning they are not market transaction rates. The logic behind including "estimated borrowing rates" was to avoid reporting only actual transactions, as many banks may not conduct actual transactions in all maturities and currencies each day. As a result, the origin of the rate submitted by each bank becomes, to some degree, discretionary.

Secondly, banks—specifically money-market and derivative traders within the banks—have a number of interests that may be impacted by borrowing costs reported by the bank that day. One such example can be found in the concerns of banks in the interbank market in September 2008, when the credit crisis was in full-bloom. A bank reporting that other banks were demanding it pay a higher rate that day would, in effect, be self-reporting the market's assessment that it was increasingly risky. In the words of one analyst, akin "to hanging a sign around one's neck that I am carrying a contagious disease." Market analysts are now estimating that many of the banks in the LIBOR panel were reporting borrowing rates which were anywhere from 30 to 40 basis points lower than actual rates throughout the financial crisis. As one financial reform advocate so sharply stated it, "the issue is Lie More, not Libor."

Court documents continue to shed light on the depth of the market's manipulation, although it is not really known to what degree attempts at manipulation have been successful.

Hi Guys, We got a big position in 3m libor for the next 3 days. Can we please keep the libor fixing at 5.39 for the next few days. It would really help.

— Barclays New York trader email, September 13, 2006, as reported in Barclays PLC, Barclays Bank PLC, and Barclays Capital Inc., CFTC Docket No. 12-25, CFTC, p.10.

In December 2013, a collection of banks in London and New York agreed to pay $2.3 billion in fines to the European Commission for LIBOR manipulation. And more lawsuits, accusations, and regulations are sure to come.

The Market for Currencies

The price of any one country's currency in terms of another country's currency is called a *foreign currency exchange rate*. For example, the exchange rate between the U.S. dollar ($ or USD) and the European euro (€ or EUR) may be stated as "1.3654 dollar per euro" or simply abbreviated as $1.3654/€. This is the same exchange rate as when stated "EUR1.00 = USD1.3654." Since most international business activities require at least one of the two parties in a business transaction to either pay or receive payment in a currency that is different from their own, an understanding of exchange rates is critical to the conduct of global business.

Currency Symbols. As noted, USD and EUR are often used as the symbols for the U.S. dollar and the European Union's euro. These are the computer symbols (ISO-4217 codes) used today on the world's digital networks. The field of international finance, however, has a rich history of using a variety of different symbols in the financial press, and a variety of different abbreviations are commonly used. For example, the British pound sterling may be £ (the pound symbol), GBP (Great Britain pound), STG (British pound sterling), ST£ (pound sterling), or UKL (United Kingdom pound). This book uses the simpler common symbols—the $ (dollar), the € (euro), the ¥ (yen), the £ (pound)—but be warned and watchful when reading the business press!

Exchange Rate Quotations and Terminology. Exhibit 1.2 lists currency exchange rates for January 13, 2014, as would be quoted in New York or London. The exchange rate listed is for a specific country's currency—for example, the Argentina peso against the U.S. dollar is Peso 6.6580/$, against the European euro is Peso 9.0905/€, and against the British pound is Peso 10.9078/£. The rate listed is termed a "mid-rate" because it is the middle or average of the rates at which currency traders buy currency (bid rate) and sell currency (offer rate).

The U.S. dollar has been the focal point of most currency trading since the 1940s. As a result, most of the world's currencies have been quoted against the dollar—Mexican pesos per dollar, Brazilian real per dollar, Hong Kong dollars per dollar, etc. This quotation convention is also followed against the world's major currencies, as listed in Exhibit 1.2. For example, the Japanese yen is commonly quoted as ¥103.365/$, ¥141.129/€, and 169.343/£.

Quotation Conventions. Several of the world's major currency exchange rates, however, follow a specific quotation convention that is the result of tradition and history. The exchange rate between the U.S. dollar and the euro is always quoted as "dollars per euro" or $/€. For example, $1.3654 listed in Exhibit 1.2 under "United States." Similarly, the exchange rate between the U.S. dollar and the British pound is always quoted as "dollars per pound" or $/£. For example, $1.6383 listed under "United States" in Exhibit 1.2. In addition, countries that were formerly members of the British Commonwealth will often be quoted against the U.S. dollar, as in U.S. dollars per Australian dollar or U.S. dollars per Canadian dollar.

EXHIBIT 1.2   Selected Global Currency Exchange Rates

January 13, 2014 Country	Currency	Symbol	Code	Currency to Equal 1 U.S. Dollar	Currency to Equal 1 Euro	Currency to Equal 1 Pound
Argentina	peso	Ps	ARS	6.6580	9.0905	10.9078
Australia	dollar	A$	AUD	1.1043	1.5078	1.8092
Bahrain	dinar	—	BHD	0.3770	0.5148	0.6177
Bolivia	boliviano	Bs	BOB	6.9100	9.4346	11.3207
Brazil	real	R$	BRL	2.3446	3.2012	3.8411
Canada	dollar	C$	CAD	1.0866	1.4836	1.7801
Chile	peso	$	CLP	526.980	719.512	863.351
China	yuan	¥	CNY	6.0434	8.2514	9.9009
Colombia	peso	Col$	COP	1,924.70	2,627.89	3,153.24
Costa Rica	colon	₡	CRC	499.475	681.959	818.291
Czech Republic	koruna	Kc	CZK	20.0425	27.3650	32.8356
Denmark	krone	Dkr	DKK	5.4656	7.4624	8.9542
Egypt	pound	£	EGP	6.9562	9.4977	11.3964
Hong Kong	dollar	HK$	HKD	7.7547	10.5878	12.7045
Hungary	forint	Ft	HUF	218.680	298.575	358.264
India	rupee	₹	INR	61.5750	84.0715	100.8780
Indonesia	rupiah	Rp	IDR	12,050.0	16,452.5	19,741.5
Iran	rial	—	IRR	12,395.5	16,924.2	20,307.5
Israel	shekel	Shk	ILS	3.4882	4.7627	5.7148
Japan	yen	¥	JPY	103.365	141.129	169.343
Kenya	shilling	KSh	KES	86.250	117.761	141.303
Kuwait	dinar	—	KWD	0.2824	0.3856	0.4627
Malaysia	ringgit	RM	MYR	3.2635	4.4559	5.3466
Mexico	new peso	$	MXN	12.9745	17.7148	21.2561
New Zealand	dollar	NZ$	NZD	1.1957	1.6326	1.9590
Nigeria	naira	₦	NGN	159.750	218.115	261.718
Norway	krone	NKr	NOK	6.1216	8.3581	10.0290
Pakistan	rupee	Rs.	PKR	105.535	144.092	172.898
Peru	new sol	S/.	PEN	2.7965	3.8182	4.5816
Phillippines	peso	₱	PHP	44.5950	60.8878	73.0600
Poland	zloty	—	PLN	3.0421	4.1535	4.9839
Romania	new leu	L	RON	3.3133	4.5238	5.4281
Russia	ruble	₽	RUB	33.2660	45.4198	54.4997
Saudi Arabia	riyal	SR	SAR	3.7505	5.1207	6.1444
Singapore	dollar	S$	SGD	1.2650	1.7272	2.0725
South Africa	rand	R	ZAR	10.7750	14.7117	17.6527
South Korea	won	W	KRW	1,056.65	1,442.70	1,731.11
Sweden	krona	SKr	SEK	6.4986	8.8728	10.6466
Switzerland	franc	Fr.	CHF	0.9026	1.2324	1.4788
Taiwan	dollar	T$	TWD	30.0060	40.9687	49.1588
Thailand	baht	B	THB	32.9750	45.0224	54.0230
Tunisia	dinar	DT	TND	1.6548	2.2593	2.7110
Turkey	lira	₺	TRY	2.1773	2.9728	3.5671
Ukraine	hrywnja	—	UAH	8.3125	11.3495	13.6184
United Arab Emirates	dirham	—	AED	3.6730	5.0149	6.0175
United Kingdom	pound	£	GBP	0.6104	0.8334	—
United States	dollar	$	USD	—	1.3654	1.6383
Uruguay	peso	$U	UYU	21.6050	29.4984	35.3955
Venezuela	bolivar fuerte	Bs	VEB	6.2921	8.5910	10.3084
Vietnam	dong	₫	VND	21,090.0	28,795.2	34,551.8
Euro	euro	€	EUR	0.7324	—	1.1999
Special Drawing Right	—	—	SDR	0.6509	0.8887	1.0663

Notes: A number of different currencies use the same symbol (for example both China and Japan have traditionally used the ¥ symbol, yen or yuan, meaning round or circle). That is one of the reasons why most of the world's currency markets today use the three-digit currency code for clarity of quotation. All quotes are mid-rates, and are drawn from the *Financial Times*, January 14, 2014. The British pound and euro are quoted here in the identical terms — per dollar, per euro, per pound — as are all other country currencies. However, the *Financial Times*, which is the original source for these currency quotations, will quote the pound and euro in the reciprocal form as is industry practice for these currencies.

Eurocurrencies and LIBOR

One of the major linkages of global money and capital markets is the eurocurrency market and its interest rate, which is LIBOR. *Eurocurrencies* are domestic currencies of one country on deposit in a second country for a period ranging from overnight to more than a year or longer. Certificates of deposit are usually for three months or more and in million-dollar increments. A eurodollar deposit is not a *demand deposit*—it is not created on the bank's books by writing loans against required fractional reserves, and it cannot be transferred by a check drawn on the bank having the deposit. Eurodollar deposits are transferred by wire or cable transfer of an underlying balance held in a correspondent bank located within the United States. In most countries, a domestic analogy would be the transfer of deposits held in nonbank savings associations. These are transferred when the association writes its own check on a commercial bank.

Any convertible currency can exist in "euro-" form. Note that this use of "euro-" should not be confused with the new common European currency called the euro. The eurocurrency market includes eurosterling (British pounds deposited outside the United Kingdom); euroeuros (euros on deposit outside the eurozone); euroyen (Japanese yen deposited outside Japan) and eurodollars (U.S. dollars deposited outside the U.S.).

Eurocurrency markets serve two valuable purposes: 1) eurocurrency deposits are an efficient and convenient money market device for holding excess corporate liquidity; and 2) the eurocurrency market is a major source of short-term bank loans to finance corporate working capital needs, including the financing of imports and exports. Banks in which eurocurrencies are deposited are called eurobanks. A *eurobank* is a financial intermediary that simultaneously bids for time deposits and makes loans in a currency other than that of its home currency. Eurobanks are major world banks that conduct a eurocurrency business in addition to all other banking functions. Thus, the eurocurrency operation that qualifies a bank for the name eurobank is, in fact, a department of a large commercial bank, and the name springs from the performance of this function.

The modern eurocurrency market was born shortly after World War II. Eastern European holders of dollars, including the various state trading banks of the Soviet Union, were afraid to deposit their dollar holdings in the United States because those deposits might be attached by U.S. residents with claims against communist governments. Therefore, Eastern European holders deposited their dollars in Western Europe, particularly with two Soviet banks: the Moscow Narodny Bank in London, and the Banque Commerciale pour l'Europe du Nord in Paris. These banks redeposited the funds in other Western banks, especially in London. Additional dollar deposits were received from various central banks in Western Europe, which elected to hold part of their dollar reserves in this form to obtain a higher yield. Commercial banks also placed their dollar balances in the market because specific maturities could be negotiated in the eurodollar market. Such companies found it financially advantageous to keep their dollar reserves in the higher-yielding eurodollar market. Various holders of international refugee funds also supplied funds.

Although the basic causes of the growth of the eurocurrency market are economic efficiencies, many unique institutional events during the 1950s and 1960s contributed to its growth.

- In 1957, British monetary authorities responded to a weakening of the pound by imposing tight controls on U.K. bank lending in sterling to nonresidents of the United Kingdom. Encouraged by the Bank of England, U.K. banks turned to dollar lending as the only alternative that would allow them to maintain their leading position in world finance. For this they needed dollar deposits.

- Although New York was "home base" for the dollar and had a large domestic money and capital market, international trading in the dollar centered in London because of that city's expertise in international monetary matters and its proximity in time and distance to major customers.

■ Additional support for a European-based dollar market came from the balance of payments difficulties of the U.S. during the 1960s, which temporarily segmented the U.S. domestic capital market.

Ultimately, however, the eurocurrency market continues to thrive because it is a large international money market relatively free from governmental regulation and interference.

Eurocurrency Interest Rates. The reference rate of interest in the eurocurrency market is the London Interbank Offered Rate, or LIBOR. LIBOR is the most widely accepted rate of interest used in standardized quotations, loan agreements or financial derivatives valuations. The use of interbank offered rates, however, is not confined to London. Most major domestic financial centers construct their own interbank offered rates for local loan agreements. Examples of such rates include PIBOR (Paris Interbank Offered Rate), MIBOR (Madrid Interbank Offered Rate), SIBOR (Singapore Interbank Offered Rate), and FIBOR (Frankfurt Interbank Offered Rate), to name but a few.

The key factor attracting both depositors and borrowers to the eurocurrency loan market is the narrow interest rate spread within that market. The difference between deposit and loan rates is often less than 1%. Interest spreads in the eurocurrency market are small for many reasons. Low lending rates exist because the eurocurrency market is a wholesale market, where deposits and loans are made in amounts of $500,000 or more on an unsecured basis. Borrowers are usually large corporations or government entities that qualify for low rates because of their credit standing and because the transaction size is large. In addition, overhead assigned to the eurocurrency operation by participating banks is small.

Deposit rates are higher in the eurocurrency markets than in most domestic currency markets because the financial institutions offering eurocurrency activities are not subject to many of the regulations and reserve requirements imposed on traditional domestic banks and banking activities. With these costs removed, rates are subject to more competitive pressures, deposit rates are higher, and loan rates are lower. A second major area of cost avoided in the eurocurrency markets is the payment of deposit insurance fees (such as the Federal Deposit Insurance Corporation, FDIC) and assessments paid on deposits in the United States.

The Theory of Comparative Advantage

The theory of comparative advantage provides a basis for explaining and justifying international trade in a model world assumed to enjoy free trade, perfect competition, no uncertainty, costless information, and no government interference. The theory's origins lie in the work of Adam Smith, and particularly with his seminal book, *The Wealth of Nations*, published in 1776. Smith sought to explain why the division of labor in productive activities, and subsequently international trade of those goods, increased the quality of life for all citizens. Smith based his work on the concept of *absolute advantage*, with every country specializing in the production of those goods for which it was uniquely suited. More would be produced for less. Thus, with each country specializing in products for which it possessed absolute advantage, countries could produce more in total and trade for goods that were cheaper in price than those produced at home.

In his work, *On the Principles of Political Economy and Taxation*, published in 1817, David Ricardo sought to take the basic ideas set down by Adam Smith a few logical steps further. Ricardo noted that even if a country possessed *absolute advantage* in the production of two goods, it might still be relatively more efficient than the other country in one good's production than the production of the other good. Ricardo termed this *comparative advantage*. Each country would then possess comparative advantage in the production of one of the two products, and both countries would then benefit by specializing completely in one product and trading for the other.

Although international trade might have approached the comparative advantage model during the nineteenth century, it certainly does not today, for a variety of reasons. Countries do not appear to specialize only in those products that could be most efficiently produced by that country's particular factors of production. Instead, governments interfere with comparative advantage for a variety of economic and political reasons, such as to achieve full employment, economic development, national self-sufficiency in defense-related industries, and protection of an agricultural sector's way of life. Government interference takes the form of tariffs, quotas, and other non-tariff restrictions.

At least two of the factors of production—capital and technology—now flow directly and easily between countries, rather than only indirectly through traded goods and services. This direct flow occurs between related subsidiaries and affiliates of multinational firms, as well as between unrelated firms via loans and license and management contracts. Even labor flows between countries, such as immigrants into the United States (legal and illegal), immigrants within the European Union, and other unions.

Modern factors of production are more numerous than in this simple model. Factors considered in the location of production facilities worldwide include local and managerial skills, a dependable legal structure for settling contract disputes, research and development competence, educational levels of available workers, energy resources, consumer demand for brand name goods, mineral and raw material availability, access to capital, tax differentials, supporting infrastructure (roads, ports, and communication facilities), and possibly others.

Although the terms of trade are ultimately determined by supply and demand, the process by which the terms are set is different from that visualized in traditional trade theory. They are determined partly by administered pricing in oligopolistic markets.

Comparative advantage shifts over time as less-developed countries become more developed and realize their latent opportunities. For example, over the past 150 years comparative advantage in producing cotton textiles has shifted from the United Kingdom to the United States, to Japan, to Hong Kong, to Taiwan, and to China. The classical model of comparative advantage also did not really address certain other issues such as the effect of uncertainty and information costs, the role of differentiated products in imperfectly competitive markets, and economies of scale.

Nevertheless, although the world is a long way from the classical trade model, the general principle of comparative advantage is still valid. The closer the world gets to true international specialization, the more world production and consumption can be increased, provided that the problem of equitable distribution of the benefits can be solved to the satisfaction of consumers, producers, and political leaders. Complete specialization, however, remains an unrealistic limiting case, just as perfect competition is a limiting case in microeconomic theory.

Global Outsourcing of Comparative Advantage

Comparative advantage is still a relevant theory to explain why particular countries are most suitable for exports of goods and services that support the global supply chain of both MNEs and domestic firms. The comparative advantage of the twenty-first century, however, is one that is based more on services, and their cross-border facilitation by telecommunications and the Internet. The source of a nation's comparative advantage, however, still is created from the mixture of its own labor skills, access to capital, and technology.

For example, India has developed a highly efficient and low-cost software industry. This industry supplies not only the creation of custom software, but also call centers for customer support, and other information technology services. The Indian software industry is composed of subsidiaries of MNEs and independent companies. If you own a Hewlett-Packard computer and call the customer support center number for help, you are likely to reach a call center in India. Answering your call will be a knowledgeable Indian software engineer or programmer who will "walk you through" your problem. India has a large number of well-educated, English-speaking technical experts who are paid only a fraction of the salary and overhead earned by their U.S. counterparts. The overcapacity and low cost of international telecommunication networks today further enhances the comparative advantage of an Indian location.

The extent of global outsourcing is already reaching out to every corner of the globe. From financial back-offices in Manila, to information technology engineers in Hungary, modern telecommunications now take business activities to labor rather than moving labor to the places of business.

What Is Different about International Financial Management?

Exhibit 1.3 details some of the main differences between international and domestic financial management. These component differences include institutions, foreign exchange and political risks, and the modifications required of financial theory and financial instruments.

Multinational financial management requires an understanding of cultural, historical, and institutional differences such as those affecting corporate governance. Although both domestic firms and MNEs are exposed to foreign exchange risks, MNEs alone face certain unique risks, such as political risks, that are not normally a threat to domestic operations.

MNEs also face other risks that can be classified as extensions of domestic finance theory. For example, the normal domestic approach to the cost of capital, sourcing debt and equity,

EXHIBIT 1.3	What Is Different about International Financial Management?	
Concept	**International**	**Domestic**
Culture, history, and institutions	Each foreign country is unique and not always understood by MNE management	Each country has a known base case
Corporate governance	Foreign countries' regulations and institutional practices are all uniquely different	Regulations and institutions are well known
Foreign exchange risk	MNEs face foreign exchange risks due to their subsidiaries, as well as import/export and foreign competitors	Foreign exchange risks from import/export and foreign competition (no subsidiaries)
Political risk	MNEs face political risk because of their foreign subsidiaries and high profile	Negligible political risks
Modification of domestic finance theories	MNEs must modify finance theories like capital budgeting and the cost of capital because of foreign complexities	Traditional financial theory applies
Modification of domestic financial instruments	MNEs utilize modified financial instruments such as options, forwards, swaps, and letters of credit	Limited use of financial instruments and derivatives because of few foreign exchange and political risks

---

GLOBAL FINANCE IN PRACTICE 1.2

Corporate Responsibility and Corporate Sustainability

Sustainable development is development that meets the needs of the present without compromising the ability of future generations to meet their own needs.

—*Brundtland Report*, 1987, p. 54.

What is the purpose of the corporation? It is accepted that the purpose of the corporation is to certainly create profits and value for its stakeholders, but the responsibility of the corporation is to do so in a way that inflicts no costs on society, including the environment. As a result of globalization, this growing responsibility and role of the corporation in society has added a level of complexity to the leadership challenges faced by the multinational firm.

This developing controversy has been somewhat hampered to date by conflicting terms and labels—*corporate goodness, corporate responsibility, corporate social responsibility* (CSR), *corporate philanthropy,* and *corporate sustainability,* to list but a few. Confusion can be reduced by using a guiding principle—that sustainability is a goal, while responsibility is an obligation. It follows that the obligation of leadership in the modern multinational is to pursue profit, social development, and the environment, all along sustainable principles.

The term *sustainability* has evolved greatly within the context of global business in the past decade. A traditional primary objective of the family-owned business has been the "sustainability of the organization"—the long-term ability of the company to remain commercially viable and provide security and income for future generations. Although narrower in scope, the concept of *environmental sustainability* shares a common core thread—the ability of a company, a culture, or even the earth, to survive and renew over time.

---

capital budgeting, working capital management, taxation, and credit analysis needs to be modified to accommodate foreign complexities. Moreover, a number of financial instruments that are used in domestic financial management have been modified for use in international financial management. Examples are foreign currency options and futures, interest rate and currency swaps, and letters of credit.

The main theme of this book is to analyze how an MNE's financial management evolves as it pursues global strategic opportunities and new constraints emerge. In this chapter, we will take a brief look at the challenges and risks associated with Trident Corporation (Trident), a company evolving from domestic in scope to becoming truly multinational. The discussion will include constraints that a company will face in terms of managerial goals and governance as it becomes increasingly involved in multinational operations. But first we need to clarify the unique value proposition and advantages that the MNE was created to exploit. And as noted by *Global Finance in Practice 1.2*, the objectives and responsibilities of the modern multinational have grown significantly more complex in the twenty-first century.

Market Imperfections: A Rationale for the Existence of the Multinational Firm

MNEs strive to take advantage of imperfections in national markets for products, factors of production, and financial assets. Imperfections in the market for products translate into market opportunities for MNEs. Large international firms are better able to exploit such competitive factors as economies of scale, managerial and technological expertise, product differentiation, and financial strength than are their local competitors. In fact, MNEs thrive best in markets characterized by international oligopolistic competition, where these factors are particularly critical. In addition, once MNEs have established a physical presence abroad, they are in a better position than purely domestic firms to identify and implement market opportunities through their own internal information network.

Why Do Firms Become Multinational?

Strategic motives drive the decision to invest abroad and become an MNE. These motives can be summarized under the following categories:

1. *Market seekers* produce in foreign markets either to satisfy local demand or to export to markets other than their home market. U.S. automobile firms manufacturing in Europe for local consumption are an example of market-seeking motivation.

2. *Raw material seekers* extract raw materials wherever they can be found, either for export or for further processing and sale in the country in which they are found—the host country. Firms in the oil, mining, plantation, and forest industries fall into this category.

3. *Production efficiency seekers* produce in countries where one or more of the factors of production are underpriced relative to their productivity. Labor-intensive production of electronic components in Taiwan, Malaysia, and Mexico is an example of this motivation.

4. *Knowledge seekers* operate in foreign countries to gain access to technology or managerial expertise. For example, German, Dutch, and Japanese firms have purchased U.S.-located electronics firms for their technology.

5. *Political safety seekers* acquire or establish new operations in countries that are considered unlikely to expropriate or interfere with private enterprise. For example, Hong Kong firms invested heavily in the United States, United Kingdom, Canada, and Australia in anticipation of the consequences of China's 1997 takeover of the British colony.

These five types of strategic considerations are not mutually exclusive. Forest products firms seeking wood fiber in Brazil, for example, may also find a large Brazilian market for a portion of their output.

In industries characterized by worldwide oligopolistic competition, each of the above strategic motives should be subdivided into proactive and defensive investments. Proactive investments are designed to enhance the growth and profitability of the firm itself. Defensive investments are designed to deny growth and profitability to the firm's competitors. Examples of the latter are investments that try to preempt a market before competitors can get established in it, or capture raw material sources and deny them to competitors.

The Globalization Process

Trident is a hypothetical U.S.-based firm that will be used as an illustrative example throughout the book to demonstrate the globalization process—the structural and managerial changes and challenges experienced by a firm as it moves its operations from domestic to global.

Global Transition I: Trident Moves from the Domestic Phase to the International Trade Phase

Trident is a young firm that manufactures and distributes an array of telecommunication devices. Its initial strategy is to develop a sustainable competitive advantage in the U.S. market. Like many other young firms, it is constrained by its small size, competitors, and lack of access to cheap and plentiful sources of capital. The top half of Exhibit 1.4 shows Trident in its early domestic phase.

Trident sells its products in U.S. dollars to U.S. customers and buys its manufacturing and service inputs from U.S. suppliers, paying U.S. dollars. The creditworth of all suppliers and buyers is established under domestic U.S. practices and procedures. A potential

---

EXHIBIT 1.4 **Trident Corp: Initiation of the Globalization Process**

Phase One: Domestic Operations

| U.S. Suppliers (domestic) | All payments in U.S. dollars. All credit risk under U.S. law. | U.S. Buyers (domestic) |

Trident Corporation (Los Angeles, USA)

| Mexican Suppliers | | Canadian Buyers |

Are Mexican suppliers dependable? Will Trident pay US$ or Mexican pesos?

Are Canadian buyers creditworthy? Will payment be made in US$ or C$?

Phase Two: Expansion into International Trade

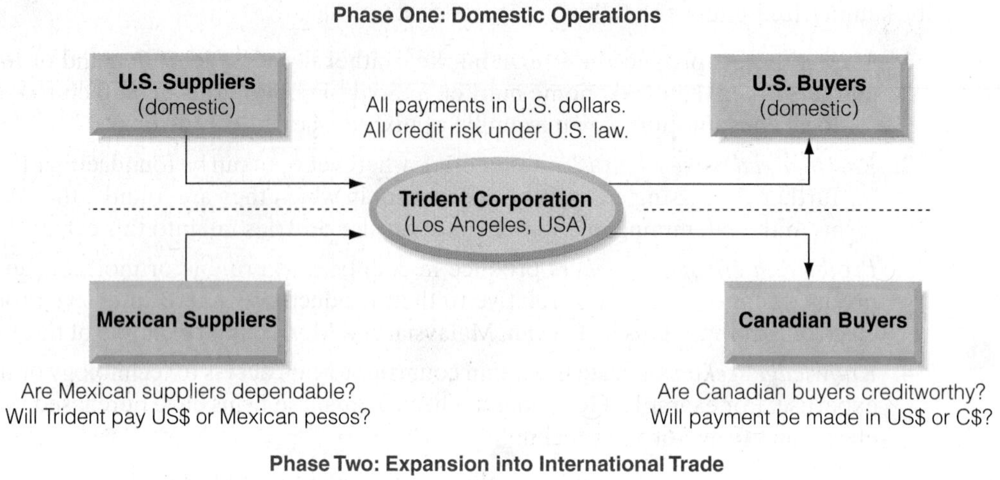

issue for Trident at this time is that although Trident is not international or global in its operations, some of its competitors, suppliers, or buyers may be. This is often the impetus to push a firm like Trident into the first phase of the globalization process—into international trade. Trident was founded by James Winston in Los Angeles in 1948 to make telecommunications equipment. The family-owned business expanded slowly but steadily over the following 40 years. The demands of continual technological investment in the 1980s, however, required that the firm raise additional equity capital in order to compete. This need led to its initial public offering (IPO) in 1988. As a U.S.-based publicly traded company on the New York Stock Exchange, Trident's management sought to create value for its shareholders.

As Trident became a visible and viable competitor in the U.S. market, strategic opportunities arose to expand the firm's market reach by exporting product and services to one or more foreign markets. The North American Free Trade Area (NAFTA) made trade with Mexico and Canada attractive. This second phase of the globalization process is shown in the lower half of Exhibit 1.4. Trident responded to these globalization forces by importing inputs from Mexican suppliers and making export sales to Canadian buyers. We define this phase of the globalization process as the International Trade Phase.

Exporting and importing products and services increases the demands of financial management over and above the traditional requirements of the domestic-only business in two ways. First, direct foreign exchange risks are now borne by the firm. Trident may now need to quote prices in foreign currencies, accept payment in foreign currencies, or pay suppliers in foreign currencies. As the values of currencies change from minute to minute in the global marketplace, Trident will increasingly experience significant risks from the changing values associated with these foreign currency payments and receipts.

Second, the evaluation of the credit quality of foreign buyers and sellers is now more important than ever. Reducing the possibility of non-payment for exports and non-delivery of imports becomes a key financial management task during the international trade phase. This credit risk management task is much more difficult in international business, as buyers and suppliers are new, subject to differing business practices and legal systems, and generally more challenging to assess.

Global Transition II: The International Trade Phase to the Multinational Phase

If Trident is successful in its international trade activities, the time will come when the globalization process will progress to the next phase. Trident will soon need to establish foreign sales and service affiliates. This step is often followed by establishing manufacturing operations abroad or by licensing foreign firms to produce and service Trident's products. The multitude of issues and activities associated with this second larger global transition is the real focus of this book.

Trident's continued globalization will require it to identify the sources of its competitive advantage, and with that knowledge, expand its intellectual capital and physical presence globally. A variety of strategic alternatives are available to Trident—the foreign direct investment sequence—as shown in Exhibit 1.5. These alternatives include the creation of foreign sales offices, the licensing of the company name and everything associated with it, and the manufacturing and distribution of its products to other firms in foreign markets.

As Trident moves farther down and to the right in Exhibit 1.5, the degree of its physical presence in foreign markets increases. It may now own its own distribution and production facilities, and ultimately, may want to acquire other companies. Once Trident owns assets and enterprises in foreign countries it has entered the multinational phase of its globalization.

The Limits to Financial Globalization

The theories of international business and international finance introduced in this chapter have long argued that with an increasingly open and transparent global marketplace in which capital may flow freely, capital will increasingly flow and support countries and companies

---

EXHIBIT 1.5 | **Trident's Foreign Direct Investment Sequence**

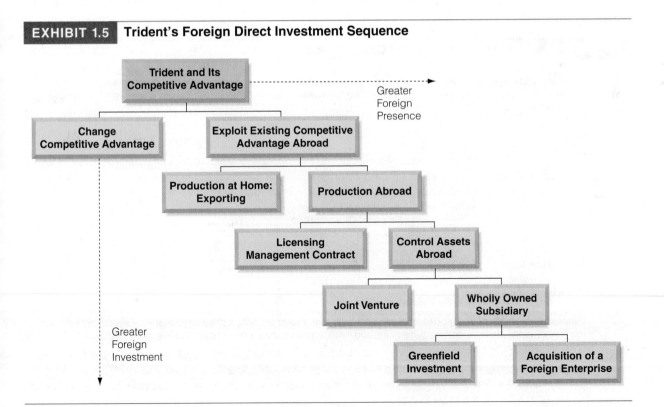

based on the theory of comparative advantage. Since the mid-twentieth century, this has indeed been the case as more and more countries have pursued more open and competitive markets. But the past decade has seen the growth of a new kind of limit or impediment to financial globalization: the growth in the influence and self-enrichment of organizational insiders.

One possible representation of this process can be seen in Exhibit 1.6. If influential insiders in corporations and sovereign states continue to pursue the increase in firm value, there will be a definite and continuing growth in financial globalization. But, if these same influential insiders pursue their own personal agendas, which may increase their personal power and influence or personal wealth, or both, then capital will not flow into these sovereign states and corporations. The result is the growth of financial inefficiency and the segmentation of globalization outcomes—creating winners and losers. As we will see throughout this book, this barrier to international finance may indeed be increasingly troublesome.

This growing dilemma is also something of a composite of what this book is about. The three fundamental elements—financial theory, global business, and management beliefs and actions—combine to present either the problem or the solution to the growing debate over the benefits of globalization to countries and cultures worldwide. The Mini-Case sets the stage for our debate and discussion. Are the controlling family members of this company creating value for themselves or for their shareholders?

We close this chapter—and open this book—with the simple words of one of our colleagues in a recent conference on the outlook for global finance and global financial management.

> *Welcome to the future. This will be a constant struggle. We need leadership, citizenship, and dialogue.*

> —Donald Lessard, in Global Risk, *New Perspectives and Opportunities*, 2011, p. 33.

EXHIBIT 1.6   The Limits of Financial Globalization

There is a growing debate over whether many of the insiders and rulers of organizations with enterprises globally are taking actions consistent with creating firm value or consistent with increasing their own personal stakes and power.

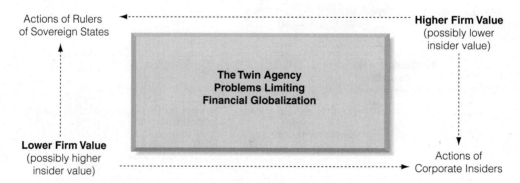

If these influential insiders are building personal wealth over that of the firm, it will indeed result in preventing the flow of capital across borders, currencies, and institutions to create a more open and integrated global financial community.

Source: Constructed by authors based on "The Limits of Financial Globalization," Rene M. Stulz, *Journal of Applied Corporate Finance*, Vol. 19, No. 1, Winter 2007, pp. 8–15.

Summary Points

- The creation of value requires combining three critical elements: 1) an open marketplace; 2) high-quality strategic management; and 3) access to capital.

- The theory of comparative advantage provides a basis for explaining and justifying international trade in a model world assumed to enjoy free trade, perfect competition, no uncertainty, costless information, and no government interference.

- International financial management requires an understanding of cultural, historical, and institutional differences, such as those affecting corporate governance.

- Although both domestic firms and MNEs are exposed to foreign exchange risks, MNEs alone face certain unique risks, such as political risks, that are not normally a threat to domestic operations.

- MNEs strive to take advantage of imperfections in national markets for products, factors of production, and financial assets.

- Large international firms are better able to exploit such competitive factors as economies of scale, managerial and technological expertise, product differentiation, and financial strength than are their local competitors.

- A firm may first enter into international trade transactions, then international contractual arrangements, such as sales offices and franchising, and ultimately the acquisition of foreign subsidiaries. At this final stage it truly becomes a multinational enterprise (MNE).

- The decision whether or not to invest abroad is driven by strategic motives and may require the MNE to enter into global licensing agreements, joint ventures, cross-border acquisitions, or greenfield investments.

- If influential insiders in corporations and sovereign states pursue their own personal agendas, which may increase their personal power, influence, or wealth, then capital will not flow into these sovereign states and corporations. This will, in turn, create limitations to globalization in finance.

MINI-CASE

Bitcoin—Cryptocurrency or Commodity?[1]

The difference is that established fiat currencies—ones where the bills and coins, or their digital versions, get their value by dint of regulation or law—are underwritten by the state which is, in principle at least, answerable to its citizens. Bitcoin, on the other hand, is a community currency. It requires self-policing on the part of its users. To some, this is a feature, not a bug. But, in the grand scheme of things, the necessary open-source engagement remains a niche pursuit. Most people would rather devolve this sort of responsibility to the authorities. Until this mindset changes, Bitcoin will be no rival to real-world dosh.

— "Bits and bob," *The Economist*, June 13, 2011.

Bitcoin is an open-source, peer-to-peer, digital currency. It is a *cryptocurrency*, a digital currency that is created and managed using advanced encryption techniques known as *cryptography*. And it may be the world's first completely decentralized digital-payments system. The unofficial three letter currency code for Bitcoin is BTC, and its singular currency symbol is shown above.

But is Bitcoin a true currency? Is it, or can it become, money? In January 2014 a number of major regulatory bodies across the world—the U.S. Federal Reserve, the European Central Bank, the People's Bank of China—were all trying to decide whether Bitcoin was something to be prohibited, regulated, or simply left alone. Perspectives on Bitcoin use varied dramatically, and in many cases, unexpectedly so. But the *regulators* were only one stakeholder interest; *users* and *producers* had their own perspectives on the potential of Bitcoin.

Producing and Using Bitcoins

Bitcoin was invented in 2009 by a man claiming to be Satoshi Nakamoto. Nakamoto published, via the Internet, a nine-page paper outlining how the Bitcoin system would work. He also provided the open-source code needed to both produce the digital coins (*mine* in Bitcoin terminology) and trade Bitcoins digitally as money. (Nakamoto is not thought to be a real person, likely being a *nome de plume* for some relatively small working group. Nakamoto disappeared from the Internet in 2012.)

Mining. The actual mining of Bitcoins is a mathematical process. The *miner* must find a sequence of data (called a *block*) that produces a particular pattern when the Bitcoin

[1]Copyright © 2014 Thunderbird School of Global Management. All rights reserved. This case was prepared by Professor Michael H. Moffett for the purpose of classroom discussion only and not to indicate either effective or ineffective management.

hash algorithm is applied to it. When a match is found, the miner obtains a bounty—an allocation—of Bitcoins. This repetitive guessing, conducted by increasingly complex computers, is called *hashing*. The motivation for mining is clear: to make and earn money.

The Bitcoin software system is designed to release a 25-coin reward to the miner in the worldwide network (any-one, anywhere, can theoretically be a part of the network) who succeeds in solving the mathematical problem. Once solved, the solution is broadcast network-wide, and com-petition for the next 25-coin reward begins. The system's protocol is designed to release a new block of Bitcoins every 10 minutes until all 21 million are released, with the blocks getting smaller as time goes on. If the miners in the net-work take more than 10 minutes to find the correct code, the Bitcoin program adapts to make the mathematics easier. If the miners solve the problems in less than 10 minutes, the mathematical code becomes harder.

The difficulty of the search continually increases over time with mining. This creates an ever-increasing scarcity over time, similar to what many believe about gold when gold was the basis of currency values. But ultimately the Bitcoin system is limited in both time (every 10 minutes) and total issuance (21 million). Theoretically the last of the 21 million Bitcoins would be mined in 2140.

Within a few short years Bitcoin mining has become a big business of its own. Whereas in the early stages an individual could have theoretically mined Bitcoins on a laptop, or theo-retically without a computer at all, that is no longer the case. By 2014, Bitcoin mining had become the object of multi-million dollar investments in computer systems by busi-ness startups from Iceland to Austin in what one journalist described as a "computational arms race." Eleven million of the total potential 21 million coins had been mined.

Users. Once mined, Bitcoins are considered a *pseudonymous*—nearly anonymous—cryptocurrency.[2] Bit-coins are initially issued to the successful miners, who are then able to buy things with them or sell them to non-miners who wish to use digital currency for purchases or speculate on its future value.

Ownership of each and every coin is verified and regis-tered through a digital chain timestamp across the thousands of network nodes. Like cash, this prevents double spend-ing, since every Bitcoin exchange is authenticated across the decentralized Bitcoin network (currently estimated at 20,000 nodes). Unlike cash, every transaction that has ever occurred in the Bitcoin system is recorded in terms of the two public keys (the transactors, the *Bitcoin addresses*) in the system. This record, called the *block chain*, includes the time, amount, and the two near-anonymous IP addresses (public keys are not tied to any person's identity). And unlike credit cards or PayPal, there is no third-party facili-tator. It is true peer-to-peer.

The Bitcoin Foundation, a nonprofit organization, runs the global system. The current Bitcoin Foundation chief scientist is Gavin Andresen, who is paid a salary. The Foun-dation is funded mainly through grants made by for-profit companies (like the Linux Foundation) who either mine or use the Bitcoin system.

Value Drivers and Concerns

Traditional currencies are issued by governments through central banks. They regulate the growth of the currency, its supply, and they also implicitly guarantee its value in some way. Bitcoin has no such guarantor, no insurer, no lender-of-last-resort. If a Bitcoin user were to lose or erase their records of ownership, there would be no support or insurer—no one to sue, no institution to apply to for recourse.[3] The value of a Bitcoin is completely dependent on what users and investors are willing to pay for it at any point in time. This makes it similar in nature to both a cur-rency and a commodity.

Bitcoin is a rather complex composite of currency sys-tems. A gold standard like that used in the first part of the twentieth century, is a system based on *specie*; it has some fixed link to a scarce metal of some intrinsic value. Bitcoin does have digital scarcity, and ultimately a fixed limit on its availability. But Bitcoins have no intrinsic value; they are not composed of a precious metal; they are nothing more than digital code. Their value reflects the supply and demand by those in the marketplace who believe in its value—a *fiat currency*—similar to the world's major currencies today. As illustrated in Exhibit A, that value has been very volatile. After spending several years trading at less than $10 per Bitcoin (using U.S. dollar values, like an exchange rate), its price skyrocketed to $1238 per coin in December 2013—and then plummeted.

The reasons behind Bitcoin's price volatility in 2013 pro-vide some insight into its potential uses. A bank crisis in November 2013 in Cyprus resulted in many Cypriot citizens putting their money into Bitcoins (bidding the price up) in an effort to keep their money out of the hands of gov-ernment. Similarly, in late 2013 Bitcoins surged in interest and use in China. Chinese residents, in search of a way to invest their money outside of China despite Chinese capital controls (restrictions on taking money out of the country), purchased Bitcoins through a number of different Bitcoin exchanges in China, using Chinese renminbi, and then used the Bitcoins to invest abroad. Chinese authorities moved

---

[2]Bitcoin is not the only cryptocurrency or *altcoin*. Competitors include *Litecoin, Ripple, MintChip, Anoncoin, Peercoin*, and *Zerocoin*.
[3]Physical bitcoins, called *Casascius coins*, can be purchased from casascius.com. These coins contain a private key on a card embedded in the coin and sealed with a tamper-evident hologram.

EXHIBIT A   **Bitcoin Price in U.S. Dollars**

Daily close: January 1, 2013 – January 19, 2014

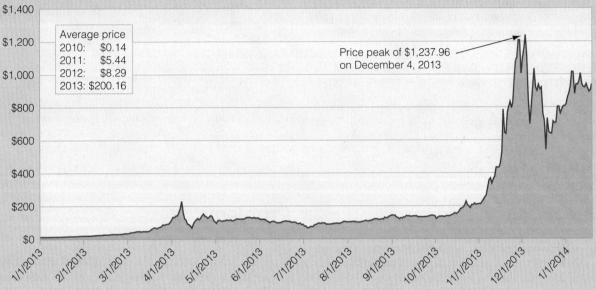

Average price	
2010:	$0.14
2011:	$5.44
2012:	$8.29
2013:	$200.16

Price peak of $1,237.96 on December 4, 2013

---

quickly to shut down the Bitcoin exchanges by prohibiting them from accepting deposits in Chinese renminbi, the local currency.

This ability of Bitcoin to bypass authorities has led to concerns about the potential use of Bitcoin for illicit trade, the laundering of money associated with illegal drugs and other illegal business activity globally. Global government response to this concern has been varied. The German government has officially labeled Bitcoin a *unit of account*. India has raided a number of exchanges thought to be conducting illicit trade using Bitcoin. The United Kingdom has left it alone, as has the EU, to date. South Korea announced that it does not recognize Bitcoin as *legal tender*. Bitcoins are not illegal in the U.S., as the U.S. Constitution actually only prevents the *states* from coining money, but not private parties. The United States Federal Reserve Chairman, Ben Bernanke, when speaking to Congress in November 2013, noted that online currencies "may hold long-term promise, particularly if the innovations promote a faster, more secure, and more efficient payment system."

Examples of expanding acceptance continue to grow: The Pembury Tavern in London; the EVR bar in New York; Cups and Cakes Bakery in San Francisco all accept Bitcoin for purchases. The Sacramento Kings of the National Basketball Association in the U.S. have told their customers that they will start accepting Bitcoin for purchases of tickets and merchandise. Yet, these are still anecdotal examples and in no way constitute acceptance and use as common. Meanwhile many of the world's established financial institutions, banks, have stayed away from digital currency involvement as legal issues over their use worldwide continue to evolve. Wells Fargo, a major U.S. bank, has asked for a 'summit' with Bitcoin activists to learn more.

Bitcoin's promise has had its highs and lows. One low was seen when Bitcoin became the primary currency for sales on *Silk Road*, an underground Web site for illegal drug trafficking. Although eventually shut down by the U.S. government, Bitcoin's potential use for illegal activities has impacted the public's perception of its potential. Others, however, see promise. For example many see the introduction of Bitcoin into Africa as a means of providing institution-free access to financial services for Africa's poor (termed the "Impala Revolution"), removing one of the major barriers to economic development.

So is Bitcoin a currency or a commodity? Is it money? Many, see it as a way to break the rules, others as an opening to a "tsunami of openness." Traditionalists, including the *Financial Times*, do not believe it will work.

Nonetheless, Nakamoto missed a crucial point. A good currency must hold its value over long periods. It must also be readily exchangeable for the goods and services that people actually want. Combining those two functions in a single instrument requires a delicate balance.

If issuance is too tight, there is not enough money moving around to meet the payment needs of the economy. This can lead to deflation and recession. Yet if too much money is issued the result will be inflation, which erodes the currency's value. This is the dilemma that "private money", the creation of banks rather than government authorities, has never been able to solve.

— "Beware the mania for Bitcoin, the tulip of the 21st century," *Financial Times*, January 16, 2014.

Proponents are quick to explain that it does not have to replace all currencies, globally, to be successful. Time will tell.

CASE QUESTIONS

1. What are the costs and benefits of using Bitcoins for transactions?

2. According to economic theory, a true currency must be capable of serving as a unit of account, a medium of exchange, and a store of value. Does Bitcoin fulfill these criteria?

3. Currencies have always been expected to grow, as money, with real economic output. If they were to grow too fast, they fuel inflation; too slow, deflation. What would be Bitcoin's impact, if any, over time?

Questions

1. **MNEs and Operation in Global Markets.** What are the factors that influence the decisions of multinational enterprises to operate in global markets?

2. **Eurocurrencies and Eurocurrency Markets.** What are the major eurocurrencies? What is meant by a eurocurrency market?

3. **MNEs and LIBOR.** Most MNEs either take loans in eurocurrencies or issue eurobonds with a floating coupon rate tied to the LIBOR. Explain how MNEs were affected by the LIBOR scandal.

4. **Theory of Comparative Advantage.** Define and explain the theory of comparative advantage.

5. **Export Subsidies and Comparative Advantage.** Nations often introduce export subsidies in order to support their balance of payments. Explain how export subsidies affect comparative advantage.

6. **Trident's Globalization.** After reading the chapter's description of Trident's globalization process, how would you explain the distinctions between international, multinational, and global companies?

7. **Trident, the MNE.** At what point in the globalization process did Trident become a multinational enterprise (MNE)?

8. **Trident's Advantages.** What are the main advantages that Trident gains by developing a multinational presence?

9. **Trident's Phases.** What are the main phases that Trident passed through as it evolved into a truly global firm? What are the advantages and disadvantages of each?

10. **Financial Globalization.** How do the motivations of individuals, both inside and outside the organization or business, define the limits of financial globalization?

Problems

Comparative Advantage

Problems 1–5 illustrate an example of trade induced by comparative advantage. They assume that China and France each have 1,000 production units. With one unit of production (a mix of land, labor, capital, and technology), China can produce either 10 containers of toys or 7 cases of wine. France can produce either 2 cases of toys or 7 cases of wine. Thus, a production unit in China is five times as efficient compared to France when producing toys, but equally efficient when producing wine. Assume at first that no trade takes place. China allocates 800 production units to building toys and 200 production units to producing wine. France allocates 200 production units to building toys and 800 production units to producing wine.

1. **Production and Consumption.** What is the production and consumption of China and France without trade?

2. **Specialization.** Assume complete specialization, where China produces only toys and France produces only wine. What would be the effect on total production?

3. **Trade at China's Domestic Price.** China's domestic price is 10 containers of toys equals 7 cases of wine. Assume China produces 10,000 containers of toys and exports 2,000 to France. Assume France produces 7,000 cases of wine and exports 1,400 cases to China. What happens to total production and consumption?

4. **Trade at France's Domestic Price.** France's domestic price is 2 containers of toys equals 7 cases of wine. Assume China produces 10,000 containers of toys and exports 400 containers to France. Assume France in turn produces 7,000 cases of wine and exports 1,400 cases to China. What happens to total production and consumption?

5. Trade at Negotiated Mid-Price. The mid-price for exchange between France and China can be calculated as follows. What happens to total production and consumption?

Assumptions	Toys (containers/unit)	Wine (cases/unit)
China—output per unit of production input	10	7
France—output per unit of production input	2	7
China—total production inputs	1,000	
France—total production inputs	1,000	

EuroVirtual

Problems 6–10 are based on EuroVirtual, a French-based multinational IT firm. In addition to its home operations in France, EuroVirtual owns and operates subsidiaries in Switzerland, the United Kingdom, and Denmark. It has 650,000 shares currently outstanding on the pan-European stock exchange, Euronext. The following table summarizes the business performance of EuroVirtual:

	French Parent Company (euros, €)	Swiss Subsidiary (Swiss franc, CHF)	U.K. Subsidiary (British Pound, GBP)	Danish Subsidiary (Danish krone, DKK)
Earnings before taxes (EBT) in 000s of domestic currency	EUR2,500	CHF400	GBP2,100	DKK4,500
Corporate income tax rate	33.3%	25%	20%	23%
Average cross rate per EUR1	—	1.0335	0.7415	7.4642

6. EuroVirtual's Consolidated Earnings. EuroVirtual pays different tax rates for each of its country operations.
   a. What are its earnings per share in EUR after deducting taxes?
   b. What is the proportion of EuroVirtual's consolidated EBT that arises from each country?
   c. What is the proportion of income generated outside France?

7. EuroVirtual's EPS Sensitivity to Exchange Rates (A). On January 15, 2015 the Swiss National Bank (SNB) decided to unpeg the franc, which was fixed at CHF1.20/€ since 2011. Suppose the SNB was to reverse its decision and readopt the previous peg. How would this affect the consolidated EPS of EuroVirtual if all other exchange rates, tax rates, and earnings remain unchanged?

8. EuroVirtual's EPS Sensitivity to Exchange Rates (B). Assume a major weather crisis hits Switzerland, reducing its agricultural and food industries and subsequently leading to a macroeconomic recession, and by extension weakening the Swiss franc. What would be the impact on EuroVirtual's consolidated EPS if, in addition to the fall in the value of the franc to CHF 1.2/€, earnings before taxes in Switzerland fell as a result of the recession by half?

9. EuroVirtual's EPS and Euro Appreciation/ Depreciation. Since its introduction in 2003, the euro has been fluctuating against major global currencies.
   a. What is the impact of 15% appreciation of all major currencies against the euro on the consolidated EPS of EuroVirtual?
   b. What is the impact of 20% depreciation of all major currencies against the euro on the consolidated EPS of EuroVirtual?

10. EuroVirtual's Global Taxation and Effective Tax Rate. All MNEs attempt to minimize their global tax liabilities. Return to the original set of baseline assumptions and answer the following questions regarding EuroVirtual's global tax liabilities:
   a. What is the total corporate income tax that EuroVirtual pays for all its operations in euros?
   b. What is its effective tax rate (total taxes paid as a percentage of pre-tax earnings)?
   c. Suppose the United Kingdom decides to reduce its corporate tax rate to 10%, leading to a rise in EuroVirtual's British subsidiary's earnings before tax to GBP3,000,000. What would be the impact on EuroVirtual's EPS?

Internet Exercises

1. International Capital Flows: Public and Private. Major multinational organizations (some of which are listed next) attempt to track the relative movements and magnitudes of global capital investment. Using these Web pages and others you may find, prepare a two-page executive briefing on the question of whether capital generated in the industrialized countries is finding its way to the less-developed and emerging markets. Is there some critical distinction between "less-developed" and "emerging"?

The World Bank	www.worldbank.org
OECD	www.oecd.org
European Bank for Reconstruction and Development	www.ebrd.org

2. **External Debt.** The World Bank regularly compiles and analyzes the external debt of all countries globally. As part of their annual publication on World Development Indicators (WDI), they provide summaries of the long-term and short-term external debt obligations of selected countries online like that of Poland shown here. Go to their Web site and find the decomposition of external debt for Brazil, Mexico, and the Russian Federation.

| The World Bank | www.worldbank.org/data |

3. **World Economic Outlook.** The International Monetary Fund (IMF) regularly publishes its assessment of the prospects for the world economy. Choose a country of interest and use the IMF's current analysis to form your own expectations of its immediate economic prospects.

| IMF Economic Outlook | www.imf.org/external/index .htm |

4. ***Financial Times* Currency Global Macromaps.** The *Financial Times* provides a very helpful real-time global map of currency values and movements online. Use it to track the movements in currency.

| *Financial Times* | http://markets.ft.com/ research/Markets/Currencies |

The International Monetary System

The price of every thing rises and falls from time to time and place to place; and with every such change the purchasing power of money changes so far as that thing goes. —Alfred Marshall.

CHAPTER 2

LEARNING OBJECTIVES

- Learn how the international monetary system has evolved from the days of the gold standard to today's eclectic currency arrangement
- Analyze the characteristics of an ideal currency
- Explain the currency regime choices faced by emerging market countries
- Examine how the euro, a single currency for the European Union, was created

This chapter begins with a brief history of the international monetary system, from the days of the classical gold standard to the present time. The first section describes contemporary currency regimes and their construction and classification, fixed versus flexible exchange rate principles, and what we would consider the theoretical core of the chapter—the attributes of the ideal currency. The second section describes the introduction of the euro and the path toward monetary unification, including the continuing expansion of the European Union. The third section analyzes the regime choices of emerging markets. The fourth and final section analyzes the trade-offs between exchange rate regimes based on rules, discretion, cooperation, and independence. The chapter concludes with the Mini-Case, *Russian Ruble Roulette*, which examines the recent change in how one country manages its currency's value.

History of the International Monetary System

Over the centuries, currencies have been defined in terms of gold, silver, and other items of value, all within a variety of different agreements between nations to recognize these varying definitions. A review of the evolution of these systems—or eras as we refer to them in Exhibit 2.1—provides a useful perspective against which to understand today's rather eclectic system of fixed rates, floating rates, crawling pegs, and others, and it helps us to evaluate weaknesses in and challenges for governments and business enterprises conducting global business.

The Gold Standard, 1876–1913

Since the days of the pharaohs (about 3000 B.C.), gold has served as a medium of exchange and a store of value. The Greeks and Romans used gold coins, and they passed on this tradition through the mercantile era to the nineteenth century. The great increase in trade

| EXHIBIT 2.1 | The Evolution of Capital Mobility |

Exchange Rate Era	The Gold Standard	The Inter-War Years	The Bretton Woods Era	The Floating Era	The Emerging Era
Cross-Border Political Economy	Growing openness in trade, with growing, but limited, capital mobility	Protectionism and isolationism	Growing belief in the benefits of open economies	Industrialized (primary) nations open; emerging states (secondary) restrict capital flows to maintain economic control	More and more emerging nations open their markets to capital at the expense of reduced economic independence
Implication	Trade dominates capital in total influence on exchange rates	Rising barriers to the movement of both trade and capital	Trade increasingly dominated by capital; era ends as capital flows	Capital flows dominate trade; emerging nations suffer devaluations	Capital flows increasingly drive economic growth and health

1860 → 1914 → 1945 → 1971 → 1997 → Present

The last 150 years has seen periods of increasing and decreasing political and economic openness between countries. Beginning with the Bretton Woods Era, global markets have moved toward increasing open exchange of goods and capital, making it increasingly difficult to maintain fixed or even stable rates of exchange between currencies. The most recent era, characterized by the growth and development of emerging economies is likely to be even more challenging.

during the free-trade period of the late nineteenth century led to a need for a more formalized system for settling international trade balances. One country after another set a par value for its currency in terms of gold and then tried to adhere to the so-called "rules of the game." This later came to be known as the classical gold standard. The *gold standard*, as an international monetary system, gained acceptance in Western Europe in the 1870s. The United States was something of a latecomer to the system, not officially adopting the gold standard until 1879.

Under the gold standard, the "rules of the game" were clear and simple: Each country set the rate at which its currency unit (paper or coin) could be converted to a given weight of gold. The United States, for example, declared the dollar to be convertible to gold at a rate of $20.67 per ounce (this rate was in effect until the beginning of World War I). The British pound was pegged at £4.2474 per ounce of gold. As long as both currencies were freely convertible into gold, the dollar/pound exchange rate was

$$\frac{\$20.67/\text{Ounce of Gold}}{£4.2474/\text{Ounce of Gold}} = \$4.8665/£$$

Because the government of each country on the gold standard agreed to buy or sell gold on demand at its own fixed parity rate, the value of each individual currency in terms of gold, and therefore exchange rates between currencies, was fixed. Maintaining reserves of gold that were sufficient to back its currency's value was very important for a country under this system. The system also had the effect of implicitly limiting the rate at which any individual country could expand its money supply. Growth in the money supply was limited to the rate at which official authorities (government treasuries or central banks) could acquire additional gold.

The gold standard worked adequately until the outbreak of World War I interrupted trade flows and the free movement of gold. This event caused the main trading nations to suspend operation of the gold standard.

The Interwar Years and World War II, 1914–1944

During World War I and through the early 1920s, currencies were allowed to fluctuate over fairly wide ranges in terms of gold and in relation to each other. Theoretically, supply and demand for a country's exports and imports caused moderate changes in an exchange rate about a central equilibrium value. This was the same function that gold had performed under the previous gold standard. Unfortunately, such flexible exchange rates did not work in an equilibrating manner. On the contrary: international speculators sold the weak currencies short, causing them to fall further in value than warranted by real economic factors. *Selling short* is a speculation technique in which an individual speculator sells an asset, such as a currency, to another party for delivery at a future date. The speculator, however, does not yet own the asset and expects the price of the asset to fall before the date by which the speculator must purchase the asset in the open market for delivery.

The reverse happened with strong currencies. Fluctuations in currency values could not be offset by the relatively illiquid forward exchange market, except at exorbitant cost. The net result was that the volume of world trade did not grow in the 1920s in proportion to world gross domestic product. Instead, it declined to a very low level with the advent of the Great Depression in the 1930s.

The United States adopted a modified gold standard in 1934 when the U.S. dollar was devalued to $35 per ounce of gold from the $20.67 per ounce price in effect prior to World War I. Contrary to previous practice, the U.S. Treasury traded gold only with foreign central banks, not private citizens. From 1934 to the end of World War II, exchange rates were theoretically determined by each currency's value in terms of gold. During World War II and its chaotic aftermath, however, many of the main trading currencies lost their convertibility into other currencies. The dollar was one of the few currencies that continued to be convertible.

Bretton Woods and the International Monetary Fund, 1944

As World War II drew to a close in 1944, the Allied Powers met at Bretton Woods, New Hampshire, to create a new postwar international monetary system. The Bretton Woods Agreement established a U.S. dollar-based international monetary system and provided for two new institutions: the International Monetary Fund and the World Bank. The *International Monetary Fund* (IMF) aids countries with balance of payments and exchange rate problems. The *International Bank for Reconstruction and Development (World Bank)* helped fund postwar reconstruction and has since supported general economic development. *Global Finance in Practice 2.1* provides some insight into the debates at Bretton Woods.

The IMF was the key institution in the new international monetary system, and it has remained so to the present day. The IMF was established to render temporary assistance to member countries trying to defend their currencies against cyclical, seasonal, or random occurrences. It also assists countries having structural trade problems if they promise to take adequate steps to correct their problems. If persistent deficits occur, however, the

GLOBAL FINANCE IN PRACTICE 2.1

Hammering Out an Agreement at Bretton Woods

The governments of the Allied powers knew that the devastating impacts of World War II would require swift and decisive policies. In the summer of 1944 (July 1–22), a full year before the end of the war, representatives of all 45 allied nations met at Bretton Woods, New Hampshire, for the United Nations Monetary and Financial Conference. Their purpose was to plan the postwar international monetary system. It was a difficult process, and the final synthesis was shaded by pragmatism.

The leading policymakers at Bretton Woods were the British and the Americans. The British delegation was led by Lord John Maynard Keynes, known as "Britain's economic heavyweight." The British argued for a postwar system that would be more flexible than the various gold standards used before the war. Keynes argued, as he had after World War I, that attempts to tie currency values to gold would create pressures for deflation in many of the war-ravaged economies.

The American delegation was led by the director of the U.S. Treasury's monetary research department, Harry D. White, and the U.S. Secretary of the Treasury, Henry Morgenthau, Jr. The Americans argued for stability (fixed exchange rates) but not a return to the gold standard itself. In fact, although the U.S. at that time held most of the gold of the Allied powers, the U.S. delegates argued that currencies should be fixed in parities,[1] but that redemption of gold should occur only between official authorities like central banks.

On the more pragmatic side, all parties agreed that a postwar system would be stable and sustainable only if there was sufficient credit available for countries to defend their currencies in the event of payment imbalances, which they knew to be inevitable in a reconstructing world order.

The conference divided into three commissions for weeks of negotiation. One commission, led by U.S. Treasury Secretary Morgenthau, was charged with the organization of a fund of capital to be used for exchange rate stabilization. A second commission, chaired by Lord Keynes, was charged with the organization of a second "bank" whose purpose would be for long-term reconstruction and development. A third commission was to hammer out details such as what role silver would have in any new system.

After weeks of meetings, the participants came to a three-part agreement—the Bretton Woods Agreement. The plan called for: 1) fixed exchange rates, termed an "adjustable peg," among members; 2) a fund of gold and constituent currencies available to members for stabilization of their respective currencies, called the International Monetary Fund (IMF); and 3) a bank for financing long-term development projects (eventually known as the World Bank). One proposal resulting from the meetings, which was not ratified by the United States, was the establishment of an international trade organization to promote free trade.

[1]*Fixed in parities* is an old expression in this field, which means that the value of currencies should be set or fixed at rates that equalize their value, typically purchasing power.

IMF cannot save a country from eventual devaluation. In recent years, it has attempted to help countries facing financial crises. It has provided massive loans as well as advice to Russia and other former Russian republics, Brazil, Indonesia, and South Korea, to name but a few.

Under the original provisions of the Bretton Woods Agreement, all countries fixed the value of their currencies in terms of gold but were not required to exchange their currencies for gold. Only the dollar remained convertible into gold (at $35 per ounce). Therefore, each country established its exchange rate vis-à-vis the dollar, and then calculated the gold par value of its currency to create the desired dollar exchange rate. Participating countries agreed to try to maintain the value of their currencies within 1% (later expanded to 2.25%) of par by buying or selling foreign exchange or gold as needed. Devaluation was not to be used as a competitive trade policy, but if a currency became too weak to defend, devaluation of up to 10% was allowed without formal approval by the IMF. Larger devaluations required IMF approval. This became known as the *gold-exchange standard.*

An additional innovation introduced by the Bretton Woods Agreement was the creation of the *Special Drawing Right* or SDR. The SDR is an international reserve asset created by the IMF to supplement existing foreign exchange reserves. It serves as a unit of account for the IMF and other international and regional organizations. It is also the base against which some countries peg the exchange rate for their currencies. Initially defined in terms of a fixed quantity of gold, the SDR is currently the weighted average of four major currencies: the U.S. dollar, the euro, the Japanese yen, and the British pound. The weights assigned to each currency are updated every five years by the IMF. Individual countries hold SDRs in the form of deposits in the IMF. These holdings are part of each country's international monetary reserves, along with its official holdings of gold, its foreign exchange, and its reserve position at the IMF. Member countries may settle transactions among themselves by transferring SDRs.

Fixed Exchange Rates, 1945–1973

The currency arrangement negotiated at Bretton Woods and monitored by the IMF worked fairly well during the post-World War II period of reconstruction and rapid growth in world trade. However, widely diverging national monetary and fiscal policies, differential rates of inflation, and various unexpected external shocks eventually resulted in the system's demise. The U.S. dollar was the main reserve currency held by central banks and was the key to the web of exchange rate values. Unfortunately, the United States ran persistent and growing deficits in its balance of payments. A heavy capital outflow of dollars was required to finance these deficits and to meet the growing demand for dollars from investors and businesses. Eventually, the heavy overhang of dollars held by foreigners resulted in a lack of confidence in the ability of the United States to meet its commitment to convert dollars to gold.

This lack of confidence came to a head in the first half of 1971. In a little less than seven months, the United States suffered the loss of nearly one-third of its official gold reserves as global confidence in the value of the dollar plummeted. Exchange rates between most major currencies and the U.S. dollar began to float, and thus indirectly, their values relative to gold. A year and a half later, the U.S. dollar once again came under attack, thereby forcing a second devaluation on February 12, 1973; this time by 10% to $42.22 per ounce of gold. By late February 1973, a fixed-rate system no longer appeared feasible given the speculative flows of currencies. The major foreign exchange markets were actually closed for several weeks in March 1973. When they reopened, most currencies were allowed to float to levels determined by market forces. Par values were left unchanged. The dollar floated downward an average of another 10% by June 1973.

The Floating Era, 1973–1997

Since March 1973, exchange rates have become much more volatile and less predictable than they were during the "fixed" exchange rate period, when changes occurred infrequently. Exhibit 2.2 illustrates the wide swings exhibited by the nominal exchange rate index of the U.S. dollar since 1964. Clearly, volatility has increased for this currency measure since 1973.

Exhibit 2.3 summarizes the key events and external shocks that have affected currency values since August 1971. The most important shocks in recent years have been the *European*

EXHIBIT 2.2   **The BIS Exchange Rate Index of the Dollar**

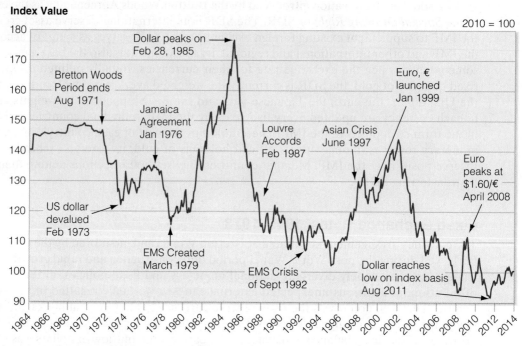

Source: BIS.org. Nominal exchange rate index for the U.S. dollar.

Monetary System (EMS) restructuring in 1992 and 1993; the emerging market currency crises, including that of Mexico in 1994, Thailand (and a number of other Asian currencies) in 1997, Russia in 1998, and Brazil in 1999; the introduction of the euro in 1999; and the currency crises and changes in Argentina and Venezuela in 2002.

The Emerging Era, 1997–Present

The period following the Asian Crisis of 1997 has seen growth in both breadth and depth of emerging market economies and currencies. We may end up being proven wrong on this count, but the final section of this chapter argues that the global monetary system has already begun embracing—for over a decade now—a number of major emerging market currencies, beginning with the Chinese renminbi. Feel free to disagree.

IMF Classification of Currency Regimes

The global monetary system—if there is indeed a singular "system"—is an eclectic combination of exchange rate regimes and arrangements. Although there is no single governing body, the International Monetary Fund (IMF) has at least played the role of "town crier" since World War II. We present its current classification system of currency regimes here.

EXHIBIT 2.3	World Currency Events, 1971–2014

Date	Event	Impact
August 1971	Dollar floated	Nixon closes the U.S. gold window, suspending purchases or sales of gold by U.S. Treasury; temporary imposition of 10% import surcharge
December 1971	Smithsonian Agreement	Group of Ten reaches compromise whereby the US$ is devalued to $38/oz. of gold; most other major currencies are appreciated versus US$
February 1973	U.S. dollar devalued	Devaluation pressure increases on US$, forcing further devaluation to $42.22/oz. of gold
February–March 1973	Currency markets in crisis	Fixed exchange rates no longer considered defensible; speculative pressures force closure of international foreign exchange markets for nearly two weeks; markets reopen on floating rates for major industrial currencies
June 1973	U.S. dollar depreciation	Floating rates continue to drive the now freely floating US$ down by about 10% by June
Fall 1973–1974	OPEC oil embargo	Organization of Petroleum Exporting Countries (OPEC) impose oil embargo, eventually quadrupling the world price of oil; because world oil prices are stated in US$, value of US$ recovers some former strength
January 1976	Jamaica Agreement	IMF meeting in Jamaica results in the "legalization" of the floating exchange rate system already in effect; gold is demonetized as a reserve asset
1977–1978	U.S. inflation rate rises	Carter administration reduces unemployment at the expense of inflation increases; rising U.S. inflation causes continued depreciation of the US$
March 1979	EMS created	The European Monetary System (EMS) is created, establishing a cooperative exchange rate system for participating members of the European Economic Community (EEC)
Summer 1979	OPEC raises prices	OPEC nations raise price of oil again
Spring 1980	U.S. dollar begins rise	Worldwide inflation and early signs of recession coupled with real interest differential advantages for dollar-denominated assets contribute to increased demand for dollars
August 1982	Latin American debt crisis	Mexico informs U.S. Treasury on Friday 13, 1982, that it will be unable to make debt service payments; Brazil and Argentina follow within months
February 1985	U.S. dollar peaks	The US$ peaks against most major industrial currencies, hitting record highs against the deutsche mark and other European currencies
September 1985	Plaza Agreement	Group of Ten members meet at the Plaza Hotel in New York City to sign an international cooperative agreement to control the volatility of world currency markets and to establish target zones
February 1987	Louvre Accords	Group of Six members state they will "intensify" economic policy coordination to promote growth and reduce external imbalances
December 1991	Maastricht Treaty	European Union concludes a treaty to replace all individual currencies with a single currency—the euro
September 1992	EMS crisis	High German interest rates induce massive capital flows into deutsche mark-denominated assets, causing the withdrawal of the Italian lira and British pound from the EMS common float
July 1993	EMS realignment	EMS adjusts allowable deviation band for all member countries (except the Dutch guilder); US$ continues to weaken; Japanese yen reaches ¥ 100.25/$
1994	EMI founded	European Monetary Institute (EMI), the predecessor to the European Central Bank, is founded in Frankfurt, Germany
December 1994	Peso collapse	Mexican peso suffers major devaluation as a result of increasing pressure on the managed devaluation policy; peso falls from Ps3.46/$ to Ps5.50/$ within days; the peso's collapse results in a fall in most major Latin American exchanges in a contagion process—the "tequila effect"
August 1995	Yen peaks	Japanese yen reaches an all-time high versus the US$ of ¥79/$; yen slowly depreciates over the following two-year period, rising to over ¥130/$

(continued)

| EXHIBIT 2.3 | World Currency Events, 1971–2014 (continued) |

Date	Event	Impact
June 1997	Asian crisis	The Thai baht is devalued in July, followed soon after by the Indonesian rupiah, Korean won, Malaysian ringgit, and Philippine peso; following the initial exchange rate devaluations, the Asian economy plummets into recession
August 1998	Russian crisis	On Monday, August 17, the Russian Central Bank devalues the ruble by 34%; the ruble continues to deteriorate in the following days, sending the already weak Russian economy into recession
January 1999	Euro launched	Official launch date for the euro, the single European currency; 11 European Union member states elect to participate in the system, which irrevocably locks their individual currencies rates among them
January 1999	Brazilian reais crisis	The reais, initially devalued 8.3% by the Brazilian government on January 12, is allowed to float against the world's currencies
January 2002	Euro coinage	Euro coins and notes are introduced in parallel with home currencies; national currencies are phased out during the six-month period beginning January 1
January 8, 2002	Argentine peso crisis	The Argentine peso, its value fixed to the US$ at 1:1 since 1991 through a currency board, is devalued to Ps1.4/$, then floated
February 13, 2002	Venezuelan bolivar floated	The Venezuelan bolivar, fixed to the US$ since 1996, is floated as a result of increasing economic crisis
Feburary 14, 2004	Venezuelan bolivar devalued	Venezuela devalues the bolivar by 17% versus the US$, to deal with its growing fiscal deficit
May 2004	EU enlargement	Ten more countries join the European Union, thereby enlarging it to 25 members; in the future, when they qualify, most of these countries are expected to adopt the euro
July 21, 2005	Yuan reform	The Chinese government and the People's Bank of China abandon the peg of the Chinese yuan (renminbi) to the US$, announcing that it will be instantly revalued from Yuan8.28/$ to Yuan8.11/$, and reform the exchange rate regime to a managed float in the future; Malaysia announces a similar change to its exchange rate regime
April 2008	Euro peaks	The euro peaks in strength against the US$ at $1.60/€. In the following months the euro falls substantially, hitting $1.25/€ by late 2008
Fall 2011	Greek/EU debt crisis	Rising fears over the future of the euro revolve around the mounting public debt levels of Greece, Portugal, and Ireland
January 2014	Emerging market downgrades	Multitude of emerging markets currencies (Argentina, Venezuela, India, and Libya) suffer significant capital flight as US$ interest rates rise and emerging market economies slow

Brief Classification History

The IMF was for many years the central clearinghouse for exchange rate classifications. Member states submitted their exchange rate policies to the IMF, and those submissions were the basis for its categorization of exchange rate regimes. However, that all changed in 1997–1998 with the Asian Financial Crisis. During the Asian Financial Crisis, many countries began following very different exchange rate practices than those they had committed to with the IMF. Their actual practices—their *de facto* systems—were not what they had publicly and officially committed to—their *de jure* systems.

Beginning in 1998 the IMF changed its practice and stopped collecting regime classification submissions from member states. Instead, it confined its regime classifications and reports to analysis performed in-house.[1] As a global institution, which is in principle apolitical, the

[1]This included the cessation of publishing its *Annual Report on Exchange Arrangements and Exchange Restrictions*, a document on which much of the financial industry depended for decades.

IMF's analysis today is focused on classifying currencies on the basis of an *ex post* analysis of how the currency's value was based in the recent past. This analysis focuses on observed behavior, not on official government policy pronouncements.

The IMF's 2009 *de facto* System

The IMF's methodology of classifying exchange rate regimes today, in effect since January 2009, is presented in Exhibit 2.4. It is based on actual observed behavior, *de facto* results, and not on the official policy statements of the respective governments, *de jure*

EXHIBIT 2.4   IMF Exchange Rate Classifications

Rate Classification	2009 *de facto* System	Description and Requirements	Countries
Hard Pegs	Arrangement with no separate legal tender	The currency of another country circulates as the sole legal tender (formal *dollarization*), as well as members of a monetary or currency union in which the same legal tender is shared by the members.	10
	Currency board arrangement	A monetary arrangement based on an explicit legislative commitment to exchange domestic currency for a specific foreign currency at a fixed exchange rate, combined with restrictions on the issuing authority. Restrictions imply that domestic currency will be issued only against foreign exchange and that it remains fully backed by foreign assets.	13
Soft Pegs	Conventional pegged arrangement	A country formally pegs its currency at a fixed rate to another currency or a basket of currencies of major financial or trading partners. Country authorities stand ready to maintain the fixed parity through direct or indirect intervention. The exchange rate may vary $\pm 1\%$ around a central rate, or may vary no more than 2% for a six-month period.	45
	Stabilized arrangement	A spot market rate that remains within a margin of 2% for six months or more and is not floating. Margin stability can be met by either a single currency or basket of currencies (assuming statistical measurement). Exchange rate remains stable as a result of official action.	22
	Intermediate pegs:		
	Crawling peg	Currency is adjusted in small amounts at a fixed rate or in response to changes in quantitative indicators (e.g., inflation differentials).	5
	Crawl-like arrangement	Exchange rate must remain with a narrow margin of 2% relative to a statistically defined trend for six months or more. Exchange rate cannot be considered floating. Minimum rate of change is greater than allowed under a stabilized arrangement.	3
	Pegged exchange rate within horizontal bands	The value of the currency is maintained within certain margins of fluctuation of at least $\pm 1\%$ around a fixed central rate, or the margin between the maximum and minimum value of the exchange rate exceeds 2%. This includes countries which are today members of the Exchange Rate Mechanism II (ERM II) system.	3
Floating Arrangements	Floating	Exchange rate is largely market determined without an ascertainable or predictable path. Market intervention may be direct or indirect, and serves to moderate the rate of change (but not targeting). Rate may exhibit more or less volatility.	39
	Free floating	A floating rate is freely floating if intervention occurs only exceptionally, and confirmation of intervention is limited to at most three instances in a six-month period, each lasting no more than three business days.	36
Residual	Other managed arrangements	This category is residual, and is used when the exchange rate does not meet the criteria for any other category. Arrangements characterized by frequent shifts in policies fall into this category.	12

Source: "Revised System for the Classification of Exchange Rate Arrangements," by Karl Habermeier, Anamaria Kokenyne, Romain Veyrune, and Harald Anderson, IMF Working Paper WP/09/211, International Monetary Fund, November 17, 2009. Classification includes 188 countries at the time of publication.

classification.[2] The classification process begins with the determination of whether the exchange rate of the country's currency is dominated by markets or by official action. Although the classification system is a bit challenging, there are four basic categories.

Category 1: Hard Pegs. These countries have given up their own sovereignty over monetary policy. This category includes countries that have adopted other country's currencies (e.g., Zimbabwe's adoption of the U.S. dollar, *dollarization*), and countries utilizing a currency board structure that limits monetary expansion to the accumulation of foreign exchange.

Category 2: Soft Pegs. This general category is colloquially referred to as *fixed exchange rates*. The five subcategories of soft peg regimes are differentiated on the basis of what the currency is fixed to, whether that fix is allowed to change—and if so under what conditions, what types, magnitudes, and frequencies of intervention are allowed/used, and the degree of variance about the fixed rate.

Category 3: Floating Arrangements. Currencies that are predominantly market-driven are further subdivided into free floating with values determined by open market forces without governmental influence or intervention, and simple floating or floating with intervention, where government occasionally does intervene in the market in pursuit of some rate goals or objectives.

Category 4: Residual. As one would suspect, this category includes all exchange rate arrangements that do not meet the criteria of the previous three categories. Country systems demonstrating frequent shifts in policy typically make up the bulk of this category.

Exhibit 2.5 provides a glimpse as to what these major regime categories translate into in the global market—fixed or floating. (The IMF's category 4 is truly *residual*, often characterized as 'who knows?', and is not explicitly shown in the exhibit.) The vertical dashed line, the *crawling peg*, is the zone some currencies move into and out of depending on their relative currency stability. Although the classification regimes appear clear and distinct, the distinctions are often more difficult to distinguish in practice in the market. For example, in January 2014, the Bank of Russia announced it would no longer conduct intervention activities with regard to the value of the ruble and that it planned to allow the ruble to trade freely, with no intervention, by 2015. Time will tell.

A Global Eclectic

Despite the IMF's attempt to lend rigor to regime classifications, the global monetary system today is indeed a global eclectic in every sense of the term. As Chapter 5 will describe in detail, the current global market in currency is dominated by two major currencies, the U.S. dollar and the European euro, and after that, a multitude of systems, arrangements, currency areas, and zones.

The euro itself is an example of a rigidly fixed system, acting as a single currency for its member countries. However, the euro is also an independently floating currency against all other currencies. Other examples of rigidly fixed exchange regimes include Ecuador, Panama, and Zimbabwe, which use the U.S. dollar as their official currency; the Central African Franc (CFA) zone, in which countries such as Mali, Niger, Senegal, Cameroon, and Chad among others use a single common currency (the franc, which is tied to the euro); and the Eastern Caribbean Currency Union (ECCU), a set of countries that use the Eastern Caribbean dollar.

---

[2]"Revised System for the Classification of Exchange Rate Arrangements," by Karl Habermeier, Annamaria Kokenyne, Romain Veyrune, and Harald Anderson, Monetary and Capital Markets Department, IMF Working Paper 09/211, November 17, 2009. The system presented is a revision of the IMF's 1998 revision to a *de facto* system.

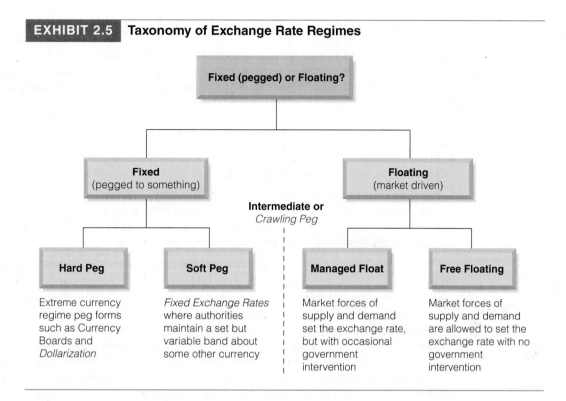

EXHIBIT 2.5   Taxonomy of Exchange Rate Regimes

At the other extreme are countries with independently floating currencies. These include many of the most developed countries, such as Japan, the United States, the United Kingdom, Canada, Australia, New Zealand, Sweden, and Switzerland. However, this category also includes a number of unwilling participants—emerging market countries that tried to maintain fixed rates but were forced by the marketplace to let them float. Among these are Korea, the Philippines, Brazil, Indonesia, Mexico, and Thailand.

It is important to note that only the last two categories, managed floats and free floats (applying to only half of the 188 countries covered), are actually "floating" to any real degree. Although the contemporary international monetary system is typically referred to as a "floating regime," it is clearly not the case for the majority of the world's nations. And as illustrated by the press release in *Global Finance in Practice 2.2* regarding the Swiss franc, even the world's most stable currencies have to "manage" their values on occasion.

GLOBAL FINANCE IN PRACTICE 2.2

Swiss National Bank Sets Minimum Exchange Rate for the Franc

The current massive overvaluation of the Swiss franc (symbol CHF) poses an acute threat to the Swiss economy and carries the risk of a deflationary development. The Swiss National Bank (SNB) is therefore aiming for a substantial and sustained weakening of the Swiss franc. With immediate effect, it will no longer tolerate a EUR/CHF exchange rate below the minimum rate of CHF 1.20. The SNB will enforce this minimum rate with the utmost determination and is prepared to buy foreign currency in unlimited quantities.

Even at a rate of CHF 1.20 per euro, the Swiss franc is still high and should continue to weaken over time. If the economic outlook and deflationary risks so require, the SNB will take further measures.

Source: "Swiss National Bank sets minimum exchange rate at CHF 1.20 per euro," Communications Press Release, Swiss National Bank, Zurich, 6 September 2011.

Fixed versus Flexible Exchange Rates

A nation's choice as to which currency regime to follow reflects national priorities about all facets of the economy, including inflation, unemployment, interest rate levels, trade balances, and economic growth. The choice between fixed and flexible rates may change over time as priorities change. At the risk of overgeneralizing, the following points partly explain why countries pursue certain exchange rate regimes. They are based on the premise that, other things being equal, countries would prefer fixed exchange rates.

■ Fixed rates provide stability in international prices for the conduct of trade. Stable prices aid in the growth of international trade and lessen risks for all businesses.

■ Fixed exchange rates are inherently anti-inflationary, requiring the country to follow restrictive monetary and fiscal policies. This restrictiveness, however, can often be a burden to a country wishing to pursue policies that alleviate continuing internal economic problems, such as high unemployment or slow economic growth.

Fixed exchange rate regimes necessitate that central banks maintain large quantities of international reserves (hard currencies and gold) for use in the occasional defense of the fixed rate. As international currency markets have grown rapidly in size and volume, increasing reserve holdings has become a significant burden to many nations.

Fixed rates, once in place, may be maintained at levels that are inconsistent with economic fundamentals. As the structure of a nation's economy changes, and as its trade relationships and balances evolve, the exchange rate itself should change. Flexible exchange rates allow this to happen gradually and efficiently, but fixed rates must be changed administratively—usually too late, with too much publicity, and at too large a one-time cost to the nation's economic health.

The terminology associated with changes in currency values is also technically specific. When a government officially declares its own currency to be worth less or more relative to other currencies, it is termed a *devaluation* or *revaluation*, respectively. This obviously applies to currencies whose value is controlled by government. When a currency's value is changed in the open currency market—not directly by government—it is called a *depreciation* (with a fall in value) or *appreciation* (with an increase in value).

The Impossible Trinity

If the ideal currency existed in today's world, it would possess the following three attributes (illustrated in Exhibit 2.6), often referred to as the impossible trinity:

1. **Exchange rate stability**. The value of the currency would be fixed in relationship to other major currencies, so traders and investors could be relatively certain of the foreign exchange value of each currency in the present and into the near future.

2. **Full financial integration**. Complete freedom of monetary flows would be allowed, so traders and investors could easily move funds from one country and currency to another in response to perceived economic opportunities or risks.

3. **Monetary independence**. Domestic monetary and interest rate policies would be set by each individual country to pursue desired national economic policies, especially as they might relate to limiting inflation, combating recessions, and fostering prosperity and full employment.

These qualities are termed the *impossible trinity* (also referred to as the *trilemma of international finance*) because the forces of economics do not allow a country to simultaneously achieve all three goals: monetary independence, exchange rate stability, and full financial integration.

EXHIBIT 2.6   **The Impossible Trinity**

All countries must implicitly decide which of the Trinity Elements they wish to pursue, and therefore which element they must give up (you can't have all three).

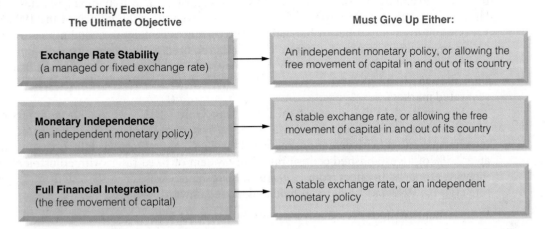

Trinity Element: The Ultimate Objective	Must Give Up Either:
Exchange Rate Stability (a managed or fixed exchange rate)	An independent monetary policy, or allowing the free movement of capital in and out of its country
Monetary Independence (an independent monetary policy)	A stable exchange rate, or allowing the free movement of capital in and out of its country
Full Financial Integration (the free movement of capital)	A stable exchange rate, or an independent monetary policy

In recent years, with the increasing deregulation of capital markets and capital controls around the globe, more countries are opting to pursue *Full Financial Integration*. The results are as theory would predict: more currency volatility and less independence in the conduct of monetary policy.

As described in Exhibit 2.6, the consensus of many experts is that the force of increased capital mobility has been pushing more and more countries toward full financial integration in an attempt to stimulate their domestic economies and feed the capital appetites of their own MNEs. As a result, their currency regimes are being "cornered" into being either purely floating (like the United States) or integrated with other countries in monetary unions (like the European Union). *Global Finance in Practice 2.3* drives this debate home.

GLOBAL FINANCE IN PRACTICE 2.3

Who Is Choosing What in the Trinity/ Trilemma?

The global financial crisis of 2008–2009 sparked much debate over the value of currencies—in some cases invoking what one academic termed "currency wars." With most of the non-Chinese world suffering very slow economic growth, and under heavy pressure to stimulate their economies and alleviate high unemployment rates, there have been increasing arguments and efforts favoring a weak or undervalued currency. Although that may sound logical, the impossible trinity makes it very clear that each economy must choose its own medicine. The table shows what many argue are the choices of three of the main global economic powers.

The choices facing the EU are clearly the more complex. As a combination of different sovereign states, the EU has pursued integration of a common currency, the euro, and free movement of labor and capital. The result, according to the impossible trinity, is that EU member states had to give up independent monetary policy, replacing individual central banks with the *European Central Bank* (ECB). The recent fiscal deficits and near-collapses of government debt issuances in Greece, Portugal, and Ireland have raised questions over the efficacy of the arrangement.

	Choice #1	Choice #2	Implied Condition #3
United States	Independent monetary policy	Free movement of capital	Currency value floats
China	Independent monetary policy	Fixed rate of exchange	Restricted movement of capital
Europe (EU)	Free movement of capital	Fixed rate of exchange	Integrated monetary policy

A Single Currency for Europe: The Euro

Beginning with the Treaty of Rome in 1957 and continuing with the Single European Act of 1987, the Maastricht Treaty of 1991–1992, and the Treaty of Amsterdam of 1997, a core set of European countries worked steadily toward integrating their individual countries into one larger, more efficient, domestic market. However, even after the launch of the 1992 Single Europe program, a number of barriers to true openness remained, including the use of different currencies. The use of different currencies required both consumers and companies to treat the individual markets separately. Currency risk of cross-border commerce still persisted. The creation of a single currency was seen as the way to move beyond these last vestiges of separated markets.

The original 15 members of the European Union (EU) were also members of the European Monetary System. The EMS formed a system of fixed exchange rates amongst the member currencies, with deviations managed through bilateral responsibility to maintain rates at $\pm 2.5\%$ of an established central rate. This system of fixed rates, with adjustments along the way, remained in effect from 1979–1999. Its resiliency was seriously tested with exchange rate crises in 1992 and 1993, but it held and moved onward.

The Maastricht Treaty and Monetary Union

In December 1991, the members of the EU met at Maastricht, the Netherlands, and concluded a treaty that changed Europe's currency future. The Maastricht Treaty specified a timetable and a plan to replace all individual EMS member currencies with a single currency—eventually named the euro. Other aspects of the treaty were also adopted that would lead to a full *European Economic and Monetary Union* (EMU). According to the EU, the EMU is a single-currency area within the the singular EU market, now known informally as the *eurozone*, in which people, goods, services, and capital are allowed to move without restrictions.

The integration of separate country monetary systems is not, however, a minor task. To prepare for the EMU, the Maastricht Treaty called for the integration and coordination of the member countries' monetary and fiscal policies. The EMU would be implemented by a process called *convergence*.

Before becoming a full member of the EMU, each member country was expected to meet the following *convergence criteria* in order to integrate systems that were at the same relative performance levels: 1) nominal inflation should be no more than 1.5% above the average for the three members of the EU that had the lowest inflation rates during the previous year; 2) long-term interest rates should be no more than 2% above the average of the three members with the lowest interest rates; 3) individual government budget deficits—fiscal deficits—should be no more than 3% of gross domestic product; and 4) government debt outstanding should be no more than 60% of gross domestic product. The convergence criteria were so tough that few, if any, of the members could satisfy them at that time, but 11 countries managed to do so just prior to 1999 (Greece was added two years later).

The European Central Bank (ECB)

The cornerstone of any monetary system is a strong, disciplined, central bank. The Maastricht Treaty established this single institution for the EMU, the European Central Bank (ECB), which was established in 1998. (The EU created the European Monetary Institute (EMI) in 1994 as a transitional step in establishing the European Central Bank.) The ECB's structure and functions were modeled after the German Bundesbank, which in turn had been modeled after the U.S.

Federal Reserve System. The ECB is an independent central bank that dominates the activities of the individual countries' central banks. The individual central banks continue to regulate banks resident within their borders, but all financial market intervention and the issuance of the single currency is the sole responsibility of the ECB. The single most important mandate of the ECB is its charge to promote price stability within the European Union.

The Launch of the Euro

On January 4, 1999, 11 member states of the EU initiated the EMU. They established a single currency, the euro, which replaced the individual currencies of the participating member states. The 11 countries were Austria, Belgium, Finland, France, Germany, Ireland, Italy, Luxembourg, the Netherlands, Portugal, and Spain. Greece did not qualify for EMU participation at the time, but joined the euro group later, in 2001. On December 31, 1998, the final fixed rates between the 11 participating currencies and the euro were put into place. On January 4, 1999, the euro was officially launched.

The United Kingdom, Sweden, and Denmark chose to maintain their individual currencies. The United Kingdom has been skeptical of increasing EU infringement on its sovereignty, and has opted not to participate. Sweden, which has failed to see significant benefits from EU membership (although it is one of the newest members), has also been skeptical of EMU participation. Denmark, like the United Kingdom, Sweden, and Norway has so far opted not to participate. (Denmark is, however, a member of ERM II, the *Exchange Rate Mechanism II*, which effectively allows Denmark to keep its own currency and monetary sovereignty, but fixes the value of its currency, the krone, to the euro.)

The official currency symbol of the euro, EUR, was registered with the International Standards Organization. The official symbol of the euro is €. According to the EU, the € symbol was inspired by the Greek letter *epsilon* (ϵ), simultaneously referring to Greece's ancient role as the source of European civilization and recalling the first letter of the word Europe.

The euro would generate a number of benefits for the participating states: 1) Countries within the eurozone enjoy cheaper transaction costs; 2) Currency risks and costs related to exchange rate uncertainty are reduced; and 3) All consumers and businesses both inside and outside the eurozone enjoy price transparency and increased price-based competition. The primary "cost" of adopting the euro, the loss of monetary independence, would be a continuing challenge for the members for years to come.

GLOBAL FINANCE IN PRACTICE   2.4

The Euro and the Greek/EU Debt Crisis

The European Monetary Union is a complex organism compared to the customary country structure of fiscal and monetary policy institutions and policies described in a typical Economics 101 course. The members of the EU do not have the ability to conduct independent monetary policy. When the EU moved to a single currency with the adoption of the euro, its member states agreed to use a single currency (exchange rate stability), allow the free movement of capital in and out of their economies (financial integration), but give up individual control of their own money supply (monetary independence). Once again, a choice was made among the three competing dimensions of the impossible trinity; in this case, to form a single monetary policy body—the European Central Bank (ECB)—to conduct monetary policy on behalf of all EU members.

But fiscal and monetary policies are still somewhat intertwined. Government deficits that are funded by issuing debt to the international financial markets still impact monetary policy. Proliferating sovereign debt—debt issued by Greece, Portugal, and Ireland, for example—may be euro-denominated, but it is the debt obligation of each individual government. However, if one or more of these governments flood the market with debt, this may result in increased cost and decreased availability of capital to other member states. In the end, if monetary independence is not preserved, then one or both of the other elements of the impossible trinity may fail—capital mobility or exchange rate stability.

On January 4, 1999, the euro began trading on world currency markets. Its introduction was a smooth one. The euro's value slid steadily following its introduction, however, primarily as a result of the robustness of the U.S. economy and U.S. dollar, and sluggish economic sectors in the EMU countries. Beginning in 2002, the euro appreciated versus the dollar. Since that time, as illustrated in Exhibit 2.7, it had remained in a range of roughly $1.20 to $1.50 per euro. It has, however, demonstrated significant volatility.

The use of the euro has continued to expand since its introduction. As of January 2012, the euro was the official currency for 17 of the 27 member countries in the European Union, as well as five other countries (Montenegro, Andorra, Monaco, San Marino, and the Vatican) that may eventually join the EU. The 17 countries that currently use the euro—the so-called eurozone—are Austria, Belgium, Cyprus, Estonia, Finland, France, Germany, Greece, Ireland, Italy, Luxembourg, Malta, the Netherlands, Portugal, Slovakia, Slovenia, and Spain. Although all members of the EU are expected eventually to replace their currencies with the euro, recent years have seen growing debates and continual postponements by new members in moving toward full euro adoption. The continuing issues with European sovereign debt, as discussed in *Global Finance in Practice 2.4*, also continue to pose serious challenges to further euro expansion.

Emerging Markets and Regime Choices

The 1997–2005 period specifically saw increasing pressures on emerging market countries to choose among more extreme types of exchange rate regimes. The increased capital mobility pressures noted in the previous section have driven a number of countries to choose between a free-floating exchange rate (as in Turkey in 2002) or, at the opposite extreme, a fixed-rate regime—such as a currency board (as in Argentina throughout the 1990s and detailed in the

EXHIBIT 2.7   **The U.S. Dollar/Euro Exchange Rate**

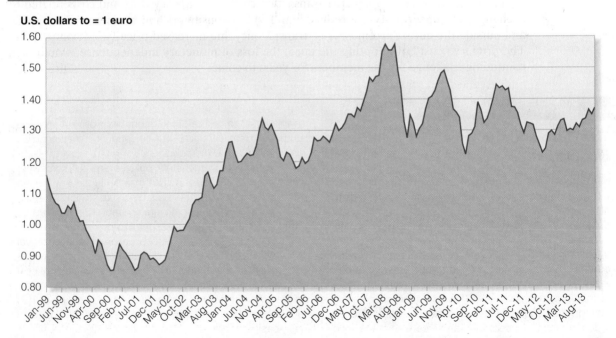

following section) or even dollarization (as in Ecuador in 2000). These systems deserve a bit more time and depth in our discussions.

Currency Boards

A *currency board* exists when a country's central bank commits to back its monetary base—its money supply—entirely with foreign reserves at all times. This commitment means that a unit of domestic currency cannot be introduced into the economy without an additional unit of foreign exchange reserves being obtained first. Eight countries, including Hong Kong, utilize currency boards as a means of fixing their exchange rates.

Argentina. In 1991, Argentina moved from its previous managed exchange rate of the Argentine peso to a currency board structure. The currency board structure pegged the Argentine peso's value to the U.S. dollar on a one-to-one basis. The Argentine government preserved the fixed rate of exchange by requiring that every peso issued through the Argentine banking system be backed by either gold or U.S. dollars held on account in banks in Argentina. This 100% reserve system made the monetary policy of Argentina dependent on the country's ability to obtain U.S. dollars through trade or investment. Only after Argentina had earned these dollars through trade could its money supply be expanded. This requirement eliminated the possibility of the nation's money supply growing too rapidly and causing inflation.

Argentina's system also allowed all Argentines and foreigners to hold dollar-denominated accounts in Argentine banks. These accounts were in actuality Eurodollar accounts, dollar-denominated deposits in non-U.S. banks. These accounts provided savers with the ability to choose whether or not to hold pesos.

From the very beginning there was substantial doubt in the market that the Argentine government could maintain the fixed exchange rate. Argentine banks regularly paid slightly higher interest rates on peso-denominated accounts than on dollar-denominated accounts. This interest differential represented the market's assessment of the risk inherent in the Argentine financial system. Depositors were rewarded for accepting risk—for keeping their money in peso-denominated accounts.

The market proved to be correct. In January 2002, after months of economic and political turmoil and nearly three years of economic recession, the Argentine currency board was ended. The peso was first devalued from Peso1.00/$ to Peso1.40/$, then it was floated completely. It fell in value dramatically within days. The Argentine decade-long experiment with a rigidly fixed exchange rate was over.

Dollarization

Several countries have suffered currency devaluation for many years, primarily as a result of inflation, and have taken steps toward dollarization. *Dollarization* is the use of the U.S. dollar as the official currency of the country. Panama has used the dollar as its official currency since 1907. Ecuador, after suffering a severe banking and inflationary crisis in 1998 and 1999, adopted the U.S. dollar as its official currency in January 2000. One of the primary attributes of dollarization was summarized well by *BusinessWeek* in a December 11, 2000, article entitled "The Dollar Club":

> One attraction of dollarization is that sound monetary and exchange-rate policies no longer depend on the intelligence and discipline of domestic policymakers. Their monetary policy becomes essentially the one followed by the U.S., and the exchange rate is fixed forever.

The arguments for dollarization follow logically from the previous discussion of the impossible trinity.

A country that dollarizes removes any currency volatility (against the dollar) and would theoretically eliminate the possibility of future currency crises. Additional benefits are expectations of greater economic integration with other dollar-based markets, both product and financial. This last point has led many to argue in favor of regional dollarization, in which several countries that are highly economically integrated may benefit significantly from dollarizing together.

Three major arguments exist against dollarization. The first is the loss of sovereignty over monetary policy. This is, however, the point of dollarization. Second, the country loses the power of *seigniorage*, the ability to profit from its ability to print its own money. Third, the central bank of the country, because it no longer has the ability to create money within its economic and financial system, can no longer serve the role of lender of last resort. This role carries with it the ability to provide liquidity to save financial institutions that may be on the brink of failure during times of financial crisis.

Ecuador. Ecuador officially completed the replacement of the Ecuadorian sucre with the U.S. dollar as legal tender in September 2000. This step made Ecuador the largest national adopter of the U.S. dollar, and in many ways made Ecuador a test case of dollarization for other emerging market countries to watch closely. As shown in Exhibit 2.8, this was the last stage of a massive depreciation of the sucre in a brief two-year period.

During 1999, Ecuador suffered a rising rate of inflation and a falling level of economic output. In March 1999, the Ecuadorian banking sector was hit with a series of devastating "bank runs," financial panics in which all depositors attempted to withdraw all of their funds simultaneously. Although there were severe problems in the Ecuadorian banking system, the truth was that even the healthiest financial institution would fail under the strain of this financial drain. Ecuador's president immediately froze all deposits (this was termed a *bank holiday* in the United States in the 1930s when banks closed their doors). The value of the Ecuadorian sucre plummeted in early March, inducing the country to default on more than $13 billion in foreign debt in 1999 alone. Ecuador's president moved quickly to propose dollarization to save the failing Ecuadorian economy.

EXHIBIT 2.8	Ecuadorian Sucre/U.S. Dollar Exchange Rate

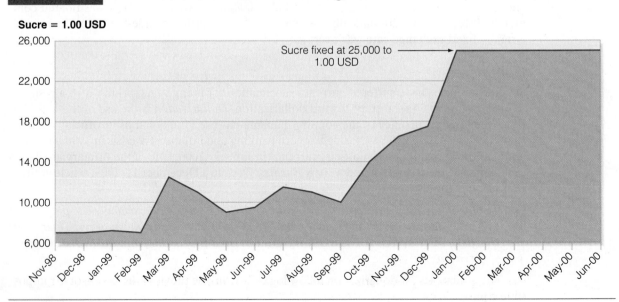

By January 2000, when the next president took office (after a rather complicated military coup and subsequent withdrawal), the sucre had fallen in value to Sucre25,000/$. The new president continued the dollarization initiative. Although unsupported by the U.S. government and the IMF, Ecuador completed its replacement of its own currency with the dollar over the next nine months. The results of dollarization in Ecuador are still unknown. Today, many years later, Ecuador continues to struggle to find both economic and political balance with its new currency regime.

Currency Regime Choices for Emerging Markets

There is no doubt that for many emerging markets the choice of a currency regime may lie somewhere between the extremes of a hard peg (a currency board or dollarization) or free-floating. However, many experts have argued for years that the global financial marketplace will drive more and more emerging market nations toward one of these extremes. As shown in Exhibit 2.9, there is a distinct lack of middle ground between rigidly fixed and free-floating extremes. But is the so-called "bi-polar choice" inevitable?

There is general consensus that three common features of emerging market countries make any specific currency regime choice difficult: 1) weak fiscal, financial, and monetary institutions; 2) tendencies for commerce to allow currency substitution and the denomination of liabilities in dollars; and 3) the emerging market's vulnerability to sudden stoppages of outside capital flows. Calvo and Mishkin may have said it best:[3]

EXHIBIT 2.9   **Regime Choices for Emerging Markets**

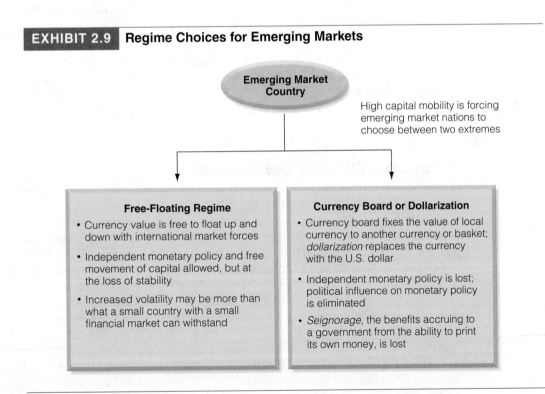

[3]"The Mirage of Exchange Rate Regimes for Emerging Market Countries," Guillermo A. Calvo and Frederic S. Mishkin, *The Journal of Economic Perspectives*, Vol. 17, No. 4, Autumn 2003, pp. 99–118.

Indeed, we believe that the choice of exchange rate regime is likely to be one second order importance to the development of good fiscal, financial and monetary institutions in producing macroeconomic success in emerging market countries. Rather than treating the exchange rate regime as a primary choice, we would encourage a greater focus on institutional reforms like improved bank and financial sector regulation, fiscal restraint, building consensus for a sustainable and predictable monetary policy and increasing openness to trade.

In anecdotal support of this argument, a poll of the general population in Mexico in 1999 indicated that 9 out of 10 people would prefer dollarization over a floating-rate peso. Clearly, many in the emerging markets have little faith in their leadership and institutions to implement an effective exchange rate policy.

Globalizing the Chinese Renminbi

Logically, it would be reasonable to expect China to make the RMB fully convertible before embarking on the ultimate goal of internationalizing the currency. But China appears to have put "the horse before the cart" by creating an offshore market to promote the currency's use in international trade and investments first. And this offshore trade has taken the lead over the onshore market.

—"RMB to Be a Globally Traded Currency by 2015," John McCormick,
RBS, in the May 3, 2013 *China Briefing*.

The Chinese *renminbi* (RMB) or *yuan* (CNY) is going global.[4] Although trading in the RMB is closely controlled by the People's Republic of China (PRC)—with all trading inside China between the RMB and foreign currencies (primarily the U.S. dollar) being conducted only according to Chinese regulations—its reach is spreading. The RMB's value, as illustrated in Exhibit 2.10, has been carefully controlled but allowed to gradually revalue against the dollar. It is now quickly moving toward what most think is an inevitable role as a true international currency.

Two-Market Currency Development

The RMB continues to develop along a segmented onshore/offshore two-market structure regulated by the PRC, as seen in Exhibit 2.11. The *onshore market* (carrying the official ISO code for the Chinese RMB, CNY) is a two-tier market, with retail exchange and an interbank wholesale exchange. The currency has, since mid-2005, been a managed float regime. Internally, the currency is traded through the China Foreign Exchange Trade System (CFETS), in which the People's Bank of China sets a daily central parity rate against the dollar (*fixing*). Actual trading is allowed to range within ±1% of the parity rate on a daily basis. This internal market continues to be gradually deregulated, with banks now being allowed to exchange negotiable certificates of deposit amongst themselves, with fewer and fewer interest rate restrictions. Nine different currencies are traded daily in the market against the RMB and themselves.

The *offshore market* for the RMB has grown out of a Hong Kong base (accounts labeled CNH, an unofficial symbol). This offshore market has enjoyed preferred access to the onshore market by government regulators, both in acquiring funds and re-injecting

---

[4]The People's Republic of China officially recognizes the terms *renminbi* (RMB) and *yuan* (CNY) as names of its official currency. *Yuan* is used in reference to the unit of account, while the physical currency is termed the *renminbi*.

EXHIBIT 2.10   **The Gradual Revaluation of the RMB**

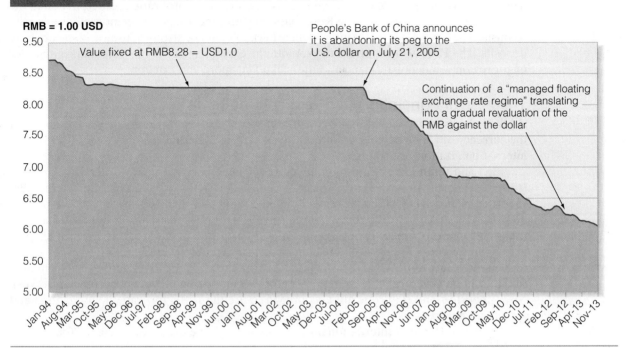

EXHIBIT 2.11   **Structure of the Chinese Renminbi Market**

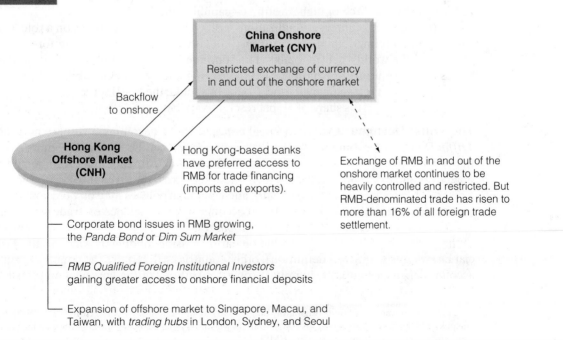

funds (termed *backflow*). Growth in this market has been fueled by the issuance of RMB-denominated debt, so-called Panda Bonds, by McDonald's Corporation, Caterpillar, and the World Bank, among others. Hong Kong-based institutional investors are now allowed access to onshore financial deposits (interest bearing), allowing a stronger use of these offshore deposits. The PRC also continues to promote the expansion of the offshore market to other major regional and global financial centers like Singapore and London.

Theoretical Principles and Practical Concerns

As the world's largest commercial trader and second-largest economy, it is inevitable that the currency of China become an international currency. But there is a variety of degrees of internationalization.

First and foremost, an international currency must become readily accessible for trade (this is technically described as *Current Account* use, to be described in detail in the next chapter). As noted in Exhibit 2.11, it is estimated that more than 16% of all Chinese trade is now denominated in RMB, which although small, is a radical increase from just 1% a mere four years ago. A Chinese exporter was typically paid in U.S. dollars, and was not allowed to keep those dollar proceeds in any bank account. Exporters were required to exchange all foreign currencies for RMB at the official exchange rate set by the PRC, and to turn them over to the Chinese government (resulting in a gross accumulation of foreign currency reserves). Now, importers and exporters are encouraged to use the RMB for trade denomination and settlement purposes.

A second degree of internationalization occurs with the use of the currency for international investment—capital account/market activity. This is an area of substantial concern and caution for the PRC at this time. The Chinese marketplace is the focus of many of the world's businesses, and if they were allowed free and open access to the market and its currency there is fear that the value of the RMB could be driven up, decreasing Chinese export competitiveness. Simultaneously, as major capital markets like the dollar and euro head into stages of rising interest rates, there is a concern that large quantities of Chinese savings could flow out of the country in search of higher returns—capital flight.

A third degree of internationalization occurs when a currency takes on a role as a *reserve currency* (also termed an *anchor currency*), a currency to be held in the foreign exchange reserves of the world's central banks. The continued dilemma of fiscal deficits in the United States and the European Union has led to growing unease over the ability of the dollar and euro to maintain their value over time. Could, or should, the RMB serve as a reserve currency? Forecasts of the RMB's share of global reserves vary between 15% and 50% by the year 2020.

The Triffin Dilemma. One theoretical concern about becoming a reserve currency is the *Triffin Dilemma* (or sometimes called the *Triffin Paradox*). The Triffin Dilemma is the potential conflict in objectives that may arise between domestic monetary and currency policy objectives and external or international policy objectives when a country's currency is used as a reserve currency.[5] Domestic monetary and economic policies may on occasion require both contraction and the creation of a current account surplus (balance on trade surplus).

If a currency rises to the status of a *global reserve currency*, in which it is considered one of the two or three key stores of value on earth (possibly finding its way into the IMF's Special Drawing Right [SDR] definition), other countries will require the country to run current account deficits, essentially dumping growing quantities of the currency on global markets.

---

[5]The theory is the namesake of its originator, Belgian-American economist Robert Triffin (1911–1963), who was an outspoken critic of the Bretton Woods Agreement, as well as a strong advocate and collaborated in the development of the European Monetary System (EMS).

This means that the country needs to become internationally indebted as part of its role as a reserve currency country. In short, when the world adopts a currency as a reserve currency, demands are placed on the use and availability of that currency, which many countries would prefer not to deal with. In fact, both Japan and Switzerland both worked for decades to prevent their currencies from gaining wider international use, partially because of these complex issues. The Chinese RMB, however, may eventually find that it has no choice—the global market may choose.

Exchange Rate Regimes: What Lies Ahead?

All exchange rate regimes must deal with the trade-off between rules and discretion, as well as between cooperation and independence. Exhibit 2.12 illustrates the trade-offs between exchange rate regimes based on rules, discretion, cooperation, and independence.

1. Vertically, different exchange rate arrangements may dictate whether a country's government has strict intervention requirements (rules) or if it may choose whether, when, and to what degree to intervene in the foreign exchange markets (discretion).

2. Horizontally, the trade-off for countries participating in a specific system is between consulting and acting in unison with other countries (cooperation) or operating as a member of the system, but acting on their own (independence).

Regime structures like the gold standard required no cooperative policies among countries, only the assurance that all would abide by the "rules of the game." Under the gold standard, in effect prior to World War II, this assurance translated into the willingness of governments to buy or sell gold at parity rates on demand. The Bretton Woods Agreement, the system in place between 1944 and 1973, required more in the way of cooperation, in that

EXHIBIT 2.12   **Exchange Rate Regime Trade-Offs**

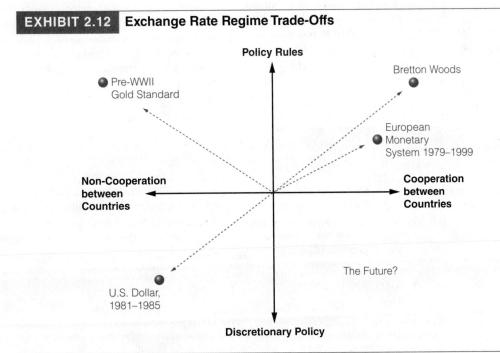

gold was no longer the "rule," and countries were required to cooperate to a higher degree to maintain the dollar-based system. Exchange rate systems, like the European Monetary System's (EMS) fixed exchange rate band system used from 1979 to 1999, were hybrids of these cooperative and rule regimes.

The present international monetary system is characterized by no rules, with varying degrees of cooperation. Although there is no present solution to the continuing debate over what form a new international monetary system should take, many believe that it will succeed only if it combines cooperation among nations with individual discretion to pursue domestic social, economic, and financial goals.

Summary Points

- Under the gold standard (1876–1913), the "rules of the game" were that each country set the rate at which its currency unit could be converted to a weight of gold.

- During the inter-war years (1914–1944), currencies were allowed to fluctuate over fairly wide ranges in terms of gold and each other. Supply and demand forces determined exchange rate values.

- The Bretton Woods Agreement (1944) established a U.S. dollar-based international monetary system. Under the original provisions of the Bretton Woods Agreement, all countries fixed the value of their currencies in terms of gold but were not required to exchange their currencies for gold. Only the dollar remained convertible into gold (at $35 per ounce).

- A variety of economic forces led to the suspension of the convertibility of the dollar into gold in August 1971. Exchange rates of most of the leading trading countries were then allowed to float in relation to the dollar and thus indirectly in relation to gold.

- If the ideal currency existed in today's world, it would possess three attributes: a fixed value, convertibility, and independent monetary policy. However, in both theory and practice, it is impossible for all three attributes to be simultaneously maintained.

- Emerging market countries must often choose between two extreme exchange rate regimes: a free-floating regime or an extremely fixed regime, such as a currency board or dollarization.

- The members of the European Union are also members of the European Monetary System (EMS). This group has tried to form an island of fixed exchange rates among themselves in a sea of major floating currencies. Members of the EMS rely heavily on trade with each other, so the day-to-day benefits of fixed exchange rates between them are perceived to be great.

- The euro affects markets in three ways: 1) Countries within the eurozone enjoy cheaper transaction costs; 2) Currency risks and costs related to exchange rate uncertainty are reduced; and 3) All consumers and businesses both inside and outside the eurozone enjoy price transparency and increased price-based competition.

MINI-CASE

Mini-Case: Russian Ruble Roulette[1]

The Russian ruble has experienced a multitude of regime shifts since the opening of the Russian economy under Perestroika in 1991.[2] After a number of years of a highly controlled official exchange rate accompanied by tight capital controls, the 1998 economic crisis prompted a movement to a heavily managed float. Using both direct intervention and interest rate policy, the ruble held surprisingly steady until 2008. But all of that stopped in 2008 when the global credit crisis, which started in the United States, spread to Russia. As illustrated by Exhibit A, the impact on the value of the ruble proved disastrous.

In an effort to protect the value of the ruble, the Bank of Russia spent $200 billion—a full one-third of its foreign exchange reserves—throughout 2008 and into 2009.

[1]Copyright © 2014 Thunderbird School of Global Management. All rights reserved. This case was prepared by Professor Michael H. Moffett for the purpose of classroom discussion only and not to indicate either effective or ineffective management.
[2]There is no established correct English spelling for the Russian currency—the *ruble* or the *rouble*. There is a journalistic tradition that most North American publications use *ruble*, while European organizations favor *rouble*, as does the *Oxford English Dictionary*.

EXHIBIT A   Russian Ruble/U.S. Dollar Exchange Rate

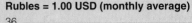

Rubles = 1.00 USD (monthly average)

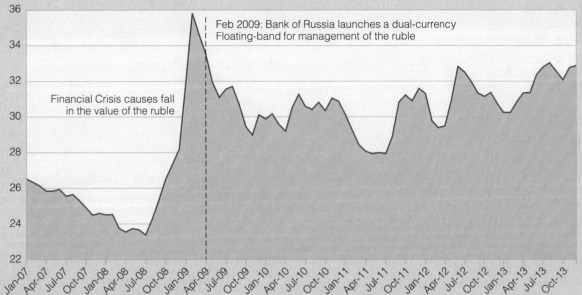

Feb 2009: Bank of Russia launches a dual-currency
Floating-band for management of the ruble

Financial Crisis causes fall
in the value of the ruble

Although the market began to calm in early 2009, the Bank decided to introduce a new more flexible exchange rate regime for the management of the ruble.

The new system was a *dual-currency floating rate band* for the ruble. A *dual-currency basket* was formed from two currencies, the U.S. dollar (55%) and the euro (45%), for the calculation of the central ruble rate. Around this basket rate, a *neutral zone* was established in which no currency intervention would be undertaken. This initial neutral zone was 1.00 ruble versus the basket. Around the neutral zone, a set of *operational band boundaries* were established, an *upper band* and *lower band*, for intervention purposes.

If the ruble remained in the neutral zone, no intervention would be made. If, however, the ruble's value hit either operational band, the Bank of Russia would intervene by buying rubles (upper band) or selling rubles (lower band) to stabilize its value. The Bank was allowed a maximum of $700 million per day in purchases of rubles. Once hitting that limit, the Bank was to move the band(s) in increments of 5 kopecks (100 kopecks = 1.00 ruble).[3]

As illustrated in Exhibit B, the ruble continued to slide (appreciating) against the basket throughout 2009 and into 2010. The dual-currency band was continually adjusted—downward—in an effort to put a

'moving floor' underneath the currency. Finally, in late-2010, the ruble stabilized.

As part of a continual program to allow the ruble to grow as a global currency, the distance between the upper and lower bands has been repeatedly increased over time. Starting with a floating band (the spread between the upper band and lower band in Exhibit B) that was only 2 rubles per basket value, the band had been continually expanded to reach 7 rubles by early 2014. Unfortunately, and frustratingly for Russian authorities, after a number of years of growing strength the ruble was now growing weaker against the dollar and euro basket.

The ruble's new found relative stability was rewarded in October 2013 when the Bank of Russia announced that it was expanding the neutral 'no-intervention' zone from 1 ruble to 3.1 rubles. This was followed by an announcement in January 2014 that the Bank would begin moving to end daily intervention, eventually ending all intervention sometime in 2015. (Daily intervention in recent months had averaged about $60 million, a relatively small amount given history.) If, however, the ruble did hit either of its bands, the Bank acknowledged that it was prepared to reenter the market to preserve stability.

The impetus for moving to a freely-floating ruble was to both allow the changes in the currency's value to "absorb"

[3]The daily foreign exchange intervention limit has been adjusted downwards a number of times since the dual-currency band was instituted. In January 2014 the limit had contracted to $350 million per day.

EXHIBIT B   Russian Ruble Floating Band

Rubles versus dual-currency basket

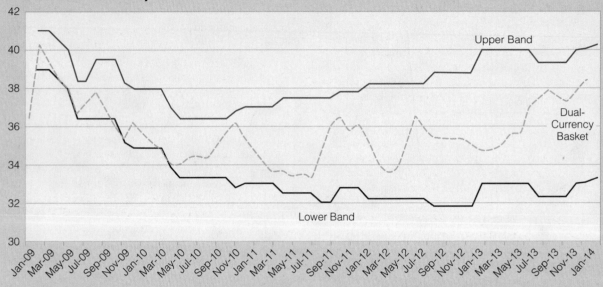

Dual-currency basket calculated by authors (monthly average exchange rates).

global economic changes, and allow the central bank to increase its focus on controlling inflationary forces. Russian inflation has been stubbornly high in recent years, and with the U.S. Federal Reserve announcing that it would be slowing/stopping its loose money policy in the wake of the financial crisis of 2008–2009, inflationary pressures were sure to continue.

The Bank of Russia was clearly continuing to implement its long-term currency strategy, which had first been put in-place back in 2009. It obviously believed that if it increasingly targeted inflation rather the ruble's exchange value, the long-term economic prospects for Russia and the ruble would be improved, and the ruble could move from being a

simple "emerging market currency" to a regional currency, and ultimately, someday, a reserve currency.

CASE QUESTIONS

1. How would you classify the exchange rate regime used by Russia for the ruble over the 1991–2014 period?

2. What did the establishment of *operational bands* do to the expectations of ruble speculators? Would these expectations be stabilizing or destabilizing in your opinion?

3. What would a depreciating ruble mean for Russia's commercial trade and its war on inflation?

Questions

1. **The Gold Standard and the Money Supply.** Under the gold standard, all national governments promised to follow the "rules of the game." This meant defending a fixed exchange rate. What did this promise imply about a country's money supply?

2. **Causes of Devaluation.** If a country follows a fixed exchange rate regime, what macroeconomic variables could cause the fixed exchange rate to be devalued?

3. **Fixed Exchange Rate.** Why do many emerging market economies prefer to adopt a fixed exchange rate?

4. **The Impossible Trinity.** With reference to the *impossible trinity*, what are the possible policy mixes that a nation could have?

5. **Currency Boards.** What is the difference between central banks and currency boards?

6. **Emerging Market Regimes.** High capital mobility is forcing emerging market nations to choose between free-floating regimes and currency board or dollarization regimes. What are the main outcomes of each of

these regimes from the perspective of emerging market nations?

7. **Argentine Currency Board.** How did the Argentine currency board function from 1991 to January 2002 and why did it collapse?

8. **The Euro.** On January 4, 1999, 11 member states of the European Union initiated the European Monetary Union (EMU) and established a single currency, the euro, which replaced the individual currencies of participating member states. Describe three of the main ways that the euro affects the members of the EMU.

9. **Mavericks.** The United Kingdom, Denmark, and Sweden have chosen not to adopt the euro but rather to maintain their individual currencies. What are the motivations of each of these three European Union member countries?

10. **International Monetary Fund (IMF).** The IMF was established by the Bretton Woods Agreement (1944). What were the original objectives of the IMF?

11. **Special Drawing Rights.** What are Special Drawing Rights?

12. **Exchange Rate Regime Classifications.** The IMF classifies all exchange rate regimes into four specific categories that are summarized in this chapter. Under which exchange rate regime would you classify the following countries?
    a. France
    b. The United States
    c. Japan
    d. Thailand

13. **The Ideal Currency.** What are the attributes of the ideal currency?

14. **Bretton Woods Failure.** Why did the fixed exchange rate regime of 1945–1973 eventually fail?

Problems

1. **Albert's Trip to Canada.** Albert visits Toronto and buys 1.74 Canadian dollars (CAD) for one British pound (GBP). When he returns home to the U.K., he converts CAD1 into GBP0.59. Is the new exchange rate favorable or unfavorable?

2. **Lottery winner.** Aisha lives in Melbourne, Australia. She wins €150 in an online lottery on Thursday and wishes to convert the amount into Australian dollars (AUD). If the exchange rate is 0.5988 euros per AUD, how many AUD does she get, and what is the value date of the AUD payment?

3. **Gilded Question.** In 1923, one ounce of gold costs 380 French francs (FRF). If at the same time one ounce of gold could be purchased in Britain for GBP4.50, what was the exchange rate between the French franc and the British pound?

4. **Brent oil.** In 2015 one barrel of Brent oil traded for GBP42.5 and South Africa rands (ZAR) 790. What is the exchange rate between the pound and the rand? How would the exchange rate change if the oil price jumps to GBP50 per barrel (assume no change in the price in South Africa)?

5. **Toyota Exports to the United Kingdom.** Toyota manufactures in Japan most of the vehicles it sells in the United Kingdom. The base platform for the Toyota Tundra truck line is ¥1,650,000. The spot rate of the Japanese yen against the British pound has recently moved from ¥197/£ to ¥190/£. How does this change the price of the Tundra to Toyota's British subsidiary in British pounds?

6. **Online shopping.** Tamara lives in Egypt and has placed a bundle of items in her Amazon.co.uk account basket. She has the choice to pay in Egyptian pounds (EGP 1844) or in GBP (151.17). What is the exchange rate between both currencies? In which currency should she pay?

7. **Israeli Shekel Changes Value.** One British Pound (GBP) traded against Israeli Shekels (ILS) 5.82 in 2013, but the exchange rate rose to 6.78 in late 2014. What is the percentage change of the ILS? Has the shekel depreciated or appreciated?

8. **Hong Kong Dollar and the Chinese Yuan.** The Hong Kong dollar has long been pegged to the U.S. dollar at HK$7.80/$. When the Chinese yuan was revalued in July 2005 against the U.S. dollar from Yuan8.28/$ to Yuan8.11/$, how did the value of the Hong Kong dollar change against the yuan?

9. **Chinese Yuan Revaluation.** Many experts believe that the Chinese currency should not only be revalued against the U.S. dollar as it was in July 2005, but also be revalued by 20% or 30%. What would be the new exchange rate value if the yuan was revalued an additional 20% or 30% from its initial post-revaluation rate of Yuan8.11/$?

10. **TEXPAK (Pakistan) in the United Kingdom.** TEXPAK is a Pakistani-based textile firm that is facing increasing competition from other manufacturers in emerging markets selling in Europe. All garments are produced in Pakistan, with costs and pricing initially stated in Pakistani rupees (PKR), but converted to British pounds (GBP) for distribution and sale in the United Kingdom. In 2014, one suit was priced at PKR 11,000 with a British pound price set at GBP95. In 2015, the GBP appreciated in value

versus the PKR, averaging PKR120/GBP. In order to preserve the GBP price and product profit margin in rupees, what should the new rupee price be set at?

11. **Vietnamese Coffee Coyote.** Many people were surprised when Vietnam became the second largest coffee producing country in the world in recent years, second only to Brazil. The Vietnamese dong, VND or d, is managed against the U.S. dollar but is not widely traded. If you were a traveling coffee buyer for the wholesale market (a "coyote" by industry terminology), which of the following currency rates and exchange commission fees would be in your best interest if traveling to Vietnam on a buying trip?

12. **Chunnel Choices.** The Channel Tunnel or "Chunnel" passes underneath the English Channel between Great Britain and France, a land-link between the Continent and the British Isles. One side is therefore an economy of British pounds, the other euros. If you were to check the Chunnel's rail ticket Internet rates you would find that they would be denominated in U.S. dollars (USD). For example, a first class round trip fare for a single adult from London to Paris via the Chunnel through RailEurope may cost USD170.00. This currency neutrality, however, means that customers on both ends of the Chunnel pay differing rates in their home currencies from day to day. What is the British pound and euro denominated prices for the USD170.00 round trip fare in local currency if purchased on the following dates at the accompanying spot rates drawn from the *Financial Times*?

Date of Spot Rate	British Pound Spot Rate (£/$)	Euro Spot Rate (€/$)
Monday	0.5702	0.8304
Tuesday	0.5712	0.8293
Wednesday	0.5756	0.8340

13. **Middle East Exports.** Oriol Díez Miguel S.R.L., a manufacturer of heavy duty machine tools near Barcelona, ships an order to a buyer in Jordan. The purchase price is €425,000. Jordan imposes a 13% import duty on all products purchased from the European Union. The Jordanian importer then re-exports the product to a Saudi Arabian importer, but only after imposing its own resale fee of 28%. Given the following spot exchange rates on April 11, 2010, what is the total cost to the Saudi Arabian importer in Saudi Arabian riyal, and what is the U.S. dollar equivalent of that price?

Internet Exercises

1. **International Monetary Fund's Special Drawing Rights.** Use the IMF's Web site to find the current weights and valuation of the SDR.

   International Monetary Fund   www.imf.org/external/np/ tre/sdr/sdrbasket.htm

2. **Malaysian Currency Controls.** The institution of currency controls by the Malaysian government in the aftermath of the Asian currency crisis is a classic response by government to unstable currency conditions. Use the following Web site to increase your knowledge of how currency controls work.

   International Monetary Fund   www.imf.org/external/pubs/ ft/bl/rr08.htm

3. **Personal Transfers.** As anyone who has traveled internationally learns, the exchange rates available to private retail customers are not always as attractive as those accessed by companies. The OzForex Web site possesses a section on "customer rates" that illustrates the difference. Use the site to calculate what the percentage difference between Australian dollar/U.S. dollar spot exchange rates are for retail customers versus interbank rates.

   OzForex   www.ozforex.com.au/ exchange-rate

4. **Exchange Rate History.** Use the Pacific Exchange Rate database and plot capability to track value changes of the British pound, the U.S. dollar, and the Japanese yen against each other over the past 15 years.

   Pacific Exchange Rate Service   fx.sauder.ubc.ca

The Balance of Payments

The sort of dependence that results from exchange, i.e., from commercial transactions, is a reciprocal dependence. We cannot be dependent upon a foreigner without his being dependent on us. Now, this is what constitutes the very essence of society. To sever natural interrelations is not to make oneself independent, but to isolate oneself completely. —Frederic Bastiat.

LEARNING OBJECTIVES

- Learn how nations measure their own levels of international economic activity, and how that activity is measured by the balance of payments

- Examine the economic relationships underlying the two basic subcomponents of the balance of payments—the current account and financial account balances

- Consider the financial dimensions of international economic activity, and how they differ between merchandise and services trade

- Identify balance of payment activities by nations in the pursuit of domestic economic and political policies

- Examine how exchange rate changes and volatility influence trade balances over time

- Evaluate the history of capital mobility, and the conditions that lead, in times of crisis, to capital flight

The measurement of all international economic transactions that take place between the residents of a country and foreign residents is called the *balance of payments* (BOP). This chapter provides a sort of navigational map to aid in understanding the balance of payments and the multitude of economic, political, and business issues that it involves. But our emphasis is far from descriptive, as a deep understanding of trade and capital flows is integral to the management of multinational enterprises. In fact, the second half of the chapter emphasizes a more detailed analysis of how elements of the balance of payments affect trade volumes and prices, as well as how capital flows, capital controls, and capital flight alter the cost and ability to do business internationally. The chapter concludes with a Mini-Case, *Global Remittances*, which is an area of the current account that has only recently been explored in depth by governments as they try to monitor and sometimes control capital flows.

Home-country and host-country BOP data are important to business managers, investors, consumers, and government officials because the data simultaneously influences and is influenced by other key macroeconomic variables, such as gross domestic product (GDP), employment levels, price levels, exchange rates, and interest rates. Monetary and fiscal policy must take the BOP into account at the national level. Business managers and investors need

BOP data to anticipate changes in host-country economic policies that might be driven by BOP events. BOP data is also important for the following reasons:

- The BOP is an important indicator of pressure on a country's foreign exchange rate, and thus of the potential for a firm trading with or investing in that country to experience foreign exchange gains or losses. Changes in the BOP may predict the imposition or removal of foreign exchange controls.

- Changes in a country's BOP may signal the imposition or removal of controls over payment of dividends and interest, license fees, royalty fees, or other cash disbursements to foreign firms or investors.

- The BOP helps to forecast a country's market potential, especially in the short run. A country experiencing a serious trade deficit is not as likely to expand imports as it would be if running a surplus. It may, however, welcome investments that increase its exports.

Typical Balance of Payments Transactions

International transactions take many forms. Each of the following examples is an international economic transaction that is counted and captured in the U.S. balance of payments:

- A U.S.-based firm, Fluor Corporation, manages the construction of a major water treatment facility in Bangkok, Thailand.

- The U.S. subsidiary of a French firm, Saint Gobain, pays profits back to its parent firm in Paris.

- An American tourist purchases a small Lapponia necklace in Finland.

- The U.S. government finances the purchase of military equipment for its military ally, Norway.

- A Mexican lawyer purchases a U.S. corporate bond through an investment broker in Cleveland.

This is a small sample of the hundreds of thousands of international transactions that occur each year. The BOP provides a systematic method for classifying these transactions. This rule of thumb always aids the understanding of BOP accounting: *Follow the cash flow*.

The BOP is composed of a number of subaccounts that are watched quite closely by groups as diverse as investment bankers, farmers, politicians, and corporate executives. These groups track and analyze the major subaccounts—the current account, the capital account, and the financial account—continually.

Fundamentals of BOP Accounting

The BOP must balance. If it does not, something has not been counted or has been counted improperly. Therefore, it is incorrect to state that "the BOP is in disequilibrium." It cannot be. The supply and demand for a country's currency may be imbalanced, but that is not the same thing as the BOP. A subacccount of the BOP, such as the *balance on goods and services* (a subaccount of any country's current account), may be imbalanced (in surplus or deficit), but the entire BOP of a single country is always balanced.

Exhibit 3.1 illustrates that the BOP does indeed balance, in this case for the United States from 2005 through 2012. The five balances listed in Exhibit 3.1—*current account, capital account, financial account, net errors and omissions*, and *reserves and related*—do indeed sum to zero.

EXHIBIT 3.1   The U.S. Balance of Payments Accounts, Summary

Balance	2005	2006	2007	2008	2009	2010	2011	2012
Current Account Balance	−740	−798	−713	−681	−382	−449	−458	−440
Capital Account Balance	13	−2	0	6	0	0	−1	7
Financial Account Balance	687	807	617	735	283	440	568	444
Net Errors and Omissions	26	−9	96	−55	151	11	−93	−6
Official Reserves Account	14	2	0	−5	−52	−2	−16	−5

Source: *Balance of Payments Statistics Yearbook: 2013*, International Monetary Fund, December 2013.

There are three main elements of the actual process of measuring international economic activity: 1) identifying what is and is not an international economic transaction; 2) understanding how the flow of goods, services, assets, and money creates debits and credits to the overall BOP; and 3) understanding the bookkeeping procedures for BOP accounting.

Defining International Economic Transactions

Identifying international transactions is ordinarily not difficult. The export of merchandise — goods such as trucks, machinery, computers, telecommunications equipment, and so forth — is obviously an international transaction. Imports such as French wine, Japanese cameras, and German automobiles are also clearly international transactions. But this merchandise trade is only a portion of the thousands of different international transactions that occur in the United States and other countries each year.

Many other international transactions are not so obvious. The purchase of a good, like a glass figure in Venice, Italy, by a U.S. tourist is classified as a U.S. merchandise import. In fact, all expenditures made by U.S. tourists around the globe for services provided by, for example, restaurants and hotels are recorded in the U.S. balance of payments as imports of travel services in the current account.

The BOP as a Flow Statement

The BOP is often misunderstood because many people infer from its name that it is a *balance sheet*, whereas in fact it is a *cash flow statement*. By recording all international transactions over a period of time such as a year, the BOP tracks the continuing flows of purchases and payments between a country and all other countries. It does not add up the value of all assets and liabilities of a country on a specific date like a balance sheet does for an individual firm (that is, in fact, the *Net International Investment* position of a country, described in a later section). Two types of business transactions dominate the balance of payments:

1. **Exchange of *real assets*.** The exchange of goods (e.g., automobiles, computers, textiles) and services (e.g., banking, consulting, and travel services) for other goods and services (barter) or for money

2. **Exchange of *financial assets*.** The exchange of financial claims (e.g., stocks, bonds, loans, and purchases or sales of companies) for other financial claims or money

Although assets can be identified as real or financial, it is often easier to think of all assets as goods that can be bought and sold. The purchase of a hand-woven area rug in a shop in Bangkok by a U.S. tourist is not all that different from a Wall Street banker buying a British government bond for investment purposes.

BOP Accounting

The measurement of all transactions in and out of a country is a daunting task. Mistakes, errors, and statistical discrepancies will occur. The primary problem is that double-entry book-keeping is employed in theory, but not in practice. Individual purchase and sale transactions should—in theory—result in financing entries in the balance of payments that match. In reality, current, capital, and financial account entries are recorded independently of one another, not together as double-entry bookkeeping would prescribe. Thus, there will be discrepancies (to use a nice term for it) between debits and credits.

The Accounts of the Balance of Payments

The balance of payments is composed of three major subaccounts: the current account, the capital account, and the financial account. In addition, the official reserves account tracks government currency transactions, and a fifth statistical subaccount, the net errors and omissions account, is produced to preserve the balance in the BOP.

The Current Account

The current account includes all international economic transactions with income or payment flows occurring within the year, the current period. The current account consists of four subcategories:

1. **Goods trade**. The export and import of goods is known as the goods trade. Merchandise trade is the oldest and most traditional form of international economic activity. Although many countries depend on imports of goods (as they should, according to the theory of comparative advantage), they also normally work to preserve either a balance of goods trade or even a surplus.

2. **Services trade**. The export and import of services is known as the services trade. Common international services are financial services provided by banks to foreign importers and exporters, travel services of airlines, and construction services of domestic firms in other countries. For the major industrial countries, this subaccount has shown the fastest growth in the past decade.

3. **Income**. This is predominantly current income associated with investments that were made in previous periods. If a U.S. firm created a subsidiary in South Korea to produce metal parts in a previous year, the proportion of net income that is paid back to the parent company in the current year (the dividend) constitutes current investment income. Additionally, wages and salaries paid to nonresident workers are also included in this category.

4. **Current transfers**. The financial settlements associated with the change in ownership of real resources or financial items are called current transfers. Any transfer between countries that is one-way—a gift or grant—is termed a current transfer. For example, funds provided by the U.S. government to aid in the development of a less-developed nation would be a current transfer. Transfer payments made by migrant or guest workers back to their home countries, the subject of this chapter's Mini-Case, is another example of a current transfer.

All countries possess some amount of trade, most of which is merchandise. Many less-developed countries have little in the way of service trade, or items that fall under the income or transfers subaccounts. The current account is typically dominated by the first component described, the export and import of merchandise. For this reason, the balance of trade (BOT), which is so widely quoted in the business press, refers to the balance of exports and imports of goods trade only. If the country is a larger industrialized country, however, the BOT is somewhat misleading, in that service trade is not included.

Goods Trade. Exhibit 3.2 presents the two major components of the U.S. current account for the 2000–2012 period: 1) goods trade and 2) services trade and investment income. The first and most striking message is the magnitude of the goods trade deficit. The balance on services and income, although not large in comparison to net goods trade, has run a small but consistent surplus over the past two decades.

Merchandise trade is the original core of international trade. The manufacturing of goods was the basis of the industrial revolution and the focus of the *theory of comparative advantage in international trade*. Manufacturing is traditionally the sector of the economy that employs most of a country's workers. Declines in the U.S. BOT attributed to specific sectors, such as steel, automobiles, automotive parts, textiles, and shoe manufacturing, caused massive economic and social disruption.

Understanding merchandise import and export performance is much like understanding the market for any single product. The demand factors that drive both are income, the economic growth rate of the buyer, and price of the product in the eyes of the consumer after passing through an exchange rate. U.S. merchandise imports reflect the income level of U.S. consumers and growth of industry. As income rises, so does the demand for imports.

EXHIBIT 3.2   U.S. Trade Balances on Goods and Services

Billions of U.S. dollars

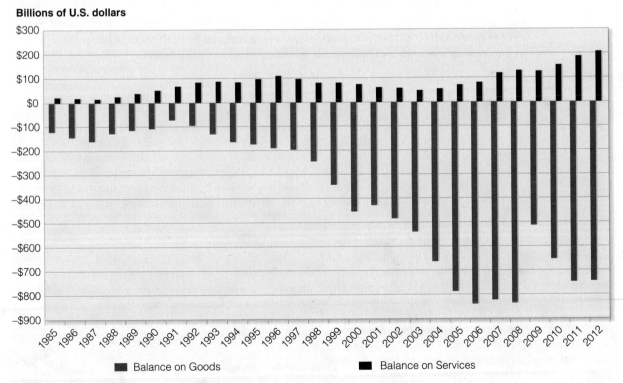

Source: *Balance of Payments Statistics Yearbook: 2013*, International Monetary Fund, December 2013, p. 1032.

Exports follow the same principles, but in the reverse. U.S. manufacturing exports depend not on the incomes of U.S. residents, but on the incomes of buyers of U.S. products in all other countries around the world. When these economies are growing, the demand for U.S. products is growing.

As illustrated in Exhibit 3.2, the United States has consistently run a surplus in services trade income. The major categories of services include travel and passenger fares; transportation services; expenditures by U.S. students abroad, foreign students studying in the U.S.; telecommunications services; and financial services.

The Capital and Financial Accounts

The capital and financial accounts of the balance of payments measure all international economic transactions of financial assets. The capital account is made up of transfers of financial assets and the acquisition and disposal of nonproduced/nonfinancial assets. This account has been introduced as a separate component in the IMF's balance of payments only recently. The magnitude of capital transactions covered by the Capital Account is relatively minor, and we will include it in principle in all of the following discussions of the financial account. But as noted in *Global Finance in Practice 3.1*, some mysteries in global accounts remain!

Financial Account

The financial account consists of four components: direct investment, portfolio investment, net financial derivatives, and other asset investment. Financial assets can be classified in a number of different ways, including by the length of the life of the asset (its maturity) and the nature of the ownership (public or private). The financial account, however, uses *degree of control* over assets or operations to classify financial assets. *Direct investment* is defined as investment that has a long-term life or maturity and in which the investor exerts some explicit degree of control over the assets. In contrast, *portfolio investment* is defined as both short-term in maturity and as an investment in which the investor has no control over the assets.

GLOBAL FINANCE IN PRACTICE 3.1

The Global Current Account Surplus

There are three kinds of lies: lies, damned lies and statistics.

—Author unknown, though frequently attributed to Lord Courtney, Sir Charles Dilke, or Mark Twain.

One country's surplus is another country's deficit. That is, individual countries may and do run current account deficits and surpluses, but it should be, theoretically, a zero sum game. But according to the IMF's most recent World Economic Outlook, however, the world is running a current account surplus. At least that is what the statistics say.*

The rational explanation is that the statistics, as reported to the IMF by its member countries, are in error. The errors are most likely both accidental and intentional. The IMF believed for many years that the most likely explanation was under-reporting of foreign investment income by residents of the wealthier industrialized countries, as well as under-reporting of transportation and freight charges.

Many alternative explanations focus on intentional misreporting of international current account activities. Over- or under-invoicing has long been a ploy used in international trade to avoid taxes, capital controls, or purchasing restrictions. Other arguments, like under-reporting of foreign income for tax avoidance and the complexity of intracompany transactions and transfer prices, are all potential partial explanations.

But in the end, while the theory says it can't be, the numbers say it is. As noted by the *Economist*, planet Earth appears to be running a current account surplus in its trade with extraterrestrials ("Are aliens buying Louis Vuitton handbags?").**

*World Economic Outlook: Slowing Growth, Rising Risks, International Monetary Fund, September 2011.
**Economics Focus, Exports to Mars," *The Economist*, November 12, 2011, p. 90.

Direct Investment. This investment measure is the net balance of capital dispersed from and into a country like the United States for the purpose of exerting control over assets. If a U.S. firm builds a new automotive parts facility in another country or purchases a company in another country, this is a direct investment in the U.S. balance of payments accounts. When the capital flows out of the U.S., it enters the balance of payments as a negative cash flow. If, however, a foreign firm purchases a firm in the U.S., it is a capital inflow and enters the balance of payments positively.

Foreign resident purchases of assets in a country are always somewhat controversial. The focus of concern over foreign investment in any country, including the United States, is on two issues: control and profit. Some countries place restrictions on what foreigners may own in their country. This rule is based on the premise that domestic land, assets, and industry in general should be owned by residents of the country. The U.S., however, has traditionally had few restrictions on what foreign residents or firms can own or control in the country (with the exception of national security concerns). Unlike the case in the traditional debates over whether international trade should be free, there is no consensus on international investment.

The second major focus of concern over foreign direct investment is who receives the profits from the enterprise. Foreign companies owning firms in the U.S. will ultimately profit from the activities of those firms — or to put it another way, foreign companies will profit from the efforts of U.S. workers. In spite of evidence that indicates foreign firms in the U.S. reinvest most of their profits in their U.S. businesses (in fact, at a higher rate than do domestic firms), the debate on possible profit drains has continued. Regardless of the actual choices made, workers of any nation feel that the profits of their work should remain in their own hands in their own country.

The choice of words used to describe foreign investment can also influence public opinion. If these massive capital inflows are described as "*capital investments from all over the world showing their faith in the future of U.S. industry,*" the net capital surplus is represented as decidedly positive. If, however, the net capital surplus is described as resulting in "*the United States being the world's largest debtor nation,*" the negative connotation is obvious. Both are essentially spins on the economic principles at work.

Capital, whether short-term or long-term, flows to where the investor believes it can earn the greatest return for the level of risk. And although in an accounting sense this is "international debt," when the majority of the capital inflow is in the form of direct investment, a long-term commitment to jobs, production, services, technological, and other competitive investments, the impact on the competitiveness of industry located within a country is increased. Net direct investment cash flows for the U.S. are shown in Exhibit 3.3.

Portfolio Investment. This is the net balance of capital that flows into and out of a country but that does not reach the 10% ownership threshold of direct investment. If a U.S. resident purchases shares in a Japanese firm but does not attain the 10% threshold, we define the purchase as a portfolio investment (and an outflow of capital). The purchase or sale of debt securities (like U.S. Treasury bills) across borders is also classified as portfolio investment, because debt securities by definition do not provide the buyer with ownership or control.

Portfolio investment is capital invested in activities that are purely profit-motivated (return), rather than activities to control or manage the investment. Purchases of debt securities, bonds, interest-bearing bank accounts, and the like are intended only to earn a return. They provide no vote or control over the party issuing the debt. Purchases of debt issued by the U.S. government (U.S. Treasury bills, notes, and bonds) by foreign investors constitute net portfolio investment in the United States. It is worth noting that most U.S. debt purchased by foreigners is U.S. dollar-denominated in the currency of the issuing country (dollars). Much of the foreign debt issued by countries such as Russia, Brazil, and Southeast Asian countries

EXHIBIT 3.3	The U.S. Financial Accounts

Billions of U.S. dollars

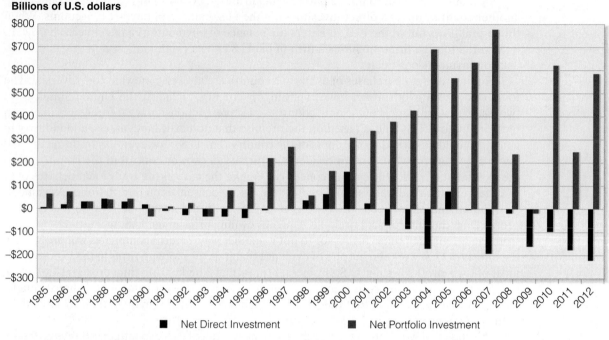

Net Direct Investment   Net Portfolio Investment

Source: Balance of Payments Statistics Yearbook: 2013, International Monetary Fund, 2013.

is also U.S. dollar-denominated, and is therefore the currency of a foreign country. The foreign country must then earn dollars to repay its foreign-held debt, typically through exports.

As illustrated in Exhibit 3.3, portfolio investment has shown much more volatile behavior than net foreign direct investment has over the past decade. Many U.S. debt securities, such as U.S. Treasury securities and corporate bonds, are consistently in high demand by foreign investors of all kinds. The motivating forces for portfolio investment flows are always the same: return and risk. These same debt securities have also been influential in a different measure of international investment activity, as described in *Global Finance in Practice 3.2*.

Other Asset Investment. This final component of the financial account consists of various short-term and long-term trade credits, cross-border loans from all types of financial institutions, currency deposits and bank deposits, and other accounts receivable and payable related to cross-border trade.

GLOBAL FINANCE IN PRACTICE 3.2

A Country's Net International Investment Position (NIIP)

The *net international investment position* (NIIP) of a country is an annual measure of the assets owned abroad by its citizens, its companies, and its government, less the assets owned by foreigners, public and private, in their

country. Whereas a country's balance of payments is often described as a country's international cash flow statement, the NIIP may be interpreted as the country's international balance sheet. NIIP is a country's stock of foreign assets minus its stock of foreign liabilities.

In the same way company cash flows are related to a company's balance sheet, the NIIP is based upon and categorized by the same capital and financial accounts used in the balance of payments: direct investment, portfolio

U.S. Net International Position (NIIP)

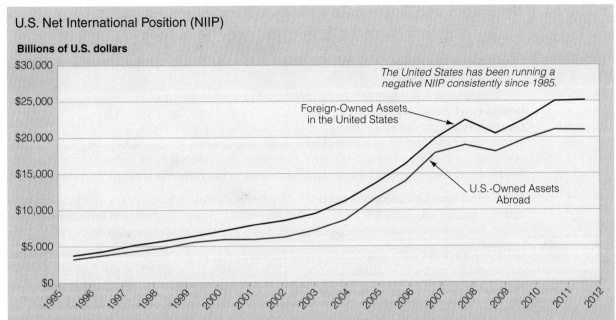

Billions of U.S. dollars

The United States has been running a negative NIIP consistently since 1985.

Foreign-Owned Assets in the United States

U.S.-Owned Assets Abroad

Source: Congressional Research Service.

investment, other investment and reserve assets. As international capital has found it easier and easier to move between currencies and cross borders in recent years, ownership of assets and securities has clearly boomed.

One common method of putting a country's NIIP into perspective is to measure it as a percentage of the total economic size of the nation—the Gross Domestic Product (GDP) of the country. As illustrated here, the NIIP of the U.S. has clearly seen a dramatic increase since 2005, now averaging 25% of U.S. GDP.

Although some observers have seen this growing percentage as a risk to the U.S. economy (calling the U.S. the world's largest debtor nation), these investments in assets of all kinds in many ways represent the faith foreign investors have in the future of the nation and its economy. A large part of this investment is the purchase of U.S. government securities, Treasury notes and bonds, issued in part to finance the U.S. government's growing deficits. These foreign purchasers have therefore aided in the financing of the U.S. government's budget deficit.

U.S. NIIP as Percentage of Gross Domestic Product

The U.S. NIIP as a percentage of GDP has been growing steadily and rapidly over the past 16 years.

A large part of this growth has resulted from foreign investors purchasing U.S. government notes and bonds—U.S. Treasuries. This has aided in the financing of the U.S. government budget deficit while keeping the cost of that financing from rising rapidly.

Net Errors and Omissions and Official Reserves Accounts

Exhibit 3.4 illustrates the current account balance and the capital/financial account balances for the United States over recent years. The exhibit shows one of the basic economic and accounting relationships of the balance of payments: the *inverse relation* between the current and financial accounts.

This inverse relationship is not accidental. The methodology of the balance of payments, double-entry bookkeeping requires that the current and financial accounts be offsetting unless the country's exchange rate is being highly manipulated by governmental authorities. The next section on China describes one very high profile case in which government policy has thwarted economics—the twin surpluses of China. Countries experiencing large current account deficits fund these deficits through equally large surpluses in the financial account, and vice versa.

Net Errors and Omissions Account. As previously noted, because current and financial account entries are collected and recorded separately, errors or statistical discrepancies will occur. The net errors and omissions account ensures that the BOP actually balances.

Official Reserves Account. The Official Reserves Account is the total reserves held by official monetary authorities within a country. These reserves are normally composed of the major currencies used in international trade and financial transactions (so-called "hard currencies" like the U.S. dollar, European euro, and Japanese yen; gold; and special drawing rights, SDRs).

The significance of official reserves depends generally on whether a country is operating under a fixed exchange rate regime or a floating exchange rate system. If a country's currency is fixed, the government of the country officially declares that the currency is convertible into a fixed

---

EXHIBIT 3.4   **Current and Combined Financial /Capital Account Balances for the United States**

Billions of U.S. dollars

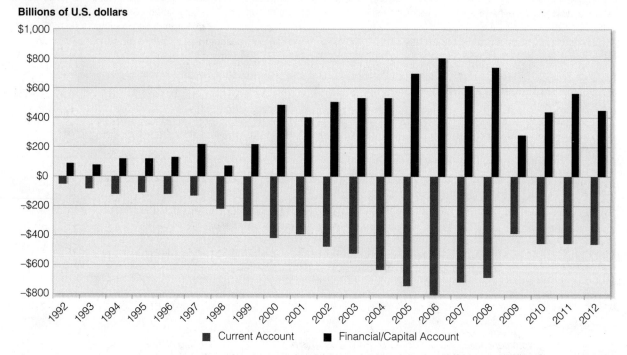

Source: *Balance of Payments Statistics Yearbook: 2013*, International Monetary Fund, December 2013, p. 1032.

amount of some other currency. For example, the Chinese yuan was fixed to the U.S. dollar for many years. It was the Chinese government's responsibility to maintain this fixed rate, also called *parity rate*. If for some reason there was an excess supply of yuan on the currency market, to prevent the value of the yuan from falling, the Chinese government would have to support the yuan's value by purchasing yuan on the open market (by spending its hard currency reserves) until the excess supply was eliminated. Under a floating rate system, the Chinese government possesses no such responsibility and the role of official reserves is diminished. But as described in the following section, the Chinese government's foreign exchange reserves are now the largest in the world, and if need be, it probably possesses sufficient reserves to manage the yuan's value for years to come.

Breaking the Rules: China's Twin Surpluses

Exhibit 3.5 documents one of the more astounding BOP behaviors seen globally in many years—the twin surplus balances enjoyed by China in recent years. China's surpluses in both the current and financial accounts—termed the *twin surplus* in the business press—is highly unusual. Ordinarily, for example, in the cases of the United States, Germany, and Great Britain, a country will demonstrate an inverse relationship between the two accounts. This inverse relationship is not accidental, and typically illustrates that most large, mature, industrial countries "finance" their current account deficits through equally large surpluses in the financial account. For some countries like Japan, it is the inverse; a current account surplus is matched against a financial account deficit.

China, however, has experienced a massive current account surplus and a marginal financial account surplus simultaneously. This is highly unusual, and an indicator of just how

EXHIBIT 3.5   **China's Twin Surplus**

Billions of U.S. dollars

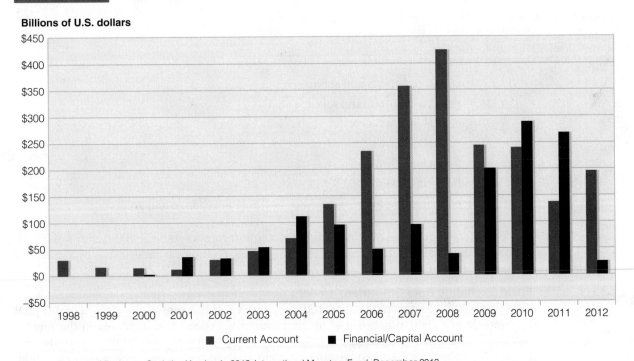

Source: *Balance of Payments Statistics Yearbook: 2013*, International Monetary Fund, December 2013.

exceptional the growth of the Chinese economy has been. Although current account surpluses of this magnitude would ordinarily always create a financial account deficit, the positive prospects of the Chinese economy have drawn such massive capital inflows into China in recent years that the financial account too is in surplus.

The rise of the Chinese economy has been accompanied by a rise in its current account surplus, and subsequently, its accumulation of foreign exchange reserves. China's foreign exchange reserves increased by a factor of 16 from 2001 to 2011—from $200 billion to nearly $3,200 billion. There is no real precedent for this build-up in foreign exchange reserves in global financial history. These reserves allow the Chinese government to manage the value of the Chinese yuan and its impact on Chinese competitiveness in the world economy. The magnitude of these reserves will allow the Chinese government to maintain a relatively stable managed fixed rate of the yuan against other major currencies like the U.S. dollar as long as it chooses.

BOP Impacts on Key Macroeconomic Rates

A country's balance of payments both impacts and is impacted by the three macroeconomic rates of international finance: exchange rates, interest rates, and inflation rates.

The BOP and Exchange Rates

A country's BOP can have a significant impact on the level of its exchange rate and vice versa, depending on that country's exchange rate regime. The relationship between the BOP and exchange rates can be illustrated by using a simplified equation that summarizes BOP data:

Current Account Balance	Capital Account Balance	Financial Account Balance	Reserve Balance	Balance of Payments
$(X - M)$ +	$(CI - CO)$ +	$(FI - FO)$ +	FXB =	BOP

$$X = \text{exports of goods and services}$$
$$M = \text{imports of goods and services}$$
$$CI = \text{capital inflows}$$
$$CO = \text{capital outflows}$$
$$FI = \text{financial inflows}$$
$$FO = \text{financial outflows}$$
$$FXB = \text{official monetary reserves such as foreign exchange and gold.}$$

The effect of an imbalance in the BOP of a country works somewhat differently depending on whether that country has fixed exchange rates, floating exchange rates, or a managed exchange rate system.

Fixed Exchange Rate Countries.   Under a fixed exchange rate system, the government bears the responsibility to ensure that the BOP is near zero. If the sum of the current and capital accounts do not approximate zero, the government is expected to intervene in the foreign exchange market by buying or selling official foreign exchange reserves. If the sum of the first two accounts is greater than zero, a surplus demand for the domestic currency exists in the world.

To preserve the fixed exchange rate, the government must then intervene in the foreign exchange market and sell domestic currency for foreign currencies or gold in order to bring the BOP back to near zero.

If the sum of the current and capital accounts is negative, an excess supply of the domestic currency exists in world markets. Then the government must intervene by buying the domestic currency with its reserves of foreign currencies and gold. It is obviously important for a government to maintain significant foreign exchange reserve balances, sufficient to allow it to intervene effectively. If the country runs out of foreign exchange reserves, it will be unable to buy back its domestic currency and will be forced to devalue its currency.

Floating Exchange Rate Countries. Under a floating exchange rate system, the government of a country has no responsibility to peg its foreign exchange rate. The fact that the current and capital account balances do not sum to zero will automatically—in theory—alter the exchange rate in the direction necessary to obtain a BOP near zero. For example, a country running a sizable current account deficit and a capital and financial accounts balance of zero will have a net BOP deficit. An excess supply of the domestic currency will appear on world markets. Like all goods in excess supply, the market will rid itself of the imbalance by lowering the price. Thus, the domestic currency will fall in value, and the BOP will move back toward zero.

Exchange rate markets do not always follow this theory, particularly in the short to intermediate term. This delay is known as the *J-curve* (detailed in an upcoming section). The deficit gets worse in the short run, but moves back toward equilibrium in the long run.

Managed Floats. Although still relying on market conditions for day-to-day exchange rate determination, countries operating with managed floats often find it necessary to take action to maintain their desired exchange rate values. They often seek to alter the market's valuation of their currency by influencing the motivations of market activity, rather than through direct intervention in the foreign exchange markets.

The primary action taken by such governments is to change relative interest rates, thus influencing the economic fundamentals of exchange rate determination. In the context of the equation presented earlier, a change in domestic interest rates is an attempt to alter the term $(CI - CO)$, especially the short-term portfolio component of these capital flows, in order to restore an imbalance caused by the deficit in the current account.

The power of interest rate changes on international capital and exchange rate movements can be substantial. A country with a managed float that wishes to defend its currency may choose to raise domestic interest rates to attract additional capital from abroad. This step will alter market forces and create additional market demand for the domestic currency. In this process, the government signals to the markets that it intends to take measures to preserve the currency's value within certain ranges. The process also raises the cost of local borrowing for businesses, however, so the policy is seldom without domestic critics.

The BOP and Interest Rates

Apart from the use of interest rates to intervene in the foreign exchange market, the overall level of a country's interest rates compared to other countries has an impact on the financial account of the balance of payments. Relatively low real interest rates should normally stimulate an outflow of capital seeking higher interest rates in other country currencies. However, in the case of the United States, the opposite effect has occurred. Despite relatively low real interest rates and large BOP deficits on the current account, the U.S. BOP financial account has experienced offsetting financial inflows due to relatively attractive U.S. growth rate prospects, high levels of productive innovation, and perceived political safety. Thus, the financial account inflows have helped the United States to maintain its lower interest rates and to finance its exceptionally large fiscal deficit. However, it is beginning to appear that the favorable inflow on the financial account is diminishing while the U.S. balance on the current account is worsening.

The BOP and Inflation Rates

Imports have the potential to lower a country's inflation rate. In particular, imports of lower-priced goods and services place a limit on what domestic competitors charge for comparable goods and services. Thus, foreign competition substitutes for domestic competition to maintain a lower rate of inflation than might have been the case without imports.

On the other hand, to the extent that lower-priced imports substitute for domestic production and employment, gross domestic product will be lower and the balance on the current account will be more negative.

Trade Balances and Exchange Rates

A country's import and export of goods and services is affected by changes in exchange rates. The transmission mechanism is in principle quite simple: changes in exchange rates change relative prices of imports and exports, and changing prices in turn result in changes in quantities demanded through the price elasticity of demand. Although the theory seems straightforward, real global business is more complex.

Trade and Devaluation

Countries occasionally devalue their own currencies as a result of persistent and sizable trade deficits. Many countries in the not-too-distant past have intentionally devalued their currencies in an effort to make their exports more price-competitive on world markets. These competitive devaluations are often considered self-destructive, however, as they also make imports relatively more expensive. So what is the logic and likely results of intentionally devaluing the domestic currency to improve the trade balance?

The J-Curve Adjustment Path

International economic analysis characterizes the trade balance adjustment process as occurring in three stages: 1) the currency contract period; 2) the pass-through period; and 3) the quantity adjustment period. These three stages are illustrated in Exhibit 3.6. Assuming that the trade balance is already in deficit prior to the devaluation, a devaluation at time t_1 results initially in a further deterioration in the trade balance before an eventual improvement. The path of adjustment, as shown, takes on the shape of a flattened "j."

In the first period, the *currency contract period*, a sudden unexpected devaluation of the domestic currency has a somewhat uncertain impact, simply because all of the contracts for exports and imports are already in effect. Firms operating under these agreements are required to fulfill their obligations, regardless of whether they profit or suffer losses. Assume that the United States experienced a sudden fall in the value of the U.S. dollar. Most exports were priced in U.S. dollars but most imports were contracts denominated in foreign currency. The result of a sudden depreciation would be an increase in the size of the trade deficit at

---

EXHIBIT 3.6   **Trade Balance Adjustment to Exchange Rate Changes: The J-Curve**

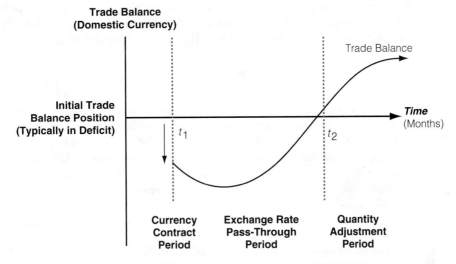

If export products are predominantly priced and invoiced in domestic currency, and imports are predominantly priced and invoiced in foreign currency, a sudden devaluation of the domestic currency can possibly result—initially—in a deterioration of the balance on trade. After exchange rate changes are passed through to product prices, and markets have time to respond to price changes by altering market demands, the trade balance will improve. The currency contract period may last from three to six months, with pass-through and quality adjustment following for an additional three to six months.

---

time t_1 because the cost to U.S. importers of paying their import bills would rise as they spent more dollars to buy the foreign currency they needed, while the revenues earned by U.S. exporters would remain unchanged. There is little reason, however, to believe that most U.S. imports are denominated in foreign currency and most exports in dollars.

The second period of the trade balance adjustment process is termed the *pass-through period*. As exchange rates change, importers and exporters eventually must pass these exchange rate changes through to their own product prices. For example, a foreign producer selling to the U.S. market after a major fall in the value of the U.S. dollar will have to cover its own domestic costs of production. This need will require that the firm charge higher dollar prices in order to earn its own local currency in large enough quantities. The firm must raise its prices in the U.S. market. U.S. import prices then rise, eventually passing the full exchange rate changes through to prices. Similarly, the U.S. export prices are now cheaper compared to foreign competitors' because the dollar is cheaper. Unfortunately for U.S. exporters, many of the inputs for their final products may actually be imported, dampening the positive impact of the fall of the dollar.

The third and final period, the *quantity adjustment period*, achieves the balance of trade adjustment that is expected from a domestic currency devaluation or depreciation. As the import and export prices change as a result of the pass-through period, consumers both in the United States and in the U.S. export markets adjust their demands to the new prices. Imports are relatively more expensive; therefore the quantity demanded decreases. Exports are relatively cheaper; therefore the quantity demanded increases. The balance of trade—the expenditures on exports less the expenditures on imports—improves.

Unfortunately, these three adjustment periods do not occur overnight. Countries like the U.S. that have experienced major exchange rate changes, have also seen this adjustment take place over a prolonged period. Empirical studies have concluded that for industrial countries, the total time elapsing between time t_1 and t_2 can vary from 3 to 12 months. To complicate the process, new exchange rate changes often occur before the adjustment is completed.

Trade Balance Adjustment Path: The Equation

A country's trade balance is essentially the net of import and export revenues, where each is a multiple of price—$P_x^\$$ and P_m^{fc}—the prices of exports and imports, respectively. Export prices are assumed to be denominated in U.S. dollars, and import prices are denominated in foreign currency. The quantity of exports and the quantity of imports are denoted as Q_x and Q_m, respectively. Import expenditures are then expressed in U.S. dollars by multiplying the foreign currency denominated expenditures by the spot exchange rate, $S^{\$/fc}$. The U.S. trade balance, expressed in U.S. dollars, is then expressed as follows:

$$\text{U.S. Trade Balance} = (P_x^\$ Q_x) - (S^{\$/fc} P_M^{fc} Q_M)$$

The immediate impact of a devaluation of the domestic currency is to increase the value of the spot exchange rate $S^{\$/fc}$, resulting in an immediate deterioration in the trade balance (currency contract period). Only after a period in which the current contracts have matured, and new prices reflecting partial to full pass-through have been instituted, would improvement in the trade balance been evident (pass-through period). In the final stage, in which the price elasticity of demand has time to take effect (quantity adjustment period), is the actual trade balance which is expected to rise above where it started in Exhibit 3.7.

EXHIBIT 3.7 **The Evolution of Capital Mobility**

Exchange Rate Era	The Gold Standard	The Inter-War Years	The Bretton Woods Era	The Floating Era	The Emerging Era
Cross-Border Political Economy	Growing openness in trade, with growing, but limited, capital mobility	Protectionism & isolationism	Growing belief in the benefits of open economies	Industrialized (primary) nations open; emerging states (secondary) restrict capital flows to maintain economic control	More and more emerging nations open their markets to capital at the expense of reduced economic independence
Implication	Trade dominates capital in total influence on exchange rates	Rising barriers to the movement of both trade & capital	Trade increasingly dominated by capital; era ends as capital flows	Capital flows dominate trade; emerging nations suffer devaluations	Capital flows increasingly drive economic growth and health
	1860	1914	1945	1971	1997 Present

The last 150 years has seen periods of increasing and decreasing political and economic openness between countries. Beginning with the Bretton Woods Era, global markets have moved toward increasing open exchange of goods and capital, making it increasingly difficult to maintain fixed or even stable rates of exchange between currencies. The most recent era, characterized by the growth and development of emerging economies is likely to be even more challenging.

Capital Mobility

The degree to which capital moves freely cross-border is critically important to a country's balance of payments. We have already seen how the U.S. has suffered a deficit in its current account balance over the past 20 years while running a surplus in the financial account, and how China has enjoyed a surplus in both the current and financial accounts over the last decade. But these are only two country cases, and may not reflect the challenges that changing balances in trade and capital may mean for many countries, particularly smaller ones or emerging markets.

Current Account versus Financial Account Capital Flows

Capital inflows can contribute significantly to an economy's development. Capital inflows can increase the availability of capital for new projects, new infrastructure development, and productivity improvements. All of which may stimulate general economic growth and job creation. For domestic holders of capital, the ability to invest outside the domestic economy may reap greater investment returns, portfolio diversification, and extend the commercial development of domestic enterprises.

That said, the free flow of capital in and out of an economy can potentially destabilize economic activity. Although the benefits of free capital flows have been known for centuries, so have the negatives. For this very reason, the creators of the Bretton Woods system were very careful to promote and require the free movement of capital for current account transactions—foreign exchange, bank deposits, money market instruments—but they did not require such free transit for capital account transactions—foreign direct investment and equity investments.

Experience has shown that current account-related capital flows can be more volatile, with capital flowing in and out of an economy and a currency on the basis of short-term interest rate differentials and exchange rate expectations. This volatility is somewhat compartmentalized, not directly impacting real asset investments, employment, or long-term economic growth. Longer-term capital flows reflect more fundamental economic expectations, including growth prospects and perceptions of political stability.

The complexity of issues, however, is apparent when you consider the plight of many emerging market countries. Recall the *impossible trinity* from Chapter 2—the theoretical structure which states that no country can maintain a fixed exchange rate, allow complete capital mobility (both in and out of the country), and conduct independent monetary policy simultaneously. Many emerging market countries have continued to develop by maintaining a near-fixed (soft peg) exchange rate regime—a strictly independent monetary policy—while restricting capital inflows and outflows. With the growth of current account business activity (exports and imports of goods and services), more current account-related capital flows are deregulated. If, however, the country experiences significant volatility in these short-term capital movements, capital flows potentially impacting either exchange rate pegs or monetary policy objectives, authorities are often quick to re-institute capital controls.

The growth in capital openness in the 1970s, 1980s, and first half of the 1990s resulted in a significant increase in political pressures for more countries to open up more of their financial account sectors to international capital. But the devastation of the Asian Financial Crisis of 1997/1998 brought much of that to a halt. Smaller economies, no matter how successful their growth and development may have been under export-oriented trade strategies, found themselves still subject to sudden and destructive capital outflows in times of economic crisis and financial contagion.

Historical Patterns of Capital Mobility

Before leaving our discussion of the balance of payments, we need to gain additional insights into the history of capital mobility and the contribution of capital outflows—capital flight—to balance of payments crises. Has capital always been free to move in and out of a country? Definitely not. The ability of foreign investors to own property, buy businesses, or purchase stocks and bonds in other countries has been controversial.

Exhibit 3.7, first presented in Chapter 2, is helpful once again in categorizing the last 150 years of economic history into five distinct exchange rate eras and their associated implications for capital mobility (or lack thereof). These exchange rate eras obviously reflect the exchange rate regimes we discussed and detailed in Chapter 2, but also reflect the evolution of political economy beliefs and policies of both industrialized and emerging market nations over this period.

The Gold Standard (1860–1914). Although an era of growing capital openness in which trade and capital began to flow more freely, it was an era dominated by industrialized nation economies that were dependent on gold convertibility to maintain confidence in the system.

The Inter-War Years (1914–1945). An era of retrenchment, in which major economic powers returned to policies of isolationism and protectionism, restricting trade and nearly eliminating capital mobility. The devastating results included financial crisis, a global depression, and rising international political and economic disputes that drove nations into a second world war.

The Bretton Woods Era (1945–1971). The dollar-based fixed exchange rate system under Bretton Woods gave rise to a long period of economic recovery and growing openness of both international trade and capital flows in and out of countries. Many researchers (for example Obstfeld and Taylor, 2001) believe it was the rapid growth in the speed and volume of capital flows that ultimately led to the failure of Bretton Woods—global capital could no longer be held in check.

The Floating Era (1971–1997). The Floating Era, saw the rise of a growing schism between the industrialized and emerging market nations. The industrialized nations (primary currencies) moved to—or were driven to—floating exchange rates by capital mobility. The emerging markets (secondary currencies), in an attempt to both promote economic development and maintain control over their economies and currencies, opened trade but maintained restrictions on capital flows. Despite these restrictions, the era ended with the onslaught of the Asian Financial Crisis in 1997.

The Emerging Era (1997–Present). The emerging economies, led by China and India, attempt to gradually open their markets to global capital. But, as the impossible trinity taught the industrial nations in previous years, the increasing mobility of capital now requires that they give up either the ability to manage their currency values or to conduct independent monetary policies. By 2011 and 2012 an increasing number of emerging market currencies "suffer" appreciation (or fight appreciation) as capital flows grow in magnitude and speed.

The 2008–2014 period reinforced what some call the double-edged sword of global capital movements. The credit crisis of 2008–2009, beginning in the United States, quickly spread to the global economy, pulling and pushing down industrial and emerging market economies alike. But in the post credit crisis period, global capital now flowed toward the emerging markets. Although funding and fueling their rapid economic recoveries, it came—in the words of

EXHIBIT 3.8   Purposes of Capital Controls

Control Purpose	Method	Capital Flow Controlled	Example
General Revenue/Finance War Effort	Controls on capital outflows permit a country to run higher inflation with a given fixed-exchange rate and also hold down domestic interest rates.	Outflows	Most belligerents in WWI and WWII
Financial Repression/Credit Allocation	Governments that use the financial system to reward favored industries or to raise revenue, may use capital controls to prevent capital from going abroad to seek higher returns.	Outflows	Common in developing countries
Correct a Balance of Payments Deficit	Controls on outflows reduce demand for foreign assets without contractionary monetary policy or devaluation. This allows a higher rate of inflation than otherwise would be possible.	Outflows	US interest equalization tax 1963–1974
Correct a Balance of Payments Surplus	Controls on inflows reduce foreign demand for domestic assets without expansionary monetary policy or revaluation. This allows a lower rate of inflation than would otherwise be possible.	Inflows	German Bardepot Scheme 1972–1974
Prevent Potentially Volatile Inflows	Restricting inflows enhances macroeconomic stability by reducing the pool of capital that can leave a country during a crisis.	Inflows	Chilean *encaje* 1991–1998
Prevent Financial Destabilization	Capital controls can restrict or change the composition of international capital flows that can exacerbate distorted incentives in the domestic financial system.	Inflows	Chilean *encaje* 1991–1998
Prevent Real Appreciation	Restricting inflows prevents the necessity of monetary expansion and greater domestic inflation that would cause a real appreciation of the currency.	Inflows	Chilean *encaje* 1991–1998
Restrict Foreign Ownership of Domestic Assets	Foreign ownership of certain domestic assets —especially natural resources—can generate resentment.	Inflows	Article 27 of the Mexican Constitution
Preserve Savings for Domestic Use	The benefits of investing in the domestic economy may not fully accrue to savers so the economy as a whole can be made better off by restricting the outflow of capital.	Outflows	—
Protect Domestic Financial Firms	Controls that temporarily segregate domestic financial sectors from the rest of the world may permit domestic firms to attain economies of scale to compete in world markets.	Inflows and Outflows	—

Source: "An Introduction to Capital Controls," Christopher J. Neely, *Federal Reserve Bank of St. Louis Review*, November/December 1999, p. 16.

one journalist—"with luggage." The increasing pressure on emerging market currencies to appreciate is partially undermining their export competitiveness. But then, just as suddenly as the capital came, it went. In late 2013, the U.S. Federal Reserve announced that it would be slowing money supply growth and allowing U.S. interest rates to rise. Capital once again moved; this time out of the emerging markets into the more traditional industrial countries like the U.S. and Europe.

Capital Controls

A *capital control* is any restriction that limits or alters the rate or direction of capital movement into or out of a country. Capital controls may take many forms, sometimes dictating which parties may undertake which types of capital transactions for which purposes—the who, what, when, where, and why of investment.

It is in many ways the bias of the journalistic and academic press that believes that capital has been able to move freely across boundaries. Free movement of capital in and out of a country is more the exception than the rule. The United States has been relatively open to capital inflows and outflows for many years, while China has been one of the most closed over that same period. When it comes to moving capital, the world is full of requirements, restrictions, taxes, and documentation approvals.

There is a wide spectrum of motivations for capital controls, with most associated with either insulating the domestic monetary and financial economy from outside markets or political motivations over ownership and access interests. As illustrated in Exhibit 3.8, capital controls are just as likely to occur over capital inflows as they are over capital outflows. Although there is a tendency for a negative connotation to accompany capital controls (possibly the bias of the word "control" itself), the impossible trinity requires that capital flows be controlled if a country wishes to maintain a fixed exchange rate and an independent monetary policy.

Capital controls may take a variety of forms that mirror restrictions on trade. They may simply be a tax on a specific transaction, they may limit the quantity or magnitude of specific capital transactions, or they may prohibit transactions altogether. The controls themselves have tended to follow the basic dichotomy of the balance of payments current account transactions versus financial account transactions.

In some cases capital controls are intended to stop or thwart capital outflows and currency devaluation or depreciation. The case of Malaysia during the Asian Crisis of 1997–1998 is one example. As the Malaysian currency came under attack and capital started to exit the Malaysian economy, the government imposed a series of capital controls that were intended to stop short-term capital movements, in or out, but not hinder trade and not restrict long-term inward investment. All trade-related requests for access to foreign exchange were granted, allowing current account-related capital flows to continue. But access to foreign exchange for inward or outward money market or capital market investments were restricted. Foreign residents wishing to invest in Malaysian assets—real assets not financial assets—had open access.

Capital controls can be implemented in the opposite case, in which the primary fear is that large rapid capital inflows will both cause currency appreciation (and therefore harm export competitiveness) and complicate monetary policy (capital inflows flooding money markets and bank deposits). Chile in the 1990s provides an example. Newfound political and economic soundness started attracting international capital. The Chilean government responded with its *encaje* program, which imposed taxes and restrictions on short-term (less than one year) capital inflows, as well as restrictions on the ability of domestic financial institutions to extend credits or loans in foreign currency. Although credited with achieving its goals of maintaining domestic monetary policy and preventing a rapid appreciation in the Chilean peso, this program came at substantial cost to Chilean firms, particularly smaller ones.

A similar use of capital controls to prevent domestic currency appreciation is the so-called case of *Dutch Disease*. With the rapid growth of the natural gas industry in the Netherlands in the 1970s, there was growing fear that massive capital inflows would drive up the demand for the Dutch guilder and cause a substantial currency appreciation. A more expensive guilder would harm other Dutch manufacturing industries, causing them to decline relative to the natural resource industry. This is a challenge faced by a number of resource-rich economies of relatively modest size and with relatively small export sectors in recent years, including oil and gas development in Azerbaijan, Kazakhstan, and Nigeria, to name but a few.

Capital Flight. An extreme problem that has raised its head a number of times in international financial history is *capital flight*, one of the problems that capital controls are designed to control. Although defining capital flight is a bit difficult, the most common definition is the rapid outflow of capital in opposition to or in fear of domestic political and economic conditions and policies. Although it is not limited to heavily indebted countries, the rapid and sometimes illegal transfer of convertible currencies out of a country poses significant economic and political problems. Many heavily indebted countries have suffered significant capital flight, compounding their problems of debt service.

There are a number of mechanisms used for moving money from one country to another—some legal, some not. Transfers via the usual international payments mechanisms (regular bank transfers) are obviously the easiest and lowest cost, and are legal. Most economically healthy countries allow free exchange of their currencies, but of course for such countries "capital flight" is not a problem. The opposite, transfer of physical currency by bearer (the proverbial smuggling out of cash in the false bottom of a suitcase) is more costly and, for transfers out of many countries, illegal. Such transfers may be deemed illegal for balance of payments reasons or to make difficult the movement of money from the drug trade or other illegal activities.

And there are other more creative solutions. One is to move cash via collectibles or precious metals, which are then transferred across borders. *Money laundering* is the cross-border purchase of assets that are then managed in a way that hides the movement of money and its ownership. And finally, *false invoicing* of international trade transactions occurs when capital is moved through the under-invoicing of exports or the over-invoicing of imports, where the difference between the invoiced amount and the actual agreed upon payment is deposited in banking institutions in a country of choice.

Globalization of Capital Flows

Notwithstanding these benefits, many EMEs [emerging market economies] are concerned that the recent surge in capital inflows could cause problems for their economies. Many of the flows are perceived to be temporary, reflecting interest rate differentials, which may be at least partially reversed when policy interest rates in advanced economies return to more normal levels. Against this backdrop, capital controls are again in the news.

A concern has been that massive inflows can lead to exchange rate overshooting (or merely strong appreciations that significantly complicate economic management) or inflate asset price bubbles, which can amplify financial fragility and crisis risk. More broadly, following the crisis, policymakers are again reconsidering the view that unfettered capital flows are a fundamentally benign phenomenon and that all financial flows are the result of rational investing/borrowing/lending decisions. Concerns that foreign investors may be subject to herd behavior, and suffer from excessive optimism, have grown stronger; and even when flows are fundamentally sound, it is recognized that they may contribute to collateral damage, including bubbles and asset booms and busts.

—"Capital Inflows: The Role of Controls," Jonathan D. Ostry, Atish R. Ghosh, Karl Habermeier, Marcos Chamon, Mahvash S. Qureshi, and Dennis B.S. Reinhardt, IMF Staff Position Note, SPN/10/04, February 19, 2010, p. 3.

Traditionally, the primary concern over capital inflows is that they are short-term in duration, may flow out with short notice, and are characteristics of the politically and economically unstable emerging markets. But as described in the preceding quote, two of the largest capital flow crises in recent years have occurred within the largest, most highly developed, mature capital markets—the United States and Western Europe.

The 2008 global credit crisis, which had the United States as its core, and the current 2011–2012 Greece/European Union sovereign debt crisis, both occurred within markets that have long been considered the most mature, the most sophisticated, and the "safest."

Summary Points

- The BOP is the summary statement—a cash flow statement—of all international transactions between one country and all other countries over a period of time, typically a year.

- Although in theory the BOP must always balance, in practice there are substantial imbalances as a result of statistical errors and misreporting of current account and financial/capital account flows.

- The two subaccounts of the BOP that receive the most attention are the current account and the financial account. These accounts summarize the current trade and international capital flows of the country, respectively.

- The current account and financial account are typically inverse on balance, one in surplus and the other in deficit.

- Although most nations strive for current account surpluses, it is not clear that a balance on current or financial account, or a surplus on current account, is either sustainable or desirable.

- Although merchandise trade is more easily observed (e.g., goods flowing through ports of entry), today, the growth of services trade is more significant to the balance of payments for many of the world's largest industrialized countries.

- Monitoring the various subaccounts of a country's BOP activity is helpful to decision-makers and policymakers, on all levels of government and industry, in detecting the underlying trends and movements of fundamental economic forces driving a country's international economic activity.

- Changes in exchange rates affect relative prices of imports and exports, and changing prices in turn result in changes in quantities demanded through the price elasticity of demand.

- A devaluation results initially in a further deterioration of the trade balance before an eventual improvement—the path of adjustment taking on the shape of a flattened "j."

- The ability of capital to move instantaneously and massively cross-border has been one of the major factors in the severity of recent currency crises. In cases such as Malaysia in 1997 and Argentina in 2001, the national governments concluded that they had no choice but to impose drastic restrictions on the ability of capital to flow.

- Although not limited to heavily indebted countries, the rapid and sometimes illegal transfer of convertible currencies out of a country poses significant economic and political problems. Many heavily indebted countries have suffered significant capital flight, which has compounded their problems of debt service.

MINI-CASE

Global Remittances

"Remittances are a vital source of financial support that directly increases the income of migrants' families," said Hans Timmer, director of development prospects at the World Bank. "Remittances lead to more investments in health, education, and small business. With better tracking of migration and remittance trends, policy makers can make informed decisions to protect and leverage this massive capital inflow which is triple the size of official aid flows," Timmer said.

— "Remittances to Developing Countries Resilient in the Recent Crisis," Press Release No. 2011/168DEC, The World Bank, November 8, 2010.

One area within the balance of payments that has received intense interest in the past decade is that of remittances. The term remittance is a bit tricky. According to the International Monetary Fund (IMF), remittances are international transfers of funds sent by migrant workers from the country where they are working to people, typically family members, in the country from which they originated.[1]

According to the IMF, a *migrant* is a person who comes to a country and stays, or intends to stay, for a year or more. As shown in Exhibit A, a brief overview of global remittances would include the following:

- The World Bank estimates that $414 billion was remitted in 2009, with $316 billion of that going to developing countries. These remittance transactions were made by more than 190 million people, roughly 3% of the world's population.

- The top remittance-sending countries in 2009 were the United States, Saudi Arabia, Switzerland, Russia, and Germany. Worldwide, the top recipient countries in 2009 were India, China, Mexico, the Philippines, and France.

- Remittances make up a very small, often negligible cash outflow from sending countries like the United States. They do, however, represent a more significant volume, for example as a percent of GDP, for smaller developing recipient countries, sometimes more than 25%. In many cases, this is greater than all development capital and aid flowing to these same countries.

The historical record on global remittances is short. As illustrated in Exhibit A, remittances have shown dramatic growth in the post-2000 period, until suffering a first real decline with the global financial crisis 2008–2009.

Remittances largely reflect the income that is earned by migrant or guest workers in one country (source country) and then transferred to families or related parties in the workers' home countries (receiving countries). Therefore, it is not surprising that although there are more migrant worker flows between developing countries, the high-income developed economies remain the main source of remittances. The global economic recession of 2009 resulted in reduced economic activities like construction and manufacturing in the major source countries; as a result, remittance cash flows fell in 2009 but rebounded slightly in 2010.

Most remittances are frequent small payments made through wire transfers or a variety of informal channels (some even carried by hand). The United States Bureau of Economic Analysis (BEA), which is responsible for the compilation and reporting of U.S. balance of payments statistics, classifies migrant remittances as "current transfers" in the current account. Wider definitions of remittances may

EXHIBIT A   Global Remittances – World Inflows

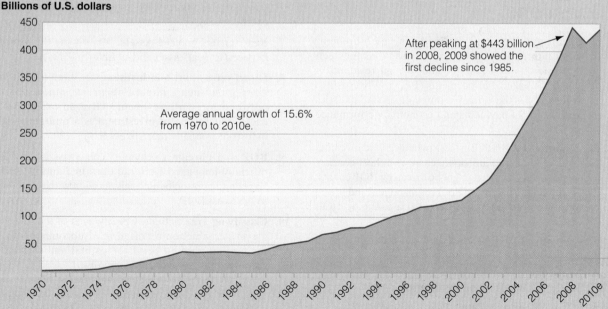

Billions of U.S. dollars

After peaking at $443 billion in 2008, 2009 showed the first decline since 1985.

Average annual growth of 15.6% from 1970 to 2010e.

Source: The World Bank.

[1] "Remittances: International Payments by Migrants," Congressional Budget Office, May 2005.

also include capital assets that migrants bring with them to host countries, and similar assets that they take back with them to their home countries.

All these values, when compiled, are generally reported under the financial account of the balance of payments. However, the definition of a "migrant" is also an area of some debate. Transfers back to his or her home country made by an individual who may be working in another country (for example, an expat working for an MNE) but who is not considered a "resident," may also be considered global remittances under current transfers in the current account.

Growing Controversies

With the growth in global remittances has come a growing debate as to what role they do or should play in a country's balance of payments, and more importantly, its economic development. In some cases, like India, there is growing resistance from the central bank and other banking institutions to allow online payment services like PayPal to process remittances. In other countries, like Honduras, Guatemala, and Mexico, there is growing debate on whether the bulk of remittances flow to families or if they are mostly payments to a variety of Central American smugglers—human trafficking smugglers.

In Mexico for example, remittances now make up the second largest source of foreign exchange earnings, second only to oil exports. The Mexican government has increasingly viewed remittances as an integral component of its balance of payments, and in some ways, a "plug" to replace declining export competition and dropping foreign direct investment. But there is also growing evidence that remittances flow to those who need it most, the lowest income component of the Mexican population, and therefore mitigate poverty and support consumer spending. Former President Vicente Fox was quoted as saying that Mexico's workers in other countries remitting income home to Mexico are "heroes."

CASE QUESTIONS

1. Where are remittances across borders included within the balance of payments? Are they current or financial account components?

2. Under what conditions are remittances significant contributors to the economy and overall balance of payments?

3. What role do remittances play in the economy of a country like Mexico?

Questions

1. **Balance of Payments Defined.** The measurement of all international economic transactions between the residents of a country and foreign residents is called the balance of payments (BOP). What institution provides the primary source of similar statistics for balance of payments and economic performance worldwide?

2. **Importance of BOP.** Business managers and investors need BOP data to anticipate changes in host-country economic policies that might be driven by BOP events. From the perspective of business managers and investors, list three specific signals that a country's BOP data can provide.

3. **Economic Activity.** What data can a nation's BOP provide about a country's economy?

4. **Balance.** If the BOP always "balances," then how do countries run a BOP deficit or surplus?

5. **Official Reserve Account.** Why does the central bank of a nation hold official reserve assets? What are its major components?

6. **Current Account Surpluses.** Explain the main causes behind the current account surpluses that Asian emerging economies have maintained during the last two decades.

7. **Real versus Financial Assets.** What is the difference between a "real" asset and a "financial" asset?

8. **Direct versus Portfolio Investments.** What is the difference between a direct foreign investment and a portfolio foreign investment? Give an example of each. Which type of investment is a multinational industrial company more likely to make?

9. **BOP and Foreign Exchange.** The Swiss franc was officially unpegged from the euro in January 2015. Explain the reason behind this decision with reference to the Swiss BOP.

10. **Classifying Transactions.** Classify each of the following as a transaction reported in a subcomponent of the current account or of the capital and financial accounts of the two countries involved:
    a. A U.S. food chain imports wine from Chile.
    b. A U.S. resident purchases a euro-denominated bond from a German company.
    c. Singaporean parents pay for their daughter to study at a U.S. university.
    d. A U.S. university gives a tuition grant to a foreign student from Singapore.

e. A British Company imports Spanish oranges, paying with eurodollars on deposit in London.

f. The Spanish orchard deposits half its proceeds in a eurodollar account in London.

g. A London-based insurance company buys U.S. corporate bonds for its investment portfolio.

h. An American multinational enterprise buys insurance from a London insurance broker.

i. A London insurance firm pays for losses incurred in the United States because of an international terrorist attack.

j. Cathay Pacific Airlines buys jet fuel at Los Angeles International Airport so it can fly the return segment of a flight back to Hong Kong.

k. A California-based mutual fund buys shares of stock on the Tokyo and London stock exchanges.

l. The U.S. army buys food for its troops in South Asia from local venders.

m. A Yale graduate gets a job with the International Committee of the Red Cross in Bosnia and is paid in Swiss francs.

n. The Russian government hires a Norwegian salvage firm to raise a sunken submarine.

o. A Colombian drug cartel smuggles cocaine into the United States, receives a suitcase of cash, and flies back to Colombia with that cash.

p. The U.S. government pays the salary of a foreign service officer working in the U.S. embassy in Beirut.

q. A Norwegian shipping firm pays U.S. dollars to the Egyptian government for passage of a ship through the Suez Canal.

r. A German automobile firm pays the salary of its executive working for a subsidiary in Detroit.

s. An American tourist pays for a hotel in Paris with his American Express card.

t. A French tourist from the provinces pays for a hotel in Paris with his American Express card.

u. A U.S. professor goes abroad for a year on a Fulbright grant.

11. **Current Account Deficits.** A deficit on the current account increases foreign liabilities. Explain why this is more of a concern to the Eurozone than a country like Brazil.

12. **Hot Money.** Hot money is the flow of foreign investors' funds to earn short-term profits. How does this impact the BOP and the economy at large?

13. **Treasury Bonds.** Especially after the global financial crisis, sovereign and portfolio investors from emerging market economies have purchased significant volumes of European treasury bonds. Discuss the impact on the European BOPs in both the short run and the long run.

14. **Capital Mobility — Brazil.** Brazil has experienced periodic depreciation of its currency over the past 20 years despite occasionally running a current account surplus. Why has this phenomenon occurred?

15. **BOP Transactions.** Identify the correct BOP account for each of the following transactions:

a. A German-based pension fund buys U.S. government 30-year bonds for its investment portfolio.

b. Scandinavian Airlines System (SAS) buys jet fuel at Newark Airport for its flight to Copenhagen.

c. Hong Kong students pay tuition to the University of California, Berkeley.

d. The U.S. Air Force buys food in South Korea to supply its air crews.

e. A Japanese auto company pays the salaries of its executives working for its U.S. subsidiaries.

f. A U.S. tourist pays for a restaurant meal in Bangkok.

g. A Colombian citizen smuggles cocaine into the United States, receives cash, and smuggles the dollars back into Colombia.

h. A U.K. corporation purchases a euro-denominated bond from an Italian MNE.

Problems

Australia's Current Account

Use the following balance of payments data for Australia from the IMF to answer Problems 1–4.

Assumptions (million US$)	2000	2001	2002	2003	2004	2005	2006	2007	2008	2009	2010	2011	2012
Goods, credit (exports)	64,052	63,676	65,099	70,577	87,207	107,011	124,913	142,421	189,057	154,777	213,782	271,677	257,754
Goods, debit (imports)	−68,865	−61,890	−70,530	−85,946	−105,238	−120,383	−134,509	−160,205	−193,972	−159,216	−196,303	−242,915	−262,966
Services, credit (exports)	18,677	16,689	17,906	21,205	26,362	31,047	33,088	40,496	45,240	40,814	46,968	51,852	52,672

(continued)

Assumptions (million US$)	2000	2001	2002	2003	2004	2005	2006	2007	2008	2009	2010	2011	2012
Services, debit (imports)	−18,388	−16,948	−18,107	−21,638	−27,040	−30,505	−32,219	−39,908	−48,338	−42,165	−51,313	−60,994	−64,389
Primary income: credit	8,984	8,063	8,194	9,457	13,969	16,445	21,748	32,655	37,320	27,402	35,711	42,965	42,097
Primary income: debit	−19,516	−18,332	−19,884	−24,245	−35,057	−44,166	−54,131	−73,202	−76,719	−65,809	−84,646	−94,689	−80,778
Secondary income: credit	2,622	2,242	2,310	2,767	3,145	3,333	3,698	4,402	4,431	4,997	5,813	7,389	7,357
Secondary income: debit	−2,669	−2,221	−2,373	−2,851	−3,414	−3,813	−4,092	−4,690	−4,805	−5,799	−7,189	−8,920	−8,783

Note: The IMF has recently adjusted their line item nomenclature. *Exports* are all now noted as *credits*, *imports* as *debits*.

1. What is Australia's balance on goods?
2. What is Australia's balance on services?
3. What is Australia's balance on goods and services?
4. What is Australia's current account balance?

India's Current Account

Use the following balance of payments data for India from the IMF to answer Problems 5–9.

Assumptions (million US$)	2000	2001	2002	2003	2004	2005	2006	2007	2008	2009	2010	2011	2012
Goods, credit (exports)	43,247	44,793	51,141	60,893	77,939	102,175	123,768	153,530	199,065	167,958	230,967	307,847	298,321
Goods, debit (imports)	−53,887	−51,212	−54,702	−68,081	−95,539	−134,692	−166,572	−208,611	−291,740	−247,908	−324,320	−428,021	−450,249
Services, credit (exports)	16,684	17,337	19,478	23,902	38,281	52,527	69,730	86,552	106,054	92,889	117,068	138,528	145,525
Services, debit (imports)	−19,187	−20,099	−21,039	−24,878	−35,641	−47,287	−58,696	−70,175	−87,739	−80,349	−114,739	−125,041	−129,659
Primary income: credit	2,521	3,524	3,188	3,491	4,690	5,646	8,199	12,650	15,593	13,733	9,961	10,147	9,899
Primary income: debit	−7,414	−7,666	−7,097	−8,386	−8,742	−12,296	−14,445	−19,166	−20,958	−21,272	−25,563	−26,191	−30,742
Secondary income: credit	13,548	15,140	16,789	22,401	20,615	24,512	30,015	38,885	52,065	50,526	54,380	62,735	68,611
Secondary income: debit	−114	−407	−698	−570	−822	−869	−1,299	−1,742	−3,313	−1,764	−2,270	−2,523	−3,176

5. What is India's balance on goods?
6. What is India's balance on services?
7. What is India's balance on goods and services?
8. What is India's balance on goods, services, and income?
9. What is India's current account balance?

China's (Mainland) Balance of Payments

Use the following balance of payments data for China (Mainland) from the IMF to answer Problems 10–13.

Assumptions (million US$)	2000	2001	2002	2003	2004	2005	2006	2007	2008	2009	2010	2011	2012
A. Current account balance	20,518	17,401	35,422	45,875	68,659	134,082	232,746	353,183	420,569	243,257	237,810	136,097	193,139
B. Capital account balance	−35	−54	−50	−48	−69	4,102	4,020	3,099	3,051	3,958	4,630	5,446	4,272

(continued)

Assumptions (million US$)	2000	2001	2002	2003	2004	2005	2006	2007	2008	2009	2010	2011	2012
C. Financial account balance	1,958	34,832	32,341	52,774	110,729	96,944	48,629	91,132	37,075	194,494	282,234	260,024	21,084
D. Net errors and omissions	−11,748	−4,732	7,504	17,985	10,531	15,847	−745	13,237	18,859	−41,181	−53,016	−13,768	−79,773
E. Reserves and related items	−10,693	−47,447	−75,217	−116,586	−189,849	−250,975	−284,651	−460,651	−479,553	−400,508	−471,659	−387,799	−96,555

10. Is China experiencing a net capital inflow or outflow?

11. What is China's total for Groups A and B?

12. What is China's total for Groups A through C?

13. What is China's total for Groups A through D?

Russia's (Russian Federation's) Balance of Payments

Use the following balance of payments data for Russia (Russian Federation) from the IMF to answer Problems 14–17.

Assumptions (million US$)	2000	2001	2002	2003	2004	2005	2006	2007	2008	2009	2010
A. Current account balance	46,839	33,935	29,116	35,410	59,512	84,602	94,686	77,768	103,530	48,605	70,253
B. Capital account balance	10,676	−9,378	−12,396	−993	−1,624	−12,764	191	−10,224	496	−11,869	73
C. Financial account balance	−34,295	−3,732	921	3,024	−5,128	1,025	3,071	94,730	−131,674	−31,648	−25,956
D. Net errors and omissions	−9,297	−9,558	−6,078	−9,179	−5,870	−7,895	9,518	−13,347	−11,271	−1,724	−7,621
E. Reserves and related items	−13,923	−11,266	−11,563	−28,262	−46,890	−64,968	−107,466	−148,928	38,919	−3,363	−36,749

14. Is Russia experiencing a net capital inflow?

15. What is Russia's total for Groups A and B?

16. What is Russia's total for Groups A through C?

17. What is Russia's total for Groups A through D?

Euro Area Balance of Payments

Use the following balance of payments data for the Euro Area from the IMF to answer Problems 18–21.

Assumptions (billion US$)	2000	2001	2002	2003	2004	2005	2006	2007	2008	2009	2010
A. Current account balance	−81.8	−19.7	44.5	24.9	81.2	19.2	−0.3	24.9	−198.2	−31.3	−53.6
B. Capital account balance	8.4	5.6	10.3	14.3	20.5	14.2	11.7	5.4	13.2	8.5	8.2
C. Financial account balance	50.9	−41.2	−15.3	−47.6	−122.9	−71.4	−27.9	−1.9	204.4	70.3	77.3
D. Net errors and omissions	6.4	38.8	−36.5	−24.4	5.6	15.0	19.0	−22.7	−14.5	12.4	−18.3
E. Reserves and related items	16.2	16.4	−3.0	32.8	15.6	23.0	−2.6	−5.7	−4.9	−59.8	−13.6

18. Is the Euro Area experiencing a net capital inflow?

19. What is the Euro Area's total for Groups A and B?

20. What is the Euro Area's total for Groups A through C?

21. What is the Euro Area's total for Groups A through D?

22. **Trade Deficits and J-Curve Adjustment Paths.**
Assume that the United Arab Emirates has the following import/export volumes and prices. It undertakes a major "devaluation" of the UAE Dirham (AED) by 6% on average against all major trading partner currencies. What is the pre-devaluation and post-devaluation trade balance?

Initial cross exchange rate (AED/€)	4.2
Price of exports (AED)	100 billion
Price of imports, euro (€)	112 billion
Quantity of exports, units	300
Quantity of imports, units	200
Percentage devaluation of the AED	6%
Price elasticity of demand, imports	−0.85

Internet Exercises

1. **World Organizations and the Economic Outlook.** The IMF, World Bank, and United Nations are only a few of the major world organizations that track, report, and aid international economic and financial development. Using these Web sites and others that may be linked, briefly summarize the economic outlook for the developed and emerging nations of the world. For example, Chapter 1 of the *World Economic Outlook* published annually by the World Bank is available through the IMF's Web page.

International Monetary Fund	www.imf.org/
United Nations	www.unsystem.org/
The World Bank Group	www.worldbank.org/
Europa (EU) Homepage	europa.eu/
Bank for International Settlements	www.bis.org/

2. **St. Louis Federal Reserve.** The Federal Reserve Bank of St. Louis provides a large amount of recent open-economy macroeconomic data online. Use the following addresses to track down recent BOP and GDP data.

Recent international economic data	research.stlouisfed.org/publications/iet/
Balance of payments statistics	research.stlouisfed.org/fred2/categories/125

3. **U.S. Bureau of Economic Analysis.** Use the following Bureau of Economic Analysis (U.S. government) and the Ministry of Finance (Japanese government) Web sites to find the most recent balance of payments statistics for both countries.

Bureau of Economic Analysis	www.bea.gov/international/
Ministry of Finance	www.mof.go.jp/

4. **World Trade Organization and Doha.** Visit the WTO's Web site and find the most recent evidence presented by the WTO on the progress of talks on issues including international trade in services and international recognition of intellectual property at the WTO.

World Trade Organization	www.wto.org

5. **Global Remittances Worldwide.** The World Bank's Web site on global remittances is a valuable source for new and developing studies and statistics on cross-border remittance activity.

World Bank	http://remittanceprices.worldbank.org/

Financial Goals and Corporate Governance

Gerald L. Storch, CEO of Toys 'R' Us, says all CEOs share the same fundamental goals: enhance the value for the customer, maximize return to the shareholders, and develop a sustainable competitive advantage. "Largely, I believe that the differences are more subtle than what I've read in many articles. On a day-to-day basis, I do the same thing. I get to work every morning. I try to make the company better." —"Public Vs. Private," *Forbes*, September 1, 2006.

LEARNING OBJECTIVES

- Examine the different ownership structures for businesses globally and how this impacts the separation between ownership and management—the agency problem

- Evaluate the distinctions between the two major forms of management goals—stockholder wealth maximization versus stakeholder capitalism

- Distinguish differences in operational goals pursued by management depending on whether the company is operated by owners or professional management

- Analyze the goals and forms of corporate governance in use in the global marketplace today, and whether that attracts or deters cross-border investment

- Examine how trends in corporate governance are altering the competitive landscape for multinational enterprises

This chapter examines how legal, cultural, political, and institutional differences affect a firm's choice of financial goals and corporate governance. The owner of a commercial enterprise, and his or her specific personal and professional interests, has a significant impact on the goals of the corporation and its governance. We therefore examine business ownership, goals, and corporate governance in turn. We then explore how governance failures have led to different approaches around the world to improve governance, by both regulatory and other means. The chapter concludes with the Mini-Case, *Luxury Wars—LVMH vs. Hermès*, the recent struggle by Hermès of France to remain family controlled.

Who Owns the Business?

We begin our discussion of corporate financial goals by asking two basic questions:

1. Who owns the business?
2. Do the owners of the business manage the business themselves?

In global business today the ownership and control of organizations varies dramatically across countries and cultures. To understand how and why those businesses operate, one must first understand the many different ownership structures.

Types of Ownership

The terminology associated with the ownership of a business can be confusing. A business owned by a government, the state, is a *public enterprise*. A business that is owned by a private individual, a private company, or simply a non-government entity, is a *private enterprise*.

A second distinction on ownership clouds the terminology. A business owned by a private party, or a small group of private individuals, a private enterprise, is termed *privately held*. If those owners, however, wish to sell a portion of their ownership in the business in the capital markets, for example by listing and trading the company's shares on a stock exchange, the firm's shares are then *publicly traded*. It is important, therefore, to be clear in understanding that shares in a publicly traded firm can be purchased and owned by private parties — publicly traded between private parties. Exhibit 4.1 provides a brief overview of these ownership distinctions.

Ownership can be held by a variety of different groups or organizations as well. A business may be owned by a single person (*sole proprietorship*), two or more people (*partnership*), a

---

EXHIBIT 4.1   **Business Ownership**

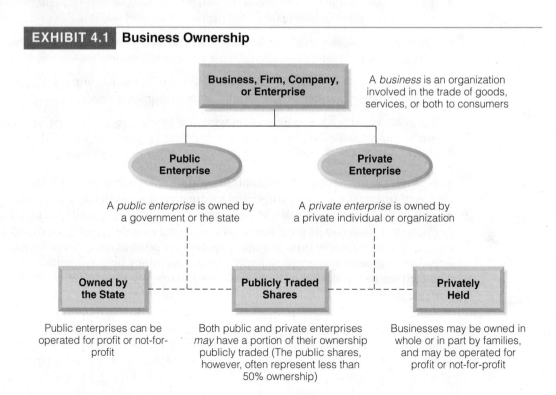

family (*family-owned business*), two other companies (*joint venture*), thousands of individuals (*publicly traded company*), a government (*state-owned enterprise*), or some combination.

The following three multinational enterprises are examples of how ownership differs in global business, as well as how it may evolve within any single enterprise over time.

■ Petróleo Brasileiro S.A., or Petrobras, is the national oil company of Brazil. Founded in 1953, it was originally 100% owned by the Brazilian government, and was therefore a *state-owned enterprise*. Over time, however, it sold portions of its ownership to the public, becoming publicly traded on the Sao Paulo stock exchange. Today the Brazilian government owns approximately 64% of the shares of Petrobras, with the remaining 36% in the hands of private investors—shareholders—all over the world.

■ Apple was founded in 1976 as a partnership of Steve Jobs, Steve Wozniak, and Ronald Wayne. On January 3, 1977, Apple was incorporated in the United States, with Ronald Wayne selling his ownership interest to his two partners. In 1980 Apple sold shares to the public for the first time in an *initial public offering* (IPO), with its shares listed (traded) on the NASDAQ Stock Market. Today Apple has roughly 900 million shares outstanding, and is considered "widely held" as no single investor holds 5% of its shares. In recent years Apple has periodically been the world's most valuable publicly traded company, as calculated by *market capitalization* (shares outstanding multiplied by the share price).

■ Hermès International is a French multinational producer of luxury goods. Founded by Thierry Hermès in 1837, it has been owned and operated by the Hermès family for most of its history, making it a family-owned business. In 1993 the company "went public" for the first time, selling 27% of its interest to the general public. The family, however, retained 73% and therefore the control of the company. (The Mini-Case at the end of this chapter details the battle fought by the family in 2010 to retain its control.)

Once the ownership of the business is established, it is then easier to understand where control lies, as ownership and control are separate concepts. Petrobras is a publicly traded Brazilian business that is controlled by the Brazilian government. Hermès International is a publicly traded family-controlled French-based business. Apple is a publicly traded and widely held business, so control rests with its Board of Directors and the senior leadership team hired by the Board to run the company. Individual investors who hold shares in Apple may vote on issues presented to them on an annual basis, so they have a degree of high-level influence, but the daily strategy, tactics, operations, and governance of Apple is under the control of the senior management team and the Board.

Any business, whether initially owned by the state, a family, or a private individual or institution, may choose to have a portion of its ownership traded as shares in the public marketplace, as noted in Exhibit 4.1. (Note that we say a *portion*, as a 100% publicly traded firm can no longer be either state-owned or privately held by definition.) For example many SOEs are also publicly traded. China National Petroleum Corporation (CNPC), the state-owned parent company of PetroChina, is one example, having shares traded on stock exchanges in Shanghai, Hong Kong, and New York, yet majority ownership and control still rests with the government of China.

If a firm's ownership decides to sell a portion of ownership to the public market, it conducts an initial public offering, or IPO. Typically only a relatively small percentage of the company is initially sold to the public, anywhere from 10% to 20%, resulting in a company that may still be controlled by a small number of private investors, a family, or a government, but now with a portion of its ownership traded publicly. Over time, a company may sell more and more of its equity interest into the public marketplace, eventually becoming totally publicly traded. Alternatively, a private owner or family may choose to retain a major share, but may not retain control. It is also possible for the controlling interest in a firm to reverse its pubic share position, reducing the number of shares outstanding by repurchasing shares.

The acquisition of one firm by another demonstrates yet another way ownership and control can change. For example, in 2005 a very large private firm, Koch Industries (U.S.), purchased all outstanding shares of Georgia-Pacific (U.S.), a very large publicly traded forest products company. Koch took Georgia-Pacific private.

Even if a firm is publicly traded, it may still be controlled by a single investor or small group of investors, including major institutional investors. This means that the control of a publicly traded company is much like that of a privately held company, reflecting the interests and goals of the controlling individual investor or family. A continuing characteristic of many emerging markets is the dominance of family-controlled firms, although many are simultaneously publicly traded. Many family-controlled firms may outperform publicly traded firms. The Mini-Case at the end of this chapter highlights one such family-based controlled enterprise.

As discussed later in this chapter, there is another significant implication of an initial sale of shares to the public: The firm becomes subject to many of the increased legal, regulatory, and reporting requirements (present in most countries) related to the sale and trading of securities. In the U.S., for example, going public means the firm must disclose a sizable degree of financial and operational detail, publish this information at least quarterly, comply with Securities and Exchange Commission (SEC) rules and regulations, and comply with all the specific operating and reporting requirements of the specific exchange on which its shares are traded.

Separation of Ownership from Management

One of the most challenging issues in the financial management of the enterprise is the possible separation of ownership from management. Hired or professional management may be present under any ownership structure, however it is most often observed in SOEs and widely held publicly traded companies. This separation of ownership from management raises the possibility that the two entities may have different business and financial objectives. This is the so-called *principal agent problem* or simply the *agency problem*. There are several strategies available for aligning shareholder and management interests, the most common of which is for senior management to own shares or share options. What is then good for the managers' own personal wealth is similar to that of general shareholders.

The United States and United Kingdom are two country markets characterized by widespread ownership of shares. Management may own some small portion of stock in their firms, but largely management is a hired *agent* that is expected to represent the interests of shareholders. In contrast, many firms in many other global markets are characterized by controlling shareholders such as government, institutions (e.g., banks in Germany), family (e.g., in France, Italy, and throughout Asia and Latin America), and consortiums of interests (e.g., keiretsus in Japan and chaebols in South Korea). A business that is owned and managed by the same entity does not suffer the agency problem.

In many of these cases, control is enhanced by ownership of shares with dual voting rights, interlocking directorates, staggered election of the board of directors, takeover safeguards, and other techniques that are not used in the Anglo-American markets. However, the recent emergence of huge equity funds and hedge funds in the United States and the United Kingdom has led to the privatization of some very prominent publicly traded firms around the world.

The Goal of Management

As companies become more deeply committed to multinational operations, a new constraint develops—one that springs from divergent worldwide opinions and practices as to just what the firms' overall goal should be from the perspective of top management, as well as the role of corporate governance.

> *What do investors want? First, of course, investors want performance: strong predictable earnings and sustainable growth. Second, they want transparency, accountability, open communications and effective corporate governance. Companies that fail to move toward international standards in each of these areas will fail to attract and retain international capital.*
>
> —"The Brave New World of Corporate Governance," *LatinFinance*, May 2001.

An introductory course in finance is usually taught based on the assumption that maximizing shareholder wealth is the goal of management. In fact, every business student memorizes the concept of maximizing shareholder wealth sometime during his or her college education. Maximizing shareholder wealth, however, has at least two major challenges: 1) It is not necessarily the accepted goal of management across countries to maximize the wealth of shareholders—other stakeholders may have substantial influence; and 2) It is extremely difficult to carry out. Creating shareholder wealth is—like so many lofty goals— much easier said than done.

Although the idea of maximizing shareholder wealth is probably realistic both in theory and in practice in the Anglo-American markets, it is not always exclusive elsewhere. Some basic differences in corporate and investor philosophies exist between the Anglo-American markets and those in the rest of the world.

The Shareholder Wealth Maximization Model

The Anglo-American markets have a philosophy that a firm's objective should follow the *shareholder wealth maximization* (SWM) model. More specifically, the firm should strive to maximize the return to shareholders, as measured by the sum of capital gains and dividends, for a given level of risk. Alternatively, the firm should minimize the risk to shareholders for a given rate of return.

The SWM theoretical model assumes, as a universal truth, that the stock market is efficient. This means that the share price is always correct because it captures all the expectations of return and risk as perceived by investors. It quickly incorporates new information into the share price. Share prices, in turn, are deemed the best allocators of capital in the macro economy.

The SWM model also treats its definition of risk as a universal truth. Risk is defined as the added probability of varying returns that the firm's shares bring to a diversified portfolio. The *operational risk*, the risk associated with the business-line of the individual firm, can be eliminated through portfolio diversification by investors. Therefore the *unsystematic risk*, the risk of the individual security, should not be a prime concern for management unless it increases the possibility of bankruptcy. On the other hand, *systematic risk*, the risk of the market in general, cannot be eliminated through portfolio diversification and is risk that the share price will be a function of the stock market.

Agency Theory. The field of *agency theory* is the study of how shareholders can motivate management to accept the prescriptions of the SWM model.[1] For example, liberal use of stock

---

[1]Michael Jensen and W. Meckling, "Theory of the Firm: Managerial Behavior, Agency Costs, and Ownership Structure," *Journal of Financial Economics*, No. 3, 1976, and Michael C. Jensen, "Agency Cost of Free Cash Flow, Corporate Finance and Takeovers, *American Economic Review*, 76, 1986, pp. 323–329.

options should encourage management to think like shareholders. Whether these inducements succeed is open to debate. However, if management deviates from the SWM objectives of working to maximize shareholder returns, then it is the responsibility of the board to replace management. In cases where the board is too weak or ingrown to take this action, the discipline of equity markets could do it through a takeover. This discipline is made possible by the one-share-one-vote rule that exists in most Anglo-American markets.

Long-Term versus Short-Term Value Maximization. During the 1990s, the economic boom and rising stock prices in most of the world's markets exposed a flaw in the SWM model, especially in the United States. Instead of seeking long-term value maximization, several large U.S. corporations sought short-term value maximization (e.g., the continuing debate about meeting the market's expected quarterly earnings). This strategy was partly motivated by the overly generous use of stock options to motivate top management.

This short-term focus sometimes created distorted managerial incentives. In order to maximize growth in short-term earnings and to meet inflated expectations by investors, firms such as Enron, Global Crossing, Health South, Adelphia, Tyco, Parmalat, and WorldCom undertook risky, deceptive, and sometimes dishonest practices for the recording of earnings and/or obfuscation of liabilities, which ultimately led to their demise. It also led to highly visible prosecutions of their CEOs, CFOs, accounting firms, legal advisers, and other related parties. This destructive short-term focus by both management and investors has been correctly labeled *impatient capitalism*. This point of debate is also sometimes referred to as the firm's *investment horizon* in reference to how long it takes the firm's actions, its investments and operations, to result in earnings. In contrast to impatient capitalism is *patient capitalism*, which focuses on long-term shareholder wealth maximization. Legendary investor Warren Buffett, through his investment vehicle Berkshire Hathaway, represents one of the best of the patient capitalists. Buffett has become a billionaire by focusing his portfolio on mainstream firms that grow slowly but steadily with the economy, such as Coca Cola.

The Stakeholder Capitalism Model

In the non-Anglo-American markets, controlling shareholders also strive to maximize long-term returns to equity. However, they are more constrained by other powerful stakeholders. In particular, outside the Anglo-American markets, labor unions are more powerful and governments interfere more in the marketplace to protect important stakeholder groups, such as local communities, the environment, and employment. In addition, banks and other financial institutions are more important creditors than securities markets. This model has been labeled the *stakeholder capitalism model* (SCM).

Market Efficiency. The SCM model does not assume that equity markets are either efficient or inefficient. It does not really matter because the firm's financial goals are not exclusively shareholder-oriented since they are constrained by the other stakeholders. In any case, the SCM model assumes that long-term "loyal" shareholders, typically controlling shareholders, should influence corporate strategy rather than the transient portfolio investor.

Risk. The SCM model assumes that total risk, that is, operating risk, does count. It is a specific-corporate objective to generate growing earnings and dividends over the long run with as much certainty as possible, given the firm's mission statement and goals. Risk is measured more by product market variability than by short-term variation in earnings and share price.

Single versus Multiple Goals. Although the SCM model typically avoids a flaw of the SWM model, namely, impatient capital that is short-run oriented, it has its own flaw. Trying to meet the desires of multiple stakeholders leaves management without a clear signal about the trade-offs. Instead, management tries to influence the trade-offs through written and oral disclosures and complex compensation systems.

The Score Card. In contrast to the SCM model, the SWM model requires a single goal of value maximization with a well-defined score card. According to the theoretical model of SWM described by Michael Jensen, the objective of management is to maximize the total market value of the firm.[2] This means that corporate leadership should be willing to spend or invest more money or capital if each additional dollar creates more than one dollar in the market value of the company's equity, debt, or any other contingent claims on the firm.

Although both models have their strengths and weaknesses, in recent years two trends have led to an increasing focus on the shareholder wealth form (SWM). First, as more of the non-Anglo-American markets have increasingly privatized their industries, a shareholder wealth focus is seemingly needed to attract international capital from outside investors, many of whom are from other countries. Second, and still quite controversial, many analysts believe that shareholder-based MNEs are increasingly dominating their global industry segments. Nothing attracts followers like success.

Operational Goals

It is one thing to say "maximize value," but it is another to actually do it. The management objective of maximizing profit is not as simple as it sounds, because the measure of profit used by ownership/management differs between the privately held firm and the publicly traded firm. In other words, is management attempting to maximize current income, capital appreciation, or both?

The return to a shareholder in a publicly traded firm combines current income in the form of dividends and capital gains from the appreciation of share price:

$$\text{Shareholder Return} = \frac{D_2}{P_1} + \frac{P_2 - P_1}{P_1}$$

where the initial price, P_1 is the beginning price, the initial investment by the shareholder, P_2 is the price of the share at the end of period, and D_2 is the dividend paid at the end of the period. The shareholder theoretically receives income from both components. For example, over the past 50 or 60 years in the U.S. marketplace, a diversified investor may have received a total average annual return of 14%, split roughly between dividends, 2%, and capital gains, 12%.

Management generally believes it has the most direct influence over the first component—the dividend yield. Management makes strategic and operational decisions that grow sales and generate profits. Then it distributes those profits to ownership in the form of dividends. Capital gains—the change in the share price as traded in the equity markets—is much more complex, and reflects many forces that are not in the direct control of management. Despite growing market share, profits, or any other traditional measure of business success, the market may not reward these actions directly with share price appreciation. Many top executives believe that stock markets move in mysterious ways and are not always consistent in their valuations. In the end, leadership in the publicly traded firm typically concludes that it is its own growth—growth in top-line sales and bottom-line profits—that is its great hope for driving share price upward.

A privately held firm has a much simpler shareholder return objective function: maximize current and sustainable income. The privately held firm does not have a share price (it does have a value, but this is not a definitive market-determined value in the way in which we believe markets work). It therefore simply focuses on generating current income, dividend income, to generate the returns to its ownership. If the privately held ownership is a family,

[2]Michael C. Jensen, "Value Maximization, Stakeholder Theory, and the Corporate Objective Function," *Journal of Applied Corporate Finance*, Fall 2001, Vol. 14, No. 3, pp. 8–21, p. 12.

EXHIBIT 4.2   Public versus Private Ownership

Organizational Characteristic	Publicly Traded	Privately Held
Entrepreneurial	No; stick to core competencies	Yes; do anything the owners wish
Long-term or short-term focus	Short-term focus on quarterly earnings	Long-term focus
Focused on profitable growth	Yes; growth in earnings is critical	No; needs defined by owners earnings need
Adequately financed	Good access to capital and capital markets	Limited in the past but increasingly available
Quality of leadership	Professional; hiring from both inside & outside	Highly variable; family-run firms are lacking
Role of Earnings (Profits)	Earnings to signal the equity markets	Earnings to support owners and family
Leadership are owners	Minimal interests; some have stock options	Yes; ownership and mgmt often one and the same

the family may also place a great emphasis on the ability to sustain those earnings over time while maintaining a slower rate of growth, which can be managed by the family itself. Without a share price, "growth" is not of the same strategic importance in the privately held firm. It is therefore critical that ownership and ownership's specific financial interests be understood from the very start if we are to understand the strategic and financial goals and objectives of management. Exhibit 4.2 provides an overview of the variety of distinctive financial and managerial differences between publicly traded and privately held firms.

The privately held firm may also be less aggressive (take fewer risks) than the publicly traded firm. Without a public share price, and therefore the ability of outside investors to speculate on the risks and returns associated with company business developments, the privately held firm—its owners and operators—may choose to take fewer risks. This may mean that it will not attempt to grow sales and profits as rapidly, and therefore may not require the capital (equity and debt) needed for rapid growth. A recent study by McKinsey found that privately held firms consistently used significantly lower levels of debt (averaging 5% less debt-to-equity) than publicly traded firms. Interestingly, these same private firms also enjoyed a lower cost of debt, roughly 30 basis points lower based on corporate bond issuances.[3]

Operational Goals for MNEs. The MNE must be guided by operational goals suitable for various levels of the firm. Even if the firm's goal is to maximize shareholder value, the manner in which investors value the firm is not always obvious to the firm's top management. Therefore, most firms hope to receive a favorable investor response to the achievement of operational goals that can be controlled by the way in which the firm performs, and then hope—if we can use that term—that the market will reward their results. The MNE must determine the proper balance between three common operational financial objectives:

1. Maximization of consolidated after-tax income
2. Minimization of the firm's effective global tax burden
3. Correct positioning of the firm's income, cash flows, and available funds as to country and currency

These goals are frequently incompatible, in that the pursuit of one may result in a less desirable outcome of another. Management must make decisions about the proper trade-offs between goals (which is why managers are people and not computers).

Consolidated Profits. The primary operational goal of the MNE is to maximize consolidated profits, after-tax. Consolidated profits are the profits of all the individual units of the firm,

---

[3]"The five attributes of enduring family businesses," Christian Caspar, Ana Karina Dias, and Heinz-Peter Elstrodt, *McKinsey Quarterly*, January 2010, p. 6.

originating in many different currencies, and expressed in the currency of the parent company. This is not to say that management is not striving to maximize the present value of all future cash flows. It is simply the case that most of the day-to-day decision-making in global management is about current earnings. The leaders of the MNE, the management team who are implementing the firm's strategy, must think far beyond current earnings.

For example, foreign subsidiaries have their own set of traditional financial statements: 1) a statement of income, summarizing the revenues and expenses experienced by the unit over the year; 2) a balance sheet, summarizing the assets employed in generating the unit's revenues, and the financing of those assets; and 3) a statement of cash flows, summarizing those activities of the unit that generate and then use cash flows over the year. These financial statements are expressed initially in the local currency of the unit for tax and reporting purposes to the local government, but they must also be consolidated with the parent company's financial statements for reporting to shareholders.

Public/Private Hybrids. The global business environment is, as one analyst termed it, "a messy place," and the ownership of companies of all kinds, including MNEs, is not necessarily purely public or purely private. One recent study of global business found that fully one-third of all companies in the S&P 500 were technically family businesses. And this was not just the case for the U.S.; roughly 40% of the largest firms in France and Germany were heavily influence by family ownership and leadership.

In other words, the firm may be publicly traded, but a family still wields substantial power over the strategic and operational decisions of the firm. This may prove to be a good thing. As illustrated in Exhibit 4.3, the financial performance of publicly traded family-controlled businesses (as measured by total returns to shareholders) in five different regions of the globe were superior to their nonfamily publicly traded counterparts.

EXHIBIT 4.3   **The Superior Performance of Family**

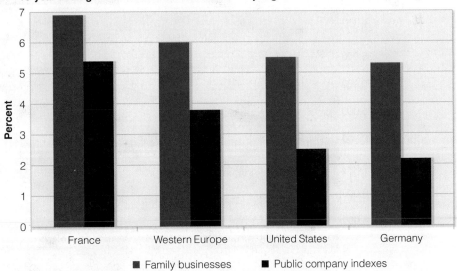

10-year average total returns to shareholders by region

■ Family businesses   ■ Public company indexes

Source: Author presentation based on data presented in "The Five Attributes of Enduring Family Businesses," Christian Caspar, Ana Karina Dias, and Heinz-Peter Elstrodt, *McKinsey Quarterly*, January 2010, p. 7. Index of public companies by region: France, SBF120; Western Europe, MSCI Europe; United States, S&P500; Germany, HDAX.

Why do family-influenced businesses seemingly perform better than others? According to Credit Suisse, there are three key catalysts for the performance of *stocks with significant family influence* (SSFI): 1) management with a longer-term focus; 2) better alignment between management and shareholder interests; and 3) stronger focus on the core business of the firm.

Publicly Traded versus Privately Held: The Global Shift

Today, the public company is in trouble: the organisation that has been at the heart of capitalism for the past 150 years faces a loss of confidence in its Anglo-Saxon heartland and the rise of powerful challengers abroad. The number of companies listed on the major American stock exchanges has been declining relentlessly in recent years … America needs 360 new listings a year merely to maintain a steady state. But it has averaged only 170 a year since 2000—and even a Facebook-fuelled IPO boom is not going to make up the difference.

—"Varied Company," The World in 2012, *The Economist*,
December 2011, p. 31.

Is the future of the publicly traded firm really at risk, or is it just that U.S.-based publicly traded shares are on the decline? Exhibit 4.4 provides a broad overview of global equity listings, separating the number of listings between those on U.S. exchanges and all others.

EXHIBIT 4.4   **Global Equity Share Listings**

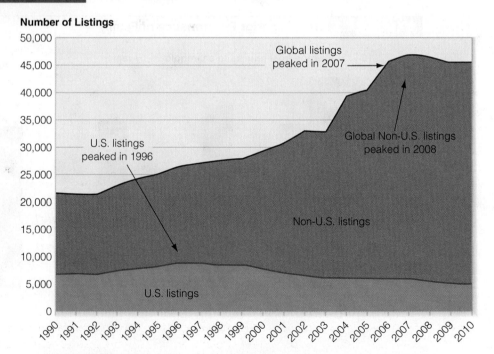

Source: Derived by authors from statistics collected by the World Federation of Exchanges (WFE), www.world-exchanges.org.

Exhibit 4.4, based on listings data from the World Federation of Exchanges, raises a number of questions about trends and tendencies across the global equity markets:

- Although global equity listings grew significantly over the past 20 years, they peaked in 2008. Although the true residual impact of the 2008–2009 global financial crisis is yet unknown, it is clear that the crisis, amid other factors, has stopped the growth of public share listings. At least for now.

- The U.S. share of global equity listings has declined dramatically and steadily since the mid-1990s. At the end of 2010, of the 45,508 equities listed on 54 stock exchanges globally, U.S. listings comprised 5,016 of the total, or 11.0%. That was a dramatic decline from 1996, the peak year of total U.S. listings, when the U.S. comprised 8,783 of the global total of 26,368 listings, or 33.3%.

- U.S. public share listings fell by 3,767 (from 8,783 in 1996 to 5,016 in 2010), 42.9% over the 14-year period since its peak. Clearly, the attraction of being a publicly traded firm on a U.S. equity exchange had declined dramatically.

Listings Measurement

New listings on a stock exchange is the net result of listing additions (new companies joining the exchange) reduced by delistings (companies exiting the exchange).

Listing Additions. Stock exchange listing additions arise from four sources: 1) initial public offerings (IPOs); 2) movements of share listings from one exchange to another; 3) spinouts from larger firms; and 4) new listings from smaller nonexchanges such as bulletin boards. Since movements between exchanges typically are a zero sum within a country, and spinouts and bulletin board movements are few in number, real growth in listings comes from IPOs.

Delistings. Delisted shares fall into three categories: 1) forced delistings, in which the equity no longer meets exchange requirements on share price or financial valuation; 2) mergers, in which two firms combine eliminating a listing; and 3) acquisitions, where the purchase results in the reduction of a listing. Companies entering into bankruptcy, or being major acquisition targets, make up a great proportion of delisting activity. Companies that are delisted are not necessarily bankrupt, and may continue trading over the counter.

Possible Causes in the Decline of Publicly Traded Shares

The decline of share listings in the United States has led to considerable debate over whether these trends represent a fundamental global business shift away from the publicly traded corporate form, or something that is more U.S.-centric combined with the economic times.

The U.S. market itself may reflect a host of country specific factors. The cost and anti-competitive effects of Sarbanes-Oxley are now well known. Compliance with it and a variety of additional restrictions and requirements on public issuances in the U.S. have reduced the attractiveness of public listings. This, combined with the continued development and growth of the private equity markets, where companies may find other forms of equity capital without a public listing, are likely major contributors to the fall in U.S. listings.

One recent study argued that it was not really the increasingly burdensome U.S. regulatory environment that was to blame, but rather a proliferation of factors that caused the decline in market making, sales, and research support for small and medium-sized equities. Beginning with the introduction of online brokerage in 1996 and online trading rules in 1997, more and more equity trading in the United States shifted to ECNs, electronic communication networks, which allowed all market participants to trade directly with the exchange order books, and not through brokers or brokerage houses. Although this increased competition reduced transaction costs dramatically, it also undermined the profitability of the retail brokerage houses, which had always supported research, market making, and sales and promotion of the small- to medium-sized equities. Without this financial support, the smaller stocks were no longer covered and promoted by the major equity houses. Without that research, marketing, promotion and coverage, their trading volumes and values fell.

Corporate Governance

Although the governance structure of any company—domestic, international, or multinational—is fundamental to its very existence, this subject has become the lightning rod of political and business debate in the past few years as failures in governance in a variety of forms has led to corporate fraud and failure. Abuses and failures in corporate governance have dominated global business news in recent years. Beginning with the accounting fraud and questionable ethics of business conduct at Enron culminating in its bankruptcy in the fall of 2001, failures in corporate governance have raised issues about the ethics and culture of business conduct.

The Goal of Corporate Governance

The single overriding objective of corporate governance in the Anglo-American markets is the optimization over time of the returns to shareholders. In order to achieve this, good governance practices should focus the attention of the board of directors of the corporation on this objective by developing and implementing a strategy for the corporation that ensures corporate growth and equity value creation. At the same time, it should ensure an effective relationship with stakeholders. A variety of organizations, including the Organization for Economic Cooperation and Development (OECD), have continued to refine their recommendations regarding five primary areas of governance:

1. **Shareholder rights**. Shareholders are the owners of the firm, and their interests should take precedence over other stakeholders.

2. **Board responsibilities**. The board of the company is recognized as the individual entity with final full legal responsibility for the firm, including proper oversight of management.

3. **Equitable treatment of shareholders**. Equitable treatment is specifically targeted toward domestic versus foreign residents as shareholders, as well as majority and minority interests.

4. **Stakeholder rights**. Governance practices should formally acknowledge the interests of other stakeholders—employees, creditors, community, and government.

5. **Transparency and disclosure**. Public and equitable reporting of firm operating and financial results and parameters should be done in a timely manner, and should be made available to all interests equitably.

These principles obviously focus on several key areas—shareholder rights and roles, disclosure and transparency, and the responsibilities of boards—which we will discuss in more detail.

The Structure of Corporate Governance

Our first challenge is to understand what people mean when they use the expression "corporate governance." Exhibit 4.5 provides an overview of the various parties and their responsibilities associated with the governance of the modern corporation. The modern corporation's actions and behaviors are directed and controlled by both internal and external forces.

EXHIBIT 4.5   **The Structure of Corporate Governance**

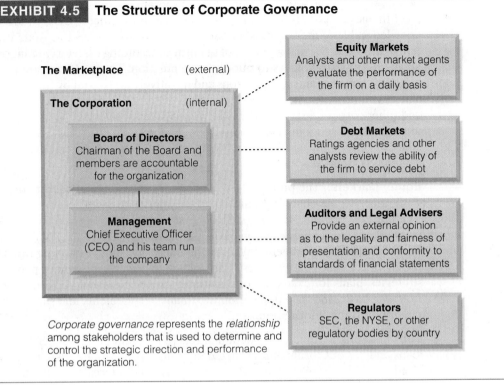

Corporate governance represents the *relationship* among stakeholders that is used to determine and control the strategic direction and performance of the organization.

The internal forces—the officers of the corporation (such as the chief executive officer or CEO) and the board of directors of the corporation (including the chairman of the board)—are those directly responsible for determining both the strategic direction and the execution of the company's future. But they are not acting within a vacuum; the internal forces are subject to the constant prying eyes of the external forces in the marketplace, who question the validity and soundness of the decisions and performance of internal forces. External forces include the equity market (stock exchanges) on which the company's shares are traded, the investment banking analysts who cover and critique the company shares, the creditors of the companies, the credit rating agencies that assign credit ratings to the company's debt or equity securities, the auditors and legal advisers who testify to the fairness and legality of the company's financial statements, and the multitude of regulators who oversee the company's actions—all in an attempt to assure the validity of information presented to investors.

Board of Directors. The legal body that is accountable for the governance of the corporation is its board of directors. The board is composed of both employees of the organization (inside members) and senior and influential nonemployees (outside members). Areas of debate surrounding boards include the following: 1) the proper balance between inside and outside members; 2) the means by which board members are compensated; and 3) the actual ability of a board to monitor and manage a corporation adequately when board members are spending few days a year in board activities. Outside members, often the current or retired chief executives of other major companies, may bring with them a healthy sense of distance and impartiality, which although refreshing, may also result in limited understanding of the true issues and events within the company.

Management. The senior officers of the corporation—the chief executive officer (CEO), the chief financial officer (CFO), and the chief operating officer (COO)—are not only the most knowledgeable of the business, but also the creators and directors of its strategic and operational direction. The management of the firm is, according to theory, acting as a contractor—as an agent—of shareholders to pursue value creation. These officers are positively motivated by salary, bonuses, and stock options and negatively motivated by the risk of losing their jobs. They may, however, have biases of self-enrichment or personal agendas, which the board and other corporate stakeholders are responsible for overseeing and policing. Interestingly, in more than 80% of the companies in the Fortune 500, the CEO is also the chairman of the board. This is, in the opinion of many, a conflict of interest and not in the best interests of the company and its shareholders.

Equity Markets. The publicly traded company, regardless of country of residence, is highly susceptible to the changing opinion of the marketplace. The equity markets themselves, whether they are the New York Stock Exchange or the Mexico City Bolsa, should reflect the market's constant evaluation of the promise and performance of the individual company. The analysts are experts employed by the many investment banking firms that also trade in the client company shares. These analysts are expected (sometimes naïvely) to evaluate the strategies, plans for execution of the strategies, and financial performance of the firms on a real-time basis, and they depend on the financial statements and other public disclosures of the firm for their information.

Debt Markets. Although the debt markets (banks and other financial institutions providing loans and various forms of securitized debt like corporate bonds) are not specifically interested in building shareholder value, they are indeed interested in the financial health of the company. Their interest, specifically, is in the company's ability to repay its debt in a timely manner. Like equity markets, they must rely on the financial statements and other disclosures (public and private in this case) of the companies with which they work.

Auditors and Legal Advisers. Auditors and legal advisers are responsible for providing an external professional opinion as to the fairness, legality, and accuracy of corporate financial statements. In this process, they attempt to determine whether the firm's financial records and practices follow what in the United States is termed generally accepted accounting principles (GAAP) in regard to accounting procedures. But auditors and legal advisers are hired by the firms they are auditing, leading to a rather unique practice of policing their employers. The additional difficulty that has arisen in recent years is that the major accounting firms pursued the development of large consulting practices, often leading to a conflict of interest.

Regulators. Publicly traded firms in the United States and elsewhere are subject to the regulatory oversight of both governmental organizations and nongovernmental organizations. In the United States, the Securities and Exchange Commission (SEC) is a careful watchdog of the publicly traded equity markets, both of the behavior of the companies themselves in those markets and of the various investors participating in those markets. The SEC and other similar authorities outside of the United States require a regular and orderly disclosure process of corporate performance so that all investors may evaluate the company's investment value with adequate, accurate, and fairly distributed information. This regulatory oversight is often focused on when and what information is released by the company, and to whom.

A publicly traded firm in the United States is also subject to the rules and regulations of the exchange upon which they are traded (New York Stock Exchange/Euronext, American Stock Exchange, and NASDAQ are the largest). These organizations, typically categorized as self-regulatory in nature, construct and enforce standards of conduct for both their member companies and themselves in the conduct of share trading.

EXHIBIT 4.6	Comparative Corporate Governance Regimes	
Regime Basis	**Characteristics**	**Examples**
Market-based	Efficient equity markets; Dispersed ownership	United States, United Kingdom, Canada, Australia
Family-based	Management and ownership is combined; Family/majority and minority shareholders	Hong Kong, Indonesia, Malaysia, Singapore, Taiwan,
Bank-based	Government influence in bank lending; Lack of transparency; Family control	Korea, Germany
Government-affiliated	State ownership of enterprise; Lack of transparency; No minority influence	China, Russia

Source: Based on "Corporate Governance in Emerging Markets: An Asian Perspective," by J. Tsui and T. Shieh, in *International Finance and Accounting Handbook*, Third Edition, Frederick D.S. Choi, editor, Wiley, 2004, pp. 24.4–24.6.

Comparative Corporate Governance

The origins of the need for a corporate governance process arise from the separation of ownership from management, and from the varying views by culture of who the stakeholders are and of their significance.[4] This assures that corporate governance practices will differ across countries, economies, and cultures. As seen in Exhibit 4.6, corporate governance regimes may be classified by the evolution of business ownership over time.

Market-based regimes, like those of the United States, Canada, and the United Kingdom, are characterized by relatively efficient capital markets in which the ownership of publicly traded companies is widely dispersed. Family-based regimes, like those characterized in many of the emerging markets, Asian markets, and Latin American markets, not only started with strong concentrations of family ownership (as opposed to partnerships or small investment groups that are not family-based), but have also continued to be largely controlled by families even after going public. Bank-based and government-based regimes are those reflecting markets in which government ownership of property and industry has been a constant over time, resulting in only marginal public ownership of enterprise, and even then, subject to significant restrictions on business practices.

All exchange rate regimes are therefore a function of at least four major factors in the evolution of corporate governance principles and practices globally: 1) the financial market development; 2) the degree of separation between management and ownership; 3) the concept of disclosure and transparency; and 4) the historical development of the legal system.

Financial Market Development. The depth and breadth of capital markets is critical to the evolution of corporate governance practices. Country markets that have had relatively slow growth, as in the emerging markets, or have industrialized rapidly utilizing neighboring capital markets (for example, Western Europe), may not form large public equity market systems. Without significant public trading of ownership shares, high concentrations of ownership are preserved and few disciplined processes of governance are developed.

Separation of Management and Ownership. In countries and cultures where the ownership of the firm has continued to be an integral part of management, agency issues and failures have been less problematic. In countries like the United States, in which ownership has become largely separated from management (and widely dispersed), aligning the goals of management and ownership is much more difficult.

[4]For a summary of comparative corporate governance see R. La Porta, F. Lopez-de-Silanes, and A. Schleifer, "Corporate Ownership Around the World," *Journal of Finance*, 54, 1999, pp. 471–517. See also A. Schleifer and R. Vishny, "A Survey of Corporate Governance," *Journal of Finance*, 52, 1997, pp. 737–783, and the Winter 2007 issue, Vol. 19, No. 1, of the *Journal of Applied Corporate Finance*.

Disclosure and Transparency. The extent of disclosure regarding the operations and financial results of a company vary dramatically across countries. Disclosure practices reflect a wide range of cultural and social forces, including the degree to which ownership is public, the degree to which government feels the need to protect investor's rights versus ownership rights, and the extent to which family-based and government-based business remains central to the culture. Transparency, a parallel concept to disclosure, reflects the visibility of decision-making processes within the business organization.

Historical Development of the Legal System. Investor protection is typically better in countries where English common law is the basis of the legal system, compared to the codified civil law that is typical in France and Germany (the so-called Code Napoleon). English common law is typically the basis of the legal systems in the United Kingdom and former colonies of the United Kingdom, including the United States and Canada. The Code Napoleon is typically the basis of the legal systems in former French colonies and the European countries that Napoleon once ruled, such as Belgium, Spain, and Italy. In countries with weak investor protection, controlling shareholder ownership is often a substitute for a lack of legal protection. Note that we have not mentioned *ethics*. All of the principles and practices described so far have assumed that the individuals in roles of responsibility and leadership pursue them truly and fairly. That, however, has not always been the case.

Family Ownership and Corporate Governance

Although much of the discussion about corporate governance concentrates on the market-based regimes (see Exhibit 4.6), family-based regimes are arguably more common and more important worldwide. For example, in a study of 5,232 corporations in 13 Western European countries, family-controlled firms represented 44% of the sample compared to 37% that were widely held.[5]

Global Finance in Practice 4.1 highlights some of the history of family power, the family cartel that controlled Italy for nearly 60 years.

GLOBAL FINANCE IN PRACTICE 4.1

Italian Cross-Shareholding and the End of the *Salatto Buono*

Italy, in the years following World War II, was a country teetering on collapse. In an effort to stabilize industrial activity, the powerful families of the north—the Agnellis (of Fiat fame), the Pesentis, the Pirellis, the Ligrestis, and later the Benettons—formed *salotto buono*—"the fine drawing room"—to control Italian finance, industry, and media, through relatively small stakes. At the core of the relationship was that each family business held significant ownership and control in the other in an interlocking or cross-shareholding structure that assured that no outsiders could gain ownership or influence.

The creator of *salotto buono* was Enrico Cuccia, the founder of Mediobanca, the Milan-based investment bank. One man in particular, Cesare Geronzi, rose to the top of Italian finance. And every step of the way, he took three scarlet chairs with him. The chairs sat in his waiting room at Mediobanca and eventually Generali, Italy's largest financial group. Geronzi rose to the pinnacle of power despite twice being the target of major financial and accounting fraud cases, including Parmalat. Over the following half-century anyone wishing to gain influence had to pass through the "three chairs," the *salotto buono*.

But, alas, the global financial crisis of 2008–2009 broke down many of the world's last bastions of private power. One such casualty was *salotto buono*, as more and more of its vested families fell further into debt and bankruptcy.

---

[5]Mara Faccio and Larry H.P. Lang, "The Ultimate Ownership of Western European Corporations," *Journal of Financial Economics*, 65 (2002), p. 365. See also: Torben Pedersen and Steen Thomsen, "European Patterns of Corporate Ownership," *Journal of International Business Studies*, Vol. 28, No. 4, Fourth Quarter, 1997, pp. 759–778.

Failures in Corporate Governance

Failures in corporate governance have become increasingly visible in recent years. The Enron scandal in the United States is well known. In addition to Enron, other firms that have revealed major accounting and disclosure failures, as well as executive looting, are WorldCom, Parmalat, Tyco, Adelphia, and HealthSouth.

In each case, prestigious auditing firms, such as Arthur Andersen, missed the violations or minimized them possibly because of lucrative consulting relationships or other conflicts of interest. Moreover, security analysts and banks urged investors to buy the shares and debt issues of these and other firms that they knew to be highly risky or even close to bankruptcy. Even more egregious, most of the top executives who were responsible for the mismanagement that destroyed their firms walked away (initially) with huge gains on shares sold before the downfall, and even overly generous severance packages.

Good Governance and Corporate Reputation

Does good corporate governance matter? This is actually a difficult question, and the realistic answer has been largely dependent on outcomes historically. For example, as long as Enron's share price continued to rise, questions over transparency, accounting propriety, and even financial facts were largely overlooked by all of the stakeholders of the corporation. Yet, eventually, the fraud, deceit, and failure of the multitude of corporate governance practices resulted in bankruptcy. It not only destroyed the wealth of investors, but the careers, incomes, and savings of so many of its own employees. Ultimately, good governance should matter.

One way in which companies may signal good governance to the investor markets is to adopt and publicize a fundamental set of governance policies and practices. Nearly all publicly traded firms have adopted this approach, as becomes obvious when visiting corporate Web sites. This has also led to a standardized set of common principles, as described in Exhibit 4.7, which might be considered a growing consensus on good governance practices.

EXHIBIT 4.7   **The Growing Consensus on Good Corporate Governance**

Although there are many different cultural and legal approaches used in corporate governance worldwide, there is a growing consensus on what constitutes good corporate governance.

- **Composition of the Board of Directors.**   A board of directors that has both internal and external members. More importantly, it should be staffed by individuals of true experience and knowledge of not only their own rules and responsibilities, but of the nature and conduct of the corporate business.

- **Management Compensation.**   A management compensation system that is aligned with corporate performance (financial and otherwise) and has significant oversight from the board and open disclosure to shareholders and investors.

- **Corporate Auditing.**   Independent auditing of corporate financial results on a meaningful real-time basis. An audit process with oversight by a Board committee composed primarily of external members would be an additional significant improvement.

- **Public Reporting and Disclosure.**   Timely public reporting of both financial and nonfinancial operating results that may be used by investors to assess the investment outlook. This should also include transparency and reporting around potentially significant liabilities.

A final international note of caution: The quality and credibility of all internal corporate practices on good governance are still subject to the quality of a country's corporate law, its protection of both creditor and investor rights (including minority shareholders), and the country's ability to provide adequate and appropriate enforcement.

Those practices—board composition, management compensation structure and oversight, corporate auditing practices, and public disclosure—have been widely accepted.

In principle, the idea is that good governance (at both the country and corporate levels) is linked to cost of capital (lower), returns to shareholders (higher), and corporate profitability (higher). An added dimension of interest is the role of country governance, as it may influence the country in which international investors may choose to invest. Curiously, however, not only have corporate rankings been highly uncorrelated across ranking firms, but a number of academic studies have also indicated little linkage between a firm's corporate governance ranking and its future likelihood of restating earnings, shareholder lawsuits, return on assets, and a variety of measures of stock price performance.

An additional way to signal good corporate governance, in non-Anglo-American firms, is to elect one or more Anglo-American board members. This was shown to be true for a select group of Norwegian and Swedish firms in a study by Oxelheim and Randøy.[6] The firms had superior market values. The Anglo-American board members suggested a governance system that would show better monitoring opportunities and enhanced investor recognition. A follow-up study of the same firms found that CEO pay increased because of the perceived reduction in tolerance for bad performance and increased monitoring required.[7]

Corporate Governance Reform

Within the United States and the United Kingdom, the main corporate governance problem is the one addressed by agency theory: With widespread share ownership, how can a firm align management's interest with that of the shareholders? Since individual shareholders do not have the resources or the power to monitor management, the U.S. and U.K. markets rely on regulators to assist in the monitoring of agency issues and conflicts of interest. Outside the U.S. and the U.K., large controlling shareholders (including Canada) are in the majority. They are able to monitor management in some ways better than regulators. However, controlling shareholders pose a different agency problem. It is extremely difficult to protect the interests of minority shareholders (investors holding small numbers of share and therefore little voting power) against the power of controlling shareholders, whether the controlling shareholders are major institutions, large wealthy private investors, or even controlling families.

In recent years, reform in the United States and Canada has been largely regulatory. Reform elsewhere has been largely focused on the adoption of principles rather than stricter legal regulations. The principles approach is softer, less costly, and less likely to conflict with other existing regulations.

Sarbanes-Oxley Act. The U.S. Congress passed the Sarbanes-Oxley Act (SOX) in July 2002. Named after its two primary congressional sponsors, SOX had four major requirements: 1) CEOs and CFOs of publicly traded firms must vouch for the veracity of the firm's published financial statements; 2) corporate boards must have audit and compensation committees drawn from independent (outside) directors; 3) companies are prohibited from making loans to corporate officers and directors; and 4) companies must test their internal financial controls against fraud.

The first provision—the so-called *signature clause*—has already had significant impacts on the way in which companies prepare their financial statements. The provision was intended to instill a sense of responsibility and accountability in senior management (and to therefore

[6]Lars Oxelheim and Trond Randøy, "The Impact of Foreign Board Membership on Firm Value," *Journal of Banking and Finance*, Vol. 27, No. 12, 2003, pp. 2369–2392.
[7]Lars Oxelheim and Trond Randøy, "The Anglo-American Financial Influence on CEO Compensation in Non-Anglo-American Firms," *Journal of International Business Studies*, Vol. 36, No. 4, July 2005, pp. 470–483.

reduce management explanations of "the auditors signed off on it"). The companies them-selves have pushed the same procedure downward in their organizations, often requiring busi-ness unit managers and directors at lower levels to sign their financial statements. Regardless of the form of corporate government reform, as discussed in *Global Finance in Practice 4.2*, the definition of *good governance* is still under debate.

Poor performance of management usually requires changes in management, ownership, or both. Exhibit 4.8 illustrates some of the alternative paths available to shareholders when they are dissatisfied with firm performance. Depending on the culture and accepted practices, it is not unusual for many investors to—for an extended time—remain quietly disgruntled regarding share price performance. A more active response is to sell their shares. It is with the third and fourth possible actions, changing management and initiating a takeover, that management hears a much louder dissatisfied "voice."

GLOBAL FINANCE IN PRACTICE   4.2

Is Good Governance Good Business Globally?

The term "good governance" is, in many instances, a highly politically charged term. When talking to the press, many directors and executives argue that the pursuit of good governance practices is good for business glob-ally. However, those same officials may also argue that stringent reporting and disclosure requirements, like those imposed by the United States under Sarbanes-Oxley, harm business competition and growth and, ultimately,

the attractiveness of listing and trading their securities in the United States. In the end, the devil may indeed be in the detail.

One size may not fit all, however. Culture has an enor-mous impact on business conduct, and many countries are finding their own way without necessarily following U.S. or European practices. For example, a number of Japanese leaders note that the Japanese corporate governance system differs from the Western system and has evolved while preserving Japanese culture and history. They argue that cultural background and history should not be ignored when developing and implementing global standards, regu-lations, and oversight.

EXHIBIT 4.8   Potential Responses to Shareholder Dissatisfaction

What counts is that the management of a publicly quoted company, and its board of directors, know that the company can become the subject of a hostile takeover bid if they fail to perform. The growth of equity and hedge funds in the United States and elsewhere in recent years has strengthened this threat as leveraged buyouts are once again common.

Summary Points

- Most commercial enterprises have their origins with either entrepreneurs (private enterprise) or governments (public enterprise). Regardless of origin, if they remain commercial in focus, they may over time choose to go public (in whole or in part) via an initial public offering (IPO).

- The U.S. and U.K. stock markets are characterized by widespread ownership of shares. In the rest of the world, ownership is usually characterized by controlling shareholders. Typical controlling shareholders are government, institutions, families, and consortiums.

- When a firm becomes widely owned, it is typically managed by hired professionals. Professional managers' interests may not be aligned with the interests of owners, thus creating an agency problem.

- The Anglo-American markets subscribe to a philosophy that a firm's objective should follow the shareholder wealth maximization (SWM) model. More specifically, the firm should strive to maximize the return to shareholders, as measured by the sum of capital gains and dividends, for a given level of risk.

- In the non-Anglo-American markets, controlling shareholders also strive to maximize long-term returns to equity. However, they also consider the interests of other stakeholders, including employees, customers, suppliers, creditors, government, and community. This is known as stakeholder capitalism.

- The return to a shareholder in a publicly traded firm combines current income in the form of dividends and capital gains from the appreciation of share price. A privately held firm tries to maximize current and sustainable income since it has no share price.

- The MNE must determine for itself the proper balance between three common operational objectives: maximization of consolidated after-tax income; minimization of the firm's effective global tax burden; and correct positioning of the firm's income, cash flows, and available funds as to country and currency.

- The relationship among stakeholders used to determine the strategic direction and performance of an organization is termed corporate governance. Dimensions of corporate governance include agency theory; composition and control of boards of directors; and cultural, historical and institutional variables.

- A trend exists for firms resident in non-Anglo-American markets to move toward being more "shareholder friendly," while firms from the Anglo-American markets may be moving toward being more "stakeholder friendly."

- A number of initiatives in governance practices in the United States, the United Kingdom, and the European Union—including board structure and compensation, transparency, auditing, and minority shareholder rights—are spreading to a number of today's major emerging markets.

- These governance practices are seen, in some countries and cultures, as overly intrusive and occasionally are viewed as damaging to the competitive capability of the firm. The result is an increasing reluctance to go public in selective markets.

MINI-CASE

Luxury Wars—LVMH vs. Hermès[1]

The basic rule is to be there at the right moment, at the right place, to seize a promising opportunity in an environment guaranteeing sufficient longer-term growth.
— Bernard Arnault, Chairman and CEO, LVMH.

Patrick Thomas focused intently on not letting his hands shake as he quietly ended the call. He had been riding his bicycle in rural Auvergne, in south-central France, when his cell phone buzzed. He took a long deep breath and tried to think. He had spent most of his professional life working at Hermès International, SA and had assumed the position of CEO in 2006 after the retirement of Jean-Louis Dumas. The first nonfamily CEO to run the company was now facing the biggest threat to the family-controlled company in its 173-year history.

The LVMH Position
The man on the other end of the phone had been none other than Bernard Arnault, Chairman and CEO of LVMH (Moët Hennessy Louis Vuitton), the world's largest luxury

[1]Copyright 2011 © Thunderbird School of Global Management. All rights reserved. This case was prepared by Joe Kleinberg, MBA 2011 and Peter Macy, MBA 2011, under the direction of Professor Michael Moffett for the purpose of classroom discussion only, and not to indicate either effective or ineffective management.

EXHIBIT A   **LVMH becomes a Shareholder of Hermès International**

LVMH Moët Hennessy Louis Vuitton, the world's leading luxury products group, announces that it holds 15 016 000 shares of Hermès International, representing 14.2% of the share capital of the company. The objective of LVMH is to be a long-term shareholder of Hermès and to contribute to the preservation of the family and French attributes which are at the heart of the global success of this iconic brand.

LVMH fully supports the strategy implemented by the founding family and the management team, who have made the brand one of the jewels of the luxury industry. LVMH has no intention of launching a tender offer, taking control of Hermès nor seeking Board representation. LVMH holds derivative instruments over 3 001 246 Hermès International shares and intends to request their conversion.

LVMH would then hold a total of 18 017 246 Hermès International shares, or 17.1% of its capital. The total cost of this shareholding would, in this case, be €1.45 billion.

Source: Press Release, October 23, 2010, LVMH.com. Reproduced by permission of LVMH Companies.

---

brand company, the richest man in France, and a major competitor. Arnault was calling to inform Thomas that LVMH would be announcing in two hours that they had acquired a 17.1% interest in Hermès (Exhibit A). Thomas had simply not believed Arnault for the first few minutes, thinking it impossible that LVMH could have gained control of that significant a stake without his knowledge. Arnault assured Thomas it was no joke and that he looked forward to participating in the company's continued success as a shareholder. Patrick Thomas began assessing the potential threat, if it was indeed a threat.

Hermès International. Hermès International, SA is a multibillion-dollar French company that makes and sells luxury goods across a number of different product categories including women's and men's apparel, watches, leather goods, jewelry, and perfume. Thierry Hermès, who was known for making the best saddles and harnesses in Paris, founded the company in 1837. The company's reputation soared as it began to provide its high-end products to nobility throughout Europe, North Africa, Russia, Asia, and the Americas. As the years passed, the company began to expand its product line to include the finest leather bags and silk scarves on the market, all while passing the company down through generations and maintaining family control.

Despite going public in 1993, roughly 60 direct descendants of Thierry Hermès, comprising the 5th and 6th generations, still controlled approximately 73% of the company. In 2006, the job of CEO was assumed, for the first time, by a nonfamily member, Patrick Thomas.

Bernard Arnault

Arnault is a shrewd man. He has reviewed his portfolio and sees what he is missing—a company that still produces true luxury—and he is going after it.
                    —Anonymous luxury brand CEO speaking
                            on the LVMH announcement.

Bernard Arnault had made a very profitable career out of his penchant for taking over vulnerable family-owned businesses (earning him the colorful nickname of "the wolf in cashmere"). Born in Roubaix, France, to an upper class family, Arnault excelled as a student and graduated from France's prestigious engineering school, Ecole Polytechnique, before working as an engineer and taking over his family's construction business. When the French government began looking for someone to acquire the bankrupt company, Boussac (and its luxury line, Christian Dior), Arnault promptly bought the company. It proved the first step in building what would eventually become the luxury titan, LVMH, and propelling Arnault to the title of France's wealthiest man.

From that point on, Arnault began assembling what his competitors referred to as "the evil empire," by preying on susceptible family-owned companies with premium names. His takeover of Louis Vuitton was said to have gotten so personal and vicious that, after the last board meeting, the Vuitton family packed their belongings and left the building in tears. In addition to Louis Vuitton, Arnault had spent the last three decades forcibly acquiring such family-owned luxury brands as Krug (champagne), Pucci (fashion), Chateau d'Yquem (vineyard), and Celine (fashion), among others.

Arnault's only failure had been his attempted takeover of Gucci in 1999, when he was beaten by Francois Pinault, whose company PPR served as the white knight for Gucci and stole the deal out from under Arnault. It marked the one time in LVMH's history that it had failed in a takeover bid.

Autorité des Marchés Financiers (AMF). Arnault's announcement of LVMH's ownership stake in Hermès came as a shock to both the fashion industry and the family shareholders of Hermès. Exhibit B is Hermès public response to LVMH's initiative. The French stock market regulator, the Autorité des Marchés Financiers (AMF), required any investor gaining a 5% or greater stake in a publicly traded company to file their ownership percentage publicly, as well as a document of intent. But no such notice had yet been filed.

In the days following the October 23 press release, LVMH confirmed that the company had complied with

---

EXHIBIT B   **Hermès Response via Press Release: October 24, 2010**

Hermès has been informed that LVMH has acquired a 17% stake in the Company. In 1993, the shareholders of Hermès International, all descendants from Emile Hermès, decided to enlist the Company on the Paris stock exchange. This decision was made with two objectives in mind: 1) support the long term development of the Company; 2) make shares easier to trade for the shareholders.

Over the last 10 years, the Hermès group has delivered an average annual growth rate of 10% of its net result and currently holds a very strong financial position with over M€ 700 of free cash. Today, Hermès Family shareholders have a strong majority control of nearly 3/4 of the shares. They are fully united around a common business vision. Their long term control of Hermès International is guaranteed by its financial status as limited partnership by shares and the family shareholders have confirmed that they are not contemplating any significant selling of shares. The public listing of shares, allows investors who want to become minority shareholders to do so. As a Family Company Hermès has treated and will always treat its shareholders with utmost respect.

The Executive Management,
Sunday October 24th, 2010

Source: Hermes.com.

---

all current rules and regulations in the transactions, and that it would file all the necessary documentation within the allotted time. The AMF announced that it would investigate LVMH's acquisition of the Hermès stock. This, however, was little consolation to Thomas and the Hermès family. Even if violations were found, the only penalty LVMH could suffer would be the loss of voting rights for two years.

Equity Swaps. LVMH had, it turns out, acquired its large ownership position under the radar of the Hermès family, company management, and industry analysts through the use of *equity swaps*. *Equity swaps* are derivative contracts where two parties agree to swap future cash flows at a preset date. The cash flows are referred to as "legs" of the swap. In most equity swaps, one leg is tied to a floating rate like LIBOR (the floating leg), and the other leg is tied to the performance of a stock or stock index (the equity leg). Under current French law, a company must acknowledge when they attain a 5% or more equity stake in another company, or the rights to purchase a 5% or more stake via derivatives like equity swaps.

But there was a loophole. The swaps could be structured so that their value was tied to the equity instrument only; at closeout the contract may be settled in cash, not shares. Using this structure, the swap holder is not required to file with the AMF, since they will never actually own the stock.

The LVMH Purchase. It was widely known that Arnault had long coveted Hermès as a brand. In fact, Mr. Arnault had previously owned 15% of Hermès when he first took over LVMH in the 1990s. At the time, Mr. Arnault had his hands full with reorganizing and redirecting LVMH after his takeover of the company, so he agreed to sell the shares to then Hermès CEO Jean-Louis Dumas when Dumas wanted to take the company public.

But things had changed for LVMH and Arnault since then. Mr. Arnault had grown his company to the largest luxury conglomerate in the world, with over $55 billion in annual sales. He accomplished this through organic growth of brands and strategic purchases. Known for his patience and shrewd business acumen, when he saw an opportunity to target a long coveted prize, he took advantage.

The attack on Hermès shares was one of Arnault's most closely kept secrets, with only three people in his empire aware of the equity swap contracts. Arnault began making his move in 2008 when three blocks of Hermès shares—totaling 12.8 million shares—were quietly placed on the market by three separate French banks. The origins of these shares were unknown, but many suspected they had come from Hermès family members.

It is believed that Arnault was contacted by the banks and was given 24 hours to decide whether he would like to purchase them or not. Arnault was hesitant to take such a large ownership stake in Hermès, particularly one requiring registration with the AMF. Arnault and the banks then developed the strategy whereby he would hold rights to the shares via equity swaps, but only as long as he put up the cash. At contract maturity, LVMH would realize the profit/loss on any movement in the share price. As part of the agreement with the banks, however, LVMH would have the option to take the shares instead. Had the contracts required share settlement, under French law LVMH would have had to acknowledge its potential equity position in Hermès publicly.

The design of the contracts prevented LVMH from actually holding the shares until October 2010, when they publicly announced their ownership stake in Hermès. During this period Hermès share price floated between €60 and €102. This explained how LVMH was able to acquire its shares in Hermès at an average price of €80 per share, nearly a 54% discount on the closing price of €176.2 on Friday, October 22.

LVMH could have actually held its swap contracts longer and postponed settlement and disclosure, but the rapid rise in Hermès share price over the previous months forced the decision (which many analysts attributed to market speculations of an LVMH takeover plot). If LVMH had postponed settlement, it would have had to account for €2 billion in paper profit, earned on the contracts when publishing their year-end accounts in February 2011.

The Battle Goes Public

Although the original press release by LVMH made it clear that the company had no greater designs on controlling Hermès, Hermès management did not believe it, and moved quickly. After a quick conference call amongst Hermès leadership, Hermès CEO Thomas and Executive Chairman Puech gave an interview with *Le Figaro* on October 27.

> It's clear his [Mr. Arnault] intention is to take over the company and the family will resist that.
> —Patrick Thomas, CEO Hermès, *Le Figaro*, October 27, 2010.

> We would like to convince him [Mr. Arnault] that this is not the right way to operate and that it's not friendly. If he entered in a friendly way, then we would like him to leave in a friendly way.
> —Mr. Puech, Executive Chairman of Emile Hermès SARL, *Le Figaro*, October 27, 2010.

Arnault wasted no time in responding in an interview given to the same newspaper the following day:

> I do not see how the head of a listed company can be qualified to ask a shareholder to sell his shares. On the contrary he is supposed to defend the interests of all shareholders.
> —Bernard Arnault, CEO LVMH, *Le Figaro*, October 28, 2010.

Pierre Godé, Vice President LVMH. On November 10, after much speculation regarding LVMH's intent, Pierre Godé, an LVMH Vice President, gave an interview with *Les Echos* newspaper (itself owned by LVMH) to discuss how and why the transactions took place the way they did, as well as to dispel media speculation about a potential hostile takeover attempt from LVMH. In the interview, Godé was questioned about why LVMH chose to purchase the equity swap contracts against Hermès in the first place, and why LVMH chose to close those contracts in Hermès shares rather than in cash.

Godé confided that LVMH had begun looking at Hermès in 2007 when the financial crisis started and the stock exchange began to fall. LVMH was looking for financial investments in the luxury industry—as that is where their expertise lies—and concluded that Hermès would weather the financial crisis better than other potential investments. It was for this reason alone that LVMH chose to purchase equity swaps with Hermès shares as the equity leg.

Godé argued that equity swaps with cash payment and settlement were trendy at that time, and virtually every bank offered this derivative. Even though LVMH already had just under a 5% stake of Hermès stock at the time the derivatives were being set up, Godé stated that LVMH never even considered the possibility of closing out the swaps in shares. For one thing, it was something they could not do contractually (according to Godé), nor did LVMH want to ask the banks for equity settlements. But by 2010, the situation had changed, prompting LVMH to reassess their Hermès equity swap contracts. The contracts themselves were running out, and LVMH had a premium of nearly €1 billion on them. According to Godé, the banks that had covered their contracts with LVMH were now tempted to sell the shares, which represented 12% of Hermès' capital.

Godé explained that selling the shares, in and of itself, did not concern LVMH. What LVMH did worry about however, was where the shares might end up. Godé stressed that at that time there were rumors that both a "powerful group from another industry" and Chinese investment funds were interested in the Hermès shares. LVMH management felt the rising share price of Hermès lent support to these rumors. Additionally, the market had been improving and LVMH had the financial means to be able to pay for the contracts and settle in shares. As a result, LVMH spoke with the banks to assess their position, and after, several weeks of talks, LVMH reached an agreement with the banks in October for part of the shares.

At this time, Godé explained, "the Board had to choose between receiving a considerable amount on the equity swaps or take a minority participation in this promising group but where our power would be very limited as the family controlled everything. There was an intense debate and finally the Board chose to have share payments." Godé completed the interview by stating that LVMH was surprised by the strong negative response from Hermès, especially considering that LVMH had owned a 15% stake in the company in the early 1990s.

Evolution of Hermès International and Its Control. Hermès was structured as a Société en Commandite, the French version of a limited partnership in the United States. In the case of Hermès, this structure concentrates power in the hands of a ruling committee, which is controlled by the family.

In addition to the Société en Commandite structure of the company, former Hermès CEO Jean-Louis Dumas established a partner company, Hermès SARL, in 1989. This company represented the interests of family shareholders (only direct Hermès descendants could be owners), and was the sole authority to appoint management and set company strategy. This unusual structure provided the Hermès family with the ability to retain decision-making power even if only one family member remained as a shareholder. The structure had been adopted as protection against a hostile takeover after Dumas saw the way Bernard Arnault had dealt with the Vuitton family when he acquired their company.

In a further attempt to placate family members and minimize family infighting, Dumas listed 25% of Hermès SA on the French stock market in 1993. This was done to provide family members with a means to value their stake in the company as well as partially cash out if they felt their family dividends were not enough (several family members were known to live large, and Dumas feared their lifestyles might exceed their means). Dumas believed—at least at that time—that his two-tier structure would insulate Hermès from a potential hostile takeover.

However, analysts were now speculating that Hermès SARL might only provide protection through the 6th generation, and that with just a 0.1% stake in the company being worth approximately €18 million at current market prices, there was reason to fear some family members "defecting." This concern was made all the more real when it became known through AMF filings that Laurent Mommeja, brother to Hermès supervisory board member Renaud fe, sold €1.8 million worth of shares on October 25 at a share price of €189 per share.

After considerable debate, the Hermès family decided to consolidate their shares into a trust in the form of a holding company that would insure their 73% ownership stake would always vote as one voice and ultimately secure the family's continued control of the company (Exhibit C). On December 21, LVMH announced that it had raised its total stake in Hermès to 20.21% and that it had filed all required documents with AMF upon passing the 20% threshold. LVMH also reiterated that it had no intention of taking control of Hermès or making a public offer for its shares. Under French law, once LVMH reached one-third share ownership it would have to make a public tender for all remaining shares.

CASE QUESTIONS

1. Hermès International was a family-owned business for many years. Why did it then list its shares on a public market? What risks and rewards come from a public listing?

2. Bernard Arnault and LVMH acquired a large position in Hermès shares without anyone knowing. How did they do it and how did they avoid the French regulations requiring disclosure of such positions?

3. The Hermès family defended themselves by forming a holding company of their family shares. How will this work and how long do you think it will last?

EXHIBIT C　**Hermès Family Confirms Its Long-Term Commitment**

Creation of a holding company owning over 50% of Hermès International's share capital

Paris, 5 December 2010—Following a meeting on 3 December 2010, members of the Hermès family reasserted their unity and their confidence in the solidity of their current control of Hermès International, partly via the Emile Hermès family company, sole general partner responsible for determining the company's strategy and management, and via its shareholding.

The family has decided to confirm its long-term unity by creating a family holding company separate from Emile Hermès SARL, which will hold the shares transferred by family members representing over 50% of Hermès International's share capital. The family's commitment to create this majority holding company is irrevocable. The new family-owned company will benefit from preferential rights to shares still directly owned by the family.

This internal reclassification of shares will not impact the family's stake in Hermès International or the powers of the general partner. The plan will be submitted to the Autorité des Marchés Financiers for definitive approval before it is implemented.

Source: Press Release, December 5, 2010, Hermes.com.

Questions

1. **Ownership of the Business.** How does ownership alter the goals and governance of a business?

2. **Separation of Ownership and Management.** Why is this separation so critical to the understanding of how businesses are structured and led?

3. **Corporate Goals: Shareholder Wealth Maximization.** Explain the assumptions and objectives of the shareholder wealth maximization model.

4. **Corporate Governance Models.** What is corporate governance? How do corporate governance models differ from one country to the other?

5. **Corporate Governance.** Define the following terms:
   a. Corporate governance
   b. Agency theory
   c. Stakeholder capitalism model

6. **Operational Goals.** How do operational goals of MNEs differ from those of local firms?

7. **Knowledge Assets.** "Knowledge assets" are a firm's intangible assets, the sources and uses of its intellectual talent—its competitive advantage. What are some of the most important "knowledge assets" that create shareholder value?

8. **Labor Unions.** In Germany and Scandinavia, among others, labor unions have representation on boards of directors or supervisory boards. How might such union representation be viewed under the two different models of management goals, shareholder wealth maximization and stakeholder capitalism?

9. **Interlocking Directorates.** In an interlocking directorate, members of the board of directors of one firm also sit on the board of directors of other firms. How would interlocking directorates be viewed by the shareholder wealth maximization model compared to the stakeholder capitalization model?

10. **Leveraged Buyouts.** A leveraged buyout is a financial strategy in which a group of investors gain voting control of a firm and then liquidate its assets in order to repay the loans used to purchase the firm's shares. How would leveraged buyouts be viewed within the shareholder wealth maximization model compared to the stakeholder capitalization model?

11. **High Leverage.** How would a high degree of leverage (debt/assets) be viewed by the shareholder wealth maximization model compared to the stakeholder capitalization model?

12. **Conglomerates.** Conglomerates are firms that have diversified into unrelated fields. How would a policy of conglomeration be viewed by the shareholder wealth maximization model compared to the stakeholder capitalization model?

13. **Risk.** How is risk defined in the shareholder wealth maximization model compared to the stakeholder capitalization model?

14. **Stock Options.** How would stock options granted to a firm's management and employees be viewed by the shareholder wealth maximization model compared to the stakeholder capitalization model?

15. **Shareholder Dissatisfaction**. What alternative actions can shareholders take if they are dissatisfied with their company?

16. **Dual Classes of Common Stock.** In many countries, it is common for a firm to have two or more classes of common stock with differential voting rights. In the United States, the norm is for a firm to have one class of common stock with one-share-one-vote. What are the advantages and disadvantages of each system?

17. **Emerging Markets Corporate Governance Failures.** It has been claimed that failures in corporate governance have hampered the growth and profitability of some prominent firms located in emerging markets. What are some typical causes of these failures in corporate governance?

18. **Corporate Governance in Emerging Markets.** Investors usually pay more attention to corporate governance especially during the processes of mergers and acquisitions. Assume you are a management consultant who is advising a MNE whether to make an offer to acquire a firm in an emerging market. How can you evaluate the corporate governance performance of this firm?

19. **Developed Markets Corporate Governance Failures.** What have been the main causes of recent corporate governance failures in the United States and Europe?

20. **Family Ownership.** What are the key differences in the goals and motivations of family business ownership as opposed to the widely held publicly traded business?

21. **Value of Good Governance.** Do markets appear to be willing to pay for good governance?

22. **Compliance with Corporate Governance.** In the wake of a series of corporate scandals, the United States introduced the Sarbanes-Oxley Act in order to enhance corporate governance mechanisms. But most other nations lack such legislations and depend on non-binding corporate governance codes. How may these codes be enhanced to have a coercive effect?

Problems

Use the following formula to answer problems on shareholder returns, where P_t is the share price at time t, and D_t is the dividend paid at time t.

$$\text{Shareholder Return} = \frac{D_2}{P_1} + \frac{P_2 - P_1}{P_1}$$

1. **BritMart's Return.** Since its listing last year on FTSE 100, the market value of BritMart rose from £21 to £23.5. For each of the following cases calculate the rate of return, distinguishing the dividend yield from the capital gain:

   a. BritMart pays no dividend

   b. BritMart decides to pay a dividend of £0.85 per share.

   c. BritMart paid the dividend, but the total return to the shareholder is separated into the dividend yield and the capital gain.

2. **Vaniteux's Returns (A).** Spencer Grant is a New York-based investor. He has been closely following his investment in 100 shares of Vaniteux, a French firm that went public in February 2010. When he purchased his 100 shares at €17.25 per share, the euro was trading at $1.360/€. Currently, the share is trading at €28.33 per share, and the dollar has fallen to $1.4170/€.

   a. If Spencer sells his shares today, what percentage change in the share price would he receive?

   b. What is the percentage change in the value of the euro versus the dollar over this same period?

   c. What would be the total return Spencer would earn on his shares if he sold them at these rates?

3. **Vaniteux's Returns (B).** Spencer Grant chooses not to sell his shares at the time described in Problem 2. He waits, expecting the share price to rise further after the announcement of quarterly earnings. His expectations are correct, and the share price rises to €31.14 per share after the announcement. He now wishes to recalculate his returns. The current spot exchange rate is $1.3110/€.

4. **Vaniteux's Returns (C).** Using the same prices and exchange rates as in Problem 3, Vaniteux (B), what would be the total return on the Vaniteux investment by Laurent Vuagnoux, a Paris-based investor?

5. **Building Society's Dividend.** The following table shows the market share price for a British building society. Since its launch in September 2004, the

Date	Share Price
Sep-04	GBP 200
Sep-05	GBP 205
Sep-06	GBP 216
Sep-07	GBP 196
Sep-08	GBP 150
Sep-09	GBP 193

management intends to pay a fixed annual dividend of £0.50 per share. How would this constant dividend per year have changed the building society's return to its shareholders over this period?

6. **Deutschelander's Rate of Return.** Deutschlander Motor Co. issues new stocks and promises to pay an annual dividend of €1.5. Financial forecasters predict that its market share price will rise from €100 to €120 after one year. Investors expect German automobile firms to reap a rate of return of 12%. Supposing that you intend to hold the stock in your portfolio for one year, should you invest in this equity?

7. **Pharma Acquisitions.** The price/earnings ratio (P/E) is one of the tools used to compare companies in the same sector. A high P/E ratio means that investors pay more for each Swiss franc of net income, especially if they believe that it has future potential. Due to high research and development expenses incurred by pharmaceutical firms, their P/E is usually higher than those of other industries.

SmallPhar and EuroPhar are hypothetical pharmaceutical firms registered on the Swiss Exchange in Zurich. EuroPhar is considering acquiring SmallPhar to take advantage of its future growth and potential new drug production. The table at the bottom of the page summarizes the financial situation of both firms.

EuroPhar wants to acquire SmallPhar. It offers 2,500,000 shares of EuroPhar, with a current market value of CHF75,000,000 and a 7.14% premium on SmallPhar's shares, for all of SmallPhar's shares.

   a. What is the total number of outstanding shares that EuroPhar will have after acquiring SmallPhar?

   b. Calculate the consolidated earnings after the acquisition.

   c. If the P/E ratio after the capitalization stays at 20, what would be the new market value of EuroPhar?

   d. What would be EuroPhar's new EPS?

   e. What is the new market price of EuroPhar's share?

   f. By how much would EuroPhar's stock price increase?

   g. Assume that the market takes a negative view of the acquisition and lowers EuroPhar's P/E ratio to 10. What would be the new market price per share of stock? What would be its percentage loss?

Problem 7.

Company	P/E Ratio	Number of Shares	Market Value per Share	Earnings	EPS	Total Market Value
SmallPhar	35	2,000,000	CHF 35	CHF 2,000,000	CHF 1.0	CHF 70,000,000
EuroPhar	20	10,000,000	CHF 30	CHF 15,000,000	CHF 1.5	CHF 300,000,000

8. Corporate Governance: Overstating Earnings. After the numerous cases of frauds and scandals, a number of firms had to lower their previously reported earnings due to accounting errors or fraud. Assume that EuroPhar in the previous problem had to lower its earnings to CHF 10,000,000 from the previously reported CHF15,000,000. What might be its new market value prior to the acquisition? Could it still do the acquisition?

9. Bertrand Manufacturing (A). Dual classes of common stock are common in a number of countries. Assume that Bertrand Manufacturing has the following capital structure at book value. The A-shares have ten votes per share and the B-shares have one vote per share.

Bertrand Manufacturing	Local Currency (millions)
Long-term debt	200
Retained earnings	300
Paid-in common stock: 1 million A-shares	100
Paid-in common stock: 4 million B-shares	400
Total long-term capital	1,000

a. What proportion of the total long-term capital has been raised by A-shares?
b. What proportion of voting rights is represented by A-shares?
c. What proportion of the dividends should the A-shares receive?

10. Bertrand Manufacturing (B). Assume all of the same debt and equity values for Bertrand Manufacturing in Problem 9, with the sole exception that both A-shares and B-shares have the same voting rights—one vote per share.
a. What proportion of the total long-term capital has been raised by A-shares?
b. What proportion of voting rights is represented by A-shares?
c. What proportion of the dividends should the A-shares receive?

11. Kingdom Enterprises (A): European Sales. Kingdom Enterprises is a Hong Kong-based exporter of consumer electronics and files all of its financial statements in Hong Kong dollars (HK$). The company's European sales director, Phillipp Bosse, has been criticized for his performance. He disagrees, arguing that sales in Europe have grown steadily in recent years. Who is correct?

	2008	2009	2010
Total net sales, HK$	171,275	187,500	244,900
Percent of total sales from Europe	48%	44%	39%
Total European sales, HK$	___	___	___
Average exchange rate, HK$/€	11.5	11.7	10.3
Total European sales, euros	___	___	___
Growth rate of European sales	___	___	___

12. Kingdom Enterprises (B): Japanese Yen Debt. Kingdom Enterprises of Hong Kong borrowed Japanese yen under a long-term loan agreement several years ago. The company's new CFO believes, however, that what was originally thought to have been relatively "cheap debt" is no longer true. What do you think?

	2008	2009	2010
Annual yen payments on debt agreement (¥)	12,000,000	12,000,000	12,000,000
Average exchange rate, ¥/HK$	12.3	12.1	11.4
Annual yen debt service, HK$	___	___	___

13. Mattel's Global Performance. Mattel (U.S.) achieved significant sales growth in its major international regions between 2001 and 2004. In its filings with the United States Security and Exchange Commission (SEC), it reported both the amount of regional sales and the percentage change in those sales resulting from exchange rate changes. Refer to table at the top of p. 124.
a. What was the percentage change in sales, in U.S. dollars, by region?
b. What were the percentage change in sales by region net of currency change impacts?
c. What impact did currency changes have on the level and growth of consolidated sales between 2001 and 2004?

14. Chinese Sourcing and the Yuan. Harrison Equipment of Denver, Colorado, purchases all of its hydraulic tubing from manufacturers in mainland China. The company has recently completed a corporate-wide initiative in six sigma/lean manufacturing. Completed oil field hydraulic system costs were reduced 4% over a one-year period, from $880,000 to $844,800.

Problem 13.

Mattel's Global Sales

(thousands of US$)	2001 Sales ($)	2002 Sales ($)	2003 Sales ($)	2004 Sales ($)
Europe	$ 933,450	$ 1,126,177	$ 1,356,131	$ 1,410,525
Latin America	471,301	466,349	462,167	524,481
Canada	155,791	161,469	185,831	197,655
Asia Pacific	119,749	136,944	171,580	203,575
Total International	$ 1,680,291	$ 1,890,939	$ 2,175,709	$ 2,336,236
United States	3,392,284	3,422,405	3,203,814	3,209,862
Sales Adjustments	(384,651)	(428,004)	(419,423)	(443,312)
Total Net Sales	$ 4,687,924	$ 4,885,340	$ 4,960,100	$ 5,102,786

	Impact of Change in Currency Rates		
Region	2001–2002	2002–2003	2003–2004
Europe	7.0%	15.0%	8.0%
Latin America	−9.0%	−6.0%	−2.0%
Canada	0.0%	11.0%	5.0%
Asia Pacific	3.0%	13.0%	6.0%

Source: Mattel, Annual Report, 2002, 2003, 2004.

The company is now worried that all of the hydraulic tubing that goes into the systems (making up 20% of their total costs) will be hit by the potential revaluation of the Chinese yuan—if some in Washington get their way. How would a 12% revaluation of the yuan against the dollar impact total system costs?

Internet Exercises

1. **Multinational Firms and Global Assets/Income.** The differences between MNEs is striking. Using a sample of firms such as the following, pull from their individual Web pages the proportions of their incomes that are earned outside their countries of incorporation. (Note how Nestlé calls itself a "transnational company.")

Walt Disney	disney.go.com
Nestlé S.A.	www.nestle.com
Intel	www.intel.com
Mitsubishi Motors	www.mitsubishi.com
Nokia	www.nokia.com
Royal Dutch/Shell	www.shell.com

Also note the way in which international business is now conducted via the Internet. Several of the home pages listed allow the user to choose the language of the presentation viewed.

2. **Corporate Governance.** There is no hotter topic in business today than corporate governance. Use the following site to view recent research, current events and news items, and other information related to the relationships between a business and its stakeholders.

Corporate Governance Net   www.corpgov.net

3. **Fortune Global 500.** *Fortune* magazine is relatively famous for its listing of the Fortune 500 firms in the global marketplace. Use Fortune's Web site to find the most recent listing of the global firms in this distinguished club.

Fortune   www.fortune.com/fortune

4. **Financial Times.** The *Financial Times*, based in London—the global center of international finance—has a Web site with a wealth of information. After going to the home page, go to "Markets" and then to the "Markets Data" page. Examine the recent stock market activity around the globe. Note the similarity in movement on a daily basis among the world's major equity markets.

Financial Times   www.ft.com

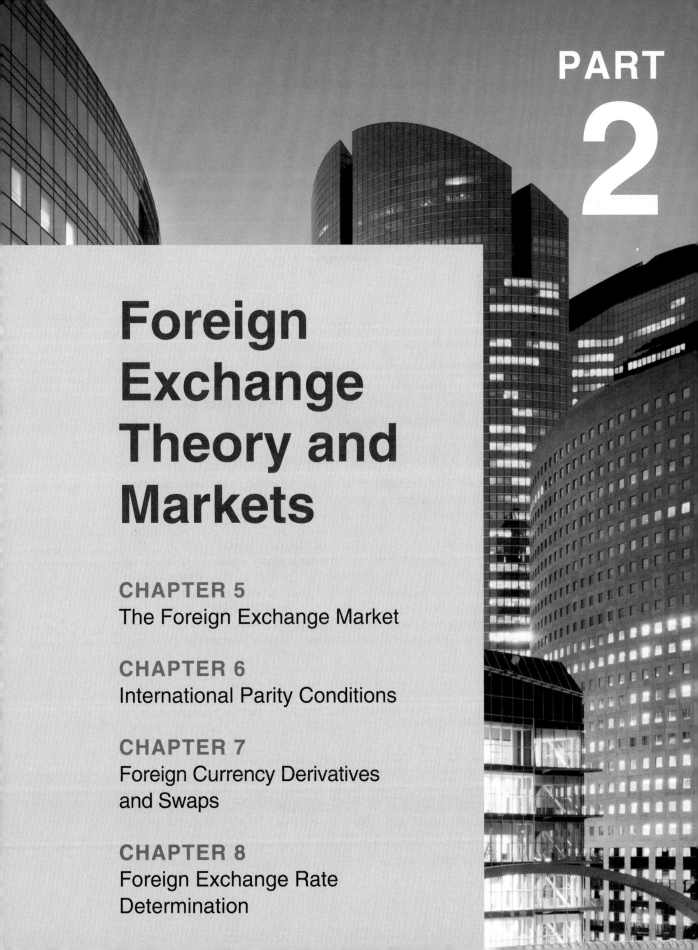

PART 2

Foreign Exchange Theory and Markets

CHAPTER 5

The Foreign Exchange Market

The best way to destroy the capitalist system is to debauch the currency. By a continuing process of inflation, governments can confiscate, secretly and unobserved, an important part of the wealth of their citizens. —John Maynard Keynes.

LEARNING OBJECTIVES

- Examine the what, when, where, and why of currency trading in the global marketplace
- Understand the definitions and distinctions between spot, forward, swap, and other types of foreign exchange financial instruments
- Learn the forms of currency quotations used by currency dealers, financial institutions, and agents of all kinds when conducting foreign exchange transactions
- Analyze the interaction between changing currency values and cross exchange rates, and the opportunities arising from intermarket arbitrage

The *foreign exchange market* provides the physical and institutional structure through which the money of one country is exchanged for that of another country—the rate of exchange between currencies is determined and foreign exchange transactions are physically completed. *Foreign exchange* means the money of a foreign country; that is, foreign currency bank balances, banknotes, checks, and drafts. A *foreign exchange transaction* is an agreement between a buyer and seller that a fixed amount of one currency will be delivered for some other currency at a specified rate. This chapter describes the following features of the foreign exchange market:

- Its three main functions
- Its participants
- Its immense daily transaction volume
- Its geographic extent
- Types of transactions, including spot, forward, and swap transactions
- Exchange rate quotation practices

The chapter concludes with the Mini-Case, *The Venezuelan Bolivar Black Market*, which describes a businessman's challenge in accessing hard-currency in a restricted exchange market.

Functions of the Foreign Exchange Market

Money is an object that is accepted as payment for goods, services, and in some cases, past debt. There are typically three functions of money: a unit of account, a store of value, a medium of exchange. The foreign exchange market is the mechanism by which participants transfer purchasing power between countries by exchanging money, obtain or provide credit for international trade transactions, and minimize exposure to the risks of exchange rate changes.

- The transfer of purchasing power is necessary because international trade and capital transactions normally involve parties living in countries with different national currencies. Usually each party wants to deal in its own currency, but the trade or capital transaction can be invoiced in only one currency. Hence, one party must deal in a foreign currency.

- Because the movement of goods between countries takes time, inventory in transit must be financed. The foreign exchange market provides a source of credit. Specialized instruments, such as bankers' acceptances and letters of credit are available to finance international trade.

- The foreign exchange market provides "hedging" facilities for transferring foreign exchange risk to someone else more willing to carry risk.

Structure of the Foreign Exchange Market

The foreign exchange market has, like all markets, evolved dramatically over time. Beginning with money changing hands in stalls on the streets of Florence and Venice, to the trading rooms in London and New York in the twentieth century, the market is based on supply and demand, market information and expectations, and negotiating strength.

The global foreign exchange market today is undergoing seismic change. That change involves every dimension of the market—the time, the place, the participants, the purpose, the instruments. The forces driving change in the foreign exchange market are fundamental: electronic trading platforms, algorithmic trading programs and routines, and the increasing role of currencies as an asset class. These forces and other facilitators have combined to expand the depth, breadth, and reach of the foreign exchange market.

Time of Day and Currency Trading

The foreign exchange market spans the globe, with prices moving and currencies trading—somewhere—every hour of every business day. As illustrated in Exhibit 5.1, the world's trading day starts each morning in Sydney and Tokyo; moves west to Hong Kong and Singapore; passes on to the Middle East; shifts to the main European markets of Frankfurt, Zurich, and London; jumps the Atlantic to New York; continues west to Chicago; and ends in San Francisco and Los Angeles. Many large international banks operate foreign exchange trading rooms in each major geographic trading center in order to serve both their customers and themselves (so-called proprietary trading) on a 24-hour-a-day basis.

Although global currency trading is indeed a 24-hour-a-day process, there are segments of the 24-hour day that are busier than others. Historically, the major financial centers of the 19th and 20th centuries dominated—London and New York. But as is the case with much of global commerce today, the Far East, represented by Tokyo and Hong Kong, are now threatening that dominance. When these city-based trading centers overlap, the global currency markets exhibit the greatest depth and liquidity.

EXHIBIT 5.1   Global Currency Trading: The Trading Day

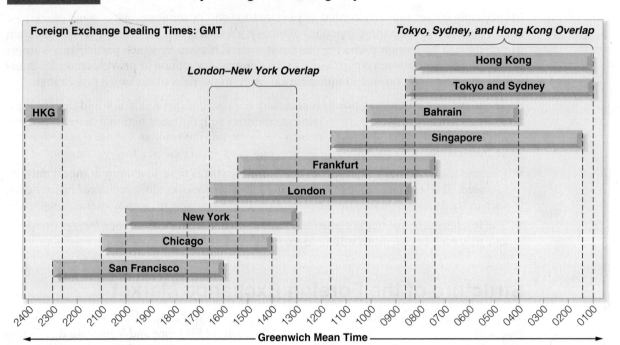

The currency trading day literally extends 24 hours per day. The busiest time of the day, which used to be when London and New York overlapped, has now started shifting 'further East,' to the Tokyo–Hong Kong dominated part of the day.

Trading Platforms and Processes

Currency trading is conducted in a variety of ways including individual-to-individual personal transactions, on official trading floors by open bidding, and increasingly by electronic platforms. Although continuous trading is indeed possible and increasingly prevalent, a "closing price" is often needed for a variety of record keeping and contractual purposes. These closing prices are often published as the official price, or "fixing," for the day, and certain commercial and investment transactions are based on this official price. Business firms in countries with exchange controls, like mainland China, often must surrender foreign exchange earned from exports to the central bank at the daily fixing price.

Currency traders are connected by highly sophisticated telecommunications networks, with dealers and brokers exchanging currency quotes instantaneously. A growing part of the industry is automated trading, electronic platforms in which corporate buyers and sellers trade currencies through Internet-based systems provided or hosted by major trading institutions. Although some of the largest currency transactions are still handled by humans via telephone, the use of computer trading has grown dramatically in recent years. The largest traditional providers of foreign exchange rate information and trading systems—Reuters, Telerate, EBS, and Bloomberg—are still substantial, but there has been a host of new service providers flooding the foreign exchange markets in recent years.

Market Participants

One of the biggest changes in the foreign exchange market in the past decade has been its shift from a two-tier market (the interbank or wholesale market, and the client or retail market) to a single-tier market. Electronic platforms and the development of sophisticated trading algorithms have facilitated market access by traders of all kinds and sizes.

Participants in the foreign exchange market can be simplistically divided into two major groups, those trading currency for commercial purposes, *liquidity seekers*, and those trading for profit, *profit seekers*. Although the foreign exchange market began as a market for liquidity purposes, facilitating the exchange of currency for the conduct of commercial trade and investment purposes, the exceptional growth in the market has been largely based on the expansion of profit-seeking agents. As might be expected, the profit seekers are typically much better informed about the market, looking to profit from its future movements, while liquidity seekers simply wish to secure currency for transactions. As a result, the profit seekers generally profit from the liquidity seekers.

Five broad categories of institutional participants operate in the market: 1) bank and nonbank foreign exchange dealers; 2) individuals and firms conducting commercial or investment transactions; 3) speculators and arbitragers; 4) central banks and treasuries; and 5) foreign exchange brokers.

Bank and Nonbank Foreign Exchange Dealers

Bank and nonbank traders and dealers profit from buying foreign exchange at a "bid" price and reselling it at a slightly higher "offer" (also called an "ask") price. Competition among dealers worldwide narrows the spread between bids and offers and so contributes to making the foreign exchange market "efficient" in the same sense as are securities markets.

Dealers in the foreign exchange departments of large international banks often function as "market makers." Such dealers stand willing at all times to buy and sell those currencies in which they specialize and thus maintain an "inventory" position in those currencies. They trade with other banks in their own monetary centers and with other centers around the world in order to maintain inventories within the trading limits set by bank policy. Trading limits are important because foreign exchange departments of many banks operate as profit centers, and individual dealers are compensated on a profit incentive basis.

Currency trading is quite profitable for many institutions. Many of the major currency-trading banks in the United States derive on average between 10% and 20% of their annual net income from currency trading. Currency trading is also very profitable for the bank's traders who typically earn a bonus based on the profitability to the bank of their individual trading activities.

Small- to medium-size banks and institutions are likely to participate but not to be market makers in the interbank market. Instead of maintaining significant inventory positions, they often buy from and sell to larger institutions in order to offset retail transactions with their own customers or to seek short-term profits for their own accounts. *Global Finance in Practice 5.1* describes a typical foreign exchange dealer's day on the job.

Individuals and Firms Conducting Commercial and Investment Transactions

Importers and exporters, international portfolio investors, multinational corporations, tourists, and others use the foreign exchange market to facilitate execution of commercial or investment transactions. Their use of the foreign exchange market is necessary, but incidental, to their underlying commercial or investment purpose. Some of these participants use the market to hedge foreign exchange risk as well.

GLOBAL FINANCE IN PRACTICE 5.1

FX Market Manipulation: Fixing the Fix

Following the turmoil surrounding the setting of LIBOR rates in the interbank market, similar allegations arose over the possible manipulation of benchmarks in the foreign exchange markets in 2013 and 2014.

Much of the focus was on the *London fix*, the 4pm daily benchmark rate used by a multitude of institutions and indices for marking value. Market analysts had noted steep spikes in trading just prior to the 4pm fix, spikes that were not sustained in the hours and days that followed. Traders were alleged to be exchanging emails, using social networking sites, and even phone calls, to collaborate on market movements and price quotes at key times. After-hours personal trading by currency traders, an area of only marginal concern before, was also under review.

Moving from voice-trading (telephone) to electronic trading was thought to be one possible fix, but the currency markets had long been something of an enigma when it came to electronic trading. *FICC trading*—fixed income, currencies, and commodities—was one of the first sectors to adopt electronic trading in the mid-1990s, but the market had proven slow to change.

But change had finally come. By 2014, nearly 75% of all currency trading was electronic. The logic of the fix was simple: computer algorithms were less likely to pursue fraudulent trading for fixing. And research had shown strong evidence that electronic trading was more stabilizing than voice-trading, as most of the algorithmic codes were based on reversion to the mean—to the market averages—over time.

But as is the case with many technological fixes, the fix did not eliminate the problem, it had possibly just changed it. E-trading might still facilitate market manipulation, just of a more sophisticated kind. For example there was a rumor of software in development that could detect mouse movements by other currency traders on some of the largest electronic platforms, allowing one computer (human attached) to detect the trader's mouse hovering over the *bid* or *ask* button prior to execution. Alas, it appeared there would always be the human element in trading, for better or for worse.

Speculators and Arbitragers

Speculators and arbitragers seek to profit from trading within the market itself. True profit seekers, they operate in their own interest, without a need or obligation to serve clients or to ensure a continuous market. Whereas dealers seek profit from the spread between bids and offers in addition to what they might gain from changes in exchange rates, speculators seek all of their profit from exchange rate changes. Arbitragers try to profit from simultaneous exchange rate differences in different markets.

Traders employed by those banks conduct a large proportion of speculation and arbitrage on behalf of major banks. Thus, banks act both as exchange dealers and as speculators and arbitragers. (Banks seldom admit to speculating, instead characterizing themselves as "taking an aggressive position"!) As described in *Global Finance in Practice 5.2*, however, trading is not for the weak of heart.

Central Banks and Treasuries

Central banks and treasuries use the market to acquire or spend their country's foreign exchange reserves as well as to influence the price at which their own currency is traded, a practice known as *foreign exchange intervention*. They may act to support the value of their own currency because of national policies or because of commitments to other countries under exchange rate relationships or regional currency agreements. Consequently, the motive is not to earn a profit as such, but rather to influence the foreign exchange value of their currency in a manner that will benefit the interests of their citizens. In many instances, they do their job best when they willingly take a loss on their foreign exchange transactions. As willing loss takers, central banks and treasuries differ in motive and behavior from all other market participants.

GLOBAL FINANCE IN PRACTICE 5.2

My First Day of Foreign Exchange Trading

For my internship I was working for the Treasury Front and Back Office of a major investment bank's New York branch on Wall Street. I was, for the first half of my internship, responsible for the timely input and verification of all foreign exchange, money market, securities, and derivative products. The second half was more interesting. I received training in currency trading.

I started on the spot desk, worked there for two weeks, and then moved to the swap desk for the remaining three weeks of my internship. From the first day I knew I would have to stay on my toes. The first two weeks of my training I was assigned to the spot desk where my supervisor was a senior trader who was very young (only 23 years old) and extremely ambitious.

On the very first day, about 11 a.m., she bet on the rise of the Japanese yen after the elections of the new Japanese Prime Minister. She had a long position on the yen and was short on the dollar. Unfortunately she lost $700,000 in less than 10 minutes. It is still unclear for me why she made such a bet. The *Wall Street Journal* and the *Financial Times*

(both papers were used heavily in the trading room) were very negative regarding the new Prime Minister's ability to reverse the financial crisis in Japan. It was clear that her position was based purely on emotions, instinct, savvy—anything but fundamentals.

To understand the impact of a $700,000 loss, you must understand that every trader on a spot desk has to make eight times his or her wage in commission. Let's say that my supervisor was making $80,000 a year. She would then need to make $640,000 in commission on spreads during that year to keep her job. A loss of $700,000 put her in a very bad position, and she knew it. But to her credit, she remained quite confident and did not appear shaken.

But after my first day I was pretty shaken. I understood after this experience that being a trader was not my cup of tea. It is not because of the stress of the job—and it is obviously very stressful. It was more that most of the skills of the job had nothing to do with what I had been learning in school for many years. And when I saw and experienced how hard these people partied up and down the streets of New York many nights—then trading hundreds of millions of dollars in minutes the following day, well, I just did not see this as my career track.

Source: Reminiscences of an anonymous intern.

Foreign Exchange Brokers

Foreign exchange brokers are agents who facilitate trading between dealers without themselves becoming principals in the transaction. They charge a small commission for this service. They maintain instant access to hundreds of dealers worldwide via open telephone lines. At times, a broker may maintain a dozen or more such lines to a single client bank, with separate lines for different currencies and for spot and forward markets.

It is a broker's business to know at any moment exactly which dealers want to buy or sell any currency. This knowledge enables the broker to find an opposite party for a client without revealing the identity of either party until after a transaction has been agreed upon. Dealers use brokers to expedite the transaction and to remain anonymous, since the identity of participants may influence short-term quotes.

Continuous Linked Settlement

In 2002, the *Continuous Linked Settlement* (CLS) system was introduced. The CLS system eliminates losses if either party of a foreign exchange transaction is unable to settle with the other party. It links the number of settlement systems, which operate on a real-time basis, and is expected to eventually result in same-day settlement, replacing the traditional two-day transaction period.

The CLS system should help counteract fraud in the foreign exchange markets as well. In the United States, the responsibility for regulating foreign exchange trading is assigned to the *U.S. Commodity Futures Trading Commission* (CFTC).

Transactions in the Foreign Exchange Market

Transactions in the foreign exchange market can be executed on a spot, forward, or swap basis.[1]

Spot Transactions

A *spot transaction* in the interbank market is the purchase of foreign exchange with delivery and payment between banks taking place normally on the second following business day. The Canadian dollar settles with the U.S. dollar on the first following business day. Exhibit 5.2 provides a time-map of the three major types of over-the-counter currency transactions typically executed in the global foreign exchange market: *spot transactions, forward transactions*, and *swap transactions*. Although there are a number of deviations on these types, some of which are described in the section that follows, all transactions are defined by their future date for delivery. (Note that we are not including futures transactions here; they parallel the time footprint of forwards, but are not executed over-the-counter.)

The date of settlement is referred to as the *value date*. On the value date, most dollar transactions in the world are settled through the computerized *Clearing House Interbank Payments System* (CHIPS) in New York, which calculates net balances owed by any one bank to

---

EXHIBIT 5.2   Foreign Exchange Transactions and Settlement

Foreign exchange operations are defined by the timing—*the future date*—set for delivery. There are in principle three major categories of over-the-counter transactions categorized by future delivery: *spot* (which may be *overnight*), *forward* (including *outright forward*), and *swap transactions*.

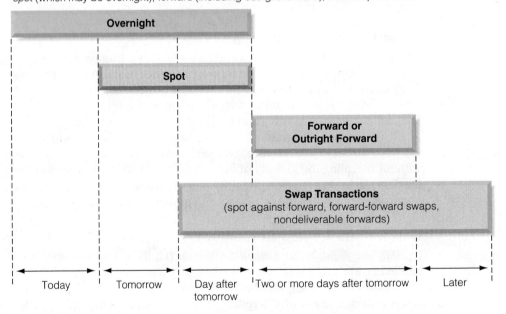

---

[1]A broader definition of the foreign exchange market includes foreign currency options, futures, and swaps, covered in Chapter 7.

another and which facilitates payment of those balances by 6:00 p.m. that same day in Federal Reserve Bank of New York funds. Other central banks and settlement services providers operate similarly in other currencies around the world.

A typical spot transaction in the interbank market might involve a U.S. bank contracting on a Monday for the transfer of £10,000,000 to the account of a London bank. If the spot exchange rate were $1.8420 to each British pound (£), the U.S. bank would transfer £10,000,000 to the London bank on Wednesday, and the London bank would transfer $18,420,000 to the U.S. bank at the same time. A spot transaction between a bank and its commercial customer would not necessarily involve a wait of two days for settlement.

Outright Forward Transactions

A *forward transaction* (or more formally, an *outright forward transaction*) requires delivery at a future value date of a specified amount of one currency for a specified amount of another currency. The exchange rate is established at the time of the agreement, but payment and delivery are not required until maturity. Forward exchange rates are normally quoted for value dates of one, two, three, six, and twelve months. Actual contracts can be arranged for other numbers of months or, on occasion, for periods of more than one year. Payment is on the second business day after the even-month anniversary of the trade. Thus, a two-month forward transaction entered into on March 18 will be for a value date of May 20, or the next business day if May 20 falls on a weekend or holiday.

Note that as a matter of terminology we can speak of "buying forward" or "selling forward" to describe the same transaction. A contract to deliver dollars for euros in six months is both "buying euros forward for dollars" and "selling dollars forward for euros."

Swap Transactions

A *swap transaction* in the interbank market is the simultaneous purchase and sale of a given amount of foreign exchange for two different value dates. Both purchase and sale are conducted with the same counterparty. There are several types of swap transactions.

Spot Against Forward. The most common type of swap is a "spot against forward." The dealer buys a currency in the spot market (at the spot rate) and simultaneously sells the same amount back to the same bank in the forward market (at the forward exchange rate). Since this is executed as a single transaction, with just one counterparty, the dealer incurs no unexpected foreign exchange risk. Swap transactions and outright forwards combined made up more than half of all foreign exchange market activity in recent years.

Forward-Forward Swaps. A more sophisticated swap transaction is called a *forward-forward swap*. For example, a dealer sells £20,000,000 forward for dollars for delivery in, say, two months at $1.8420/£ and simultaneously buys £20,000,000 forward for delivery in three months at $1.8400/£. The difference between the buying price and the selling price is equivalent to the interest rate differential, which is the interest rate parity described in Chapter 6, between the two currencies. Thus, a swap can be viewed as a technique for borrowing another currency on a fully collateralized basis.

Nondeliverable Forwards (NDFs). Created in the early 1990s, the *nondeliverable forward* (NDF), is now a relatively common derivative offered by the largest providers of foreign exchange derivatives. NDFs possess the same characteristics and documentation requirements as traditional forward contracts, except that they are settled only in U.S. dollars; the foreign currency being sold forward or bought forward is not delivered. The dollar-settlement feature reflects the fact that NDFs are contracted offshore, for example in New York for a Mexican investor, and so are beyond the reach and regulatory frameworks of the home country governments (Mexico in this case). NDFs are traded internationally using standards set by the *International Swaps and Derivatives Association* (ISDA). Although originally envisioned to be a method of currency hedging, it is now estimated that more than 70% of all NDF trading is for speculation purposes.

NDFs are used primarily for emerging market currencies or currencies subject to significant exchange controls, like Venezuela. Emerging market currencies often do not have open spot market currency trading, liquid money markets, or quoted Eurocurrency interest rates. Although most NDF trading focused on Latin America in the 1990s, many Asian currencies—including the Chinese renminbi—have been very widely traded in recent years. In general, NDF markets normally develop for country currencies having large cross-border capital movements, but still being subject to convertibility restrictions.

Pricing of NDFs reflects basic interest differentials, as with regular forwards, plus some additional premium charged by the bank for dollar settlement. If, however, there is no accessible or developed money market for interest rate setting, the pricing of the NDF takes on a much more speculative element. Without true interest rates, traders often price NDFs based on what they believe spot rates may be at the time of settlement.

NDFs are traded and settled outside the country of the subject currency, and therefore are beyond the control of the country's government. In the past, this has created a difficult situation, in which the NDF market serves as something of a gray market in the trading of that currency. For example, in late 2001, Argentina was under increasing pressure to abandon its fixed exchange rate regime of one peso equaling one U.S. dollar. The NDF market began quoting rates of ARS1.05/USD and ARS1.10/USD, in effect a devalued peso, for NDFs settling within the next year. This led to increasing speculative pressure against the peso (to the ire of the Argentine government).

NDFs, however, have proven to be something of an imperfect replacement for traditional forward contracts. The problems with the NDF typically involve its "fixing of spot rate on the fixing date," the spot rate at the end of the contract used to calculate the settlement. In times of financial crisis, for example with the Venezuelan bolivar in 2003, the government of the subject currency may suspend foreign exchange trading in the spot market for an extended period. Without an official fixing rate, the NDF cannot be settled. In the case of Venezuela, the problem was compounded when a new official "devalued bolivar" was announced, but was still not traded.

Size of the Foreign Exchange Market

The *Bank for International Settlements* (BIS), in conjunction with central banks around the world, conducts a survey of currency trading activity every three years. The most recent survey, conducted in April 2013, estimated daily global net turnover in the foreign exchange market to be $5.3 trillion. The BIS data for surveys between 1989 and 2013 is shown in Exhibit 5.3.

Global foreign exchange turnover in Exhibit 5.3 is divided into the three categories of currency instruments discussed previously (spot transactions, forward transactions, and swap transactions) plus a fourth category of options and other variable-value foreign exchange derivatives. Growth has been dramatic; since 1989, the foreign exchange market has grown at an average annual rate of 9.6% per year.

EXHIBIT 5.3   **Global Foreign Exchange Market Turnover, 1989–2013** (average daily turnover in April)

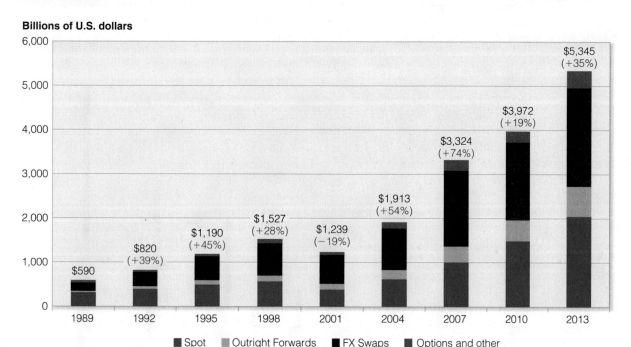

Billions of U.S. dollars

Legend: ■ Spot   ■ Outright Forwards   ■ FX Swaps   ■ Options and other

Source: Bank for International Settlements, "Triennial Central Bank Survey: Foreign Exchange and Derivatives Market Activity in April 2013: Preliminary Results," December 2013, www.bis.org.

As of 2013 (daily trading in April), trading in the foreign exchange market was at an all-time high of $5.3 trillion per day. Although the global recession in 2000–2001 clearly dampened market activity, the global financial crisis of 2008–2009 did not. According to the BIS, the organization that collects and deciphers this data, the primary driver of rapid foreign exchange growth in recent years is the increasing profit seeker activity facilitated by electronic trading and access to the greater market.

Geographical Distribution

Exhibit 5.4 shows the proportionate share of foreign exchange trading for the most important national markets in the world between 1992 and 2013. (Note that although the data is collected and reported on a national basis, the "United States" and "United Kingdom" should largely be interpreted as "New York" and "London," respectively, because the majority of foreign exchange trading takes place in each country's major financial city.)

The United Kingdom (London) continues to be the world's major foreign exchange market in traditional foreign exchange market activity with 40.9% of the global market. The United Kingdom is followed by the United States with 18.9%, Singapore with 5.7%, Japan (Tokyo) with 5.6%, Switzerland with 3.2%, and Hong Kong now reaching 4.1% of global trading. Indeed, the United Kingdom and United States together make up nearly 60% of daily currency trading. The relative growth of currency trading in Asia versus Europe over the past

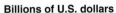

EXHIBIT 5.4   **Top 10 Geographic Trading Centers in the Foreign Exchange Market, 1992–2013**
(average daily turnover in April)

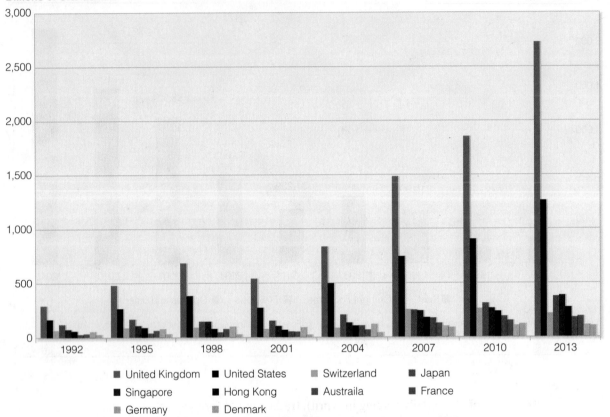

Billions of U.S. dollars

Legend:
■ United Kingdom   ■ United States   ■ Switzerland   ■ Japan
■ Singapore   ■ Hong Kong   ■ Austraila   ■ France
■ Germany   ■ Denmark

Source: Bank for International Settlements, "Triennial Central Bank Survey: Foreign Exchange and Derivatives Market Activity in April 2013: Preliminary Results," December 2013, www.bis.org.

15 years is pronounced, as the growth of the Asian economies and markets has combined with the introduction of the euro to shift currency exchange activity.

Currency Composition

The currency composition of trading for the 2001–2013 period, as shown in Exhibit 5.5, also indicates significant global shifts. Because all currencies are traded against some other currency-pairs, all percentages shown in Exhibit 5.5 are for that currency versus another. The dollar continues to dominate global trading, ultimately involved in 85.9% of all currency trading. The USD/EUR makes up 24.1% of trading, followed by the USD/JPY with 18.3%, the USD/GBP with 8.8%, and the USD/AUD at 6.8%. According to the BIS, the "big three" (dollar, euro, and yen) continue to dominate global currency trades, totaling roughly 92% of all trading surveyed.

There is, however, growing awareness of the rapid development of several major emerging market currencies, namely the Mexican peso, the Chinese renminbi, and the Russian ruble. It may not be long before several of these (most analysts are betting on the renminbi) become prominent currencies in the global market.

| EXHIBIT 5.5 | Daily FX Trading by Currency Pair (percent of total) |

Currency Pair	Versus Dollar	2001	2004	2007	2010	2013
USD/EUR	Euro	30.0	28.0	26.8	27.7	24.1
USD/JPY	Japanese yen	20.2	17.0	13.2	14.3	18.3
USD/GBP	British pound	10.4	13.4	11.6	9.1	8.8
USD/AUD	Australian dollar	4.1	5.5	5.6	6.3	6.8
USD/CAD	Canadian dollar	4.3	4.0	3.8	4.6	3.7
USD/CHF	Swiss franc	4.8	4.3	4.5	4.2	3.4
Subtotal		73.8	72.2	65.5	66.2	65.1
USD/MXN	Mexican peso	—	—	—	—	2.4
USD/CNY	Chinese renminbi	—	—	—	0.8	2.1
USD/NZD	New Zealand dollar	—	—	—	—	1.5
USD/RUB	Russian ruble	—	—	—	—	1.5
Subtotal		73.8	72.2	65.5	67.0	72.6
Other/USD	USD versus others	16.0	15.9	16.7	18.8	13.3
Dollar Total		89.8	88.1	82.2	85.8	85.9
Currency Pair	Versus Euro					
EUR/JPY	Japanese yen	2.9	3.2	2.6	2.8	2.8
EUR/GBP	British pound	2.1	2.4	2.1	2.7	1.9
EUR/CHF	Swiss franc	1.1	1.6	1.9	1.8	1.3
EUR/SEK	Swedish krona	—	—	0.7	0.9	0.5
Other	Other versus other	4.1	4.7	11.2	6.9	8.1
Non-dollar total		10.2	11.9	17.8	14.2	14.1
Global Total		100.0	100.0	100.0	100.0	100.0

Source: Constructed by authors based on data presented in Table 3, p. 11, of Triennial Central Bank Survey, Foreign exchange turnonver in April 2013: preliminary global results, Bank for International Settlements, Monetary and Economic Department, September 2013.

Foreign Exchange Rates and Quotations

A *foreign exchange rate* is the price of one currency expressed in terms of another currency. A foreign exchange quotation (or quote) is a statement of willingness to buy or sell at an announced rate. As we delve into the terminology of currency trading, keep in mind basic pricing, say the price of an orange. If the price is $1.20/orange, the "price" is $1.20, the "unit" is the orange.

Currency Symbols

Quotations may be designated by traditional currency symbols or by ISO codes.[2] The codes were developed for use in electronic communications. Both traditional symbols and currency

[2]ISO (International Organization for Standardization) is the world's largest developer of voluntary International Standards. ISO 4217 is the International Standard for currency codes. The most recent edition is ISO 4217:2008.

codes are given in full at the end of this book, but the major ones used throughout this chapter are the following:

Currency	Traditional Symbol	ISO 4217 Code
U.S. dollar	$	USD
European euro	€	EUR
Great Britain pound	£	GBP
Japanese yen	¥	JPY
Mexican peso	Ps	MXN

Today, all electronic trading of currencies between institutions in the global marketplace uses the three-letter ISO codes. Although there are no hard and fast rules in the retail markets and in business periodicals, European and American periodicals have a tendency to use the traditional currency symbols, while many publications in Asia and the Middle East have embraced the use of ISO codes. The paper currency (banknotes) of most countries continues to be represented using the country's traditional currency symbol. As illustrated in *Global Finance in Practice 5.3*, some countries like Russia are trying to return to traditional symbol use.

Exchange Rate Quotes

Foreign exchange quotations follow a number of principles, which at first may seem a bit confusing or non-intuitive. Every currency exchange involves two currencies, currency 1 (CUR1) and currency 2 (CUR2):

$$\text{CUR1 / CUR2}$$

The currency to the left of the slash is called the *base currency* or the *unit currency*. The currency to the right of the slash is called the *price currency* or *quote currency*. The quotation always indicates the number of units of the price currency, CUR2, required in exchange for receiving one unit of the base currency, CUR1.

For example, the most commonly quoted currency exchange is that between the U.S. dollar and the European euro. For example, a quotation of

$$\text{EUR / USD 1.2174}$$

GLOBAL FINANCE IN PRACTICE 5.3

Russian Symbolism

During an era in which currencies have increasingly been identified by their 3-digit ISO codes, the Russian government has decided that it is time for the Russian *ruble* (or *rouble* depending on your preference) to have its own symbol.

 In December 2013, the Bank of Russia had a contest, a popular vote, to choose among five different symbolic choices to be the new face of the currency. The winner (at left), with 61% of the vote, was the Russian letter R. The new symbol, in the words of the Governor of the Bank of Russia, "embodied the stability and reliability of the currency." When asked if the new ruble symbol may end up being confused with the Latin letter P, the Governor said it wasn't a problem because the dollar sign looks like the letter S.

The ruble's new symbol now joins that historical list of symbols—the $ (U.S. dollar), £ (British pound sterling), ¥ (Japanese yen), and the relatively youthful € (European Union euro)—as a declaration of currency value. More and more countries of late have promoted their own currency symbols in a show of nationalistic pride. India announced a new symbol for the rupee in 2010 (₹), and Turkey's lira got its own new symbol in 2012 (₺).

designates the euro (EUR) as the base currency, the dollar (USD) as the price currency, and the exchange rate is USD 1.2174 = EUR 1.00. If you can remember that the currency quoted on the left of the slash is always the base currency, and always a single unit, you can avoid confusion. Exhibit 5.6 provides a brief overview of the multitude of terms often used around the world to quote currencies, through an example using the European euro and U.S. dollar.

Market Conventions

The international currency market, although the largest financial market in the world, is steeped in history and convention.

European Terms. European terms, the quoting of the quantity of a specific currency per one U.S. dollar, has been market practice for most of the past 60 years or more. Globally, the base currency used to quote a currency's value has typically been the U.S. dollar. Termed *European terms*, this means that whenever a currency's value is quoted, it is quoted in terms of number of units of currency to equal one U.S. dollar.

For example, if a trader in Zurich, whose home currency is the Swiss franc (CHF), were to request a quote from an Oslo-based trader on the Norwegian krone (NOK), the Norwegian trader would quote the value of the NOK against the USD, not the CHF. The result is that most currencies are quoted per U.S. dollar—Japanese yen per U.S. dollar, Norwegian krone per U.S. dollar, Mexican pesos per U.S. dollar, Brazilian real per U.S. dollar, Malaysian ringgit per U.S. dollar, Chinese renminbi per U.S. dollar, and so on.

American Terms. There are two major exceptions to this rule of using European terms: the euro and the U.K. pound sterling. Both are normally quoted in *American terms*—the U.S. dollar price of one euro and the U.S. dollar price of one pound sterling.[3] Additionally, Australian dollars and New Zealand dollars are normally quoted on American terms.

For centuries, the British pound sterling consisted of 20 shillings, each of which equaled 12 pence. Multiplication and division with the nondecimal currency were difficult. The custom

---

EXHIBIT 5.6 **Foreign Currency Quotations**

European terms Foreign currency price of one dollar (USD)	**American terms** U.S. dollar price of one euro (EUR)
USD/EUR 0.8214 or **USD 1.00 = EUR 0.8214**	**EUR/USD 1.2174** or **EUR 1.00 = USD 1.2174**
USD is the *base* or *unit currency* **EUR is the *quote* or *price currency***	**EUR is the *base* or *unit currency*** **USD is the *quote* or *price currency***

$$\frac{1}{\text{EUR } 0.8214 \,/\, \text{USD}} = \text{USD } 1.2714 \,/\, \text{EUR}$$

---

[3]Sterling is quoted as the foreign currency price of one pound for historical reasons.

evolved for foreign exchange prices in London, then the undisputed financial capital of the world, to be stated in foreign currency units per pound. This practice remained even after sterling changed to decimals in 1971.

The euro was first introduced as a substitute or replacement for domestic currencies like the Deutsche mark and French franc. To make the transition simple for residents and users of these historical currencies, all quotes were made on a "domestic currency per euro" basis. This held true for its quotation against the U.S. dollar; hence, "U.S. dollars per euro" is the common quotation used today.

American terms are also used in quoting rates for most foreign currency options and futures, as well as in retail markets that deal with tourists and personal remittances. Again, this is largely a result of established practices that have been perpetuated over time, rather than some basic law of nature or finance.

Currency Nicknames. Foreign exchange traders may also use nicknames for major currencies. "Cable" means the exchange rate between U.S. dollars and U.K. pounds sterling, the name dating from the time when transactions in dollars and pounds were carried out over the Transatlantic telegraph cable. A Canadian dollar is a "loonie," named after the water fowl on Canada's one-dollar coin. "Kiwi" stands for the New Zealand dollar, "Aussie" for the Australian dollar, "Swissie" for Swiss francs, and "Sing dollar" for the Singapore dollar.

Direct and Indirect Quotations. A *direct quote* is the price of a foreign currency in domestic currency units. An *indirect quote* is the price of the domestic currency in foreign currency units.

In retail exchange in many countries (such as currency exchanged in hotels or airports), it is common practice to quote the home currency as the price and the foreign currency as the unit. A woman walking down the Avenue des Champs-Elysèes in Paris might see the following quote:

$$\text{EUR } 0.8214 = \text{USD } 1.00$$

Since in France the *home currency* is the euro (the price) and the *foreign currency* is the dollar (the unit), in Paris this quotation is a *direct quote on the dollar* or a *price quote on the dollar*. Verbally, she might say to herself, "0.8214 euros per dollar," or "it will cost me 0.8214 euros to get one dollar." These are European terms.

At the same time a man walking down Broadway in New York City may see the following quote in a bank window:

$$\text{USD } 1.2174 = \text{EUR } 1.00$$

Since in the U.S. the *home currency* is the dollar (the price) and the *foreign currency* is the euro (the unit), in New York this would be a *direct quote on the euro* (the home currency price of one unit of foreign currency) and an *indirect quote on the dollar* (the foreign currency price of one unit of home currency). The man might say to himself, "I will pay $1.2174 dollars per euro." These are American terms.

The two quotes are obviously equivalent (at least to four decimal places), one being the reciprocal of the other:

$$\frac{1}{\textbf{EUR 0.8214/USD}} = \textbf{USD1.2174/EUR}$$

Bid and Ask Rates. Although a newspaper or magazine article will state an exchange rate as a single value, the market for buying and selling currencies, whether it be retail or wholesale, uses two different rates, one for buying and one for selling. Exhibit 5.7 provides a sample of how these quotations may be seen in the market for the dollar/euro.

EXHIBIT 5.7   Bid, Ask, and Mid-Point Quotation

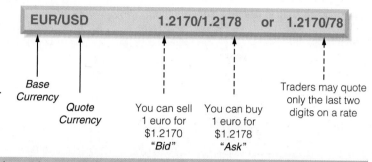

For example, the *Wall Street Journal* would quote the following currencies as follows:				
	Last Bid			**Last Bid**
Euro (EUR/USD)	1.2170	Brazilian Real (USD/BRL)		1.6827
Japanese Yen (USD/JPY)	83.16	Canadian Dollar (USD/CAD)		0.9930
U.K. Pound (GBP/USD)	1.5552	Mexican Peso (USD/MXN)		12.2365

A *bid* is the price (i.e., exchange rate) in one currency at which a dealer will buy another currency. An *ask* is the price (i.e., exchange rate) at which a dealer will sell the other currency. Dealers bid (buy) at one price and ask (sell) at a slightly higher price, making their profit from the spread between the prices. The bid-ask spread may be quite large for currencies that are traded infrequently, in small volumes, or both.

Bid and ask quotations in the foreign exchange markets are superficially complicated by the fact that the bid for one currency is also the offer for the opposite currency. A trader seeking to buy dollars with euros is simultaneously offering to sell euros for dollars.

Closing rates for 47 currencies (plus the SDR) as quoted by the *Wall Street Journal* are presented in Exhibit 5.8.

The *Wall Street Journal* gives American terms quotes under the heading "USD equivalent" and European terms quotes under the heading "Currency per USD." Quotes are given on an outright basis for spot, with forwards of one, three, and six months provided for a few select currencies. Quotes are for trading among banks in amounts of $1 million or more, as quoted at 4 p.m. EST by Reuters. The *Journal* does not state whether these are bid, ask, or mid-rate (an average of the bid and ask) quotations.

The order of currencies in quotations used by traders can be confusing (at least the authors of this book think so). As noted by one major international banking publication, *The notation EUR/USD is the system used by traders, although mathematically it would be more correct to express the exchange rate the other way around, as it shows how many USD have to be paid to obtain EUR 1.*

This is why the currency quotes in Exhibit 5.7—like EUR/USD, USD/JPY, or GBP/USD—are quoted and used in business and the rest of this text as $1.2170/€, ¥83.16/$, and $1.5552/£. International finance is not for the weak of heart!

EXHIBIT 5.8   Exchange Rates: New York Closing Snapshot

U.S.-dollar foreign-exchange rates in late New York trading, Friday, January 3, 2014

Country	Currency	Symbol	Code	USD equivalent	Currency per USD
Americas					
Argentina*	peso	Ps	ARS	0.1526	6.5547
Brazil	real	R$	BRL	0.4208	2.3764
Canada	dollar	C$	CAD	0.9403	1.0635
Chile	peso	$	CLP	0.001889	529.4
Colombia	peso	Col$	COP	0.000516	1937.98
Ecuador	U.S. dollar	$	USD	1	1
Mexico*	new peso	$	MXN	0.0763	13.1073
Peru	new sol	S/.	PEN	0.3562	2.8075
Uruguay[†]	peso	$U	UYU	0.04739	21.102
Venezuela	boliviar fuerte	Bs	VND	0.15748031	6.35
Asia-Pacific					
Australia	dollar	A$	AUD	0.8947	1.1177
1-month forward				0.8929	1.12
3-months forward				0.8894	1.1244
6-months forward				0.8841	1.1311
China	yuan	¥	CNY	0.1652	6.0516
Hong Kong	dollar	HK$	HKG	0.129	7.7541
India	rupee	₹	INR	0.01606	62.25495
Indonesia	rupiah	Rp	IDR	0.0000826	12110
Japan	yen	¥	JPY	0.00954	104.85
1-month forward				0.00954	104.84
3-months forward				0.00954	104.81
6-months forward				0.00955	104.75
Malaysia[§]	ringgit	RM	MYR	0.3032	3.2985
New Zealand	dollar	NZ$	NZD	0.8272	1.2088
Pakistan	rupee	Rs.	PKR	0.00951	105.205
Philippines	peso	?	PHP	0.0224	44.641
Singapore	dollar	S$	SGD	0.7892	1.267
South Korea	won	W	KRW	0.0009476	1055.3
Taiwan	dollar	T$	TWD	0.03339	29.949
Thailand	baht	B	THB	0.03031	32.992
Vietnam	dong	d	VND	0.00005	21095
Europe					
Czech Republic**	koruna	Kc	CZK	0.0493	20.283
Denmark	krone	Dkr	DKK	0.1822	5.4892
Euro area	euro	€	EUR	1.3588	0.7359
Hungary	forint	Ft	HUF	0.00454644	219.95
Norway	krone	NKr	NOK	0.1626	6.1516
Poland	zloty	—	PLN	0.3259	3.068
Romania	leu	L	RON	0.3023	3.3081
Russia[‡]	ruble	P	RUB	0.03015	33.173
Sweden	krona	SKr	SEK	0.1532	6.5258
Switzerland	franc	Fr.	CHF	1.1044	0.9054
1-month forward				1.1047	0.9052
3-months forward				1.1052	0.9048
6-months forward				1.1062	0.904
Turkey**	lira	₺	TRY	0.4592	2.1779
United Kingdom	pound	£	GBP	1.6417	0.6091
1-month forward				1.6414	0.6092
3-months forward				1.6407	0.6095
6-months forward				1.6394	0.61
Middle East/Africa					
Bahrain	dinar	—	BHD	2.6527	0.377
Egypt*	pound	£	EGP	0.1437	6.9578
Israel	shekel	Shk	ILS	0.2852	3.5064
Jordan	dinar	—	JOD	1.4147	0.7069
Kenya	shilling	KSh	KES	0.01151	86.906
Kuwait	dinar	—	KWD	3.5428	0.2823
Lebanon	pound	—	LBP	0.0006654	1502.95
Saudi Arabia	riyal	SR	SAR	0.2666	3.7505
South Africa	rand	R	ZAR	0.0937	10.675
United Arab Emirates	dirham	—	AED	0.2723	3.6731

Notes: *Floating rate †Financial §Government rate and ‡Russian Central Bank rate **Commercial rate ††Special Drawing Rights (SDR); from the International Monetary Fund; based on exchange rates for U.S., British and Japanese currencies. Note: Based on trading among banks of $1 million and more, as quoted at 4 p.m. ET by Reuters. Rates are drawn from the *Wall Street Journal* for January 4, 2014.

Cross Rates

Many currency pairs are only inactively traded, so their exchange rate is determined through their relationship to a widely traded third currency. For example, a Mexican importer needs Japanese yen to pay for purchases in Tokyo. Both the Mexican peso (MXN or the old peso symbol, Ps) and the Japanese yen (JPY or ¥) are commonly quoted against the U.S. dollar (USD or $). Using the following quotes from Exhibit 5.8,

		Currency per USD
Japanese yen	USD/JPY	104.85
Mexican peso	USD/MXN	13.1073

the Mexican importer can buy one U.S. dollar for MXN 13.1073, and with that dollar can buy JPY 104.85. The *cross rate* calculation would be as follows:

$$\frac{\text{Japanese Yen} = 1 \text{ U.S. Dollar}}{\text{Mexican Peso} = 1 \text{ U.S. Dollar}} = \frac{¥104.85/\$}{Ps13.1073/\$} = ¥7.9994/Ps$$

The cross rate could also be calculated as the reciprocal, with the USD/MXN rate divided by the USD/JPY rate, yielding Ps0.1250/¥.

Cross rates often appear in various financial publications in the form of a matrix to simplify the math. Exhibit 5.9 calculates a number of key cross rates from the quotes presented in Exhibit 5.8, including the Mexican peso/Japanese yen calculation just described (the Ps0.1250/¥ rate).

Intermarket Arbitrage

Cross rates can be used to check on opportunities for intermarket arbitrage. Suppose the following exchange rates are quoted:

Citibank quotes U.S. dollars per euro	USD1.3297/EUR
Barclays Bank quotes U.S. dollars per pound sterling	USD1.5585/GBP
Dresdner Bank quotes euros per pound sterling	EUR1.1722/GBP

EXHIBIT 5.9   **Key Currency Cross Rate Calculations for January 3, 2014**

	Dollar	Euro	Pound	SFranc	Peso	Yen	CdnDlr
				Calculated			
Canada	1.0635	1.4452	1.746	1.1746	0.0811	0.0101	—
Japan	104.8503	142.4790	172.140	115.8055	7.9994	—	98.5898
Mexico	13.1073	17.8113	21.5191	14.4768	—	0.1250	12.3247
Switzerland	0.9054	1.2303	1.4865	—	0.0691	0.0086	0.8513
U.K.	0.6091	0.8277	—	0.6727	0.0465	0.0058	0.5727
Euro	0.7359	—	1.2082	0.8128	0.0561	0.007	0.692
U.S.	—	1.3589	1.6418	1.1045	0.0763	0.0095	0.9403

Note: Cross rates are calculated from the quotes presented in the first column "Dollar," drawn from Exhibit 5.8.

The cross rate between Citibank and Barclays Bank is

$$\frac{USD1.5585/GBP}{USD1.3297/EUR} = EUR1.1721/GBP$$

Note that the calculated cross rate is *not the same* as Dresdner Bank's quotation of EUR1.1722/GBP, so an opportunity exists to profit from arbitrage between the three markets. Exhibit 5.10 shows the steps in what is called triangular arbitrage.

A market trader at Citibank New York, with USD1,000,000, can sell that sum spot to Barclays Bank for USD1,000,000 ÷ USD1.5585/GBP = GBP641,643. Simultaneously, these pounds can be sold to Dresdner Bank for GBP641,643 × EUR1.1722/GBP = EUR752,133, and the trader can then immediately sell these euros to Citibank for dollars: EUR752,133 × USD1.3297/EUR = USD1,000,112.

The profit on one such "turn" is a risk-free USD112 ($1,000,112 − $1,000,000; not much, but it's digital!). Such triangular arbitrage can continue until exchange rate equilibrium is reestablished; that is, until the calculated cross rate equals the actual quotation, less any tiny margin for transaction costs.

Percentage Change in Spot Rates

Assume that the Mexican peso has recently changed in value from USD/MXN 10.00 to 11.00. Your home currency is the U.S. dollar. What is the percent change in the value of the Mexican peso? The calculation depends upon the designated home currency.

Foreign Currency Terms. When the foreign currency price (the price, Ps) of the home currency (the unit, $) is used, Mexican pesos per U.S. dollar in this case, the formula for the percent change (%Δ) in the foreign currency becomes

$$\%\Delta = \frac{\text{Beginning Rate} - \text{Ending Rate}}{\text{Ending Rate}} \times 100 = \frac{\text{Ps}10.00/\$ - \text{Ps}11.00/\$}{\text{Ps}11.00/\$} \times 100 = -9.09\%$$

EXHIBIT 5.10   **Triangular Arbitrage by a Market Trader**

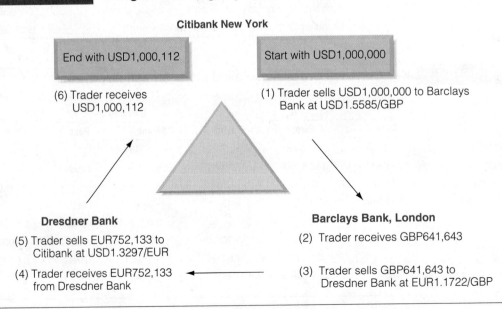

Citibank New York

End with USD1,000,112

Start with USD1,000,000

(6) Trader receives
USD1,000,112

(1) Trader sells USD1,000,000 to Barclays
Bank at USD1.5585/GBP

Dresdner Bank

(5) Trader sells EUR752,133 to
Citibank at USD1.3297/EUR

(4) Trader receives EUR752,133
from Dresdner Bank

Barclays Bank, London

(2) Trader receives GBP641,643

(3) Trader sells GBP641,643 to
Dresdner Bank at EUR1.1722/GBP

The Mexican peso fell in value 9.09% against the dollar. Note that it takes more pesos per dollar, and the calculation resulted in a negative value, both characteristics of a fall in value.

Home Currency Terms. When the home currency price (the price) for a foreign currency (the unit) is used—the reciprocals of the numbers above—the formula for the percent change in the foreign currency is:

$$\%\Delta = \frac{\text{Ending Rate} - \text{Beginning Rate}}{\text{Beginning Rate}} \times 100 = \frac{\$0.09091/\text{Ps} - \$0.1000/\text{Ps}}{\$0.1000/\text{Ps}} \times 100 = -9.09\%$$

The calculation yields the identical percentage change, a fall in the value of the peso by 9.09%. Although many people find the second calculation, the home currency term calculation, to be the more "intuitive" because it reminds them of many percentage change calculations, one must be careful to remember that these are exchanges of currency for currency, and the currency that is designated as home currency is significant.

Forward Quotations

Although spot rates are typically quoted on an outright basis (meaning all digits expressed), forward rates are, depending on the currency, typically quoted in terms of points or *pips*, the last digits of a currency quotation. Forward rates of one year or less maturity are termed cash rates; for longer than one-year they are called swap rates. A forward quotation expressed in points is not a foreign exchange rate as such. Rather it is the *difference* between the forward rate and the spot rate. Consequently, the spot rate itself can never be given on a points basis.

Consider the spot and forward point quotes in Exhibit 5.11. The bid and ask spot quotes are outright quotes, but the forwards are stated as points from the spot rate. The three-month

EXHIBIT 5.11   Spot and Forward Quotations for the Euro and Japanese Yen

		Euro: Spot and Forward ($/€)				Japanese Yen: Spot and Forward (¥/$)			
		Bid		Ask		Bid		Ask	
	Term	Points	Rate	Points	Rate	Points	Rate	Points	Rate
	Spot		1.0897		1.0901		118.27		118.37
Cash	1 week	3	1.0900	4	1.0905	−10	118.17	−9	118.28
rates	1 month	17	1.0914	19	1.0920	−51	117.76	−50	117.87
	2 months	35	1.0932	36	1.0937	−95	117.32	−93	117.44
	3 months	53	1.0950	54	1.0955	−143	116.84	−140	116.97
	4 months	72	1.0969	76	1.0977	−195	116.32	−190	116.47
	5 months	90	1.0987	95	1.0996	−240	115.87	−237	116.00
	6 months	112	1.1009	113	1.1014	−288	115.39	−287	115.50
	9 months	175	1.1072	177	1.1078	−435	113.92	−429	114.08
	1 year	242	1.1139	245	1.1146	−584	112.43	−581	112.56
Swap	2 years	481	1.1378	522	1.1423	−1150	106.77	−1129	107.08
rates	3 years	750	1.1647	810	1.1711	−1748	100.79	−1698	101.39
	4 years	960	1.1857	1039	1.1940	−2185	96.42	−2115	97.22
	5 years	1129	1.2026	1276	1.2177	−2592	92.35	−2490	93.47

points quotations for the Japanese yen in Exhibit 5.11 are −143 bid and −140 ask. The first number (−143) refers to points away from the spot bid, and the second number (−140) refers to points away from the spot ask. Given the outright quotes of 118.27 bid and 118.37 ask, the outright three-month forward rates are calculated as follows:

	Bid	Ask
Outright spot	JPY118.27	JPY118.37
Plus points (3 months)	1.43	1.40
Outright forward	JPY116.84	JPY116.97

The forward bid and ask quotations in Exhibit 5.11 of two years and longer are called swap rates. As mentioned earlier, many forward exchange transactions in the interbank market involve a simultaneous purchase for one date and sale (reversing the transaction) for another date. This "swap" is a way to borrow one currency for a limited time while giving up the use of another currency for the same time. In other words, it is a short-term borrowing of one currency combined with a short-term loan of an equivalent amount of another currency. The two parties could, if they wanted, charge each other interest at the going rate for each of the currencies. However, it is easier for the party with the higher-interest currency to simply pay the net interest differential to the other. The swap rate expresses this net interest differential on a points basis rather than as an interest rate.

Forward Quotations in Percentage Terms

The percent per annum deviation of the forward from the spot rate is termed the *forward premium*. However, as with the calculation of percentage changes in spot rates, the forward premium—which may be either a positive (a premium) or negative value (a discount)—depends upon the designated home (or base) currency. Assume the following spot rate for our discussion of foreign currency terms and home currency terms.

	Foreign currency (price)/ home currency (unit)	Home currency (price)/ foreign currency (unit)
Spot rate	¥118.27/$	USD/JPY 0.0084552
3-month forward	¥116.84/$	USD/JPY 0.0085587

Foreign Currency Terms. Using the foreign currency as the price of the home currency (the unit), JPY/USD spot and forward rates, and 90 days forward, the forward premium on the yen (f^{JPY}) is calculated as follows:

$$f^{JPY} = \frac{\text{Spot} - \text{Forward}}{\text{Forward}} \times \frac{360}{90} \times 100 = \frac{118.27 - 116.84}{116.84} \times \frac{360}{90} \times 100 = +4.90\%$$

The sign is positive indicating that the Japanese yen is selling forward at a premium of 4.90% against the U.S. dollar.

Home Currency Terms. Using the home currency (the dollar) as the price for the foreign currency (the yen) and the reciprocals of the spot and forward rates from the previous calculation, the forward premium on the yen (f^{JPY}) is calculated as follows:

$$f^{\text{JPY}} = \frac{\text{Spot} - \text{Forward}}{\text{Forward}} \times \frac{360}{90} \times 100 = \frac{\dfrac{1}{116.84} - \dfrac{1}{118.27}}{\dfrac{1}{118.27}} \times \frac{360}{90} \times 100$$

such that

$$f^{\text{JPY}} = \frac{\text{Forward} - \text{Spot}}{\text{Spot}} \times \frac{360}{90} \times 100 = \frac{0.0085587 - 0.0084552}{0.0084552} \times \frac{360}{90} \times 100 = +4.90\%$$

Again, the result is identical to the previous premium calculation: a positive 4.90% premium of the yen against the dollar.

Summary Points

- The three functions of the foreign exchange market are to transfer purchasing power, provide credit, and minimize foreign exchange risk.

- One of the biggest changes in the foreign exchange market in the past decade has been in its shift from a two-tier market (the interbank or wholesale market, and the client or retail market) to a single-tier market. Electronic platforms and the development of sophisticated trading algorithms have facilitated market access by traders of all kinds and sizes.

- Geographically the foreign exchange market spans the globe, with prices moving and currencies traded somewhere every hour of every business day.

- A foreign exchange rate is the price of one currency expressed in terms of another currency. A foreign exchange quotation is a statement of willingness to buy or sell currency at an announced price.

- Transactions within the foreign exchange market are executed either on a spot basis, requiring settlement two days after the transaction, or on a forward or swap basis, which requires settlement at some designated future date.

- European terms quotations are the foreign currency price of a U.S. dollar. American terms quotations are the dollar price of a foreign currency.

- Quotations can also be direct or indirect. A direct quote is the home currency price of a unit of foreign currency, while an indirect quote is the foreign currency price of a unit of home currency.

- Direct and indirect are not synonyms for American and European terms, because the home currency will change depending on who is doing the calculation, while European terms are always the foreign currency price of a dollar.

- A cross rate is an exchange rate between two currencies, calculated from their common relationships with a third currency. When cross rates differ from the direct rates between two currencies, intermarket arbitrage is possible.

MINI-CASE

The Venezuelan Bolivar Black Market[1]

"Rumor has it that during the year and a half that Venezuelan President Hugo Chávez spent in jail for his role in a 1992 coup attempt against the government, he was a voracious reader. Too bad his prison syllabus seems to have been so skimpy on economics and so heavy on Machiavelli."

—"Money Fun in the Venezuela of Hugo Chávez,"
The Economist, February 13, 2004.

It's late afternoon on March 10th, 2004, and Santiago opens the window of his office in Caracas, Venezuela. Immediately he is hit with the sounds rising from the plaza—cars honking, protesters banging their pots and pans, street vendors hawking their goods. Since the imposition of a new set of economic policies by President Hugo Chávez in 2002, such sights and sounds had become a fixture of city life in Caracas. Santiago sighed as he yearned for the simplicity of life in the old Caracas.

Santiago's once-thriving pharmaceutical distribution business had hit hard times. Since capital controls were

[1]Copyright © 2004 Thunderbird School of Global Management. All rights reserved. This case was prepared by Nina Camera, Thanh Nguyen, and Jay Ward under the direction of Professor Michael H. Moffett for the purpose of classroom discussion only and not to indicate either effective or ineffective management. Names of principals involved in the case have been changed to preserve confidentiality.

implemented in February of 2003, dollars had been hard to come by. He had been forced to pursue various methods—methods that were more expensive and not always legal—to obtain dollars, causing his margins to decrease by 50%. Adding to the strain, the Venezuelan currency, the bolivar (Bs), had been recently devalued (repeatedly). This had instantly squeezed his margins as his costs had risen directly with the exchange rate. He could not find anyone to sell him dollars. His customers needed supplies and they needed them quickly, but how was he going to come up with the $30,000—the hard currency—to pay for his most recent order?

Political Chaos

Hugo Chávez's tenure as President of Venezuela had been tumultuous at best since his election in 1998. After repeated recalls, resignations, coups, and re-appointments, the political turmoil had taken its toll on the Venezuelan economy as a whole, and its currency in particular. The short-lived success of the anti-Chávez coup in 2001, and his nearly immediate return to office, had set the stage for a retrenchment of his isolationist economic and financial policies.

On January 21st, 2003, the bolivar closed at a record low—Bs1853/$. The next day President Hugo Chávez suspended the sale of dollars for two weeks. Nearly instantaneously, an unofficial or *black market* for the exchange of Venezuelan bolivars for foreign currencies (primarily U.S. dollars) sprouted. As investors of all kinds sought ways to exit the Venezuelan market, or simply obtain the hard-currency needed to continue to conduct their businesses (as was the case for Santiago), the escalating capital flight caused the black market value of the bolivar to plummet to Bs2500/$ in weeks. As markets collapsed and exchange values fell, the Venezuelan inflation rate soared to more than 30% per annum.

Capital Controls and CADIVI

To combat the downward pressures on the bolivar, the Venezuelan government announced on February 5th, 2003, the passage of the *2003 Exchange Regulations Decree*. The Decree took the following actions:

1. Set the official exchange rate at Bs1596/$ for purchase (*bid*) and Bs1600/$ for sale (*offer*);

2. Established the Comisión de Administración de Divisas (CADIVI) to control the distribution of foreign exchange; and

3. Implemented strict price controls to stem inflation triggered by the weaker bolivar and the exchange control-induced contraction of imports.

CADIVI was both the official means and the cheapest means by which Venezuelan citizens could obtain foreign currency. In order to receive an authorization from CADIVI to obtain dollars, an applicant was required to complete a series of forms. The applicant was then required to prove that they had paid taxes the previous three years, provide proof of business and asset ownership and lease agreements for company property, and document the current payment of Social Security.

Unofficially, however, there was an additional unstated requirement for permission to obtain foreign currency: authorizations would be reserved for Chávez supporters. In August 2003 an anti-Chávez petition had gained widespread circulation. One million signatures had been collected. Although the government ruled that the petition was invalid, it had used the list of signatures to create a database of names and social security numbers that CADIVI utilized to cross-check identities on hard currency requests. President Chávez was quoted as saying "Not one more dollar for the *putschits*; the bolivars belong to the people."[2]

Santiago's Alternatives

Santiago had little luck obtaining dollars via CADIVI to pay for his imports. Because he had signed the petition calling for President Chávez's removal, he had been listed in the CADIVI database as anti-Chávez, and now could not obtain permission to exchange bolivar for dollars.

The transaction in question was an invoice for $30,000 in pharmaceutical products from his U.S.-based supplier. Santiago intended to resell these products to a large Venezuelan customer who would distribute the products. This transaction was not the first time that Santiago had been forced to search out alternative sources for meeting his U.S. dollar-obligations. Since the imposition of capital controls, his search for dollars had become a weekly activity for Santiago. In addition to the official process—through CADIVI—he could also obtain dollars through the gray or black markets.

The Gray Market: CANTV Shares

In May 2003, three months following the implementation of the exchange controls, a window of opportunity had opened up for Venezuelans—an opportunity that

[2]"Venezuela Girds for Exchange Controls," the *Wall Street Journal* (Eastern edition), February 5, 2003, p. A14.

allowed investors in the Caracas stock exchange to avoid the tight foreign exchange curbs. This loophole circumvented the government-imposed restrictions by allowing investors to purchase local shares of the leading telecommunications company CANTV on the Caracas' bourse, and to then convert those shares into dollar-denominated American Depositary Receipts (ADRs) traded on the NYSE.

The sponsor for CANTV ADRs on the NYSE was the Bank of New York, the leader in ADR sponsorship and management in the U.S. The Bank of New York had suspended trading in CANTV ADRs in February after the passage of the Decree, wishing to determine the legality of trading under the new Venezuelan currency controls. On May 26th, after concluding that trading was indeed legal under the Decree, trading resumed in CANTV shares. CANTV's share price and trading volume both soared in the following week.[3]

The share price of CANTV quickly became the primary method of calculating the implicit gray market exchange rate. For example, CANTV shares closed at Bs7945/share on the Caracas bourse on February 6, 2004. That same day, CANTV ADRs closed in New York at $18.84/ADR. Each New York ADR was equal to seven shares of CANTV in Caracas. The implied gray market exchange rate was then calculated as follows:

$$\text{Implicit Gray Market Rate} = \frac{7 \times \text{Bs7945/Share}}{\$18.84/\text{ADR}} = \text{Bs2952/\$}$$

The official exchange rate on that same day was Bs1598/$. This meant that the gray market rate was quoting the bolivar about 46% weaker against the dollar than what the Venezuelan government officially declared its currency to be worth. Exhibit A illustrates both the official exchange rate and the gray market rate (calculated using CANTV shares) for the January 2002 to March 2004 period. The divergence between the official and gray market rates beginning in February 2003 coincided with the imposition of capital controls.[4]

The Black Market

A third method of obtaining hard currency by Venezuelans was through the rapidly expanding black market. The black market was, as is the case with black markets all over the world, essentially unseen and illegal. It was, however, quite sophisticated, using the services of a stockbroker or banker in Venezuela who simultaneously held U.S. dollar accounts offshore. The choice of a black market broker was a critical one; in the event of a failure to complete the transaction properly there was no legal recourse.

If Santiago wished to purchase dollars on the black market, he would deposit bolivars in his broker's account in Venezuela. The agreed upon black market exchange rate was determined on the day of the deposit, and usually was within a 20% band of the gray market rate derived from the CANTV share price. Santiago would then be given access to a dollar-denominated bank account outside of Venezuela in the agreed amount. The transaction took, on average, two business days to settle. The unofficial black market rate was Bs3300/$.

In early 2004 President Chávez had asked Venezuela's Central Bank to give him "a little billion"—*millardito*—of its $21 billion in foreign exchange reserves. Chávez argued that the money was actually the people's, and he wished to invest some of it in the agricultural sector. The Central Bank refused. Not to be thwarted in its search for funds, the Chávez government announced on February 9, 2004, another devaluation. The bolivar was devalued 17%, falling in official value from Bs1600/$ to Bs1920/$ (see Exhibit A). With all Venezuelan exports of oil being purchased in U.S. dollars, the devaluation of the bolivar meant that the country's proceeds from oil exports grew by the same 17% as the devaluation itself.

The Chávez government argued that the devaluation was necessary because the bolivar was "a variable that cannot be kept frozen, because it prejudices exports and pressures the balance of payments" according to Finance Minister Tobias Nobriega. Analysts, however, pointed out that Venezuelan government actually had significant control over its balance of payments: oil was the primary export, the government maintained control over the official access to hard currency necessary for imports, and the Central Bank's foreign exchange reserves were now over $21 billion.

It's not clear whether Mr. Chávez understands what a massive hit Venezuelans take when savings and earnings in dollar terms are cut in half in just three years. Perhaps the political-science student believes that more devalued bolivars

---

[3]In fact CANTV's share price continued to rise over the 2002 to 2004 period as a result of its use as an exchange rate mechanism. The use of CANTV ADRs as a method of obtaining dollars by Venezuelan individuals and organizations was typically described as "not illegal."

[4]Morgan Stanley Capital International (MSCI) announced on November 26, 2003, that it would change its standard spot rate for the Venezuelan bolivar to the notional rate based on the relationship between the price of CANTV Telefonos de Venezuela D in the local market in bolivars and the price of its ADR in U.S. dollars.

EXHIBIT A   Official and Gray Market Exchange Rates, Venezuelan Bolivar/U.S. Dollar

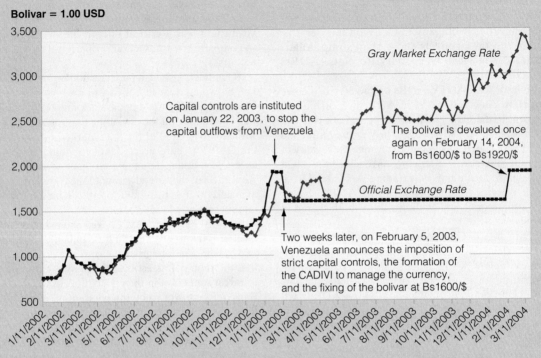

Note: All prices and rates are Friday closing values.

makes everyone richer. But one unavoidable conclusion is that he recognized the devaluation as a way to pay for his Bolivarian "missions," government projects that might restore his popularity long enough to allow him to survive the recall, or survive an audacious decision to squelch it.

— "Money Fun in the Venezuela of Hugo Chávez,"
the *Wall Street Journal* (eastern edition),
February 13, 2004, p. A13.

Time Was Running Out

Santiago received confirmation from CADIVI on the afternoon of March 10th that his latest application for dollars was approved and that he would receive $10,000 at the official exchange rate of Bs1920/$. Santiago attributed his good fortune to the fact that he paid a CADIVI insider an extra 500 bolivars per dollar to expedite his request. Santiago noted with a smile that "the Chávistas need to make money too."

The noise from the street seemed to be dying with the sun. It was time for Santiago to make some decisions.

None of the alternatives were *bonita*, but if he was to preserve his business, bolivars—at some price—had to be obtained.

CASE QUESTIONS

1. Why does a country like Venezuela impose capital controls?

2. In the case of Venezuela, what is the difference between the *gray market* and the *black market*?

3. Create a financial analysis of Santiago's choices. Use it to recommend a solution to his problem.

Post Script. Although President Chávez died in 2013, and the Venezuelan bolivar has been devalued repeatedly and renamed the *bolivar fuerte* since the time of this case, it remains a currency that is overvalued by its government and restricted in its exchange, therefore it continues to lead a double life—officially and unofficially.

Questions

1. **Definitions.** Define the following terms:
   a. Foreign exchange market
   b. Foreign exchange transaction
   c. Foreign exchange

2. **Functions of the Foreign Exchange Market.** What are the three major functions of the foreign exchange market?

3. **Market Participants.** For each of the foreign exchange market participants, identify their motive for buying or selling foreign exchange.

4. **Transaction.** Define each of the following types of foreign exchange transactions:
   a. Spot
   b. Outright forward
   c. Forward-forward swaps

5. **Foreign Exchange Market Characteristics.** With reference to foreign exchange turnover in 2001, rank the following:
   a. The relative size of spot, forwards, and swaps as of 2001
   b. The five most important geographic locations for foreign exchange turnover
   c. The three most important currencies of denomination

6. **Foreign Exchange Rate Quotations.** Define and give an example of the following:
   a. Bid rate quote
   b. Ask rate quote

7. **Reciprocals.** Suppose that Australia is the home country. Determine whether the following quotes are direct or indirect, and convert indirect (direct) quotes to direct (indirect) quotes:
   a. Euro: AUD1.4462/EUR.
   b. Canada: CAD0.9812/AUD.

8. **Geographical Extent of the Foreign Exchange Market.** Answer the following:
   a. What is the geographical location of the foreign exchange market?
   b. What are the two main types of trading systems for foreign exchange?
   c. How are foreign exchange markets connected for trading activities?

9. **Organization.** Explain the change in the foreign exchange market from a two-tier (interbank/wholesale and client/retail) market to a single-tier market.

10. **Cross Rates.** Calculate the cross rates for the following currencies:
    a. Find the cross rate JPY/CAD from the spot rates JPY104.8/USD and CAD1.06/USD.
    b. Find the cross rate MXN/BRL from the spot rates MXN2.81/USD and USD0.42/BRL.

Problems

1. **Visiting Guatemala.** Isaac Díez Peris lives in Rio de Janeiro. While attending school in Spain he meets Juan Carlos Cordero from Guatemala. Over the summer holiday Isaac decides to visit Juan Carlos in Guatemala City for a couple of weeks. Isaac's parents give him some spending money, R$4,500. Isaac wants to exchange it for Guatemalan quetzals (GTQ). He collects the following rates:

   Spot rate on the GTQ/€ cross rate   GTQ 10.5799/€
   Spot rate on the €/R$ cross rate   €0.4462/R$

   a. What is the Brazilian reais/Guatemalan quetzal cross rate?
   b. How many quetzals will Isaac get for his reais?

2. **Forward Premiums on the Japanese Yen.** Use the following spot and forward bid-ask rates for the Japanese yen/U.S. dollar (¥/$) exchange rate from October 1, 2014, to answer the following questions:
   a. What is the mid-rate for each maturity?
   b. What is the annual forward premium for all maturities?
   c. Which maturities have the smallest and largest forward premiums?

Period	¥/$ Bid	¥/$ Ask
spot	109.30	109.32
1 month	109.05	109.09
2 months	108.80	108.90
3 months	107.97	108.34
6 months	107.09	107.40
12 months	103.51	104.19
24 months	96.82	97.35

3. **Munich to Moscow.** On your post-graduation celebratory trip you decide to travel from Munich, Germany, to Moscow, Russia. You leave Munich with 15,000 euros in your wallet. Wanting to exchange all of them for Russian rubles, you obtain the following quotes:

   Spot rate on the dollar/euro cross rate $1.3214/€
   Spot rate on the ruble/dollar cross rate   Rbl 30.96/$

   a. What is the Russian ruble/euro cross rate?
   b. How many rubles will you obtain for your euros?

4. **Jumping to Japan.** After spending a week in London you get an email from your friend in Japan. He can get you a very good deal on a plane ticket and wants you to meet him in Osaka next week to continue your post-graduation celebratory trip. You have GBP2,000 left in your purse. In preparation for the trip you want to exchange your British pounds for Japanese yen, and you get the following quotes:

Spot rate on the pound/dollar cross rate   £0.6178/$

Spot rate on the yen/dollar cross rate   ¥109.31/$

a. What is the yen/pound cross rate?
b. How many yen will you obtain for your pound?

5. **Vancouver Exports.** A Canadian exporter, Vancouver Exports, will be receiving six payments of €12,000, ranging from now to 12 months in the future. Since the company keeps cash balances in both Canadian dollars and U.S. dollars, it can choose which currency to exchange the euros for at the end of the various periods. Which currency appears to offer the better rates in the forward market?

Period	Days Forward	C$/euro	US$/euro
spot	—	1.3360	1.3221
1 month	30	1.3368	1.3230
2 months	60	1.3376	1.3228
3 months	90	1.3382	1.3224
6 months	180	1.3406	1.3215
12 months	360	1.3462	1.3194

6. **Crisis in the Pacific.** The Asian financial crisis that began in July 1997 wreaked havoc throughout the currency markets of East Asia.

a. Which of the following currencies had the largest depreciations or devaluations during the July to November period?
b. Which seemingly survived the first five months of the crisis with the least impact on their currencies?

Country	Currency	July 1997 (per US$)	November 1997 (per US$)
China	yuan	8.40	8.40
Hong Kong	dollar	7.75	7.73
Indonesia	rupiah	2,400	3,600
Korea	won	900	1,100
Malaysia	ringgit	2.50	3.50
Philippines	peso	27	34
Singapore	dollar	1.43	1.60
Taiwan	dollar	27.80	32.70
Thailand	baht	25.0	40.0

7. **Bloomberg Currency Cross Rates.** Use the table at the bottom of the page from Bloomberg to calculate each of the following:
a. Japanese yen per U.S. dollar?
b. U.S. dollars per Japanese yen?
c. U.S. dollars per euro?
d. Euros per U.S. dollar?
e. Japanese yen per euro?
f. Euros per Japanese yen?
g. Canadian dollars per U.S. dollar?
h. U.S. dollars per Canadian dollar?
i. Australian dollars per U.S. dollar?
j. U.S. dollars per Australian dollar?
k. British pounds per U.S. dollar?
l. U.S. dollars per British pound?
m. U.S. dollars per Swiss franc?
n. Swiss francs per U.S. dollar?

Problem 7.

Currency	USD	EUR	JPY	GBP	CHF	CAD	AUD	HKD
HKD	7.7736	10.2976	0.0928	12.2853	7.9165	7.6987	7.6584	—
AUD	1.015	1.3446	0.0121	1.6042	1.0337	1.0053	—	0.1306
CAD	1.0097	1.3376	0.0121	1.5958	1.0283	—	0.9948	0.1299
CHF	0.9819	1.3008	0.0117	1.5519	—	0.9725	0.9674	0.1263
GBP	0.6328	0.8382	0.0076	—	0.6444	0.6267	0.6234	0.0814
JPY	83.735	110.9238	—	132.3348	85.2751	82.9281	82.4949	10.7718
EUR	0.7549	—	0.009	1.193	0.7688	0.7476	0.7437	0.0971
USD	—	1.3247	0.0119	1.5804	1.0184	0.9904	0.9852	0.1286

8. **Forward Premiums on the Dollar/Euro ($/€).** Use the following spot and forward bid-ask rates for the U.S. dollar/euro (US$/€) from December 10, 2010, to answer the following questions:
   a. What is the mid-rate for each maturity?
   b. What is the annual forward premium for all maturities?
   c. Which maturities have the smallest and largest forward premiums?

Period	US$/€ Bid Rate	US$/€ Ask Rate
spot	1.3231	1.3232
1 month	1.3230	1.3231
2 months	1.3228	1.3229
3 months	1.3224	1.3227
6 months	1.3215	1.3218
12 months	1.3194	1.3198
24 months	1.3147	1.3176

9. **Trading in Zurich.** Andreas Broszio just started as an analyst for Credit Suisse in Zurich, Switzerland. He receives the following quotes for Swiss francs against the dollar for spot, 1 month forward, 3 months forward, and 6 months forward.

   Spot exchange rate:

Bid rate	SF1.2575/$
Ask rate	SF1.2585/S
1 month forward	10 to 15
3 months forward	14 to 22
6 months forward	20 to 30

   a. Calculate outright quotes for bid and ask and the number of points spread between each.
   b. What do you notice about the spread as quotes evolve from spot toward 6 months?
   c. What is the 6-month Swiss bill rate?

10. **Triangular Arbitrage Using the Swiss Franc.** The following exchange rates are available to you. (You can buy or sell at the stated rates.) Assume you have an initial SF12,000,000. Can you make a profit via triangular arbitrage? If so, show the steps and calculate the amount of profit in Swiss francs.

Mt. Fuji Bank	¥ 92.00/$
Mt. Rushmore Bank	SF1.02/$
Mt. Blanc Bank	¥ 90.00/SF

11. **Forward Premiums on the Australian Dollar.** Use the following spot and forward bid-ask rates for the U.S. dollar/Australian dollar (US$/A$) exchange rate from December 10, 2010, to answer the following questions:
    a. What is the mid-rate for each maturity?
    b. What is the annual forward premium for all maturities?
    c. Which maturities have the smallest and largest forward premiums?

Period	US$/A$ Bid Rate	US$/A$ Ask Rate
spot	0.98510	0.98540
1 month	0.98131	0.98165
2 months	0.97745	0.97786
3 months	0.97397	0.97441
6 months	0.96241	0.96295
12 months	0.93960	0.94045
24 months	0.89770	0.89900

12. **Transatlantic Arbitrage.** A corporate treasury working out of Vienna with operations in New York simultaneously calls Citibank in New York City and Barclays in London. The banks give the following quotes on the euro simultaneously.

Citibank NYC	Barclays London
$1.2624–25/€	$1.2622–23/€

Using $1 million or its euro equivalent, determine whether the corporate treasury could make geographic arbitrage profit with the two different exchange rate quotes.

13. **Venezuelan Bolivar (A).** The Venezuelan government officially floated the Venezuelan bolivar (Bs) in February 2002. Within weeks, its value had moved from the pre-float fix of Bs778/$ to Bs1025/$.
    a. Is this a devaluation or a depreciation?
    b. By what percentage did the value change?

14. **Venezuelan Bolivar (B).** The Venezuelan political and economic crisis deepened in late 2002 and early 2003. On January 1, 2003, the bolivar was trading

at Bs1400/$. By February 1, its value had fallen to Bs1950/$. Many currency analysts and forecasters were predicting that the bolivar would fall an additional 40% from its February 1 value by early summer 2003.

a. What was the percentage change in January?

b. What is the forecast value for June 2003?

15. **Indirect Quotation on the Dollar.** Calculate the forward premium on the dollar (the dollar is the home currency) if the spot rate is €1.3300/$ and the 3-month forward rate is €1.3400/$.

16. **Direct Quotation on the Dollar.** Calculate the forward discount on the dollar (the dollar is the home currency) if the spot rate is $1.5800/£ and the 6-month forward rate is $1.5550/£.

17. **Around the Horn (A).** Assuming the following quotes, calculate how a market trader at Citibank with $1,000,000 can make an intermarket arbitrage profit.

Banks	Spot Rates
Citibank	$1.6194/£
National Westminster	€1.2834/£
Deutschebank	$1.2615/€

18. **Around the Horn (B).** Assume the following bid-ask quotes and calculate how the market trader can now make an intermarket arbitrage profit.

Banks	Spot Rates
Citibank	$1.6192–96/£
National Westminster	€1.2833–35/£
Deutschebank	$1.2614–16/€

19. **Around the Horn.** Assuming the following quotes, calculate how a market trader at Citibank with $1,000,000 can make an intermarket arbitrage profit.

Citibank quotes U.S. dollar per pound	$1.5900/£
National Westminster quotes euros per pound	€1.2000/£
Deutschebank quotes U.S. dollar per euro	$0.7550/€

20. **Great Pyramids.** Inspired by his recent trip to the Great Pyramids, Citibank trader Ruminder Dhillon wonders if he can make an intermarket arbitrage profit using Libyan dinars and Saudi riyals. He has $1,000,000 to work with so he gathers the following quotes. Is there an opportunity for an arbitrage profit?

Citibank quotes U.S. dollar per Libyan dinar	$1.9324/LYD
National Bank of Kuwait quotes Saudi riyal per Libyan dinar	SAR1.9405/LYD
Barclay quotes U.S. dollar per Saudi riyal	$0.2667/SAR

Internet Exercises

1. **Bank for International Settlements.** The Bank for International Settlements (BIS) publishes a wealth of effective exchange rate indices. Use its database and analyses to determine the degree to which the dollar, the euro, and the yen (the "big three currencies") are currently overvalued or undervalued.

   Bank for International Settlements   www.bis.org/statistics/eer/index.htm

2. **Bank of Canada Exchange Rate Index (CERI).** The Bank of Canada regularly publishes an index of the Canadian dollar's value, the CERI. The CERI is a multilateral trade-weighted index of the Canadian dollar's value against other major global currencies relevant to the Canadian economy and business landscape. Use the CERI from the Bank of Canada's Web site to evaluate the relative strength of the loonie in recent years.

   Bank of Canada exchange rates   www.bankofcanada.ca/rates/exchange/ceri/

3. **Forward Quotes.** FXStreet foreign exchange services provides representative forward rates on a multitude of currencies online. Use the following Web site to search out forward exchange rate quotations on a variety of currencies.

   FXStreet   www.fxstreet.com/rates-charts/forward-rates/

4. **Federal Reserve Statistical Release.** The United States Federal Reserve provides daily updates of the value of the major currencies traded against the U.S. dollar on its Web site. Use the Fed's Web site to determine the relative weights used by the Fed to determine the index of the dollar's value.

   Federal Reserve   www.federalreserve.gov/releases/h10/update/

5. **Daily Market Commentary.** Many different online currency trading and consulting services provide daily assessments of global currency market activity. Use the following GCI site to find the market's current assessment of how the euro is trading against both the U.S. dollar and the Canadian dollar.

   GCI Financial Ltd.   www.gcitrading.com/fxnews/

6. **Pacific Exchange Rate Service.** The Pacific Exchange Rate Service Web site, managed by Professor Werner Antweiler of the University of British Columbia, possesses a wealth of current information on currency exchange rates and related statistics. Use the service to plot the recent performance of currencies that have recently suffered significant devaluations or depreciations, such as the Argentine peso, the Venezuelan bolivar, the Turkish lira, and the Egyptian pound.

   Pacific Exchange Rate Service   fx.sauder.ubc.ca/plot.html

International Parity Conditions

… if capital freely flowed towards those countries where it could be most profitably employed, there could be no difference in the rate of profit, and no other difference in the real or labour price of commodities, than the additional quantity of labour required to convey them to the various markets where they were to be sold.

—David Ricardo, *On the Principles of Political Economy and Taxation,* 1817, Chapter 7.

LEARNING OBJECTIVES

- Examine how price levels and price level changes (inflation) in countries determine the exchange rates at which their currencies are traded

- Show how interest rates reflect inflationary forces within each country and currency

- Explain how forward markets for currencies reflect expectations held by market participants about the future spot exchange rate

- Analyze how, in equilibrium, the spot and forward currency markets are aligned with interest differentials and differentials in expected inflation

What are the determinants of exchange rates? Are changes in exchange rates predictable? Managers of MNEs, international portfolio investors, importers and exporters, and government officials must deal with these fundamental questions every day. This chapter describes the core financial theories surrounding the determination of exchange rates. Chapter 8 will introduce two other major theoretical schools of thought regarding currency valuation and combine the three different theories in a variety of real-world applications.

The economic theories that link exchange rates, price levels, and interest rates are called international *parity conditions*. In the eyes of many, these international parity conditions form the core of the financial theory that is considered unique to the field of international finance. These theories do not always work out to be "true" when compared to what students and practitioners observe in the real world, but they are central to any understanding of how multinational business is conducted and funded in the world today. And, as is often the case, the mistake is not always in the theory itself, but in the way it is interpreted or applied in practice. This chapter concludes with a Mini-Case, *Mrs. Watanabe and the Japanese Yen Carry Trade*, that demonstrates how both the theory and practice of international parity conditions sometimes combine to form unusual opportunities for profit—for those who are willing to bear the risk!

Prices and Exchange Rates

If identical products or services can be sold in two different markets, and no restrictions exist on the sale or transportation of product between markets, the product's price should be the same in both markets. This is called the *law of one price*.

A primary principle of competitive markets is that prices will equalize across markets if frictions or costs of moving the products or services between markets do not exist. If the two markets are in two different countries, the product's price may be stated in different currency terms, but the price of the product should still be the same. Comparing prices would require only a conversion from one currency to the other. For example,

$$P^\$ \times S = P^\yen$$

where the price of the product in U.S. dollars ($P^\$$), multiplied by the spot exchange rate (S, yen per U.S. dollar), equals the price of the product in Japanese yen ($P^\yen$). Conversely, if the prices of the two products were stated in local currencies, and markets were efficient at competing away a higher price in one market relative to the other, the exchange rate could be deduced from the relative local product prices:

$$S = \frac{P^\yen}{P^\$}$$

Purchasing Power Parity and the Law of One Price

If the law of one price were true for all goods and services, the *purchasing power parity* (PPP) exchange rate could be found from any individual set of prices. By comparing the prices of identical products denominated in different currencies, one could determine the "real" or PPP exchange rate that should exist if markets were efficient. This is the absolute version of purchasing power parity. *Absolute purchasing power parity* states that the spot exchange rate is determined by the relative prices of similar baskets of goods.

The "Big Mac Index," as it has been christened by *The Economist* (see Exhibit 6.1) and calculated regularly since 1986, is a prime example of the law of one price. Assuming that the Big Mac is indeed identical in all countries listed, it serves as one form of comparison of whether currencies are currently trading at market rates that are close to the exchange rate implied by Big Macs in local currencies.

For example, using Exhibit 6.1, in China a Big Mac costs Yuan 16.0 (local currency), while in the United States the same Big Mac costs $4.56. The actual spot exchange rate was Yuan6.1341/$ at this time. The price of a Big Mac in China in U.S. dollar terms was therefore

$$\frac{\text{Price of Big Mac in China in Yuan}}{\text{Yuan/\$ Spot Rate}} = \frac{\text{Yuan16.0}}{\text{Yuan6.1341/\$}} = \$2.61$$

This is the value in column 3 of Exhibit 6.1 for China. We then calculate the implied *purchasing power parity rate of exchange* using the actual price of the Big Mac in China (Yuan16.0) over the price of the Big Mac in the United States in U.S. dollars ($4.56):

$$\frac{\text{Price of Big Mac in China in Yuan}}{\text{Price of Big Mac in the U.S. in \$}} = \frac{\text{Yuan16.0}}{\$4.56} = \text{Yuan3.509/\$}$$

This is the value in column 4 of Exhibit 6.1 for China. In principle, this is what the Big Mac Index is saying the exchange rate between the Yuan and the dollar should be according to the theory.

EXHIBIT 6.1   Selected Rates from the Big Mac Index

Country and Currency		(1) Big Mac Price in Local Currency	(2) Actual Dollar Exchange Rate July 2013	(3) Big Mac Price in Dollars	(4) Implied PPP of the Dollar	(5) Under/Overvaluation Against Dollar**
United States	$	4.56	—	4.56	—	—
Britain	£	2.69	1.4945*	4.02	1.695*	−11.8%
Canada	C$	5.53	1.0513	5.26	1.213	15.4%
China	Yuan	16.0	6.1341	2.61	3.509	−42.8%
Denmark	DK	28.5	5.8006	4.91	6.250	7.7%
Euro area	€	3.62	1.2858*	4.66	1.258*	2.2%
India	₹	90.0	59.9800	1.50	19.737	−67.1%
Japan	¥	320	100.11	3.20	70.175	−29.9%
Norway	kr	46.00	6.1281	7.51	10.088	64.6%
Peru	Sol	10.0	2.7830	3.59	2.193	−21.2%
Russia	P	87.0	32.9389	2.64	19.079	−42.1%
Switzerland	SFr	6.50	0.9674	6.72	1.425	47.3%
Thailand	Baht	89.0	31.2750	2.85	19.518	−37.6%

* These exchange rates are stated in US$ per unit of local currency, $/£ and $/€.
** Percentage under/overvaluation against the dollar is calculated as (Implied-Actual)/(Actual), except for the Britain and Euro area calculations, which are (Actual-Implied)/(Implied).

Source: Data for columns (1) and (2) drawn from "The Big Mac Index," *The Economist*, July 2013.

Now comparing this implied PPP rate of exchange, Yuan 3.509/$, with the actual market rate of exchange at that time, Yuan 6.1341/$, the degree to which the yuan is either *undervalued* (−%) or *overvalued* (+%) versus the U.S. dollar is calculated as follows:

$$\frac{\text{Implied Rate} - \text{Actual Rate}}{\text{Actual Rate}} = \frac{\text{Yuan}3.509/\$ - \text{Yuan}6.1341/\$}{\text{Yuan}6.1341/\$} \approx -42.8\%$$

In this case, the Big Mac Index indicates that the Chinese yuan is undervalued by 42.8% versus the U.S. dollar as indicated in column 5 for China in Exhibit 6.1. *The Economist* is also quick to note that although this indicates a sizable undervaluation of the *managed value* of the Chinese yuan versus the dollar, the theory of purchasing power parity is supposed to indicate where the value of currencies should go over the long-term, and not necessarily its value today.

It is important to understand why the Big Mac may be a good candidate for the application of the law of one price and measurement of under or overvaluation. First, the product itself is nearly identical in each market. This is the result of product consistency, process excellence, and McDonald's brand image and pride. Second, and just as important, the product is a result of predominantly local materials and input costs. This means that its price in each country is representative of domestic costs and prices and not imported ones, which would be influenced by exchange rates themselves. The index, however, still possesses limitations. Big Macs cannot be traded across borders, and costs and prices are influenced by a variety of other factors in each country market, such as real estate rental rates and taxes.

A less extreme form of this principle would be that in relatively efficient markets the price of a basket of goods would be the same in each market. Replacing the price of a single product with a price index allows the PPP exchange rate between two countries to be stated as

$$S = \frac{PI^{¥}}{PI^{\$}}$$

where $PI^{¥}$ and $PI^{\$}$ are price indices expressed in local currency for Japan and the United States, respectively. For example, if the identical basket of goods cost ¥1,000 in Japan and $10 in the United States, the PPP exchange rate would be

$$\frac{¥1000}{\$10} = ¥100/\$$$

Just in case you are starting to believe that PPP is just about numbers, *Global Finance in Practice 6.1* reminds you of the human side of the equation.

Relative Purchasing Power Parity

If the assumptions of the absolute version of PPP theory are relaxed a bit, we observe what is termed *relative purchasing power parity*. Relative PPP holds that PPP is not particularly helpful in determining what the spot rate is today, but that the relative change in prices between two countries over a period of time determines the change in the exchange rate over that period. More specifically, *if the spot exchange rate between two countries starts in equilibrium,*

GLOBAL FINANCE IN PRACTICE   6.1

The Immiseration of the North Korean People—The "Revaluation" of the North Korean Won

The principles of purchasing power are not just theoretical, they can also capture the problems, poverty, and misery of a people. The devaluation of the North Korean won (KPW) in November 2009 was one such case.

The North Korean government has been trying to stop the growth and activity in the street markets of its country for decades. For many years the street markets have been the sole opportunity for most of the Korean people to earn a living. Under the communist state's stewardship, the quality of life for its 24 million people has continued to deteriorate. Between 1990 and 2008, the country's infant mortality rate had increased 30%, and life expectancy had fallen by three years. The United Nations estimated that one in three children under the age of five suffered malnutrition. Although most of the working population worked officially for the government, many were underpaid (or in many cases not paid at all). They often bribed their bosses to allow them to leave work early to try to scrape out a living in the street markets of the underground economy.

But it was this very basic market economy that President Kim Jong-il (now deceased) and the governing regime wished to stamp out. On November 30, 2009, the Korean government made a surprise announcement to its people: a new, more valuable Korean won would replace the old one. "You have until the end of the day to exchange your old won for new won." All old 1,000 won notes would be replaced with 10 won notes, knocking off two zeros from the officially recognized value of the currency. This meant that everyone holding old won, their cash and savings, would now officially be worth 1/100th of what it was previously. Exchange was limited to 100,000 old won. People who had worked and saved for decades to accumulate what was roughly $200 or $300 in savings outside of North Korea were wiped out; their total life savings were essentially worthless. By officially denouncing the old currency, the North Korean people would be forced to exchange their holdings for new won. The government would indeed undermine the underground economy.

The results were devastating. After days of street protests, the government raised the 100,000 ceiling to 150,000. By late January 2010, inflation was rising so rapidly that Kim Jong-il apologized to the people for the revaluation's impact on their lives. The government administrator who had led the revaluation was arrested, and in February 2010, executed "for his treason."

any change in the differential rate of inflation between them tends to be offset over the long run by an equal but opposite change in the spot exchange rate.

Exhibit 6.2 shows a general case of relative PPP. The vertical axis shows the percentage change in the spot exchange rate for foreign currency, and the horizontal axis shows the percentage difference in expected rates of inflation (foreign relative to home country). The diagonal parity line shows the equilibrium position between a change in the exchange rate and relative inflation rates. For instance, point P represents an equilibrium point at which inflation in the foreign country, Japan, is 4% lower than in the home country, the United States. Therefore, relative PPP predicts that the yen will appreciate by 4% per annum with respect to the U.S. dollar. If current market expectations led to either point W or S in Exhibit 6.2, the home currency would be considered either *weak* (point W) or *strong* (point S), and the market would not be in equilibrium.

The logic behind the application of PPP to changes in the spot exchange rate is that if a country experiences inflation rates higher than those of its main trading partners, and its exchange rate does not change, its exports of goods and services become less competitive with comparable products produced elsewhere. Imports from abroad become more price-competitive with higher-priced domestic products. These price changes lead to a deficit on the current account in the balance of payments unless offset by capital and financial flows.

Empirical Tests of Purchasing Power Parity

There has been extensive testing of both the absolute and relative versions of purchasing power parity and the law of one price.[1] These tests have, for the most part, not proved PPP to be accurate in predicting future exchange rates. Goods and services do not in reality move at zero cost between countries, and in fact many services are not "tradable," for example,

EXHIBIT 6.2 **Relative Purchasing Power Parity**

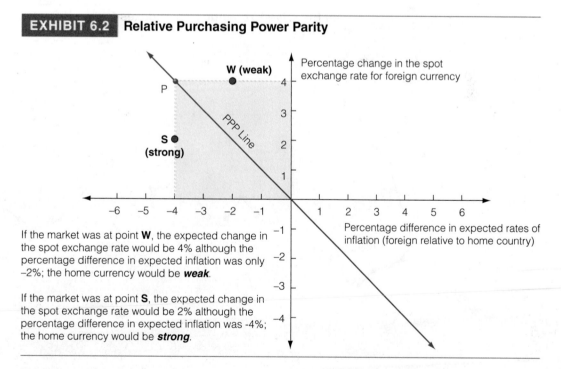

If the market was at point **W**, the expected change in the spot exchange rate would be 4% although the percentage difference in expected inflation was only −2%; the home currency would be **weak**.

If the market was at point **S**, the expected change in the spot exchange rate would be 2% although the percentage difference in expected inflation was -4%; the home currency would be **strong**.

[1]See for example, Kenneth Rogoff, "The Purchasing Power Parity Puzzle," *Journal of Economic Literature*, Vol. 34, No. 2, June 1996, 647–668; and Barry K. Goodwin, Thomas Greenes, and Michael K. Wohlgenant, "Testing the Law of One Price When Trade Takes Time," *Journal of International Money and Finance*, March 1990, pp. 21–40.

for haircuts. Many goods and services are not of the same quality across countries, reflecting differences in the tastes and resources of the countries of their manufacture and consumption.

Two general conclusions can be made from these tests: 1) PPP holds up well over the very long run but poorly for shorter time periods; and 2) The theory holds better for countries with relatively high rates of inflation and underdeveloped capital markets.

Exchange Rate Indices: Real and Nominal

Because any single country trades with numerous partners, we need to track and evaluate its individual currency value against all other currency values in order to determine relative purchasing power. The objective is to discover whether its exchange rate is "overvalued" or "undervalued" in terms of PPP. One of the primary methods of dealing with this problem is the calculation of *exchange rate indices*. These indices are formed by trade-weighting the bilateral exchange rates between the home country and its trading partners.

The *nominal effective exchange rate index* uses actual exchange rates to create an index, on a weighted average basis, of the value of the subject currency over time. It does not really indicate anything about the "true value" of the currency or anything related to PPP. The nominal index simply calculates how the currency value relates to some arbitrarily chosen base period, but it is used in the formation of the real effective exchange rate index. The *real effective exchange rate index* indicates how the weighted average purchasing power of the currency has changed relative to some arbitrarily selected base period. Exhibit 6.3 plots the real effective exchange rate indexes for Japan, the euro area, and the U.S. for the 1980–2012 period.

EXHIBIT 6.3   **Real Effective Exchange Rate Indexes for the U.S., Japan, and the Euro Area**

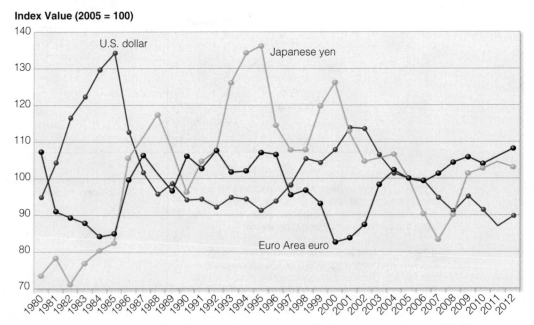

Source: International Financial Statistics, IMF, annual, CPI-weighted real effective exchange rates, series RECZF.

The real effective exchange rate index for the U.S. dollar, $E_R^\$$, is found by multiplying the nominal effective exchange rate index, $E_N^\$$, by the ratio of U.S. dollar costs, $C^\$$ over foreign currency costs, C^{FC}, both in index form:

$$E_R^\$ = E_N^\$ \times \frac{C^\$}{C^{FC}}$$

If changes in exchange rates just offset differential inflation rates—if purchasing power parity holds—all the real effective exchange rate indices would stay at 100. If an exchange rate strengthened more than was justified by differential inflation, its index would rise above 100. If the real effective exchange rate index were above 100, the currency would be considered "overvalued" from a competitive perspective. An index value below 100 would suggest an "undervalued" currency.

Exhibit 6.3 shows how the real effective exchange rate of the U.S. dollar, Japanese yen, and the European euro have changed over the past three decades. The dollar's index value was substantially above 100 in the early 1980s (overvalued), falling below 100 during the 1988–1997 period (undervalued), then rising above 100 again. According to this index, the dollar has consistently been undervalued since 2006. In this same post-2006 period, the euro has consistently been above 100, while the Japanese yen has bounced upwards from being significantly undervalued to slightly overvalued in recent years.

Apart from measuring deviations from PPP, a country's real effective exchange rate is an important tool for management when predicting upward or downward pressure on a country's balance of payments and exchange rate, as well as an indicator of whether producing for export in that country could be highly competitive.

Exchange Rate Pass-Through

Incomplete *exchange rate pass-through* is one reason that a country's real effective exchange rate index can deviate for lengthy periods from its PPP-equilibrium level of 100. The degree to which the prices of imported and exported goods change as a result of exchange rate changes is termed exchange rate pass-through. Although PPP implies that all exchange rate changes are passed through by equivalent changes in prices to trading partners, empirical research in the 1980s questioned this long-held assumption. For example, sizable current account deficits of the United States in the 1980s and 1990s did not respond to changes in the value of the dollar.

To illustrate exchange rate pass-through, assume that BMW produces an automobile in Germany and pays all production expenses in euros. When the firm exports the auto to the United States, the price of the BMW in the U.S. market should simply be the euro value converted to dollars at the spot exchange rate:

$$P_{BMW}^\$ = P_{BMW}^\euro \times S^{\$/\euro}$$

where $P_{BMW}^\$$ is the BMW price in dollars, $P_{BMW}^\euro$ is the BMW price in euros, and $S^{\$/\euro}$ is the spot exchange rate in number of dollars per euro. If the euro appreciated 10% versus the U.S. dollar, the new spot exchange rate should result in the price of the BMW in the United States rising a proportional 10%. If the price in dollars increases by the same percentage change as the exchange rate, the pass-through of exchange rate changes is complete (or 100%).

However, if the price in dollars rises by less than the percentage change in exchange rates (as is often the case in international trade), the pass-through is partial, as illustrated in Exhibit 6.4. The 71% pass-through (U.S. dollar prices rose only 14.29% when the euro

---

EXHIBIT 6.4   **Exchange Rate Pass-Through**

Exchange rate pass-through is the measure of response of imported and exported product prices to exchange rate changes. Assume that the price in U.S. dollars and Euros of a BMW automobile produced in Germany and sold in the United States at the spot exchange rate is calculated as follows:

$$P^{\$}_{BMW} = P^{€}_{BMW} \times S^{\$/€} = €35{,}000 \times \$1.00/€ = \$35{,}000$$

If the euro were to appreciate 20% versus the U.S. dollar, from $1.00/€ to $1.20/€, the price of the BMW in the U.S. market should theoretically rise to $42,000. But if the price of the BMW in the U.S. does not rise by 20%, for example rising to only $40,000, then the degree of exchange rate pass-through is only partial.

$$\frac{P^{\$}_{BMW,2}}{P^{\$}_{BMW,1}} \quad \frac{\$40{,}000}{\$35{,}000} = 1.1429, \text{ or a 14.29\% increase}$$

The *degree of exchange rate pass-through* is measured by the proportion of the exchange rate change reflected in the final price, in this case, the final U.S. dollar price of the BMW. In this example, the dollar price of the BMW rose only 14.29%, not 20% ([$42,000 ÷ $35,000] − 1), resulting in a pass-through of 71% (14.29% ÷ 20.00%). This means that only 71% of the exchange rate change was passed-through to the U.S. dollar price. The remaining 29% of the exchange rate change was absorbed in a reduced margin by BMW.

---

appreciated 20%) implies that BMW is absorbing a portion of the adverse exchange rate change. This absorption could result from smaller profit margins, cost reductions, or both.

For example, components and raw materials imported to Germany cost less in euros when the euro appreciates. It is also likely that some time may pass before all exchange rate changes are finally reflected in the prices of traded goods, including the period over which previously signed contracts are delivered upon. It is obviously in the interest of BMW to keep the appreciation of the euro from raising the price of its automobiles in major export markets.

The concept of *price elasticity of demand* is useful when determining the desired level of pass-through. Recall that the price elasticity of demand for any good is the percentage change in quantity of the good demanded as a result of the percentage change in the good's price:

$$\text{Price elasticity of demand} = e_p = \frac{\%\Delta Q_d}{\%\Delta P}$$

where Q_d is quantity demanded and P is product price. If the absolute value of e_p is less than 1.0, then the good is relatively "inelastic." If it is greater than 1.0, the good is relatively "elastic."

A German product that is relatively price-inelastic, meaning that the quantity demanded is relatively unresponsive to price changes, may often demonstrate a high degree of pass-through. This is because a higher dollar price in the United States market would have little noticeable effect on the quantity of the product demanded by consumers. Dollar revenue would increase, but euro revenue would remain the same. However, products that are relatively price-elastic would respond in the opposite way. If the 20% euro appreciation resulted in 20% higher dollar prices, U.S. consumers would decrease the number of BMWs purchased. If the price elasticity of demand for BMWs in the United States were greater than one, total dollar sales revenue of BMWs would decline.

Interest Rates and Exchange Rates

We have already seen how prices of goods in different countries should be related through exchange rates. We now consider how interest rates are linked to exchange rates.

The Fisher Effect

The *Fisher effect*, named after economist Irving Fisher, states that nominal interest rates in each country are equal to the required real rate of return plus compensation for expected inflation. More formally, this is derived from $(1 + r)(1 + \pi) - 1$ as:

$$i = r + \pi + r\pi$$

where i is the nominal rate of interest, r is the real rate of interest, and π is the expected rate of inflation over the period of time for which funds are to be lent. The final compound term, $r\pi$, is frequently dropped from consideration due to its relatively minor value. The Fisher effect then reduces to (approximate form):

$$i = r + \pi$$

The Fisher effect applied to the United States and Japan would be as follows:

$$i^\$ = r^\$ + \pi^\$; \ i^¥ = r^¥ + \pi^¥$$

where the superscripts $\$$ and $¥$ pertain to the respective nominal (i), real (r), and expected inflation (π) components of financial instruments denominated in dollars and yen, respectively. We need to forecast the future rate of inflation, not what inflation has been. Predicting the future is, well, difficult.

Empirical tests using *ex-post* national inflation rates have shown that the Fisher effect usually exists for short-maturity government securities such as Treasury bills and notes. Comparisons based on longer maturities suffer from the increased financial risk inherent in fluctuations of the market value of the bonds prior to maturity. Comparisons of private sector securities are influenced by unequal creditworthiness of the issuers. All the tests are inconclusive to the extent that recent past rates of inflation are not a correct measure of future expected inflation.

The International Fisher Effect

The relationship between the percentage change in the spot exchange rate over time and the differential between comparable interest rates in different national capital markets is known as the *international Fisher effect*. "Fisher-open," as it is often termed, states that the spot exchange rate should change in an equal amount but in the opposite direction to the difference in interest rates between two countries. More formally,

$$\frac{S_1 - S_2}{S_2} = i^\$ - i^¥$$

where $i^\$$ and $i^¥$ are the respective national interest rates, and S is the spot exchange rate using indirect quotes (an indirect quote on the dollar is, for example, $¥/\$$) at the beginning of the period (S_1) and the end of the period (S_2). This is the approximation form commonly used in industry. The precise formulation is as follows:

$$\frac{S_1 - S_2}{S_2} = \frac{i^\$ - i^¥}{1 + i^¥}$$

Justification for the international Fisher effect is that investors must be rewarded or penalized to offset the expected change in exchange rates. For example, if a dollar-based investor buys a 10-year yen bond earning 4% interest, instead of a 10-year dollar bond earning 6% interest, the investor must be expecting the yen to appreciate *vis-à-vis* the dollar by at least 2% per year during the 10 years. If not, the dollar-based investor would be better off remaining in dollars. If the yen appreciates 3% during the 10-year period, the dollar-based investor would earn a bonus of 1% higher return. However, the international Fisher effect predicts that, with unrestricted capital flows, an investor should be indifferent to whether his bond is in dollars or yen—because investors worldwide would see the same opportunity and compete it away.

Empirical tests lend some support to the relationship postulated by the international Fisher effect, although considerable short-run deviations occur. A more serious criticism has been posed, however, by recent studies that suggest the existence of a foreign exchange risk premium for most major currencies. Also, speculation in uncovered interest arbitrage creates distortions in currency markets. Thus, the expected change in exchange rates might consistently be greater than the difference in interest rates.

The Forward Rate

A *forward rate* (or *outright forward* as described in Chapter 5) is an exchange rate quoted today for settlement at some future date. A forward exchange agreement between currencies states the rate of exchange at which a foreign currency will be "bought forward" or "sold forward" at a specific date in the future (typically after 30, 60, 90, 180, 270, or 360 days).

The forward rate is calculated for any specific maturity by adjusting the current spot exchange rate by the ratio of euro currency interest rates of the same maturity for the two subject currencies. For example, the 90-day forward rate for the Swiss franc/U.S. dollar exchange rate ($F^{SF/\$}$) is found by multiplying the current spot rate ($S^{SF/\$}$) by the ratio of the 90-day euro-Swiss franc deposit rate (i^{SF}) over the 90-day eurodollar deposit rate ($i^{\$}$):

$$F_{90}^{SF/\$} = S^{SF/\$} \times \frac{\left[1 + \left(i^{SF} \times \dfrac{90}{360}\right)\right]}{\left[1 + \left(i^{\$} \times \dfrac{90}{360}\right)\right]}$$

Assuming a spot rate of SF1.4800/$, a 90-day euro Swiss franc deposit rate of 4.00% per annum, and a 90-day eurodollar deposit rate of 8.00% per annum, the 90-day forward rate is SF1.4655/$:

$$F_{90}^{SF/\$} = \text{SF1.4800/\$} \times \frac{\left[1 + \left(0.0400 \times \dfrac{90}{360}\right)\right]}{\left[1 + \left(0.0800 \times \dfrac{90}{360}\right)\right]} = \text{SF1.4800/\$} \times \frac{1.01}{1.02} = \text{SF1.4655/\$}$$

The forward premium or discount is the percentage difference between the spot and forward exchange rate, stated in annual percentage terms. When the foreign currency price of the home currency is used, as in this case of SF/$, the formula for the percent-per-annum premium or discount becomes:

$$f^{SF} = \frac{\text{Spot} - \text{Forward}}{\text{Forward}} \times \frac{360}{\text{Days}} \times 100$$

| EXHIBIT 6.5 | Currency Yield Curves and the Forward Premium |

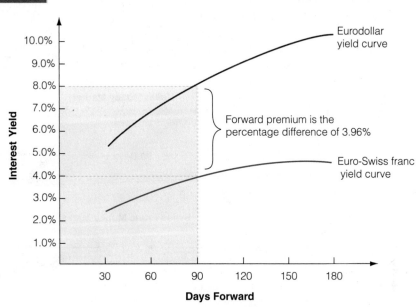

Substituting the SF/$ spot and forward rates, as well as the number of days forward (90),

$$f^{SF} = \frac{SF1.4800/\$ - SF1.4655/\$}{SF1.4655/\$} \times \frac{360}{90} \times 100 = +3.96\% \text{ per annum}$$

The sign is positive, indicating that the Swiss franc is *selling forward* at a 3.96% per annum premium over the dollar (it takes 3.96% more dollars to get a franc at the 90-day forward rate).

As illustrated in Exhibit 6.5, the forward premium on the eurodollar forward arises from the differential between eurodollar interest rates and Swiss franc interest rates. Because the forward rate for any particular maturity utilizes the specific interest rates for that term, the forward premium or discount on a currency is visually obvious—the currency with the higher interest rate (in this case the U.S. dollar) will sell forward at a discount, and the currency with the lower interest rate (here the Swiss franc) will sell forward at a premium.

The forward rate is calculated from three observable data items—the spot rate, the foreign currency deposit rate, and the home currency deposit rate—and is not a forecast of the future spot exchange. It is, however, frequently used by managers as a forecast, with mixed results, as the following section describes.

Interest Rate Parity (IRP)

The theory of *interest rate parity* (IRP) provides the link between the foreign exchange markets and the international money markets. The theory states: *The difference in the national interest rates for securities of similar risk and maturity should be equal to, but opposite in sign to, the forward rate discount or premium for the foreign currency, except for transaction costs.*

Exhibit 6.6 shows how the theory of interest rate parity works. Assume that an investor has $1,000,000 and several alternative but comparable Swiss franc (SF) monetary investments. If the investor chooses to invest in a dollar money market instrument, the investor would earn

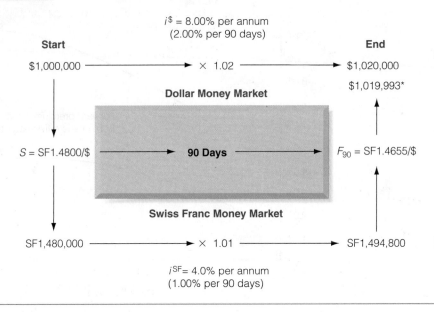

EXHIBIT 6.6   Interest Rate Parity (IRP)

$i^\$ = 8.00\%$ per annum
(2.00% per 90 days)

Start		End
\$1,000,000	⟶ × 1.02 ⟶	\$1,020,000
		\$1,019,993*

Dollar Money Market

$S = \text{SF}1.4800/\$$ ⟶ **90 Days** ⟶ $F_{90} = \text{SF}1.4655/\$$

Swiss Franc Money Market

| SF1,480,000 | ⟶ × 1.01 ⟶ | SF1,494,800 |

$i^{SF} = 4.0\%$ per annum
(1.00% per 90 days)

the dollar rate of interest. This results in $(1 + i^\$)$ at the end of the period, where $i^\$$ is the dollar rate of interest in decimal form.

The investor may, however, choose to invest in a Swiss franc money market instrument of identical risk and maturity for the same period. This action would require that the investor exchange the dollars for francs at the spot rate, invest the francs in a money market instrument, sell the francs forward (in order to avoid any risk that the exchange rate would change), and at the end of the period convert the resulting proceeds back to dollars.

A dollar-based investor would evaluate the relative returns of starting in the top-left corner and investing in the dollar market (straight across the top of the box) compared to investing in the Swiss franc market (going down and then around the box to the top-right corner). The comparison of returns would be as follows:

$$(1 + i^\$) = S^{SF/\$} \times (1 + i^{SF}) \times \frac{1}{F^{SF/\$}}$$

where S = spot rate of exchange and F = the forward rate of exchange. Substituting in the spot rate (SF1.4800/\$) and forward rate (SF1.4655/\$) and respective interest rates from Exhibit 6.6, the interest rate parity condition is as follows:

$$(1 + 0.02) = 1.4800 \times (1 + 0.01) \times \frac{1}{1.4655}$$

The left-hand side of the equation is the gross return the investor would earn by investing in dollars. The right-hand side is the gross return the investor would earn by exchanging dollars for Swiss francs at the spot rate, investing the franc proceeds in the Swiss franc money market, and simultaneously selling the principal plus interest in Swiss francs forward for dollars at the current 90-day forward rate.

Ignoring transaction costs, if the returns in dollars are equal between the two alternative money market investments, the spot and forward rates are considered to be at IRP.

The transaction is "covered," because the exchange rate back to dollars is guaranteed at the end of the 90-day period. Therefore, as shown in Exhibit 6.6, in order for the two alternatives to be equal, any differences in interest rates must be offset by the difference between the spot and forward exchange rates (in approximate form):

$$\frac{F}{S} = \frac{(1 + i^{SF})}{(1 + i^{\$})}, \text{ or } \frac{SF1.4655/\$}{SF1.4800/\$} = \frac{1.01}{1.02} = 0.9902 \approx 1\%$$

Covered Interest Arbitrage (CIA)

The spot and forward exchange markets are not constantly in the state of equilibrium described by interest rate parity. When the market is not in equilibrium, the potential for "riskless" or arbitrage profit exists. The arbitrager who recognizes such an imbalance will move to take advantage of the disequilibrium by investing in whichever currency offers the higher return on a covered basis. This is called *covered interest arbitrage* (CIA).

Exhibit 6.7 describes the steps that a currency trader, most likely working in the arbitrage division of a large international bank, would implement to perform a CIA transaction. The currency trader, Fye Hong, may utilize any of a number of major Eurocurrencies that his bank holds to conduct arbitrage investments. The morning conditions indicate to Fye Hong that a CIA transaction that exchanges 1 million U.S. dollars for Japanese yen, invested in a six month euroyen account and sold forward back to dollars, will yield a profit of $4,638 ($1,044,638−$1,040,000) over and above the profit available from a eurodollar investment. Conditions in the exchange markets and euromarkets change rapidly however, so if Fye Hong waits even a few minutes, the profit opportunity may disappear.

Fye Hong now executes the following transaction:

Step 1: Convert $1,000,000 at the spot rate of ¥106.00/$ to ¥106,000,000 (see "Start" in Exhibit 6.7).

Step 2: Invest the proceeds, ¥106,000,000, in a euroyen account for six months, earning 4.00% per annum, or 2% for 180 days.

EXHIBIT 6.7   Covered Interest Arbitrage (CIA)

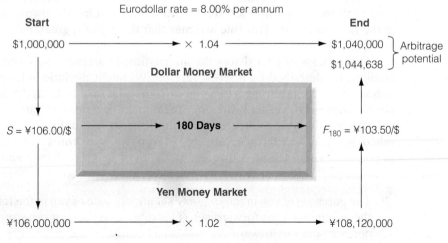

Step 3: Simultaneously sell the future yen proceeds (¥108,120,000) forward for dollars at the 180-day forward rate of ¥103.50/$. This action "locks in" gross dollar revenues of $1,044,638 (see "End" in Exhibit 6.7).

Step 4: Calculate the cost (opportunity cost) of funds used at the eurodollar rate of 8.00% per annum, or 4% for 180 days, with principal and interest then totaling $1,040,000. Profit on CIA ("End") is $4,638 ($1,044,638−$1,040,000).

Note that all profits are stated in terms of the currency in which the transaction was initialized, but that a trader may conduct investments denominated in U.S. dollars, Japanese yen, or any other major currency.

Rule of Thumb. All that is required to make a covered interest arbitrage profit is for interest rate parity not to hold. Depending on the relative interest rates and forward premium, Fye Hong would have started in Japanese yen, invested in U.S. dollars, and sold the dollars forward for yen. The profit would then end up denominated in yen. But how would Fye Hong decide in which direction to go around the box in Exhibit 6.7?

The key to determining whether to start in dollars or yen is to compare the differences in interest rates to the forward premium on the yen (the cost of cover). For example, in Exhibit 6.7, the difference in 180-day interest rates is 2.00% (dollar interest rates are higher by 2.00%). The premium on the yen for 180 days forward is as follows:

$$f^{¥} = \frac{\text{Spot} - \text{Forward}}{\text{Forward}} \times \frac{360}{180} \times 100 = \frac{¥106.00/\$ - ¥103.50/\$}{¥103.50/\$} \times 200 = 4.8309\%$$

In other words, by investing in yen and selling the yen proceeds forward at the forward rate, Fye Hong earns more on the combined interest rate arbitrage and forward premium than if he continues to invest in dollars.

> **Arbitrage Rule of Thumb:** *If the difference in interest rates is greater than the forward premium (or expected change in the spot rate), invest in the higher interest yielding currency. If the difference in interest rates is less than the forward premium (or expected change in the spot rate), invest in the lower interest yielding currency.*

Using this rule of thumb should enable Fye Hong to choose in which direction to go around the box in Exhibit 6.7. It also guarantees that he will always make a profit if he goes in the right direction. This rule assumes that the profit is greater than any transaction costs incurred.

This process of CIA drives the international currency and money markets toward the equilibrium described by interest rate parity. Slight deviations from equilibrium provide opportunities for arbitragers to make small riskless profits. Such deviations provide the supply and demand forces that will move the market back toward parity (equilibrium).

Covered interest arbitrage opportunities continue until interest rate parity is reestablished, because the arbitragers are able to earn risk-free profits by repeating the cycle as often as possible. Their actions, however, nudge the foreign exchange and money markets back toward equilibrium for the following reasons:

1. The purchase of yen in the spot market and the sale of yen in the forward market narrows the premium on the forward yen. This is because the spot yen strengthens from the extra demand and the forward yen weakens because of the extra sales. A narrower premium on the forward yen reduces the foreign exchange gain previously captured by investing in yen.

2. The demand for yen-denominated securities causes yen interest rates to fall, and the higher level of borrowing in the United States causes dollar interest rates to rise. The net result is a wider interest differential in favor of investing in the dollar.

Uncovered Interest Arbitrage (UIA)

A deviation from covered interest arbitrage is *uncovered interest arbitrage* (UIA), wherein investors borrow in countries and currencies exhibiting relatively low interest rates and convert the proceeds into currencies that offer much higher interest rates. The transaction is "uncovered," because the investor does not sell the higher yielding currency proceeds forward, choosing to remain uncovered and accept the currency risk of exchanging the higher yield currency into the lower yielding currency at the end of the period. Exhibit 6.8 demonstrates the steps an uncovered interest arbitrager takes when undertaking what is termed the "yen carry-trade."

The "yen carry-trade" is an age-old application of UIA. Investors, from both inside and outside Japan, take advantage of extremely low interest rates in Japanese yen (0.40% per annum) to raise capital. Investors exchange the capital they raise for other currencies like U.S. dollars or euros. Then they reinvest these dollar or euro proceeds in dollar or euro money markets where the funds earn substantially higher rates of return (5.00% per annum in Exhibit 6.8). At the end of the period—a year, in this case—they convert the dollar proceeds back into Japanese yen in the spot market. The result is a tidy profit over what it costs to repay the initial loan.

The trick, however, is that the spot exchange rate at the end of the year must not change significantly from what it was at the beginning of the year. If the yen were to appreciate significantly against the dollar, as it did in late 1999, moving from ¥120/$ to ¥105/$, these "uncovered" investors would suffer sizable losses when they convert their dollars into yen to repay the yen they borrowed. Higher return at higher risk.

The Mini-Case at the end of this chapter details one of the most frequent carry trade structures, the Australian dollar/Japanese yen cross rate. *Global Finance in Practice 6.2* also demonstrates how foreign-currency home mortgages can turn an innocent homeowner into a foreign currency speculator.

EXHIBIT 6.8   **Uncovered Interest Arbitrage (UIA): The Yen Carry Trade**

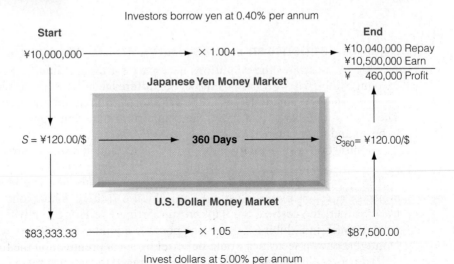

GLOBAL FINANCE IN PRACTICE   6.2

Hungarian Mortgages

No one has learned the linkage between interest rates and currencies better than Hungarian homeowners. Given the choice of taking mortgages in local currency (Hungarian forint) or foreign currency (Swiss francs for example), many chose francs because the interest rates were lower.

But regardless of the actual interest rate itself, the fall in the value of the forint against the franc by more than 40% has resulted in radically increasing mortgage debt service payments. These borrowers are now trying to have their own mortgages declared "unconstitutional" in order to get out from under their rising debt burdens.

Hungarian forint = 1.00 Swiss franc (monthly, January 2000–January 2014)

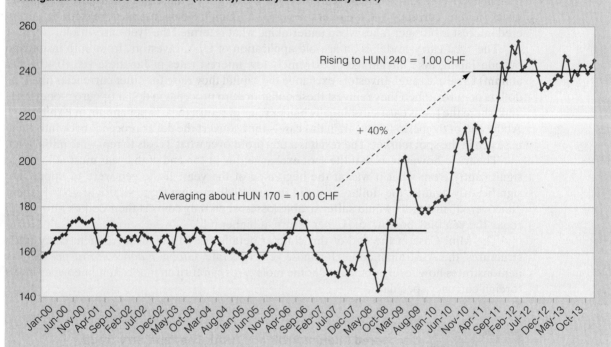

Equilibrium between Interest Rates and Exchange Rates

Exhibit 6.9 illustrates the conditions necessary for equilibrium between interest rates and exchange rates. The vertical axis shows the difference in interest rates in favor of the foreign currency, and the horizontal axis shows the forward premium or discount on that currency. The interest rate parity line shows the equilibrium state, but transaction costs cause the line to be a band rather than a thin line.

Transaction costs arise from foreign exchange and investment brokerage costs on buying and selling securities. Typical transaction costs in recent years have been in the range of 0.18% to 0.25% on an annual basis. For individual transactions, like Fye Hong's covered interest arbitrage (CIA) activities illustrated in Exhibit 6.7, there is no explicit transaction cost per trade; rather, the costs of the bank in supporting Fye Hong's activities are the transaction costs. Point X in Exhibit 6.9 shows one possible equilibrium position, where a 4% lower rate of interest on yen securities would be offset by a 4% premium on the forward yen.

The disequilibrium situation, which encouraged the interest rate arbitrage in the previous CIA example of Exhibit 6.7, is illustrated in Exhibit 6.9 by point U. Point U is located off the

EXHIBIT 6.9 **Interest Rate Parity and Equilibrium**

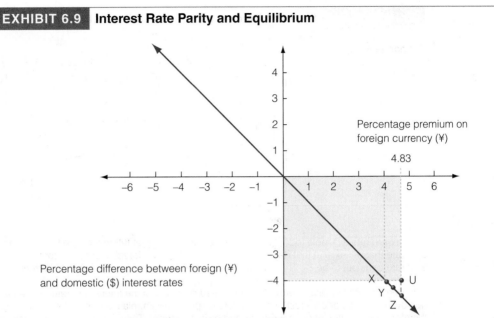

interest rate parity line because the lower interest on the yen is 4% (annual basis), whereas the premium on the forward yen is slightly over 4.8% (annual basis). Using the formula for forward premium presented earlier, we can find the premium on the yen as follows:

$$\frac{¥106.00/\$ - 103.50/\$}{¥103.50/\$} \times \frac{360 \text{ Days}}{180 \text{ Days}} \times 100 = 4.83\%$$

The situation depicted by point U is unstable, because all investors have an incentive to execute the same covered interest arbitrage. Except for a bank failure, the arbitrage gain is virtually risk-free.

Some observers have suggested that political risk does exist, because one of the governments might apply capital controls that would prevent execution of the forward contract. This risk is fairly remote for covered interest arbitrage between major financial centers of the world, especially because a large portion of funds used for covered interest arbitrage is in eurodollars. The concern may be valid for pairings with countries not noted for political and fiscal stability.

The net result of the disequilibrium is that fund flows will narrow the gap in interest rates and/or decrease the premium on the forward yen. In other words, market pressures will cause point U in Exhibit 6.9 to move toward the interest rate parity band. Equilibrium might be reached at point Y, or at any other locus between X and Z, depending on whether forward market premiums are more or less easily shifted than interest rate differentials.

Forward Rate as an Unbiased Predictor of the Future Spot Rate

Some forecasters believe that foreign exchange markets for the major floating currencies are "efficient" and forward exchange rates are unbiased predictors of future spot exchange rates.

Exhibit 6.10 demonstrates the meaning of "unbiased prediction" in terms of how the forward rate performs in estimating future spot exchange rates. If the forward rate is an unbiased

| EXHIBIT 6.10 | Forward Rate as an Unbiased Predictor for Future Spot Rate |

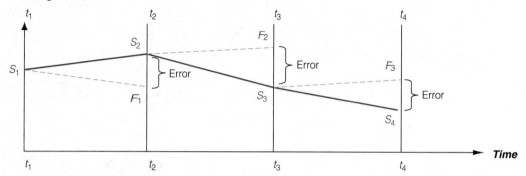

The forward rate available today (F_t, $t+1$), time t, for delivery at future time $t+1$, is used as a "predictor" of the spot rate that will exist at that day in the future. Therefore, the forecast spot rate for time S_{t2} is F_1 ; the actual spot rate turns out to be S_2. The vertical distance between the prediction and the actual spot rate is the forecast error.

When the forward rate is termed an "unbiased predictor of the future spot rate," it means that the forward rate overestimates or underestimates the future spot rate with relatively equal frequency and amount. It therefore "misses the mark" in a regular and orderly manner. The sum of the errors equals zero.

predictor of the future spot rate, the expected value of the future spot rate at time 2 equals the present forward rate for time 2 delivery, available now, $E_1 (S_2) = F_{1,2}$.

Intuitively, this means that the distribution of possible actual spot rates in the future is centered on the forward rate. The fact that it is an unbiased predictor, however, does not mean that the future spot rate will actually be equal to what the forward rate predicts. Unbiased prediction simply means that the forward rate will, on average, overestimate and underestimate the actual future spot rate in equal frequency and degree. The forward rate may, in fact, never actually equal the future spot rate.

The rationale for this relationship is based on the hypothesis that the foreign exchange market is reasonably efficient. Market efficiency assumes that 1) All relevant information is quickly reflected in both the spot and forward exchange markets; 2) Transaction costs are low; and 3) Instruments denominated in different currencies are perfect substitutes for one another.

Empirical studies of the efficient foreign exchange market hypothesis have yielded conflicting results. Nevertheless, a consensus is developing that rejects the efficient market hypothesis. It appears that the forward rate is not an unbiased predictor of the future spot rate and that it does pay to use resources to attempt to forecast exchange rates.

If the efficient market hypothesis is correct, a financial executive cannot expect to profit in any consistent manner from forecasting future exchange rates, because current quotations in the forward market reflect all that is presently known about likely future rates. Although future exchange rates may well differ from the expectation implicit in the present forward market quotation, we cannot know today which way actual future quotations will differ from today's forward rate. The expected mean value of deviations is zero. The forward rate is therefore an "unbiased" estimator of the future spot rate.

Tests of foreign exchange market efficiency, using longer time periods of analysis, conclude that either exchange market efficiency is untestable or, if it is testable, that the market is not efficient. Furthermore, the existence and success of foreign exchange forecasting services suggest that managers are willing to pay a price for forecast information even though they can use the forward rate as a forecast at no cost. The "cost" of buying this information is, in many circumstances, an "insurance premium" for financial managers who might get fired for using their own forecast, including forward rates, when that forecast proves incorrect. If they "bought" professional advice that turned out wrong, the fault was not in their forecast!

If the exchange market is not efficient, it is sensible for a firm to spend resources on forecasting exchange rates. This is the opposite conclusion to the one in which exchange markets are deemed efficient.

Prices, Interest Rates, and Exchange Rates in Equilibrium

Exhibit 6.11 illustrates all of the fundamental parity relations simultaneously, in equilibrium, using the U.S. dollar and the Japanese yen. The forecasted inflation rates for Japan and the United States are 1% and 5%, respectively—a 4% differential. The nominal interest rate in the U.S. dollar market (1-year government security) is 8%—a differential of 4% over the Japanese nominal interest rate of 4%. The spot rate is ¥104/\$, and the 1-year forward rate is ¥100/\$.

Relation A: Purchasing Power Parity (PPP). According to the relative version of purchasing power parity, the spot exchange rate one year from now, S_2, is expected to be ¥100/\$:

$$S_2 = S_1 \times \frac{1 + \pi^{¥}}{1 + \pi^{\$}} = ¥104/\$ \times \frac{1.01}{1.05} = ¥100/\$$$

This is a 4% change and equal, but opposite in sign, to the difference in expected rates of inflation (1% − 5%, or −4%).

Relation B: The Fisher Effect. The real rate of return is the nominal rate of interest less the expected rate of inflation. Assuming efficient and open markets, the real rates of return should be equal across currencies. Here, the real rate is 3% in U.S. dollar markets ($r = i - \pi = 8\% - 5\%$) and in Japanese yen markets (4% − 1%). Note that the 3% real rate of return is not in Exhibit 6.11, but rather the Fisher effect's relationship—that nominal interest rate differentials equal the difference in expected rates of inflation, −4%.

Relation C: International Fisher Effect. The forecast change in the spot exchange rate, in this case 4%, is equal to, but opposite in sign to, the differential between nominal interest rates:

$$\frac{S_1 - S_2}{S_2} \times 100 = i^{¥} - i^{\$} = -4\%$$

Relation D: Interest Rate Parity (IRP). According to the theory of interest rate parity, the difference in nominal interest rates is equal to, but opposite in sign to, the forward premium. For this numerical example, the nominal yen interest rate (4%) is 4% less than the nominal dollar interest rate (8%):

$$i^{¥} - i^{\$} = 1\% - 5\% = -4\%$$

and the forward premium, $f^{¥}$, is a positive 4%:

$$f^{¥} = \frac{S_1 - F}{F} \times 100 = \frac{¥104/\$ - ¥100/\$}{¥100/\$} \times 100 = 4\%$$

Relation E: Forward Rate as an Unbiased Predictor. Finally, the 1-year forward rate on the Japanese yen, F, if assumed to be an unbiased predictor of the future spot rate, also forecasts ¥100/\$.

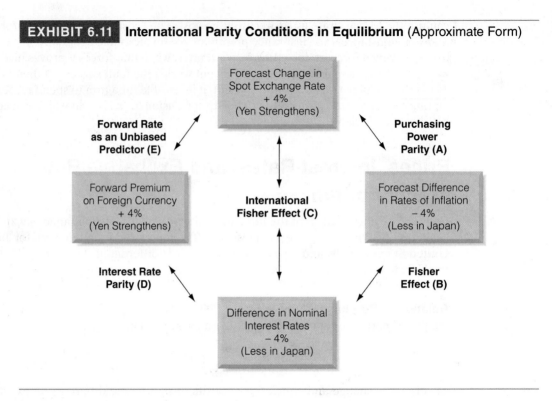

EXHIBIT 6.11   International Parity Conditions in Equilibrium (Approximate Form)

Summary Points

■ Parity conditions have traditionally been used by economists to help explain the long-run trend in an exchange rate.

■ Under conditions of freely floating rates, the expected rate of change in the spot exchange rate, differential rates of national inflation and interest, and the forward discount or premium are all directly proportional to each other and mutually determined. A change in one of these variables has a tendency to change all of them with a feedback on the variable that changes first.

■ If the identical product or service can be sold in two different markets, and there are no restrictions on its sale or transportation costs of moving the product between markets, the product's price should be the same in both markets. This is called the law of one price.

■ The absolute version of purchasing power parity states that the spot exchange rate is determined by the relative prices of similar baskets of goods.

■ The relative version of purchasing power parity states that if the spot exchange rate between two countries starts in equilibrium, any change in the differential rate of inflation between them tends to be offset over the long run by an equal but opposite change in the spot exchange rate.

■ The Fisher effect, named after economist Irving Fisher, states that nominal interest rates in each country are equal to the required real rate of return plus compensation for expected inflation.

■ The international Fisher effect, "Fisher-open" as it is often termed, states that the spot exchange rate should change in an equal amount, but in the opposite direction, to the difference in interest rates between two countries.

■ The theory of interest rate parity (IRP) states that the difference in the national interest rates for securities of similar risk and maturity should be equal to, but opposite in sign to, the forward rate discount or premium for the foreign currency, except for transaction costs.

■ When the spot and forward exchange markets are not in equilibrium as described by interest rate parity, the potential for "riskless" or arbitrage profit exists. This is called covered interest arbitrage (CIA).

■ Some forecasters believe that for the major floating currencies, foreign exchange markets are "efficient" and forward exchange rates are unbiased predictors of future spot exchange rates.

MINI-CASE

Mrs. Watanabe and the Japanese Yen Carry Trade[1]

At more than ¥1,500,000bn (some $16,800bn), these savings are considered the world's biggest pool of investable wealth. Most of it is stashed in ordinary Japanese bank accounts; a surprisingly large amount is kept at home in cash, in tansu savings, named for the traditional wooden cupboards in which people store their possessions. But from the early 2000s, the housewives—often referred to collectively as "Mrs. Watanabe", a common Japanese surname—began to hunt for higher returns.

—"Shopping, Cooking, Cleaning… Playing The Yen Carry Trade," *Financial Times*, February 21, 2009.

Over the past 20 years, Japanese yen interest rates have remained extremely low by global standards. For years the monetary authorities at the Bank of Japan have worked tirelessly fighting equity market collapses, deflationary pressures, liquidity traps, and economic recession, all by keeping yen-denominated interests rates hovering at around 1% per annum or lower. Combined with a sophisticated financial industry of size and need, these low interest rates have spawned an international financial speculation termed *the yen carry trade*.

In the textbooks, this trading strategy is categorized more formally, as uncovered interest arbitrage (UIA). It is a fairly simple speculative position: borrow money where it is cheap and invest it in a different currency market with higher interest returns. The only real trick is to time the market correctly so that when the currency in the high-yield market is converted back to the original currency, the exchange rate has either stayed the same or moved in favor of the speculator. "In favor of" means that the high-yielding currency has strengthened against the borrowed currency. And as Shakespeare stated, "ay, there's the rub."

Yen Availability

But why the focus on Japan? Aren't there other major currency markets in which interest rates are periodically low? Japan and the Japanese yen turn out to have a number of uniquely attractive characteristics to investors and speculators pursuing carry trade activities.

First, Japan has consistently demonstrated one of the world's highest savings rates for decades. This means that an enormous pool of funds has accumulated in the hands of private savers, savers who are traditionally very conservative. Those funds, whether stuffed in the mattress or placed in savings accounts, earn little in return. (In fact, given the extremely low interest rates offered, there is little effective difference between the mattress and the bank.)

A second factor facilitating the yen carry trade is the sheer size and sophistication of the Japanese financial sector. Not only is the Japanese economy one of the largest industrial economies in the world, it is one that has grown and developed with a strong international component. One only has to consider the size and global reach of Toyota or Sony to understand the established and developed infrastructure surrounding business and international finance in Japan. The Japanese banking sector, however, has been continuously in search of new and diverse investments with which to balance the often despondent domestic economy. It has therefore sought out foreign investors and foreign borrowers who are attractive customers. Multinational companies have found ready access to yen-denominated debt for years—debt which is, once again, available at extremely low interest.

A third expeditor of the yen carry trade is the value of the Japanese yen itself. The yen has long been considered the most international of Asian currencies, and is widely traded. It has, however, also been exceedingly volatile over time. But it is not volatility alone, as volatility itself could undermine interest arbitrage overnight. The key has been in the relatively long trends in value change of the yen against other major currencies like the U.S. dollar, or as in the following example, the Australian dollar.

The Australian Dollar/Japanese Yen Exchange Rate

Exhibit A illustrates the movement of the Japanese yen/Australian dollar exchange rate over a 13-year period, from 2000 through 2013. This spot rate movement and long-running periodic trends have offered a number of extended periods in which interest arbitrage was highly profitable.

The two periods of Aussie dollar appreciation are clear. During those periods, an investor who was short yen and long Aussie dollars (and enjoying relatively higher Aussie dollar interest) could and did enjoy substantial returns. At least it is obvious after-the-fact!

But what about shorter holding periods, say a year, in which the speculator does not have a crystal ball over the long-term trend of the spot rate—but only a guess? Consider the one-year speculation detailed in Exhibit B. An investor looking at the exchange rate in January 2009 (Exhibit A) would see a yen that had reached a recent historical "low"—a strong position against the Aussie dollar. Betting that the yen would likely bounce, weakening once again against the Aussie dollar, she could borrow

[1]Copyright 2014 © Thunderbird School of Global Management. All rights reserved. This case was prepared by Professor Michael Moffett for the purpose of classroom discussion only, and not to indicate either effective or ineffective management.

EXHIBIT A   The Trending JPY and AUD Spot Rate

Japanese yen = 1.00 Australian dollar (monthly)

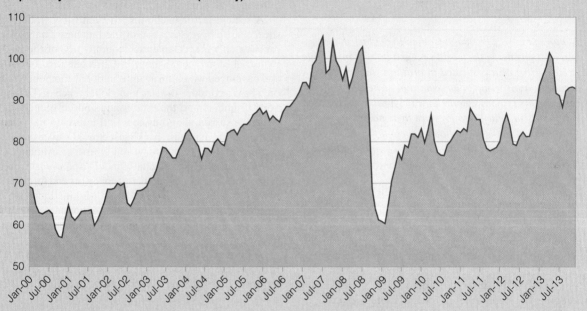

¥50 million at 1.00% interest per annum for one year. She could then exchange the ¥50 million yen for Australian dollars at ¥60.91/A$, and then deposit the A$820,883 proceeds for one year at the Australian interest rate of 4.50% per annum. The investor could even have rationalized that

even if the exchange rate did not change, she would earn a 3.50% per annum interest differential.

As it turned out, the spot exchange rate one year later, in January 2010, saw a much weaker Japanese yen against the Aussie dollar, ¥83.19/A$. The one-year Aussie-Yen carry

EXHIBIT B   The Aussie-Yen Carry Trade

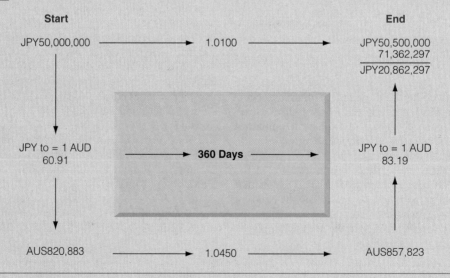

trade position would then have earned a very healthy profit of ¥20,862,296.83 on a one-year investment of ¥50,000,000, a 41.7% rate of return.

Post 2009 Financial Crisis

The global financial crisis of 2008–2009 has left a marketplace in which the U.S. Federal Reserve and the European Central Bank have pursued easy money policies. Both central banks, in an effort to maintain high levels of liquidity and to support fragile commercial banking systems, have kept interest rates at near-zero levels. Now global investors who see opportunities for profit in an anemic global economy are using those same low-cost funds in the U.S. and Europe to fund uncovered interest arbitrage activities. But what is making this "emerging market carry trade" so unique is not the interest rates, but the fact that investors are shorting two of the world's core currencies: the dollar and the euro.

Consider the strategy outlined in Exhibit B. An investor borrows EUR 20 million at an incredibly low rate, say 1.00% per annum or 0.50% for 180 days. The EUR 20 million are then exchanged for Indian rupees (INR), the current spot rate being INR 60.4672 = EUR 1.00. The resulting INR 1,209,344,000 are put into an interest-bearing deposit with any of a number of Indian banks attempting to attract capital. The rate of interest offered, 2.50%, is not particularly high, but is greater than that available in the dollar, euro, or even yen markets. But the critical component of the strategy is not to earn the higher rupee interest (although that does help), it is the expectations of the investor regarding the direction of the INR per EUR exchange rate.

CASE QUESTIONS

1. Why are interest rates so low in the traditional core markets of USD and EUR?

2. What makes this "emerging market carry trade" so different from traditional forms of uncovered interest arbitrage?

3. Why are many investors shorting the dollar and the euro?

Questions

1. **Purchasing Power Parity.** Define the following terms:
   a. The law of one price
   b. Absolute purchasing power parity
   c. Relative purchasing power parity

2. **Nominal Effective Exchange Rate Index.** Explain how a nominal effective exchange rate index is constructed.

3. **Real Effective Exchange Rate Index.** What formula is used to convert a nominal effective exchange rate index into a real effective exchange rate index?

4. **Real Effective Exchange Rates: Japan and the United States.** Exhibit 6.3 compares the real effective exchange rates for the United States and Japan. If the comparative real effective exchange rate was the main determinant, does the United States or Japan have a competitive advantage in exporting? Which of the two has an advantage in importing? Explain why.

5. **Exchange Rate Pass-Through.** Incomplete exchange rate pass-through is one reason that a country's real effective exchange rate can deviate for lengthy periods from its purchasing power equilibrium level of 100. What is meant by the term exchange rate pass-through?

6. **The Fisher Effect.** Define the Fisher effect. What would it say about real interest rates if markets are open and efficient?

7. **The International Fisher Effect.** Define the international Fisher effect. Would it discourage local investors from capitalizing on higher foreign interest rates?

8. **Interest Rate Parity.** Define interest rate parity. What would it say about interest rates if spot rates and forward rates were the same?

9. **Covered Interest Arbitrage.** Ignoring transaction costs, under what conditions will covered interest arbitrage be plausible?

10. **Forward Rate as an Unbiased Predictor of the Future Spot Rate.** Some forecasters believe that foreign exchange markets for the major floating currencies are "efficient" and forward exchange rates are unbiased predictors of future spot exchange rates. What is meant by "unbiased predictor" in terms of how the forward rate performs in estimating future spot exchange rates?

Problems

1. **Pulau Penang Island Resort.** Theresa Nunn is planning a 30-day vacation on Pulau Penang, Malaysia, one year from now. The present charge for a luxury suite plus meals in Malaysian ringgit (RM) is RM1,000/day. The Malaysian ringgit presently trades at RM5.2522/GBP. She determines that the pound cost today for a 30-day stay would be about GBP6,000. The hotel informs her that any increase in its room charges will be limited to an increase in the Malaysian cost of living. Malaysian inflation is expected to be 3% per annum, while U.K. inflation is expected to be 1%.
   a. How many pounds might Theresa expect to need one year hence to pay for her 30-day vacation?
   b. By what percent will the pound cost have gone up? Why?

2. **Crisis at the Heart of Carnaval.** The Argentine peso was fixed through a currency board at Ps1.00/$ throughout the 1990s. In January 2002, the Argentine peso was floated. On January 29, 2003, it was trading at Ps3.20/$. During that one-year period, Argentina's inflation rate was 20% on an annualized basis. Inflation in the United States during that same period was 2.2% annualized.
   a. What should have been the exchange rate in January 2003 if PPP held?
   b. By what percentage was the Argentine peso undervalued on an annualized basis?
   c. What were the probable causes of undervaluation?

3. **Japanese/Australia Parity Conditions.** William Leon is attempting to determine whether Japanese and Australian financial conditions are at parity. The current spot rate is a flat ¥108.33/A$, while the one-year forward rate is ¥106.50/A$. Forecast inflation is 5.00% for Japan and 6.80% for the Australia. The one-year Japanese yen deposit rate is 7.85%, and the one-year Australian dollar deposit rate is 9.70%.
   a. Draw a diagram and calculate whether international parity conditions hold between Japan and Australia.
   b. Find the forecasted change in the Japanese yen/Australian dollar (¥/A$) exchange rate one year from now.

4. **Traveling Down Under.** Terry Lamoreaux owns homes in Sydney, Australia, and Phoenix, Arizona. He travels between the two cities at least twice a year. Because of his frequent trips, he wants to buy some new high-quality luggage. He has done his research and has decided to purchase a Briggs and Riley three-piece luggage set. There are retail stores in Phoenix and Sydney. Terry was a finance major and wants to use purchasing power parity to determine if he is paying the same price regardless of where he makes his purchase.
   a. If the price of the three-piece luggage set in Phoenix is $850 and the price of the same three-piece set in Sydney is A$930, using purchasing power parity, is the price of the luggage truly equal if the spot rate is A$1.0941/$?
   b. If the price of the luggage remains the same in Phoenix one year from now, determine the price of the luggage in Sydney in one year's time if PPP holds true. The U.S. inflation rate is 1.15% and the Australian inflation rate is 3.13%.

5. **Starbucks in Croatia.** Starbucks opened its first store in Zagreb, Croatia in October 2010. In Zagreb, the price of a tall vanilla latte is 25.70kn. In New York City, the price of a tall vanilla latte is $2.65. The exchange rate between Croatian kunas (kn) and U.S. dollars is kn5.6288/$. According to purchasing power parity, is the Croatian kuna overvalued or undervalued?

6. **Corolla Exports and Pass-Through.** Assume that the export price of a Toyota Corolla from Osaka, Japan is ¥2,150,000. The exchange rate is ¥87.60/$. The forecast rate of inflation in the United States is 2.2% per year and in Japan it is 0.0% per year. Use this data to answer the following questions on exchange rate pass-through.
   a. What was the export price for the Corolla at the beginning of the year expressed in U.S. dollars?
   b. Assuming purchasing power parity holds, what should be the exchange rate at the end of the year?
   c. Assuming 100% exchange rate pass-through, what will be the dollar price of a Corolla at the end of the year?
   d. Assuming 75% exchange rate pass-through, what will be the dollar price of a Corolla at the end of the year?

7. **Takeshi Kamada—CIA Japan (A).** Takeshi Kamada, a foreign exchange trader at Credit Suisse (Tokyo), is exploring covered interest arbitrage possibilities. He wants to invest $5,000,000 or its yen equivalent, in a covered interest arbitrage between U.S. dollars and Japanese yen. He faced the following exchange rate and interest rate quotes. Is CIA profit possible? If so, how?

Arbitrage funds available	$5,000,000
Spot rate (¥/$)	118.60
180-day forward rate (¥/$)	117.80
180-day U.S. dollar interest rate	4.800%
180-day Japanese yen interest rate	3.400%

8. **Takeshi Kamada—UIA Japan (B).** Takeshi Kamada, Credit Suisse (Tokyo), observes that the ¥/$ spot rate has been holding steady, and that both dollar and yen interest rates have remained relatively fixed over the past week. Takeshi wonders if he should try an uncovered interest arbitrage (UIA) and thereby save the cost of forward cover. Many of Takeshi's research associates—and their computer models—are predicting the spot rate to remain close to ¥118.00/$ for the coming 180 days. Using the same data as in Problem 7, analyze the UIA potential.

9. **Copenhagen Covered (A).** Heidi Høi Jensen, a foreign exchange trader at JPMorgan Chase, can invest $5 million, or the foreign currency equivalent of the bank's short-term funds, in a covered interest arbitrage with Denmark. Using the following quotes, can Heidi make a covered interest arbitrage (CIA) profit?

Arbitrage funds available	$5,000,000
Spot exchange rate (kr/$)	6.1720
3-month forward rate (kr/$)	6.1980
U.S. dollar 3-month interest rate	3.000%
Danish kroner 3-month interest rate	5.000%

10. **Copenhagen Covered (B).** Heidi Høi Jensen is now evaluating the arbitrage profit potential in the same market after interest rates change. (Note that any time the difference in interest rates does not exactly equal the forward premium, it must be possible to make a CIA profit one way or another.)

Arbitrage funds available	$5,000,000
Spot exchange rate (kr/$)	6.1720
3-month forward rate (kr/$)	6.1980
U.S. dollar 3-month interest rate	4.000%
Danish kroner 3-month interest rate	5.000%

11. **Copenhagen Covered (C).** Heidi Høi Jensen is again evaluating the arbitrage profit potential in the same market after another change in interest rates. (Remember that any time the difference in interest rates does not exactly equal the forward premium, it must be possible to make a CIA profit one way or another.)

Arbitrage funds available	$5,000,000
Spot exchange rate (kr/$)	6.1720
3-month forward rate (kr/$)	6.1980
U.S. dollar 3-month interest rate	3.000%
Danish kroner 3-month interest rate	6.000%

12. **Casper Landsten—CIA (A).** Casper Landsten is a foreign exchange trader for a bank in New York. He has $1 million (or its Swiss franc equivalent) for a short-term money market investment. Given the following quotes, should he invest in U.S. dollars for 90 days or make a covered interest arbitrage (CIA) investment in the Swiss franc?

Funds available	$1,000,000
Spot exchange rate (SFr/$)	0.9502
90-day forward rate (SFr/$)	0.9410
U.S. dollar 90-day interest rate	3.80%
Swiss franc 90-day interest rate	5.30%

13. **Casper Landsten—UIA (B).** Using the same values and assumptions as in Problem 12, Casper Landsten decides to seek the full 3.80% return available in U.S. dollars by not covering his forward dollar receipts—an uncovered interest arbitrage (UIA) transaction. Assess this decision.

14. **Casper Landsten—Thirty Days Later.** One month after the events described in Problems 12 and 13, Casper Landsten once again has $1 million (or its Swiss franc equivalent) to invest for 90 days. He now faces the following foreign exchange and interest rates. Should he again enter into a CIA investment?

Funds available	$1,000,000
Spot exchange rate (SFr/$)	0.9452
90-day forward rate (SFr/$)	0.9410
Swiss franc 90-day interest rate	4.30%
U.S. dollar 90-day interest rate	6.80%

15. **Statoil of Norway's Arbitrage.** Statoil, the national oil company of Norway, is a large, sophisticated, and active participant in both the currency and petrochemical markets. Although it is a Norwegian company, because it operates within the global oil market, it considers the U.S. dollar, rather than the Norwegian krone, as its functional currency. Ari Karlsen is a currency trader for Statoil and has immediate use of either $3 million (or the Norwegian krone equivalent). He is faced with the following market rates and wonders whether he can make some arbitrage profits in the coming 90 days.

Arbitrage funds available	$3,000,000
Spot exchange rate (Nok/$)	6.0312
3-month forward rate (Nok/$)	6.0186
U.S. dollar 3-month interest rate	5.000%
Norwegian krone 3-month interest rate	4.450%

16. **Separated by the Atlantic.** Separated by more than 3,000 nautical miles and five time zones, money and foreign exchange markets in both London and New York are very efficient. The following information has been collected from the respective areas:

Assumptions	London	New York
Spot exchange rate ($/€)	1.3264	1.3264
1-year Treasury bill rate	3.900%	4.500%
Expected inflation rate	Unknown	1.250%

a. What do the financial markets suggest for inflation in Europe next year?

b. Estimate today's 1-year forward exchange rate between the dollar and the euro?

17. **Chamonix Chateau Rentals.** You are planning a ski vacation to Mt. Blanc in Chamonix, France, one year from now. You are negotiating the rental of a chateau. The chateau's owner wishes to preserve his real income against both inflation and exchange rate changes, and so the present weekly rent of €9,800 (Christmas season) will be adjusted upward or downward for any change in the French cost of living between now and then. You are basing your budgeting on purchasing power parity (PPP). French inflation is expected to average 3.5% for the coming year, while U.S. dollar inflation is expected to be 2.5%.

The current spot rate is \$1.3620/€. What should you budget as the U.S. dollar cost of the 1-week rental?

Spot exchange rate (\$/€)	\$1.3620
Expected U.S. inflation for coming year	2.500%
Expected French inflation for coming year	3.500%
Current chateau nominal weekly rent (€)	9,800.00

18. **East Asiatic Company—Thailand.** The East Asiatic Company (EAC), a Danish company with subsidiaries throughout Asia, has been funding its Bangkok subsidiary primarily with U.S. dollar debt because of the cost and availability of dollar capital as opposed to Thai baht-denominated (B) debt. The treasurer of EAC-Thailand is considering a 1-year bank loan for \$250,000. The current spot rate is B32.06/\$, and the dollar-based interest is 6.75% for the 1-year period. 1-year loans are 12.00% in baht.

   a. Assuming expected inflation rates for the coming year of 4.3% and 1.25% in Thailand and the United States, respectively, according to purchase power parity, what would be the effective cost of funds in Thai baht terms?

   b. If EAC's foreign exchange advisers believe strongly that the Thai government wants to push the value of the baht down against the dollar by 5% over the coming year (to promote its export competitiveness in dollar markets), what might be the effective cost of funds in baht terms?

   c. If EAC could borrow Thai baht at 13% per annum, would this be cheaper than either part (a) or part (b)?

19. **Maltese Falcon.** Imagine that the mythical solid gold falcon, initially intended as a tribute by the Knights of Malta to the King of Spain in appreciation for his gift of the island of Malta to the order in 1530, has recently been recovered. The falcon is 14 inches high and solid gold, weighing approximately 48 pounds. Assume that gold prices have risen to \$440/ounce, primarily as a result of increasing political tensions. The falcon is currently held by a private investor in Istanbul, who is actively negotiating with the Maltese government on its purchase and prospective return to its island home. The sale and payment are to take place one year from now, and the parties are negotiating over the price and currency of payment. The investor has decided, in a show of goodwill, to base the sales price only on the falcon's specie value—its gold value.

The current spot exchange rate is 0.39 Maltese lira (ML) per 1.00 U.S. dollar. Maltese inflation is expected to be about 8.5% for the coming year, while U.S. inflation, on the heels of a double-dip recession, is expected to come in at only 1.5%. If the investor bases value in the U.S. dollar, would he be better off receiving Maltese lira in one year (assuming purchasing power parity) or receiving a guaranteed dollar payment (assuming a gold price of \$420 per ounce one year from now).

20. **Malaysian Risk.** Clayton Moore is the manager of an international money market fund managed out of London. Unlike many money funds that guarantee their investors a near risk-free investment with variable interest earnings, Clayton Moore's fund is a very aggressive fund that searches out relatively high interest earnings around the globe, but at some risk. The fund is pound-denominated. Clayton is currently evaluating a rather interesting opportunity in Malaysia. Since the Asian Crisis of 1997, the Malaysian government enforced a number of currency and capital restrictions to protect and preserve the value of the Malaysian ringgit. The ringgit was fixed to the U.S. dollar at RM3.80/\$ for seven years. In 2005, the Malaysian government allowed the currency to float against several major currencies. The current spot rate today is RM3.13485/\$. Local currency time deposits of 180-day maturities are earning 8.900% per annum. The London eurocurrency market for pounds is yielding 4.200% per annum on similar 180-day maturities. The current spot rate on the British pound is \$1.5820/£, and the 180-day forward rate is \$1.5561/£.

21. **The Beer Standard.** In 1999, *The Economist* reported the creation of an index, or standard, for the evaluation of African currency values using the local prices of beer. Beer, instead of Big Macs, was chosen as the product for comparison because McDonald's had not penetrated the African continent beyond South Africa, and beer met most of the same product and market characteristics required for the construction of a proper currency index. Investec, a South African investment banking firm, has replicated the process of creating a measure of purchasing power parity (PPP) like that of the Big Mac Index of *The Economist*, for Africa.

The index compares the cost of a 375 milliliter bottle of clear lager beer across Sub-Saharan Africa. As a measure of PPP, the beer needs to be relatively homogeneous in quality across countries, and must possess substantial elements of local manufacturing, inputs, distribution, and service in order to actually provide a measure of relative purchasing power. The beer is first priced in local currency (purchased in the taverns of the locals, and not in the high-priced tourist centers). The price is then converted to South African rand and the rand-price compared to the local currency price as one measure of whether the local currency is undervalued or overvalued versus the South African rand. Use the data in the table and complete the calculation of whether the individual currencies are undervalued or overvalued.

Country	Beer	Beer Prices			Implied PPP Rate	Spot Rate
		Local Currency	Price in Currency	Price in Rand		
South Africa	Castle	Rand	2.30	—	—	—
Botswana	Castle	Pula	2.20	2.94	0.96	0.75
Ghana	Star	Cedi	1,200.00	3.17	521.74	379.10
Kenya	Tusker	Shilling	41.25	4.02	17.93	10.27
Malawi	Carlsberg	Kwacha	18.50	2.66	8.04	6.96
Mauritius	Phoenix	Rupee	15.00	3.72	6.52	4.03
Namibia	Windhoek	N$	2.50	2.50	1.09	1.00
Zambia	Castle	Kwacha	1,200.00	3.52	521.74	340.68
Zimbabwe	Castle	Z$	9.00	1.46	3.91	6.15

Internet Exercises

1. **Big Mac Index Updated.** Use *The Economist*'s Web site to find the latest edition of the Big Mac Index of currency overvaluation and undervaluation. (You will need to do a search for "Big Mac Currencies.") Create a worksheet to compare how the British pound, the euro, the Swiss franc, and the Canadian dollar have changed from the version presented in this chapter.

   The Economist   www.economist.com/markets-data

2. **Purchasing Power Parity Statistics.** The Organization for Economic Cooperation and Development (OECD) publishes detailed measures of prices and purchasing power for its member countries. Go to the OECD's Web site and download the spreadsheet file with the historical data for purchasing power for the member countries.

   OECD   www.oecd.org/std/prices-ppp/

3. **International Interest Rates.** A number of Web sites publish current interest rates by currency and maturity. Use the *Financial Times* Web site listed here to isolate the interest rate differentials between the U.S. dollar, the British pound, and the euro for all maturities up to and including one year.

   Financial Times   markets.ft.com/RESEARCH/
   Markets/Interest-Rates

Data Listed by the *Financial Times*:

   - International money rates (bank call rates for major currency deposits)
   - Money rates (LIBOR and CD rates, etc.)
   - 10-year spreads (individual country spreads versus the euro and U.S. 10-year treasuries). Note: Which countries actually have lower 10-year government bond rates than the United States and the euro? Probably Switzerland and Japan. Check.
   - Benchmark government bonds (sampling of representative government issuances by major countries and recent price movements). Note which countries are showing longer maturity benchmark rates.
   - Emerging market bonds (government issuances, Brady bonds, etc.)
   - Eurozone rates (miscellaneous bond rates for assorted European-based companies; includes debt ratings by Moodys and S&P)

4. **World Bank's International Comparison Program.** The World Bank has an ongoing research program that focuses on the relative purchasing power of 107 different economies globally, specifically in terms of household consumption. Download the latest data tables and highlight which economies seem to be showing the greatest growth in recent years in relative purchasing power. Search the Internet for the World Bank's ICP program site.

CHAPTER 6 APPENDIX
An Algebraic Primer to International Parity Conditions

The following is a purely algebraic presentation of the parity conditions explained in this chapter. It is offered to provide those students who desire additional theoretical detail and definition ready access to the step-by-step derivation of the various conditions.

The Law of One Price

The *law of one price* refers to the state in which — in the presence of free trade, perfect substitutability of goods, and costless transactions — the equilibrium exchange rate between two currencies is determined by the ratio of the price of any commodity i denominated in two different currencies. For example,

$$S_t = \frac{P_{i,t}^{\$}}{P_{i,t}^{SF}}$$

where $P_i^{\$}$ and P_i^{SF} refer to the prices of the same commodity i, at time t, denominated in U.S. dollars and Swiss francs, respectively. The spot exchange rate, S_t, is simply the ratio of the two currency prices.

Purchasing Power Parity

The more general form in which the exchange rate is determined by the ratio of two price indexes is termed the absolute version of *purchasing power parity* (PPP). Each price index reflects the currency cost of the identical "basket" of goods across countries. The exchange rate that equates purchasing power for the identical collection of goods is then stated as follows:

$$S_t = \frac{P_t^{\$}}{P_t^{SF}}$$

where $P_t^{\$}$ and P_t^{SF} are the price index values in U.S. dollars and Swiss francs at time t, respectively. If $\pi^{\$}$ and π^{SF} represent the rates of inflation in each currency respectively, then the spot exchange rate at time $t + 1$ would be

$$S_{t+1} = \frac{P_t^{\$}(1 + \pi^{\$})}{P_t^{SF}(1 + \pi^{SF})} = S_t \left[\frac{(1 + \pi^{\$})}{(1 + \pi^{SF})} \right]$$

The change from period t to $t + 1$ is then

$$\frac{S_{t+1}}{S_t} = \frac{\dfrac{P_t^{\$}(1 + \pi^{\$})}{P_t^{SF}(1 + \pi^{SF})}}{\dfrac{P_t^{\$}}{P_t^{SF}}} = \frac{S_t\left[\dfrac{(1 + \pi^{\$})}{(1 + \pi^{SF})}\right]}{S_t} = \frac{(1 + \pi^{\$})}{(1 + \pi^{SF})}$$

Isolating the percentage change in the spot exchange rate between periods t and $t + 1$ is then

$$\frac{S_{t+1} - S_t}{S_t} = \frac{S_t\left[\dfrac{(1 + \pi^{\$})}{(1 + \pi^{SF})}\right] - S_t}{S_t} = \frac{(1 + \pi^{\$}) - (1 + \pi^{SF})}{(1 + \pi^{SF})}$$

This equation is often approximated by dropping the denominator of the right-hand side if it is considered to be relatively small. It is then stated as

$$\frac{S_{t+1} - S_t}{S_t} = (1 + \pi^{\$}) - (1 + \pi^{SF}) = \pi^{\$} - \pi^{SF}$$

Forward Rates

The *forward exchange rate* is the contractual rate that is available to private agents through banking institutions and other financial intermediaries who deal in foreign currencies and debt instruments. The annualized percentage difference between the forward rate and the spot rate is termed the *forward premium*,

$$f^{SF} = \left[\frac{F_{t,t+1} - S_t}{S_t}\right] \times \left[\frac{360}{n_{t,t+1}}\right]$$

where f^{SF} is the forward premium on the Swiss franc, $F_{t,t+1}$ is the forward rate contracted at time t for delivery at time $t + 1$, S_t is the current spot rate, and $n_{t,t+1}$ is the number of days between the contract date (t) and the delivery date ($t + 1$).

Covered Interest Arbitrage (CIA) and Interest Rate Parity (IRP)

The process of *covered interest arbitrage* is when an investor exchanges domestic currency for foreign currency in the spot market, invests that currency in an interest-bearing instrument, and signs a forward contract to "lock in" a future exchange rate at which to convert the foreign currency proceeds (gross) back to domestic currency. The net return on CIA is

$$\text{Net Return} = \left[\frac{(1 + i^{SF})F_{t,t+1}}{S_t}\right] - (1 + i^{\$})$$

where S_t and $F_{t,t+1}$ are the spot and forward rates ($/SF), i^{SF} is the nominal interest rate (or yield) on a Swiss franc-denominated monetary instrument, and $i^{\$}$ is the nominal return on a similar dollar-denominated instrument.

If they possess exactly equal rates of return—that is, if CIA results in zero riskless profit—*interest rate parity* (IRP) holds, and appears as

$$(1 + i^\$) = \left[\frac{(1 + i^{SF})F_{t,t+1}}{S_t} \right]$$

or alternatively as

$$\frac{(1 + i^\$)}{(1 + i^{SF})} = \frac{F_{t,t+1}}{S_t}$$

If the percent difference of both sides of this equation is found (the percentage difference between the spot and forward rate is the *forward premium*), then the relationship between the forward premium and relative interest rate differentials is

$$\frac{F_{t,t+1} - S_t}{S_t} = f^{SF} = \frac{i^\$ - i^{SF}}{1 + i^{SF}}$$

If these values are not equal (thus, the markets are not in equilibrium), there exists a potential for riskless profit. The market will then be driven back to equilibrium through CIA by agents attempting to exploit such arbitrage potential—until CIA yields no positive return.

Fisher Effect

The *Fisher effect* states that all nominal interest rates can be decomposed into an implied real rate of interest (return) and an expected rate of inflation:

$$i^\$ = [(1 + r^\$)(1 + \pi^\$)] - 1$$

where $r^\$$ is the real rate of return and $\pi^\$$ is the expected rate of inflation for dollar-denominated assets. The subcomponents are then identifiable:

$$i^\$ = r^\$ + \pi^\$ + r^\$\pi^\$$$

As with PPP, there is an approximation of this function that has gained wide acceptance. The cross-product term of $r^\$\pi^\$$ is often very small and therefore dropped altogether:

$$i^\$ = r^\$ + \pi^\$$$

International Fisher Effect

The *international Fisher effect* is the extension of this domestic interest rate relationship to the international currency markets. If capital, by way of covered interest arbitrage (CIA), attempts to find higher rates of return internationally resulting from current interest rate differentials, the real rates of return between currencies are equalized (e.g., $r^\$ = r^{SF}$):

$$\frac{S_{t+1} - S_t}{S_t} = \frac{(1 + i^\$) - (1 + i^{SF})}{(1 + i^{SF})} = \frac{i^\$ - i^{SF}}{(1 + i^{SF})}$$

If the nominal interest rates are then decomposed into their respective real and expected inflation components, the percentage change in the spot exchange rate is

$$\frac{S_{t+1} - S_t}{S_t} = \frac{(r^\$ + \pi^\$ + r^\$\pi^\$) - (r^{SF} + \pi^{SF} + r^{SF}\pi^{SF})}{1 + r^{SF} + \pi^{SF} + r^{SF}\pi^{SF}}$$

The international Fisher effect has a number of additional implications if the following requirements are met: (1) capital markets can be freely entered and exited; (2) capital markets possess investment opportunities that are acceptable substitutes; and (3) market agents have complete and equal information regarding these possibilities.

Given these conditions, international arbitragers are capable of exploiting all potential riskless profit opportunities until real rates of return between markets are equalized ($r^\$ = r^{SF}$). Thus, the expected rate of change in the spot exchange rate reduces to the differential in the expected rates of inflation:

$$\frac{S_{t+1} - S_t}{S_t} = \frac{\pi^\$ + r^\$\pi^\$ - \pi^{SF} - r^{SF}\pi^{SF}}{1 + r^{SF} + \pi^{SF} + r^{SF}\pi^{SF}}$$

If the approximation forms are combined (through the elimination of the denominator and the elimination of the interactive terms of r and π), the change in the spot rate is simply

$$\frac{S_{t+1} - S_t}{S_t} = \pi^\$ - \pi^{SF}$$

Note the similarity (identical in equation form) of the approximate form of the international Fisher effect to purchasing power parity discussed previously—the only potential difference is that between *ex post* and *ex ante* (expected) inflation.

CHAPTER 7

Foreign Currency Derivatives and Swaps

Unless derivatives contracts are collateralized or guaranteed, their ultimate value also depends on the creditworthiness of the counterparties to them. In the meantime, though, before a contract is settled, the counterparties record profits and losses—often huge in amount—in their current earnings statements without so much as a penny changing hands. The range of derivatives contracts is limited only by the imagination of man (or sometimes, so it seems, madmen).

—Warren Buffett, *Berkshire Hathaway Annual Report*, 2002.

LEARNING OBJECTIVES

- Explain how foreign currency futures are quoted, valued, and used for speculation purposes

- Illustrate how foreign currency futures differ from forward contracts

- Analyze how foreign currency options are quoted and used for speculation purposes

- Consider the distinction between buying options and writing options in terms of whether profits and losses are limited or unlimited

- Explain how foreign currency options are valued

- Define interest rate risk and demonstrate how it can be managed

- Explain interest rate swaps and how they can be used to manage interest rate risk

- Analyze how interest rate swaps and cross-currency swaps can be used to manage both foreign exchange risk and interest rate risk simultaneously

Financial management of the multinational enterprise in the twenty-first century will certainly include the use of *financial derivatives*. These derivatives, so named because their values are derived from an underlying asset like a stock or a currency, are powerful tools used in business today for two very distinct management objectives, *speculation* and *hedging*. The financial manager of an MNE may purchase financial derivatives in order to take positions in the expectation of profit—speculation—or may use these instruments to reduce the risks associated with the everyday management of corporate cash flow—hedging. Before these financial instruments can be used effectively, however, the financial manager must understand certain basics about their structure and pricing.

In this chapter, we cover the primary foreign currency financial derivatives used today in multinational financial management: *foreign currency futures*, *foreign currency options*, *interest rate swaps*, and *cross-currency interest rate swaps*. We focus on the fundamentals of their valuation and use for speculative purposes. Chapter 9 will describe how these foreign currency derivatives can be used to hedge commercial transactions—hedging. The Mini-Case at the end of this chapter, *McDonald's Corporation's British Pound Exposure* illustrates how one major multinational company, McDonald's, has used currency derivatives quite successfully over time.

A word of caution—of reservation—before proceeding further. Financial derivatives are powerful tools in the hands of careful and competent financial managers. They can also be destructive devices when used recklessly and carelessly. The history of finance is littered with cases in which financial managers—either intentionally or unintentionally—took huge positions resulting in significant losses for their companies, and occasionally, their outright collapse. In the right hands and with the proper controls, however, financial derivatives may provide management with opportunities to enhance and protect their corporate financial performance. User beware.

Foreign Currency Futures

A *foreign currency futures contract* is an alternative to a forward contract that calls for future delivery of a standard amount of foreign exchange at a fixed time, place, and price. It is similar to futures contracts that exist for commodities (hogs, cattle, lumber, etc.), interest-bearing deposits, and gold.

Most world money centers have established foreign currency futures markets. In the United States, the most important market for foreign currency futures is the *International Monetary Market* (IMM) of Chicago, a division of the Chicago Mercantile Exchange.

Contract Specifications

Contract specifications are established by the exchange on which futures are traded. Using the Chicago IMM as an example, the major features of standardized futures trading can be illustrated by the Mexican peso futures traded on the *Chicago Mercantile Exchange* (CME), as shown in Exhibit 7.1.

Each futures contract is for 500,000 Mexican pesos. This is the *notional principal*. Trading in each currency must be done in an even multiple of currency units. The method of stating exchange rates is in American terms, the U.S. dollar cost (price) of a foreign currency (unit),

EXHIBIT 7.1   Mexican Peso (CME) (MXN 500,000; $ per 10MXN)

| Maturity | Open | High | Low | Settle | Change | Lifetime | | Open Interest |
						High	Low	
Mar	0.10953	0.10988	0.10930	0.10958	...	0.11000	0.09770	34,481.00
June	0.10790	0.10795	0.10778	0.10773	...	0.10800	0.09730	3,405.00
Sept	0.10615	0.10615	0.10610	0.10573	...	0.10615	0.09930	1,481.00

All contracts are for 500,000 Mexican pesos. "Open" means the opening price on the day. "High" means the high price on the day. "Low" indicates the lowest price on the day. "Settle" is the closing price on the day. "Change" indicates the change in the settle price from the previous day's close. "High" and "Low" to the right of Change indicate the highest and lowest prices this specific contract (as defined by its maturity) has experienced over its trading history. "Open Interest" indicates the number of contracts outstanding.

$/MXN, where the CME is mixing the old dollar symbol with the ISO 4217 code for the peso, MXN. In Exhibit 7.1 this is U.S. dollars per Mexican peso. Contracts mature on the third Wednesday of January, March, April, June, July, September, October, or December. Contracts may be traded through the second business day prior to the Wednesday on which they mature. Unless holidays interfere, the last trading day is the Monday preceding the maturity date.

One of the defining characteristics of futures is the requirement that the purchaser deposit a sum as an initial *margin* or *collateral*. This requirement is similar to requiring a performance bond, and it can be met by a letter of credit from a bank, Treasury bills, or cash. In addition, a *maintenance margin* is required. The value of the contract is marked to market daily, and all changes in value are paid in cash daily. *Marked to market* means that the value of the contract is revalued using the closing price for the day. The amount to be paid is called the *variation margin*.

Only about 5% of all futures contracts are settled by the physical delivery of foreign exchange between buyer and seller. More often, buyers and sellers offset their original position prior to delivery date by taking an opposite position. That is, an investor will normally close out a futures position by selling a futures contract for the same delivery date. The complete buy/sell or sell/buy is called a "round turn."

Customers pay a commission to their broker to execute a round turn and a single price is quoted. This practice differs from that of the interbank market, where dealers quote a bid and an offer and do not charge a commission. All contracts are agreements between the client and the exchange clearinghouse, rather than between the two clients involved. Consequently, clients need not worry that a specific counterparty in the market will fail to honor an agreement (*counterparty risk*). The clearinghouse is owned and guaranteed by all members of the exchange.

Using Foreign Currency Futures

Any investor wishing to speculate on the movement of the Mexican peso versus the U.S. dollar could pursue one of the following futures strategies. Keep in mind the principle of a futures contract: A speculator who buys a futures contract is locking in the price at which she must buy that currency on the specified future date. A speculator who sells a futures contract is locking in the price at which she must sell that currency on that future date.

Short Positions. If Amber McClain, a speculator working for International Currency Traders, believes that the Mexican peso will fall in value versus the U.S. dollar by March, she could sell a March futures contract, taking a short position. By selling a March contract, Amber locks in the right to sell 500,000 Mexican pesos at a set price. If the price of the peso falls by the maturity date as she expects, Amber has a contract to sell pesos at a price above their current price on the spot market. Hence, she makes a profit.

Using the quotes on Mexican peso (MXN) futures in Exhibit 7.1, Amber sells one March futures contract for 500,000 pesos at the closing price, termed the settle price, of $.10958 /MXN. The value of her position at maturity—at the expiration of the futures contract in March—is then

$$\text{Value at Maturity (Short Position)} = -\text{Notional Principal} \times (\text{Spot} - \text{Futures})$$

Note that the short position is entered into the valuation as a negative notional principal. If the spot exchange rate at maturity is $.09500/MXN, the value of her position on settlement is

$$\text{Value} = -\text{MXN } 500{,}000 \times (\$.09500/\text{MXN} - \$.10958/\text{MXN}) = \$7{,}290$$

Amber's expectation proved correct; the Mexican peso fell in value versus the U.S. dollar. We could say, "Amber ends up buying at $.09500 and sells at $.10958 per peso."

All that was really required of Amber to speculate on the Mexican peso's value was for her to form an opinion on the Mexican peso's future exchange value versus the U.S. dollar. In this case, she opined that it would fall in value by the March maturity date of the futures contract.

Long Positions.   If Amber McClain expected the peso to rise in value versus the dollar in the near term, she could take a long position, by buying a March future on the Mexican peso. Buying a March future means that Amber is locking in the price at which she must buy Mexican pesos at the future's maturity date. Amber's futures contract at maturity would have the following value:

$$\text{Value at Maturity (Long Position)} = \text{Notional Principal} \times (\text{Spot} - \text{Futures})$$

Again using the March settle price on Mexican peso futures in Exhibit 7.1, $.10958/MXN, if the spot exchange rate at maturity is $.1100/MXN, Amber has indeed guessed right. The value of her position on settlement is then

$$\text{Value} = \text{MXN } 500{,}000 \times (\$.11000/\text{MXN} - \$.10958/\text{MXN}) = \$210$$

In this case, Amber makes a profit in a matter of months of $210 on the single futures contract. We could say, "Amber buys at $.10958 and sells at $.11000 per peso."

But what happens if Amber's expectation about the future value of the Mexican peso proves wrong? For example, if the Mexican government announces that the rate of inflation in Mexico has suddenly risen dramatically, and the peso falls to $.08000/MXN by the March maturity date, the value of Amber's futures contract on settlement is

$$\text{Value} = \text{MXN } 500{,}000 \times (\$.08000/\text{MXN} - \$.10958/\text{MXN}) = (\$14{,}790)$$

In this case, Amber McClain suffers a speculative loss.

Futures contracts could obviously be used in combinations to form a variety of more complex positions. When we combine contracts, valuation is fairly straightforward and additive in character.

Foreign Currency Futures versus Forward Contracts

Foreign currency futures contracts differ from forward contracts in a number of important ways. Individuals find futures contracts useful for speculation because they usually do not have access to forward contracts. For businesses, futures contracts are often considered inefficient and burdensome because the futures position is marked to market on a daily basis over the life of the contract. Although this does not require the business to pay or receive cash daily, it does result in more frequent margin calls from its financial service providers than the business typically wants.

Currency Options

A *foreign currency option* is a contract that gives the option purchaser (the buyer) the right, but not the obligation, to buy or sell a given amount of foreign exchange at a fixed price per unit for a specified time period (until the maturity date). A key phrase in this definition is "but not the obligation," which means that the owner of an option possesses a valuable choice.

In many ways, buying an option is like buying a ticket to a benefit concert. The buyer has the right to attend the concert, but is not obliged to. The buyer of the concert ticket risks nothing more than what she pays for the ticket. Similarly, the buyer of an option cannot lose more than what he pays for the option. If the buyer of the ticket decides later not to attend the concert — prior to the day of the concert, the ticket can be sold to someone else who wishes to go.

Option Fundamentals

There are two basic types of options, *calls* and *puts*. A *call* is an option to buy foreign currency, and a *put* is an option to sell foreign currency. The buyer of an option is termed the *holder*, while the seller of an option is referred to as the *writer* or *grantor*.

Every option has three different price elements: 1) the *exercise* or *strike price*, the exchange rate at which the foreign currency can be purchased (call) or sold (put); 2) the *premium*, which is the cost, price, or value of the option itself; and 3) the underlying or actual spot exchange rate in the market.

An *American option* gives the buyer the right to exercise the option at any time between the date of writing and the expiration or maturity date. A *European option* can be exercised only on its expiration date, not before. Nevertheless, American and European options are priced almost the same because the option holder would normally sell the option itself before maturity. The option would then still have some "time value" above its "intrinsic value" if exercised (explained later in this chapter).

The premium or option price is the cost of the option, usually paid in advance by the buyer to the seller. In the *over-the-counter market* (options offered by banks), premiums are quoted as a percentage of the transaction amount. Premiums on exchange-traded options are quoted as a domestic currency amount per unit of foreign currency.

An option whose exercise price is the same as the spot price of the underlying currency is said to be *at-the-money* (ATM). An option that would be profitable, excluding the cost of the premium, if exercised immediately is said to be *in-the-money* (ITM). An option that would not be profitable, again excluding the cost of the premium, if exercised immediately is referred to as *out-of-the-money* (OTM).

Foreign Currency Options Markets

In the past three decades, the use of foreign currency options as a hedging tool and for speculative purposes has blossomed into a major foreign exchange activity. A number of banks in the United States and other capital markets offer flexible foreign currency options on transactions of $1 million or more. The bank market, or over-the-counter market as it is called, offers custom-tailored options on all major trading currencies for any period up to one year, and in some cases, two to three years.

The Philadelphia Stock Exchange introduced trading in standardized foreign currency option contracts in the United States in 1982. The Chicago Mercantile Exchange and other exchanges in the U.S. and abroad have followed suit. Exchange-traded contracts are particularly appealing to speculators and individuals who do not normally have access to the over-the-counter market. Banks also trade on the exchanges because it is one of several ways they can offset the risk of options they may have transacted with clients or other banks.

Increased use of foreign currency options is a reflection of the explosive growth in the use of other kinds of options and the resultant improvements in option pricing models. The original option-pricing model developed by Fischer Black and Myron Scholes in 1973[1] has been

---

[1]Fischer Black and Myron Scholes, "The Pricing of Options and Corporate Liabilities," *Journal of Political Economy*, Vol. 81, No. 3, May–June, 1973, pp. 637–654.

expanded, adapted, and commercialized in hundreds of forms since that time. One wonders if Black and Scholes truly appreciated what a monster they may have created!

Options on the Over-the-Counter Market. *Over-the-counter* (OTC) options are most frequently written by banks for U.S. dollars against British pounds sterling, Canadian dollars, Japanese yen, Swiss francs, or the euro.

The main advantage of OTC options is that they are tailored to the specific needs of the firm. Financial institutions are willing to write or buy options that vary by amount (notional principal), strike price, and maturity. Although the OTC markets were relatively illiquid in the early years, these markets have grown to such proportions that liquidity is now quite good. On the other hand, the buyer must assess the writing bank's ability to fulfill the option contract. Termed *counterparty risk*, the financial risk associated with the counterparty is a growing issue in international markets as a result of the increasing use of financial contracts like options and swaps by MNE management. Exchange-traded options are more the territory of individuals and financial institutions than of business firms.

If an investor wishes to purchase an option in the OTC market, the investor will normally place a call to the currency option desk of a major money center bank, specify the currencies, maturity, strike rate(s), and ask for an *indication*—a bid-offer quote. The bank will normally take a few minutes to a few hours to price the option and return the call.

Options on Organized Exchanges. Options on the physical (underlying) currency are traded on a number of organized exchanges worldwide, including the Philadelphia Stock Exchange (PHLX) and the Chicago Mercantile Exchange. Exchange-traded options are settled through a clearinghouse, so that buyers do not deal directly with sellers. The clearinghouse is the counterparty to every option contract and it guarantees fulfillment. Clearinghouse obligations are in turn the obligation of all members of the exchange, including a large number of banks. In the case of the Philadelphia Stock Exchange, clearinghouse services are provided by the *Options Clearing Corporation* (OCC).

Currency Option Quotations and Prices

Typical quotes in the *Wall Street Journal* for options on Swiss francs are shown in Exhibit 7.2. The *Journal's* quotes refer to transactions completed on the Philadelphia Stock Exchange on the previous day. Although a multitude of strike prices and expiration dates are quoted

| EXHIBIT 7.2 | **Swiss Franc Option Quotations** (U.S. cents/SF) |

Option and Underlying	Strike Price	Calls – Last			Puts – Last		
		Aug	Sep	Dec	Aug	Sep	Dec
58.51	56.0	—	—	2.76	0.04	0.22	1.16
58.51	56.5	—	—	—	0.06	0.30	—
58.51	57.0	1.13	—	1.74	0.10	0.38	1.27
58.51	57.5	0.75	—	—	0.17	0.55	—
58.51	58.0	0.71	1.05	1.28	0.27	0.89	1.81
58.51	58.5	0.50	—	—	0.50	0.99	—
58.51	59.0	0.30	0.66	1.21	0.90	1.36	—
58.51	59.5	0.15	0.40	—	2.32	—	—
58.51	60.0	—	0.31	—	2.32	2.62	3.30

Each option = 62,500 Swiss francs. The August, September, and December listings are the option maturities or expiration dates.

(shown in the exhibit), not all were actually traded the previous trading day, hence no premium price is shown. Currency option strike prices and premiums on the U.S. dollar are typically quoted as direct quotations on the U.S. dollar and indirect quotations on the foreign currency ($/SF, $/¥, etc.).

Exhibit 7.2 illustrates the three different prices that characterize any foreign currency option. The three prices that characterize an "August 58.5 call option" (highlighted in Exhibit 7.2) are the following:

1. **Spot rate**. "Option and Underlying" in the exhibit means that 58.51 cents, or $0.5851, was the spot dollar price of one Swiss franc at the close of trading on the preceding day.

2. **Exercise price**. The *exercise price*, or "Strike Price" in the exhibit, means the price per franc that must be paid if the option is exercised. The August call option on francs of 58.5 means $0.5850/SF. Exhibit 7.2 lists nine different strike prices, ranging from $0.5600/SF to $0.6000/SF, although more were available on that date than are listed.

3. **Premium**. The *premium* is the cost or price of the option. The price of the August 58.5 call option on Swiss francs was 0.50 U.S. cents per franc, or $0.0050/SF. There was no trading of the September and December 58.5 call on that day. The premium is the market value of the option, and therefore the terms *premium*, *cost*, *price*, and *value* are all interchangeable when referring to an option.

The August 58.5 call option premium is 0.50 cents per franc, and in this case, the August 58.5 put's premium is also 0.50 cents per franc. Since one option contract on the Philadelphia Stock Exchange consists of 62,500 francs, the total cost of one option contract for the call (or put in this case) is SF62,500 × $0.0050/SF = $312.50.

Buyer of a Call

Options differ from all other types of financial instruments in the patterns of risk they produce. The option owner, the holder, has the choice of exercising the option or allowing it to expire unused. The owner will exercise it only when exercising is profitable, which means only when the option is in the money. In the case of a call option, as the spot price of the underlying currency moves up, the holder has the possibility of unlimited profit. On the down side, however, the holder can abandon the option and walk away with a loss never greater than the premium paid.

Hans Schmidt is a currency speculator in Zurich. The position of Hans as a buyer of a call is illustrated in Exhibit 7.3. Assume he purchases the August call option on Swiss francs described previously, the one with a strike price of $0.585, and a premium of $0.005 /SF. The vertical axis measures profit or loss for the option buyer at each of several different spot prices for the franc up to the time of maturity.

At all spot rates below the strike price of $0.585, Hans would choose not to exercise his option. This is obvious because at a spot rate of $0.580 for example, he would prefer to buy a Swiss franc for $0.580 on the spot market over exercising his option to buy a franc at $0.585. If the spot rate were to remain at $0.580 or below until August when the option expired, Hans would not exercise the option. His total loss would be limited to only what he paid for the option, the $0.005/SF purchase price. Regardless of how far the spot rate were to fall, his loss would be limited to the original $0.005/SF cost.

Alternatively, at all spot rates above the strike price of $0.585, Hans would exercise the option, paying only the strike price for each Swiss franc. For example, if the spot rate were $0.595 per franc at maturity, he would exercise his call option, buying Swiss francs for $0.585 each instead of purchasing them on the spot market at $0.595 each. He could sell the Swiss

EXHIBIT 7.3   Profit and Loss for the Buyer of a Call Option

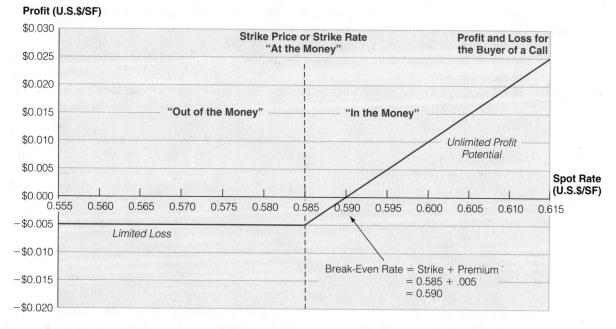

The buyer of a call option has unlimited profit potential (*in the money*), and limited loss potential, the amount of the premium (*out of the money*).

francs immediately in the spot market for $0.595 each, pocketing a gross profit of $0.010/SF, or a net profit of $0.005/SF after deducting the original cost of the option of $0.005/SF. Hans' profit, if the spot rate is greater than the strike price, with strike price $0.585, a premium of $0.005, and a spot rate of $0.595, is

$$\begin{aligned} \text{Profit} &= \text{Spot Rate} - (\text{Strike Price} + \text{Premium}) \\ &= \$0.595/\text{SF} - (\$0.585/\text{SF} + \$0.005/\text{SF}) \\ &= \$0.005/\text{SF} \end{aligned}$$

More likely, Hans would realize the profit through executing an offsetting contract on the options exchange rather than taking delivery of the currency. Because the dollar price of a franc could rise to an infinite level (off the upper right-hand side of Exhibit 7.3), maximum profit is unlimited. The buyer of a call option thus possesses an attractive combination of outcomes: limited loss and unlimited profit potential.

Note that *break-even price* of $0.590/SF is the price at which Hans neither gains nor loses on exercising the option. The premium cost of $0.005, combined with the cost of exercising the option of $0.585, is exactly equal to the proceeds from selling the francs in the spot market at $0.590. Hans will still exercise the call option at the break-even price. This is because by exercising it he at least recoups the premium paid for the option. At any spot price above the exercise price but below the break-even price, the gross profit earned on exercising the option and selling the underlying currency covers part (but not all) of the premium cost.

Writer of a Call

The position of the writer (seller) of the same call option is illustrated in Exhibit 7.4. If the option expires when the spot price of the underlying currency is below the exercise price of $0.585, the option holder does not exercise. What the holder loses, the writer gains. The writer keeps as profit the entire premium paid of $0.005/SF. Above the exercise price of 58.5, the writer of the call must deliver the underlying currency for $0.585/SF at a time when the value of the franc is above $0.585. If the writer wrote the option "naked," that is, without owning the currency, then the writer will need to buy the currency at spot and, in this scenario, take the loss. The amount of such a loss is unlimited and increases as the price of the underlying currency rises.

Once again, what the holder gains, the writer loses, and vice versa. Even if the writer already owns the currency, the writer will experience an opportunity loss, surrendering against the option the same currency that could have been sold for more in the open market.

For example, the profit to the writer of a call option of strike price $0.585, premium $0.005, a spot rate of $0.595/SF is

$$\text{Profit} = \text{Premium} - (\text{Spot Rate} - \text{Strike Price})$$
$$= \$0.005/\text{SF} - (\$0.595/\text{SF} - \$0.585/\text{SF})$$
$$= \$0.005/\text{SF}$$

but only if the spot rate is greater than or equal to the strike rate. At spot rates less than the strike price, the option will expire worthless and the writer of the call option will keep the premium earned. The maximum profit that the writer of the call option can make is limited to the premium. The writer of a call option has a rather unattractive combination of potential

---

EXHIBIT 7.4   **Profit and Loss for the Writer of a Call Option**

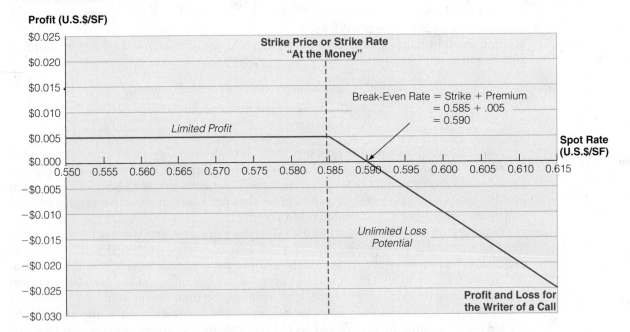

The writer of a call option has unlimited loss potential and limited profit potential, the amount of the premium.

outcomes: limited profit potential and unlimited loss potential—but there are ways to limit such losses through other offsetting techniques that we will discuss later in this chapter.

Buyer of a Put

Hans' position as buyer of a put is illustrated in Exhibit 7.5. The basic terms of this put are similar to those we just used to illustrate a call. The buyer of a put option, however, wants to be able to sell the underlying currency at the exercise price when the market price of that currency drops (rather than when it rises as in the case of a call option). If the spot price of a franc drops to, say, $0.575/SF, Hans will deliver francs to the writer and receive $0.585/SF. The francs can now be purchased on the spot market for $0.575 each, and the cost of the option was $0.005/SF, so he will have a net gain of $0.005/SF.

Explicitly, the profit to the holder of a put option if the spot rate is less than the strike price, with a strike price $0.585/SF, premium of $0.005/SF, and a spot rate of $0.575/SF, is

$$\text{Profit} = \text{Strike Price} - (\text{Spot Rate} + \text{Premium})$$
$$= \$0.585/SF - (\$0.575/SF + \$0.005/SF)$$
$$= \$0.005/SF$$

The break-even price for the put option is the strike price less the premium, or $0.580/SF in this case. As the spot rate falls further and further below the strike price, the profit potential would continually increase, and Hans' profit could be up to a maximum of $0.580/SF, when the price of a franc would be zero. At any exchange rate above the strike price of 58.5, Hans would not exercise the option, and so would lose only the $0.005/SF premium paid for the put

EXHIBIT 7.5   Profit and Loss for the Buyer of a Put Option

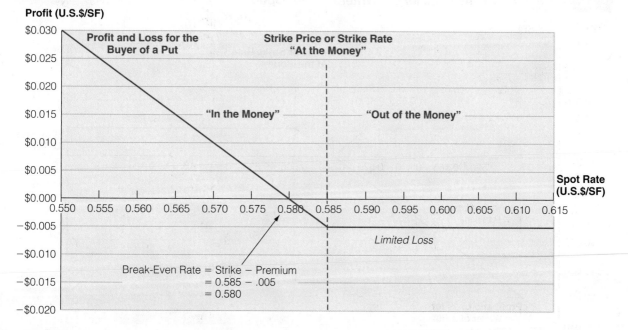

The buyer of a put option has unlimited profit potential (*in the money*), and limited loss potential, the amount of the premium (*out of the money*).

option. The buyer of a put option has an almost unlimited profit potential with a limited loss potential. Like the buyer of a call, the buyer of a put can never lose more than the premium paid up front.

Writer of a Put

The position of the writer who sold the put to Hans is shown in Exhibit 7.6. Note the symmetry of profit/loss, strike price, and break-even prices between the buyer and the writer of the put. If the spot price of francs drops below $0.585 per franc, Hans will exercise the option. Below a price of $0.585 per franc, the writer will lose more than the premium received from writing the option ($0.005/SF), falling below breakeven. Between $0.580/SF and $0.585/SF the writer will lose part, but not all, of the premium received. If the spot price is above $0.585/SF, Hans will not exercise the option, and the option writer will pocket the entire premium of $0.005/SF.

The profit (loss) earned by the writer of a $0.585 strike price put, premium $0.005, at a spot rate of $0.575, is

$$\text{Profit (Loss)} = \text{Premium} - (\text{Strike Price} - \text{Spot Rate}$$
$$= \$0.005/SF - (\$0.585/SF - \$0.575/SF)$$
$$= \$0.005/SF$$

but only for spot rates that are less than or equal to the strike price. At spot rates greater than the strike price, the option expires out-of-the-money and the writer keeps the premium. The writer of the put option has the same combination of outcomes available to the writer of a call: limited profit potential and loss potential.

EXHIBIT 7.6   **Profit and Loss for the Writer of a Put Option**

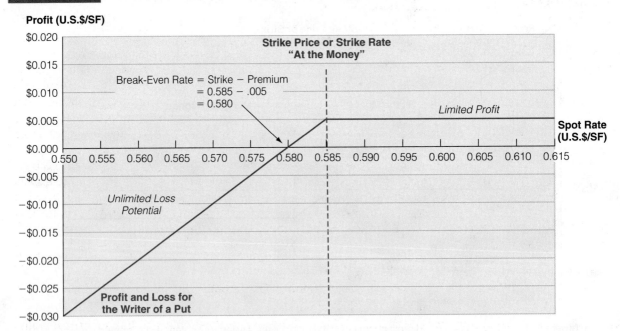

The writer of a put option has limited profit potential, the premium, and an unlimited loss potential.

GLOBAL FINANCE IN PRACTICE 7.1

The New Zealand Kiwi, Key, and Krieger

In 1987 Andrew Krieger was a 31-year-old currency trader for Bankers Trust of New York (BT). Following the U.S. stock market crash in October 1987, the world's currency markets moved rapidly to exit the dollar. Many of the world's other currencies—including small ones that were in stable, open, industrialized markets, like that of New Zealand—became the subject of interest. As the world's currency traders dumped dollars and bought kiwis, the value of the kiwi rose sharply.

Krieger believed that the markets were overreacting. He took a short position on the kiwi, betting on its eventual fall. And he did so in a big way, combining spot, forward, and options positions. (Krieger supposedly had approval for positions rising to nearly $700 million in size, while all other BT traders were restricted to $50 million.) Krieger, on behalf of BT, is purported to have shorted 200 million kiwi—more than the entire New Zealand money supply at the time. His view proved correct. The kiwi fell, and Krieger was able to earn millions in currency gains for BT. Ironically, only months later, Krieger resigned from BT when annual bonuses were announced and he was reportedly awarded only $3 million on the more than $300 million profit.

Eventually, the New Zealand central bank lodged complaints with BT, in which the CEO at the time, Charles S. Sanford Jr., seemingly added insult to injury when he reportedly remarked "We didn't take too big a position for Bankers Trust, but we may have taken too big a position for that market."

Global Finance in Practice 7.1 describes one of the largest, and most successful, currency option speculations ever made—that by Andrew Krieger against the New Zealand kiwi.

Option Pricing and Valuation

Exhibit 7.7 illustrates the profit/loss profile of a European-style call option on British pounds. The call option allows the holder to buy British pounds at a strike price of $1.70/£. It has a 90-day maturity. The value of this call option is actually the sum of two components:

$$\text{Total Value (Premium)} = \text{Intrinsic Value} + \text{Time Value}$$

The pricing of any currency option combines six elements. For example, this European-style call option on British pounds has a premium of $0.033/£ (3.3 cents per pound) at a spot rate of $1.70/£. This premium is calculated using the following assumptions: a spot rate of $1.70/£, a 90-day maturity, a $1.70/£ forward rate, both U.S. dollar and British pound interest rates of 8.00% per annum, and an option volatility for the 90-day period of 10.00% per annum.

Intrinsic value is the financial gain if the option is exercised immediately. It is shown by the solid line in Exhibit 7.7, which is zero until it reaches the strike price, then rises linearly (1 cent for each 1-cent increase in the spot rate). Intrinsic value will be zero when the option is *out-of-the-money*—that is, when the strike price is above the market price—as no gain can be derived from exercising the option. When the spot rate rises above the strike price, the intrinsic value becomes positive because the option is always worth at least this value if exercised. On the date of maturity, an option will have a value equal to its intrinsic value (zero time remaining means zero time value).

Exhibit 7.7 illustrates the intrinsic value of time value elements of the $1.70/£ strike price rate call option on British pounds at three different ending spot rates:

■ When the spot rate is $1.74/£, the option is in-the-money and has an intrinsic value of $1.74−$1.70/£, or 4 cents per pound.

■ When the spot rate is $1.70/£, the option is at-the-money and has an intrinsic value of $1.70−$1.70/£, or zero cents per pound.

■ When the spot rate is $1.66/£, the option is out-of-the-money and has no intrinsic value. This is shown by the intrinsic value lying on the horizontal axis. Only a fool would exercise this call option at this spot rate instead of buying pounds more cheaply on the spot market.

EXHIBIT 7.7 **Option Intrinsic Value, Time Value, and Premium (Total Value)**

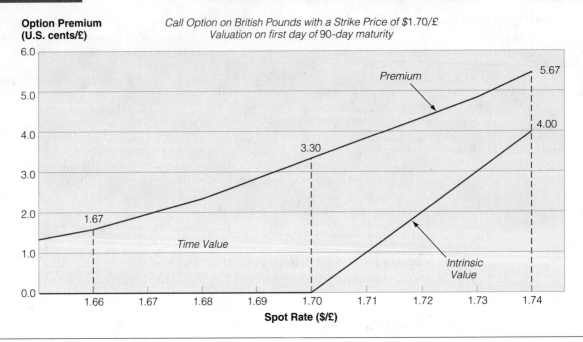

The *time value* of an option exists because the price of the underlying currency, the spot rate, can potentially move further and further into the money before the option's expiration. Time value is shown in Exhibit 7.7 as the area between the *total value* of the option and its intrinsic value. An investor will pay something today for an out-of-the-money option (i.e., zero intrinsic value) on the chance that the spot rate will move far enough before maturity put the option in-the-money. Consequently, the price of an option is always somewhat greater than its intrinsic value, since there is always some chance that the intrinsic value will rise by the expiration date.

If currency options are to be used effectively, either for the purposes of speculation or risk management (covered in Chapters 9 and 10), the individual trader needs to know how option values—premiums—react to their various components. Exhibit 7.8 summarizes six basic sensitivities.

Although rarely noted, standard foreign currency options are priced around the forward rate because the current spot rate and both the domestic and foreign interest rates (home currency and foreign currency rates) are included in the option premium calculation. Regardless of the specific strike rate chosen and priced, the forward rate is central to valuation. The option-pricing formula calculates a subjective probability distribution centered on the forward rate. This approach does not mean that the market expects the forward rate to be equal to the future spot rate, it is simply a result of the arbitrage—pricing structure of options.

The forward rate focus also provides helpful information for the trader managing a position. When the market prices a foreign currency option, it does so without any bullish or bearish sentiment on the direction of the foreign currency's value relative to the domestic currency. If the trader has specific expectations about the future spot rate's direction, those expectations can be put to work. A trader will not be inherently betting against the market.

| EXHIBIT 7.8 | Summary of Option Premium Components |

Greek	Definition	Interpretation
Delta	Expected change in the option premium for a small change in the spot rate	The higher the delta, the more likely the option will move in-the-money
Theta	Expected change in the option premium for a small change in time to expiration	Premiums are relatively insensitive until the final 30 or so days
Lambda	Expected change in the option premium for a small change in volatility	Premiums rise with increases in volatility
Rho	Expected change in the option premium for a small change in the domestic interest	Increases in domestic interest rates cause increasing call option premiums
Phi	Expected change in the option premium for a small change in the foreign interest rate	Increases in foreign interest rates cause decreasing call option premiums

Interest Rate Risk

All firms—domestic or multinational, small or large, leveraged or unleveraged—are sensitive to interest rate movements in one way or another. Although a variety of interest rate risks exist in theory and industry, this book focuses on the financial management of the nonfinancial firm. Hence, our discussion is limited to the interest rate risks associated with the multinational firm. The interest rate risks of financial firms, such as banks, are not covered here.

The single largest interest rate risk of the nonfinancial firm is debt service. The debt structure of the MNE will possess differing maturities of debt, different interest rate structures (such as fixed versus floating-rate), and different currencies of denomination. Interest rates are currency-specific. Each currency has its own interest rate yield curve and credit spreads for borrowers. Therefore, the multicurrency dimension of interest rate risk for the MNE is a serious concern. As illustrated in Exhibit 7.9, even the interest rate calculations vary on occasion across currencies and countries. *Global Finance in Practice 7.2* provides additional evidence on the use of fixed versus floating-rate instruments in today's marketplace.

The second most prevalent source of interest rate risk for the MNE lies in its holdings of interest-sensitive securities. Unlike debt, which is recorded on the right-hand-side of the firm's balance sheet, the marketable securities portfolio of the firm appears on the left-hand-side. Marketable securities represent potential earnings or interest inflows to the firm. Ever-increasing competitive pressures have pushed financial managers to tighten their management of both the left and right sides of the firm's balance sheet.

| EXHIBIT 7.9 | International Interest Rate Calculations |

International interest rate calculations differ by the number of days used in the period's calculation and their definition of how many days there are in a year (for financial purposes). The following example highlights how the different methods result in different one-month payments of interest on a $10 million loan, 5.500% per annum interest, for an exact period of 28 days.

Practice	Day Count in Period	Days/Year	$10 Million @ 5.500% per Annum	
			Days Used	Interest Payment
International	Exact number of days	360	28	$42,777.78
British	Exact number of days	365	28	$42,191.78
Swiss (Eurobond)	Assumed 30 days/month	360	30	$45,833.33

GLOBAL FINANCE IN PRACTICE 7.2

A Fixed-Rate or Floating-Rate World?

The *BIS Quarterly Review* of March 2009 provides a detailed statistical breakdown of the types of international notes and bonds newly issued and outstanding, listing them by issuer, by type of instrument, and by currency of denomination. The data provides some interesting insights into the international securities market.

■ At the end of year 2008, there were $22.7 trillion outstanding in international notes and bonds issued by all types of institutions.

■ The market continues to be dominated by issuances of financial institutions. The issuers by dollar value were as follows: financial institutions, $17.9 trillion or 79%; governments, $1.8 trillion or 8%; international organizations, $0.6 trillion or 3%; and corporate issuers, $2.4 trillion or 10% of the total outstanding.

■ The instruments are still largely fixed-rate issuances, with 64% of all outstanding issuances being fixed-rate, 34% floating-rate, and roughly 2% equity-related.

■ The euro continues to dominate international note and bond issuances, making up more than 48% of the total. The euro is followed by the dollar with 36%, the pound sterling with 8%, the Japanese yen with 3%, and the Swiss franc with 2%.

The data continues to support two long-standing fundamental properties of the international debt markets.

■ The euro's domination reflects the long-term use of the international security markets by the institutions in the countries constituting the euro-Western Europe.

■ Fixed-rate issuances are still the foundation of the market. Although floating-rate issuances did rise marginally in the 2003–2006 period, the international credit crisis of 2008–2009 and the response by central banks to push interest rates downward created new opportunities for the issuance of longer-term, fixed-rate issuances by issuers of all kinds.

Source: Data drawn from Table 13B, *BIS Quarterly Review*, March 2009, p. 91, www.bis.org/statistics/secstats.htm.

Credit Risk and Repricing Risk

Prior to describing the management of the most common interest rate pricing risks, it is important to distinguish between credit risk and repricing risk. *Credit risk*, sometimes termed *rollover risk*, is the possibility that a borrower's creditworthiness, at the time of renewing a credit, is reclassified by the lender. This can result in changing fees, changing interest rates, altered credit line commitments, or even denial. *Repricing risk* is the risk of changes in interest rates charged (earned) at the time a financial contract's rate is reset.

Consider the following debt strategies being considered by a corporate borrower. Each is intended to provide $1 million in financing for a three-year period.

Strategy 1:   Borrow $1 million for three years at a fixed rate of interest.

Strategy 2:   Borrow $1 million for three years at a floating rate, LIBOR + 2% to be reset annually.

Strategy 3:   Borrow $1 million for one year at a fixed rate, then renew the credit annually.

Although the lowest cost of funds is always a major selection criterion, it is not the only one. If the firm chooses Strategy 1, it assures itself of the funding for the full three years at a known interest rate. It has maximized the predictability of cash flows for the debt obligation. What it has sacrificed, to some degree, is the ability to enjoy a lower interest rate in the event that interest rates fall over the period. Of course, it has also eliminated the risk that interest rates could rise over the period, thereby increasing debt servicing costs.

Strategy 2 offers what Strategy 1 did not — flexibility (repricing risk). It too assures the firm of full funding for the three-year period. This eliminates credit risk. Repricing risk is, however, alive and well in Strategy 2. If LIBOR changes dramatically by the second or third year, the LIBOR rate change is passed through completely to the borrower. The spread, however, remains fixed (reflecting the credit standing that has been locked in for the full three years). Flexibility comes at a cost in this case, the risk that interest rates can go up as well as down.

Strategy 3 offers more flexibility and more risk. First, the firm is borrowing at the shorter end of the yield curve. If the yield curve is positively sloped, as is commonly the case in major industrial markets, the base interest rate should be lower. But the short end of the yield curve is also the more volatile. It responds to short-term events in a much more pronounced fashion than longer-term rates. The strategy also exposes the firm to the possibility that its credit rating may change dramatically by the time for credit renewal, for better or worse. Noting that credit ratings in general are established on the premise that a firm can meet its debt-service obligations under worsening economic conditions, firms that are highly creditworthy (investment-rated grades) may view Strategy 3 as a more relevant alternative than do firms of lower quality (speculative grades). This is not a strategy for financially weak firms.

Although the previous example gives only a partial picture of the complexity of funding decisions within the firm, it demonstrates the many ways credit risks and repricing risks are inextricably intertwined. The expression "interest rate exposure" is a complex concept, and the proper measurement of the exposure prior to its management is critical. We now proceed to describe the interest rate risk of the most common form of corporate debt, floating-rate loans.

Interest Rate Derivatives

Like foreign currency, interest rates have derivatives, such as futures, forwards, and options. In addition, and likely of more importance, is the interest rate swap.

Interest Rate Futures

Unlike foreign currency futures, interest rate futures are relatively widely used by financial managers and treasurers of nonfinancial companies. Their popularity stems from the relatively high liquidity of the interest rate futures markets, their simplicity in use, and the rather standardized interest rate exposures most firms possess. The two most widely used futures contracts are the eurodollar futures traded on the Chicago Mercantile Exchange (CME) and the U.S. Treasury Bond Futures of the Chicago Board of Trade (CBOT). To illustrate the use of futures for managing interest rate risks, we will focus on the three-month eurodollar futures contracts. Exhibit 7.10 presents eurodollar futures for two years (they actually trade 10 years into the future).

EXHIBIT 7.10   Eurodollar Futures Prices

Maturity	Open	High	Low	Settle	Yield	Open Interest
June 10	94.99	95.01	94.98	95.01	4.99	455,763
Sept	94.87	94.97	94.87	94.96	5.04	535,932
Dec	94.60	94.70	94.60	94.68	5.32	367,036
March 11	94.67	94.77	94.66	94.76	5.24	299,993
June	94.55	94.68	94.54	94.63	5.37	208,949
Sept	94.43	94.54	94.43	94.53	5.47	168,961
Dec	94.27	94.38	94.27	94.36	5.64	130,824

Typical presentation by the *Wall Street Journal*. Only regular quarterly maturities shown. All contracts are for $1 million; points of 100%. Open interest is number of contracts outstanding.

The yield of a futures contract is calculated from the settlement price, which is the closing price for that trading day. For example, a financial manager examining the eurodollar quotes in Exhibit 7.10 for a March 2011 contract would see that the *settlement price* on the previous day was 94.76, an annual yield of 5.24%:

$$\text{Yield} = (100.00 - 94.76) = 5.24\%$$

Since each contract is for a three-month period (quarter) and a notional principal of $1 million, each basis point is actually worth $2,500 (.01 $\times$ $1,000,000 $\times$ 90/360).

If a financial manager were interested in hedging a floating-rate interest payment due in March 2011, she would need to sell a future, to take a short position. This strategy is referred to as a *short position* because the manager is selling something she does not own (as in shorting common stock). If interest rates rise by March—as the manager fears—the futures price will fall and she will be able to close the position at a profit. This profit will roughly offset the losses associated with rising interest payments on her debt. If the manager is wrong, however, and interest rates actually fall by the maturity date, causing the futures price to rise, she will suffer a loss that will wipe out the "savings" derived from making a lower floating-rate interest payment than she expected. So by selling the March 2011 futures contract, the manager will be locking in an interest rate of 5.24%.

Obviously, interest rate futures positions could be—and are on a regular basis—purchased purely for speculative purposes. Although that is not the focus of the managerial context here, the example shows how any speculator with a directional view on interest rates could take positions in expectations of profit.

As mentioned previously, the most common interest rate exposure of the nonfinancial firm is interest payable on debt. Such exposure is not, however, the only interest rate risk. As more and more firms aggressively manage their entire balance sheet, the interest earnings from the left-hand-side are under increasing scrutiny. If financial managers are expected to earn higher interest on interest-bearing securities, they may well find a second use for the interest rate futures market—to lock in future interest earnings. Exhibit 7.11 provides an overview of these two basic interest rate exposures and the strategies needed to manage interest rate futures.

Forward Rate Agreements

A *forward rate agreement* (FRA) is an interbank-traded contract to buy or sell interest rate payments on a notional principal. These contracts are settled in cash. The buyer of an FRA obtains the right to lock in an interest rate for a desired term that begins at a future date. The contract specifies that the seller of the FRA will pay the buyer the increased interest expense

EXHIBIT 7.11	Interest Rate Futures Strategies for Common Exposures		
Exposure or Position	**Futures Action**	**Interest Rates**	**Position Outcome**
Paying interest on future date	Sell a Futures (short position)	If rates go up	Futures price falls; short earns a profit
		If rates go down	Futures price rises; short earns a loss
Earning interest on future date	Buy a Futures (long position)	If rates go up	Futures price falls; long earns a loss
		If rates go down	Futures price rises; long earns a profit

on a nominal sum (the notional principal) of money if interest rates rise above the agreed rate, but the buyer will pay the seller the differential interest expense if interest rates fall below the agreed rate. Maturities available are typically 1, 3, 6, 9, and 12 months, much like traditional forward contracts for currencies.

Like foreign currency forward contracts, FRAs are useful on individual exposures. They are contractual commitments of the firm that allow little flexibility to enjoy favorable movements, such as when LIBOR is falling as described in the previous section. Firms also use FRAs if they plan to invest in securities at future dates but fear that interest rates might fall prior to the investment date. Because of the limited maturities and currencies available, however, FRAs are not widely used outside the largest industrial economies and currencies.

Interest Rate Swaps

Swaps are contractual agreements to exchange or swap a series of cash flows. These cash flows are most commonly the interest payments associated with debt service, such as the floating-rate loan described in the previous section. The following three key concepts clarify the differences between swap agreements:

- If the agreement is for one party to swap its fixed interest rate payment for the floating interest rate payments of another, it is termed an *interest rate swap*.
- If the agreement is to swap currencies of debt service obligation—for example, Swiss franc interest payments in exchange for U.S. dollar interest payments—it is termed a *currency swap*.
- A single swap may combine elements of both interest rate and currency swaps.

In all cases, the swap serves to alter the firm's cash flow obligations, as in changing floating-rate payments into fixed-rate payments associated with an existing debt obligation. The swap itself is not a source of capital, but rather an alteration of the cash flows associated with payment. What is often termed the "plain vanilla swap" is an agreement between two parties to exchange fixed-rate for floating-rate financial obligations. This type of swap forms the largest single financial derivative market in the world.

The two parties may have various motivations for entering into the agreement. For example, a very common position is as follows: A corporate borrower of good credit standing has existing floating-rate debt service payments. The borrower, after reviewing current market conditions and forming expectations about the future, may conclude that interest rates are about to rise. In order to protect the firm against rising debt-service payments, the company's treasury may enter into a swap agreement to pay fixed/receive floating. This means the firm will now make fixed interest rate payments and receive from the swap counterparty floating interest rate payments. The floating-rate payments that the firm receives are used to service the debt obligation of the firm, so the firm, on a net basis, is now making fixed interest rate payments. Using derivatives it has synthetically changed floating-rate debt into fixed-rate debt. It has done so without going through the costs and intricacies of refinancing existing debt obligations.

Similarly, a firm with fixed-rate debt that expects interest rates to fall can change fixed-rate debt to floating-rate debt. In this case, the firm would enter into a plain vanilla interest rate swap to pay floating and receive fixed. Exhibit 7.12 presents a summary table of the recommended interest rate swap strategies for firms holding either fixed-rate debt or floating-rate debt.

The cash flows of an interest rate swap are interest rates applied to a set amount of capital (*notional principal*). For this reason, they are also referred to as coupon swaps. Firms entering into interest rate swaps set the notional principal so that the cash flows resulting from the interest rate swap cover their interest rate management needs.

EXHIBIT 7.12	Interest Rate Swap Strategies	
Position	**Interest Rate Expectation**	**Swap Strategy**
Fixed Rate Debt	Rates to go up	Do nothing
	Rates to go down	Pay floating and Receive fixed
Floating Rate Debt	Rates to go up	Pay fixed and Receive floating
	Rates to go down	Do nothing

Interest rate swaps are contractual commitments between a firm and a swap dealer and are completely independent of the interest rate exposure of the firm. That is, the firm may enter into a swap for any reason it sees fit and then swap a notional principal that is less than, equal to, or even greater than the total position being managed. For example, a firm with a variety of floating-rate loans on its books may, if it wishes, enter into interest rate swaps for only 70% of the existing principal. The reason for entering into a swap and the swap position the firm enters into, is purely at management's discretion. It should also be noted that the interest rate swap market is filling a gap in market efficiency. If all firms had free and equal access to capital markets, regardless of interest rate structure or currency of denomination, the swap market would most likely not exist. The fact that the swap market not only exists but also flourishes and provides benefits to all parties is in some ways the proverbial "free lunch."

Currency Swaps

Since all swap rates are derived from the yield curve in each major currency, the fixed-to-floating-rate interest rate swap existing in each currency allows firms to swap across currencies. Exhibit 7.13 lists typical swap rates for the euro, the U.S. dollar, the Japanese yen, and the Swiss franc. These swap rates are based on the government security yields in each of the individual currency markets, plus a credit spread applicable to investment grade borrowers in the respective markets.

Note that the swap rates in Exhibit 7.13 are not rated or categorized by credit ratings. This is because the swap market itself does not carry the credit risk associated with individual borrowers. Individual borrowers with obligations priced at LIBOR plus a spread will keep the spread. The fixed spread, a credit risk premium, is still borne by the firm itself. For example, lower-rated firms may pay spreads of 3% or 4% over LIBOR, while some of the world's largest and most financially sound MNEs may actually raise capital at LIBOR rates. The swap market does not differentiate the rate by the participant; all swap at fixed rates versus LIBOR in the respective currency.

The usual motivation for a currency swap is to replace cash flows scheduled in an undesired currency with flows in a desired currency. The desired currency is probably the currency in which the firm's future operating revenues will be generated. Firms often raise capital in currencies in which they do not possess significant revenues or other natural cash flows. The reason they do so is cost; specific firms may find capital costs in specific currencies attractively priced to them under special conditions. Having raised the capital, however, the firm may wish to swap its repayment into a currency in which it has future operating revenues.

The utility of the currency swap market to an MNE is significant. An MNE wishing to swap a 10-year fixed 6.04% U.S. dollar cash flow stream could swap to 4.46% fixed in euros, 3.30% fixed in Swiss francs, or 2.07% fixed in Japanese yen. It could swap from fixed dollars not only to fixed rates, but also to floating LIBOR rates in the various currencies as well. All are possible at the rates quoted in Exhibit 7.13.

| EXHIBIT 7.13 | Interest Rate and Currency Swap Quotes | | | | | | | |

	Euro €		Swiss Franc		U.S. Dollar		Japanese Yen	
Years	Bid	Ask	Bid	Ask	Bid	Ask	Bid	Ask
1	2.99	3.02	1.43	1.47	5.24	5.26	0.23	0.26
2	3.08	3.12	1.68	1.76	5.43	5.46	0.36	0.39
3	3.24	3.28	1.93	2.01	5.56	5.59	0.56	0.59
4	3.44	3.48	2.15	2.23	5.65	5.68	0.82	0.85
5	3.63	3.67	2.35	2.43	5.73	5.76	1.09	1.12
6	3.83	3.87	2.54	2.62	5.80	5.83	1.33	1.36
7	4.01	4.05	2.73	2.81	5.86	5.89	1.55	1.58
8	4.18	4.22	2.91	2.99	5.92	5.95	1.75	1.78
9	4.32	4.36	3.08	3.16	5.96	5.99	1.90	1.93
10	4.42	4.46	3.22	3.30	6.01	6.04	2.04	2.07
12	4.58	4.62	3.45	3.55	6.10	6.13	2.28	2.32
15	4.78	4.82	3.71	3.81	6.20	6.23	2.51	2.56
20	5.00	5.04	3.96	4.06	6.29	6.32	2.71	2.76
25	5.13	5.17	4.07	4.17	6.29	6.32	2.77	2.82
30	5.19	5.23	4.16	4.26	6.28	6.31	2.82	2.88
LIBOR	3.0313	3.0938	1.3125	1.4375	4.9375	5.0625	0.1250	0.2188

Typical presentation by the *Financial Times*. Bid and ask spreads as of close of London business. US$ is quoted against 3-month LIBOR; Japanese yen against 6-month LIBOR; Euro and Swiss franc against 6-month LIBOR.

Prudence in Practice

In the following chapters we will illustrate how derivatives can be used to reduce the risks associated with the conduct of multinational financial management. It is critical, however, that the user of any financial tool or technique—including financial derivatives—follow sound principles and practices. Many a firm has been ruined as a result of the misuse of derivatives. A word to the wise: Do not fall victim to what many refer to as the gambler's dilemma—confusing luck with talent.

Major corporate financial disasters related to financial derivatives continue to be a problem in global business. As is the case with so many issues in modern society, technology is not at fault, rather human error in its use.

Summary Points

- Foreign currency futures contracts are standardized forward contracts. Unlike forward contracts, however, trading occurs on the floor of an organized exchange rather than between banks and customers. Futures also require collateral and are normally settled through the purchase of an offsetting position.

- Corporate financial managers typically prefer foreign currency forwards over futures out of simplicity of use and position maintenance. Financial speculators typically prefer foreign currency futures over forwards because of the liquidity of the futures markets.

- Foreign currency options are financial contracts that give the holder the right, but not the obligation, to buy (in the case of calls) or sell (in the case of puts) a specified amount of foreign exchange at a predetermined price on or before a specified maturity date.

- The use of a currency option as a speculative device for the buyer of an option arises from the fact that an option gains in value as the underlying currency rises (for calls) or falls (for puts). The amount of loss when the underlying currency moves opposite to the desired direction is limited to the option premium.

- The use of a currency option as a speculative device for the writer (seller) of an option arises from the option premium. If the option—either a put or call—expires out-of-the-money (valueless), the writer of the option has earned, and retains, the entire premium.

- Speculation is an attempt to profit by trading on expectations about prices in the future. In the foreign exchange market, one speculates by taking a position in a foreign currency and then closing that position afterwards; a profit results only if the rate moves in the direction that the speculator expected.

- Currency option valuation, the determination of the option's premium, is a complex combination of the current spot rate, the specific strike rate, the forward rate (which itself is dependent on the current spot rate and interest differentials), currency volatility, and time to maturity.

- The total value of an option is the sum of its intrinsic value and time value. Intrinsic value depends on the relationship between the option's strike price and the current spot rate at any single point in time, whereas time value estimates how intrinsic value may change—for the better—prior to maturity.

- The single largest interest rate risk of the nonfinancial firm is debt-service. The debt structure of the MNE will possess differing maturities of debt, different interest rate structures (such as fixed versus floating-rate), and different currencies of denomination.

- The increasing volatility of world interest rates, combined with the increasing use of short-term and variable-rate debt by firms worldwide, has led many firms to actively manage their interest rate risks.

- The primary sources of interest rate risk to a multinational nonfinancial firm are short-term borrowing, short-term investing, and long-term debt service.

- The techniques and instruments used in interest rate risk management in many ways resemble those used in currency risk management. The primary instruments used for interest rate risk management include forward rate agreements (FRAs), forward swaps, interest rate futures, and interest rate swaps.

- The interest rate and currency swap markets allow firms that have limited access to specific currencies and interest rate structures to gain access at relatively low costs. This in turn allows these firms to manage their currency and interest rate risks more effectively.

- A cross-currency interest rate swap allows a firm to alter both the currency of denomination of cash flows in debt service and the fixed-to-floating or floating-to-fixed interest rate structure.

MINI-CASE

McDonald's Corporation's British Pound Exposure

McDonald's Corporation has investments in more than 100 countries. It considers its equity investment in foreign affiliates capital that is at risk, subject to hedging depending on the individual country, currency, and market.

British Subsidiary as an Exposure
McDonald's parent company has three different pound-denominated exposures arising from its ownership and operation of its British subsidiary.

1. The British subsidiary has equity capital, which is a pound-denominated asset of the parent company.

2. In addition to the equity capital invested in the British affiliate, the parent company provides intracompany debt in the form of a four-year £125 million loan. The loan is denominated in British pounds and carries a fixed 5.30% per annum interest payment.

3. The British subsidiary pays a fixed percentage of gross sales in royalties to the parent company. This too is pound-denominated.

These three different exposures sum to a significant exposure problem for McDonald's.

An additional technical detail further complicates the situation. When the parent company makes an intracompany loan to the British subsidiary, it must designate—according to U.S. accounting and tax law practices—whether the loan is considered to be permanently invested in that country. (Although on the surface it seems illogical to consider four years "permanent," the loan itself could simply be continually rolled over by the parent company and never actually be repaid.) If not considered permanent, the foreign exchange gains and losses related to the loan flow directly to the parent company's profit and loss statement (P&L), according to FAS #52. If, however, the loan is designated as permanent, the foreign exchange gains and losses related to the intracompany loan would flow only to the CTA (cumulative translation adjustment) on the consolidated balance sheet. To date, McDonald's has chosen to designate the loan as permanent. The functional currency of the British affiliate for consolidation purposes is the local currency, the British pound.

Anka Gopi is both the Manager for Financial Markets/Treasury and a McDonald's shareholder. She is currently reviewing the existing hedging strategy employed by McDonald's against the pound exposure. The company has been hedging the pound exposure by entering into a cross-currency U.S. dollar/British pound sterling swap. The current swap is a seven-year swap to receive dollars and pay pounds. Like all cross-currency swaps, the agreement requires

McDonald's (U.S.) to make regular pound-denominated interest payments and a bullet principal repayment (notional principal) at the end of the swap agreement. McDonald's considers the large notional principal payment a hedge against the equity investment in its British affiliate.

According to accounting practice, a company may elect to take the interest associated with a foreign currency-denominated loan and carry that directly to the parent company's P&L. This has been done in the past, and McDonald's has benefited from the inclusion of this interest payment.

FAS #133, Accounting for Derivative Instruments and Hedging Activities, issued in June 1998, was originally intended to be effective for all fiscal quarters within fiscal years beginning after June 15, 1999 (for most firms this meant January 1, 2000). The new standard, however, was so complex and potentially of such material influence to U.S.-based MNEs, that the Financial Accounting Standards Board has been approached by dozens of major firms and asked to postpone mandatory implementation. The standard's complexity, combined with the workloads associated with Y2K (year 2000) risk controls, persuaded the Financial Accounting Standards Board to delay FAS #133's mandatory implementation date indefinitely.

Issues for Discussion
Anka Gopi, however, still wishes to consider the impact of FAS #133 on the hedging strategy currently employed.

Under FAS #133, the firm will have to mark-to-market the entire cross-currency swap position, including principal, and carry this to other comprehensive income (OCI). OCI, however, is actually a form of income required under U.S. GAAP and reported in the footnotes to the financial statements, but not the income measure used in reported earnings per share. Although McDonald's has been carrying the interest payments on the swap to income, it has not previously had to carry the present value of the swap principal to OCI. In Anka Gopi's eyes, this poses a substantial material risk to OCI.

Anka Gopi also wishes to reconsider the current strategy. She begins by listing the pros and cons of the current strategy, comparing these to alternative strategies, and then deciding what if anything should be done about it at this time.

CASE QUESTIONS

1. How does the cross-currency swap effectively hedge the three primary exposures McDonald's has relative to its British subsidiary?

2. How does the cross-currency swap hedge the long-term equity position in the foreign subsidiary?

3. Should Anka—and McDonald's—worry about OCI?

Questions

1. **Options versus Futures.** Explain the difference between foreign currency options and futures and when either might be most appropriately used.

2. **Trading Location for Futures.** Check the *Wall Street Journal* to find where in the United States foreign exchange future contracts are traded.

3. **Futures Terminology.** Explain the meaning and probable significance for international business of the following contract specifications:
   a. notional principal
   b. margin
   c. marked to market

4. **A Futures Trade.** A newspaper shows the prices below for the previous day's trading in U.S. dollar-euro currency futures. What do the terms shown indicate?

Month:	December
Open:	0.9124
Settlement:	0.9136
Change:	+0.0027
High:	0.9147
Low:	0.9098
Estimated volume	29,763
Open interest:	111,360
Contract size:	€125,000

5. **Hedging with Futures.** What are the disadvantages of using futures contracts to hedge a firm's exposure?

6. **Put Contract Elements.** The CME exchange-traded American put option has a contract size of €125,000; the December puts with a strike price of 1.2900 are now quoted at 0.0297. Explain what these figures mean for a put buyer.

7. **The Option Cost.** Assuming that you have the same information as in Question 6, what premium does a buyer pay for the December put option? What happens to this premium?

8. **Exercising Option.** You have the same information as in Question 6. Will an owner of the American December put exercise the option if the spot rate is $1.3501/€? What is the gain in this case?

9. **Writing Options.** Why would anyone write an option, knowing that the gain from receiving the option premium is fixed but the loss if the underlying price goes in the wrong direction can be extremely large?

10. **Option Valuation.** The value of an option is stated to be the sum of its intrinsic value and its time value. Explain what is meant by these terms.

11. **Credit and Repricing Risk.** From the point of view of a borrowing corporation, what are credit and repricing risks? Explain steps a company might take to minimize both.

12. **Forward Rate Agreement.** How can a business firm that has borrowed on a floating rate basis use a forward rate agreement to reduce interest rate risk?

13. **Eurodollar Futures.** A newspaper reports that a given June eurodollar futures settled at 93.55. What was the annual yield? How many dollars does this represent?

14. **Defaulting on an Interest Rate Swap.** Smith Company and Jones Company enter into an interest rate swap, with Smith paying fixed interest to Jones, and Jones paying floating interest to Smith. Smith now goes bankrupt and so defaults on its remaining interest payments. What is the financial damage to Jones Company?

15. **Currency Swaps.** Why would one company, with interest payments due in pounds sterling, want to swap those payments for interest payments due in U.S. dollars?

16. **Counterparty Risk.** How does exchange trading in swaps remove any risk that the counterparty in a swap agreement will not complete the agreement?

Problems

1. **Amber McClain.** Amber McClain, the currency speculator we met in the chapter, sells eight June futures contracts for 500,000 pesos at the closing price quoted in Exhibit 7.1.
   a. What is the value of her position at maturity if the ending spot rate is $0.12000/Ps?
   b. What is the value of her position at maturity if the ending spot rate is $0.09800/Ps?
   c. What is the value of her position at maturity if the ending spot rate is $0.11000/Ps?

2. **Peleh's Puts.** Peleh writes a put option on the Australian dollar (A$) with a strike price of $0.9100/A$ at a premium of $0.0245/A$ and with an expiration date six months from now. The option is for A$100,000. What is Peleh's profit or loss at maturity if the ending spot rates are $0.8500/A$, $0.8800/A$, $0.9100/A$, $0.9400/A$, and $0.9700/A$?

3. **Ventosa Investments.** Jamie Rodriguez, a currency trader for Chicago-based Ventosa Investments, uses the following futures quotes on the British pound (£) to speculate on the value of the pound.

   a. If Jamie buys 5 June pound futures, and the spot rate at maturity is $1.3980/£, what is the value of her position?
   b. If Jamie sells 12 March pound futures, and the spot rate at maturity is $1.4560/£, what is the value of her position?
   c. If Jamie buys 3 March pound futures, and the spot rate at maturity is $1.4560/£, what is the value of her position?
   d. If Jamie sells 12 June pound futures, and the spot rate at maturity is $1.3980/£, what is the value of her position?

4. **Sallie Schnudel.** Sallie Schnudel trades currencies for Keystone Funds in Jakarta. She focuses nearly all of her time and attention on the U.S. dollar/Singapore dollar ($/S$) cross-rate. The current spot rate is $0.6000/S$. After considerable study, she has concluded that the Singapore dollar will appreciate versus the U.S. dollar in the coming 90 days, probably to about $0.7000/S$. She has the following options on the Singapore dollar to choose from:

Option	Strike Price	Premium
Put on Sing $	$0.6500/S$	$0.00003/S$
Call on Sing $	$0.6500/S$	$0.00046/S$

   a. Should Sallie buy a put on Singapore dollars or a call on Singapore dollars?
   b. What is Sallie's break-even price on the option purchased in part (a)?
   c. Using your answer from part (a), what is Sallie's gross profit and net profit (including premium) if the spot rate at the end of 90 days is indeed $0.7000/S$?
   d. Using your answer from part (a), what is Sallie's gross profit and net profit (including premium) if the spot rate at the end of 90 days is $0.8000/S$?

5. **Blade Capital (A).** Christoph Hoffeman trades currency for Blade Capital of Geneva. Christoph has $10 million to begin with, and he must state all profits at the end of any speculation in U.S. dollars. The spot rate on the euro is $1.3358/€, while the 30-day forward rate is $1.3350/€.
   a. If Christoph believes the euro will continue to rise in value against the U.S. dollar, so that he expects the spot rate to be $1.3600/€ at the end of 30 days, what should he do?

Problem 3.

British Pound Futures, US$/Pound (CME)						Contract = 62,500 Pounds	
Maturity	Open	High	Low	Settle	Change	High	Open Interest
March	1.4246	1.4268	1.4214	1.4228	0.0032	1.4700	25,605
June	1.4164	1.4188	1.4146	1.4162	0.0030	1.4550	809

b. If Christoph believes the euro will depreciate in value against the U.S. dollar, so that he expects the spot rate to be $1.2800/€ at the end of 30 days, what should he do?

6. **Blade Capital (B).** Christoph Hoffeman of Blade Capital now believes the Swiss franc will appreciate versus the U.S. dollar in the coming 3-month period. He has $100,000 to invest. The current spot rate is $0.5820/SF, the 3-month forward rate is $0.5640/SF, and he expects the spot rates to reach $0.6250/SF in three months.
   a. Calculate Christoph's expected profit assuming a pure spot market speculation strategy.
   b. Calculate Christoph's expected profit assuming he buys or sells SF three months forward.

7. **Chavez S.A.** Chavez S.A., a Venezuelan company, wishes to borrow $10,000,000 for 18 weeks. Potential lenders in New York, Switzerland, and London using, respectively, international, Swiss (eurobond), and British definitions of interest (day count conventions) quote rates, respectively, of 8.25%, 8.30%, and 8.35% per annum. From which source should Chavez borrow?

8. **Botany Bay Corporation.** The Botany Bay Corporation of Australia seeks to borrow US$50,000,000 in the eurodollar market. Funding is needed for two years. Investigation leads to three possibilities.
   a. Borrow the US$50,000,000 for two years at a fixed 5.50% rate of interest.
   b. Borrow the US$50,000,000 at LIBOR + 0.50%, and the rate would be reset every six months.
   c. Borrow the US$50,000,000 for one year only at 5.25%. At the end of the first year, Botany Bay Corporation would have to negotiate for a new 1-year loan.
   Compare the alternatives and make a recommendation. Assume that LIBOR is currently 5.00% for all maturities.

9. **Vatic Capital.** Cachita Haynes works as a currency speculator for Vatic Capital of Los Angeles. Her latest speculative position is to profit from her expectation that the U.S. dollar will rise significantly against the Japanese yen. The current spot rate is ¥120.00/$. She must choose between the following 90-day options on the Japanese yen:

Option	Strike Price	Premium
Put on yen	¥125/$	$0.00003/S$
Call on yen	¥125/$	$0.00046/S$

   a. Should Cachita buy a put on yen or a call on yen?
   b. What is Cachita's break-even price on the option purchased in part (a)?
   c. Using your answer from part (a), what is Cachita's gross profit and net profit (including premium) if the spot rate at the end of 90 days is ¥140/$?

10. **Calling All Profits.** Consider an American call option on New Zealand dollars (NZ$) with a strike price of $0.8100/NZ$ traded at a premium of $0.0192 per NZ$ and with an expiration date three months from now. The option is for NZ$100,000.
   a. Suppose that you have bought such a call option. Plot your profit or loss on a graph should you exercise before maturity at a time when the NZ$ is traded spot at between $0.7000/NZ$ and $0.9200/NZ$. Find the break-even exchange rate.
   b. Repeat (a) if you have sold such a call option.

11. **Mystery at Baker Street.** Arthur Doyle is a currency trader for Baker Street, a private investment house in London. Baker Street's clients are a collection of wealthy private investors who, with a minimum stake of £250,000 each, wish to speculate on the movement of currencies. The investors expect annual returns in excess of 25%. Although officed in London, all accounts and expectations are based in U.S. dollars.

Arthur is convinced that the British pound will slide significantly—possibly to $1.3200/£—in the coming 30 to 60 days. The current spot rate is $1.4260/£. Arthur wishes to buy a put on pounds, which will yield the 25% return expected by his investors. Which of the following put options would you recommend he purchase? Prove your choice is the preferable combination of strike price, maturity, and up-front premium expense.

Strike Price	Maturity	Premium
$1.36/£	30 days	$0.00081/£
$1.34/£	30 days	$0.00021/£
$1.32/£	30 days	$0.00004/£
$1.36/£	60 days	$0.00333/£
$1.34/£	60 days	$0.00150/£
$1.32/£	60 days	$0.00060/£

12. **Contrarious Calandra.** Calandra Panagakos works for CIBC Currency Funds in Toronto. Calandra is something of a contrarian—as opposed to most of the forecasts, she believes the Canadian dollar (C$) will appreciate versus the U.S. dollar over the coming 90 days. The current spot rate is $0.6750/C$. Calandra may choose between the following options on the Canadian dollar.

Option	Strike Price	Premium
Put on C$	$0.7000	$0.00003/S$
Call on C$	$0.7000	$0.00049/S$

a. Should Calandra buy a put on Canadian dollars or a call on Canadian dollars?

b. What is Calandra's break-even price on the option purchased in part (a)?

c. Using your answer from part (a), what is Calandra's gross profit and net profit (including premium) if the spot rate at the end of 90 days is indeed $0.7600?

d. Using your answer from part (a), what is Calandra's gross profit and net profit (including premium) if the spot rate at the end of 90 days is $0.8250?

13. **Raid Gauloises.** Raid Gauloises is a rapidly growing French sporting goods and adventure racing outfitter. The company has decided to borrow €20,000,000 via a euro-euro floating rate loan for four years. Raid must decide between two competing loan offers from two of its banks.

Banque de Paris has offered the 4-year debt with an up-front initiation fee of 1.8%. Banque de Sorbonne, however, has offered a higher spread, but with no loan initiation fees up front, for the same term and principal. Both banks reset the interest rate at the end of each year.

Euro-LIBOR is currently 4.00%. Raid's economist forecasts that LIBOR will rise by 0.5 percentage points each year. Banque de Sorbonne, however, officially forecasts euro-LIBOR to begin trending upward at the rate of 0.25 percentage points per year. Raid Gauloises' cost of capital is 11%. Which loan proposal do you recommend for Raid Gauloises?

14. **Schifano Motors.** Schifano Motors of Italy recently took out a 4-year €5 million loan on a floating rate basis. It is now worried, however, about rising interest costs. Although it had initially believed interest rates in the eurozone would be trending downward when taking out the loan, recent economic indicators show growing inflationary pressures. Analysts are predicting that the European Central Bank will slow monetary growth driving interest rates up.

Schifano is now considering whether to seek some protection against a rise in euro-LIBOR, and is considering a forward rate agreement (FRA) with an insurance company. According to the agreement, Schifano would pay to the insurance company at the end of each year the difference between its initial interest cost at (6.50%) and any fall in interest cost due to a fall in LIBOR. Conversely, the insurance company would pay to Schifano 70% of the difference between Schifano's initial interest cost and any increase in interest costs caused by a rise in LIBOR.

Purchase of the floating rate agreement will cost €100,000, paid at the time of the initial loan. What are Schifano's annual financing costs now if LIBOR rises and if LIBOR falls? Schifano uses 12% as its weighted

average cost of capital. Do you recommend that Schifano purchase the FRA?

15. **Chrysler LLC.** Chrysler LLC, the now privately held company sold by DaimlerChrysler, must pay a floating rate interest three months from now. It wants to lock in these interest payments using interest rate futures contracts. Interest rate futures for three months from now settled at 96.77, for a yield of 3.23% per annum.

a. Should Chrysler buy or sell the interest rate futures contract?

b. If the floating interest rate three months from now is either 3.00% or 3.50%, what did Daimler-Chrysler gain or lose in each case?

16. **CB Solutions.** Heather O'Reilly, the treasurer of CB Solutions, believes interest rates are going to rise, so she wants to swap her future floating rate interest payments for fixed rates. Presently, she is paying per annum on $5,000,000 of debt for the next two years, with payments due semiannually. LIBOR is currently 4.00% per annum. Heather has just made an interest payment today, so the next payment is due six months from today.

Heather finds that she can swap her current floating rate payments for fixed payments of 7.00% per annum. (CB Solution's weighted average cost of capital is 12%, which Heather calculates to be 6% per 6-month period, compounded semiannually).

a. If LIBOR rises at the rate of 50 basis points per 6-month period, starting tomorrow, how much does Heather save or cost her company by making this swap?

b. If LIBOR falls at the rate of 25 basis points per 6-month period, starting tomorrow, how much does Heather save or cost her company by making this swap?

17. **Lluvia and Paraguas.** Lluvia Manufacturing and Paraguas Products both seek funding at the lowest possible cost. Lluvia would prefer the flexibility of floating rate borrowing, while Paraguas wants the security of fixed rate borrowing. Lluvia is the more creditworthy company. They face the following rate structure. Lluvia, with the better credit rating, has lower borrowing costs in both types of borrowing.

Lluvia wants floating rate debt, so it could borrow at LIBOR + 1%. However, it could borrow fixed at 8% and swap for floating rate debt. Paraguas wants fixed rate debt, so it could borrow fixed at 12%. However, it could borrow floating at LIBOR + 2% and swap for fixed rate debt. What should they do?

18. **Trident's Cross-Currency Swap: SFr for US$.** Trident Corporation entered into a 3-year cross-currency interest rate swap to receive U.S. dollars and pay Swiss francs. Trident, however, decided to unwind the swap after one year—thereby having two years left on the

settlement costs of unwinding the swap after one year. Repeat the calculations for unwinding, but assume that the rates shown below now apply.

Assumptions	Values
Notional principal	$ 10,000,000
Spot exchange rate, SFr/$	1.5000
Spot exchange rate, $/euro	1.1200

Swap Rates	3-Year Bid	3-Year Ask
U.S. dollar	5.56%	5.59%
Swiss franc-SFr	1.93%	2.01%

19. **Trident's Cross-Currency Swap: Yen for Euros.** Use the table of swap rates in the chapter (Exhibit 7.13), and assume Trident enters into a swap agreement to receive euros and pay Japanese yen, on a notional principal of €5,000,000. The spot exchange rate at the time of the swap is ¥104/€.
   a. Calculate all principal and interest payments, in both euros and Swiss francs, for the life of the swap agreement.
   b. Assume that one year into the swap agreement Trident decides it wants to unwind the swap agreement and settle it in euros. Assuming that a 2-year fixed rate of interest on the Japanese yen is now 0.80%, and a 2-year fixed rate of interest on the euro is now 3.60%, and the spot rate of exchange is now ¥114/€, what is the net present value of the swap agreement? Who pays whom what?

20. **Falcor.** Falcor is the U.S.-based automotive parts supplier that was spun-off from General Motors in 2000. With annual sales of over $26 billion, the company has expanded its markets far beyond traditional automobile manufacturers in the pursuit of a more diversified sales base. As part of the general diversification effort, the company wishes to diversify the currency of denomination of its debt portfolio as well. Assume Falcor enters into a $50 million 7-year cross-currency interest rate swap to do just that—pay euros and receive dollars. Using the data in Exhibit 7.13,
   a. Calculate all principal and interest payments in both currencies for the life of the swap.
   b. Assume that three years later Falcor decides to unwind the swap agreement. If 4-year fixed rates of interest in euros have now risen to 5.35%, 4-year fixed rate dollars have fallen to 4.40%, and the current spot exchange rate is $1.02/€, what is the net present value of the swap agreement? Explain the payment obligations of the two parties precisely.

Pricing Your Own Options

An Excel workbook entitled FX Option Pricing is downloadable from this book's Web site. The workbook has five spreadsheets constructed for pricing currency options for the following five currency pairs (dollar/euro shown here): U.S. dollar/euro, U.S. dollar/Japanese yen, euro/Japanese yen, U.S. dollar/British pound, and euro/British pound. Use the appropriate spreadsheet from the workbook to answer Problems 21–25.

Pricing Currency Options on the Euro

	A U.S.-based firm wishing to buy or sell euros (the foreign currency)		A European firm wishing to buy or sell dollars (the foreign currency)	
	Variable	Value	Variable	Value
Spot rate (domestic/foreign)	S_0	$1.2480	S_0	€0.8013
Strike rate (domestic/foreign)	X	$1.2500	X	€0.8000
Domestic interest rate (% p.a.)	r_d	1.453%	r_d	2.187%
Foreign interest rate (% p.a.)	r_f	2.187%	r_f	1.453%
Time (years, 365 days)	T	1.000	T	1.000
Days equivalent		365.00		365.00
Volatility (% p.a.)	s	10.500%	s	10.500%
Call option premium (per unit fc)	c	$0.0461	c	€0.0366
Put option premium (per unit fc)	p	$0.0570	p	€0.0295
(European pricing)				
Call option premium (%)	c	3.69%	c	4.56%
Put option premium (%)	p	4.57%	p	3.68%

21. U.S. Dollar/Euro. The table above indicates that a 1-year call option on euros at a strike rate of $1.25/€ will cost the buyer $0.0632/€, or 4.99%. But that assumed a volatility of 12.000% when the spot rate was $1.2674/€. What would that same call option cost if the volatility was reduced to 10.500% when the spot rate fell to $1.2480/€?

22. U.S. Dollar/Japanese Yen. What would be the premium expense, in home currency, for a Japanese firm to purchase an option to sell 750,000 U.S. dollars, assuming the initial values listed in the FX Option Pricing workbook?

23. Euro/Japanese Yen. A French firm is expecting to receive JPY 10.4 million in 90 days as a result of an export sale to a Japanese semiconductor firm. What will it cost, in total, to purchase an option to sell the yen at €0.0072/JPY?

24. U.S. Dollar/British Pound. Assuming the same initial values for the dollar/pound cross rate in the FX Option Pricing workbook, how much more would a call option on pounds be if the maturity was doubled from 90 to 180 days? What percentage increase is this for twice the length of maturity?

25. Euro/British Pound. How would the call option premium change on the right to buy pounds with euros if the euro interest rate changed to 4.000% from the initial values listed in the FX Option Pricing workbook?

Internet Exercises

1. Financial Derivatives and the ISDA. The International Swaps and Derivatives Association (ISDA) publishes a wealth of information about financial derivatives, their valuation and their use, in addition to providing master documents for their contractual use between parties. Use the following ISDA Internet site to find the definitions to 31 basic financial derivative questions and terms:

ISDA   www.isda.org/educat/faqs.html

2. Risk Management of Financial Derivatives. If you think this book is long, take a look at the freely downloadable U.S. Comptroller of the Currency's handbook on risk management related to the care and use of financial derivatives!

Comptroller of the Currency   www.occ.gov/publications/publications-by-type/comptrollers-handbook/deriv.pdf

3. Option Pricing. OzForex Foreign Exchange Services is a private firm with an enormously powerful foreign currency derivative-enabled Web site. Use the following site to evaluate the various "Greeks" related to currency option pricing.

OzForex   www.ozforex.com.au/forex-tools/tools/fx-options-calculator

4. Garman-Kohlhagen Option Formulation. For those brave of heart and quantitatively adept, check out the following Internet site's detailed presentation of the Garman-Kohlhagen option formulation used widely in business and finance today.

Riskglossary.com   www.riskglossary.com/link/garman_kohlhagen_1983.htm

5. Chicago Mercantile Exchange. The Chicago Mercantile Exchange trades futures and options on a variety of currencies, including the Brazilian real. Use the following site to evaluate the uses of these currency derivatives:

Chicago Mercantile Exchange   www.cmegroup.com/trading/fx/

6. Implied Currency Volatilities. The single unobservable variable in currency option pricing is the volatility, since volatility inputs are the expected standard deviation of the daily spot rate for the coming period of the option's maturity. Use the New York Federal Reserve's Web site to obtain current implied currency volatilities for major trading cross-rate pairs.

Federal Reserve Bank of New York   www.ny.frb.org/markets/impliedvolatility.html

7. Montreal Exchange. The Montreal Exchange is a Canadian exchange devoted to the support of financial derivatives in Canada. Use its Web site to view the latest on MV volatility—the volatility of the Montreal Exchange Index itself—in recent trading hours and days.

Montreal Exchange   www.m-x.ca/marc_options_en.php

Foreign Exchange Rate Determination

The herd instinct among forecasters makes sheep look like independent thinkers. —Edgar R. Fiedler.

LEARNING OBJECTIVES

- Examine how the supply and demand for any currency can be viewed as an asset choice issue within the portfolio of investors

- Explore how the three major approaches to exchange rate determination—parity conditions, the balance of payments, and the asset approach—combine to explain, in part, numerous emerging market currency crises

- Detail how direct and indirect foreign exchange market intervention is conducted by central banks

- Observe how forecasters combine technical analysis with the three major theoretical approaches to forecasting exchange rates

What determines the exchange rate between currencies? This has proven to be a very difficult question to answer. Companies and agents need foreign currency for buying imports, or they may earn foreign currency by exporting. Investors need foreign currency to invest in interest-bearing instruments in foreign countries and currencies, fixed-income securities like bonds, shares in publicly traded companies, or other new types of hybrid instruments in foreign markets. Tourists, migrant workers, speculators on currency movements—all of these economic agents buy and sell and supply and demand currencies every day. This chapter offers a basic theoretical framework with which to organize these elements, forces, and principles.

Chapter 6 described the international parity conditions that integrate exchange rates with inflation and interest rates and provided a theoretical framework for both the global financial markets and the management of international financial business. Chapter 3 provided a detailed analysis of how an individual country's international economic activity, its balance of payments, can impact exchange rates. This chapter builds on those discussions of exchange rate determination schools of thought and looks at a third school of thought—the asset market approach. The chapter then turns to government intervention in the foreign exchange market. In the third and final section, we discuss a number of approaches to foreign exchange forecasting in practice. The chapter concludes with the Mini-Case entitled *The Japanese Yen Intervention of 2010*—a study in how the Japanese government has repeatedly tried to intervene in the foreign exchange market.

Exhibit 8.1 provides an overview of the many determinants of exchange rates. This roadmap is first organized by the three major schools of thought (parity conditions, balance of payments approach, asset market approach) and second by the individual drivers within those approaches. At first glance, the idea that there are three theories may appear daunting, but it is important to remember that these are not competing theories, but rather complementary theories. Without the depth and breadth of the various approaches combined, our ability to capture the complexity of the global market for currencies is lost.

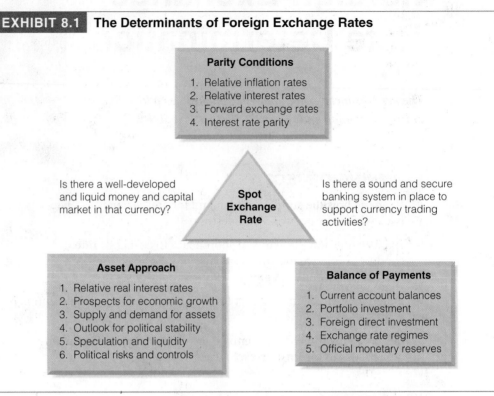

EXHIBIT 8.1 The Determinants of Foreign Exchange Rates

Parity Conditions

1. Relative inflation rates
2. Relative interest rates
3. Forward exchange rates
4. Interest rate parity

Is there a well-developed and liquid money and capital market in that currency?

Spot Exchange Rate

Is there a sound and secure banking system in place to support currency trading activities?

Asset Approach

1. Relative real interest rates
2. Prospects for economic growth
3. Supply and demand for assets
4. Outlook for political stability
5. Speculation and liquidity
6. Political risks and controls

Balance of Payments

1. Current account balances
2. Portfolio investment
3. Foreign direct investment
4. Exchange rate regimes
5. Official monetary reserves

Finally, note that most determinants of the spot exchange rate are also affected by changes in the spot rate. In other words, they are not only linked but also mutually determined.

Exchange Rate Determination: The Theoretical Thread

> *There are basically three views of the exchange rate. The first takes the exchange rate as the relative price of monies (the monetary approach); the second, as the relative price of goods (the purchasing-power-parity approach); and the third, the relative price of bonds.*
>
> —Rudiger Dornbusch, "Exchange Rate Economics: Where Do We Stand?,"
> *Brookings Papers on Economic Activity* 1, 1980, pp. 143–194.

Professor Dornbusch's tripartite categorization of exchange rate theory is a good starting point, but in some ways not robust enough—in our humble opinion—to capture the multitude of theories and approaches. So, in the spirit of both tradition and completeness, we have amended Dornbusch's three categories with several additional streams of thought in the following discussion. The next section will provide a brief overview of the many different, but related, theories of exchange rate determination, and their relative usefulness in forecasting for business purposes.

Purchasing Power Parity Approaches

> *Under the skin of an international economist lies a deep-seated belief in some variant of the PPP theory of the exchange rate.*
>
> —Paul Krugman, 1976.

The most widely accepted of all exchange rate determination theories, the theory of purchasing power parity (PPP) states that the long-run equilibrium exchange rate is determined by the ratio of domestic prices relative to foreign prices, as explained in Chapter 6. PPP is both the oldest and most widely followed of the exchange rate theories, and most theories of exchange rate determination have PPP elements embedded within their frameworks.

There are a number of different versions of PPP: the Law of One Price, Absolute Purchasing Power Parity, and Relative Purchasing Power Parity (discussed in detail in Chapter 6). The latter of the three theories, Relative Purchasing Power Parity, is thought to be the most relevant to possibly explaining what drives exchange rate values. In essence, it states that changes in relative prices between countries drive the change in exchange rates over time.

If, for example, the current spot exchange rate between the Japanese yen and U.S. dollar was ¥90.00 = $1.00, and Japanese and U.S. prices were to change at 2% and 1% over the coming period, respectively, the spot exchange rate next period would be ¥90.89/$.

$$S_{t+1} = S_t \times \frac{1 + \Delta \text{ in Japanese Prices}}{1 + \Delta \text{ in U.S. Prices}} = ¥90.00/\$ \times \frac{1.02}{1.01} = ¥90.89/\$$$

Although PPP seems to possess a core element of common sense, it has proven to be quite poor at forecasting exchange rates. The problems are both theoretical and empirical. The theoretical problems lie primarily with its basic assumption that the only thing that matters is relative price changes. Yet many currency supply and demand forces are driven by other forces, including investment incentives and economic growth. The empirical issues are primarily in deciding which measures or indexes of prices to use across countries, in addition to the ability to provide a "predicted change in prices" with the chosen indexes.

Balance of Payments (Flows) Approaches

After PPP, the most frequently used theoretical approach to exchange rate determination is probably that involving the supply and demand for currencies in the foreign exchange market. These exchange rate flows reflect current account and financial account transactions recorded in a nation's balance of payments, as described in Chapter 3. The basic *balance of payments approach* argues that the equilibrium exchange rate is found when the net inflow (outflow) of foreign exchange arising from current account activities matches the net outflow (inflow) of foreign exchange arising from financial account activities.

The balance of payments approach continues to enjoy widespread appeal, as balance of payments transactions are among the most frequently captured and reported of international economic activity. Trade surpluses and deficits, current account growth in service activity, and, recently, the growth and significance of international capital flows continue to fuel this theoretical fire.

Criticisms of the balance of payments approach arise from the theory's emphasis on flows of currency and capital rather than on stocks of money or financial assets. Relative stocks of money or financial assets play no role in exchange rate determination in this theory, a weakness explored in the following discussion of monetary and asset market approaches. Curiously, while the balance of payments approach is largely dismissed by the academic community today, the practitioner public—market participants including currency traders themselves—still rely on different variations of this theory for much of their decision making.

Monetary Approaches

The *monetary approach* in its simplest form states that the exchange rate is determined by the supply and demand for national monetary stocks, as well as the expected future levels and rates of growth of monetary stocks. Other financial assets, such as bonds, are not considered relevant for exchange rate determination as both domestic and foreign bonds are viewed as perfect substitutes. It is all about money stocks.

The monetary approach focuses on changes in the supply and demand for money as the primary determinant of inflation. Changes in relative inflation rates in turn are expected to alter exchange rates through a purchasing power parity effect. The monetary approach then assumes that prices are flexible in the short run as well as the long run, so that the transmission mechanism of inflationary pressure is immediate in impact.

A weakness of monetary models of exchange rate determination is that real economic activity is relegated to a role in which it only influences exchange rates through changes in the demand for money. The monetary approach is also criticized for its omission of a number of factors that are generally agreed upon by area experts as important to exchange rate determination, including 1) the failure of PPP to hold in the short- to medium-term; 2) money demand appears to be relatively unstable over time; and 3) the level of economic activity and the money supply appear to be interdependent, not independent.

Asset Market Approach (Relative Price of Bonds)

The *asset market approach*, sometimes called the *relative price of bonds or portfolio balance approach*, argues that exchange rates are determined by the supply and demand for financial assets of a wide variety. Shifts in the supply and demand for financial assets alter exchange rates. Changes in monetary and fiscal policy alter expected returns and perceived relative risks of financial assets, which in turn alter rates.

Many of the macroeconomic theoretical developments in recent years focused on how monetary and fiscal policy changes altered the relative perceptions of return and risk to the stocks of financial assets driving exchange rate changes. The frequently cited works of Mundell-Fleming are in this genre. Theories of *currency substitution*, the ability of individual and commercial investors to alter the composition of their portfolios, follow the same basic premises of the portfolio balance and re-balance framework.

Unfortunately, for all of the good work and research over the past 50 years, the ability to forecast exchange rate values in the short term to long term is—in the words of the authors below—sorry. Although academics and practitioners alike agree that in the long run fundamental principles such as purchasing power and external balances drive currency values, none of the fundamental theories have proven to be very useful in the short- to medium-term.

> . . . *the case for macroeconomic determinants of exchange rates is in a sorry state [The] results indicate that no model based on such standard fundamentals like money supplies, real income, interest rates, inflation rates and current account balances will ever succeed in explaining or predicting a high percentage of the variation in the exchange rate, at least at short- or medium-term frequencies.*
>
> —Jeffrey A. Frankel and Andrew K. Rose, "A Survey of Empirical Research on Nominal Exchange Rates," *NBER Working Paper* No. 4865, 1994.

Technical Analysis

The forecasting inadequacies of fundamental theories has led to the growth and popularity of technical analysis, the belief that the study of past price behavior provides insights into future price movements. The primary feature of technical analysis is the assumption that exchange rates, or for that matter all market-driven prices, follow trends. And those trends may be analyzed and projected to provide insights into short-term and medium-term price movements in the future.

Most theories of technical analysis differentiate *fair value* from *market value*. *Fair value* is the true long-term value that the price will eventually retain. The *market value* is subject to a multitude of changes and behaviors arising from widespread market participant perceptions and beliefs—at the time.

The Asset Market Approach to Forecasting

The asset market approach assumes that whether foreigners are willing to hold claims in monetary form depends on an extensive set of investment considerations or drivers. These drivers, as previously depicted in Exhibit 8.1, include the following elements:

- Relative real interest rates are a major consideration for investors in foreign bonds and short-term money market instruments.

- Prospects for economic growth and profitability are an important determinant of cross-border equity investment in both securities and foreign direct investment.

- Capital market liquidity is particularly important to foreign institutional investors. Cross-border investors are not only interested in the ease of buying assets, but also in the ease of selling those assets quickly for fair market value if desired.

- A country's economic and social infrastructure is an important indicator of its ability to survive unexpected external shocks and to prosper in a rapidly changing world economic environment.

- Political safety is exceptionally important to both foreign portfolio and direct investors. The outlook for political safety is usually reflected in political risk premiums for a country's securities and for purposes of evaluating foreign direct investment in that country.

- The credibility of corporate governance practices is important to cross-border portfolio investors. A firm's poor corporate governance practices can reduce foreign investors' influence and cause subsequent loss of the firm's focus on shareholder wealth objectives.

- Contagion is defined as the spread of a crisis in one country to its neighboring countries and other countries with similar characteristics—at least in the eyes of cross-border investors. Contagion can cause an "innocent" country to experience capital flight with a resulting depreciation of its currency.

- Speculation can either cause a foreign exchange crisis or make an existing crisis worse. We will observe this effect through the three illustrative cases—the Asian crisis, Russian crisis, and Argentine crisis—discussed later in this chapter.

Foreign investors are willing to hold securities and undertake foreign direct investment in highly developed countries based primarily on relative real interest rates and the outlook for economic growth and profitability. All the other drivers described in Exhibit 8.1 are assumed to be satisfied.

For example, during the 1981–1985 period, the U.S. dollar strengthened despite growing current account deficits. This strength was due partly to relatively high real interest rates in the United States. Another factor, however, was the heavy inflow of foreign capital into the U.S. stock market and real estate, motivated by good long-run prospects for growth and profitability in the United States.

The same cycle was repeated in the United States in the period between 1990 and 2000. Despite continued worsening balances on the current account, the U.S. dollar strengthened in both nominal and real terms due to foreign capital inflow motivated by rising stock and real estate prices, a low rate of inflation, high real interest returns, and a seemingly endless "irrational exuberance" about future economic prospects. This time the "bubble" burst following the September 11, 2001, terrorist attacks on the United States. The attacks and their aftermath caused a negative reassessment of long-term growth and profitability prospects in the United States (as well as a newly formed level of political risk for the United States itself). This negative outlook was reinforced by a very sharp drop in the U.S. stock markets based on lower expected earnings. Further damage to the economy was caused by a series of revelations about failures in corporate governance by several large corporations (including overstatement of earnings, insider trading, and self-serving executives).

Loss of confidence in the U.S. economy led to a large withdrawal of foreign capital from U.S. security markets. As would be predicted by both the balance of payments and asset market approaches, the U.S. dollar depreciated. Indeed, its nominal rate depreciated by 18% between mid-January and mid-July 2002 relative to the euro alone.

The experience of the United States, as well as other highly developed countries, illustrates why some forecasters believe that exchange rates are more heavily influenced by economic prospects than by the current account. One scholar summarizes this belief using an interesting anecdote.

> *Many economists reject the view that the short-term behavior of exchange rates is determined in flow markets. Exchange rates are asset prices traded in an efficient financial market. Indeed, an exchange rate is the relative price of two currencies and therefore is determined by the willingness to hold each currency. Like other asset prices, the exchange rate is determined by expectations about the future, not current trade flows.*
>
> *A parallel with other asset prices may illustrate the approach. Let's consider the stock price of a winery traded on the Bordeaux stock exchange. A frost in late spring results in a poor harvest, in terms of both quantity and quality. After the harvest the wine is finally sold, and the income is much less than the previous year. On the day of the final sale there is no reason for the stock price to be influenced by this flow. First, the poor income has already been discounted for several months in the winery stock price. Second, the stock price is affected by future, in addition to current, prospects. The stock price is based on expectations of future earnings, and the major cause for a change in stock price is a revision of these expectations.*
>
> *A similar reasoning applies to exchange rates: Contemporaneous international flows should have little effect on exchange rates to the extent they have already been expected. Only news about future economic prospects will affect exchange rates. Since economic expectations are potentially volatile and influenced by many variables, especially variables of a political nature, the short-run behavior of exchange rates is volatile.*
>
> —Bruno Solnik, *International Investments*, 3rd Edition, Reading, MA:
> Addison Wesley, 1996, p. 58. Reprinted with permission of Pearson Education, Inc.

The asset market approach to forecasting is also applicable to emerging markets. In this case, however, a number of additional variables contribute to exchange rate determination. These variables are, as described previously, illiquid capital markets, weak economic and social infrastructure, political instability, corporate governance, contagion effects, and speculation. These variables will be illustrated in the section detailing major currency crises later in this chapter.

Currency Market Intervention

A fundamental problem with exchange rates is that no commonly accepted method exists to estimate the effectiveness of official intervention into foreign exchange markets. Many interrelated factors affect the exchange rate at any given time, and no quantitative model exists that is able to provide the magnitude of any causal relationship between intervention and an exchange rate when so many interdependent variables are acting simultaneously.

—"Japan's Currency Intervention: Policy Issues," Dick K. Nanto, CRS Report to Congress, July 13, 2007, CRS-7.

The value of a country's currency is of significant interest to an individual government's economic and political policies and objectives. Those interests sometimes extend beyond the individual country, but may actually reflect some form of collective country interest. Although many countries have moved from fixed exchange rate values long ago, the governments and central bank authorities of the multitude of floating rate currencies still privately and publicly profess what value their currency "should hold" in their eyes, regardless of whether the market for that currency agrees at that time. *Foreign currency intervention*—the active management, manipulation, or intervention in the market's valuation of a country's currency—is a component of currency valuation and forecast that cannot be overlooked.

Motivations for Intervention

There is a long-standing saying that "what worries bankers is inflation, but what worries elected officials is unemployment." The principle is actually quite useful in understanding the various motives for currency market intervention. Depending upon whether a country's central bank is an independent institution (e.g., the U.S. Federal Reserve), or a subsidiary of its elected government (as the Bank of England was for many years), the bank's policies may either fight inflation or fight slow economic growth, but rarely can do both.

Historically, a primary motive for a government to pursue currency value change was to keep the country's currency cheap so that foreign buyers would find its exports cheap. This policy, long referred to as "beggar-thy-neighbor," gave rise to many competitive devaluations over the years. It has not, however, fallen out of fashion. The slow economic growth and continuing employment problems in many countries in 2012 and 2013 led to some governments, the United States and the European Union being prime examples, working to hold their currency values down.

Alternatively, the fall in the value of the domestic currency will sharply reduce the purchasing power of its people. If the economy is forced, for a variety of reasons, to continue to purchase imported products (e.g., petroleum imports because of no domestic substitute), a currency devaluation or depreciation may prove highly inflationary—and in the extreme, impoverish the country's people (as in the case of Venezuela).

It is frequently noted that most countries would like to see stable exchange rates and to avoid the entanglements associated with manipulating currency values. Unfortunately, that would also imply that they are also happy with the current exchange rate's impact on country-level competitiveness. One must look no further than the continuing highly public debate between the United States and China over the value of the yuan. The U.S. believes the yuan is undervalued, making Chinese exports to the United States overly cheap, which in turn, results in a growing current account deficit for the United States and current account surplus for China.

The International Monetary Fund, as one of its basic principles (Article IV), encourages members to avoid pursuing "currency manipulation" to gain competitive advantages over other members. The IMF defines manipulation as "protracted large-scale intervention in one direction in the exchange market." It seems that many governments often choose to ignore the IMF's advice.

Intervention Methods

There are many ways in which an individual or collective set of governments and central banks can alter the value of their currencies. It should be noted, however, that the methods of market intervention used are very much determined by the size of the country's economy, the magnitude of global trading in its currency, and the depth and breadth of development in its domestic financial markets. A short list of the intervention methods would include *direct intervention*, *indirect intervention*, and *capital controls*.

Direct Intervention. This is the active buying and selling of the domestic currency against foreign currencies. This traditionally required a central bank to act like any other trader in the currency market—albeit a big one. If the goal were to increase the value of the domestic currency, the central bank would purchase its own currency using its foreign exchange reserves, at least to the acceptable limits that it could endure depleting its reserves.

If the goal were to decrease the value of its currency—to fight an appreciation of its currency's value on the foreign exchange market—it would sell its own currency in exchange for foreign currency, typically a major hard currency like the dollar and euro. Although there are no physical limits to its ability to sell its own currency (it could theoretically continue to "print money" endlessly), central banks are cautious in the degree to which they may potentially change their monetary supplies through intervention.

Direct intervention was the primary method used for many years, but beginning in the 1970s, the world's currency markets grew enough that any individual player, even a central bank, could find itself with insufficient resources to move the market. As one trader stated a number of years ago, "We at the bank found ourselves little more than a grain of sand on the beach of the market."

One solution to the market size challenge has been the occasional use of coordinated intervention, in which several major countries, or a collective such as the G8 of industrialized countries, agree that a specific currency's value is out of alignment with their collective interests. In that situation, the countries may work collectively to intervene and push a currency's value in a desired direction. The September 1985 Plaza Agreement, an agreement signed at the Plaza Hotel in New York City by the members of the Group of Ten, was one such coordinated intervention agreement. The members, collectively, had concluded that currency values had become too volatile or too extreme in movement for sound economic policy management. The problem with coordinated intervention is, of course, achieving agreement between nations. This has proven to be a major sticking point in the principle's use.

Indirect Intervention. This is the alteration of economic or financial fundamentals that are thought to be drivers of capital to flow in and out of specific currencies. This was a logical development for market manipulation given the growth in size of the global currency markets relative to the financial resources of central banks.

The most obvious and widely used factor here is interest rates. Following the financial principles outlined in the previous discussion of parity conditions, higher real rates of interest attract capital. If a central bank wishes to "defend its currency" for example, it might follow a restrictive monetary policy, which would drive real rates of interest up. The method is therefore no longer limited to the quantity of foreign exchange reserves held by the country. Instead, it is limited only by the country's willingness to suffer the domestic impacts of higher real interest rates in order to attract capital inflows and therefore drive up the demand for its currency.

Alternatively, in a country wishing for its currency to fall in value, particularly when confronted with a continual appreciation of its value against major trading partner currencies, the central bank may work to lower real interest rates, reducing the returns to capital.

Because indirect intervention uses tools of monetary policy, a fundamental dimension of economic policy, the magnitude and extent of impacts may reach far beyond currency value. Overly stimulating economic activity, or increasing money supply growth beyond real economic activity, may prove inflationary. The use of such broad-based tools like interest rates to manipulate currency values requires a determination of importance, which in some cases may involve a choice to pursue international economic goals at the expense of domestic economic policy goals.

Turkish Crisis of 2014. It is also important to remember that intervention may—and often does—fail. The Turkish currency crisis of 2014 is a classic example of a drastic indirect intervention that ultimately only slowed the rate of capital flight and currency collapse. Turkey had enjoyed some degree of currency stability throughout 2012 and 2013. But the Turkish economy (one of the so-called "Fragile Five" countries, along with South Africa, India, Indonesia, and Brazil) was suffering a widening current account deficit and rising inflation. With the increasing anxieties in emerging markets in the fourth quarter of 2013 over the U.S. Federal Reserve's announcement that it would be slowing its bond purchasing (the Taper Program, essentially a tighter monetary policy), capital began exiting Turkey. The Turkish lira came under increasing downward pressure as illustrated in Exhibit 8.2.

Turkey, however, was also under a great deal of domestic political strife, as the president of Turkey believed that the central bank should be stimulating the Turkish economy by lowering interest rates. Lower rates provided additional incentive for short-term capital flight. Pressures intensified in early January 2014, resulting in a sudden increase in the Turkish one-week

---

EXHIBIT 8.2   **The Turkish Lira Crisis of 2014**

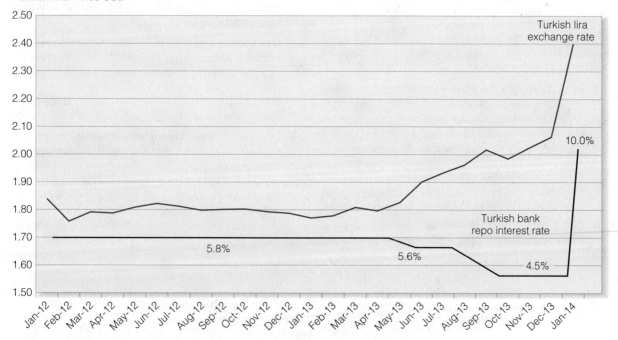

Turkish lira = 1.00 USD

bank repurchase interest rate (or "repo rate") from 4.5% to 10.0%. Although the first few hours indicated some relief with the lira returning to a slightly stronger value versus the dollar (and euro), within days it was trading weaker once again. Indirect intervention in this case had not only proven a failure, but the attempted cure may in the end have worsened both political and economic instability for Turkey in the near-term.[1]

Capital Controls. This is the restriction of access to foreign currency by government. This involves limiting the ability to exchange domestic currency for foreign currency. When access and exchange is permitted, trading often takes place only with official designees of the government or central bank, and only at dictated exchange rates.

Often, governments will limit access to foreign currencies to commercial trade: for example, allowing access to hard currency for the purchase of imports only. Access for investment purposes—particularly for short-term portfolios in which investors are moving in and out of interest-bearing accounts, purchasing or selling securities or other funds—is often prohibited or limited. The Chinese regulation of access and trading of the Chinese yuan is a prime example of the use of capital controls over currency value. In addition to the government's setting the daily rate of exchange, access to the exchange is limited by a difficult and timely bureaucratic process for approval, and limited to commercial trade transactions.

Understanding the motivations and methods for currency market intervention is critical to any analysis of the determination of future exchange rates. And although it is often impossible to determine, in the end, whether subtle intervention was successful, it appears to be an area of growing market activity, particularly for countries trying to "emerge" to higher levels of economic income and wealth. *Global Finance in Practice 8.1* provides a short list of possible best practices for effective intervention.

GLOBAL FINANCE IN PRACTICE 8.1

Rules of Thumb for Effective Intervention

There are a number of factors, features, and tactics, according to many currency traders that determine the effectiveness of an intervention effort.

- **Don't Lean into the Wind.** Markets that are moving significantly in one direction, like the strengthening of the Japanese yen in the fall of 2010, are very tough to turn. Termed "leaning into the wind," intervention during a strong market movement will most likely result in a very expensive failure. Currency traders argue that central banks should time their intervention very carefully, choosing moments when trading volumes are light and direction nearly flat. Don't lean into the wind, read it.

- **Coordinate Timing and Activity.** Use traders or associates in a variety of geographic markets and trading centers, possibly other central banks, if possible. The markets are much more likely to be influenced if they believe the intervention activity is reflecting a grass-roots movement, and not the singular activity of a single trading entity or bank.

- **Use Good News.** Particularly when trying to quell a currency fall, time the intervention to coincide with positive economic, financial, or business news closely associated with a country's currency market. Traders often argue that "markets wish to celebrate good news," and currencies may be no different.

- **Don't Be Cheap. Overwhelm Them.** Traders fear missing the moment, and a large, coordinated, well-timed intervention can make them fear they are leaning in the wrong direction. A successful intervention is in many ways a battle of psychology; play on insecurities. If it appears the intervention is gradually having the desired impact, throw ever-increasing assets into the battle. Don't get cheap.

---

[1]One of the most famous failures occurred in 1992 when the United Kingdom attempted to defend the value of the British pound. The Bank of England, in an attempt to defend the value of the pound within the European Monetary System, increased key interest rates three times in six hours, eventually exiting the EMS. The United Kingdom was said to have suffered a "humiliating defeat," although it was a currency war, not a military one.

Disequilibrium: Exchange Rates in Emerging Markets

Although the three different schools of thought on exchange rate determination (parity conditions, balance of payments approach, and asset approach) described earlier make understanding exchange rates appear to be straightforward, that is rarely the case. The large and liquid capital and currency markets follow many of the principles outlined so far relatively well in the medium to long term. The smaller and less liquid markets, however, frequently demonstrate behaviors that seemingly contradict theory. The problem lies not in the theory, but in the relevance of the assumptions underlying the theory. An analysis of the emerging market crises illustrates a number of these seeming contradictions.

After a number of years of relative global economic tranquility, the second half of the 1990s was racked by a series of currency crises that shook all emerging markets. The Asian crisis of July 1997, the Russian ruble's collapse in August 1998, and the fall of the Argentine peso in 2002 provide a spectrum of emerging market economic failures, each with its own complex causes and unknown outlooks. These crises also illustrated the growing problem of capital flight and short-run international speculation in currency and securities markets. We will use each of the individual crises to focus on a specific dimension of the causes and consequences.

The Asian Crisis of 1997

At a 1998 conference sponsored by the Milken Institute, a speaker noted that the world's preoccupation with the economic problems of Indonesia was incomprehensible because "the total gross domestic product of Indonesia is roughly the size of North Carolina." The following speaker observed, however, that the last time he had checked, "North Carolina did not have a population of 220 million people."

The roots of the Asian currency crisis extended from a fundamental change in the economics of the region, the transition of many Asian nations from being net exporters to net importers. Starting as early as 1990 in Thailand, the rapidly expanding economies of the Far East began importing more than they exported, requiring major net capital inflows to support their currencies. As long as the capital continued to flow in—capital for manufacturing plants, dam projects, infrastructure development, and even real estate speculation—the pegged exchange rates of the region could be maintained. When the investment capital inflows stopped, however, crisis was inevitable.

The most visible roots of the crisis were in the excesses of capital inflows into Thailand. With rapid economic growth and rising profits forming the backdrop, Thai firms, banks, and finance companies had ready access to capital on the international markets, finding U.S. dollar debt cheap offshore. Thai banks continued to raise capital internationally, extending credit to a variety of domestic investments and enterprises beyond what the Thai economy could support. As capital flows into the Thai market hit record rates, financial flows poured into investments of all kinds. As the investment "bubble" expanded, some participants raised questions about the economy's ability to repay the rising debt. The baht came under attack.

Currency Collapse. In May and June 1997, more and more rumors circulated throughout the globe's currency traders that the Thai baht was weak and that a number of major investors were now speculating on its fall. The Thai government and central bank quickly intervened in the foreign exchange markets directly (using up hard currency reserves) and indirectly (by raising interest rates in an attempt to stop the outflow). Foreign capital, which had flowed into Thailand freely in the months and years previous, stopped.

EXHIBIT 8.3   **The Thai Baht and the Asian Crisis**

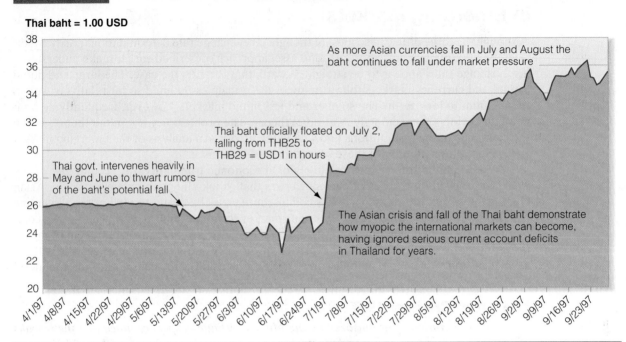

Thai baht = 1.00 USD

As more Asian currencies fall in July and August the baht continues to fall under market pressure

Thai baht officially floated on July 2, falling from THB25 to THB29 = USD1 in hours

Thai govt. intervenes heavily in May and June to thwart rumors of the baht's potential fall

The Asian crisis and fall of the Thai baht demonstrate how myopic the international markets can become, having ignored serious current account deficits in Thailand for years.

A second round of speculative attacks in late June and early July proved too much for the Thai authorities. On July 2, 1997, the Thai central bank finally allowed the baht to float (or sink in this case). The baht fell 17% against the U.S. dollar and more than 12% against the Japanese yen in a matter of hours. By November, the baht had fallen from 25 to 40 baht per dollar, a fall of about 38%, as illustrated in Exhibit 8.3.

Within days, in Asia's own version of what is called the *tequila effect*[2], a number of neighboring Asian nations, some with and some without similar characteristics to Thailand, came under speculative attack by currency traders and capital markets. The Philippine peso, the Malaysian ringgit, and the Indonesian rupiah all fell in the months following the July baht devaluation.

In late October 1997, Taiwan caught the markets off balance with a surprise competitive devaluation of 15%. The Taiwanese devaluation seemed only to renew the momentum of the crisis. Although the Hong Kong dollar survived (at great expense to its foreign exchange reserves), the Korean won (KRW) was not so lucky. In November 1997, the historically stable won also fell victim, falling from 900 Korean won per dollar to more than 1100. The only currency that had not fallen besides the Hong Kong dollar was the Chinese renminbi, which was not freely convertible.

Causal Complexities. The Asian economic crisis—for it was more than just a currency collapse—had many roots besides traditional balance of payments difficulties. The causes were different in each country, yet there were specific underlying similarities, which allow comparison: corporate socialism, corporate governance, and banking stability.

■ The rapidly growing export-led countries of Asia had known only stability. Because of the influence of government and politics in the business arena, even in the event of failure, it was believed that government would not allow firms to fail, workers to lose their jobs, or

---

[2]"Tequila effect" is the term used to describe how the Mexican peso crisis of December 1994 quickly spread to other Latin American currency and equity markets, a form of financial panic termed contagion.

banks to close. Practices that had persisted for decades without challenge, such as lifetime employment, were now no longer sustainable.

■ Many firms operating within the Far Eastern business environments were often largely controlled either by families or by groups related to the governing party or body of the country. This tendency has been labeled *cronyism*. *Cronyism* means that the interests of minority stockholders and creditors are often secondary at best to the primary motivations of corporate management.

■ The banking sector had fallen behind. Bank regulatory structures and markets had been deregulated nearly without exception across the globe. The central role played by banks in the conduct of business had largely been ignored. As firms across Asia collapsed, government coffers were emptied and banks failed. Without banks, the "plumbing" of business conduct was shut down.

The Asian economic crisis had global impacts. What started as a currency crisis quickly became a region-wide depression. The slowed economies of the region quickly caused major reductions in world demands for many products, especially commodities. World oil, metal, and agricultural products markets fell. Commodity export earnings fell, as did growth prospects for other emerging economies.

In the aftermath, the international speculator and philanthropist George Soros was the object of much criticism for being the cause of the crisis because of massive speculation by his and other hedge funds. Soros, however, was likely only the messenger. *Global Finance in Practice 8.2* details the Soros debate.

GLOBAL FINANCE IN PRACTICE 8.2

Was George Soros to Blame for the Asian Crisis?

For Thailand to blame Mr. Soros for its plight is rather like condemning an undertaker for burying a suicide.
—The Economist, August 2, 1997, p. 57.

In the weeks following the start of the Asian Crisis in July 1997, officials from a number of countries including Thailand and Malaysia blamed the international financier George Soros for causing the crisis. Particularly vocal was the Prime Minister of Malaysia, Dr. Mahathir Mohamad, who repeatedly implied that Soros had a political agenda associated with Burma's prospect of joining the Association of Southeast Asian Nations (ASEAN). Mahathir noted in a number of public speeches that Soros might have been making a political statement, and not just speculating against currency values. Mahathir argued that the poor people of Malaysia, Thailand, the Phillipines, and Indonesia would pay a great price for Soros' attacks on Asian currencies.

George Soros is probably the most famous currency speculator—and possibly the most successful—in global history. Admittedly responsible for much of the European financial crisis of 1992 and the fall of the French franc in 1993, he once again was the recipient of critical attention in 1997 following the fall of the Thai baht and Malaysian ringgit.

Nine years later, in 2006, Mahathir and Soros met for the first time. Mahathir apologized and withdrew his previous accusations. In Soros' book published in 1998, *The Crisis of Global Capitalism: Open Society Endangered* (pp. 208–209), Soros explained his role in the crisis as follows:

The financial crisis that originated in Thailand in 1997 was particularly unnerving because of its scope and severity. . . . By the beginning of 1997, it was clear to Soros Fund Management that the discrepancy between the trade account and the capital account was becoming untenable. We sold short the Thai baht and the Malaysian ringgit early in 1997 with maturities ranging from six months to a year. (That is, we entered into contracts to deliver at future dates Thai Baht and Malaysian ringgit that we did not currently hold.) Subsequently Prime Minister Mahathir of Malaysia accused me of causing the crisis, a wholly unfounded accusation. We were not sellers of the currency during or several months before the crisis; on the contrary, we were buyers when the currencies began to decline—we were purchasing ringgit to realize the profits on our earlier speculation. (Much too soon, as it turned out. We left most of the potential gain on the table because we were afraid that Mahathir would impose capital controls. He did so, but much later.)

—From *The Crisis of Global Capitalism* by George Soros, copyright © 1998. Reprinted by permission of Public Affairs, a member of The Perseus Books Group.

The Russian Crisis of 1998

The crisis of August 1998 was the culmination of a continuing deterioration in general economic conditions in Russia. During the period from 1995 to 1998, Russian borrowers—both governmental and non-governmental—had borrowed heavily on the international capital markets. Servicing this debt soon became a growing problem, as servicing dollar debt requires earning dollars. The Russian current account, a surprisingly healthy surplus, was not finding its way into internal investment and external debt service. Capital flight accelerated as hard-currency earnings flowed out as fast as they found their way in. Finally, in the spring of 1998, even Russian export earnings began to decline. Russian exports were predominantly commodity-based, and global commodity prices had been falling since the start of the Asian crisis in 1997.

The Russian currency, the ruble (RUB), operated under a managed float. This meant that the Russian Central Bank set a trading band, and then adjusted it continually. Theoretically, the exchange rate was allowed to slide daily at a 1.5% per month rate. Automatically, the Central Bank announced an official exchange rate each day at which it was willing to buy and sell rubles, always within the official band. In the event that the ruble's rate came under pressure at the limits of the band, the Central Bank intervened in the market by buying and selling rubles, usually buying, using up the country's foreign exchange reserves.

The August Collapse. On August 7, 1998, the Russian Central Bank announced that its currency reserves had fallen by $800 million in the last week of July. Prime Minister Kiriyenko said that Russia would issue an additional $3 billion in foreign bonds to help pay its rising debt, a full $1 billion more than scheduled. On August 10, Russian stocks fell more than 5% as investors feared a Chinese currency (renminbi) devaluation. The Chinese currency was the only Asian currency of size not devalued in 1997 and 1998. Analysts worldwide speculated that international markets were waiting to see if the Russian government would increase its tax revenues as it had promised the IMF throughout the year. Russian tax collections averaged $1 billion per month in 1998, less than those of New York City.

The following days saw a continuing series of press releases assuring the world that the government had everything under control. The government stated that the "panic" was psychological, not fiscal. President Boris Yeltsin promised, "There will be no devaluation—that's firm and definite. That would signify that there was a disaster and that everything was collapsing. On the contrary, everything is going as it should."

"As it should" turned out to mean devaluation. On Monday, August 17, the Russian Central Bank announced that the ruble would be allowed to fall by 34%, from 6.30 rubles per dollar to 9.50. The government then announced a 90-day moratorium on all repayment of foreign debt, debt owed by Russian banks and all private borrowers, in order to avert a banking collapse. The currency's fall continued, as illustrated in Exhibit 8.4. The Central Bank of Russia, in an attempt to defray criticism of its management of the ruble's devaluation, disclosed that it had expended $8.8 billion in the preceding eight weeks defending the ruble's value. On August 28, the Moscow currency exchange closed after 10 minutes of trading as the ruble continued to fall.

The Aftermath. It is hard to say when a crisis begins or ends, but for the Russian people and the Russian economy, the deterioration of the economic conditions continued. What is of more substantial concern is the toll taken on Russian society. For many, the collapse of the ruble and the loss of Russia's access to the international capital markets brought into question the benefits of a free-market economy, long championed by the advocates of Western-style democracy.

EXHIBIT 8.4   **The Fall of the Russian Ruble**

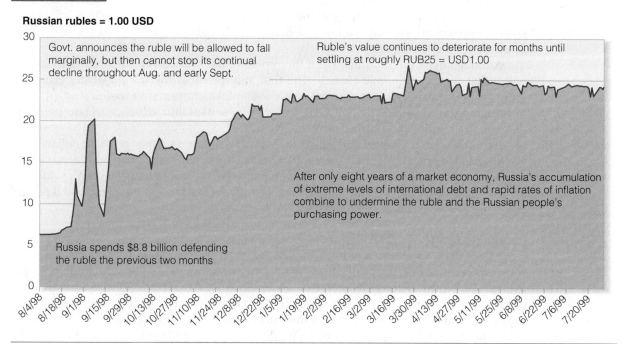

Russian rubles = 1.00 USD

Govt. announces the ruble will be allowed to fall marginally, but then cannot stop its continual decline throughout Aug. and early Sept.

Ruble's value continues to deteriorate for months until settling at roughly RUB25 = USD1.00

After only eight years of a market economy, Russia's accumulation of extreme levels of international debt and rapid rates of inflation combine to undermine the ruble and the Russian people's purchasing power.

Russia spends $8.8 billion defending the ruble the previous two months

The Argentine Crisis of 2002

Now, most Argentines are blaming corrupt politicians and foreign devils for their ills. But few are looking inward, at mainstream societal concepts such as viveza criolla, an Argentine cultural quirk that applauds anyone sly enough to get away with a fast one. It is one reason behind massive tax evasion here: One of every three Argentines does so—and many like to brag about it.

—"Once-Haughty Nation's Swagger Loses Its Currency,"
Anthony Faiola, *The Washington Post*, March 13, 2002.

Argentina's economic ups and downs have historically been tied to the health of the Argentine peso. South America's southernmost resident—which oftentimes considered itself more European than Latin American—had been wracked by hyperinflation, international indebtedness, and economic collapse in the 1980s. By 1991, the people of Argentina had had enough. Economic reform was a common goal of the Argentine people. They were not interested in quick fixes, but lasting change and a stable future. They nearly got it.

The Currency Board. In 1991, the Argentine peso had been pegged to the U.S. dollar at a one-to-one rate of exchange. The policy was a radical departure from traditional methods of fixing the rate of a currency's value. Argentina adopted a currency board, a structure—rather than merely a commitment—to limit the growth of money in the economy. Under a currency board, the central bank may increase the money supply in the banking system only with increases in its holdings of hard currency reserves. The reserves were, in this case, U.S. dollars. By removing the ability of government to expand the rate of growth of the money supply, Argentina believed it was eliminating the source of inflation that had devastated its standard of living.

The idea was simple: *limit the rate of growth in the country's money supply to the rate at which the country receives net inflows of U.S. dollars as a result of trade growth.* It was both a recipe for conservative and prudent financial management, and a decision to eliminate the power of politicians, elected and unelected, to exercise judgment both good and bad. It was an automatic and unbendable rule.

Although hyperinflation had been the problem, the "cure" was a restrictive monetary policy that slowed economic growth. The first and foremost cost of the slower economic growth was in unemployment. The country's unemployment rate rose to double-digit levels in 1994 and stayed there. The real GDP growth rate settled into recession in late 1998, and the economy continued to shrink through 2000.

Argentine banks allowed depositors to hold their money in either pesos or dollars. This was intended to provide a market-based discipline to the banking and political systems, and to demonstrate the government's unwavering commitment to maintaining the peso's value parity with the dollar. Although intended to build confidence in the system, in the end it proved disastrous to the Argentine banking system.

Economic Crisis of 2001. The 1998 recession proved to be unending. Three-and-a-half years later, Argentina was still in recession. By 2001, crisis conditions had revealed three very important underlying problems with Argentina's economy: 1) The Argentine peso was overvalued; 2) The currency board regime had eliminated monetary policy alternatives for macroeconomic policy; and 3) The Argentine government budget deficit was out of control. Inflation had not been eliminated, and the world's markets were watching.

Most of the major economies of South America now slid into recession. With slowing economic activity, imports fell. Most South American currencies now fell against the U.S. dollar, but because the Argentine peso remained pegged to the dollar, Argentine exports grew increasingly overpriced.

The Currency Board and Monetary Policy. The increasingly sluggish economic growth in Argentina warranted expansionary economic policies, argued many policymakers. But the currency board's basic premise was that the money supply to the financial system could not be expanded any further or faster than the ability of the economy to capture dollar reserves—eliminating monetary policy.

Government spending was not slowing, however. As the unemployment rate grew higher, as poverty and social unrest grew—both in Buenos Aires, the civil center of Argentina, and in the outer provinces—government was faced with growing expansionary spending needs to close the economic and social gaps. Government spending continued to increase, but tax receipts did not. Argentina turned to the international markets to aid in the financing of its government's deficit spending. The total foreign debt of the country began rising dramatically. Only a number of IMF capital injections prevented the total foreign debt of the country from skyrocketing. By the end of the 1990s, however, total foreign debt had doubled, and the economy's earning power had not.

As economic conditions continued to deteriorate, banks suffered increasing runs. Depositors, fearing that the peso would be devalued, lined up to withdraw their money—both Argentine peso and U.S. dollar cash balances. Pesos were converted to dollars, once again adding fuel to the growing fire of currency crisis. The government, fearing that the increasing financial drain on banks would cause their collapse, closed the banks. Consumers, unable to withdraw more than $250 per week, were instructed to use debit cards and credit cards to make purchases and to conduct the everyday transactions required by society.

EXHIBIT 8.5   The Collapse of the Argentine Peso

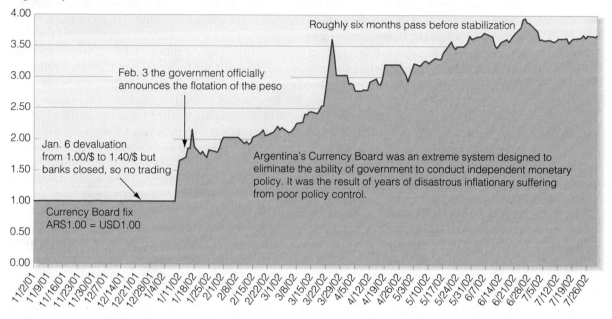

Argentine pesos = 1.00 USD

Roughly six months pass before stabilization

Feb. 3 the government officially
announces the flotation of the peso

Jan. 6 devaluation
from 1.00/$ to 1.40/$ but
banks closed, so no trading

Argentina's Currency Board was an extreme system designed to
eliminate the ability of government to conduct independent monetary
policy. It was the result of years of disastrous inflationary suffering
from poor policy control.

Currency Board fix
ARS1.00 = USD1.00

Devaluation. On Sunday, January 6, 2002, in the first act of his presidency, President Eduardo Duhalde devalued the peso from 1.00 Argentine peso per U.S. dollar to 1.40. But the economic pain continued. Two weeks after the devaluation, the banks were still closed. On February 3, 2002, the Argentine government announced that the peso would be floated, as shown in Exhibit 8.5. The government would no longer attempt to fix or manage its value to any specific level, allowing the market to find or set the exchange rate.[3]

Martin Feldstein, a former Harvard professor and member of the U.S. President's Council of Economic Advisors, summed up the hard lessons of the Argentine story in the following way:[4]

> *In reality, the Argentines understood the risk that they were taking at least as well as the IMF staff did. Theirs was a calculated risk that might have produced good results. It is true, however, that the IMF staff did encourage Argentina to continue with the fixed exchange rate and currency board. Although the IMF and virtually all outside economists believe that a floating exchange rate is preferable to a "fixed but adjustable" system, in which the government recognizes that it will have to devalue occasionally, the IMF (as well as some outside economists) came to believe that the currency board system of a firmly fixed exchange rate (a "hard peg" in the jargon of international finance) is a viable long-term policy for an economy. Argentina's experience has proved that wrong.*

[3]Unfortunately, this was not the last currency crisis for Argentina. Argentina once again suffered capital flight and a rapid deterioration in the recognized value of its currency in 2013–2014. This crisis, highlighted by capital controls and black market ("blue market") trading, was described in Chapter 2.

[4]"Argentina's Fall," Martin Feldstein, *Foreign Affairs*, March/April 2002. Reprinted by permission of FOREIGN AFFAIRS, (81, 2002). Copyright 2002 by the Council of Foreign Relations, Inc. www.ForeignAffairs.com

Forecasting in Practice

Numerous foreign exchange forecasting services exist, many of which are provided by banks and independent consultants. In addition, some multinational firms have their own in-house forecasting capabilities. Predictions can be based on econometric models, technical analysis, intuition, and a certain measure of gall.

Exhibit 8.6 summarizes the various forecasting periods, regimes, and most widely followed methodologies. (Remember, if we authors could predict the movement of exchange rates with regularity, we surely wouldn't write books.) Whether any of the forecasting services are worth their cost depends both on the motive for forecasting as well as the required accuracy. For example, long-run forecasts may be motivated by a multinational firm's desire to initiate a foreign investment in Japan, or perhaps to raise long-term funds in Japanese yen. Or a portfolio manager may be considering diversifying for the long term in Japanese securities. The longer the time horizon of the forecast, the more inaccurate, but also the less critical the forecast is likely to be.

Short-term forecasts are typically motivated by a desire to hedge a receivable, payable, or dividend for a period of perhaps three months. In this case, the long-run economic fundamentals may not be as important as technical factors in the marketplace, government intervention, news, and passing whims of traders and investors. Accuracy of the forecast is critical, since most of the exchange rate changes are relatively small even though the day-to-day volatility may be high.

Forecasting services normally undertake fundamental economic analysis for long-term forecasts, and some base their short-term forecasts on the same basic model. Others base their short-term forecasts on technical analysis similar to that conducted in security analysis. They attempt to correlate exchange rate changes with various other variables, regardless of whether there is any economic rationale for the correlation. The chances of these forecasts

EXHIBIT 8.6	Exchange Rate Forecasting in Practice	
Forecast Period	**Regime**	**Recommended Forecast Methods**
SHORT-RUN	*Fixed-Rate*	1. Assume the fixed rate is maintained 2. Indications of stress on fixed rate? 3. Capital controls; black market rates 4. Indicators of government's capability to maintain fixed-rate? 5. Changes in official foreign currency reserves

	Floating-Rate	1. Technical methods that capture trend
		2. Forward rates as forecasts
		   (a) <30 days, assume a random walk
		   (b) 30–90 days, forward rates
		   (c) 90–360 days, combine trend with fundamental analysis
		3. Fundamental analysis of inflationary concerns
		4. Government declarations and agreements regarding exchange rate goals
		5. Cooperative agreements with other countries

LONG-RUN	*Fixed-Rate*	1. Fundamental analysis 2. BOP management 3. Ability to control domestic inflation 4. Ability to generate hard currency reserves to use for intervention 5. Ability to run trade surpluses
	Floating-Rate	1. Focus on inflationary fundamentals and PPP 2. Indicators of general economic health such as economic growth and stability 3. Technical analysis of long-term trends; new research indicates possibility of long-term technical "waves"

being consistently useful or profitable depend on whether one believes the foreign exchange market is efficient. The more efficient the market is, the more likely it is that exchange rates are "random walks," with past price behavior providing no clues to the future. The less efficient the foreign exchange market is, the better the chance that forecasters may get lucky and find a key relationship that holds, at least for the short run. If the relationship is consistent, however, others will soon discover it and the market will become efficient again with respect to that piece of information.

Technical Analysis

Technical analysts, traditionally referred to as *chartists*, focus on price and volume data to determine past trends that are expected to continue into the future. The single most important element of technical analysis is that future exchange rates are based on the current exchange rate. Exchange rate movements, similar to equity price movements, can be subdivided into three periods: 1) day-to-day movement, which is seemingly random; 2) short-term movements, ranging from several days to trends lasting several months; and 3) long-term movements, characterized by up and down long-term trends. Long-term technical analysis has gained new popularity as a result of recent research into the possibility that long-term "waves" in currency movements exist under floating exchange rates.

The longer the time horizon of the forecast, the more inaccurate the forecast is likely to be. Whereas forecasting for the long run must depend on economic fundamentals of exchange rate determination, many of the forecast needs of the firm are short- to medium-term in their time horizon and can be addressed with less theoretical approaches. Time series techniques infer no theory or causality but simply predict future values from the recent past. Forecasters freely mix fundamental and technical analysis, presumably because forecasting is like playing horseshoes—getting close counts. *Global Finance in Practice 8.3* provides a short analysis of how accurate one prestigious currency forecaster, JPMorgan Chase, was over a three-year period.

Cross-Rate Consistency in Forecasting

International financial managers must often forecast their home currency exchange rates for the set of countries in which the firm operates, not only to decide whether to hedge or to make an investment, but also as part of preparing multi-country operating budgets in the home country's currency. These are the operating budgets against which the performance of foreign subsidiary managers will be judged. Checking *cross-rate consistency*—the reasonableness of the cross rates implicit in individual forecasts—acts as a reality check.

Forecasting: What to Think?

Obviously, with the variety of theories and practices, forecasting exchange rates into the future is a daunting task. Here is a synthesis of our thoughts and experience:

■ It appears, from decades of theoretical and empirical studies, that exchange rates do adhere to the fundamental principles and theories outlined in the previous sections. Fundamentals do apply in the long term. There is, therefore, something of a *fundamental equilibrium path* for a currency's value.

■ It also seems that in the short term, a variety of random events, institutional frictions, and technical factors may cause currency values to deviate significantly from their long-term fundamental path. This is sometimes referred to as *noise*. Clearly, therefore, we might expect deviations from the long-term path not only to occur, but also to occur with some regularity and relative longevity.

GLOBAL FINANCE IN PRACTICE 8.3

JPMorgan Chase Forecast of the Dollar/Euro

There are many different foreign exchange forecasting services and service providers. JPMorgan Chase (JPMC) is one of the most prestigious and widely used. A review of JPMC's forecasting accuracy for the U.S. dollar/euro spot exchange rate ($/€) for the 2002 to 2005 period, in 90-day increments, is presented in the exhibit.* The graph shows the actual spot exchange rate for the period and JPMC's forecast for the spot exchange rate for the same period.

There is good news and there is bad news. The good news is that JPMC hit the actual spot rate dead-on in both May and November 2002. The bad news is that after that,

they missed. Somewhat worrisome is when the forecast got the direction wrong. For example, in February 2004, JPMC had forecast the spot rate to move from the current rate of $1.27/€ to $1.32/€, but in fact, the dollar had appreciated dramatically in the following three-month period to close at $1.19/€. This was in fact a massive difference. Again, in November 2004, JPMC had forecast the spot rate to move from the current spot rate of $1.30/€ to $1.23/€, but in fact, the actual spot rate proved to be $1.32/€. The lesson learned is probably that regardless of how professional and prestigious a forecaster may be, and how accurate they may have been in the past, forecasting the future—by anyone about anything—is challenging to say the least.

*This analysis uses exchange rate data as published in the print edition of *The Economist*, appearing quarterly. The source of the exchange rate forecasts, as noted in *The Economist*, is JPMorgan Chase.

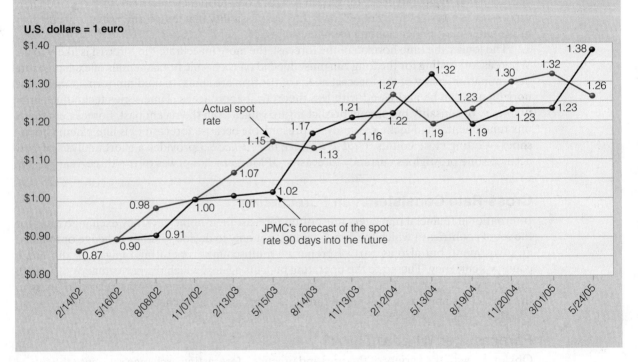

Exhibit 8.7 illustrates this synthesis of forecasting thought. The long-term equilibrium path of the currency—although relatively well-defined in retrospect—is not always apparent in the short term. The exchange rate itself may deviate in something of a cycle or wave about the long-term path.

If market participants agree on the general long-term path and possess *stabilizing expectations*, the currency's value will periodically return to the long-term path. It is critical, however, that when the currency's value rises above the long-term path, most market participants see it as being overvalued and respond by selling the currency—causing its price to fall. Similarly, when the currency's value falls below the long-term path, market participants respond by buying the currency—driving its value up. This is what is meant by *stabilizing expectations*:

EXHIBIT 8.7	Short-Term Noise versus Long-Term Trends

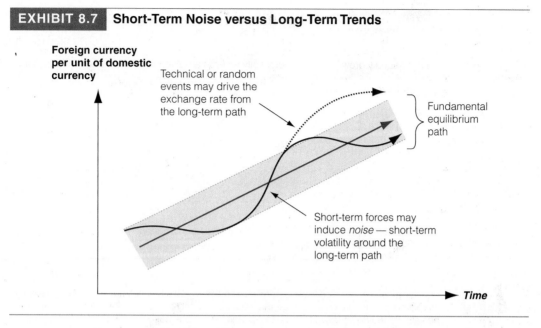

Market participants continually respond to deviations from the long-term path by buying or selling to drive the currency back to the long-term path.

If, for some reason, the market becomes unstable, as illustrated by the dotted deviation path in Exhibit 8.7, the exchange rate may move significantly away from the long-term path for longer periods of time. Causes of these destabilizing markets—weak infrastructure (such as the banking system) and political or social events that dictate economic behaviors—are often the actions of speculators and inefficient markets.

Exchange Rate Dynamics: Making Sense of Market Movements

Although the various theories surrounding exchange rate determination are clear and sound, it may appear on a day-to-day basis that the currency markets do not pay much attention to the theories—they don't read the books! The difficulty is in understanding which fundamentals are driving markets at which points in time.

One example of this relative confusion over exchange rate dynamics is the phenomenon known as *overshooting*. Assume that the current spot rate between the dollar and the euro, as illustrated in Exhibit 8.8, is S_0. The U.S. Federal Reserve announces an expansionary monetary policy that cuts U.S. dollar interest rates. If euro-denominated interest rates remain unchanged, the new spot rate expected by the exchange markets based on interest differentials is S_1. This immediate change in the exchange rate is typical of how the markets react to news, distinct economic and political events that are observable. The immediate change in the value of the dollar/euro is therefore based on interest differentials.

As time passes, however, the price impacts of the monetary policy change start working their way through the economy. As price changes occur over the medium to long term, purchasing power parity forces drive the market dynamics, and the spot rate moves from S_1 toward S_2. Although both S_1 and S_2 were rates determined by the market, they reflected the dominance of different theoretical principles. As a result, the initial lower value of the dollar of S_1 is described as *overshooting* the longer-term equilibrium value of S_2.

EXHIBIT 8.8   Exchange Rate Dynamics: Overshooting

If the U.S. Federal Reserve were to announce a change in monetary policy, an expansion in money supply growth, it could potentially result in an "overshooting" exchange rate change.

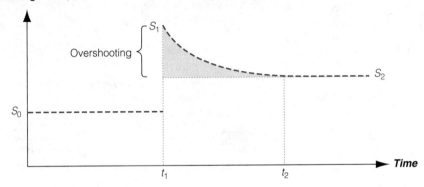

The Fed announces a monetary expansion at a time t_1. This results immediately in lower dollar interest rates. The foreign exchange markets immediately respond to the lower dollar interest rates by driving the value of the dollar down from S_0 to S_1. This new rate is based on *interest differentials*. However, in the coming days and weeks, as the fundamental price effects of the monetary policy actions work their way through the economy, *purchasing power parity* takes hold and the market moves toward a longer term valuation of the dollar—by time t_2—of S_2, a weaker dollar than S_0, but not as weak as initially set at S_1.

This is, of course, only one possible series of events and market reactions. Currency markets are subject to new news every hour of every day, making it very difficult to forecast exchange rate movements in short periods of time. In the longer term, as shown in Exhibit 8.8, the markets do customarily return to fundamentals of exchange rate determination.

Summary Points

- There are three major schools of thought to explaining the economic determinants of exchange rates: parity conditions, the balance of payments approach, and the asset market approach.

- The asset market approach to exchange rate determination suggests that whether foreigners are willing to hold claims in monetary form depends partly on relative real interest rates and partly on a country's outlook for economic growth and profitability.

- The recurrence of exchange rate crises demonstrates not only how sensitive currency values continue to be to economic fundamentals like inflation and economic growth, but also how vulnerable many emerging market currencies continue to be in an ever-expanding global financial network.

- Exchange rate forecasting is part of global business. All businesses of all kinds must form some expectation

of what the future holds. Short-term forecasting of exchange rates in practice tends to focus on time series trends and current spot rates. Longer-term forecasting, over one year, requires a return to the basic analysis of exchange rate fundamentals such as BOP, relative inflation rates, relative interest rates, and the long-run properties of purchasing power parity.

- In the short term, a variety of random events, institutional frictions, and technical factors may cause currency values to deviate significantly from their long-term fundamental path. In the long term, it does appear that exchange rates follow a fundamental equilibrium path, one consistent with the fundamental theories of exchange rate determination.

MINI-CASE

The Japanese Yen Intervention of 2010[1]

We will take decisive steps if necessary, including intervention, while continuing to closely watch currency market moves from now on.

— Yoshihiko Noda, Finance Minister of Japan,
September 13, 2010.

Japan has been the subject of continued criticism for nearly two decades over its frequent intervention in the foreign exchange markets. Trading partners have accused it of market manipulation, while Japan has argued that it is a country and economy that is inherently global in its economic structure, relying on its international competitiveness for its livelihood, and currency stability is its only desire.

The debate was renewed in September 2010 when Japan intervened in the foreign exchange markets for the first time in nearly six years. Japan reportedly bought nearly 20 billion U.S. dollars in exchange for Japanese yen in an attempt to stop the continuing appreciation of the yen. Finance Ministry officials had stated publicly that 82 yen per dollar was probably the limit of their tolerance for yen appreciation.

As illustrated in Exhibit A, the Bank of Japan intervened on September 13 as the yen approached 82 yen per dollar. (The Bank of Japan is independent in its ability to conduct Japanese monetary policy, but as the organizational subsidiary of the Japanese Ministry of Finance, it must conduct foreign exchange operations on behalf of the Japanese government.) Japanese officials reportedly notified authorities in both the United States and the European Union of their activity, but noted that they had not asked for permission or support.

The intervention resulted in public outcry from Beijing to Washington to London over the "new era of currency intervention." Although market intervention is always looked down upon by free market proponents, the move by Japan was seen as particularly frustrating as it came at a time when the United States was continuing to pressure China to

EXHIBIT A   Intervention and the Japanese Yen 2010

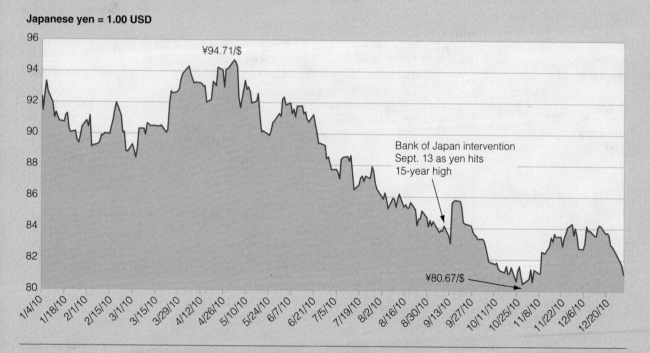

Japanese yen = 1.00 USD

¥94.71/$

Bank of Japan intervention
Sept. 13 as yen hits
15-year high

¥80.67/$

[1]Copyright © 2011 Thunderbird School of Global Management. All rights reserved. This case was prepared by Professor Michael Moffett for the purpose of classroom discussion only, and not to indicate effective or ineffective management. This Mini-Case draws from a number of sources including "Japan's Currency Intervention: Policy Issues," Dick K. Nanto, CRS Report for Congress, July 13, 2007; IMF Country Report No. 05/273, Japan: 2005 Article IV Consultation Staff Report, August 2005; "Interventions and the Japanese Economic Recovery," Takatoshi Ito, paper presented at the University of Michigan Conference on Policy Options for Japan and the United States, October 2004; "Towards a New Era of Currency Intervention," Mansoor Mohi-Uddin, *Financial Times*, September 22, 2010; "Currency Intervention's Mixed Record of Success," Russell Hotten, BBC News, September 16, 2010.

revalue its currency, the renminbi. As noted by economist Nouriel Roubini, "We are in a world where everyone wants a weak currency," a marketplace in which all countries are looking to stimulate their domestic economies through exceptionally low interest rates and corresponding weak currency values—"a global race to the bottom."

Ironically, as illustrated in Exhibit A, it appears that the intervention was largely unsuccessful. When the Bank of Japan started buying dollars in an appreciating yen market—the so-called "leaning into the wind" strategy—it was hoping to either stop the appreciation, change the direction of the spot rate movement, or both. In either pursuit, it appears to have failed. As one analyst commented, it turned out to be a "short-term fix to a long-term problem." Although the yen spiked downward (more yen per dollar) for a few days, it returned once again to an appreciating path within a week.

Japan's frequent interventions, described in Exhibit B, have been the subject of much study. In an August 2005 study by the IMF, it was noted that between 1991 and 2005, the Bank of Japan had intervened on 340 days, while the U.S. Federal Reserve intervened on 22 days, and the European Central Bank intervened only on 4 days (since its inception in 1998). Although the IMF has never found Japanese intervention to be officially "currency manipulation," an analysis by Takatoshi Ito in 2004 concluded that there was on average a one-yen per dollar change in market rates, roughly 1%, as a result of Japanese intervention over time.

It is not clear at this time whether or not Japan will "sterilize" the intervention, meaning neutralize the impact of the additional yen on the money supply by buying bonds domestically. Although this has been the tendency historically, given the current deflation forces in Japan, it may not be necessary.

Japan's interventions are not, however, a lone example of attempted market manipulation. The Swiss National Bank repeatedly intervened in 2009 to stop the appreciation of the Swiss franc against both the dollar and the euro, and recently, in January 2011, Chile aggressively sold Chilean pesos against the U.S. dollar to stop its continued appreciation.

There is no historical case in which [yen] selling intervention succeeded in immediately stopping the pre-existing long-term uptrend in the Japanese yen.

—Tohru Sasaki, Currency Strategist, JPMorgan.

CASE QUESTIONS

1. Could the Bank of Japan continually intervene to try to stop the appreciation of the yen? Is there any limit to its ability to intervene?

2. Why is a stronger yen such a bad thing for Japan? Isn't a stronger currency value an indication of confidence by the global markets in the economy and policies of a country?

3. If currency intervention has such a poor record, why do you think countries like Japan or Switzerland or Chile continue to intervene in the foreign exchange market?

EXHIBIT B   The History of Japanese Intervention

Japanese yen = 1.00 USD

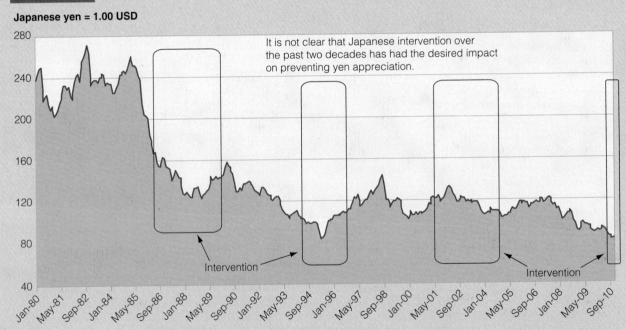

Questions

1. **Term Forecasting.** What are the major differences between short-term and long-term forecasts for a fixed exchange rate versus a floating exchange rate?

2. **Motivations for Currency Market Intervention.** Why and when do central banks intervene in currency markets?

3. **Fundamental Equilibrium.** What is meant by the term "fundamental equilibrium path" for a currency value? What is "noise"?

4. **Asset Market Approach to Forecasting.** Explain how the asset market approach can be used to forecast spot exchange rates. How does the asset market approach differ from the BOP approach to forecasting?

5. **Technical Analysis.** Explain how technical analysis can be used to forecast future spot exchange rates. How does technical analysis differ from the BOP and asset market approaches to forecasting?

6. **Forecasting Services.** Many financial forecasting firms charge their customers fees in accordance with the accuracy of their historical forecasts. Most traders diversify their portfolio into different types of financial instruments and markets. Suppose that you are keen on allocating at least half of your portfolio to emerging market instruments, what should be the requirements that determine your selection of the forecasting service provider?

7. **Cross-Rate Consistency in Forecasting.** Explain the meaning of "cross-rate consistency" as used by MNEs. How do MNEs use a check of cross-rate consistency in practice?

8. **Financial Infrastructure Weakness.** Infrastructure weakness was one of the causes of the emerging market crisis in Thailand in 1997. Define infrastructure weakness and explain how it could affect a country's exchange rate.

9. **Speculation.** The emerging market crises of 1997–2002 were worsened because of rampant speculation. Do speculators cause such crisis or do they simply respond to market signals of weakness? How can a government manage foreign exchange speculation?

10. **Foreign Direct Investment.** Swings in foreign direct investment flows into and out of emerging markets contribute to exchange rate volatility. Describe one concrete historical example of this phenomenon during the last 10 years.

11. **Thailand's Crisis of 1997.** What were the main causes of Thailand's crisis of 1997? What lessons were learned and what steps were eventually taken to normalize Thailand's economy?

12. **Russia's Crisis of 1998.** What were the main causes of Russia's crisis of 1998? What lessons were learned and what steps were taken to normalize Russia's economy?

13. **Argentina's Crisis of 2001–2002.** What were the main causes of Argentina's crisis of 2001–2002? What lessons were learned and what steps were taken to normalize Argentina's economy?

Problems

1. **Calculating Cross Exchange Rates.** On May 1, 2015, the yen/dollar and euro/dollar exchange rates were ¥120.15 and €0.8929, respectively. What is the euro/yen cross exchange rate?

2. **Fluctuations of Cross Exchange Rates.** After the Egyptian Revolution of January 2011, the value of the Egyptian Pound (EGP) massively declined. It fell from EGP1.584/United Arab Dirham (AED) on January 25, 2011, to EGP2.0803/AED on May 1, 2015. What was the percentage decline in its value?

3. **South Korean Won.** The value of 100 South Korean Won (KRW) against the Japanese Yen (JPY) rose from 9.7730 in May 2014 to 11.1710 on May 1, 2015. What was the percentage change in its value?

4. **Currencies of Emerging Market Economies.** The Indian Rupee (INR) is among the twenty most actively traded currencies in the world. Its value has been depreciating against most major currencies such as the British pound (GBP). Using the following graph of the GBP/INR exchange rate, calculate the percentage change in the value of the rupee against the pound for the following periods.
   a. 1980–1985
   b. 1985–1990
   c. 1990–1995
   d. 1995–2000
   e. 2000–2005
   f. 2010–2015
   g. 2010–2015

GBP/INR

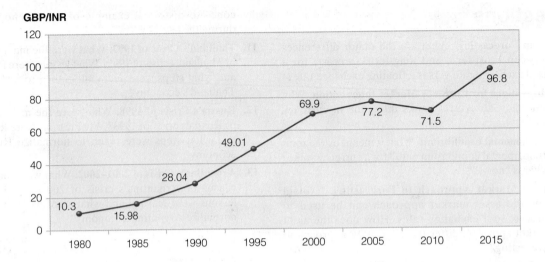

5. **Paris to Tokyo.** The Japanese yen-euro cross rate is one of the more significant currency values for global trade and commerce. The graph below shows this cross rate from when the euro was launched in January 1999 through the end-of-year 2010. Estimate the change in the value of the yen over the following three periods of change.

a. January 1999–August 2001
b. September 2001–June 2008
c. July 2008–December 2010

Monthly Average Exchange Rates:
Japanese yen = 1.00 euro

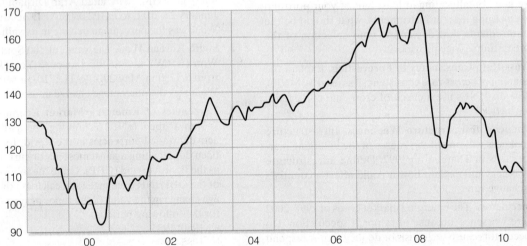

Source: PACIFIC Exchange Rates © 2010 by Prof. Werner Antweiler, University of British Columbia, Vancouver BC, Canada.

6. **Whatever is Happening to the Rand?** Since its inception in 1961, the value of the South African Rand (ZAR) has been affected by changing political and economic conditions. The political turmoil and racial discrimination led many nations to impose sanctions against South African apartheid governments, leading to gradual depreciations of the rand. By the time the first indigenous government assumed power in 1994, the value of the rand against the British Pound (GBP) reached 5.41. The most massive impacts were seen in 2002, after the 9/11 terror attacks and the land reform laws. The global financial crisis has also severely depreciated the rand.

Ever since, the rand has been declining, indicating that it is no longer a currency that traders have an appetite for. It is for this reason that the ZAR is one of the most over-sold currencies of the world.

a. What was the rate of depreciation from the time of the inception of the rand till the indigenous government assumed power?

b. What was the percentage change from 1994 till 2015?

Year	ZAR/GBP
1961–1982	2
1982–1985	1.95
1985	2.99
1986–1988	3.47
1989–1993	4.51
1994	5.41
1999	9.07
2001	21.3
2002	13.85
2005	10.2
2008	17.82
2010	12.01
2015	18.27

7. **Cada Seis Años.** Mexico was famous—or infamous—for many years for having two things every six years (cada seis años in Spanish): presidential elections and currency devaluation. This was the case in 1976, 1982, 1988, and in 1994. In its last devaluation on December 20, 1994, the value of the Mexican peso (MXN) was officially changed from MXN5.08/GBP to MXN8.46/GBP. What was the percentage devaluation?

8. **Bankruptcy.** In 2002, Argentina took a number of measures that ended in its bankruptcy. After the Argentine peso (ARS) was floated in January 2002, the bank run led to a massive devaluation from ARS1.4464 per British Pound (GBP) on January 2, 2002 to 5.3629 on December 30, 2002. What was the percentage devaluation of the peso?

9. **Forecasting the Argentine Peso.** As illustrated in the graph, the Argentine peso moved from its fixed exchange rate of Ps1.00/$ to over Ps2.00/$ in a matter of days in early January 2002. After a brief period of high volatility, the peso's value appeared to settle down to a range varying between 2.0 and 2.5 pesos per dollar. If you were forecasting the Argentine peso further into the future, how would you use the information in the graph—the value of the peso freely floating in the weeks following devaluation—to forecast its future value?

10. **Current Spot Rates.** What are the current spot exchange rates for the following cross rates?
a. Japanese yen/U.S. dollar exchange rate
b. Japanese yen/Australian dollar exchange rate
c. Australian dollar/U.S. dollar exchange rate

11. **Purchasing Power Parity Forecasts.** Assuming purchasing power parity, and assuming that the forecasted change in consumer prices is a good proxy of predicted inflation, forecast the following cross rates:
a. Japanese yen/U.S. dollar in one year
b. Japanese yen/Australian dollar in one year
c. Australian dollar/U.S. dollar in one year

12. **International Fischer Forecasts.** Assuming International Fischer applies to the coming year, forecast the following future spot exchange rates using the government bond rates for the respective country currencies:
a. Japanese yen/U.S. dollar in one year
b. Japanese yen/Australian dollar in one year
c. Australian dollar/U.S. dollar in one year

13. **Implied Real Interest Rates.** If the nominal interest rate is the government bond rate, and the current change in consumer prices is used as expected inflation, calculate the "implied real rate of interest" (the nominal rate corrected for expected inflation) by currency.
a. Australian dollar "real" rate
b. Japanese yen "real" rate
c. U.S. dollar "real" rate

Problem 9.

Forecasting the Pan-Pacific Pyramid

Use the table, which contains economic, financial, and business indicators from the October 20, 2007, issue of *The Economist* (print edition), to answer Problems 10–15.

Forecasting the Pan-Pacific Pyramid: Australia, Japan and The United States

| Country | Gross Domestic Product | | | | Industrial Production | Unemployment Rate |
	Latest Qtr	Qtr*	Forecast 2007e	Forecast 2008e	Recent Qtr	Latest
Australia	4.3%	3.8%	4.1%	3.5%	4.6%	4.2%
Japan	1.6%	−1.2%	2.0%	1.9%	4.3%	3.8%
United States	1.9%	3.8%	2.0%	2.2%	1.9%	4.7%

| Country | Consumer Prices | | | Interest Rates | |
	Year Ago	Latest	Forecast 2007e	3-Month Latest	1-Yr Govt Latest
Australia	4.0%	2.1%	2.4%	6.90%	6.23%
Japan	0.9%	−0.2%	0.0%	0.73%	1.65%
United States	2.1%	2.8%	2.8%	4.72%	4.54%

| Country | Trade Balance | Curent Account | | Current Units (per U.S.$) | |
	Last 12 Mos (billion $)	Last 12 Mos (billion $)	Forecast 07 (% of GDP)	Oct 17th	Year Ago
Australia	−13.0	−$47.0	−5.7%	1.12	1.33
Japan	98.1	$197.5	4.6%	117	119
United States	−810.7	−$793.2	−5.6%	1.00	1.00

Source: Data abstracted from *The Economist*, October 20, 2007, print edition. Unless otherwise noted, percentages are percentage changes over one year. Recent Qtr = recent quarter. Values for 2007e are estimates or forecasts.

14. **Forward Rates.** Using the spot rates and 3-month interest rates, calculate the 90-day forward rates for:
    a. Japanese yen/U.S. dollar exchange rate
    b. Japanese yen/Australian dollar exchange rate
    c. Australian dollar/U.S. dollar exchange rate

15. **Real Economic Activity and Misery.** Calculate the country's Misery Index (unemployment + inflation) and then use it like an interest differential to forecast the future spot exchange rate, one year into the future.
    a. Japanese yen/U.S. dollar exchange rate in one year
    b. Japanese yen/Australian dollar exchange rate in one year
    c. Australian dollar/U.S. dollar exchange rate in one year

Internet Exercises

1. **Recent Economic and Financial Data.** Use the following Web sites to obtain recent economic and financial data used for all approaches to forecasting presented in this chapter.

   Economist.com   www.economist.com/
   markets-data

   FT.com   www.ft.com
   EconEdLink   www.econedlink.org/
   economic-resources/focus-
   on-economic-data.php

2. **OzForex Weekly Comment.** The OzForex Foreign Exchange Services Web site provides a weekly commentary on major political and economic factors and events that move current markets. Using their Web site, see what they expect to happen in the coming week on the three major global currencies—the dollar, yen, and euro.

   OzForex   www.ozforex.com.au/
   news-commentary/weekly

3. **Exchange Rates, Interest Rates, and Global Markets.** The magnitude of market data can seem overwhelming on occasion. Use the following Bloomberg markets page to organize your mind and your global data.

   Bloomberg Financial News   www.bloomberg.com/markets

4. **Banque Canada and the Canadian Dollar Forward Market.** Use the following Web site to find the latest spot and forward quotes of the Canadian dollar against the Bahamian dollar and the Brazilian real.

   Banque Canada   www.bankofcanada.ca/rates/
   exchange/

Foreign Exchange Exposure

Transaction Exposure

*There are two times in a man's life when he should
not speculate: when he can't afford it and when he can.*
—"Following the Equator," *Pudd'nhead Wilson's New Calendar*,
Mark Twain.

LEARNING OBJECTIVES

- Distinguish between the three major foreign exchange exposures experienced by firms
- Analyze the pros and cons of hedging foreign exchange transaction exposure
- Examine the alternatives available to a firm for managing a large and significant transaction exposure
- Evaluate the institutional practices and concerns of conducting foreign exchange risk management

Foreign exchange exposure is a measure of the potential for a firm's profitability, net cash flow, and market value to change because of a change in exchange rates. An important task of the financial manager is to measure foreign exchange exposure and to manage it so as to maximize the profitability, net cash flow, and market value of the firm. This chapter provides an in-depth discussion of transaction exposure—the first category of two main accounting exposures—while the following chapters focus on translation exposure—the second category of accounting exposures—and operating exposure. The chapter concludes with a Mini-Case, *Banbury Impex (India)*, which involves a recent exposure management problem in India.

Types of Foreign Exchange Exposure

What happens to a firm when foreign exchange rates change? There are two distinct categories of foreign exchange exposure for the firm, those that are based in accounting and those that arise from economic competitiveness. The accounting exposures, specifically described as transaction exposure and translation exposure, arise from contracts and accounts being denominated in foreign currency. The economic exposure, which we will describe as operating exposure, is the potential change in the value of the firm from its changing global competitiveness as determined by exchange rates. Exhibit 9.1 shows schematically the three main types of foreign exchange exposure: transaction, translation, and operating:

- *Transaction exposure* measures changes in the value of outstanding financial obligations incurred prior to a change in exchange rates but not due to be settled until after the exchange rates change. Thus, it deals with changes in cash flows that result from existing contractual obligations.

EXHIBIT 9.1	Corporate Foreign Exchange Exposure

Resulting from Accounting	Resulting from Economics
Transaction Exposure Impact of settling outstanding obligations entered into before change in exchange rates but to be settled after change in exchange rates **Translation Exposure** Changes in income and owners' equity in consolidated financial statements caused by a change in exchange rates	**Operating Exposure** Change in expected future cash flows arising from an unexpected change in exchange rates Changes in future cash flows arising from firm and competitor firm responses

Time and Exchange Rate Changes →

■ *Translation exposure* is the potential for accounting-derived changes in owner's equity to occur because of the need to "translate" foreign currency financial statements of foreign subsidiaries into a single reporting currency to prepare worldwide consolidated financial statements.

■ *Operating exposure*, also called *economic exposure*, *competitive exposure*, or *strategic exposure*, measures the change in the present value of the firm resulting from any change in future operating cash flows of the firm caused by an unexpected change in exchange rates. The change in value depends on the effect of the exchange rate change on future sales volume, prices, and costs.

Transaction exposure and operating exposure exist because of unexpected changes in future cash flows. The difference between the two is that transaction exposure is concerned with future cash flows already contracted for, while operating exposure focuses on expected (not yet contracted for) future cash flows that might change because a change in exchange rates has altered international competitiveness.

Why Hedge?

MNEs possess a multitude of cash flows that are sensitive to changes in exchange rates, interest rates, and commodity prices. Chapters 9, 10, and 11 focus exclusively on the sensitivity of the individual firm's value and future cash flows to exchange rates. We begin by exploring the question of whether exchange rate risk should or should not be managed.

Hedging Defined

Many firms attempt to manage their currency exposures through *hedging*. Hedging requires a firm to take a position—an asset, a contract, or a derivative—that will rise or fall in the value offsetting the fall or rise in value of an existing position—the exposure. Hedging protects the owner of the existing asset from loss. However, it also eliminates any gain from an increase in the value of the asset hedged. The question remains: What is to be gained by the firm from hedging?

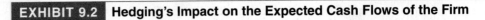

EXHIBIT 9.2   Hedging's Impact on the Expected Cash Flows of the Firm

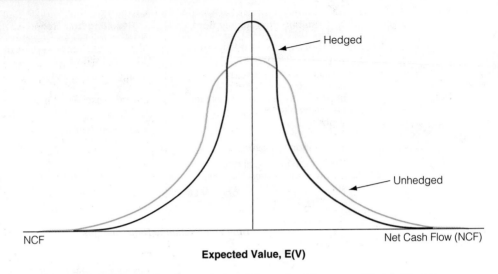

Hedging reduces the variability of expected cash flows about the mean of the distribution.
This reduction of distribution variance is a reduction of risk.

According to financial theory, the value of a firm is the net present value of all expected future cash flows. The fact that these cash flows are *expected* emphasizes that nothing about the future is certain. If the reporting currency value of many of these cash flows is altered by exchange rate changes, a firm that hedges its currency exposures reduces the variance in the value of its future expected cash flows. *Currency risk* can then be defined as the variance in expected cash flows arising from unexpected changes in exchange rates.

Exhibit 9.2 illustrates the distribution of expected net cash flows of the individual firm. Hedging these cash flows narrows the distribution of the cash flows about the mean of the distribution. Currency hedging reduces risk. Reduction of risk is not, however, the same as adding value or return. The value of the firm depicted in Exhibit 9.2 would be increased only if hedging actually shifted the mean of the distribution to the right. In fact, if hedging is not "free," meaning the firm must expend resources to hedge, then hedging will add value only if the rightward shift is sufficiently large to compensate for the cost of hedging.

The Pros and Cons of Hedging

Is a reduction in the variability of cash flows sufficient reason for currency risk management?

Pros. Proponents of hedging cite the following arguments:

■ Reduction in risk of future cash flows improves the planning capability of the firm. If the firm can more accurately predict future cash flows, it may be able to undertake specific investments or activities that it might otherwise not consider.

■ Reduction of risk in future cash flows reduces the likelihood that the firm's cash flows will fall below a level sufficient to make debt-service payments in order for its continued operation. This minimum cash flow point, often referred to as the *point of financial distress*, lies left of the center of the distribution of expected cash flows. Hedging reduces the likelihood of the firm's cash flows falling to this level.

- Management has a comparative advantage over the individual shareholder in knowing the actual currency risk of the firm. Regardless of the level of disclosure provided by the firm to the public, management always possesses an advantage in the depth and breadth of knowledge concerning the real risks.

- Markets are usually in disequilibrium because of structural and institutional imperfections, as well as unexpected external shocks (such as an oil crisis or war). Management is in a better position than shareholders to recognize disequilibrium conditions and to take advantage of single opportunities to enhance firm value through *selective hedging*—exceptional exposures or the occasional use of hedging when management has a definite expectation of the direction of exchange rates.

Cons. Opponents of currency hedging commonly make the following arguments:

- Shareholders are more capable of diversifying currency risk than is the management of the firm. If stockholders do not wish to accept the currency risk of any specific firm, they can diversify their portfolios to manage the risk in a way that satisfies their individual preferences and risk tolerance.

- Currency hedging does not increase the expected cash flows of the firm. Currency risk management does, however, consume firm resources and so reduces cash flow. The impact on value is a combination of the reduction of cash flow (which lowers value) and the reduction in variance (which increases value).

- Management often conducts hedging activities that benefit management at the expense of the shareholders. The field of finance called *agency theory* frequently argues that management is generally more risk-averse than are shareholders.

- Managers cannot outguess the market. If and when markets are in equilibrium with respect to parity conditions, the expected net present value of hedging should be zero.

- Management's motivation to reduce variability is sometimes driven by accounting reasons. Management may believe that it will be criticized more severely for incurring foreign exchange losses than for incurring even higher cash costs by hedging. Foreign exchange losses appear in the income statement as a highly visible separate line item or as a footnote, but the higher costs of protection are buried in operating or interest expenses.

- Efficient market theorists believe that investors can see through the "accounting veil" and therefore have already factored the foreign exchange effect into a firm's market valuation. Hedging would only add cost.

Measurement of Transaction Exposure

Transaction exposure measures gains or losses that arise from the settlement of existing financial obligations whose terms are stated in a foreign currency. Transaction exposure arises from any of the following:

1. Purchasing or selling on credit (on *open account*) goods or services when prices are stated in foreign currencies

2. Borrowing or lending funds when repayment is to be made in a foreign currency

3. Being a party to an unperformed foreign exchange forward contract

4. Otherwise acquiring assets or incurring liabilities denominated in foreign currencies

The most common example of transaction exposure arises when a firm has a receivable or payable denominated in a foreign currency. Exhibit 9.3 demonstrates how this exposure is born. The total transaction exposure consists of *quotation*, *backlog*, and *billing* exposures.

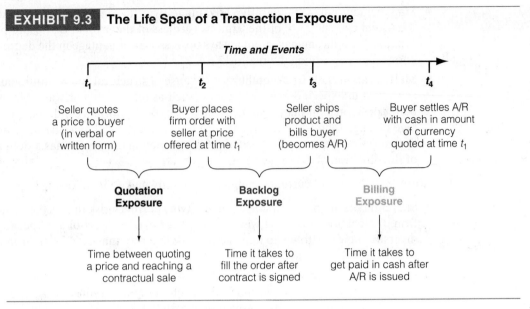

EXHIBIT 9.3   The Life Span of a Transaction Exposure

A transaction exposure is created at the first moment the seller quotes a price in foreign currency terms to a potential buyer (t_1). The quote can be either verbal, as in a telephone quote, or as a written bid or a printed price list. This is *quotation exposure*. When the order is placed (t_2), the potential exposure created at the time of the quotation (t_1) is converted into actual exposure, called *backlog exposure*, because the product has not yet been shipped or billed. Backlog exposure lasts until the goods are shipped and billed (t_3), at which time it becomes *billing exposure*. Billing exposure remains until payment is received by the seller (t_4).

Purchasing or Selling on Open Account. Suppose that Trident Corporation, a U.S. firm, sells merchandise on open account to a Belgian buyer for €1,800,000, with payment to be made in 60 days. The spot exchange rate on the date of the sale is $1.1200/€, and the seller expects to exchange the euros for €1,800,000 × $1.1200/€ = $2,016,000 when payment is received. The $2,016,000 is the value of the sale that is posted to the firm's books. Accounting practices stipulate that the foreign currency transaction be listed at the spot exchange rate in effect on the date of the transaction.

Transaction exposure arises because of the risk that Trident will receive something other than the $2,016,000 expected and booked. For example, if the euro weakens to $1.1000/€ when payment is received, the U.S. seller will receive only €1,800,000 × $1.1000/€ = $1,980,000, or some $180,000 less than what was expected at the time of sale.

$$\text{Transaction settlement: €1,800,000} \times \$1.1000/€ = \$1,980,000$$
$$\text{Transaction booked: €1,800,000} \times \$1.1200/€ \quad = \underline{\$2,016,000}$$
$$\text{Foreign exchange gain (loss) on sale} \qquad = (\$180,000)$$

If the euro should strengthen to $1.3000/€, however, Trident receives €1,800,000 × $1.3000/€ = $2,340,000, an increase of $180,000 over the amount expected. Thus, exposure is the chance of either a loss or a gain on the resulting dollar settlement versus the amount at which the sale was booked.

The U.S. seller might have avoided transaction exposure by invoicing the Belgian buyer in dollars. Of course, if the U.S. company attempted to sell only in dollars it might not have obtained the sale in the first place. Even if the Belgian buyer agrees to pay in dollars, transaction exposure is not eliminated. Instead, it is transferred to the Belgian buyer, whose dollar account payable has an unknown cost 60 days hence.

Borrowing or Lending. A second example of transaction exposure arises when funds are borrowed or loaned, and the amount involved is denominated in a foreign currency. For example, in 1994, PepsiCo's largest bottler outside of the United States was the Mexican company, Grupo Embotellador de Mexico (Gemex). In mid-December 1994, Gemex had U.S. dollar debt of $264 million. At that time, Mexico's *new peso* ("Ps") was traded at Ps3.45/$, a pegged rate that had been maintained with minor variations since January 1, 1993, when the new currency unit had been created. On December 22, 1994, the peso was allowed to float because of economic and political events within Mexico, and in one day it sank to Ps4.65/$. For most of the following January it traded in a range near Ps5.50/$.

Dollar debt in mid-December 1994: $264,000,000 × Ps3.45/$ =   Ps910,800,000

Dollar debt in mid-January 1995: $264,000,000 × Ps5.50/$ =   Ps1,452,000,000

Dollar debt increase measure in Mexican pesos   Ps541,200,000

The number of pesos needed to repay the dollar debt increased by 59%! In U.S. dollar terms, the drop in the value of the peso meant that Gemex needed the peso-equivalent of an additional $98,400,000 to repay its debt.

Unperformed Foreign Exchange Contracts. When a firm enters into a forward exchange contract, it deliberately creates transaction exposure. This risk is usually incurred to hedge an existing transaction exposure. For example, a U.S. firm might want to offset an existing obligation to purchase ¥100 million to pay for an import from Japan in 90 days. One way to offset this payment is to purchase ¥100 million in the forward market today for delivery in 90 days. In this manner any change in value of the Japanese yen relative to the dollar is neutralized. Thus, the potential transaction loss (or gain) on the account payable is offset by the transaction gain (or loss) on the forward contract.

Contractual Hedges. Foreign exchange transaction exposure can be managed by contractual, operating, and financial hedges. The main *contractual hedges* employ the forward, money, futures, and options markets. *Operating hedges* utilize operating cash flows—cash flows originating from the operating activities of the firm—and include risk-sharing agreements and leads and lags in payment strategies. *Financial hedges* utilize financing cash flows—cash flows originating from the financing activities of the firm—and include specific types of debt and foreign currency derivatives, such as swaps. These operating and financing hedges will be described in detail in later chapters.

The term *natural hedge* refers to an offsetting operating cash flow, a payable arising from the conduct of business. A *financial hedge* refers to either an offsetting debt obligation (such as a loan) or some type of financial derivative such as an interest rate swap. Care should be taken to distinguish hedges in the same way finance distinguishes cash flows—*operating* from *financing*. The following case illustrates how contractual hedging techniques may be used to protect against transaction exposure.

Transaction Exposure Management: The Case of Trident

Maria Gonzalez is the chief financial officer of Trident. She has just concluded negotiations for the sale of a turbine generator to Regency, a British firm, for £1,000,000. This single sale is quite large in relation to Trident's present business. Trident has no other current foreign customers, so the currency risk of this sale is of particular concern. The sale is made in March with payment due three months later in June. Exhibit 9.4 summarizes the financial and market information Maria has collected for the analysis of her currency exposure problem. The unknown—the *transaction exposure*—is the actual realized value of the receivable in U.S. dollars at the end of 90 days.

Trident operates on relatively narrow margins. Although Maria and Trident would be very happy if the pound appreciated versus the dollar, concerns center on the possibility that the pound will fall. When Trident had priced and budgeted this contract, it had set a very slim minimum acceptable margin at a sales price of $1,700,000; Trident wanted the deal for both financial and strategic purposes. The budget rate, the lowest acceptable dollar per pound exchange rate, was therefore established at $1.70/£. Any exchange rate below this budget rate would result in Trident realizing no profit on the deal.

Four alternatives are available to Trident to manage the exposure: 1) remain unhedged; 2) hedge in the forward market; 3) hedge in the money market; or 4) hedge in the options market.

Unhedged Position

Maria may decide to accept the transaction risk. If she believes the foreign exchange advisor, she expects to receive £1,000,000 × $1.76 = $1,760,000 in three months. However, that amount is at risk. If the pound should fall to, say, $1.65/£, she will receive only $1,650,000.

EXHIBIT 9.4   **Trident's Transaction Exposure**

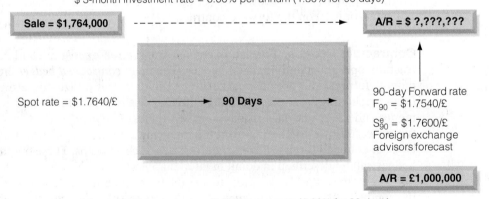

U.S. Dollar Market

Trident's weighted average cost of capital = 12.00% (3.00% for 90 days)
$ 3-month borrowing rate = 8.00% per annum (2.00% for 90 days)
$ 3-month investment rate = 6.00% per annum (1.50% for 90 days)

Sale = $1,764,000   ------------------------------→   A/R = $?,???,???

Spot rate = $1.7640/£   ——→   **90 Days**   ——→

90-day Forward rate
F_{90} = $1.7540/£

S_{90}^e = $1.7600/£
Foreign exchange
advisors forecast

A/R = £1,000,000

£ 3-month investment rate = 8.00% per annum (2.00% for 90 days)
£ 3-month borrowing rate = 10.00% per annum (2.50% for 90 days)

British Pound Market

June (3-month) put option for £1,000,000 with a strike rate of $1.75/£; premium of 1.5%

Exchange risk is not one-sided, however; if the transaction is left uncovered and the pound strengthened even more than forecast by the advisor, Trident will receive considerably more than $1,760,000. The essence of an unhedged approach is as follows:

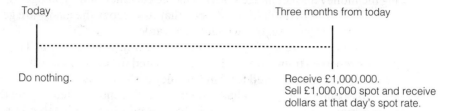

Today

Do nothing.

Three months from today

Receive £1,000,000.
Sell £1,000,000 spot and receive
dollars at that day's spot rate.

Forward Market Hedge

A *forward hedge* involves a forward (or futures) contract and a source of funds to fulfill that contract. The forward contract is entered into at the time the transaction exposure is created. In Trident's case, that would be in March, when the sale to Regency was booked as an account receivable.

When a foreign currency denominated sale such as this is made, it is booked at the spot rate of exchange existing on the booking date. In this case, the spot rate on the date of sale was $1.7640/£, so the receivable was booked as $1,764,000. Funds to fulfill the forward contract will be available in June, when Regency pays £1,000,000 to Trident. If funds to fulfill the forward contract are on hand or are due because of a business operation, the hedge is considered *covered*, *perfect*, or *square* because no residual foreign exchange risk exists. Funds on hand or to be received are matched by funds to be paid.

In some situations, funds to fulfill the forward exchange contract are not already available or due to be received later, but must be purchased in the spot market at some future date. Such a hedge is *open* or *uncovered*. It involves considerable risk because the hedger must take a chance on purchasing foreign exchange at an uncertain future spot rate in order to fulfill the forward contract. Purchase of such funds at a later date is referred to as *covering*.

Should Trident wish to hedge its transaction exposure with a forward, it will sell £1,000,000 forward today at the 3-month forward rate of $1.7540/£. This is a *covered transaction* in which the firm no longer has any foreign exchange risk. In three months the firm will receive £1,000,000 from the British buyer, deliver that sum to the bank against its forward sale, and receive $1,754,000. This would be recorded on Trident's income statement as a foreign exchange loss of $10,000 ($1,764,000 as booked, $1,754,000 as settled).

The essence of a forward hedge is as follows:

Today

Sell £1,000,000
forward @ $1.7540/£.

Three months from today

Receive £1,000,000.
Deliver £1,000,000 against forward sale.
Receive $1,754,000.

If Maria's forecast of future rates was identical to that implicit in the forward quotation, that is, $1.7540/£, expected receipts would be the same whether or not the firm hedges. However, realized receipts under the unhedged alternative could vary considerably from the certain receipts when the transaction is hedged. Never underestimate the value of predictability of outcomes (and 90 nights of solid sleep).

Money Market Hedge

Like a forward market hedge, a *money market hedge* also involves a contract and a source of funds to fulfill that contract. In this instance, the contract is a loan agreement. The firm seeking the money market hedge borrows in one currency and exchanges the proceeds for another currency. Funds to fulfill the contract—that is, to repay the loan—are generated from business operations, in this case, the account receivable.

A money market hedge can cover a single transaction, such as Trident's £1,000,000 receivable, or repeated transactions. Hedging repeated transactions is called *matching*. It requires the firm to match the expected foreign currency cash inflows and outflows by currency and maturity. For example, if Trident had numerous sales denominated in pounds to British customers over a long period of time, it would have somewhat predictable U.K. pound cash inflows. ·The appropriate money market hedge technique here would be to borrow U.K. pounds in an amount matching the typical size and maturity of expected pound inflows. Then, if the pound depreciated or appreciated, the foreign exchange effect on cash inflows in pounds would be offset by the effect on cash outflows in pounds from repaying the pound loan plus interest.

The structure of a money market hedge resembles that of a forward hedge. The difference is that the cost of the money market hedge is determined by different interest rates than the interest rates used in the formation of the forward rate. The difference in interest rates facing a private firm borrowing in two separate country markets may be different from the difference in risk-free government bill rates or eurocurrency interest rates in these same markets. In efficient markets interest rate parity should ensure that these costs are nearly the same, but not all markets are efficient at all times.

To hedge in the money market, Maria will borrow pounds in London at once, immediately convert the borrowed pounds into dollars, and repay the pound loan in three months with the proceeds from the sale of the generator. She will need to borrow just enough to repay both the principal and interest with the sale proceeds. The borrowing interest rate will be 10% per annum, or 2.5% for three months. Therefore, the amount to borrow now for repayment in three months is

$$\frac{£1,000,000}{1 + 0.025} = £975,610$$

Maria would borrow £975,610 now, and in three months repay that amount plus £24,390 of interest with the account receivable. Trident would exchange the £975,610 loan proceeds for dollars at the current spot exchange rate of $1.7640/£, receiving $1,720,976 at once.

The money market hedge, if selected by Trident, creates a pound-denominated liability, the pound loan, to offset the pound-denominated asset, the account receivable. The money market hedge works as a hedge by matching assets and liabilities according to their currency of denomination. Using a simple T-account illustrating Trident's balance sheet, the loan in British pounds is seen to offset the pound-denominated account receivable:

Assets		Liabilities and Net Worth	
Account receivable	£1,000,000	Bank loan (principal)	£975,610
		Interest payable	24,390
	£1,000,000		£1,000,000

The loan acts as a *balance sheet hedge* against the pound-denominated account receivable.

To compare the forward hedge with the money market hedge, one must analyze how Trident's loan proceeds will be utilized for the next three months. Remember that the loan proceeds are received today but the forward contract proceeds are received in three months.

For comparison purposes, one must either calculate the future value of the loan proceeds or the present value of the forward contract proceeds. Since the primary uncertainty here is the dollar value in three months, we will use future value here.

As both the forward contract proceeds and the loan proceeds are relatively certain, it is possible to make a clear choice between the two alternatives based on the one that yields the higher dollar receipts. This result, in turn, depends on the assumed rate of investment or use of the loan proceeds.

At least three logical choices exist for an assumed investment rate for the loan proceeds for the next three months. First, if Trident is cash rich, the loan proceeds might be invested in U.S. dollar money market instruments that yield 6% per annum. Second, Maria might simply use the pound loan proceeds to pay down dollar loans that currently cost Trident 8% per annum. Third, Maria might invest the loan proceeds in the general operations of the firm, in which case the cost of capital of 12% per annum would be the appropriate rate. The field of finance generally uses the company's cost of capital to move capital forward and backward in time, and we will therefore use the WACC of 12% (3% for the 90-day period here) to calculate the future value of proceeds under the money market hedge:

$$\$1,720,976 \times 1.03 = \$1,772,605$$

A break-even rate can now be calculated between the forward hedge and the money market hedge. Assume that r is the unknown 3-month investment rate (expressed as a decimal) that would equalize the proceeds from the forward and money market hedges. We have

$$\text{(Loan Proceeds)} \times (1 + \text{Rate}) = \text{(Forward Proceeds)}$$
$$\$1,720,976 \times (1 + r) = \$1,754,000$$
$$r = 0.0192$$

One can convert this 3-month (90 days) investment rate to an annual whole percentage equivalent, assuming a 360-day financial year, as follows:

$$0.0192 \times \frac{360}{90} \times 100 = 7.68\%$$

In other words, if Maria Gonzalez can invest the loan proceeds at a rate higher than 7.68% per annum, she would prefer the money market hedge. If she can only invest at a rate lower than 7.68%, she would prefer the forward hedge.

The essence of a money market hedge is as follows:

Today

Three months from today

Borrow £975,610.
Exchange £975,610 for dollars @ $1.7640/£.
Receive $1,720,976 cash.

Receive £1,000,000.
Repay £975,610 loan plus £24,390 interest, for a total of £1,000,000.

The money market hedge therefore results in cash received up-front (at the start of the period), which can then be carried forward in time for comparison with the other hedging alternatives.

Options Market Hedge

Maria Gonzalez could also cover her £1,000,000 exposure by purchasing a put option. This technique—an *option hedge*—allows her to speculate on the upside potential for appreciation of the pound while limiting downside risk to a known amount. Maria could purchase from her bank a 3-month put option on £1,000,000 at an at-the-money (ATM) strike price of $1.75/£ with a premium cost of 1.50%. The cost of the option—the premium—is

$$(\text{Size of Option}) \times (\text{Premium}) \times (\text{Spot Rate}) = \text{Cost of Option}$$
$$£1,000,000 \times 0.015 \times \$1.7640 = \$26,460$$

Because we are using future value to compare the various hedging alternatives, it is necessary to project the premium cost of the option forward three months. We will use the cost of capital of 12% per annum or 3% per quarter. Therefore the premium cost of the put option as of June would be $26,460(1.03) = $27,254. This is equal to $0.0273 per pound ($27,254 ÷ £1,000,000).

When the £1,000,000 is received in June, the value in dollars depends on the spot rate at that time. The upside potential is unlimited, the same as in the unhedged alternative. At any exchange rate above $1.75/£, Trident would allow its option to expire unexercised and would exchange the pounds for dollars at the spot rate. If the expected rate of $1.76/£ materializes, Trident would exchange the £1,000,000 in the spot market for $1,760,000. Net proceeds would be $1,760,000 minus the $27,254 cost of the option, or $1,732,746.

In contrast to the unhedged alternative, downside risk is limited with an option. If the pound depreciates below $1.75/£, Maria would exercise her option to sell (put) £1,000,000 at $1.75/£, receiving $1,750,000 gross, but $1,722,746 net of the $27,254 cost of the option. Although this downside result is worse than the downside of either the forward or money market hedges, the upside potential is unlimited.

The essence of the at-the-money (ATM) put option market hedge is as follows:

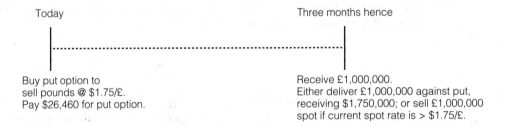

We can calculate a trading range for the pound that defines the break-even points for the option compared with the other strategies. The upper bound of the range is determined by comparison with the forward rate. The pound must appreciate enough above the $1.7540 forward rate to cover the $0.0273/£ cost of the option. Therefore, the break-even upside spot price of the pound must be $1.7540 + $0.0273 = $1.7813. If the spot pound appreciates above $1.7813, proceeds under the option strategy will be greater than under the forward hedge. If the spot pound ends up below $1.7813, the forward hedge would have been superior in retrospect.

The lower bound of the range is determined by the unhedged strategy. If the spot price falls below $1.75/£, Maria will exercise her put and sell the proceeds at $1.75/£. The net proceeds will be $1.75/£ less than the $0.0273 cost of the option, or $1.7227/£. If the spot rate falls below $1.7227/£, the net proceeds from exercising the option will be greater than the net proceeds from selling the unhedged pounds in the spot market. At any spot rate above $1.7221/£, the spot proceeds from remaining unhedged will be greater.

Foreign currency options have a variety of hedging uses. A put option is useful to construction firms or other exporters when they must submit a fixed price bid in a foreign currency without knowing until some later date whether their bid is successful. Similarly, a call option is useful to hedge a bid for a foreign firm if a potential future foreign currency payment may be required. In either case, if the bid is rejected, the loss is limited to the cost of the option.

Comparison of Alternatives

Exhibit 9.5 shows the value of Trident's £1,000,000 account receivable over a range of possible ending spot exchange rates and hedging alternatives. This exhibit makes it clear that the firm's view of likely exchange rate changes aids in the hedging choice as follows:

■ If the exchange rate is expected to move against Trident, to the left of $1.76/£, the money market hedge is the clearly preferred alternative with a guaranteed value of $1,772,605.

■ If the exchange rate is expected to move in Trident's favor, to the right of $1.76/£, the choice of the hedge is more complex, and lies between remaining unhedged, the money market hedge, or the put option.

Remaining unhedged is most likely an unacceptable choice. If Maria's expectations regarding the future spot rate proved wrong, and the spot rate fell below $1.70/£, she would not reach her budget rate. The put option offers a unique alternative. If the exchange rate moves in Trident's favor, the put option offers nearly the same upside potential as the unhedged alternative except for the up-front costs. If, however, the exchange rate moves against Trident, the put option limits the downside risk to $1,722,746.

EXHIBIT 9.5	Valuation of Cash Flows under Hedging Alternatives for Trident with Option

Value in U.S. dollars of Trident's £1,000,000 A/R

Strategy Choice and Outcome

Trident, like all firms attempting to hedge transaction exposure, must decide on a strategy before exchange rate changes occur. How will Maria Gonzalez choose among the alternative hedging strategies? She must select on the basis of two decision criteria: 1) the *risk tolerance* of Trident, as expressed in its stated policies; and 2) her own *view*, or expectation of the direction (and distance) the exchange rate will move over the coming 90-day period.

Trident's risk tolerance is a combination of management's philosophy toward transaction exposure and the specific goals of treasury activities. Many firms believe that currency risk is simply a part of doing business internationally, and therefore, begin their analysis from an unhedged baseline. Other firms, however, view currency risk as unacceptable, and either begin their analysis from a full forward contract cover baseline, or simply mandate that all transaction exposures be fully covered by forward contracts regardless of the value of other hedging alternatives. The treasury in most firms operates as a *cost* or *service center* for the firm. On the other hand, if the treasury operates as a *profit center*, it might tolerate taking more risk.

The final choice among hedges—if Maria Gonzalez does expect the pound to appreciate—combines the firm's risk tolerance, its view, and its confidence in its view. Transaction exposure management with contractual hedges requires managerial judgment.

Management of an Account Payable

The management of an account payable, where the firm would be required to make a foreign currency payment at a future date, is similar but not identical to the management of an account receivable. If Trident had a £1,000,000 account payable in 90 days, the hedging choices would appear as follows:

Remain Unhedged. Trident could wait 90 days, exchange dollars for pounds at that time, and make its payment. If Trident expects the spot rate in 90 days to be $1.7600/£, the payment would be expected to cost $1,760,000. This amount is, however, uncertain; the spot exchange rate in 90 days could be very different from that expected.

Forward Market Hedge. Trident could buy £1,000,000 forward, locking in a rate of $1.7540/£, and a total dollar cost of $1,754,000. This is $6,000 less than the expected cost of remaining unhedged, and therefore clearly preferable to the first alternative.

Money Market Hedge. The money market hedge is distinctly different for a payable as opposed to a receivable. To implement a money market hedge in this case, Trident would exchange U.S. dollars spot and invest them for 90 days in a pound-denominated interest-bearing account. The principal and interest in British pounds at the end of the 90-day period would be used to pay the £1,000,000 account payable.

In order to assure that the principal and interest exactly equal the £1,000,000 due in 90 days, Trident would discount the £1,000,000 by the pound investment interest rate of 8% for 90 days in order to determine the pounds needed today:

$$\frac{£1,000,000}{\left[1 + \left(.08 \times \frac{90}{360}\right)\right]} = £980,392.16$$

This £980,392.16 needed today would require $1,729,411.77 at the current spot rate of $1.7640/£:

$$£980,392.16 \times \$1.7640/£ = \$1,729,411.77.$$

Finally, in order to compare the money market hedge outcome with the other hedging alternatives, the $1,729,411.77 cost today must be carried forward 90 days to the same future date as the other hedge choices. If the current dollar cost is carried forward at Trident's WACC of 12%, the total cost of the money market hedge is $1,781,294.12. This is higher than the forward hedge and therefore unattractive.

$$\$1,729,411.77 \times \left[1 + \left(.12 \times \frac{90}{360} \right) \right] = \$1,781,294.12$$

Option Hedge. Trident could cover its £1,000,000 account payable by purchasing a call option on £1,000,000. A June call option on British pounds with a near at-the-money strike price of $1.75/£ would cost 1.5% (premium) or

$$£1,000,000 \times 0.015 \times \$1.7640/£ = \$26,460.$$

This premium, regardless of whether the call option is exercised or not, will be paid up-front. Its value, carried forward 90 days at the WACC of 12%, would raise its end of period cost to $27,254.

If the spot rate in 90 days is less than $1.75/£, the option would be allowed to expire and the £1,000,000 for the payable purchased on the spot market. The total cost of the call option hedge, if the option is not exercised, is theoretically smaller than any other alternative (with the exception of remaining unhedged, because the option premium is still paid and lost). If the spot rate in 90 days exceeds $1.75/£, the call option would be exercised. The total cost of the call option hedge if exercised is as follows:

Exercise call option (£1,000,000 × $1.75/£)	$1,750,000
Call option premium (carried forward 90 days)	27,254
Total maximum expense of call option hedge	$1,777,254

Payable Hedging Strategy Choice. The four hedging methods of managing a £1,000,000 account payable for Trident are summarized in Exhibit 9.6. The costs of the forward hedge

---

EXHIBIT 9.6   **Valuation of Hedging Alternatives for an Account Payable**

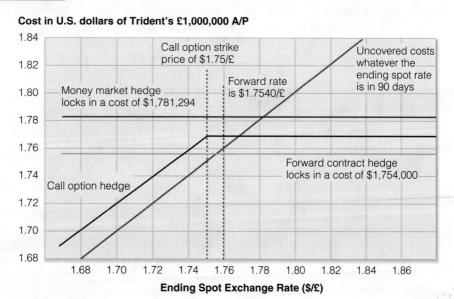

and money market hedge are certain. The cost using the call option hedge is calculated as a maximum, and the cost of remaining unhedged is highly uncertain.

As with Trident's account receivable, the final hedging choice depends on the confidence of Maria's exchange rate expectations, and her willingness to bear risk. The forward hedge provides the lowest cost of making the account payable payment that is certain. If the dollar strengthens against the pound, ending up at a spot rate less than \$1.75/£, the call option could potentially be the lowest cost hedge. Given an expected spot rate of \$1.76/£, however, the forward hedge appears the preferred alternative.

Risk Management in Practice

There are as many different approaches to exposure management as there are firms. A variety of surveys of corporate risk management practices in recent years in the United States, the United Kingdom, Finland, Australia, and Germany, indicate no real consensus exists regarding the best approach. The following is our attempt to assimilate the basic results of these surveys and combine them with our own personal experiences. But as illustrated by *Global Finance in Practice 9.1*, there are many different approaches.

Which Goals?

The treasury function of most private firms, the group typically responsible for transaction exposure management, is usually considered a cost center. It is not expected to add profit to the firm's bottom-line (which is not the same thing as saying it is not expected to add value to the firm). Currency risk managers are expected to err on the conservative side when managing the firm's money.

Which Exposures?

Transaction exposures exist before they are actually booked as foreign currency-denominated receivables and payables. However, many firms do not allow the hedging of quotation exposure or backlog exposure as a matter of policy. The reasoning is straightforward: until the transaction exists on the accounting books of the firm, the probability of the exposure actually occurring is considered to be less than 100%. Conservative hedging policies dictate that contractual hedges be placed only on existing exposures.

GLOBAL FINANCE IN PRACTICE 9.1

Hedging and the German Automobile Industry

The leading automakers in Germany have long been some of the world's biggest advocates of currency hedging. Companies like BMW, Mercedes, Porsche—and Porsche's owner Volkswagen—have aggressively hedged their foreign currency earnings for years given their structural exposure: while they manufacture in the euro-zone, they increasingly rely on sales in dollar, yen, or other foreign (non-euro) currency markets.

How the individual companies hedge, however, differs dramatically. Some companies like BMW state clearly that they "hedge to protect earnings," but do not speculate. Others, for example Porsche and Volkswagen in the past, have sometimes generated more than 40% of their earnings from their "hedges."

Hedges that earn money continue to pose difficulties for regulators, auditors, and investors worldwide. How a hedge is defined, and whether a hedge should only "cost" but not "profit," has delayed the implementation of many new regulatory efforts in the United States and Europe in the post–2008 financial crisis era. If a publicly traded company—for example an automaker—can consistently earn profits from hedging, is its core competency automobile manufacturing and assembly, or hedging/speculating on exchange rate movements?

GLOBAL FINANCE IN PRACTICE 9.2

The Credit Crisis and Option Volatilities in 2009

The global credit crisis had a number of lasting impacts on corporate foreign exchange hedging practices in late 2008 and early 2009. Currency volatilities rose to some of the highest levels seen in years, and stayed there. This caused option premiums to rise so dramatically that many companies were much more selective in their use of currency options in their risk management programs.

The dollar-euro volatility was a prime example. As recently as July 2007, the implied volatility for the most widely traded currency cross was below 7% for maturities from one week to three years. By October 31, 2008, the 1-month implied volatility had reached 29%. Although this was seemingly the peak, 1-month implied volatilities were still over 20% on January 30, 2009.

This makes options very expensive. For example, the premium on a 1-month call option on the euro with a strike rate forward-at-the-money at the end of January 2009 rose from $0.0096/€ to $0.0286/€ when volatility is 20%, not 7%. For a notional principal of €1 million, that is an increase in price from $9,580 to $28,640. That will put a hole in any treasury department's budget.

An increasing number of firms, however, are actively hedging not only backlog exposures, but also selectively hedging quotation and anticipated exposures. Anticipated exposures are transactions for which there are—at present—no contracts or agreements between parties, but are anticipated on the basis of historical trends and continuing business relationships. Although this may appear to be overly speculative on the part of these firms, it may be that hedging expected foreign-currency payables and receivables for future periods is the most conservative approach to protect the firm's future operating revenues.

Which Contractual Hedges?

As might be expected, transaction exposure management programs are generally divided along an "option-line," those that use options and those that do not. Firms that do not use currency options rely almost exclusively on forward contracts and money market hedges. *Global Finance in Practice 9.2* demonstrates how market condition may change firm hedging choices.

Many MNEs have established rather rigid transaction exposure risk management policies which mandate proportional hedging. These policies generally require the use of forward contract hedges on a percentage (e.g., 50, 60, or 70%) of existing transaction exposures. As the maturity of the exposures lengthens, the percentage forward-cover required decreases. The remaining portion of the exposure is then selectively hedged on the basis of the firm's risk tolerance, view of exchange rate movements, and confidence level. Although rarely acknowledged by the firms themselves, selective hedging is essentially speculation. A significant question remains as to whether a firm or a financial manager can consistently predict the future direction of exchange rates.

Summary Points

- MNEs encounter three types of currency exposure: transaction exposure, translation exposure, and operating exposure.

- Transaction exposure measures gains or losses that arise from the settlement of financial obligations whose terms are stated in a foreign currency.

- Translation exposure is the potential for accounting-derived changes in owner's equity to occur because of the need to "translate" foreign currency financial statements of foreign affiliates into a single reporting currency to prepare worldwide consolidated financial statements.

- Operating exposure, also called economic exposure, measures the change in the present value of the firm resulting from any change in future operating cash flows of the firm caused by an unexpected change in exchange rates.

- Considerable theoretical debate exists as to whether firms should hedge currency risk. Theoretically, hedging reduces the variability of the cash flows to the firm. It does not increase the cash flows to the firm. In fact, the costs of hedging may potentially lower them.

- Transaction exposure can be managed by contractual techniques and certain operating strategies. Contractual hedging techniques include forward, futures, money market, and option hedges.

- The choice of which contractual hedge to use depends on the individual firm's currency risk tolerance and its expectation of the probable movement of exchange rates over the transaction exposure period.

- In general, if an exchange rate is expected to move in a firm's favor, the preferred contractual hedges are probably those that allow it to participate in some up-side potential, but protect it against significant adverse exchange rate movements.

- In general, if the exchange rate is expected to move against the firm, the preferred contractual hedge is one that locks in an exchange rate, such as the forward contract hedge or money market hedge.

- Risk management in practice requires a firm's treasury department to identify its goals. Is treasury a cost center or profit center?

- Treasury must also choose which contractual hedges it wishes to use and what proportion of the currency risk should be hedged. Additionally, treasury must determine whether the firm should buy and/or sell currency options, a strategy that has historically been risky for some firms and banks.

MINI-CASE

Banbury Impex (India)[1]

As November 2010 came to a close, CEO Aadesh Lapura of Banbury Impex Private Limited, a textile company in India, sat in his office in solitude looking over his company's financial statements. It looked like 2010 would close with a small growth in sales and a small drop in profits. Although Banbury's profits were positive, the prospects of about 1.5% return on sales were simply not good enough moving forward. He now had two problems: negotiating a short-term prospective sale to a Turkish company, and increasing his overall profitability, which was a larger, long-term problem.

Lapura concluded that overall profitability—or lack thereof—was a result of two price forces. The first was the rapid rise in the price of cotton. A major cost driver in the textiles industry, cotton prices had risen dramatically in 2010. The second issue was clearly the rising value of the Indian rupee (INR) against the U.S. dollar (USD). Banbury's sales were all invoiced in U.S. dollars, and the dollar was falling. Profit margins were down, and he needed to move quickly.

Banbury Fabrics

Founded in 1997, Banbury Impex Private Ltd. was a family-owned enterprise that manufactured and exported apparel fabrics. The company expected sales close to INR 24.28 crores or USD 5.4 million (a crore, cr, is a unit in the Indian numbering system equal to 10 million) in 2010 as illustrated in Exhibit A. Sales were flat, operating income was declining, and—to be honest—prospects were bleak.

Banbury's sales were nearly all exported, mainly to the Middle East (50%), South America (30%), and Europe (10%). Banbury's products included a range of blended woven fabrics made from viscose, cotton, and wool. The company operated two weaving units based in India.

The company's sales growth had been slow over the past five years, averaging about 2.5% per year. However, management had been satisfied with 5% margins in 2006 and 2007 in a highly competitive business environment. Cash flows had remained relatively predictable as Lapura had managed foreign exchange risks by using forward contracts. Choosing to invoice all international sales in USD helped provide further stability in mitigating raw material costs, as international cotton prices were priced in USD. All things considered, Banbury's profit projections for 2011 looked disastrously low.

The Indian Textile Industry

The Indian textile industry has been a major contributor to Indian GDP over the past several years. After dismantling the quota regime in 2005, the government had hoped for textile exports to hit USD 50 billion by 2012, but as of 2010, they had reached only USD 22 billion.

The industry was both capital and labor intensive, as well as highly regulated. Companies operated on small margins in a highly competitive marketplace, and the global recession of 2008–2009 had battered the Indian industry even further. The Indian textile industry faced a number of challenges including rising raw material and labor costs, competition

---

[1]Copyright © 2010 Thunderbird, School of Global Management. All rights reserved. This case was prepared by Kyle Mineo, MBA '10; Saurabh Goyal, MBA '10; and Tim Erion, MBA '10, under the direction of Professor Michael Moffett for the purpose of classroom discussion only, and not to indicate either effective or ineffective management.

EXHIBIT A   Banbury Impex Private Ltd—Sales and Income

	2006	2007	2008	2009	Expected 2010	Forecast 2011
Sales (USD)	5,000,000	5,100,000	5,202,000	5,306,040	5,412,161	5,520,404
Average rate (INR to equal 1 USD)	44.6443	41.7548	43.6976	46.8997	44.8624	45.2500
Sales (INR)	223,221,500	212,949,480	227,314,915	248,851,684	242,802,523	249,798,282
Cost of goods sold (INR)	151,790,620	144,805,646	159,120,441	216,500,965	235,518,447	242,304,333
Cotton Costs	57,680,436	55,026,146	60,465,767	84,435,376	124,824,777	128,421,297
Direct Labor	19,732,781	28,961,129	38,188,906	47,630,212	49,458,874	48,460,867
Weaving Charges	44,019,280	40,545,581	31,824,088	47,630,212	32,972,583	33,922,607
Variable Overhead	30,358,124	20,272,790	28,641,679	36,805,164	28,262,214	31,499,563
Operating Income	71,430,880	68,143,834	68,194,475	32,350,719	7,284,076	7,493,948
Net Income	11,161,075	10,647,474	11,365,746	7,465,551	3,642,038	3,746,974
Return on Sales (% of sales)	5.0%	5.0%	5.0%	3.0%	1.5%	1.5%
COGS (% of Sales)	68%	68%	70%	87%	97%	97%
Cotton Costs (% of COGS)	38%	38%	38%	39%	53%	53%
Direct Labor (% of COGS)	13%	20%	24%	22%	21%	20%

from China and other Asian countries, and appreciation of the rupee.

Rising Raw Material and Labor Costs. The chief raw materials used in textiles were cotton and other natural and poly-based yarns. Erratic monsoons, coupled with increased exports of cotton in recent years, had caused the price of cotton to rise dramatically. During the past 12 months, cotton prices had increased more than 75%. A variety of government programs and restrictions had also contributed to a growing scarcity of skilled labor in the textile industry.

Competition from China and Other Asian Countries. India and China account for the majority of global textile production. Due to low labor costs and strong government support and infrastructure, China had been able to stay ahead in competing with the BRIC (Brazil, Russia, India, and China) countries. As a consequence, Chinese textile products were priced more competitively in the global market, and prevented Indian companies from pushing through any price increases. Indian companies were now suffering falling margins and losing orders to other countries. Much of the Indian low-value market had already shifted to Bangladesh, as costs there were 50% lower than in India.

Appreciation of the Rupee. The rupee had grown increasingly volatile in recent years against the dollar, and over the past two years, appreciated by nearly 20%. This appreciation had made countries like Bangladesh and Vietnam more competitive on the global front.

In early November, the rupee had risen to INR44/USD, the strongest in more than three years. It now hovered at INR45/USD. Further strengthening of the rupee against the dollar would most likely put many Indian textile companies out of business.

The Curious Case of High Cotton Prices. The cotton market had been nothing short of "crazy" recently. The monsoons in India had prompted many farmers to plant more cotton to meet the heightened demand. But, despite increased production, cotton prices had skyrocketed in the past year, reaching $1.50/lb, as illustrated in Exhibit B. The increased demand from China and the reduced inventories in the United States had driven the price up.

Although most market analysts continued to argue that cotton prices were abnormally high—and must fall sooner rather than later—they remained high and only seemed to go higher, even as the soothsayers predicted their fall. What frightened Lapura even more, were the market analysts who were now arguing that cotton prices had moved to a higher level—permanently.

Lapura was considering the use of cotton futures, a practice some of his competitors were already using. A recent check of futures prices had provided him some data on what prices he may be able to lock in now for cotton in the coming year, in U.S. cents per pound: 113.09 (March 2011); 102.06 (July 2011); 95.03 (October 2011). Although futures would eliminate the risk of further increases in cotton prices, he was still afraid he would be locking in the price at the top.

EXHIBIT B   Curious Case of Rising Cotton Prices

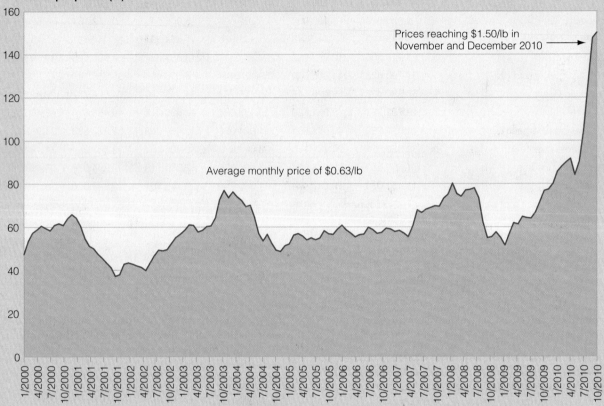

U.S. cents per pound (lb)

Prices reaching $1.50/lb in November and December 2010

Average monthly price of $0.63/lb

Currency of Invoice

As an Indian textile exporter, Lapura had never had a choice about the currency of invoice—it would be the U.S. dollar. But maybe times had changed? The dollar had been falling against the rupee for some time now (as seen in Exhibit C), and as a result, the rupees generated from export sales were less and less. The problem was that, as an exporter from what the world called an "emerging market," his hard currency choices were the U.S. dollar, the European euro, and the Japanese yen. And the rupee had been strengthening against all of them!

But what might the future bring? All three hard currencies were at record low rates of return—nominal interest rate yields—and not expected to change much in the immediate future. They were under careful watch by their central banks, with all three central banks pumping liquidity into the respective monetary systems following the credit crisis of 2008–2009. The most immediate likelihood was the rise of inflation in all three markets. Unfortunately, that would not help, as a rise in inflation would probably only drive U.S. dollar, euro, and yen values down even further against the rupee.

The Turkish Sale

Lapura's immediate problem was a $250,000 textile sale he had made to a Turkish customer. The contract allowed him to change the currency of invoice from the Turkish lira to the dollar or euro if he wished, but he had to decide by close of business day.

Expected settlement on the invoice was January 30, 2011. But regardless of which currency he chose (the rupee not being one of the choices), he still had to decide how to hedge it.

Lapura had collected a variety of forward rates from his local bank for the dollar, euro, and Turkish lira, as listed in Exhibit D. He eyed the dollar quotes the closest. The forwards would lock him into a rupee rate, which was slightly better than the current spot rate. Of course if the forwards were considered indicators of likely rate movement, they did indicate what he had long hoped for—a rise in the dollar.

| EXHIBIT C | Indian Rupee/U.S. Dollar Spot Rate |

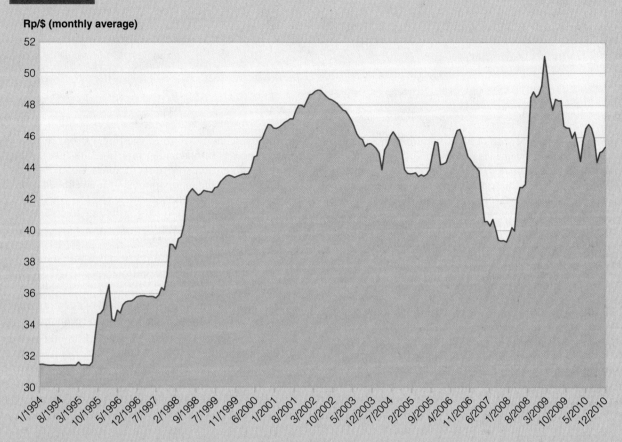

He had also considered some form of money market hedge—borrowing Turkish lira against the receivable. Although he had been selling in Turkey for over five years, he had never borrowed there, and only had one bank relationship in Ankara. If he provided sales history to the Turkish bank, he may be able to use his $250,000 receivable as collateral. Domestic loan rates in Turkey for companies with similar credit quality were about 14% according to his bankers. But his bankers also told him that as a small foreign business, the Turkish market would charge him an additional 300 basis point credit spread. But if he did indeed get the money sooner rather than later, domestic Indian deposit rates were averaging a healthy 10.4%.

Currency options had recently become a hedging alternative in India. The National Stock Exchange of India in Mumbai had opened a currency options market in October 2010.

| EXHIBIT D | Forward Rate Quotes |

Currency Cross	Symbols	Spot	Bank Quotes on Forward Rates		
			30 days	60 days	90 days
Indian rupees per U.S. dollar	USD/INR	45.8300	46.12	46.70	46.11
Indian rupees per euro	EUR/INR	60.9611	61.70	61.90	62.20
Japanese yen per rupee	INR/JPY	1.8250	1.81	1.81	1.80
Indian rupees per Turkish lira	TRY/INR	30.7192	30.96	30.95	30.87
Turkish lira per U.S. dollar	USD/TRY	1.4793	1.49	1.48	1.48

EXHIBIT E	Currency Option Quotes on the USD	

Strike Rate (Rupee/USD)	Put Premium (Rupee/USD)	Call Premium (Rupee/USD)
44.00	0.005	1.890
45.25	0.035	0.440

Quotes for 60-day maturity, USD 1000 per contract.

Source: National Stock Exchange of India, nseindia.com.

With no experience with options, Lapura wondered if an option would provide better protection than a forward contract. The options market, at least for now, was limited to INR/USD options. Although Mr. Lapura could see the upside potential that an options contract might provide, he wondered how much the contract would hurt his slim margins if he had to exercise his contract. Put and call option quotes on the dollar, considered by Mr. Lapura, are listed in Exhibit E.

Out of Time

Aadesh Lapura picked up his notes and knew it was time to call a family meeting. Times were tough and the family's livelihood was being threatened. Two things needed to be sorted out and quickly. With the last major sale of 2010 on the books—the Turkish sale—he knew he needed to protect the value of this sale from currency losses. Secondly, he needed to find a sustainable path to protecting the business over the long term. With India's continued economic growth, many analysts are forecasting a stronger Indian rupee versus USD exchange rate into the foreseeable future. Competition was fierce. Lapura wondered how much longer his Indian operations—the livelihood of the family—would be profitable.

MINI-CASE QUESTIONS

1. Which factor do you think is more threatening to Banbury's profitability, cotton prices or the rising value of the rupee?

2. Do you believe Lapura should hedge his cotton costs with cotton futures? What would you recommend?

3. Which currency of invoice do you think Lapura should choose for the Turkish sale?

4. What recommendation would you make in terms of hedging the Turkish sale receipts?

Questions

1. **Foreign Exchange.** Define the following terms:
   a. Foreign exchange exposure
   b. The three types of foreign exchange exposure

2. **Hedging and Currency Risk.** Define the following terms:
   a. hedging
   b. currency risk

3. **Arguments against Currency Risk Management.** Describe six arguments against a firm pursuing an active currency risk management program?

4. **Arguments for Currency Risk Management.** Describe four arguments in favor of a firm pursuing an active currency risk management program?

5. **Hedging versus Speculating.** What is the difference between hedging and speculating?

6. **Hedging with Forward Contracts.** Explain how a Singaporean corporation could hedge a receivable in British pounds using a forward contract. What is the cost of such a forward market hedge?

7. **Avoiding Exposure.** Can firms avoid foreign exchange exposure by using and transacting only in their home currency?

8. **Cash Balances.** Explain why foreign currency cash balances do not cause transaction exposure.

9. **Natural Hedges.** What is a natural hedge? Give an example of a natural hedge in a firm.

10. **Decision Criteria.** Ultimately, a treasurer must choose among alternative strategies to manage transaction exposure. Explain the two main decision criteria that must be used.

11. **Proportional Hedge.** Many MNEs have established transaction exposure risk management policies that mandate proportional hedging. Explain and give an example of how proportional hedging can be implemented.

Problems

1. **P&G India.** Procter and Gamble's affiliate in India, P&G India, procures much of its toiletries product line from a Vietnamese company. Because of the shortage of working capital in India, payment terms by Indian importers are typically 180 days or longer. P&G India wishes to hedge a 10 million Vietnamese dong (₫) payable. Although options are not available on the

Indian rupee (₹), forward rates are available against the dong. Additionally, a common practice in India is for companies like P&G India to work with a currency agent who will, in this case, lock in the current spot exchange rate in exchange for a 3.85% fee. Using the following exchange rate and interest rate data, recommend a hedging strategy.

Spot rate	346.49đ/₹
180-day forward rate	318.49đ/₹
Expected spot, 180 days	318.49đ/₹
180-day rupee investing rate	6.00%
180-day dong investing rate	1.80%
Currency agent's exchange rate	3.85%
P&G India's cost of capital	10.00%

2. **Siam Cement.** Siam Cement, the Bangkok-based cement manufacturer, suffered enormous losses with the coming of the Asian crisis in 1997. The company had been pursuing a very aggressive growth strategy in the mid-1990s, taking on massive quantities of foreign-currency-denominated debt (primarily U.S. dollars). When the Thai baht (B) was devalued from its pegged rate of B25.0/$ in July 1997, Siam's interest payments alone were over $900 million on its outstanding dollar debt (with an average interest rate of 8.40% on its U.S. dollar debt at that time). Assuming Siam Cement took out $50 million in debt in June 1997 at 8.40% interest, and had to repay it in one year when the spot exchange rate had stabilized at B42.0/$, what was the foreign exchange loss incurred on the transaction?

3. **BioTron Medical, Inc.** Brent Bush, CFO of a medical device distributor, BioTron Medical, Inc., was approached by a Japanese customer, Numata, with a proposal to pay cash (in yen) for its typical orders of ¥10,000,000 every other month if it were given a 5% discount. Numata's current terms are 90 days with no discounts. Using the following quotes and estimated cost of capital for Numata, Bush will compare the proposal with covering yen payments with forward contracts. Should Brent Bush accept Numata's proposal?

Spot rate	¥107.91/$
30-day forward rate	¥107.66/$
90-day forward rate	¥106.81/$
180-day forward rate	¥105.89/$
Numata's WACC	9.38%
BioTron's WACC	7.85%

4. **Embraer of Brazil.** Embraer of Brazil is one of the two leading global manufacturers of regional jets (Bombardier of Canada is the other). Regional jets are smaller than the traditional civilian airliners produced by Airbus and Boeing, seating between 50 and 100 people on average. Embraer has concluded an agreement with a regional U.S. airline to produce and deliver four aircraft one year from now for $80 million. Although Embraer will be paid in U.S. dollars, it also possesses a currency exposure of inputs—it must pay foreign suppliers $20 million for inputs one year from now (but they will be delivering the subcomponents throughout the year). The current spot rate on the Brazilian real (R$) is R$1.8240/$, but it has been steadily appreciating against the U.S. dollar over the past three years. Forward contracts are difficult to acquire and are considered expensive. Citibank Brasil has not explicitly provided Embraer a forward rate quote, but has stated that it will probably be pricing a forward off the current 4.00% U.S. dollar eurocurrency rate and the 10.50% Brazilian government bond rate. Advise Embraer on its currency exposure.

5. **Vizor Pharmaceuticals.** Vizor Pharmaceuticals, a U.S.-based multinational pharmaceutical company, is evaluating an export sale of its cholesterol-reduction drug with a prospective Indonesian distributor. The purchase would be for 1,800 million Indonesian rupiah (Rp), which at the current spot exchange rate of Rp12,215/$ translates into nearly $135,000. Although not a big sale by Vizor's standards, company policy dictates that sales must be settled for at least a minimum gross margin, in this case, a cash settlement of $133,000. The current 90-day forward rate is Rp12,472/$. Although this rate appeared unattractive, Vizor had to contact several major banks before even finding a forward quote on the rupiah. The consensus of currency forecasters at the moment, however, is that the rupiah will hold relatively steady, possibly falling to Rp12,400/$ over the coming 90 to 120 days. Analyze the prospective sale and make a hedging recommendation.

6. **Mattel Toys.** Mattel is a U.S.-based company whose sales are roughly two-thirds in dollars (Asia and the Americas) and one-third in euros (Europe). In September, Mattel delivers a large shipment of toys (primarily Barbies and Hot Wheels) to a major distributor in Antwerp. The receivable, €30 million, is due in 90 days, standard terms for the toy industry in Europe. Mattel's treasury team has collected the following currency and market quotes. The company's foreign exchange advisors believe the euro will be at about $1.4200/€ in 90 days. Mattel's management does not use currency options in currency risk management activities. Advise Mattel on which hedging alternative is probably preferable.

Current spot rate ($/€)	$1.4158
Credit Suisse 90-day forward rate ($/€)	$1.4172
Barclays 90-day forward rate ($/€)	$1.4195
Mattel Toys WACC ($)	9.600%
90-day eurodollar interest rate	4.000%
90-day euro interest rate	3.885%
90-day eurodollar borrowing rate	5.000%
90-day euro borrowing rate	5.000%

7. **Bobcat**. Bobcat, a U.S.-based manufacturer of industrial equipment, just purchased a Korean company that produces plastic nuts and bolts for heavy equipment. The purchase price was Won7,800 million. Won1,500 million has already been paid, and the remaining Won6,300 million is due in six months. The current spot rate is Won1,071.95/$, and the 6-month forward rate is Won1,103.28/$. The 6-month Korean won interest rate is 12% per annum; the 6-month U.S. dollar rate is 5% per annum. Bobcat can invest at these interest rates or borrow at 1% per annum above those rates. A 6-month call option on won with a Won1,100/$ strike rate has a 2.83% premium, while the 6-month put option at the same strike rate has a 2.48% premium.

Bobcat can invest at the rates given above, or borrow at 1% per annum above those rates. Bobcat's weighted average cost of capital is 9%. Compare alternate ways that Bobcat might deal with its foreign exchange exposure. What do you recommend and why?

8. **Aquatech.** Aquatech is a U.S.-based company that manufactures, sells, and installs water purification equipment. On April 11, the company sold a system to the City of Nagasaki, Japan, for installation in Nagasaki's famous Glover Gardens (where Puccini's Madame Butterfly waited for the return of Lt. Pinkerton). The sale was priced in yen at ¥20,000,000, with payment due in three months.

Spot exchange rate:	¥118.255/$ (closing mid-rates)
1-month forward rate:	¥117.760/$, a 5.04% per annum premium
3-month forward:	¥116.830/$, a 4.88% per annum premium
1-year forward:	¥112.450/$, a 5.16% per annum premium

Money Rates	United States	Japan	Differential
One month	4.8750%	0.09375%	4.78125%
Three months	4.9375%	0.09375%	4.84375%
Twelve months	5.1875%	0.31250%	4.87500%

Note that the interest rate differentials vary slightly from the forward discounts on the yen because of time differences for the quotes. The spot ¥118.255/$, for example, is a mid-point range. On April 11, the spot yen traded in London from ¥118.30/$ to ¥117.550/$.

Aquatech's Japanese competitors are currently borrowing yen from Japanese banks at a spread of two percentage points above the Japanese money rate. Aquatech's weighted average cost of capital is 16%, and the company wishes to protect the dollar value of this receivable.

3-month options from Kyushu Bank:

- Call option on ¥20,000,000 at exercise price of ¥118.00/$: a 1% premium.
- Put option on ¥20,000,000, at exercise price of ¥118.00/$: a 3% premium.
  a. What are the costs and benefits of alternative hedges? Which would you recommend, and why?
  b. What is the break-even reinvestment rate when comparing forward and money market alternatives?

9. **Compass Rose.** Compass Rose, Ltd., a Canadian manufacturer of raincoats, does not selectively hedge its transaction exposure. Instead, if the date of the transaction is known with certainty, all foreign currency-denominated cash flows must utilize the following mandatory forward cover formula:

Compass Rose's Mandatory Forward Cover	0–90 days	91–180 days	180 days
Paying the points forward	75%	60%	50%
Receiving the points forward	100%	90%	50%

Compass Rose expects to receive multiple payments in Danish kroner over the next year. DKr3,000,000 is due in 90 days; DKr2,000,000 is due in 180 days; and DKr1,000,000 is due in one year. Using the following spot and forward exchange rates, what would be the amount of forward cover required by company policy for each period?

Spot rate, Dkr/C$	4.70
3-month forward rate, Dkr/C$	4.71
6-month forward rate, Dkr/C$	4.72
12-month forward rate, Dkr/C$	4.74

10. **Pupule Travel.** Pupule Travel, a Honolulu, Hawaii-based 100% privately owned travel company, has signed an agreement to acquire a 50% ownership share of Taichung Travel, a Taiwan-based privately owned travel agency specializing in servicing inbound customers from the United States and Canada.

The acquisition price is 7 million Taiwan dollars (T$7,000,000) payable in cash in three months.

Thomas Carson, Pupule Travel's owner, believes the Taiwan dollar will either remain stable or decline slightly over the next three months. At the present spot rate of T$35/$, the amount of cash required is only $200,000, but even this relatively modest amount will need to be borrowed personally by Thomas Carson. Taiwanese interest-bearing deposits by nonresidents are regulated by the government, and are currently set at 1.5% per year. He has a credit line with Bank of Hawaii for $200,000 with a current borrowing interest rate of 8% per year. He does not believe that he can calculate a credible weighted average cost of capital since he has no stock outstanding and his competitors are all also privately held. Since the acquisition would use up all his available credit, he wonders if he should hedge this transaction exposure. He has the following quotes from the Bank of Hawaii:

Spot rate (T$/$)	33.40
3-month forward rate (T$/$)	32.40
3-month Taiwan dollar deposit rate	1.500%
3-month dollar borrowing rate	6.500%
3-month call option on T$	not available

Analyze the costs and risks of each alternative, and then make a recommendation as to which alternative Thomas Carson should choose.

11. **Chronos Time Pieces.** Chronos Time Pieces, a Boston-based firm, exports watches to many countries, selling in local currencies to stores and distributors. Chronos prides itself on being financially conservative. At least 75% of each individual transaction exposure is hedged, mostly in the forward market, but occasionally with options. Chronos' foreign exchange policy is such that the 75% hedge may be increased to a 125% hedge if devaluation or depreciation appears imminent. Chronos has just shipped to its major North American distributor. It has issued a 90-day invoice to its buyer for €1,800,000. The current spot rate is $1.2628/€; the 90-day forward rate is $1.2615/€. Chronos' treasurer, Manny Hernandez, has a very good track record in predicting exchange rate movements. He currently believes the euro will weaken against the dollar in the coming 90 to 120 days, possibly to around $1.2600/€.
    a. Evaluate the hedging alternatives for Chronos if Manny is right (Case 1: $1.2600/€) and if Manny is wrong (Case 2: $1.2700/€). What do you recommend?
    b. What does it mean to hedge 125% of a transaction exposure?

c. What would be considered the most conservative transaction exposure management policy by a firm? How does Chronos compare?

12. **Lucky 13.** Lucky 13 Jeans of San Antonio, Texas, is completing a new assembly plant near Guatemala City. A final construction payment of Q8,400,000 is due in six months. ("Q" is the symbol for Guatemalan quetzals.) Lucky 13 uses 20% per annum as its weighted average cost of capital. Today's foreign exchange and interest rate quotations are as follows:

Construction payment due in 6 months (A/P, quetzals)	8,400,000
Present spot rate (quetzals/$)	7.0000
6-month forward rate (quetzals/$)	7.1000
Guatemalan 6-month interest rate (per annum)	14.000%
U.S. dollar 6-month interest rate (per annum)	6.000%
Lucky 13's weighted average cost of capital (WACC)	20.000%

Lucky 13's treasury manager, concerned about the Guatemalan economy, wonders if Lucky 13 should be hedging its foreign exchange risk. The manager's own forecast is as follows:

Expected spot rate in 6-months (quetzals/$):

Highest expected rate (reflecting a significant devaluation)	8.0000
Expected rate	7.3000
Lowest expected rate (reflecting a strengthening of the quetzal)	6.4000

What realistic alternatives are available to Lucky 13 for making payments? Which method would you select and why?

13. **Burton Manufacturing.** Jason Stedman is the director of finance for Burton Manufacturing, a U.S.-based manufacturer of handheld computer systems for inventory management. Burton's system combines a low-cost active tag that is attached to inventory items (the tag emits an extremely low-grade radio frequency) with custom designed hardware and software that tracks the low-grade emissions for inventory control. Burton has completed the sale of an inventory management system to a British firm, Pegg Metropolitan (UK), for a total payment of £1,000,000. The exchange rates shown at the bottom of this page were available to Burton on the dates shown, corresponding to the events of this specific export sale. Assume each month is 30 days.
    a. What will be the amount of foreign exchange gain (loss) upon settlement?
    b. If Jason hedges the exposure with a forward contract, what will be the net foreign exchange gain (loss) on settlement?

Problem 13.

Date	Event	Spot Rate ($/£)	Forward Rate ($/£)	Days Forward
February 1	Price quotation for Pegg	1.7850	1.7771	210
March 1	Contract signed for sale	1.7465	1.7381	180
	Contract amount, pounds	£1,000,000		
June 1	Product shipped to Pegg	1.7689	1.7602	90
August 1	Product received by Pegg	1.7840	1.7811	30
September 1	Grand Met makes payment	1.7290	—	—

14. **Micca Metals, Inc.** Micca Metals, Inc. is a specialty materials and metals company located in Detroit, Michigan. The company specializes in specific precious metals and materials that are used in a variety of pigment applications in many industries including cosmetics, appliances, and a variety of high tinsel metal fabricating equipment. Micca just purchased a shipment of phosphates from Morocco for 6,000,000 dirhams, payable in six months.

Six-month call options on 6,000,000 dirhams at an exercise price of 10.00 dirhams per dollar are available from Bank Al-Maghrub at a premium of 2%. Six-month put options on 6,000,000 dirhams at an exercise price of 10.00 dirhams per dollar are available at a premium of 3%. Compare and contrast alternative ways that Micca might hedge its foreign exchange transaction exposure. What is your recommendation?

Assumptions	Values
Shipment of phosphates from Morocco, Moroccan dirhams	6,000,000
Micca's cost of capital (WACC)	14.000%
Spot exchange rate, dirhams/$	10.00
6-month forward rate, dirhams/$	10.40

15. **Maria Gonzalez and Trident.** Trident—the U.S.-based company discussed in this chapter—has concluded another large sale of telecommunications equipment to Regency (U.K.). Total payment of £3,000,000 is due in 90 days. Maria Gonzalez has also learned that Trident will only be able to borrow in the United Kingdom at 14% per annum (due to credit concerns of the British banks). Given the following exchange rates and interest rates, what transaction exposure hedge is now in Trident's best interest?

Assumptions	Value
90-day A/R in pounds	£3,000,000.00
Spot rate, US$ per pound ($/£)	$1.7620
90-day forward rate, US$ per pound ($/£)	$1.7550

(*continued*)

Problem 15. (continued)

Assumptions	Value
3-month U.S. dollar investment rate	6.000%
3-month U.S. dollar borrowing rate	8.000%
3-month U.K. investment interest rate	8.000%
3-month U.K. borrowing interest rate	14.000%
Put options on the British pound: Strike rates, US$/pound ($/£)	
Strike rate ($/£)	$1.75
Put option premium	1.500%
Strike rate ($/£)	$1.71
Put option premium	1.000%
Trident's WACC	12.000%
Maria Gonzalez's expected spot rate in 90-day, US$ per pound ($/£)	$1.7850

16. **Larkin Hydraulics.** On May 1, Larkin Hydraulics, a wholly owned subsidiary of Caterpillar (U.S.), sold a 12-megawatt compression turbine to Rebecke-Terwilleger Company of the Netherlands for €4,000,000, payable as €2,000,000 on August 1 and €2,000,000 on November 1. Larkin derived its price quote of €4,000,000 on April 1 by dividing its normal U.S. dollar sales price of $4.320,000 by the then current spot rate of $1.0800/€.

By the time the order was received and booked on May 1, the euro had strengthened to $1.1000/€, so the sale was in fact worth €4,000,000 × $1.1000/€ = $4,400,000. Larkin had already gained an extra $80,000 from favorable exchange rate movements. Nevertheless, Larkin's director of finance now wondered if the firm should hedge against a reversal of the recent trend of the euro. Four approaches were possible:

1. *Hedge in the forward market*: The 3-month forward exchange quote was $1.1060/€ and the 6-month forward quote was $1.1130/€.

2. *Hedge in the money market*: Larkin could borrow euros from the Frankfurt branch of its U.S. bank at 8.00% per annum.

3. *Hedge with foreign currency options*: August put options were available at strike price of $1.1000/€ for a premium of 2.0% per contract, and November put options were available at $1.1000/€ for a premium of 1.2%. August call options at $1.1000/€ could be purchased for a premium of 3.0%, and November call options at $1.1000/€ were available at a 2.6% premium.

4. *Do nothing*: Larkin could wait until the sales proceeds were received in August and November, hope the recent strengthening of the euro would continue, and sell the euros received for dollars in the spot market.

Larkin estimates the cost of equity capital to be 12% per annum. As a small firm, Larkin Hydraulics is unable to raise funds with long-term debt. U.S. T-bills yield 3.6% per annum. What should Larkin do?

Internet Exercises

1. **Current Volatilities.** You wish to price your own options, but you need current volatilities on the euro, British pound, and Japanese yen. Using the following Web sites, collect spot rates and volatilities in order to price forward at-the-money put options for your option pricing analysis.

Federal Reserve Bank of New York	www.newyorkfed.org/markets/foreignex.html
RatesFX.com	www.ratesfx.com/

2. **Hedging Objectives.** All multinational companies will state the goals and objectives of their currency risk management activities in their annual reports. Beginning with the following firms, collect samples of corporate "why hedge?" discussions for a contrast and comparison discussion.

Nestlé	www.nestle.com
Disney	www.disney.com
Nokia	www.nokia.com
BP	www.bp.com

3. **Changing Translation Practices: FASB.** The Financial Accounting Standards Board promulgates standard practices for the reporting of financial results by companies in the United States. It also, however, often leads the way in the development of new practices and emerging issues around the world. One major issue today is the valuation and reporting of financial derivatives and derivative agreements by firms. Use the FASB's home page and the Web pages of several of the major accounting firms and other interest groups around the world to see current proposed accounting standards and the current state of reaction to the proposed standards.

FASB home page	raw.rutgers.edu/
Treasury Management of NY	www.tmany.org/

CHAPTER

10

Translation Exposure

The pen is mightier than the sword, but no match for the accountant. —Jonathan Glancey

LEARNING OBJECTIVES

- Explain the meaning behind the designation of a foreign subsidiary's "functional currency"

- Illustrate both the theoretical and practical differences between the two primary methods of *translating* or *remeasuring* foreign currency-denominated financial statements

- Understand how an accounting-based concept like translation can have valuation impacts on multinational firms

- Analyze the costs and benefits of managing translation exposure

Translation exposure, the second category of accounting exposures, arises because financial statements of foreign subsidiaries—which are stated in foreign currency—must be restated in the parent's reporting currency for the firm to prepare consolidated financial statements. Foreign subsidiaries of U.S. companies, for example, must restate local euro, pound, yen, etc., statements in U.S. dollars so the foreign values can be added to the parent's U.S. dollar-denominated balance sheet and income statement. This accounting process is called "translation." *Translation exposure* is the potential for an increase or decrease in the parent's net worth and reported net income caused by a change in exchange rates since the last translation.

Although the main purpose of translation is to prepare consolidated statements, translated statements are also used by management to assess the performance of foreign subsidiaries. Although such assessment might be performed from the local currency statements, restatement of all subsidiary statements into the single "common denominator" of one currency facilitates management comparison.

This chapter reviews the predominate methods used in translation today, and concludes with the Mini-Case, *LaJolla Engineering Services*, illustrating how translation may arise and affect a multinational's financial performance.

Overview of Translation

There are two financial statements for each subsidiary that must be translated for consolidation: the income statement and the balance sheet. Statements of cash flow are not translated from the foreign subsidiaries. The consolidated statement of cash flow is constructed from the consolidated statement of income and consolidated balance sheet. Because the consolidated results for any multinational firm are constructed from all of its subsidiary operations, including foreign subsidiaries, the possibility of a change in consolidated net income or consolidated net worth from period to period, as a result of a change in exchange rates, is high.

For any individual financial statement, internally, if the same exchange rate were used to remeasure each and every line item on the individual statement—the income statement and balance sheet—there would be no imbalances resulting from the remeasurement. But if a different exchange rate were used for different line items on an individual statement, an imbalance would result. Different exchange rates are used in remeasuring different line items because translation principles are a complex compromise between historical and current values. The question, then, is what is to be done with the imbalance?

Subsidiary Characterization

Most countries specify the translation method to be used by a foreign subsidiary based on its business operations. For example, a foreign subsidiary's business can be categorized as either an integrated foreign entity or a self-sustaining foreign entity. An *integrated foreign entity* is one that operates as an extension of the parent company, with cash flows and general business lines that are highly interrelated with those of the parent. A *self-sustaining foreign entity* is one that operates in the local economic environment independent of the parent company. The differentiation is important to the logic of translation. A foreign subsidiary should be valued principally in terms of the currency that is the basis of its economic viability.

It is not unusual for a single company to have both types of foreign subsidiaries, integrated and self-sustaining. For example, a U.S.-based manufacturer, which produces subassemblies in the United States that are then shipped to a Spanish subsidiary for finishing and resale in the European Union, would likely characterize the Spanish subsidiary as an integrated foreign entity. The dominant currency of economic operation is likely the U.S. dollar. That same U.S. parent may also own an agricultural marketing business in Venezuela that has few cash flows or operations related to the U.S. parent company or U.S. dollar. The Venezuelan subsidiary may source all inputs and sell all products in Venezuelan bolivar. Because the Venezuelan subsidiary's operations are independent of its parent, and its functional currency is the Venezuelan bolivar, it would be classified as a self-sustaining foreign entity.

Functional Currency

A foreign subsidiary's *functional currency* is the currency of the primary economic environment in which the subsidiary operates and in which it generates cash flows. In other words, it is the dominant currency used by that foreign subsidiary in its day-to-day operations. It is important to note that the geographic location of a foreign subsidiary and its functional currency may be different. The Singapore subsidiary of a U.S. firm may find that its functional currency is the U.S. dollar (integrated subsidiary), the Singapore dollar (self-sustaining subsidiary), or a third currency such as the British pound (also a self-sustaining subsidiary).

The United States, rather than distinguishing a foreign subsidiary as either integrated or self-sustaining, requires that the functional currency of the subsidiary be determined. Management must evaluate the nature and purpose of each of its individual foreign subsidiaries to determine the appropriate functional currency for each. If a foreign subsidiary of a U.S.-based company is determined to have the U.S. dollar as its functional currency, it is essentially an extension of the parent company (equivalent to the integrated foreign entity designation used by most countries). If, however, the functional currency of the foreign subsidiary is determined to be different from the U.S. dollar, the subsidiary is considered a separate entity from the parent (equivalent to the self-sustaining entity designation).

Translation Methods

Two basic methods for translation are employed worldwide: the current rate method and the temporal method. Regardless of which method is employed, a translation method must not only designate at what exchange rate individual balance sheet and income statement items are remeasured, but also designate where any imbalance is to be recorded, either in current income or in an equity reserve account in the balance sheet.

Current Rate Method

The *current rate method* is the most prevalent in the world today. Under this method, all financial statement line items are translated at the "current" exchange rate with few exceptions.

- **Assets and liabilities.** All assets and liabilities are translated at the current rate of exchange; that is, at the rate of exchange in effect on the balance sheet date.
- **Income statement items.** All items, including depreciation and cost of goods sold, are translated at either the actual exchange rate on the dates the various revenues, expenses, gains, and losses were incurred or at an appropriately weighted average exchange rate for the period.
- **Distributions.** Dividends paid are translated at the exchange rate in effect on the date of payment.
- **Equity items.** Common stock and paid-in capital accounts are translated at historical rates. Year-end retained earnings consist of the original year-beginning retained earnings plus or minus any income or loss for the year.

  Gains or losses caused by translation adjustments are not included in the calculation of consolidated net income. Rather, translation gains or losses are reported separately and accumulated in a separate equity reserve account (on the consolidated balance sheet) with a title such as "cumulative translation adjustment" (CTA), but it depends on the country. If a foreign subsidiary is later sold or liquidated, translation gains or losses of past years accumulated in the CTA account are reported as one component of the total gain or loss on sale or liquidation. The total gain or loss is reported as part of the net income or loss for the period in which the sale or liquidation occurs.

Temporal Method

Under the *temporal method*, specific assets and liabilities are translated at exchange rates consistent with the timing of the item's creation. The temporal method assumes that a number of individual line item assets, such as inventory and net plant and equipment, are restated regularly to reflect market value. If these items were not restated, but were instead carried at historical cost, the temporal method becomes the *monetary/nonmonetary method* of translation, a form of translation that is still used by a number of countries today. Line items include the following:

- **Monetary assets** (primarily cash, marketable securities, accounts receivable, and long-term receivables) **and monetary liabilities** (primarily current liabilities and long-term debt). These are translated at current exchange rates. Nonmonetary assets and liabilities (primarily inventory and fixed assets) are translated at historical rates.
- **Income statement items.** These are translated at the average exchange rate for the period, except for items such as depreciation and cost of goods sold that are directly associated with nonmonetary assets or liabilities. These accounts are translated at their historical rate.

- **Distributions.** Dividends paid are translated at the exchange rate in effect on the date of payment.
- **Equity items.** Common stock and paid-in capital accounts are translated at historical rates. Year-end retained earnings consist of the original year-beginning retained earnings plus or minus any income or loss for the year, plus or minus any imbalance from translation.

Under the temporal method, gains or losses resulting from remeasurement are carried directly to current consolidated income, and not to equity reserves. Hence, foreign exchange gains and losses arising from the translation process do introduce volatility to consolidated earnings.

U.S. Translation Procedures

The United States differentiates foreign subsidiaries based on functional currency, not subsidiary characterization. A note on terminology: Under U.S. accounting and translation practices, use of the current rate method is termed "translation" while use of the temporal method is termed "remeasurement." The primary principles of U.S. translation are summarized as follows:

- If the financial statements of the foreign subsidiary of a U.S. company are maintained in U.S. dollars, translation is not required.
- If the financial statements of the foreign subsidiary are maintained in the local currency and the local currency is the functional currency, they are translated by the current rate method.
- If the financial statements of the foreign subsidiary are maintained in the local currency and the U.S. dollar is the functional currency, they are remeasured by the temporal method.
- If the financial statements of foreign subsidiaries are in the local currency and neither the local currency nor the dollar is the functional currency, then the statements must first be remeasured into the functional currency by the temporal method, and then translated into dollars by the current rate method.
- U.S. translation practices, summarized in Exhibit 10.1, have a special provision for translating statements of foreign subsidiaries operating in hyperinflation countries. These are countries where cumulative inflation has been 100% or more over a three-year period. In this case, the subsidiary must use the temporal method.

A final note: The selection of the functional currency is determined by the economic realities of the subsidiary's operations, and is not a discretionary management decision on preferred procedures or elective outcomes. Since many U.S.-based multinationals have numerous foreign subsidiaries, some dollar-functional and some foreign currency-functional, currency gains and losses may be passing through both current consolidated income and/or accruing in equity reserves.

International Translation Practices

Many of the world's largest industrial countries use International Accounting Standards Committee (IASC), and therefore the same basic translation procedure. A foreign subsidiary is an integrated foreign entity or a self-sustaining foreign entity; integrated foreign entities are typically remeasured using the temporal method (or some slight variation thereof); and self-sustaining foreign entities are translated at the current rate method, also termed the closing-rate method.

EXHIBIT 10.1 **Flow Chart for U.S. Translation Practices**

Purpose: *Foreign currency financial statements must be translated into U.S. dollars*

If the financial statements of the foreign subsidiary
are expressed in a foreign currency, the following
determinations need to be made.

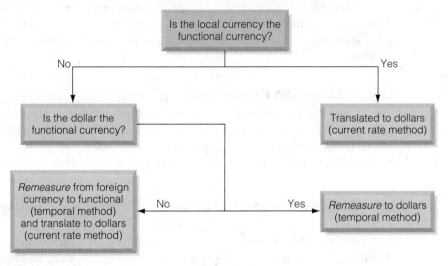

* The term "remeasure" means to translate, as to change the unit of measure, from a foreign currency
to the functional currency.

Trident Corporation's Translation Exposure

Trident Corporation, first introduced in Chapter 1 and shown in Exhibit 10.2, is a U.S.-based corporation with a U.S. business unit as well as foreign subsidiaries in both Europe and China. The company is publicly traded and its shares are traded on the New York Stock Exchange (NYSE).

Each subsidiary of Trident—the United States, Europe, and China—will have its own set of financial statements. Each set of financials will be constructed in the local currency (renminbi, dollar, euro), but the subsidiary income statements and balance sheets will also be translated into U.S. dollars, the reporting currency of the company for consolidation and reporting. As a U.S.-based corporation whose shares are traded on the NYSE, Trident will report all of its final results in U.S. dollars.

Trident Corporation's Translation Exposure: Income

Trident Corporation's sales and earnings by operating unit for 2009 and 2010 are described in Exhibit 10.3.

- **Consolidated sales.** For 2010, the company generated $300 million in sales in its U.S. unit, $158.4 million in its European subsidiary (€120 million at $1.32/€), and $89.6 million in its Chinese subsidiary (Rmb600 million at Rmb6.70/$). Total global sales for 2010 were $548.0 million. This constituted sales growth of 2.8% over 2009.

- **Consolidated earnings.** The company's earnings (profits) fell in 2010, dropping to $53.1 million from $53.2 million in 2009. Although not a large fall, Wall Street would not react favorably to a fall in consolidated earnings.

EXHIBIT 10.2   Trident Corporation: U.S. Multinational

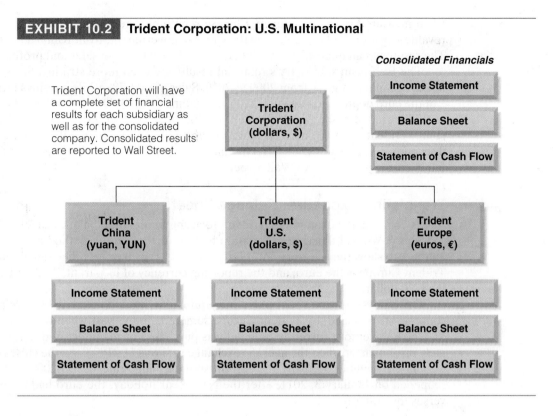

A closer look at the sales and earnings by country, however, yields some interesting insights. Sales and earnings in the U.S. unit rose, sales growing 7.1% and earnings growing 1.4%. Since the U.S. unit makes up more than half of the total company's sales and profits, this is very important. The Chinese subsidiary's sales and earnings were identical in 2009 and 2010

EXHIBIT 10.3   Trident Corporation, Selected Financial Results, 2009–2010

	Sales (millions, local currency)			Average Exchange Rate ($/€ and YUN/$)			Sales (millions of USD)		
	2009	2010	% Change	2009	2010	% Change	2009	2010	% Change
United States	$280	$300	7.1%	—	—		$280.0	$300.0	7.1%
Europe	€118	€120	1.7%	1.4000	1.3200	−5.71%	$165.2	$158.4	−4.1%
China	YUN600	YUN600	0.0%	6.8300	6.7000	1.94%	$87.8	$89.6	1.9%
Total							$533.0	$548.0	2.8%

	Earnings (millions, local currency)			Average Exchange Rate ($/€ and YUN/$)			Earnings (millions of USD)		
	2009	2010	% Change	2009	2010	% Change	2009	2010	% Change
United States	$28.2	$28.6	1.4%	—	—		$28.2	$28.6	1.4%
Europe	€10.4	€10.5	1.0%	1.4000	1.3200	−5.71%	$14.6	$13.9	−4.8%
China	YUN71.4	YUN71.4	0.0%	6.8300	6.7000	1.94%	$10.5	$10.7	1.9%
Total							$53.2	$53.1	−0.2%

when measured in local currency, Chinese renminbi. The Chinese renminbi, however, was revalued against the U.S. dollar by the Chinese government, from Rmb6.83/$ to Rmb6.70/$. The result was an increase in the dollar value of both Chinese sales and profits.

The European subsidiary's financial results are even more striking. Sales and earnings in Europe in euros grew from 2009 to 2010. Sales grew 1.7% while earnings increased 1.0%. But the euro depreciated against the dollar, falling from $1.40/€ to $1.32/€. This depreciation of 5.7% resulted in the financial results of European operations falling in dollar terms. As a result, Trident's consolidated earnings, as reported dollars, fell in 2010. One can imagine the discussion and debate within Trident, and among the analysts who follow the firm, over the fall in earnings reported to Wall Street.

Translation Exposure: Balance Sheet

Let us continue the example of Trident, focusing here on the balance sheet of its European subsidiary. We will illustrate translation by both the temporal method and the current rate method, to show the arbitrary nature of a translation gain or loss. The functional currency of Trident Europe is the euro, and the reporting currency of its parent, Trident Corporation, is the U.S. dollar.

Our analysis assumes that plant and equipment and long-term debt were acquired, and common stock issued, by Trident Europe sometime in the past when the exchange rate was $1.2760/€. Inventory currently on hand was purchased or manufactured during the immediately prior quarter when the average exchange rate was $1.2180/€. At the close of business on Monday, December 31, 2010, the current spot exchange rate was $1.2000/€. When business reopened on January 3, 2011, after the New Year holiday, the euro had dropped in value versus the dollar to $1.0000/€.

Current Rate Method. Exhibit 10.4 illustrates translation loss using the current rate method. Assets and liabilities on the pre-depreciation balance sheet are translated at the current exchange rate of $1.2000/€. Capital stock is translated at the historical rate of $1.2760/€, and retained earnings are translated at a composite rate that is equivalent to having each past year's addition to retained earnings translated at the exchange rate in effect that year.

The sum of retained earnings and the CTA account must "balance" the liabilities and net worth section of the balance sheet with the asset side. For this example, we have assumed the two amounts used for the December 31 balance sheet. As shown in Exhibit 10.4, the "just before depreciation" dollar translation reports an accumulated translation loss from prior periods of $136,800. This balance is the cumulative gain or loss from translating euro statements into dollars in prior years.

After the depreciation, Trident Corporation translates assets and liabilities at the new exchange rate of $1.0000/€. Equity accounts, including retained earnings, are translated just as they were before depreciation, and as a result, the cumulative translation loss increases to $1,736,800. The increase of $1,600,000 in this account (from a cumulative loss of $136,800 to a new cumulative loss of $1,736,800) is the translation loss measured by the current rate method.

This translation loss is a decrease in equity, measured in the parent's reporting currency, of "net exposed assets." An *exposed asset* is an asset whose value drops with the depreciation of the functional currency and rises with an appreciation of that currency. *Net exposed assets* in this context is exposed assets minus exposed liabilities. Net exposed assets are positive ("long") if exposed assets exceed exposed liabilities. They are negative ("short") if exposed assets are less than exposed liabilities.

EXHIBIT 10.4	Trident Europe's Translation Loss after Depreciation of the Euro: Current Rate Method

| | | December 31, 2010 | | January 2, 2011 | |
Assets	In Euros (€)	Exchange Rate (USD/EUR)	Translated Accounts (USD)	Exchange Rate (USD/EUR)	Translated Accounts (USD)
Cash	1,600,000	1.2000	$ 1,920,000	1.0000	$ 1,600,000
Accounts receivable	3,200,000	1.2000	3,840,000	1.0000	3,200,000
Inventory	2,400,000	1.2000	2,880,000	1.0000	2,400,000
Net plant & equipment	4,800,000	1.2000	5,760,000	1.0000	4,800,000
Total	12,000,000		$14,400,000		$ 12,000,000
Liabilities and Net Worth					
Accounts payable	800,000	1.2000	$ 960,000	1.0000	$ 800,000
Short-term bank debt	1,600,000	1.2000	1,920,000	1.0000	1,600,000
Long-term debt	1,600,000	1.2000	1,920,000	1.0000	1,600,000
Common stock	1,800,000	1.2760	2,296,800	1.2760	2,296,800
Retained earnings	6,200,000	1.2000 (a)	7,440,000	1.2000 (b)	7,440,000
Translation adjustment (CTA)	—		$ (136,800)		$ (1,736,800)
Total	12,000,000		$14,400,000		$ 12,000,000

(a) Dollar retained earnings before depreciation are the cumulative sum of additions to retained earnings of all prior years, translated at exchange rates in each year.

(b) Translated into dollars at the same rate as before depreciation of the euro.

Temporal Method. Translation of the same accounts under the temporal method shows the arbitrary nature of any gain or loss from translation. This is illustrated in Exhibit 10.5. Monetary assets and monetary liabilities in the predepreciation euro balance sheet are translated at the current rate of exchange, but other assets and the equity accounts are translated at their historic rates. For Trident Europe, the historical rate for inventory differs from that for net plant and equipment because inventory was acquired more recently.

Under the temporal method, translation losses are not accumulated in a separate equity account but passed directly through each quarter's income statement. Thus, in the dollar balance sheet translated before depreciation, retained earnings were the cumulative result of earnings from all prior years translated at historical rates in effect each year, plus translation gains or losses from all prior years. In Exhibit 10.5, no translation loss appears in the predepreciation dollar balance sheet because any losses would have been closed to retained earnings.

The effect of the depreciation is to create an immediate translation loss of $160,000. This amount is shown as a separate line item in Exhibit 10.5 to focus attention on it for this example. Under the temporal method, this translation loss of $160,000 would pass through the income statement, reducing reported net income and reducing retained earnings. Ending retained earnings would, in fact, be $7,711,200 minus $160,000, or $7,551,200. Whether gains and losses pass through the income statement under the temporal method depends upon the country.

Managerial Implications

In the case of Trident, the translation gain or loss is larger under the current rate method because inventory and net plant and equipment, as well as all monetary assets, are deemed exposed. When net exposed assets are larger, gains or losses from translation are also larger.

| EXHIBIT 10.5 | Trident Europe's Translation Loss after Depreciation of the Euro: Temporal Method |

		December 31, 2010		January 2, 2011	
Assets	In Euros (€)	Exchange Rate (USD/EUR)	Translated Accounts (USD)	Exchange Rate (USD/EUR)	Translated Accounts (USD)
Cash	1,600,000	1.2000	$ 1,920,000	1.0000	$ 1,600,000
Accounts receivable	3,200,000	1.2000	3,840,000	1.0000	3,200,000
Inventory	2,400,000	1.2180	2,923,200	1.2180	2,923,200
Net plant and equipment	4,800,000	1.2760	6,124,800	1.2760	6,124,800
Total	12,000,000		$14,808,000		$ 13,848,000
Liabilities and Net Worth					
Accounts payable	800,000	1.2000	$ 960,000	1.0000	$ 800,000
Short-term bank debt	1,600,000	1.2000	1,920,000	1.0000	1,600,000
Long-term debt	1,600,000	1.2000	1,920,000	1.0000	1,600,000
Common stock	1,800,000	1.2760	2,296,800	1.2760	2,296,800
Retained earnings	6,200,000	1.2437 (a)	7,711,200	1.2437 (b)	7,711,200
Translation gain (loss)	—			(c)	$ (160,000)
Total	12,000,000		$14,808,000		$ 13,848,000

(a) Dollar retained earnings before depreciation are the cumulative sum of additions to retained earnings of all prior years, translated at exchange rates in each year.

(b) Translated into dollars at the same rate as before depreciation of the euro.

(c) Under the temporal method, the translation loss of $160,000 would be closed into retained earnings through the income statement rather than left as a separate line item as shown here. Ending retained earnings would actually be $7,711,200−$160,000 = $7,551,200.

If management expects a foreign currency to depreciate, it could minimize translation exposure by reducing net exposed assets. If management anticipates an appreciation of the foreign currency, it should increase net exposed assets to benefit from a gain.

Depending on the accounting method, management might select different assets and liabilities for reduction or increase. Thus, "real" decisions about investing and financing might be dictated by which accounting technique is used, when in fact, accounting impacts should be neutral.

As illustrated in *Global Finance in Practice 10.1*, transaction, translation, and operating exposures can become intertwined in the valuation of business units—in this case, the valuation of a foreign subsidiary.

GLOBAL FINANCE IN PRACTICE 10.1

Foreign Subsidiary Valuation

The value contribution of a subsidiary of a multinational firm to the firm as a whole is a topic of increasing debate in global financial management. Most multinational companies report the earnings contribution of foreign operations either individually or by region when they are significant to the total earnings of the consolidated firm.

Changes in the value of a subsidiary as a result of the change in an exchange rate can be decomposed into those changes specific to the income and the assets of the subsidiary:

Δ in Value of Subsidiary = Δ in Value of Assets + Δ in Value of Earnings

Subsidiary Earnings

The earnings of the subsidiary, once remeasured into the home currency of the parent company, contributes directly to the consolidated income of the firm. An exchange rate change results in fluctuations in the value of the subsidiary's income to the global corporation. If the individual subsidiary in question constitutes a relatively significant or material component of consolidated income, the multinational firm's reported income (and earnings per share, EPS) may be seen to change purely as a result of translation.

Subsidiary Assets

Changes in the reporting currency value of the net assets of the subsidiary are passed into consolidated income or equity.

- If the foreign subsidiary was designated as "dollar functional," remeasurement results in a transaction exposure, which is passed through current consolidated income.

- If the foreign subsidiary was designated as "local currency functional," translation results in a translation adjustment and is reported in consolidated equity as a translation adjustment. It does not alter reported consolidated net income in the current period.

Managing Translation Exposure

The main technique to minimize translation exposure is called a balance sheet hedge. At times, some firms have attempted to hedge translation exposure in the forward market. Such action amounts to speculating in the forward market in the hope that a cash profit will be realized to offset the noncash loss from translation. Success depends on a precise prediction of future exchange rates, for such a hedge will not work over a range of possible future spot rates. In addition, the profit from the forward "hedge" (i.e., speculation) is taxable, but the translation loss does not reduce taxable income.

Balance Sheet Hedge

A balance sheet hedge requires an equal amount of exposed foreign currency assets and liabilities on a firm's consolidated balance sheet. If this can be achieved for each foreign currency, net translation exposure will be zero. A change in exchange rates will change the value of exposed liabilities in an equal amount but in a direction opposite to the change in value of exposed assets. If a firm translates by the temporal method, a zero net exposed position is called "monetary balance." Complete monetary balance cannot be achieved under the current rate method because total assets would have to be matched by an equal amount of debt, but the equity section of the balance sheet must still be translated at historic exchange rates.

The cost of a balance sheet hedge depends on relative borrowing costs. If foreign currency borrowing costs, after adjusting for foreign exchange risk, are higher than parent currency borrowing costs, the balance sheet hedge is costly, and vice versa. Normal operations, however, already require decisions about the magnitude and currency denomination of specific balance sheet accounts. Thus, balance sheet hedges are a compromise in which the denomination of balance sheet accounts is altered, perhaps at a cost in terms of interest expense or operating efficiency, in order to achieve some degree of foreign exchange protection.

To achieve a balance sheet hedge, Trident Corporation must either 1) reduce exposed euro assets without simultaneously reducing euro liabilities, or 2) increase euro liabilities without simultaneously increasing euro assets. One way to achieve this is to exchange existing euro cash for dollars. If Trident Europe does not have large euro cash balances, it can borrow euros and exchange the borrowed euros for dollars. Another subsidiary could also borrow euros and exchange them for dollars. That is, the essence of the hedge is for the parent or any of its subsidiaries to create euro debt and exchange the proceeds for dollars.

Current Rate Method. Under the current rate method, Trident should borrow as much as €8,000,000. The initial effect of this first step is to increase both an exposed asset (cash) and an exposed liability (notes payable) on the balance sheet of Trident Europe, with no immediate effect on net exposed assets. The required follow-up step can take two forms: 1) Trident Europe could exchange the acquired euros for U.S. dollars and hold those dollars itself, or 2) it could transfer the borrowed euros to Trident Corporation, perhaps as a euro dividend or as repayment of intracompany debt. Trident Corporation could then exchange the euros for dollars. In some countries, local monetary authorities will not allow their currency to be so freely exchanged.

An alternative would be for Trident Corporation or a sister subsidiary to borrow the euros, thus keeping the euro debt entirely off Trident's books. However, the second step is still essential to eliminate euro exposure; the borrowing entity must exchange the euros for dollars or other unexposed assets. Any such borrowing should be coordinated with all other euro borrowings to avoid the possibility that one subsidiary is borrowing euros to reduce translation exposure at the same time as another subsidiary is repaying euro debt. (Note that euros can be "borrowed," by simply delaying repayment of existing euro debt; the goal is to increase euro debt, not to borrow in a literal sense.)

Temporal Method. If translation is by the temporal method, the much smaller amount of only €800,000 need be borrowed. As before, Trident Europe could use the proceeds of the loan to acquire U.S. dollars. However, Trident Europe could also use the proceeds to acquire inventory or fixed assets in Europe. Under the temporal method, these assets are not regarded as exposed and do not drop in dollar value when the euro depreciates.

When Is a Balance Sheet Hedge Justified?

If a firm's subsidiary is using the local currency as the functional currency, the following circumstances could justify when to use a balance sheet hedge:

- The foreign subsidiary is about to be liquidated, so that value of its CTA would be realized.
- The firm has debt covenants or bank agreements that state the firm's debt/equity ratios will be maintained within specific limits.
- Management is evaluated based on certain income statement and balance sheet measures that are affected by translation losses or gains.
- The foreign subsidiary is operating in a hyperinflationary environment.

If a firm is using the parent's home currency as the functional currency of the foreign subsidiary, all transaction gains/losses are passed through to the income statement. Hedging this consolidated income to reduce its variability may be important to investors and bond rating agencies.

In the end, accounting exposure is a topic of great concern and complex choices for all multinationals. As demonstrated by *Global Finance in Practice 10.2*, despite the best of intentions and structures, business itself may dictate hedging outcomes.

GLOBAL FINANCE IN PRACTICE   10.2

When Business Dictates Hedging Results

GM Asia, a regional subsidiary of GM Corporation, U.S., held major corporate interests in a variety of countries and companies, including Daewoo Auto of South Korea. GM had acquired control of Daewoo's automobile operations in 2001. The following years had been very good for the Daewoo unit, and by 2009, GM Daewoo was selling automobile components and vehicles to more than 100 countries.

Daewoo's success meant that it had expected sales (receivables) from buyers all over the world. What was even more remarkable was that the global automobile industry now used the U.S. dollar more than ever as its currency of contract for cross-border transactions. This meant that Daewoo did not really have dozens of foreign currencies to manage, just one, the U.S. dollar. So Daewoo of Korea had, in late 2007 and early 2008, entered into a series of forward exchange contracts. These currency contracts locked in the Korean won value of the many dollar-denominated receivables the company expected to receive from international automobile sales in the coming year. In the eyes of many, this was a conservative and responsible currency hedging policy; that is, until the global financial crisis and the following collapse of global automobile sales.

The problem for Daewoo was not that the Korean won per U.S. dollar exchange rate had moved dramatically; it had not. The problem was that Daewoo's sales, like all other automobile industry participants, had collapsed. The sales had not taken place, and therefore the underlying exposures, the expected receivables in dollars by Daewoo, had not happened. But GM still had to contractually deliver on the forward contracts. It would cost GM Daewoo Won2,300 billion. GM's Daewoo unit was now broke, its equity wiped out by currency hedging gone bad. GM Asia needed money, quickly, and selling interests in its highly successful Chinese and Indian businesses was the only solution.

Summary Points

- Translation exposure results from translating foreign currency-denominated statements of foreign subsidiaries into the parent's reporting currency so the parent can prepare consolidated financial statements. Translation exposure is the potential for loss or gain from this translation process.

- A foreign subsidiary's functional currency is the currency of the primary economic environment in which the subsidiary operates and in which it generates cash flows. In other words, it is the dominant currency used by that foreign subsidiary in its day-to-day operations.

- The two basic procedures for translation used in most countries today are the current rate method and the temporal method.

- Technical aspects of translation include questions about when to recognize gains or losses in the income statement, the distinction between functional and reporting currency, and the treatment of subsidiaries in hyperinflation countries.

- Translation gains and losses can be quite different from operating gains and losses, not only in magnitude but also in sign. Management may need to determine which is of greater significance prior to deciding which exposure is to be managed first.

- The main technique for managing translation exposure is a balance sheet hedge. This calls for having an equal amount of exposed foreign currency assets and liabilities.

- Even if management chooses to follow an active policy of hedging translation exposure, it is nearly impossible to offset both transaction and translation exposure simultaneously. If forced to choose, most managers will protect against transaction losses because these are realized cash losses, rather than protect against translation losses.

MINI-CASE

LaJolla Engineering Services[1]

Meaghan O'Connor had inherited a larger set of problems in the Engineering Equipment Division than she had ever expected. After taking over as the CFO of the Division in March of 2004, Meaghan had discovered that LaJolla's Engineering Equipment Division's Latin American subsidiaries were the source of recent losses and growing income threats. The rather unusual part of the growing problem was that both the losses and the threats were arising from currency translation.

Latin American Subsidiaries

LaJolla was a multinational engineering services company with an established reputation in electrical power system design and construction. Although most of LaJolla's business was usually described as "services," and therefore used or owned few real assets, that was not the case with the Engineering Equipment Division. This specific business unit was charged with owning and operating the very high-cost and specialized heavy equipment involved in certain electrical power transmission and distribution system construction. In Meaghan's terminology, she was in charge of the "Big Iron" in a company of consultants.

LaJolla's recent activity had been focused in four countries, Argentina, Jamaica, Venezuela, and Mexico. And unfortunately, the last few years had not been kind to the value of these currencies—particularly against the U.S. dollar. Each of LaJolla's subsidiaries in these countries was local currency functional. Each subsidiary generated the majority of its revenues from local service contracts, and many of the operating expenses were also local. But each of the units had invested in some of the

[1]Copyright © 2010 Thunderbird School of Global Management. All rights reserved. This case was prepared by Professor Michael Moffett for the purpose of classroom discussion only, and not to indicate either effective or ineffective management. This case concerns a real company; names and countries have been changed to preserve confidentiality.

specialized equipment—the so-called "Big Iron"—which had led to *net exposed assets* when LaJolla had completed its consolidation of foreign activities each year for financial reporting purposes. The translation gains and losses (mostly losses in recent years as the Argentine peso, Jamaican dollar, Venezuelan bolivar, and Mexican peso had weakened against the U.S. dollar), had accumulated in the cumulative translation adjustment line item on the company's consolidated books. But the problem had become more real of late.

Ordinarily, these translation losses would not have been a large managerial issue for LaJolla and Meaghan, except for a minor document filing error in Argentina in the fall of 2003. LaJolla, like many multinational companies operating in Argentina in recent years, had simply given up on conducting any real business of promise in the severely depressed post-crisis Argentina. It had essentially closed up shop there in the summer of 2003. But its legal counsel in Buenos Aires had made a mistake. Instead of ceasing current operations and "mothballing" the existing assets of LaJolla Engineering Argentina, the local counsel had filed papers stating that LaJolla was liquidating the business. Although a minor issue in terms of distinction, according to U.S. GAAP and FAS 52, LaJolla would now have to realize in current earnings the cumulative translation losses that had grown over the years from the Argentine business. And they were substantial. It had resulted in the recognition of $7 million in losses in the fourth quarter of 2003; LaJolla's management had not been happy.

LaJolla 2004

As a result of this recent experience, LaJolla was taking a close look at all of the translation gains and losses of its various business units worldwide. Once again, the company's Latin American operations were the focal point, as collectively many of the Latin currencies had weakened recently against the dollar, although the dollar itself was quite weak against the euro. Jamaica, Venezuela, and Mexico each posed their individual problems and challenges, but all posed translation adjustment threats to LaJolla.

Jamaica

The company had been fairly concerned about the Jamaican business and its contracts from the very beginning. The company had initially agreed to take all revenues in Jamaican dollars (therefore dictating that the local currency be designated as the unit's functional currency), but after the fall of the Jamaican dollar in early 2003, it had renegotiated a risk-sharing agreement. The agreement restructured the relationship to one in which, although LaJolla would continue to be paid in local currency, the two companies would share any changes in the exchange rate beginning in the fourth quarter of 2003 when establishing the charges as invoiced. Regardless, the continuing decline of the Jamaican dollar (as seen in Exhibit A) had created substantial translation losses for LaJolla in Jamaica.

Mexico

Although the Mexican peso had been quite stable for a number of years, it clearly had started to slide against the

---

EXHIBIT A   Jamaican Dollars per U.S. Dollar

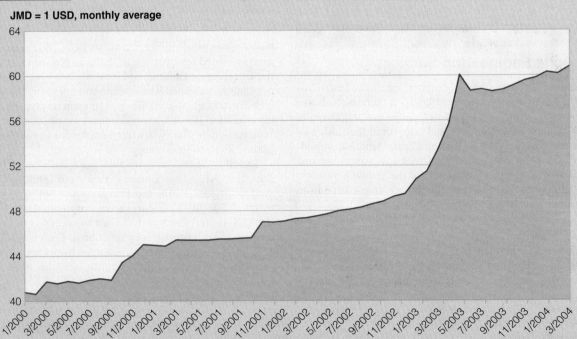

JMD = 1 USD, monthly average

dollar in 2002 and 2003, as illustrated in Exhibit B. Meaghan had become particularly frustrated with the Mexican situation the more she looked into it. LaJolla had only initiated the subsidiary's operations in Mexico in early 2000, yet the reported translation losses from Mexico had grown much more rapidly than what she would have expected.

She had also become quite alarmed when she realized that the financial reports coming from her Mexican offices were seemingly "writing-up" the translation losses every quarter. When she had asked questions, first by phone and then later in person, her local financial controller simply stopped talking (she was working through an interpreter), claiming they did not understand her questions. Meaghan was no beginner in international finance, and also knew that Mexican financial statements did regularly index foreign currency-denominated accounts in line with government published indexes of asset values related to currencies. She wondered if the indexing could be at the source of the translation losses.

Venezuela

The continuing political crisis in Venezuela surrounding the presidency of Hugo Chavez had taken its toll on the Venezuelan bolivar, as seen in Exhibit C.

Not only was LaJolla suffering declining U.S. dollar proceeds from its Venezuelan operations, but it had continued to suffer severe late payments from the various government agencies to which the company was exclusively providing services. The average invoice was now taking more than 180 days to be settled, and the bolivar's decline had added to the losses. Again, translation losses were accumulating here, again from a subsidiary whose functional currency was the local currency. The LaJolla controller in Venezuela had faxed Meaghan a proposal that would involve changing the currency used for the books in Venezuela to U.S. dollars, as well as a suggestion that they consider moving the subsidiary offshore for accounting and consolidation purposes (meaning out of Venezuela). He had suggested either the Cayman Islands or the Netherlands Antilles just off the coast.

All in all, Meaghan was beginning to think she had made a big mistake when she accepted the promotion to CFO of this division. She turned her eyes once more to look out over the Pacific to ponder what alternatives she might have to manage these exposures, and what—if anything—she should do immediately.

EXHIBIT B **Mexican Pesos per U.S. Dollar**

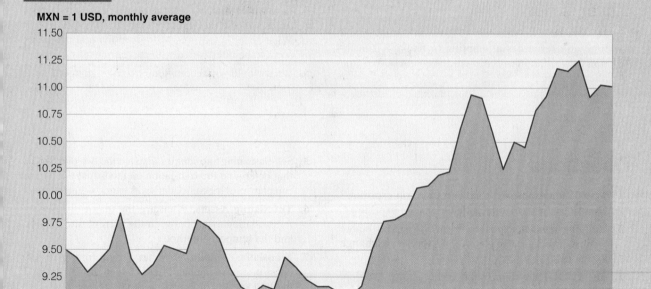

MXN = 1 USD, monthly average

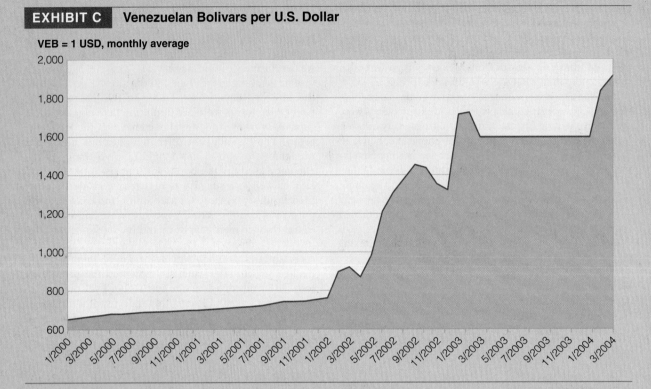

EXHIBIT C   Venezuelan Bolivars per U.S. Dollar

VEB = 1 USD, monthly average

MINI-CASE QUESTIONS

1. Do you believe Meaghan O'Connor should spend time and resources attempting to manage translation losses that many consider purely an accounting phenomenon?

2. How would you characterize or structure your analysis of each of the individual country threats to LaJolla? What specific features of their individual problems seem to be intertwined with currency issues?

3. What would you recommend that Meaghan do?

Questions

1. **Translation exposure.** What is translation exposure? How does it differ from foreign exchange exposure?

2. **Hedging against exposure.** How do MNEs hedge against translation exposure and foreign exchange exposure?

3. **The Central Problem.** What is the central problem involved in consolidating the financial statements of a foreign subsidiary?

4. **Functional Currency.** Why do subsidiaries prefer to use local currency as the functional currency? When should the functional currency be the reporting currency?

5. **Self-Sustaining Subsidiaries.** Explain the two dimensions that determine the translation methods that the parent company uses for consolidating its financial statements.

6. **Translating Assets.** What are the major differences in translating assets between the current rate method and the temporal method?

7. **Translating Liabilities.** What are the major differences in translating liabilities between the current rate method and the temporal method?

8. **Inflation and Hyperinflation.** Should MNEs be worried about inflation and hyperinflation in countries where they operate? How can they hedge against inflation?

9. **Forecasting.** MNEs closely monitor forecasts about interest rates and inflation. How can MNEs profit from such future expectations?

Problems

1. **Trident Europe (A).** Using facts in the chapter for Trident Europe, assume the exchange rate on January 2, 2006, in Exhibit 10.4 *dropped in value* from $1.2000/€ to $0.9000/€ (rather than to $1.0000/€). Recalculate Trident Europe's translated balance sheet for January 2, 2006, with the new exchange rate using the *current rate method.*
   a. What is the amount of translation gain or loss?
   b. Where should it appear in the financial statements?

2. **Trident Europe (B).** Using facts in the chapter for Trident Europe, assume as in Problem 1 that the exchange rate on January 2, 2006, in Exhibit 10.4 dropped in value from $1.2000/€ to $0.9000/€ (rather than to $1.0000/€). Recalculate Trident Europe's translated balance sheet for January 2, 2006, with the new exchange rate using the temporal rate method.
   a. What is the amount of translation gain or loss?
   b. Where should it appear in the financial statements?
   c. Why does the translation loss or gain under the temporal method differ from the loss or gain under the current rate method?

3. **Trident Europe (C).** Using facts in the chapter for Trident Europe, assume the exchange rate on January 2, 2006, in Exhibit 10.4 *appreciated* from $1.2000/€ to $1.500/€. Calculate Trident Europe's translated balance sheet for January 2, 2006, with the new exchange rate using the *current rate method.*
   a. What is the amount of translation gain or loss?
   b. Where should it appear in the financial statements?

4. **Trident Europe (D).** Using facts in the chapter for Trident Europe, assume as in Problem 3 that the exchange rate on January 2, 2006, in Exhibit 10.4 *appreciated* from $1.2000/€ to $1.5000/€. Calculate Trident Europe's translated balance sheet for January 2, 2006, with the new exchange rate using the temporal method.
   a. What is the amount of translation gain or loss?
   b. Where should it appear in the financial statements?

5. **Italianica S.A. (A)** Italiana S.A. is the Italian subsidiary of a British automobile spare parts company. The following is its balance sheet as at December 31, when the exchange rate between the euro and the British pound was €1.3749/GBP. Using the current rate method, calculate the contribution of the Italian subsidiary to the translation exposure of its parent on December 31. Assume that there was no change in Italianica's accounts since the beginning of the year.

Balance Sheet (thousands of Euros)

Assets		Liabilities and Net Worth	
Cash	€95,000	Current liabilities	€60,000
Accounts receivable	180,000	Long-term debt	110,000
Inventory	125,000	Capital stock	350,000
Net plant and equipment	250,000	Retained earnings	130,000
	€650,000		€650,000

6. **Italianica S.A. (B).** Please refer to the same balance sheet as in Problem 5. Calculate Italianica's contribution to its British parent's translation loss if the exchange rate on December 31 is €1.4/£. Assume that there are no changes in the accounts of the subsidiary in euros during the last six months.

7. **Italiana S.A. (C).** Calculate Italiana's contribution to its parent's translation gain/loss using the current rate method if the exchange rate on September 30 is €1.2/£. Assume that there are no changes in the accounts of the subsidiary in euros during the last nine months.

8. **Bangkok Instruments, Ltd.(A).** Bangkok Instruments, Ltd., the Thai subsidiary of a U.S. corporation, is a seismic instrument manufacturer. Bangkok Instruments manufactures the instruments primarily for the oil and gas industry globally, though with recent commodity price increases of all kinds—including copper—its business has begun to grow rapidly. Sales are primarily to multinational companies based in the United States and Europe. Bangkok Instruments' balance sheet in thousands of Thai bahts (B) as of March 31 is as follows:

Bangkok Instruments, Ltd.
Balance Sheet, March 1, thousands of Thai bahts

Assets		Liabilities and Net Worth	
Cash	B24,000	Accounts payable	B18,000
Accounts receivable	36,000	Bank loans	60,000
Inventory	48,000	Common stock	18,000
Net plant and equipment	60,000	Retained earnings	72,000
	B168,000		B168,000

Exchange rates for translating Siam Toy's balance sheet into U.S. dollars are:

B40.00/$ April 1st exchange rate after 25% devaluation.

B30.00/$ March 31st exchange rate, before 25% devaluation. All inventory was acquired at this rate.

B20.00/$ Historic exchange rate at which plant and equipment were acquired.

The Thai baht dropped in value from B30/$ to B40/$ between March 31 and April 1. Assuming no change in balance sheet accounts between these two days, calculate the gain or loss from translation by both the current rate method and the temporal method. Explain the translation gain or loss in terms of changes in the value of exposed accounts.

9. **Bangkok Instruments, Ltd. (B).** Using the original data provided for Bangkok Instruments, assume that the Thai baht *appreciated* in value from B30/$ to B25/$ between March 31 and April 1. Assuming no change in balance sheet accounts between those two days, calculate the gain or loss from translation by both the current rate method and the temporal method. Explain the translation gain or loss in terms of changes in the value of exposed accounts.

10. **Cairo Ingot, Ltd.** Cairo Ingot, Ltd., is the Egyptian subsidiary of Trans-Mediterranean Aluminum, a British multinational that fashions automobile engine blocks from aluminum. Trans-Mediterranean's home reporting currency is the British pound. Cairo Ingot's December 31 balance sheet is shown below. At the date of this balance sheet the exchange rate between Egyptian pounds and British pounds sterling was £E5.50/UK£.

Assets		Liabilities and New Worth	
Cash	£E16,500,000	Accounts payable	£E24,750,000
Accounts receivable	33,000,000	Long-term debt	49,500,000
Inventory	49,500,000	Invested capital	90,750,000
Net plant and equipment	66,000,000		
	£E165,000,000		£E165,000,000

What is Cairo Ingot's contribution to the translation exposure of Trans-Mediterranean on December 31, using the current rate method? Calculate the translation exposure loss to Trans-Mediterranean if the exchange rate at the end of the following quarter is £E6.00/£. Assume all balance sheet accounts are the same at the end of the quarter as they were at the beginning.

Internet Exercises

1. **Foreign Source Income.** If you are a citizen of the United States, and you receive income from outside the U.S.—foreign source income—how must you report this income? Use the following Internal Revenue Service Web site to determine current reporting practices for tax purposes.

U.S. Internal Revenue Service	www.irs.gov/Individuals/International-Taxpayers/Foreign-Currency-and-Currency-Exchange-Rates

2. **Translation in the United Kingdom.** What are the current practices and procedures for translation of financial statements in the United Kingdom? Use the following Web site to start your research.

Institute of Chartered Accountants in England and Wales	www.icaew.com/en/technical/financial-reporting/uk-gaap/uk-gaap-standards/ssap-20-foreign-currency-translation

3. **Changing Translation Practices: FASB.** The Financial Accounting Standards Board (FASB) promulgates standard practices for the reporting of financial results by companies in the United States. It also, however, often leads the way in the development of new practices and emerging issues around the world. One major issue today is the valuation and reporting of financial derivatives and derivative agreements by firms. Use the FASB and Treasury Management Association Web pages to see current proposed accounting standards and the current state of reaction to the proposed standards.

FASB home page	raw.rutgers.edu/raw/fasb/
Treasury Management Association	www.tma.org/

4. **Yearly Average Exchange Rates.** When translating foreign currency values into U.S. dollar values for individual reporting purposes in the United States, which average exchange rates should you use? Use the following Web site to find the current average rates.

U.S. Internal Revenue Service	www.irs.gov/Individuals/International-Taxpayers/Yearly-Average-Currency-Exchange-Rates

Operating Exposure

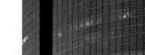

The essence of risk management lies in maximizing the areas where we have some control over the outcome while minimizing the areas where we have absolutely no control over the outcome and the linkage between effect and cause is hidden from us. —Peter Bernstein, *Against the Gods*, 1996.

LEARNING OBJECTIVES

- Examine how operating exposure arises through unexpected changes in both operating and financing cash flows

- Analyze how unexpected exchange rate changes alter the economic performance of a business unit through the sequence of volume, price, cost, and other key variable changes

- Evaluate strategic alternatives to managing operating exposure

- Detail the proactive policies firms use in managing operating exposure

This chapter examines the economic exposure of a firm over time, what we term operating exposure. *Operating exposure*, also referred to as *economic exposure*, *competitive exposure*, or *strategic exposure*, measures any change in the present value of a firm resulting from changes in future operating cash flows caused by any unexpected change in exchange rates. Operating exposure analysis assesses the impact of changing exchange rates on a firm's own operations over coming months and years and on its competitive position vis-à-vis other firms. The goal is to identify strategic moves or operating techniques the firm might wish to adopt to enhance its value in the face of unexpected exchange rate changes.

Operating exposure and transaction exposure are related in that they both deal with future cash flows. They differ in terms of which cash flows management considers and why those cash flows change when exchange rates change. We begin by revisiting the structure of our firm, Trident Corporation, and how its structure dictates its likely operating exposure. The chapter continues with a series of strategies and structures used in the management of operating exposure, and concludes with a Mini-Case, *Toyota's European Operating Exposure*.

A Multinational's Operating Exposure

The structure and operations of a multinational company determine the nature of its operating exposure. Trident Corporation's basic structure and currencies of operation are described in Exhibit 11.1. As a U.S.-based publicly traded company, ultimately all financial metrics and values have to be consolidated and expressed in U.S. dollars. That accounting exposure of the firm—translation exposure—was described in Chapter 10. Operationally, however, the functional currencies of the individual subsidiaries in combination determine the overall operating exposure of the firm in total.

| EXHIBIT 11.1 | Trident Corporation: Structure and Operations |

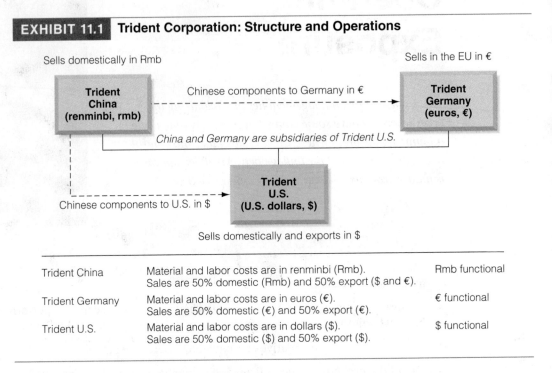

Trident China   Material and labor costs are in renminbi (Rmb).   Rmb functional
                     Sales are 50% domestic (Rmb) and 50% export ($ and €).

Trident Germany   Material and labor costs are in euros (€).   € functional
                     Sales are 50% domestic (€) and 50% export (€).

Trident U.S.   Material and labor costs are in dollars ($). $ functional
                     Sales are 50% domestic ($) and 50% export ($).

The *net operating exposure* of any individual business reflects the cash inflows and cash outflows by currency of its competitive position in the market. Accounts receivable are the cash flow proceeds from sales, and accounts payable are all ongoing operating costs associated with the purchase of labor, materials, and other inputs. The net result—in general—is in essence the lifeblood of any business and the source of value created by the firm over time.

For example, Trident Germany sells locally and exports, but all sales are invoiced in euros. All operating cash inflows are therefore in its home currency, the euro. On the cost side, labor costs are local and in euros, as well as many of its material input purchases being local and in euros. It also purchases components from Trident China, but those too are invoiced in euros. Trident Germany is clearly euro-functional, with all cash inflows and outflows in euros.

Trident Corporation U.S. is similar in structure to Trident Germany. All cash inflows from sales, domestic and international, are in U.S. dollars. All costs, labor and materials, sourced domestically and internationally, are invoiced in U.S. dollars. This includes purchases from Trident China. Trident U.S. is, therefore, obviously dollar functional.

Trident China is more complex. Cash outflows, labor and materials, are all domestic and paid in Chinese renminbi. Cash inflows, however, are generated across three different currencies as the company sells locally in renminbi, as well as exporting to both Germany in euros and the United States in dollars. On net, although having some cash inflows in both dollars and euros, the dominant currency cash flow is the renminbi.

Static versus Dynamic Operating Exposure

Measuring the operating exposure of a firm like Trident requires forecasting and analyzing all the firm's future individual transaction exposures together with the future exposures of all the firm's competitors and potential competitors worldwide. Exchange rate changes in the short term affect current and immediate contracts, generally termed transactions. But over the longer term, as prices change and competitors react, the more fundamental economic and competitive drivers of the business may alter all cash flows of all units. A simple example will clarify the point.

Assume Trident's three business units are roughly equal in size. In 2012, the dollar starts depreciating in the market against the euro. At the same time, the Chinese government continues the gradual revaluation of the renminbi. The operating exposure of each individual business unit then needs to be examined statically (transaction exposures) and dynamically (future business transactions not yet contracted for).

- **Trident China.**   Sales in U.S. dollars will result in fewer renminbi proceeds in the immediate period. Sales in euros may stay roughly the same in renminbi proceeds depending on the relative movement of the Rmb against the euro. General profitability will fall in the short run. In the longer term, depending on the markets for its products and the nature of competition, it may need to raise the price at which it sells its export products, even to its U.S. parent company.

- **Trident Germany.**   Since this business unit's cash inflows and outflows are all in euros, there is no immediate transaction exposure or change. It may suffer some rising input costs in the future if Trident China does indeed eventually push through price increases of component sales. Profitability is unaffected in the short term.

- **Trident U.S.**   Like Trident Germany, Trident U.S. has all local currency cash inflows and outflows. A fall in the value of the dollar will have no immediate impact (transaction exposure), but may change over the medium to long term as input costs from China may rise over time as the Chinese subsidiary tries to regain prior profit margins. But, like Germany, short-term profitability is unaffected.

The net result for Trident is possibly a fall in the total profitability of the firm in the short term, primarily from the fall in profits of the Chinese subsidiary; that is, the short-term transaction/operating exposure impact. The fall in the dollar in the short term, however, is likely to have a positive impact on translation exposure, as profits and earnings in renminbi and euros translate into more dollars. Wall Street would likely like results in the immediate quarter or two.

Operating and Financing Cash Flows

The cash flows of the MNE can be divided into *operating cash flows* and *financing cash flows*. *Operating cash flows* for Trident arise from intercompany (between unrelated companies) and intracompany (between units of the same company) receivables and payables, rent and lease payments for the use of facilities and equipment, royalty and license fees for the use of technology and intellectual property, and assorted management fees for services provided.

Financing cash flows are payments for the use of intercompany and intracompany loans (principal and interest) and stockholder equity (new equity investments and dividends). Each of these cash flows can occur at different time intervals, in different amounts, and in different currencies of denomination, and each has a different predictability of occurrence. We summarize cash flow possibilities in Exhibit 11.2 for Trident China and Trident U.S.

Expected versus Unexpected Changes in Cash Flow

Operating exposure is far more important for the long-run health of a business than changes caused by transaction or translation exposure. However, operating exposure is inevitably subjective because it depends on estimates of future cash flow changes over an arbitrary time horizon. Thus, it does not spring from the accounting process but rather from operating analysis.

EXHIBIT 11.2   Financial and Operating Cash Flows between Parent and Subsidiary

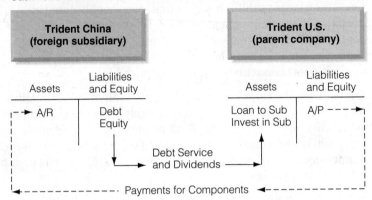

Cash flows related to the financing of the subsidiary are *Financial Cash Flows*
Cash flows related to the business activities of the subsidiary are *Operating Cash Flows*

Planning for operating exposure is a total management responsibility depending upon the interaction of strategies in finance, marketing, purchasing, and production.

An expected change in foreign exchange rates is not included in the definition of operating exposure, because both management and investors should have factored this information into their evaluation of anticipated operating results and market value. This "expected change" arises from differing perspectives as follows:

- From a management perspective, budgeted financial statements already reflect information about the effect of an expected change in exchange rates.

- From a debt service perspective, expected cash flow to amortize debt should already reflect the international Fisher effect. The level of expected interest and principal repayment should be a function of expected exchange rates rather than existing spot rates.

- From an investor's perspective, if the foreign exchange market is efficient, information about expected changes in exchange rates should be widely known and thus reflected in a firm's market value. Only unexpected changes in exchange rates, or an inefficient foreign exchange market, should cause market value to change.

- From a broader macroeconomic perspective, operating exposure is not just the sensitivity of a firm's future cash flows to unexpected changes in foreign exchange rates, but also its sensitivity to other key macroeconomic variables. This factor has been labeled as *macroeconomic uncertainty*.

We explore this further in *Global Finance in Practice 11.1*. Chapter 6 described the parity relationships among exchange rates, interest rates, and inflation rates. However, these variables are often in disequilibrium with one another. Therefore, unexpected changes in interest rates and inflation rates could also have a simultaneous but differential impact on future cash flows.

Measuring Operating Exposure

An unexpected change in exchange rates impacts a firm's expected cash flows at four levels, depending on the time horizon used, as summarized in Exhibit 11.3.

GLOBAL FINANCE IN PRACTICE 11.1

Expecting the Devaluation—Ford and Venezuela

Key to the understanding of operating exposure is that expected change in foreign exchange rates is not included in the firm's operating exposure. The assumption is that the market has already taken this value change into account. But is that assumption a sound one?

Consider the case of Ford Motor Company. In December 2013, Ford was very open and public about what it expected to happen to the Venezuelan currency—further devaluation—and what that would mean for Ford's financial results. In filings with the Securities and Exchange Commission (SEC), Ford reported that it had $802 million in investments in Venezuela, that it expected the Venezuelan bolivar to fall from 6.3 to the dollar to 12, and that it could end up suffering a $350 million financial loss as a result. The company was speaking from some experience. Earlier in the year it had lost $186 million when Venezuela devalued the bolivar to 6.3 from 4.3 per dollar.

Short Run. The first level impact is on expected cash flows in the one-year operating budget. The gain or loss depends on the currency of denomination of expected cash flows. These are both existing transaction exposures and anticipated exposures. The currency of denomination cannot be changed for existing obligations, or even for implied obligations such as purchase or sales commitments. Apart from real or implied obligations, in the short run it is difficult to change sales prices or renegotiate factor costs. Therefore, realized cash flows will differ from those expected in the budget. However, as time passes, prices and costs can be changed to reflect the new competitive realities caused by a change in exchange rates.

Medium Run: Equilibrium. The second level impact is on expected medium-run cash flows, such as those expressed in two- to five-year budgets, assuming parity conditions hold among foreign exchange rates, national inflation rates, and national interest rates. Under equilibrium conditions, the firm should be able to adjust prices and factor costs over time to maintain the expected level of cash flows. In this case, the currency of denomination of expected cash flows is not as important as the countries in which cash flows originate. National monetary, fiscal, and balance of payments policies determine whether equilibrium conditions will exist and whether firms will be allowed to adjust prices and costs.

If equilibrium exists continuously, and a firm is free to adjust its prices and costs to maintain its expected competitive position, its operating exposure may be zero. Its expected cash flows would be realized and therefore its market value unchanged since the exchange rate change was anticipated. However, it is also possible that equilibrium conditions exist but the firm is unwilling or unable to adjust operations to the new competitive environment. In such

EXHIBIT 11.3   **Operating Exposure's Phases of Adjustment and Response**

Phase	Time	Price Changes	Volume Changes	Structural Changes
Short Run	Less than 1 year	Prices are fixed/contracted	Volumes are contracted	No competitive market changes
Medium Run: Equilibrium	2 to 5 years	Complete pass-through of exchange rate changes	Volumes begin a partial response to prices	Existing competitors begin partial responses
Medium Run: Disequilibrium	2 to 5 years	Partial pass-through of exchange rate changes	Volumes begin a partial response to prices	Existing competitors begin partial responses
Long Run	More than 5 years	Completely flexible	Completely flexible	Threat of new entrants and changing competitor responses

a case, the firm would experience operating exposure because its realized cash flows would differ from expected cash flows. As a result, its market value might also be altered.

Medium Run: Disequilibrium. The third level impact is on expected medium-run cash flows assuming disequilibrium conditions. In this case, the firm may not be able to adjust prices and costs to reflect the new competitive realities caused by a change in exchange rates. The primary problem may be the reactions of existing competitors. The firm's realized cash flows will differ from its expected cash flows. The firm's market value may change because of the unanticipated results.

Long Run. The fourth level impact is on expected long-run cash flows, meaning those beyond five years. At this strategic level a firm's cash flows will be influenced by the reactions of both existing competitors and potential competitors—possible new entrants—to exchange rate changes under disequilibrium conditions. In fact, all firms that are subject to international competition, whether they are purely domestic or multinational, are exposed to foreign exchange operating exposure in the long run whenever foreign exchange markets are not continuously in equilibrium.

Measuring Operating Exposure: Trident Germany

Exhibit 11.4 presents the dilemma facing Trident as a result of an unexpected change in the value of the euro, the currency of economic consequence for the German subsidiary. Trident derives much of its reported profits—the earnings and earnings per share (EPS) as reported to Wall Street—from its European subsidiary. If the euro were to unexpectedly fall in value, how would the value of Trident Germany's business change?

EXHIBIT 11.4   **Trident and Trident Germany**

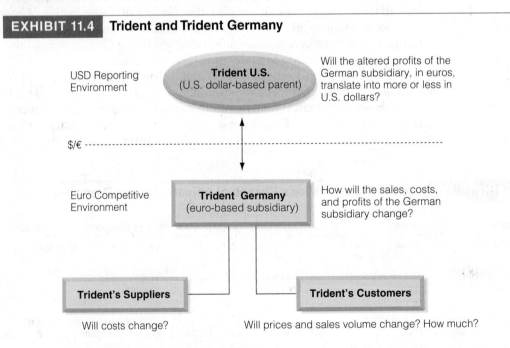

An unexpected depreciation in the value of the euro alters both the competitiveness of the subsidiary and the financial results which are consolidated with the parent company.

Value, in the world of finance, is generated by operating cash flow. If Trident wished to attempt to measure the operating exposure of Trident Germany to an unexpected exchange rate change, it would do so by evaluating the likely impact of that exchange rate on the operating cash flows of Trident Germany. Specifically, how would prices, costs, and volume sales change? How would competitors and their respective prices, costs, and volumes change? The following section illustrates how those very values might respond in the short run and medium run to a fall in the value of the euro against Trident's home currency, the dollar.

The Base Case

Trident Germany manufactures in Germany, sells domestically, and exports, and all sales are invoiced in euros. Exhibit 11.5 summarizes the current baseline forecast for Trident Germany income and operating cash flows for the 2014–2018 period (assume it is currently 2013). Sales volume is assumed to be a constant 1 million units per year, with a per unit sales price of €12.80

EXHIBIT 11.5   **Trident Germany's Valuation: Baseline Analysis**

Assumptions	2014	2015	2016	2017	2018
Sales volume (units)	1,000,000	1,000,000	1,000,000	1,000,000	1,000,000
Sales price per unit	€12.80	€12.80	€12.80	€12.80	€12.80
Direct cost per unit	€9.60	€9.60	€9.60	€9.60	€9.60
German corporate tax rate	29.5%	29.5%	29.5%	29.5%	29.5%
Exchange rate ($/€)	1.2000	1.2000	1.2000	1.2000	1.2000
Income Statement	**2014**	**2015**	**2016**	**2017**	**2018**
Sales revenue	€12,800,000	€12,800,000	€12,800,000	€12,800,000	€12,800,000
Direct cost of goods sold	−9,600,000	−9,600,000	−9,600,000	−9,600,000	−9,600,000
Cash operating expenses (fixed)	−890,000	−890,000	−890,000	−890,000	−890,000
Depreciation	−600,000	−600,000	−600,000	−600,000	−600,000
Pretax profit	€1,710,000	€1,710,000	€1,710,000	€1,710,000	€1,710,000
Income tax expense	−504,450	−504,450	−504,450	−504,450	−504,450
Net income	€1,205,550	€1,205,550	€1,205,550	€1,205,550	€1,205,550
Cash Flows for Valuation					
Net income	€1,205,550	€1,205,550	€1,205,550	€1,205,550	€1,205,550
Add back depreciation	600,000	600,000	600,000	600,000	600,000
Changes in net working capital	0	0	0	0	0
Free cash flow for valuation, in euros	€1,805,550	€1,805,550	€1,805,550	€1,805,550	€1,805,550
Cash flow from operations, in dollars	$2,166,660	$2,166,660	$2,166,660	$2,166,660	$2,166,660
Present Value @ 15%	$7,262,980				

and a per unit direct cost of €9.60. The corporate income tax rate in Germany is 29.5%, and the exchange rate is $1.20/€.[1]

These assumptions generate sales of €12,800,000, and €1,205,550 in net income. Adding net income to depreciation and changes in net working capital (which are zero in the base case) generates €1,805,550 or $2,166,660 in operating cash flow at $1.20/€. Trident's management values its subsidiaries by finding the present value of these total free cash flows over the coming five-year period, in U.S. dollars, assuming a 15% discount rate. The baseline analysis finds a present value of Trident Germany of $7,262,980.

On January 1, 2014, before any commercial activity begins, the euro unexpectedly drops from $1.2000/€ to $1.0000/€. Operating exposure depends on whether an unexpected change in exchange rates causes unanticipated changes in sales volume, sales prices, or operating costs.

Following a euro depreciation, Trident Germany might choose to maintain its domestic sales prices constant in euro terms, or it might try to raise domestic prices because competing imports are now priced higher in Europe. The firm might choose to keep export prices constant in terms of foreign currencies, in terms of euros, or somewhere in between (partial pass-through). The strategy undertaken depends to a large measure on management's opinion about the price elasticity of demand, which would also include management's assessment of competitor response. On the cost side, Trident Germany might raise prices because of more expensive imported raw material or components, or perhaps because all domestic prices in Germany have risen and labor is now demanding higher wages to compensate for domestic inflation.

Trident Germany's domestic sales and costs might also be partly determined by the effect of the euro depreciation on demand. To the extent that the depreciation, by making prices of German goods initially more competitive, stimulates purchases of European goods in import-competing sectors of the economy as well as exports of German goods, German national income should increase. This assumes that the favorable effect of a euro depreciation on comparative prices is not immediately offset by higher domestic inflation. Thus, Trident Germany might be able to sell more goods domestically because of price and income effects and internationally because of price effects.

To illustrate the effect of various post-depreciation scenarios on Trident Germany's operating exposure, consider four simple cases.

Case 1: Depreciation (all variables remain constant)

Case 2: Increase in sales volume (other variables remain constant)

Case 3: Increase in sales price (other variables remain constant)

Case 4: Sales price, cost, and volume increase

To calculate the changes in value under each of the scenarios, we will use the same five-year horizon for any change in cash flow induced by the change in the dollar/euro exchange rate.

---

[1]The analysis assumes, for simplification purposes, that Trident Germany has no debt and therefore no interest expenses. We also assume there are no additional capital expenditures required over the five years shown. We also assume no terminal value; Trident is valued on its coming expected five years of cash flow only. Net working capital requirements (accounts receivable + inventory − accounts payable) require no additions in the base case due to constant sales. In subsequent scenarios it is assumed receivables are maintained at 45 days of sales, inventory at 10 days of cost of goods sold, and accounts payable at 38 days of sales.

Case 1: Depreciation—All Variables Remain Constant

Assume that in the five years ahead no changes occur in sales volume, sales price, or operating costs. Profits for the coming year in euros will be as expected, and cash flow from operations will still be €1,805,550. There is no change in NWC because all results in euros remain the same. The exchange rate change, however, means that operating cash flows measured in U.S. dollars decline to $1,805,550. The present value of this series of operating cash flows is $6,052,483, a fall in Trident Germany's value—when measured in U.S. dollars—by $1,210,497.

Case 2: Volume Increases—Other Variables Remain Constant

Assume that, following the depreciation in the euro, sales within Europe increase by 40%, to 1,400,000 units (assume all other variables remain constant). The depreciation has now made German-made telecom components more competitive with imports. Additionally, export volume increases because German-made components are now cheaper in countries whose currencies have not weakened. The sales price is kept constant in euro terms because management of Trident Germany has not observed any change in local German operating costs and because it sees an opportunity to increase market share.

Trident Germany's net income rises to €2,107,950, and operating cash flows the first year rise to €2,504,553, after a one-time increase in net working capital of €203,397 (using a portion of the increased cash flows). Operating cash flow is €2,707,950 per year for the following four years. The present value of Trident Germany has risen by $1,637,621 over baseline to $8,900,601.

Case 3: Sales Price Increases—Other Variables Remain Constant

Assume the euro sales price is raised from €12.80 to €15.36 per unit to maintain the same U.S. dollar-equivalent price (the change offsets the depreciation of the euro) and that all other variables remain constant.

	Before	After
Price in euro	€12.80	€15.36
Exchange rate	$1.20/€	$1.00/€
Price in US$	$15.36	$15.36

Also assume that volume remains constant (the baseline 1,000,000 units) in spite of this price increase; that is, customers expect to pay the same dollar-equivalent price, and local costs do not change.

Trident Germany is now better off following the depreciation than it was before because the sales price, which is pegged to the international price level, increased. And volume did not drop. Net income rises to €3,010,350 per year, with operating cash flow rising to €3,561,254 in 2014 (after a working capital increase of €49,096) and €3,610,350 per year in the following four years. Trident Germany has now increased in value to $12,059,761.

Case 4: Price, Cost, and Volume Increases

The final case we examine, illustrated in Exhibit 11.6, is a combination of possible outcomes. Price increases by 10% to €14.08, direct cost per unit increases by 5% to €10.00, and volume rises by 10% to 1,100,000 units. Revenues rise by more than costs, and net income for Trident Germany rises to €2,113,590. Operating cash flow rises to €2,623,683 in 2014

| EXHIBIT 11.6 | Trident Germany: Case 4 – Sales Price, Volume and Costs Increase |

Assumptions	2014	2015	2016	2017	2018
Sales volume (units)	1,100,000	1,100,000	1,100,000	1,100,000	1,100,000
Sales price per unit	€14.08	€14.08	€14.08	€14.08	€14.08
Direct cost per unit	€10.00	€10.00	€10.00	€10.00	€10.00
German corporate tax rate	29.5%	29.5%	29.5%	29.5%	29.5%
Exchange rate ($/€)	1.0000	1.0000	1.0000	1.0000	1.0000
Income Statement	**2014**	**2015**	**2016**	**2017**	**2018**
Sales revenue	€15,488,000	€15,488,000	€15,488,000	€15,488,000	€15,488,000
Direct cost of goods sold	−11,000,000	−11,000,000	−11,000,000	−11,000,000	−11,000,000
Cash operating expenses (fixed)	−890,000	−890,000	−890,000	−890,000	−890,000
Depreciation	−600,000	−600,000	−600,000	−600,000	−600,000
Pretax profit	€2,998,000	€2,998,000	€2,998,000	€2,998,000	€2,998,000
Income tax expense	−884,410	−884,410	−884,410	−884,410	−884,410
Net income	€2,113,590	€2,113,590	€2,113,590	€2,113,590	€2,113,590
Cash Flows for Valuation					
Net income	€2,113,590	€2,113,590	€2,113,590	€2,113,590	€2,113,590
Add back depreciation	600,000	600,000	600,000	600,000	600,000
Changes in net working capital	−89,907	0	0	0	0
Free cash flow for valuation, in euros	€2,623,683	€2,713,590	€2,713,590	€2,713,590	€2,713,590
Cash flow from operations, in dollars	$2,623,683	$2,713,590	$2,713,590	$2,713,590	$2,713,590
Present Value @ 15%	$9,018,195				

(after NWC increase), and €2,713,590 for each of the following four years. Trident Germany's present value is now $9,018,195.

Other Possibilities

If any portion of sales revenues were incurred in other currencies, the situation would be different. Trident Germany might leave the foreign sales price unchanged, in effect raising the euro-equivalent price. Alternatively, it might leave the euro-equivalent price unchanged, thus lowering the foreign sales price in an attempt to gain volume. Of course, it could also position itself between these two extremes. Depending on elasticities and the proportion of foreign to domestic sales, total sales revenue might rise or fall.

If some or all raw material or components were imported and paid for in hard currencies, euro operating costs would increase after the depreciation of the euro. Another possibility is that local (not imported) euro costs would rise after a depreciation.

EXHIBIT 11.7 | Summary of Trident Germany Value Changes to Depreciation of the Euro

Case	Exchange Rate	Price	Volume	Cost	Valuation	Change in Value	Percent Change in Value
Baseline	$1.20/€	€12.80	1,000,000	€9.60	$7,262,980	—	
Case 1: Depreciation	$1.00/€	€12.80	1,000,000	€9.60	$6,052,483	($1,210,497)	−16.7%
Case 2: Volume increases	$1.00/€	€12.80	1,400,000	€9.60	$8,900,601	$1,637,621	22.5%
Case 3: Sales price increases	$1.00/€	€15.60	1,000,000	€9.60	$12,059,761	$4,796,781	66.0%
Case 4: Price, cost, and volume increases	$1.00/€	€14.08	1,100,000	€10.00	$9,018,195	$1,755,215	24.2%

Measurement of Loss

Exhibit 11.7 summarizes the change in Trident Germany's value across our small set of simple cases given an instantaneous and permanent change in the value of the euro from $1.20/€ to $1.00/€. These cases estimate Trident Germany's operating exposure by measuring the change in the subsidiary's value as measured by the present value of its operating cash flows over the coming five-year period.

In Case 1, in which the euro depreciates (all variables remain constant), Trident's German subsidiary's value falls by the percent change in the exchange rate, −16.7%. In Case 2, in which volume increased by 40% as a result of increasing price competitiveness, the German subsidiary's value increased 22.5%. In Case 3, in which the change in the exchange rate was completely passed-through to a higher sales price, resulting in a massive 66% increase in subsidiary value. The final case, Case 4, combined increases in all three income-drivers. The resulting change in subsidiary valuation of +24.2%, may be creeping toward a "realistic outcome," but there are obviously an infinite number of possibilities which subsidiary management should be able to narrow. In the end, although the measurement of operating exposure is indeed difficult, it is not impossible—and maybe worth the time and effort—in progressive financial management.[2]

Strategic Management of Operating Exposure

The objective of managing both operating and transaction exposure is to anticipate and influence the effect of unexpected changes in exchange rates on a firm's future cash flows, rather than merely hoping for the best. To meet this objective, management can diversify the firm's operating and financing base. Management can also change the firm's operating and financing policies if it is concerned. *Global Finance in Practice 11.2* highlights one of the challenges to management awareness—fixed exchange rates.

The key to managing operating exposure at the strategic level is for management to recognize a disequilibrium in parity conditions when it occurs and to be pre-positioned to react most appropriately. This task can best be accomplished if a firm diversifies internationally both its operating and its financing bases. Diversifying operations means diversifying sales, location of production facilities, and raw material sources. Diversifying the financing base means raising funds in more than one capital market and in more than one currency.

[2]Note that, depending on the specific scenario, net working capital requirements have to adjust as shown in the first year with sales level changes.

GLOBAL FINANCE IN PRACTICE 11.2

Do Fixed Exchange Rates Increase Corporate Currency Risk in Emerging Markets?

It has long been argued that when firms know the exchange rate cannot or will not change, they will conduct their business as if currency exposure—at least against the major currency(s) to which their home currency is fixed—will not occur. As one study of currency risk in India noted, "These results support the hypothesis that pegged exchange rates induce *moral hazard* and increase financial fragility."

Moral hazard is the concept that a party—an agent, an individual, or a firm—will take on more risk when it either knows or believes that a second party will handle, accommodate, or insure the negative repercussions of the firm's risk-taking decisions. In other words, a firm may take more risk when it knows that someone else will pick up the tab. In a fixed or managed exchange rate regime, that "someone else" is represented by the central bank, which tells all those undertaking cross-currency contractual obligations and exposures that the exchange rate will not change.

Although there is still scant research on this specific practice for most of the emerging markets, it could prove to be a significant issue in the years to come, as many emerging markets become the object of major new international capital flows—the so-called *globalization of finance*. If commercial firms in those markets are not aware of the risk that the country itself may be taking by opening the door to international capital flows, both in and out of the country, and the impact they may have on the country's exchange rate, those firms may be in for a wild ride in the immediate years to come.

Sources: "Does the currency regime shape unhedged currency exposure?," by Ila Patnaik and Ajay Shah, *Journal of International Money and Finance*, 29, 2010, pp. 760–769. See also "Moral Hazard, Financial Crises, and the Choice of Exchange Rate Regimes," Apanard Angkinand and Thomas Willett, June 2006; and "Exchange-Rate Regimes for Emerging Markets: Moral Hazard and International Borrowing," by Ronald I. McKinnon and Huw Pill, *Oxford Review of Economic Policy*, Vol. 15, No. 3, 1999.

A diversification strategy permits the firm to react either actively or passively, depending on management's risk preference, to opportunities presented by disequilibrium conditions in the foreign exchange, capital, and product markets. Such a strategy does not require management to predict disequilibrium but only to recognize it when it occurs. It does require management to consider how competitors are pre-positioned with respect to their own operating exposures. This knowledge should reveal which firms would be helped or hurt competitively by alternative disequilibrium scenarios.

Diversifying Operations

Diversification of operations is one structural strategy to pre-positioning the firm for managing operating exposure. Consider the case in which purchasing power parity is temporarily in disequilibrium. Although the disequilibrium may have been unpredictable, management can often recognize its symptoms as soon as they occur. For example, management might notice a change in comparative costs in the firm's plants located in different countries. It might also observe changed profit margins or sales volume in one area compared to another, depending on price and income elasticities of demand and competitors' reactions.

Recognizing a temporary change in worldwide competitive conditions permits management to make changes in operating strategies. Management might make marginal shifts in sourcing raw materials, components, or finished products. If spare capacity exists, production runs can be lengthened in one country and reduced in another. The marketing effort can be strengthened in export markets where the firm's products have become more price competitive because of the disequilibrium condition.

Even if management does not actively alter normal operations when exchange rates change, the firm should experience some beneficial portfolio effects. The variability of its cash flows is probably reduced by international diversification of its production, sourcing, and sales because exchange rate changes under disequilibrium conditions are likely to increase the firm's competitiveness in some markets while reducing it in others. In that case, operating exposure would be neutralized.

In contrast to the internationally diversified MNE, a purely domestic firm might be subject to the full impact of foreign exchange operating exposure even though it does not have foreign currency cash flows. For example, it could experience intense import competition in its domestic market from competing firms producing in countries with undervalued currencies.

A purely domestic firm does not have the option to react to an international disequilibrium condition in the same manner as an MNE. In fact, a purely domestic firm will not be positioned to recognize that a disequilibrium exists because it lacks comparative data from its own internal sources. By the time external data are available, it is often too late to react. Even if a domestic firm recognizes the disequilibrium, it cannot quickly shift production and sales into foreign markets in which it has had no previous presence.

Constraints exist that may limit the feasibility of diversifying production locations. The technology of a particular industry may require large economies of scale. For example, high-tech firms, such as Intel, prefer to locate in places where they have easy access to high-tech suppliers, a highly educated workforce, and one or more leading universities. Their R&D efforts are closely tied to initial production and sales activities.

Diversifying Financing

If a firm diversifies its financing sources, it will be pre-positioned to take advantage of temporary deviations from the international Fisher effect. If interest rate differentials do not equal expected changes in exchange rates, opportunities to lower a firm's cost of capital will exist. However, to be able to switch financing sources, a firm must already be well known in the international investment community, with banking contacts firmly established. Again, this is not typically an option for a domestic firm.

As we will demonstrate in Chapter 12, diversifying sources of financing, regardless of the currency of denomination, can lower a firm's cost of capital and increase its availability of capital. The ability to source capital from outside of a segmented market is especially important for firms resident in emerging markets.

Proactive Management of Operating Exposure

Operating and transaction exposures can be partially managed by adopting operating or financing policies that offset anticipated foreign exchange exposures. Five of the most commonly employed proactive policies are 1) matching currency cash flows; 2) risk-sharing agreements; 3) back-to-back or parallel loans; 4) cross-currency swaps, and 5) contractual approaches.

Matching Currency Cash Flows

One way to offset an anticipated continuous long-term exposure to a particular currency is to acquire debt denominated in that currency. Exhibit 11.8 depicts the exposure of a U.S. firm with continuing export sales to Canada. In order to compete effectively in Canadian markets, the firm invoices all export sales in Canadian dollars. This policy results in a continuing receipt of Canadian dollars month after month. If the export sales are part of a continuing supplier relationship, the long Canadian dollar position is relatively predictable and constant. This endless series of transaction exposures could of course be continually hedged with forward contracts or other contractual hedges, as discussed in Chapter 9.

But what if the firm sought out a continual use—an outflow—for its continual inflow of Canadian dollars? If the U.S. firm were to acquire part of its debt-capital in the Canadian dollar markets, it could use the relatively predictable Canadian dollar cash inflows from export sales to service the principal and interest payments on Canadian dollar debt and be cash flow matched.

EXHIBIT 11.8   Debt Financing as a Financial Hedge

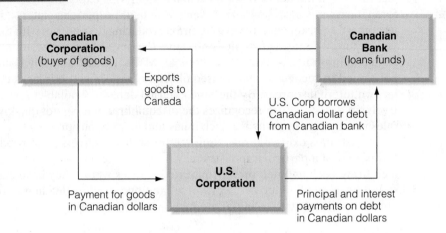

Exposure: The sale of goods to Canada creates a foreign currency exposure from the inflow of Canadian dollars.

Hedge: The Canadian dollar debt payments act as a financial hedge by requiring debt service, an outflow of Canadian dollars.

The U.S.-based firm has hedged an operational cash inflow by creating a financial cash outflow, and so it does not have to actively manage the exposure with contractual financial instruments such as forward contracts. This form of hedging, sometimes referred to as *matching*, is effective in eliminating currency exposure when the exposure cash flow is relatively constant and predictable over time.

The list of potential matching strategies is nearly endless. A second alternative would be for the U.S. firm to seek out potential suppliers of raw materials or components in Canada as a substitute for U.S. or other foreign firms. The firm would then possess both an operational Canadian dollar cash inflow—a receivable—and a Canadian dollar operational cash outflow—a payable. If the cash flows were roughly the same in magnitude and timing, the strategy would be a natural hedge. The term "natural" refers to operating-based activities of the firm.

A third alternative, often referred to as *currency switching*, would be to pay foreign suppliers with Canadian dollars. For example, if the U.S. firm imported components from Mexico, the Mexican firms themselves might welcome payment in Canadian dollars because they are short Canadian dollars in their multinational cash flow network.

Risk-Sharing Agreements

An alternative arrangement for managing a long-term cash flow exposure between firms with a continuing buyer-supplier relationship is *risk-sharing*. *Risk-sharing* is a contractual arrangement in which the buyer and seller agree to "share" or split currency movement impacts on payments between them. If the two firms are interested in a long-term relationship based on product quality and supplier reliability, and not on the whims of the currency markets, a cooperative agreement to share the burden of currency risk may be in order.

If Ford's North American operations import automotive parts from Mazda (Japan) every month, year after year, major swings in exchange rates can benefit one party at the expense of the other. (Ford is a major stockholder of Mazda, but it does not exert control over its operations. Therefore, the risk-sharing agreement is particularly appropriate; transactions between the two are both intercompany and intracompany in nature. A risk-sharing agreement solidifies the partnership.) One potential solution would be for Ford and Mazda to agree that all purchases by Ford will be made in Japanese yen at the current exchange rate, as long as the spot rate on the date of invoice is between, say, ¥115/$ and ¥125/$. If the exchange rate is between these values on the payment dates, Ford agrees to accept whatever transaction exposure exists (because it is paying in a foreign currency). If, however, the exchange rate falls outside this range on the payment date, Ford and Mazda will share the difference equally.

For example, Ford has an account payable of ¥25,000,000 for the month of March. If the spot rate on the date of invoice is ¥110/$, the Japanese yen would have appreciated versus the dollar, causing Ford's costs of purchasing automotive parts to rise. Since this rate falls outside the contractual range, Mazda would agree to accept a total payment in Japanese yen which would result from a difference of ¥5/$ (i.e., ¥115–¥110). Ford's payment would be as follows:

$$\left[\frac{\yen 25,000,000}{\yen 115.00/\$ - \left(\dfrac{\yen 5.00/\$}{2} \right)} \right] = \frac{\yen 25,000,000}{\yen 112.50/\$} = \$222,222.22$$

Ford's total payment in Japanese yen would be calculated using an exchange rate of ¥112.50/$, and saves Ford $5,050.51. At a spot rate of ¥110/$, Ford's costs for March would be $227,272.73. The risk-sharing agreement between Ford and Mazda allows Ford to pay $222,222.22, a savings of $5,050.51 over the cost without risk-sharing (this "savings" is a reduction in an increased cost, not a true cost reduction). Both parties therefore incur costs and benefits from exchange rate movements outside the specified band. Note that the movement could just as easily have been in Mazda's favor if the spot rate had moved to ¥130/$.

The risk-sharing arrangement is intended to smooth the impact on both parties of volatile and unpredictable exchange rate movements. Of course, a sustained appreciation of one currency versus the other would require the negotiation of a new sharing agreement, but the ultimate goal of the agreement is to alleviate currency pressures on the continuing business relationship. Risk-sharing agreements like these have been in use for nearly 50 years on world markets. They became something of a rarity during the 1960s when exchange rates were relatively stable under the Bretton Woods Agreement. But with the return to floating exchange rates in the 1970s, firms with long-term customer-supplier relationships across borders have returned to some old ways of maintaining mutually beneficial long-term trade.

Back-to-Back or Parallel Loans

A *back-to-back loan*, also referred to as a *parallel loan* or *credit swap*, occurs when two business firms in separate countries arrange to borrow each other's currency for a specific period of time. At an agreed terminal date they return the borrowed currencies. The operation is conducted outside the foreign exchange markets, although spot quotations may be used as the reference point for determining the amount of funds to be swapped. Such a swap creates a covered hedge against exchange loss, since each company, on its own books, borrows the same currency it repays. Back-to-back loans are also used at a time of actual or anticipated legal limitations on the transfer of investment funds to or from either country.

The structure of a typical back-to-back loan is illustrated in Exhibit 11.9. A British parent firm that wants to invest funds in its Dutch subsidiary locates a Dutch parent firm that wants to invest funds in the United Kingdom. Avoiding the exchange markets entirely, the British parent lends pounds to the Dutch subsidiary in the United Kingdom, while the Dutch parent lends euros to the British subsidiary in the Netherlands. The two loans would be for equal

EXHIBIT 11.9 Back-to-Back Loans for Currency Hedging

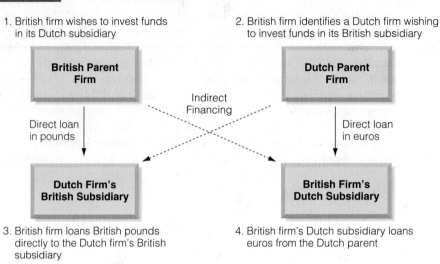

1. British firm wishes to invest funds in its Dutch subsidiary

2. British firm identifies a Dutch firm wishing to invest funds in its British subsidiary

3. British firm loans British pounds directly to the Dutch firm's British subsidiary

4. British firm's Dutch subsidiary loans euros from the Dutch parent

The back-to-back loan provides a method for parent-subsidiary cross-border financing without incurring direct currency exposure.

values at the current spot rate and for a specified maturity. At maturity, the two separate loans would each be repaid to the original lender, again without any need to use the foreign exchange markets. Neither loan carries any foreign exchange risk, and neither loan normally needs the approval of any governmental body regulating the availability of foreign exchange for investment purposes.

Parent company guarantees are not needed on the back-to-back loans because each loan carries the right of offset in the event of default of the other loan. A further agreement can provide for maintenance of principal parity in case of changes in the spot rate between the two countries. For example, if the pound dropped by more than, say, 6% for as long as 30 days, the British parent might have to advance additional pounds to the Dutch subsidiary to bring the principal value of the two loans back to parity. A similar provision would protect the British if the euro should weaken. Although this parity provision might lead to changes in the amount of home currency each party must lend during the period of the agreement, it does not increase foreign exchange risk, because at maturity all loans are repaid in the same currency loaned.

There are two fundamental impediments to widespread use of the back-to-back loan. First, it is difficult for a firm to find a partner, termed a *counterparty*, for the currency, amount, and timing desired. Second, a risk exists that one of the parties will fail to return the borrowed funds at the designated maturity—although this risk is minimized because each party to the loan has, in effect, 100% collateral, albeit in a different currency. These disadvantages have led to the rapid development and wide use of the cross-currency swap.

Cross-Currency Swaps

A *cross-currency swap* resembles a back-to-back loan except that it does not appear on a firm's balance sheet. As noted previously in Chapter 5, the term *swap* is used in a variety of ways in international finance, and care should be used to identify the exact use in a specific case.

In a *currency swap*, a firm and a swap dealer or swap bank agree to exchange an equivalent amount of two different currencies for a specified period of time. Currency swaps can be negotiated for a wide range of maturities up to 30 years in some cases. The swap dealer or swap bank acts as a middleman in setting up the swap agreement. Currency swap structures are covered in detail in Chapter 7.

A typical currency swap first requires two firms to borrow funds in markets and currencies in which they are well known. For example, a Japanese firm would typically borrow yen on a regular basis in its home market. If, however, the Japanese firm were exporting to the United States and earning U.S. dollars, it might wish to construct a matching cash flow hedge that would allow it to use the U.S. dollars earned to make regular debt-service payments on U.S. dollar debt. If, however, the Japanese firm is not well known in the U.S. financial markets, it may have no ready access to U.S. dollar debt.

One way in which this Japanese firm could, in effect, borrow dollars, is to participate in a cross-currency swap as see in Exhibit 11.10. The firm could swap its yen-denominated debt service payments with another firm that has U.S. dollar-debt service payments. This swap would have the Japanese firm "paying dollars" and "receiving yen." The Japanese firm would then have dollar-debt service without actually borrowing U.S. dollars. Simultaneously, a U.S. corporation would actually be entering into a cross-currency swap in the opposite direction—"paying yen" and "receiving dollars." The swap dealer takes the role of a middleman. Swap dealers arrange most swaps on a "blind basis," meaning that the initiating firm does not know who is on the other side of the swap arrangement—the counterparty. The initiating firm views the dealer or bank as its counterparty. Because the swap markets are dominated by the major money center banks worldwide, the counterparty risk is acceptable. Because the swap dealer's business is arranging swaps, the dealer can generally arrange for the currency, amount, and timing of the desired swap.

Accountants in the United States treat the currency swap as a foreign exchange transaction rather than as debt and they treat the obligation to reverse the swap at some later date as a forward exchange contract. Forward exchange contracts can be matched against assets,

---

EXHIBIT 11.10   Using Cross-Currency Swaps

Both the Japanese corporation and the U.S. corporation would like to enter into a cross-currency swap which would allow them to use foreign currency cash inflows to service debt.

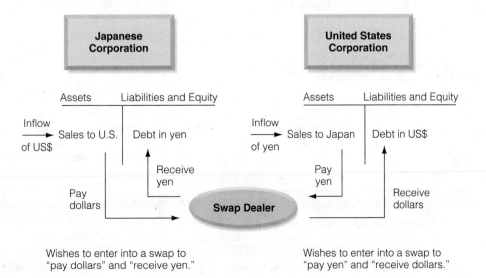

but they are entered in a firm's footnotes rather than as balance sheet items. The result is that both translation and operating exposures are avoided, and neither a long-term receivable nor a long-term debt is created on the balance sheet.

Contractual Approaches: Hedging the Unhedgeable

Some MNEs now attempt to hedge their operating exposure with contractual strategies. A number of firms like Merck (U.S.) have undertaken long-term currency option positions—hedges designed to offset lost earnings from adverse exchange rate changes. This hedging of what many of these firms refer to as strategic exposure or competitive exposure seems to fly in the face of traditional theory.

The ability of firms to hedge the "unhedgeable" is dependent upon predictability: 1) the predictability of the firm's future cash flows, and 2) the predictability of the firm's competitor's responses to exchange rate changes. Although the management of many firms may believe they are capable of predicting their own cash flows, in practice few feel capable of accurately predicting competitor response. Many firms still find timely measurement of exposure challenging.

Merck is an example of a firm whose management feels capable of both. The company possesses relatively predictable long-run revenue streams due to the product-niche nature of the pharmaceuticals industry. As a U.S.-based exporter to foreign markets, markets in which sales levels by product are relatively predictable and prices are often regulated by government, Merck can accurately predict net long-term cash flows in foreign currencies five and ten years into the future. Merck has a relatively undiversified operating structure, and it is highly centralized in terms of where research, development, and production costs are located. Merck's managers feel the company has no real alternatives but contractual hedging if it is to weather long-term unexpected exchange rate changes. Merck has purchased over-the-counter (OTC) long-term put options on foreign currencies versus the U.S. dollar as insurance against potential lost earnings from exchange rate changes.

A significant question remains as to the true effectiveness of hedging operating exposure with contractual hedges. The fact remains that even after feared exchange rate movements and put option position payoffs have occurred, the firm is competitively disadvantaged. The capital outlay required for the purchase of such sizable put option positions is capital not used for the potential diversification of operations, which in the long run might have more effectively maintained the firm's global market share and international competitiveness.

Summary Points

- Operating exposure measures the change in value of the firm that results from changes in future operating cash flows caused by an unexpected change in exchange rates.

- An unexpected change in exchange rates impacts a firm's expected cash flow at four levels: 1) short run; 2) medium run, equilibrium case; 3) medium run, disequilibrium case; and 4) long run.

- Operating strategies for the management of operating exposure emphasize the structuring of firm operations in order to create matching streams of cash flows by currency. This is termed "natural hedging."

- The objective of operating exposure management is to anticipate and influence the effect of unexpected changes in exchange rates on a firm's future cash flow, rather than being forced into passive reaction to such changes as was described in the Trident Germany case. This task can best be accomplished if a firm diversifies internationally both its operations and its financing base.

- Proactive policies include matching currency cash flows, currency risk-sharing clauses, back-to-back loan structures, and cross-currency swap agreements.

- Contractual approaches (i.e., options and forwards) have occasionally been used to hedge operating exposure but are costly and possibly ineffectual.

MINI-CASE

Toyota's European Operating Exposure[1]

It was January 2002, and Toyota Motor Europe Manufacturing (TMEM) had a problem. More specifically, Mr. Toyoda Shuhei, the new President of TMEM, had a problem. He was on his way to Toyota Motor Company's (Japan) corporate offices outside Tokyo to explain the continuing losses of the European manufacturing and sales operations. The CEO of Toyota Motor Company, Mr. Hiroshi Okuda, was expecting a proposal from Mr. Shuhei to reduce and eventually eliminate the European losses. The situation was intense given that TMEM was the only major Toyota subsidiary suffering losses.

Toyota and Auto Manufacturing

Toyota Motor Company was the number one automobile manufacturer in Japan, the third largest manufacturer in the world by unit sales (5.5 million units or one auto every six seconds), but number eight in sales in Continental Europe. The global automobile manufacturing industry had been experiencing, like many industries, continued consolidation in recent years as margins were squeezed, economies of scale and scope pursued, and global sales slowed.

Toyota was no different. It had continued to rationalize its manufacturing along regional lines. Toyota had continued to increase the amount of local manufacturing in North America. In 2001, over 60% of Toyota's North American sales were locally manufactured. But Toyota's European sales were nowhere close to this yet. Most of Toyota's automobile and truck manufacturing for Europe was still done in Japan. In 2001, only 24% of the autos sold in Europe were manufactured in Europe (including the United Kingdom). The remainder were imported from Japan (see Exhibit A).

Toyota Motor Europe sold 634,000 automobiles in 2000. This was the second largest foreign market for Toyota, second only to North America. TMEM expected significant growth in European sales, and was planning to expand European manufacturing and sales to 800,000 units by 2005. But for fiscal 2001, the unit reported operating losses of ¥9.897 billion ($82.5 million at ¥120/$). TMEM had three assembly plants in the United Kingdom, one plant in Turkey, and one plant in Portugal. In November 2000, Toyota Motor Europe announced publicly that it would not generate positive profits for the next two years due to the weakness of the euro.

Toyota had recently introduced a new model to the European market, the Yaris, which was proving very successful.

EXHIBIT A   Toyota's European Currency Operating Stucture

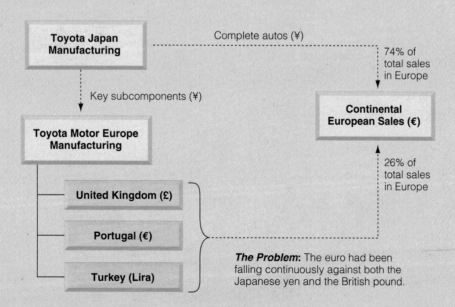

The Problem: The euro had been falling continuously against both the Japanese yen and the British pound.

---

[1]Copyright © 2005 Thunderbird School of Global Management. All rights reserved. This case was prepared by Professor Michael H. Moffett for the purpose of classroom discussion only, and not to indicate either effective or ineffective management.

The Yaris, a super-small vehicle with a 1,000cc engine, had sold more than 180,000 units in 2000. Although the Yaris had been specifically designed for the European market, the decision had been made early on to manufacture it in Japan.

Currency Exposure

The primary source of the continuing operating losses suffered by TMEM was the falling value of the euro. Over the recent two-year period, the euro had fallen in value against both the Japanese yen and the British pound. As demonstrated in Exhibit A, the cost base for most of the autos sold within the Continental European market was the Japanese yen. Exhibit B illustrates the slide of the euro against the Japanese yen.

As the yen rose against the euro, costs increased significantly when measured in euros. If Toyota wished to preserve its price competitiveness in the European market, it had to absorb most of the exchange rate changes and suffer reduced margins on both completed cars and key subcomponents shipped to its European manufacturing centers. Deciding to manufacture the Yaris in Japan had only exacerbated the situation.

Management Response

Toyota management was not sitting passively by. In 2001, they had initiated some assembly operations in Valenciennes, France. Although accounting for a relatively small percentage of total European sales as of January 2002, Toyota planned to continue to expand its European capacity and capabilities and to source about 25% of European sales by 2004. Assembly of the Yaris was scheduled to be relocated to Valenciennes in 2002. The continuing problem, however, was that it was an assembly facility, meaning that many of the expensive value-added components of the autos being assembled were still based in either Japan or the United Kingdom.

Mr. Shuhei, with the approval of Mr. Okuda, had also initiated a local sourcing and procurement program for the United Kingdom manufacturing operations. TMEM wished to decrease the number of key components imported from Toyota Japan in order to reduce the currency exposure of the U.K. unit. But again, the continuing problem of the British pound's value against the euro, as shown in Exhibit C, reduced the effectiveness of even this solution.

CASE QUESTIONS

1. Why do you think Toyota waited so long to move much of its manufacturing for European sales to Europe?

2. If the British pound were to join the European Monetary Union would the problem be resolved? How likely do you think this is?

3. If you were Mr. Shuhei, how would you categorize your problems and solutions? What was a short-term problem? What was a long-term problem?

4. What measures would you recommend that Toyota Europe take to resolve the continuing operating losses?

EXHIBIT B   Japanese Yen per Euro Spot Rate

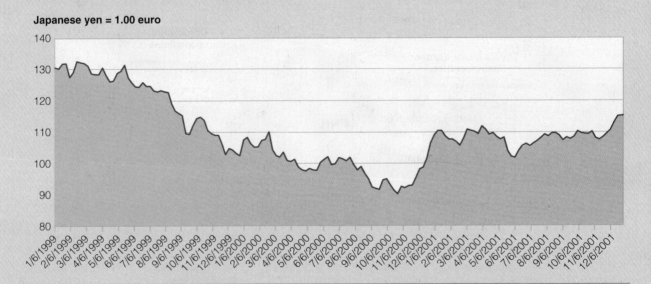

Japanese yen = 1.00 euro

EXHIBIT C **British Pounds per Euro Spot Rate**

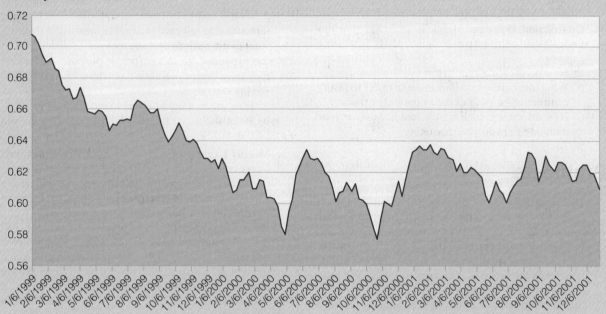

British pounds = 1.00 euro

Questions

1. **Measurement of Operating Exposure.**
   a. What is the difference between operating exposure and transaction exposure?
   b. How is operating exposure measured?
   c. Why is it difficult to measure operating exposure?

2. **Unexpected Exchange Rate Changes.**
   a. Explain why the management of MNEs finds that quantifying and hedging operational exposure are challenging tasks.
   b. Explain why exchange rate uncertainty may not expose firms to exchange risk.

3. **Economic Exposure.** Economic exposure is highest for MNEs with multiple foreign currency operations. Is economic exposure confined to MNEs or does it involve local firms as well?

4. **Strategic Exposure.** Operating or strategic exposure has become a concern of long-term corporate strategy. Which level of management is responsible for mitigating and managing strategic exposure? Explain the various policy options that the management uses to manage strategic exposure.

5. **Managing Operating Exposure.** The key to managing operating exposure at the strategic level is for management to recognize a disequilibrium in parity conditions when it occurs and to be pre-positioned to react most appropriately. How can this task best be accomplished?

6. **Diversifying Operations.**
   a. How can an MNE diversify operations?
   b. How can an MNE diversify financing?

7. **Proactive Management of Operating Exposure.** Operating and transaction exposures can be partially managed by adopting operating or financing policies that offset anticipated foreign exchange exposures. What are four of the most commonly employed proactive policies?

8. **Matching Currency Exposure.**
   a. Explain how matching currency cash flows can offset operating exposure.
   b. Give an example of matching currency cash flows.

9. **Currency Risk-Sharing.** Explain why suppliers are ready to get into currency risk-sharing deals with MNEs. How do such deals impact the financial position of both parties?

10. **Back-to-Back Loans.** Explain how back-to-back loans can hedge foreign exchange operating exposure.

11. **Currency Swaps.** Explain how currency swaps can hedge foreign exchange operating exposure. What are the accounting advantages of currency swaps?

12. **Contractual Hedging.** Merck is an MNE that has undertaken contractual hedging of its operating exposure.
    a. How do they accomplish this task?
    b. What assumptions do they make in order to justify contractual hedging of their operating exposure?
    c. How effective is such contractual hedging in your opinion? Explain your reasoning.

Problems

1. **DeMagistris Fashion Company.** DeMagistris Fashion Company, based in New York City, imports leather coats from Acuña Leather Goods, a reliable and longtime supplier, based in Buenos Aires, Argentina. Payment is in Argentine pesos. When the peso lost its parity with the U.S. dollar in January 2002, it collapsed in value to Ps4.0/$ by October 2002. The outlook was for a further decline in the peso's value. Since both DeMagistris and Acuña wanted to continue their longtime relationship, they agreed on a risk-sharing arrangement. As long as the spot rate on the date of an invoice is between Ps3.5/$ and Ps4.5/$, DeMagistris will pay based on the spot rate. If the exchange rate falls outside this range, they will share the difference equally with Acuña Leather Goods. The risk-sharing agreement will last for six months, at which time the exchange rate limits will be reevaluated. DeMagistris contracts to import leather coats from Acuña for Ps8,000,000 or $2,000,000 at the current spot rate of Ps4.0/$ during the next six months.
    a. If the exchange rate changes immediately to Ps6.00/$, what will be the dollar cost of six months of imports to DeMagistris?
    b. At Ps6.00/$, what will be the peso export sales of Acuña Leather Goods to DeMagistris Fashion Company?

2. **Mauna Loa.** Mauna Loa, a macadamia nut subsidiary of Hershey's with plantations on the slopes of its namesake volcano in Hilo, Hawaii, exports macadamia nuts worldwide. The Japanese market is its biggest export market, with average annual sales invoiced in yen to Japanese customers of ¥1,200,000,000. At the present exchange rate of ¥125/$, this is equivalent to $9,600,000. Sales are relatively equally distributed throughout the year. They show up as a ¥250,00,000 account receivable on Mauna Loa's balance sheet. Credit terms to each customer allow for 60 days before payment is due. Monthly cash collections are typically ¥100,000,000.

Mauna Loa would like to hedge its yen receipts, but it has too many customers and transactions to make it practical to sell each receivable forward. It does not want to use options because they are considered to be too expensive for this particular purpose. Therefore, they have decided to use a "matching" hedge by borrowing yen.
    a. How much should Mauna Loa borrow in yen?
    b. What should be the terms of payment on the yen loan?

3. **Murray Exports (A).** Murray Exports (U.S.) exports heavy crane equipment to several Chinese dock facilities. Sales are currently 10,000 units per year at the yuan equivalent of $24,000 each. The Chinese yuan (renminbi) has been trading at Yuan8.20/$, but a Hong Kong advisory service predicts the renminbi will drop in value next week to Yuan9.00/$, after which it will remain unchanged for at least a decade. Accepting this forecast as given, Murray Exports faces a pricing decision in the face of the impending devaluation. It may either 1) maintain the same yuan price and in effect sell for fewer dollars, in which case Chinese volume will not change; or 2) maintain the same dollar price, raise the yuan price in China to offset the devaluation, and experience a 10% drop in unit volume. Direct costs are 75% of the U.S. sales price.
    a. What would be the short-run (one year) impact of each pricing strategy?
    b. Which do you recommend?

4. **Murray Exports (B).** Assume the same facts as in Problem 3. Additionally, financial management believes that if it maintains the same yuan sales price, volume will increase at 12% per annum for eight years. Dollar costs will not change. At the end of 10 years, Murray Exports' patent expires and it will no longer export to China. After the yuan is devalued to Yuan9.20/$, no further devaluations are expected. If Murray Exports raises the yuan price so as to maintain its dollar price, volume will increase at only 1% per annum for eight years, starting from the lower initial base of 9,000 units. Again, dollar costs will not change, and at the end of eight years Murray Exports will stop exporting to China. Murray Exports' weighted average cost of capital is 10%. Given these considerations, what should be Murray Exports' pricing policy?

5. **MacLoren Automotive.** MacLoren Automotive manufactures British sports cars, a number of which are exported to New Zealand for payment in pounds sterling. The distributor sells the sports cars in New Zealand

for New Zealand dollars. The New Zealand distributor is unable to carry all of the foreign exchange risk, and would not sell MacLoren models unless MacLoren could share some of the foreign exchange risk. MacLoren has agreed that sales for a given model year will initially be priced at a "base" spot rate between the New Zealand dollar and pound sterling set to be the spot mid-rate at the beginning of that model year. As long as the actual exchange rate is within ±5% of that base rate, payment will be made in pounds sterling. That is, the New Zealand distributor assumes all foreign exchange risk. However, if the spot rate at time of shipment falls outside of this ±5% range, MacLoren will share equally (i.e., 50/50) the difference between the actual spot rate and the base rate. For the current model year the base rate is NZ$1.6400/£.

a. What are the outside ranges within which the New Zealand importer must pay at the then current spot rate?

b. If MacLoren ships 10 sports cars to the New Zealand distributor at a time when the spot exchange rate is NZ$1.7000/£, and each car has an invoice cost £32,000, what will be the cost to the distributor in New Zealand dollars? How many pounds will MacLoren receive, and how does this compare with McLoren's expected sales receipt of £32,000 per car?

c. If MacLoren Automotive ships the same 10 cars to New Zealand at a time when the spot exchange rate is NZ$1.6500/£, how many New Zealand dollars will the distributor pay? How many pounds will MacLoren Automotive receive?

d. Does a risk-sharing agreement such as this one shift the currency exposure from one party of the transaction to the other?

e. Why is such a risk-sharing agreement of benefit to MacLoren? Why is it of benefit to the New Zealand distributor?

6. **Trident Germany—All Domestic Competitors.** Using the Trident Germany analysis in Exhibit 11.5 and 11.6 where the euro depreciates, how would prices, costs, and volumes change if Trident Germany was operating in a nearly purely domestic mature market with major domestic competitors?

7. **Trident Germany—All Foreign Competitors.** Trident Germany is now competing in a number of international (export) markets, growth markets, in which most of its competitors are foreign. Now how would you expect Trident Germany's operating exposure to respond to the depreciation of the euro?

8. **Risk-Sharing at Harley Davidson.** Harley-Davidson (U.S.) reportedly uses risk-sharing agreements with its foreign subsidiaries and with independent foreign distributors. Because these foreign units typically sell to their local markets and earn local currency, Harley would like to ease their individual currency exposure problems by allowing them to pay for merchandise from Harley (U.S.) in their local functional currency.

The spot rate between the U.S. dollar and the Australian dollar on January 1 is A$1.3052/US$. Assume that Harley uses this rate as the basis for setting its central rate or base exchange rate for the year at A$1.3000/US$. Harley agrees to price all contracts to Australian distributors at this exact exchange rate as long as the current spot rate on the order date is within ±2.5% of this rate. If the spot rate falls outside of this range, but is still within ±5.0% of the central rate, Harley will "share" equally (i.e., "50/50") the difference between the new spot rate and the neutral boundary with the distributor.

a. Diagram and detail the exact exchange rates in effect for both the upper and lower boundaries of the fixed rate and sharing zones used by Harley.

b. If Harley ships a *hog* (the nickname of the Harley-Davidson motorcycle) costing US$8,500, and the spot exchange rate on the order date is A$1.3442/US$, what is the price to the Australian dealership?

c. If Harley ships a hog costing US$8,500, and the spot exchange rate on the order date is A$1.2940/US$, what is the price to the Australian dealership?

9. **Hurte-Paroxysm Products, Inc. (A).** Hurte-Paroxysm Products, Inc. (HP) of the United States, exports computer printers to Brazil, whose currency, the reais (R$) has been trading at R$3.40/US$. Exports to Brazil are currently 50,000 printers per year at the reais equivalent of $200 each. A strong rumor exists that the reais will be devalued to R$4.00/$ within two weeks by the Brazilian government. Should the devaluation take place, the reais is expected to remain unchanged for another decade. Accepting this forecast as given, HP faces a pricing decision which must be made before any actual devaluation: HP may either 1) maintain the same reais price and in effect sell for fewer dollars, in which case Brazilian volume will not change, or 2) maintain the same dollar price, raise the reais price in Brazil to compensate for the devaluation, and experience a 20% drop in volume. Direct costs in the United States are 60% of the U.S. sales price. What would be the short-run (1-year) implication of each pricing strategy? Which do you recommend?

10. **Hurte-Paroxysm Products, Inc. (B).** Assume the same facts as in Problem 9. HP also believes that if it maintains the same price in Brazilian reais as a permanent policy, volume will increase at 10% per annum for six years, costs will not change. At the end of six years,

HP's patent expires and it will no longer export to Brazil. After the reais is devalued to R$4.00/US$, no further devaluation is expected. If HP raises the price in reais so as to maintain its dollar price, volume will increase at only 4% per annum for six years, starting from the lower initial base of 40,000 units. Again, dollar costs will not change, and at the end of six years, HP will stop exporting to Brazil. HP's weighted average cost of capital is 12%. Given these considerations, what do you recommend for HP's pricing policy? Justify your recommendation.

Internet Exercises

1. **Operating Exposure: Recent Examples**. Using the following major periodicals as starting points, find a current example of a firm with a substantial operating exposure problem. To aid in your search, you might focus on businesses having major operations in countries with recent currency crises, either through depreciation or major home currency appreciation.

Financial Times	www.ft.com/
The Economist	www.economist.com/
The *Wall Street Journal*	www.wsj.com/

2. **SEC Edgar Files**. To analyze an individual firm's operating exposure more carefully, it is necessary to have more detailed information available than in the normal annual report. Choose a specific firm with substantial international operations, for example, Coca-Cola or PepsiCo, and search the Security and Exchange Commission's Edgar Files for more detailed financial reports of their international operations.

Search SEC EDGAR Archives	www.sec.gov/cgi-bin/ srch-edgar

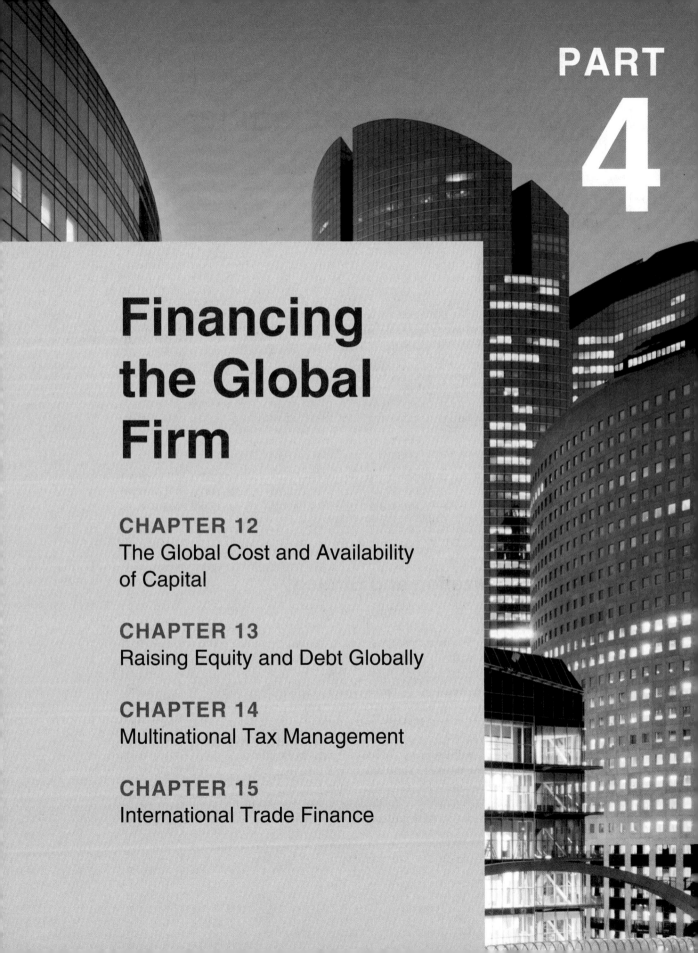

CHAPTER 12

The Global Cost and Availability of Capital

Capital must be propelled by self-interest; it cannot be enticed by benevolence. —Walter Bagehot, 1826–1877.

LEARNING OBJECTIVES

- Examine how a firm headquartered in a country with an illiquid and segmented capital market achieves a lower global cost and greater availability of capital

- Analyze the linkage between cost and availability of capital

- Evaluate the effect of market liquidity and segmentation on the cost of capital

- Compare the weighted average cost of capital for an MNE with its domestic counterpart

How can firms tap global capital markets for the purpose of minimizing their cost of capital and maximizing capital's availability? Why should they do so? Is global capital cheaper? This chapter explores these questions, concluding with a Mini-Case that details one of the most influential corporate financial strategies ever executed, *Novo Industri A/S (Novo)*.

Financial Globalization and Strategy

Global integration of capital markets has given many firms access to new and cheaper sources of funds, beyond those available in their home markets. These firms can then accept more long-term projects and invest more in capital improvements and expansion. If a firm is located in a country with illiquid and/or segmented capital markets, it can achieve this lower global cost and greater availability of capital through a properly designed and implemented strategy. The dimensions of the cost and availability of capital are presented in Exhibit 12.1.

A firm that must source its long-term debt and equity in a highly illiquid domestic securities market will probably have a relatively high cost of capital and will face limited availability of such capital, which in turn will lower its competitiveness both internationally and vis-à-vis foreign firms entering its home market. This category of firms includes both firms resident in emerging countries, where the capital market remains undeveloped, and firms too small to gain access to their own national securities markets. Many family-owned firms find themselves in this category because they choose not to utilize securities markets to source their long-term capital needs.

EXHIBIT 12.1   **Dimensions of the Cost and Availability of Capital Strategy**

Local Market Access   Global Market Access

Firm-Specific Characteristics

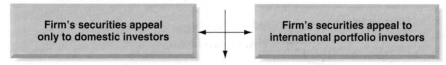

Firm's securities appeal only to domestic investors ⟷ Firm's securities appeal to international portfolio investors

Market Liquidity for Firm's Securities

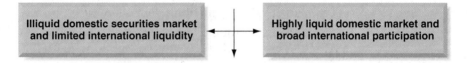

Illiquid domestic securities market and limited international liquidity ⟷ Highly liquid domestic market and broad international participation

Effect of Market Segmentation on Firm's Securities and Cost of Capital

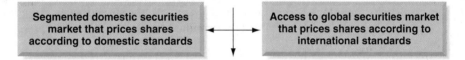

Segmented domestic securities market that prices shares according to domestic standards ⟷ Access to global securities market that prices shares according to international standards

Firms resident in industrial countries with small capital markets often source their long-term debt and equity at home in these partially liquid domestic securities markets. The firms' cost and availability of capital is better than that of firms in countries with illiquid capital markets. However, if these firms can tap the highly liquid global markets, they can also strengthen their competitive advantage in sourcing capital.

Firms resident in countries with segmented capital markets must devise a strategy to escape dependence on that market for their long-term debt and equity needs. A national capital market is *segmented* if the required rate of return on securities in that market differs from the required rate of return on securities of comparable expected return and risk traded on other securities markets. Capital markets become segmented because of such factors as excessive regulatory control, perceived political risk, anticipated foreign exchange risk, lack of transparency, asymmetric availability of information, cronyism, insider trading, and many other market imperfections. Firms constrained by any of these conditions must develop a strategy to escape their own limited capital markets and source some of their long-term capital abroad.

Cost of Capital

A domestic firm normally finds its *cost of capital* by evaluating where and from whom it will raise its capital. The cost will obviously differ on the mix of investors interested in the firm, investors willing and able to buy its equity shares, and the debt available to the firm, raised from the domestic bank and debt market.

The firm then calculates its *weighted average cost of capital* (WACC) by combining the cost of equity with the cost of debt in proportion to the relative weight of each in the firm's optimal long-term financial structure. More specifically,

$$k_{WACC} = k_e \frac{E}{V} + k_d (1 - t) \frac{D}{V}$$

where k_{WACC} = weighted average after-tax cost of capital

$\quad k_e$ = risk-adjusted cost of equity

$\quad k_d$ = before-tax cost of debt

$\quad t$ = marginal tax rate

$\quad E$ = market value of the firm's equity

$\quad D$ = market value of the firm's debt

$\quad V$ = market value of the firm's securities $(D + E)$

Cost of Equity

The most widely accepted and used method of calculating the cost of equity for a firm today is the *capital asset pricing model* (CAPM). CAPM defines the cost of equity to be the sum of a risk-free interest component and a firm-specific spread, over and above that risk-free component, as seen in the following formula:

$$k_e = k_{rf} + \beta_j(k_m - k_{rf})$$

where k_e = expected (required) rate of return on equity

$\quad k_{rf}$ = rate of interest on risk-free bonds (Treasury bonds, for example)

$\quad \beta_j$ = coefficient of *systematic risk* for the firm (beta)

$\quad k_m$ = expected (required) rate of return on the market portfolio of stocks

The key component of CAPM is *beta* (β_j), the measure of systematic risk. *Systematic risk* is a measure of how the firm's returns vary with those of the market in which it trades. Beta is calculated as a function of the total variability of expected returns of the firm's stock relative to the market index (k_m) and the degree to which the variability of expected returns of the firm is correlated to the expected returns on the market index. More formally,

$$\beta_j = \frac{\rho_{jm}\sigma_j}{\sigma_m}$$

where β_j (beta) = measure of systematic risk for security j

$\quad \rho$ (rho) = correlation between security j and the market

$\quad \sigma_j$ (sigma) = standard deviation of the return on firm j

$\quad \sigma_m$ (sigma) = standard deviation of the market return

Beta will have a value of less than 1.0 if the firm's returns are less volatile than the market, 1.0 if its returns are the same as the market, or greater than 1.0 if its returns are more volatile—or risky—than the market. CAPM analysis assumes that the required return estimated is an indication of what more is necessary to keep an investor's capital invested in the equity considered. If the equity's return does not reach the expected return, CAPM assumes that individual investors will liquidate their holdings.

CAPM's biggest challenge is that, for a beta to be most useful, it should be an indicator of the future rather than the past. A prospective investor is interested in how the individual firm's returns will vary in the coming periods. Unfortunately, since the future is not known, the beta used in any firm's estimate of equity cost is based on evidence from the recent past.

Cost of Debt

Firms acquire debt in either the form of loans from commercial banks—the most common form of debt—or as securities sold to the debt markets, such as instruments like notes and bonds. The normal procedure for measuring the cost of debt requires a forecast of interest rates for the next few years, the proportions of various classes of debt the firm expects to use, and the corporate income tax rate. The interest costs of the different debt components are then averaged according to their proportion in the debt structure. This before-tax average, k_d, is then adjusted for corporate income taxes by multiplying it by the expression $(1 - \text{tax rate})$ to obtain $k_d (1 - t)$, the weighted average after-tax cost of debt.

The weighted average cost of capital is normally used as the risk-adjusted discount rate whenever a firm's new projects are in the same general risk class as its existing projects. On the other hand, a project-specific required rate of return should be used as the discount rate if a new project differs from existing projects in business or financial risk.

International Portfolio Theory and Diversification

The potential benefits to companies from raising capital on global markets are based on international portfolio theory, the benefits of international diversification. We briefly review these principles before examining the costs and capacities for raising capital in the global market.

Portfolio Risk Reduction

The risk of a portfolio is measured by the ratio of the variance of the portfolio's return relative to the variance of the market return. This is the *beta* of the portfolio. As an investor increases the number of securities in a portfolio, the portfolio's risk declines rapidly at first, then asymptotically approaches the level of *systematic risk* of the market. The total risk of any portfolio is therefore composed of *systematic risk* (the market) and *unsystematic risk* (the individual securities). Increasing the number of securities in the portfolio reduces the unsystematic risk component but leaves the systematic risk component unchanged. A fully diversified domestic portfolio would have a beta of 1.0. This is standard—domestic—financial theory.

Exhibit 12.2 illustrates the incremental gains of diversifying both domestically and internationally. The lowest line in Exhibit 12.2 (portfolio of international stocks) represents a portfolio in which foreign securities have been added. It has the same overall risk shape as the U.S. stock portfolio, but it has a lower portfolio beta. This means that the international portfolio's market risk is lower than that of a domestic portfolio. This situation arises because the returns on the foreign stocks are not perfectly correlated with U.S. stocks.

Foreign Exchange Risk

The foreign exchange risks of a portfolio, whether it is a securities portfolio or the general portfolio of activities of the MNE, are reduced through international diversification. The construction of internationally diversified portfolios is both the same as and different from

EXHIBIT 12.2   Portfolio Risk Reduction through International Diversification

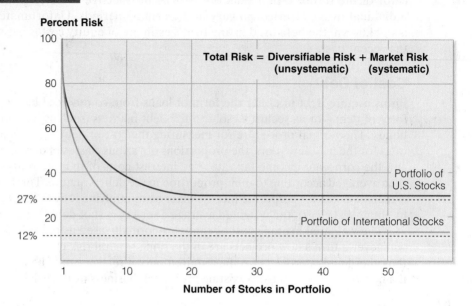

When the portfolio is diversified, the variance of the portfolio's return relative to the variance of the market's return (*beta*) is reduced to the level of *systematic risk* – the risk of the market itself. When the portfolio is diversified internationally, the portfolio's beta is lowered.

creating a traditional domestic portfolio. Internationally diversified portfolios are the same in principle because the investor is attempting to combine assets that are less than perfectly correlated, reducing the total risk of the portfolio. In addition, by adding assets outside the home market—assets that previously were not available to be averaged into the portfolio's expected returns and risks—the investor is tapping into a larger pool of potential investments.

But international portfolio construction is also different in that when the investor acquires assets or securities outside the investor's host-country market, the investor may also be acquiring a *foreign currency-denominated asset*.[1] Thus, the investor has actually acquired *two* additional assets—the currency of denomination and the asset subsequently purchased with the currency—one asset in principle, but two in expected returns and risks.

Japanese Equity Example. A numerical example can illustrate the difficulties associated with international portfolio diversification and currency risk. A U.S.-based investor takes $1,000,000 on January 1, and invests in shares traded on the Tokyo Stock Exchange (TSE). The spot exchange rate on January 1 is ¥130.00/$. The $1 million therefore yields ¥130,000,000. The investor uses ¥130,000,000 to acquire shares on the Tokyo Stock Exchange at ¥20,000 per share, acquiring 6,500 shares, and holds the shares for one year.

At the end of one year the investor sells the 6,500 shares at the market price, which is now ¥25,000 per share; the shares have risen ¥5,000 per share in price. The 6,500 shares at ¥25,000 per share yield proceeds of ¥162,500,000.

---

[1]This is not always the case. For example, many U.S.-based investors routinely purchase and hold eurodollar bonds on the secondary market only (illegal during primary issuance), which poses no currency risk to the U.S.-based investor because they are denominated in the investor's home currency.

The Japanese yen are then changed back into the investor's home currency, the U.S. dollar, at the spot rate of ¥125.00/$ now in effect. This results in total U.S. dollar proceeds of $1,300,000.00. The total return on the investment is then

$$\frac{\$1,300,000 - \$1,000,000}{\$1,000,000} = 30.00\%$$

The total U.S. dollar return is actually a combination of the return on the Japanese yen (which in this case was positive) and the return on the shares listed on the Tokyo Stock Exchange (which was also positive). This value is expressed by isolating the percentage change in the share price (r^{shares}) in combination with the percentage change in the currency value ($r^{¥/\$}$):

$$R^\$ = [(1 + r^{¥/\$})(1 + r^{shares, ¥})] - 1$$

In this case, the value of the Japanese yen, in the eyes of a U.S.-based investor, rose 4.00% (from ¥130/$ to ¥125/$—see percentage change calculation on page 144), while the shares traded on the Tokyo Stock Exchange rose 25.00%. The total investment return in U.S. dollars is therefore

$$R^\$ = [(1 + .0400)(1 + .2500)] - 1 = .3000 \text{ or } 30.00\%$$

Obviously, the risk associated with international diversification, when it includes currency risk, is inherently more complex than that of domestic investments. You should also see, however, that the presence of currency risk may alter the correlations associated with securities in different countries and currencies, providing new portfolio composition and diversification possibilities. In conclusion:

- International diversification benefits induce investors to demand foreign securities (the so-called "buy-side").
- If the addition of a foreign security to the portfolio of the investor aids in the reduction of risk for a given level of return, or if it increases the expected return for a given level of risk, then the security adds value to the portfolio.
- A security that adds value will be demanded by investors. Given the limits of the potential supply of securities, increased demand will bid up the price of the security, resulting in a lower cost of capital for the firm. The firm issuing the security, the "sell-side," is therefore able to raise capital at a lower cost.

International CAPM (ICAPM)

The traditional form of CAPM, the domestic CAPM discussed earlier, assumes the firm's equity trades in a purely domestic market. The beta and market risk premium ($k_m - k_{rf}$) used in the cost of equity calculation, therefore, were based on a purely domestic market of securities and choices. But what if globalization has opened up the global markets, integrating them, and allowing investors to choose among stocks of a global portfolio?

International CAPM (ICAPM) assumes that there is a global market in which the firm's equity trades, and estimates of the firm's beta, β_j^g, and the market risk premium, ($k_m^g - k_{rf}^g$), must then reflect this global portfolio.

$$k_e^{global} = k_{rf}^g + \beta_j^g(k_m^g - k_{rf}^g)$$

The value of the risk-free rate, k_{rf}^g, may not change (so that $k_{rf}^g = k_{rf}$), as a U.S. Treasury note may be the risk-free rate for a U.S.-based investor regardless of the domestic or international portfolio. The market return, k_m^g, will change, reflecting average expected global market returns for the coming periods. The firm's beta, β_j^g, will most assuredly change as it now will reflect the expected variations against a greater global portfolio. How that beta will change, however, depends.

Sample Calculation: Trident's Cost of Capital

Maria Gonzalez, Trident's Chief Financial Officer, wants to calculate the company's weighted average cost of capital in both forms, the traditional CAPM and also ICAPM.

Maria assumes the risk-free rate of interest (k_{rf}) as 4%, using the U.S. government 10-year Treasury bond rate. The expected rate of return of the market portfolio (k_m) is assumed to be 9%, the expected rate of return on the market portfolio held by a well-diversified domestic investor. Trident's estimate of its own systematic risk—its beta—against the domestic portfolio is 1.2. Trident's cost of equity is then

$$k_e = k_{rf} + \beta(k_m - k_{rf}) = 4.00\% + 1.2\,(9.00\% - 4.00\%) = 10.00\%$$

Trident's cost of debt (k_d), the before tax cost of debt estimated by observing the current yield on Trident's outstanding bonds combined with bank debt, is 8%. Using 35% as the corporate income tax rate for the United States, Trident's after-tax cost of debt is then

$$k_d(1 - t) = 8.00\,(1 - 0.35) = 8.00\,(0.65) = 5.20\%$$

Trident's long-term capital structure is 60% equity (E/V) and 40% debt (D/V), where V is Trident's total market value. Trident's weighted average cost of capital k_{WACC} is then

$$k_{WACC} = k_e \frac{E}{V} + k_d\,(1 - t)\frac{D}{V} = 10.00\%\,(.60) + 5.20\%\,(.40) = 8.08\%$$

This is Trident's cost of capital using the traditional domestic CAPM estimate of the cost of equity.

But Maria Gonzalez wonders if this is the proper approach for Trident. As Trident has globalized its own business activities, the investor base that owns Trident's shares has also globally diversified. Trident's shares are now listed in London and Tokyo, in addition to their home listing on the New York Stock Exchange. Over 40% of Trident's stock is now held by foreign portfolio investors, as part of their globally diversified portfolios, while Trident's U.S. investors also typically hold globally diversified portfolios.

A second calculation of Trident's cost of equity, this time using the ICAPM, yields different results. Trident's beta, when calculated against a larger global equity market index, which includes these foreign markets and their investors, is a lower 0.90. The expected market return for a larger globally integrated equity market is a lower value as well, 8.00%. The ICAPM cost of equity is a much lower value of 7.60%.

$$k_e^{global} = k_{rf}^g + \beta_j^g\,(k_m^g - k_{rf}^g) = 4.00\% + 0.90\,(8.00\% - 4.00\%) = 7.60\%$$

Maria now recalculates Trident's WACC using the ICAPM estimate of equity costs, assuming the same debt and equity proportions and the same cost of current debt. Trident's WACC is now estimated at a lower cost of 6.64%.

$$k_{WACC}^{ICAPM} = k_e^{global}\frac{E}{V} + k_d(1 - t)\frac{D}{V} = 7.60\%\,(.60) + 5.20\%\,(.40) = 6.64\%$$

Maria believes that this is a more appropriate estimate of Trident's cost of capital. It is fully competitive with Trident's main rivals in the telecommunications hardware industry segment worldwide, which are mainly headquartered in the United States, the United Kingdom,

Canada, Finland, Sweden, Germany, Japan, and the Netherlands. The key to Trident's favorable global cost and availability of capital going forward is its ability to attract and hold the international portfolio investors that own its stock.

ICAPM Considerations

In theory, the primary distinction in the estimation of the cost of equity for an individual firm using an internationalized version of the CAPM is the definition of the "market" and a recalculation of the firm's beta for that market. The three basic components of the CAPM model must then be reconsidered.

Nestlé, the Swiss-based multinational firm that produces and distributes a variety of confectionary products, serves as an excellent example of how the international investor may view the global cost of capital differently from a domestic investor, and what that means for Nestlé's estimate of its own cost of equity.[2] The numerical example for Nestlé is summarized in Exhibit 12.3.

In the case of Nestlé, a prospective Swiss investor might assume a risk-free return in Swiss francs of 3.3% — the rate of return on an index of Swiss government bond issues. That same Swiss investor might also assume an expected market return in Swiss francs of 10.2% — an average return on a portfolio of Swiss equities, the *Financial Times* Swiss index. Assuming a risk-free rate of 3.30%, an expected market return of 10.2%, and a $\beta_{\text{Nestlé}}$ of 0.885, a Swiss investor would expect Nestlé to yield 9.4065% for the coming year.

$$k_e^{\text{Nestlé}} = k_{\text{RF}} + (k_{\text{M}} - k_{\text{RF}})\beta_{\text{Nestlé}} = 3.3 + (10.2 - 3.3)\,0.885 = 9.4065\%$$

But what if Swiss investors held internationally diversified portfolios instead? Both the expected market return and the beta estimate for Nestlé itself would be defined and determined differently. For the same period as before, a global portfolio index such as the *Financial Times* index in Swiss francs (FTA-Swiss) would show a market return of 13.7% (as opposed to the domestic Swiss index return of 10.2%). In addition, a beta for Nestlé estimated on Nestlé's returns versus the global portfolio index would be much smaller, 0.585 (as opposed to the 0.885 found previously). An internationally diversified Swiss investor would expect the following return on Nestlé:

$$k_e^{\text{Nestlé}} = k_{\text{RF}} + (k_{\text{M}} - k_{\text{RF}})\beta_{\text{Nestlé}} = 3.3 + (13.7 - 3.3)\,0.585 = 9.3840\%$$

EXHIBIT 12.3   **The Cost of Equity for Nestlé of Switzerland**

Nestlé's estimate of its cost of equity will depend upon whether a Swiss investor is thought to hold a domestic portfolio of equity securities or a global portfolio.

Domestic Portfolio for Swiss Investor	Global Portfolio for Swiss Investor
k_{RF} = 3.3% (Swiss bond index yield)	k_{RF} = 3.3% (Swiss bond index yield)
k_{M} = 10.2% (Swiss market portfolio in SF)	k_{M} = 13.7% (*Financial Times* Global index in SF)
$\beta_{\text{Nestlé}}$ = 0.885 (Nestlé versus Swiss market portfolio)	$\beta_{\text{Nestlé}}$ = 0.585 (Nestlé versus FTA-Swiss index)

$$k_{\text{Nestlé}}\; k_{\text{RF}} + \beta_{\text{Nestlé}}(k_{\text{M}} - k_{\text{RF}})$$

Required return on Nestlé:	Required return on Nestlé:
$k_e^{\text{Nestlé}}$ = 9.4065%	$k_e^{\text{Nestlé}}$ = 9.3840%

Source: All values are taken from René Stulz, "The Cost of Capital in Internationally Integrated Markets: The Case of Nestlé," *European Financial Management*, Vol. 1, No. 1, March 1995, pp.11–22.

---

[2]René Stulz, "The Cost of Capital in Internationally Integrated Markets: The Case of Nestlé," *European Financial Management*, Vol. 1, No. 1, March 1995, pp. 11–22.

Admittedly, this is not a lot of difference in the end. However, given the magnitude of change in both the values of the market return average and the beta for the firm, it is obvious that the result could easily have varied by several hundred basis points. The proper construction of the investor's portfolio and the proper portrayal of the investor's perceptions of risk and opportunity cost are clearly important to identifying the global cost of a company's equity capital. In the end, it all depends on the specific case—the firm, the country-market, and the *global portfolio*.

We follow the practice here of describing the internationally diversified portfolio as the *global portfolio* rather than the *world portfolio*. The distinction is important. The *world portfolio* is an index of all securities in the world. However, even with the increasing trend of deregulation and financial integration, a number of securities markets still remain segmented or restricted in their access. Those securities actually available to an investor are the *global portfolio*.

There are, in fact, a multitude of different proposed formulations for calculating the international cost of capital. The problems with both formulation and data expand dramatically as the analysis is extended to rapidly developing or emerging markets. Harvey (2005) serves as a first place to start if you wish to expand your reading and research.[3]

Global Betas

International portfolio theory typically concludes that adding international securities to a domestic portfolio will reduce the portfolio's risks. Although this idea is fundamental to much of international financial theory, it still depends on individual firms in individual markets. Nestlé's beta went down when calculated using a global portfolio of equities, but that may not always be the case. Depending on the firm, its business line, the country it calls home, and the industry domestically and globally in which it competes, the global beta may go up or down.

One company often noted by researchers is Petrobrás, the national oil company of Brazil. Although government controlled, the company is publicly traded. Its shares are listed in São Paulo and New York. It operates in a global oil market in which prices and values are set in U.S. dollars. As a result, its domestic or home beta has been estimated at 1.3, but its global beta higher, at 1.7.[4] This is only one example of many.

Although it seems obvious to some that the returns to the individual firm should become less correlated to those of the market as the market is redefined ever-larger, it turns out to be more of a case of empirical analysis, not preconceived notions of correlation and covariance.

Equity Risk Premiums

In practice, calculating a firm's equity risk premium is much more controversial. Although the capital asset pricing model (CAPM) has now become widely accepted in global business as the preferred method of calculating the cost of equity for a firm, there is rising debate over what numerical values should be used in its application, especially the equity risk premium. The *equity risk premium* is the average annual return of the market expected by investors over and above riskless debt, the term $(k_m - k_{rf})$.

Equity Risk Premium History. The field of finance does agree that a cost of equity calculation should be forward looking, meaning that the inputs to the equation should represent what

[3]"12 Ways to Calculate the International Cost of Capital," Campbell R. Harvey, Duke University, unpublished, October 14, 2005.

[4]*The Real Cost of Capital*, Tim Ogier, John Rugman and Lucinda Spicer, Financial Times/Prentice Hall, Pearson Publishing, 2004, p. 139.

EXHIBIT 12.4	Alternative Estimates of Cost of Equity for a Hypothetical U.S. Firm Assuming $\beta = 1$ and $k_{rf} = 4\%$		
Source	Equity Risk Premium $(k_m - k_{rf})$	Cost of Equity $k_{rf} + \beta (k_m - k_{rf})$	Differential
Ibbotson	8.800%	12.800%	3.800%
Finance textbooks	8.500%	12.500%	3.500%
Investor surveys	7.100%	11.100%	2.100%
Dimson, et al.	5.000%	9.000%	Baseline

Source: Equity risk premium quotes from "Stockmarket Valuations: Great Expectations," The Economist, January 31, 2002.

is expected to happen over the relevant future time horizon. As is typically the case, however, practitioners use historical evidence as the basis for their forward-looking projections. The current debate begins with a debate over what has happened in the past.

In a large study completed in 2001 by Dimson, Marsh, and Stanton (updated in 2003), the authors estimated the equity risk premium in 16 different developed countries for the 1900–2002 period. The study found significant differences in equity returns over bill and bond returns (proxies for the risk-free rate) over time by country. For example Italy was found to have had the highest equity risk premium, 10.3%, followed by Germany with 9.4% and Japan at 9.3%. Denmark had the lowest at 3.8%.

The debate over which equity risk premium to use in practice was highlighted in this same study by looking at what equity risk premiums are being recommended for the United States by a variety of different sources. As illustrated in Exhibit 12.4, a hypothetical firm with a beta of 1.0 (estimated market risk equal to that of the market) might have a cost of equity as low as 9.000% and as high as 12.800% using this set of alternative values. Note that here the authors used geometric returns, not arithmetic returns. Fernandez and del Campo (2010), in their annual survey of market risk premiums used by analysts and academics, most recently found the average risk premium used by U.S. and Canadian analysts is 5.1%, European analysts 5.0%, and British analysts 5.6%.[5]

How important is it for a company to accurately predict its cost of equity? The corporation must annually determine which potential investments it will accept and reject due to its limited capital resources. If the company is not accurately estimating its cost of equity, and therefore its general cost of capital, it will not be accurately estimating the net present value of potential investments.

The Demand for Foreign Securities: The Role of International Portfolio Investors

Gradual deregulation of equity markets during the past three decades not only elicited increased competition from domestic players but also opened up markets to foreign competitors. International portfolio investment and cross-listing of equity shares on foreign markets have become commonplace.

What motivates portfolio investors to purchase and hold foreign securities in their portfolios? The answer lies in an understanding of "domestic" portfolio theory and how it has been extended to handle the possibility of global portfolios. More specifically, it requires an understanding of the principles of portfolio risk reduction, portfolio rate of return, and foreign currency risk.

[5]"Market Risk Premium Used in 2010 by Analysts and Companies: A Survey with 2,400 Answers," Pablo Fernandez and Javier Del Campo Baonza, IESE Business School, May 21, 2010.

Both domestic and international portfolio managers are asset allocators. Their objective is to maximize a portfolio's rate of return for a given level of risk, or to minimize risk for a given rate of return. International portfolio managers can choose from a larger bundle of assets than portfolio managers limited to domestic-only asset allocations. As a result, internationally diversified portfolios often have a higher expected rate of return, and they nearly always have a lower level of portfolio risk, since national securities markets are imperfectly correlated with one another.

Portfolio asset allocation can be accomplished along many dimensions depending on the investment objective of the portfolio manager. For example, portfolios can be diversified according to the type of securities. They can be composed of stocks only or bonds only or a combination of both. They also can be diversified by industry or by size of capitalization (small-cap, mid-cap, and large-cap stock portfolios).

For our purposes, the most relevant dimensions are diversification by country, geographic region, stage of development, or a combination of these (global). An example of diversification by country is the Korea Fund. It was at one time the only vehicle allowing foreign investors to hold South Korean securities, but foreign ownership restrictions have more recently been liberalized. A typical regional diversification would be one of the many Asian funds. These performed exceptionally well until the "bubble" burst in Japan and Southeast Asia during the second half of the 1990s. Portfolios composed of emerging market securities are examples of diversification by stage of development. They are composed of securities from different countries, geographic regions, and stage of development.

The Link Between Cost and Availability of Capital

Trident's weighted average cost of capital (WACC) was calculated assuming that equity and debt capital would always be available at the same required rate of return even if Trident's capital budget expands. This is a reasonable assumption considering Trident's excellent access through the NYSE to international portfolio investors in global capital markets. It is a bad assumption, however, for firms resident in illiquid or segmented capital markets, small domestic firms, and family-owned firms resident in any capital market. We will now examine how market liquidity and market segmentation can affect a firm's cost of capital.

Improving Market Liquidity

Although no consensus exists about the definition of *market liquidity*, we can observe market liquidity by noting the degree to which a firm can issue a new security without depressing the existing market price. In the domestic case, an underlying assumption is that total availability of capital to a firm at any time is determined by supply and demand in the domestic capital markets.

A firm should always expand its capital budget by raising funds in the same proportion as its optimal financial structure. As its budget expands in absolute terms, however, its marginal cost of capital will eventually increase. In other words, a firm can only tap the capital market for some limited amount in the short run before suppliers of capital balk at providing further funds, even if the same optimal financial structure is preserved. In the long run, this may not be a limitation, depending on market liquidity.

In the multinational case, a firm is able to improve market liquidity by raising funds in the euromarkets (money, bond, and equity), by selling security issues abroad, and by tapping local capital markets through foreign subsidiaries. Such activity should logically expand the capacity of an MNE to raise funds in the short run over what might have been raised if the firm were limited to its home capital market. This situation assumes that the firm preserves its optimal financial structure.

Market Segmentation

If all capital markets are fully integrated, securities of comparable expected return and risk should have the same required rate of return in each national market after adjusting for foreign exchange risk and political risk. This definition applies to both equity and debt, although it often happens that one or the other may be more integrated than its counterpart.

Capital *market segmentation* is a financial market imperfection caused mainly by government constraints, institutional practices, and investor perceptions. The following are the most important imperfections:

- Asymmetric information between domestic and foreign-based investors
- Lack of transparency
- High securities transaction costs
- Foreign exchange risks
- Political risks
- Corporate governance differences
- Regulatory barriers

Market imperfections do not necessarily imply that national securities markets are inefficient. A national securities market can be efficient in a domestic context and yet segmented in an international context. According to finance theory, a market is efficient if security prices in that market reflect all available relevant information and adjust quickly to any new relevant information. Therefore, the price of an individual security reflects its "intrinsic value," and any price fluctuations will be "random walks" around this value. Market efficiency assumes that transaction costs are low, that many participants are in the market, and that these participants have sufficient financial strength to move security prices. Empirical tests of market efficiency show that most major national markets are reasonably efficient.

An efficient national securities market might very well correctly price all securities traded in that market on the basis of information available to the investors who participate in that market. However, if that market is segmented, foreign investors would not be participants.

Availability of capital depends on whether a firm can gain liquidity for its debt and equity securities and a price for those securities based on international rather than national standards. In practice, this means that the firm must define a strategy to attract international portfolio investors and thereby escape the constraints of its own illiquid or segmented national market.

The Effect of Market Liquidity and Segmentation

The degree to which capital markets are illiquid or segmented has an important influence on a firm's marginal cost of capital and thus on its weighted average cost of capital. The marginal cost of capital is the weighted average cost of the next currency unit raised. This is illustrated in Exhibit 12.5, which shows the transition from a domestic to a global marginal cost of capital.

Exhibit 12.5 shows that the MNE has a given marginal return on capital at different budget levels, represented in the line MRR. This demand is determined by ranking potential projects according to net present value or internal rate of return. Percentage rate of return to both users and suppliers of capital is shown on the vertical scale. If the firm is limited to raising funds in its domestic market, the line MCC_D shows the marginal domestic cost of capital (vertical axis) at various budget levels (horizontal axis). Remember that the firm continues to maintain the same debt ratio as it expands its budget, so that financial risk does not change.

| EXHIBIT 12.5 | Market Liquidity, Segmentation, and the Marginal Cost of Capital |

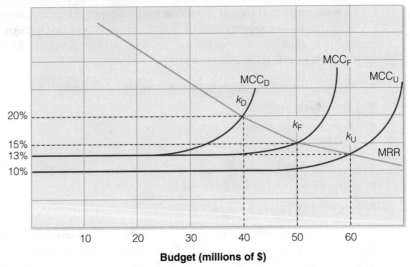

The optimal budget in the domestic case is $40 million, where the marginal return on capital (MRR) just equals the marginal cost of capital (MCC$_D$). At this budget, the marginal domestic cost of capital, k_D, would be equal to 20%.

If the MNE has access to additional sources of capital outside an illiquid domestic capital market, the marginal cost of capital should shift to the right (the line MCC$_F$). In other words, foreign markets can be tapped for long-term funds at times when the domestic market is saturated because of heavy use by other borrowers or equity issuers, or when it is unable to absorb another issue of the MNE in the short run. Exhibit 12.5 shows that by a tap of foreign capital markets the firm has reduced its marginal international cost of capital, to 15%, even while it raises an additional $10 million. This statement assumes that about $20 million is raised abroad, since only about $30 million could be raised domestically at a 15% marginal cost of capital.

If the MNE is located in a capital market that is both illiquid and segmented, the line MCC$_U$ represents the decreased marginal cost of capital if it gains access to other equity markets. As a result of the combined effects of greater availability of capital and international pricing of the firm's securities, the marginal cost of capital, k_U, declines to 13% and the optimal capital budget climbs to $60 million.

Most of the tests of market segmentation suffer from the usual problem for models— namely, the need to abstract from reality in order to have a testable model. In our opinion, a realistic test would be to observe what happens to a single security's price when, after it has been traded only in a domestic market, it is "discovered" by foreign investors, and then is traded in a foreign market. Arbitrage should keep the market price equal in both markets. However, if during the transition we observe a significant change in the security's price, uncorrelated with price movements in either of the underlying securities markets, we can infer that the domestic market was segmented.

In academic circles, tests based on case studies are often considered to be "casual empiricism," since no theory or model exists to explain what is being observed. Nevertheless, something may be learned from such cases, just as scientists learn from observing nature in an uncontrolled environment. Furthermore, case studies that preserve real-world complications may illustrate specific kinds of barriers to market integration and ways in which they might be overcome.

Unfortunately, few case studies have been documented in which a firm has "escaped" from a segmented capital market. In practice, escape usually means being listed on a foreign stock market such as New York or London, and/or selling securities in foreign capital markets. We will explore one firm's escape from a segmented market with a discussion of Novo in the Mini-Case at the end of the chapter.

Globalization of Securities Markets

During the 1980s, numerous Nordic and other European firms cross-listed on major foreign exchanges such as London and New York. They placed equity and debt issues in major securities markets. In most cases, they were successful in lowering their WACC and increasing its availability. This is the subject of this chapter's Mini-Case.

During the 1990s, national restrictions on cross-border portfolio investment were gradually eased under pressure from the Organization for Economic Cooperation and Development (OECD), a consortium of most of the world's most industrialized countries. Liberalization of European securities markets was accelerated because of the European Union's efforts to develop a single European market without barriers. Emerging nation markets followed suit, as did the former Eastern Bloc countries after the breakup of the Soviet Union. Emerging national markets have often been motivated by the need to source foreign capital to finance large-scale privatization.

Now, market segmentation has been significantly reduced, although the liquidity of individual national markets remains limited. Most observers believe that for better or for worse, we have achieved a global market for securities. The good news is that many firms have been assisted to become MNEs because they now have access to a global cost and availability of capital. The bad news is that the correlation among securities markets has increased, thereby reducing, but not eliminating, the benefits of international portfolio diversification. Globalization of securities markets has also led to more volatility and speculative behavior, as shown by the emerging market crises of the 1995–2001 period, and the 2008–2009 global credit crisis.

Corporate Governance and the Cost of Capital. Would global investors be willing to pay a premium for a share in a good corporate governance company? A recent study of Norwegian and Swedish firms measured the impact of foreign board membership (Anglo-American) on firm value. They summarized their findings as follows:[6]

> Using a sample of firms with headquarters in Norway or Sweden the study indicates a significantly higher value for firms that have outsider Anglo-American board member(s), after a variety of firm-specific and corporate governance related factors have been controlled for. We argue that this superior performance reflects the fact that these companies have successfully broken away from a partly segmented domestic capital market by "importing" an Anglo-American corporate governance system. Such an "import" signals a willingness on the part of the firm to expose itself to improved corporate governance and enhances its reputation in the financial market.

[6]Lars Oxelheim and Trond Randøy, "The impact of foreign board membership on firm value," *Journal of Banking and Finance*, Vol. 27, No. 12, 2003, p. 2369.

Strategic Alliances

Strategic alliances are normally formed by firms that expect to gain synergies from one or more joint efforts. For example, they might share the cost of developing technology or pursue complementary marketing activities. They might gain economies of scale or scope or a variety of other commercial advantages. However, one synergy that may sometimes by overlooked is the possibility for a financially strong firm to help a financially weak firm to lower its cost of capital by providing attractively priced equity or debt financing.

The Cost of Capital for MNEs Compared to Domestic Firms

Is the weighted average cost of capital for MNEs higher or lower than for their domestic counterparts? The answer is a function of the marginal cost of capital, the relative after-tax cost of debt, the optimal debt ratio, and the relative cost of equity.

Availability of Capital

Earlier in this chapter, we saw that international availability of capital to MNEs, or to other large firms that can attract international portfolio investors, may allow them to lower their cost of equity and debt compared with most domestic firms. In addition, international availability permits an MNE to maintain its desired debt ratio, even when significant amounts of new funds must be raised. In other words, an MNE's marginal cost of capital is constant for considerable ranges of its capital budget. This statement is not true for most domestic firms. They must either rely on internally generated funds or borrow in the short and medium term from commercial banks.

Financial Structure, Systematic Risk, and the Cost of Capital for MNEs

Theoretically, MNEs should be in a better position than their domestic counterparts to support higher debt ratios because their cash flows are diversified internationally. The probability of a firm's covering fixed charges under varying conditions in product, financial, and foreign exchange markets should improve if the variability of its cash flows is minimized.

By diversifying cash flows internationally, the MNE might be able to achieve the same kind of reduction in cash flow variability as portfolio investors receive from diversifying their security holdings internationally. The same argument applies to cash flow diversification—namely that returns are not perfectly correlated between countries. For example, in 2000 Japan was in recession, but the United States was experiencing rapid growth. Therefore, we might have expected returns, on either a cash flow or an earnings basis, to be depressed in Japan and favorable in the United States. An MNE with operations located in both these countries could rely on its strong U.S. cash inflow to cover debt obligations, even if its Japanese subsidiary produced weak net cash inflows.

Despite the theoretical elegance of this hypothesis, empirical studies have come to the opposite conclusion.[7] Despite the favorable effect of international diversification of cash flows, bankruptcy risk was only about the same for MNEs as for domestic firms. However, MNEs faced higher agency costs, political risk, foreign exchange risk, and asymmetric information. These have been identified as the factors leading to lower debt ratios and even a higher cost of

[7]Lee, Kwang Chul and Chuck C.Y. Kwok, "Multinational Corporations vs. Domestic Corporations: International Environmental Factors and Determinants of Capital Structure," *Journal of International Business Studies*, Summer 1988, pp. 195–217.

long-term debt for MNEs. Domestic firms rely much more heavily on short and intermediate debt, which lie at the low cost end of the yield curve.

Even more surprising, one study found that MNEs have a higher level of systematic risk than their domestic counterparts.[8] The same factors caused this phenomenon as caused the lower debt ratios for MNEs. The study concluded that the increased standard deviation of cash flows from internationalization more than offset the lower correlation from diversification.

As we stated earlier, the systematic risk term, β_j, is defined as

$$\beta_j = \frac{\rho_{jm}\sigma_j}{\sigma_m}$$

where ρ_{jm} is the correlation coefficient between security j and the market; σ_j is the standard deviation of the return on firm j; and σ_m is the standard deviation of the market return. The MNE's systematic risk could increase if the decrease in the correlation coefficient, ρ_{jm}, due to international diversification, is more than offset by an increase in σ_j, the standard deviation due to the aforementioned risk factors. This conclusion is consistent with the observation that many MNEs use a higher hurdle rate to discount expected foreign project cash flows. In essence, they are accepting projects they consider to be riskier than domestic projects, thus potentially skewing upward their perceived systematic risk. At the least, MNEs need to earn a higher rate of return than their domestic equivalents in order to maintain their market value.

Other studies have found that internationalization actually allows emerging market MNEs to carry a higher level of debt and lower their systematic risk. This occurs because the emerging market MNEs are investing in more stable economies abroad, a strategy that lowers their operating, financial, foreign exchange, and political risks. The reduction in risk more than offsets increased agency costs and allows the firms to enjoy higher leverage and lower systematic risk than their U.S.-based MNE counterparts.

The Riddle: Is the Cost of Capital Higher for MNEs?

The riddle is that the MNE is supposed to have a lower marginal cost of capital (MCC) than a domestic firm because of the MNE's access to a global cost and availability of capital. On the other hand, the empirical studies we mentioned show that the MNE's weighted average cost of capital (WACC) is actually higher than for a comparable domestic firm because of agency costs, foreign exchange risk, political risk, asymmetric information, and other complexities of foreign operations.

The answer to this riddle lies in the link between the cost of capital, its availability, and the opportunity set of projects. As the opportunity set of projects increases, eventually the firm needs to increase its capital budget to the point where its marginal cost of capital is increasing. The optimal capital budget would still be at the point where the rising marginal cost of capital equals the declining rate of return on the opportunity set of projects. However, this would be at a higher weighted average cost of capital than would have occurred for a lower level of the optimal capital budget.

To illustrate this linkage, Exhibit 12.6 shows the marginal cost of capital given different optimal capital budgets. Assume that there are two different demand schedules based on the opportunity set of projects for both the multinational enterprise (MNE) and domestic counterpart (DC).

[8]Reeb, David M., Chuck C.Y. Kwok, and H. Young Baek, "Systematic Risk of the Multinational Corporation, *Journal of International Business Studies*, Second Quarter 1998, pp. 263–279.

EXHIBIT 12.6   **The Cost of Capital for MNE and Domestic Counterpart Compared**

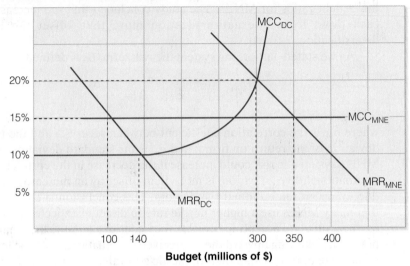

Marginal Cost of Capital
and Rate of Return (percentage)

Budget (millions of $)

The line MRR_{DC} depicts a modest set of potential projects. It intersects the line MCC_{MNE} at 15% and a $100 million budget level. It intersects the MCC_{DC} at 10% and a $140 million budget level. At these low budget levels the MCC_{MNE} has a higher MCC and probably weighted average cost of capital than its domestic counterpart (DC), as discovered in recent empirical studies.

The line MRR_{MNE} depicts a more ambitious set of projects for both the MNE and its domestic counterpart. It intersects the line MCC_{MNE} still at 15% and a $350 million budget. However, it intersects the MCC_{DC} at 20% and a budget level of $300 million. At these higher budget levels, the MCC_{MNE} has a lower MCC and probably weighted average cost of capital than its domestic counterpart, as predicted earlier in this chapter. In order to generalize this conclusion, we would need to know under what conditions a domestic firm would be willing to undertake the optimal capital budget despite its increasing the firm's marginal cost of capital. At some point the MNE might also have an optimal capital budget at the point where its MCC is rising.

Empirical studies show that neither mature domestic firms nor MNEs are typically willing to assume the higher agency costs or bankruptcy risk associated with higher MCCs and capital budgets. In fact, most mature firms demonstrate some degree of corporate wealth maximizing behavior. They are somewhat risk averse and tend to avoid returning to the market to raise fresh equity. They prefer to limit their capital budgets to what can be financed with free cash flows. Indeed, they have a so-called pecking order that determines the priority of which sources of funds they tap and in what order. This behavior motivates shareholders to monitor management more closely. They tie management's compensation to stock performance (options). They may also require other types of contractual arrangements that are collectively part of agency costs.

In conclusion, if both MNEs and domestic firms do actually limit their capital budgets to what can be financed without increasing their MCC, then the empirical findings that MNEs have higher WACC stands. If the domestic firm has such good growth opportunities that it chooses to undertake growth despite an increasing marginal cost of capital, then the MNE would have a lower WACC. Exhibit 12.7 summarizes these conclusions.

| EXHIBIT 12.7 | Do MNEs Have a Higher or Lower Cost of Capital than Their Domestic Counterparts? |

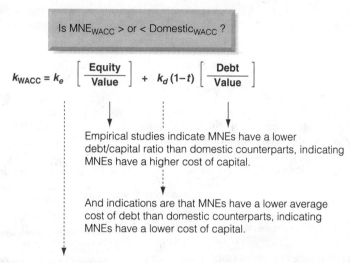

$$k_{WACC} = k_e \left[\frac{\text{Equity}}{\text{Value}} \right] + k_d (1-t) \left[\frac{\text{Debt}}{\text{Value}} \right]$$

Is MNE$_{WACC}$ > or < Domestic$_{WACC}$?

Empirical studies indicate MNEs have a lower debt/capital ratio than domestic counterparts, indicating MNEs have a higher cost of capital.

And indications are that MNEs have a lower average cost of debt than domestic counterparts, indicating MNEs have a lower cost of capital.

The cost of equity required by investors is higher for multinational firms than for domestic firms. Possible explanations are higher levels of *political risk, foreign exchange risk,* and higher *agency costs* of doing business in a multinational managerial environment. However, at relatively high levels of the optimal capital budget, the MNE would have a lower cost of capital.

Summary Points

■ Gaining access to global capital markets should allow a firm to lower its cost of capital. This can be achieved by increasing the market liquidity of its shares and by escaping from segmentation of its home capital market.

■ The cost and availability of capital is directly linked to the degree of market liquidity and segmentation. Firms having access to markets with high liquidity and a low level of segmentation should have a lower cost of capital and greater ability to raise new capital.

■ A firm is able to increase its market liquidity by raising debt in the euromarket, by selling security issues in individual national capital markets and as euroequities, and tapping local capital markets through foreign subsidiaries. Increased market liquidity causes the marginal cost of capital line to "flatten out to the right." This results in the firm being able to raise more capital at the same low marginal cost of capital, and thereby justify investing in more capital projects. The key is to attract international portfolio investors.

■ A national capital market is segmented if the required rate of return on securities in that market differs from

the required rate of return on securities of comparable expected return and risk that are traded on other national securities markets.

■ Capital market segmentation is a financial market imperfection caused by government constraints and investor perceptions. The most important imperfections are 1) asymmetric information; 2) transaction costs; 3) foreign exchange risk; 4) corporate governance differences; 5) political risk; and 6) regulatory barriers.

■ Segmentation results in a higher cost of capital and less availability of capital.

■ If a firm is resident in a segmented capital market, it can still escape from this market by sourcing its debt and equity abroad. The result should be a lower marginal cost of capital, improved liquidity for its shares, and a larger capital budget.

■ Whether or not MNEs have a lower cost of capital than their domestic counterparts depends on their optimal financial structures, systematic risk, availability of capital, and the level of the optimal capital budget.

MINI-CASE

Novo Industri A/S (Novo)[1]

Novo is a Danish multinational firm that produces industrial enzymes and pharmaceuticals (mostly insulin). In 1977, Novo's management decided to "internationalize" its capital structure and sources of funds. This decision was based on the observation that the Danish securities market was both illiquid and segmented from other capital markets. In particular, the lack of availability and high cost of equity capital in Denmark resulted in Novo having a higher cost of capital than its main multinational competitors, such as Eli Lilly (U.S.), Miles Laboratories (U.S.—a subsidiary of Bayer, Germany), and Gist Brocades (The Netherlands).

Apart from the cost of capital, Novo's projected growth opportunities signaled the eventual need to raise new long-term capital beyond what could be raised in the illiquid Danish market. Since Novo is a technology leader in its specialties, planned capital investments in plant, equipment, and research could not be postponed until internal financing from cash flow became available. Novo's competitors would preempt any markets not served by Novo.

Even if an equity issue of the size required could have been raised in Denmark, the required rate of return would have been unacceptably high. For example, Novo's price/earnings ratio was typically around 5; that of its foreign competitors was well over 10. Yet Novo's business and financial risk appeared to be about equal to that of its competitors. A price/earnings ratio of 5 appeared appropriate for Novo only within a domestic Danish context when compared with other domestic firms of comparable business and financial risk.

If Denmark's securities markets were integrated with world markets, one would expect foreign investors to rush in and buy "undervalued" Danish securities. In that case, firms like Novo would enjoy an international cost of capital comparable to that of its foreign competitors. Strangely enough, no Danish governmental restrictions existed that would have prevented foreign investors from holding Danish securities. Therefore, one must look for investor perception as the main cause of market segmentation in Denmark at that time.

At least six characteristics of the Danish equity market were responsible for market segmentation: 1) asymmetric information base of Danish and foreign investors, 2) taxation, 3) alternative sets of feasible portfolios, 4) financial risk, 5) foreign exchange risk, and 6) political risk.

Asymmetric Information

Certain institutional characteristics of Denmark caused Danish and foreign investors to lack information about one another's equity securities. The most important information barrier was a Danish regulation that prohibited Danish investors from holding foreign private sector securities. Therefore, Danish investors had no incentive to follow developments in foreign securities markets or to factor such information into their evaluation of Danish securities. As a result, Danish securities might have been priced correctly in the efficient market sense relative to one another, considering the Danish information base, but priced incorrectly considering the combined foreign and Danish information base. Another detrimental effect of this regulation was that foreign securities firms did not locate offices or personnel in Denmark, since they had no product to sell there. Lack of a physical presence in Denmark reduced the ability of foreign security analysts to follow Danish securities.

A second information barrier was that there were too few Danish security analysts following Danish securities. Only one professional Danish securities analysis service was published (Børsinformation), and that was in the Danish language. A few Danish institutional investors employed in-house analysts, but their findings were not available to the public. Almost no foreign security analysts followed Danish securities because they had no product to sell and the Danish market was too small (small-country bias).

Other information barriers included language and accounting principles. Naturally, financial information was normally published in the Danish language using Danish accounting principles. A few firms, such as Novo, published English versions, but almost none used U.S. or British accounting principles or attempted to show any reconciliation with such principles.

Taxation

Danish taxation policy had all but eliminated investment in common stock by individuals. Until a tax law change in July 1981, capital gains on shares held for over two years were taxed at a 50% rate. Shares held for less than two years, or for "speculative" purposes, were taxed at personal income tax rates, with the top marginal rate being 75%. In contrast, capital gains on bonds were tax-free. This situation resulted in bonds being issued at deep discounts because the redemption at par at maturity was considered a capital gain. Thus, most individual investors held bonds rather than stocks. This factor reduced the liquidity of the stock

[1]This is a condensed version of Arthur Stonehill and Kåre B. Dullum, *Internationalizing the Cost of Capital in Theory and Practice: The Novo Experience and National Policy Implications* (Copenhagen: Nyt Nordisk Forlag Arnold Busck, 1982; and New York: Wiley, 1982). Reprinted with permission.

market and increased the required rate of return on stocks if they were to compete with bonds.

Feasible Portfolios

Because of the prohibition on foreign security ownership, Danish investors had a very limited set of securities from which to choose a portfolio. In practice, Danish institutional portfolios were composed of Danish stocks, government bonds, and mortgage bonds. Since Danish stock price movements are closely correlated with each other, Danish portfolios possessed a rather high level of systematic risk. In addition, government policy had been to provide a relatively high real rate of return on government bonds after adjusting for inflation. The net result of taxation policies on individuals, and attractive real yields on government bonds was that required rates of return on stocks were relatively high by international standards.

From a portfolio perspective, Danish stocks provided an opportunity for foreign investors to diversify internationally. If Danish stock price movements were not closely correlated with world stock price movements, inclusion of Danish stocks in foreign portfolios would reduce those portfolios' systematic risk. Furthermore, foreign investors were not subject to the high Danish income tax rates, due to protections provided by tax treaties that typically limit foreign investor tax rates to 15% on dividends and capital gains. As a result of the international diversification potential, foreign investors might have required a lower rate of return on Danish stocks than the rate required by Danish investors, other things being equal. However, other things were not equal because foreign investors perceived Danish stocks to carry more financial, foreign exchange, and political risk than their own domestic securities.

Financial, Foreign Exchange, and Political Risks

Financial leverage utilized by Danish firms was relatively high by U.S. and U.K. standards but not abnormal for Scandinavia, Germany, Italy, or Japan. In addition, most of the debt was short term with variable interest rates. Just how foreign investors viewed financial risk in Danish firms depended on what norms they followed in their home countries. We know from Novo's experience in tapping the eurobond market in 1978, that Morgan Grenfell, Novo's British investment banker, advised Novo to maintain a debt ratio (debt/total capitalization) closer to 50% rather than the traditional Danish 65% to 70%.

Foreign investors in Danish securities are subject to foreign exchange risk. Whether this is a plus or minus factor depends on the investor's home currency, perception about the future strength of the Danish krone, and its impact on a firm's operating exposure. Through personal contacts with foreign investors and bankers, Novo's management did not believe foreign exchange risk was a factor in Novo's stock price because its operations were perceived as being well diversified internationally. Over 90% of its sales were to customers located outside of Denmark.

With respect to political risk, Denmark was perceived as a stable Western democracy but with the potential to cause periodic problems for foreign investors. In particular, Denmark's national debt was regarded as too high for comfort, although this judgment had not yet shown up in the form of risk premiums on Denmark's eurocurrency syndicated loans.

The Road to Globalization

Although Novo's management in 1977 wished to escape from the shackles of Denmark's segmented and illiquid capital market, many barriers had to be overcome. It is worthwhile to explore some of these obstacles, because they typify the barriers faced by other firms from segmented markets that wish to internationalize their capital sources.

Closing the Information Gap. Novo had been a family-owned firm from its founding in the 1920s by the two Pedersen brothers. Then in 1974, it went public and listed its "B" shares on the Copenhagen Stock Exchange. The "A" shares were held by the Novo Foundation, and these shares were sufficient to maintain voting control. However, Novo was essentially unknown in investment circles outside of Denmark. To overcome this disparity in the information base, Novo increased the level of its financial and technical disclosure in both Danish and English versions.

The information gap was further closed when Morgan Grenfell successfully organized a syndicate to underwrite and sell a $20 million convertible eurobond issue for Novo in 1978. In connection with this offering, Novo listed its shares on the London Stock Exchange to facilitate conversion and to gain visibility. These twin actions were the key to dissolving the information barrier and, of course, they also raised a large amount of long-term capital on favorable terms, which would have been unavailable in Denmark.

Despite the favorable impact of the eurobond issue on availability of capital, Novo's cost of capital actually increased when Danish investors reacted negatively to the potential dilution effect of the conversion right. During 1979, Novo's share price declined from around Dkr300 per share to around Dkr220 per share.

The Biotechnology Boom. During 1979, a fortuitous event occurred. Biotechnology began to attract the interest of the U.S. investment community, with several sensationally oversubscribed stock issues by such start-up firms as Genentech and Cetus. Thanks to the aforementioned domestic information gap, Danish investors were unaware of these events and continued to value Novo at a low price/earnings ratio of 5, compared with over 10 for its established competitors and 30 or more for these new potential competitors.

In order to profile itself as a biotechnology firm with a proven track record, Novo organized a seminar in New York City on April 30, 1980. Soon after the seminar a few sophisticated individual U.S. investors began buying Novo's shares and convertibles through the London Stock Exchange. Danish investors were only too happy to supply this foreign demand. Therefore, despite relatively strong demand from U.S. and British investors, Novo's share price increased only gradually, climbing back to the Dkr300 level by midsummer. However, during the following months, foreign interest began to snowball, and by the end of 1980 Novo's stock price had reached the Dkr600 level. Moreover, foreign investors had increased their proportion of share ownership from virtually nothing to around 30%. Novo's price/earnings ratio had risen to around 16, which was now in line with that of its international competitors but not with the Danish market. At this point one must conclude that Novo had succeeded in internationalizing its cost of capital. Other Danish securities remained locked in a segmented capital market.

Directed Share Issue in the United States. During the first half of 1981, under the guidance of Goldman Sachs and with the assistance of Morgan Grenfell and Copenhagen Handelsbank, Novo prepared a prospectus for SEC registration of a U.S. share offering and eventual listing on the New York Stock Exchange. The main barriers encountered in this effort, which would have general applicability, were connected with preparing financial statements that could be reconciled with U.S. accounting principles and the higher level of disclosure required by the SEC. In particular, industry segment reporting was a problem both from a disclosure perspective and an accounting perspective because the accounting data were not available internally in that format. As it turned out, the investment barriers in the U.S. were relatively tractable, although expensive and time consuming to overcome.

The more serious barriers were caused by a variety of institutional and governmental regulations in Denmark. The latter were never designed so that firms could issue shares at market value, since Danish firms typically issued stock at par value with preemptive rights. By this time, however, Novo's share price, driven by continued foreign buying, was so high that virtually nobody in Denmark thought it was worth the price which foreigners were willing to pay. In fact, prior to the time of the share issue in July 1981, Novo's share price had risen to over Dkr1500, before settling down to a level around Dkr1400. Foreign ownership had increased to over 50% of Novo's shares outstanding!

Stock Market Reactions. One final piece of evidence on market segmentation can be gleaned from the way Danish and foreign investors reacted to the announcement of the proposed $61 million U.S. share issue on May 29, 1981. Novo's share price dropped 156 points the next trading day in Copenhagen, equal to about 10% of its market value. As soon as trading started in New York, the stock price immediately recovered all of its loss. The Copenhagen reaction was typical for an illiquid market. Investors worried about the dilution effect of the new share issue, because it would increase the number of shares outstanding by about 8%. They did not believe that Novo could invest the new funds at a rate of return that would not dilute future earnings per share. They also feared that the U.S. shares would eventually flow back to Copenhagen if biotechnology lost its glitter.

The U.S. reaction to the announcement of the new share issue was consistent with what one would expect in a liquid and integrated market. U.S. investors viewed the new issue as creating additional demand for the shares as Novo became more visible due to the selling efforts of a large aggressive syndicate. Furthermore, the marketing effort was directed at institutional investors who were previously underrepresented among Novo's U.S. investors. They had been underrepresented because U.S. institutional investors want to be assured of a liquid market in a stock in order to be able to get out, if desired, without depressing the share price. The wide distribution effected by the new issue, plus SEC registration and a New York Stock Exchange listing, all added up to more liquidity and a global cost of capital.

Effect on Novo's Weighted Average Cost of Capital. During most of 1981 and the years thereafter, Novo's share price was driven by international portfolio investors transacting on the New York, London, and Copenhagen stock exchanges. This reduced Novo's weighted average cost of capital and lowered its marginal cost of capital. Novo's systematic risk was reduced from its previous level, which was determined by nondiversified (internationally) Danish institutional investors and the Novo Foundation. However, its appropriate debt ratio level was also reduced to match the standards expected by international portfolio investors trading in the United States, United Kingdom, and other important markets. In essence, the U.S. dollar became Novo's functional currency when being evaluated by international investors. Theoretically, its revised weighted average cost of capital should have become a new reference hurdle rate when evaluating new capital investments in Denmark or abroad.

Other firms that follow Novo's strategy are also likely to have their weighted average cost of capital become a function of the requirements of international portfolio investors. Firms resident in some of the emerging market countries have already experienced "dollarization" of trade and financing for working capital. This phenomenon might be extended to long-term financing and the weighted average cost of capital.

The Novo experience can be a model for other firms wishing to escape from segmented and illiquid home equity markets. In particular, MNEs based in emerging markets often face barriers and lack of visibility similar to what Novo faced. They could benefit by following Novo's proactive strategy employed to attract international portfolio investors. However, a word of caution is advised. Novo had an excellent operating track record and a very strong worldwide market niche in two important industry sectors, insulin and industrial enzymes. This record continues to attract investors in Denmark and abroad. Other companies aspiring to achieve similar results would also need to have such a favorable track record to attract foreign investors.

Globalization of Securities Markets. During the 1980s, numerous other Nordic and other European firms followed Novo's example. They cross-listed on major foreign exchanges such as London and New York. They placed equity and debt issues in major securities markets. In most cases, they were successful in lowering their WACC and increasing its availability.

During the 1980s and 1990s, national restrictions on cross-border portfolio investment were gradually eased under pressure from the Organization for Economic Cooperation and Development (OECD), a consortium of most of the world's most industrialized countries. Liberalization of European securities markets was accelerated because of the European Union's efforts to develop a single European market without barriers. Emerging nation markets followed suit, as did the former Eastern Bloc countries after the breakup of the Soviet Union. Emerging national markets have often been motivated by the need to source foreign capital to finance large-scale privatization.

Now, market segmentation has been significantly reduced, although the liquidity of individual national markets remains limited. Most observers believe that for better or for worse, we have achieved a global market for securities. The good news is that many firms have been assisted to become MNEs because they now have access to a global cost and availability of capital. The bad news is that the correlation among securities markets has increased, thereby reducing, but not eliminating, the benefits of international portfolio diversification. Globalization of securities markets has also led to more volatility and speculative behavior as shown by the emerging market crises of the 1995–2001 period.

CASE QUESTIONS

1. What were the impacts on Novo as a result of operating in a segmented market?

2. What were the primary causes of the market segmentation?

3. Ultimately, what actions did Novo take to escape its segmented market?

Questions

1. **Dimensions of the Cost and Availability of Capital.** Global integration has given many firms access to new and cheaper sources of funds beyond those available in their home markets. What are the dimensions of a strategy to capture this lower cost and greater availability of capital?

2. **MNEs' Capital.** When compared to domestic firms, why do MNEs enjoy more capital availability and lower capital costs?

3. **Definitions.** Define the following terms:
   a. CAPM and ICAPM
   b. Risk-free interest rate

4. **Equity risk premiums.**
   a. Why are equity risk premiums important to investors?
   b. Why is it necessary to use one consistent measurement of risk premiums?

5. **Portfolio Investors.** Both domestic and international portfolio managers are asset allocators.
   a. What is their portfolio management objective?
   b. What is the main advantage that international portfolio managers have compared to portfolio managers limited to domestic-only asset allocation?

6. **Dimensions of Asset Allocation.** Portfolio asset allocation can be accomplished along many dimensions depending on the investment objective of the portfolio manager. Identify the various dimensions.

7. **Market Liquidity.**
   a. Define what is meant by the term market liquidity.
   b. What are the main disadvantages for a firm to be located in an illiquid market?
   c. If a firm is limited to raising funds in its domestic capital market, what happens to its marginal cost of capital as it expands?
   d. If a firm can raise funds abroad what happens to its marginal cost of capital as it expands?

8. **Market Segmentation.**
   a. Define market segmentation.
   b. What are the six main causes of market segmentation?
   c. What are the main disadvantages for a firm to be located in a segmented market?

9. **Market Illiquidity and Segmentation.** Explain why illiquidity and segmentation lead to financial market imperfections. Can MNEs tackle market imperfections?

10. **Novo Industri (A).** Why did Novo believe its cost of capital was too high compared to its competitors?

Why did Novo's relatively high cost of capital create a competitive disadvantage?

11. **Novo Industri (B).** Novo believed that the Danish capital market was segmented from world capital markets. Explain the six characteristics of the Danish equity market that were responsible for its segmentation.

12. **Novo Industri A/S.**
   a. What was Novo's strategy to internationalize its cost of capital?
   b. What is the evidence that Novo's strategy succeeded?

13. **MNEs Internationalizing the Cost of Capital.** What are the factors that determine the efficiency of MNEs' strategies for internationalizing their cost of capital? Explain how such strategies have proven to be beneficial to both global and national economies as well as MNEs.

14. **Cost of Capital for MNEs Compared to Domestic Firms.** Theoretically, MNEs should be in a better position than their domestic counterparts to support higher debt ratios because their cash flows are diversified internationally. However, recent empirical studies have come to the opposite conclusion. These studies also concluded that MNEs have higher betas than their domestic counterparts. According to these empirical studies
   a. Why do MNEs have lower debt ratios than their domestic counterparts?
   b. Why do MNEs have higher betas than their domestic counterparts?

15. **The "Riddle."** The riddle is an attempt to explain under what conditions an MNE would have a higher or lower debt ratio and beta than its domestic counterpart. Explain and diagram these conditions.

16. **Emerging Market MNEs.** Explain why some firms in MNEs have managed to expand their operations outside their national borders. How can MNEs in emerging markets raise extra funds to finance their expansions?

Problems

1. **Corcovado Pharmaceuticals.** Corcovado Pharmaceutical's cost of debt is 7%. The risk-free rate of interest is 3%. The expected return on the market portfolio is 8%. After effective taxes, Corcovado's effective tax rate is 25%. Its optimal capital structure is 60% debt and 40% equity.
   a. If Corcovado's beta is estimated at 1.1, what is its weighted average cost of capital?
   b. If Corcovado's beta is estimated at 0.8, significantly lower because of the continuing profit prospects in the global energy sector, what is its weighted average cost of capital?

2. **Petro-U.K. (U.K.).** Petro-U.K. is a British energy firm that needs to raise £150 million to finance expansion projects. Suppose that Petro-U.K. is seeking a capital structure comprising 30% debt and 70% equity. The corporate tax rate in the United Kingdom is 21%. Petro-U.K. finds that it can raise finance in the domestic London stock market as follows: both debt and equity would have to be sold in multiples of £50 million (30% debt and 70% equity). For equity and debt respectively, the financing costs are 8% and 6% on the U.K. market and 10% and 8% on the Latin American market.

A consultancy firm advises Petro-U.K. that incremental finance could be raised in multiples of £50 million (maintaining the 30/70 capital structure). Each increment of cost would be influenced by the total amount of capital raised.

For equity and debt respectively, the first increment of £50 million (30% debt and 70% equity) would cost 10% and 8% on the U.K. market and 12% and 10% on the Latin American market. The second increment of £50 million would cost 12% and 10% on the U.K. market and 16% and 14% on the Latin American market.
   a. Calculate the lowest average cost of capital for each increment of £150 million of new capital, where Petro-U.K. raises £45 million in the equity market and an additional £105 million in the debt market at the same time.
   b. If Petro-U.K. plans an expansion of only £75 million, how should that expansion be financed? What will be the weighted average cost of capital for the expansion?

3. **Trident's Cost of Capital.** Maria Gonzalez now estimates the risk-free rate to be 3.60%, the company's credit risk premium is 4.40%, the domestic beta is estimated at 1.05, the international beta is estimated at 0.85, and the company's capital structure is now 30% debt. All other values remain the same as those presented in this chapter in "Sample Calculation: Trident's Cost of Capital." For both the domestic CAPM and ICAPM, calculate the following:
   a. Trident's cost of equity
   b. Trident's cost of debt
   c. Trident's weighted average cost of capital

4. **Trident and Equity Risk Premiums.** Using the original weighted average cost of capital data for Trident used in the chapter in "Sample Calculation: Trident's Cost of Capital," calculate both the CAPM and ICAPM weighted average costs of capital for the following equity risk premium estimates.
   a. 8.00%
   b. 7.00%
   c. 5.00%
   d. 4.00%

5. **Mobi-SA (South Africa).** Mobi-SA is a large mobile phone provider based in South Africa. It has not entered the Nigerian marketplace yet, but is considering establishing network and distribution facilities in Nigeria through a wholly owned subsidiary. It has approached two different investment banking advisors, Standard Chartered Bank of South Africa and First Bank of Nigeria, for estimates of what its costs of capital would be several years into the future when it planned to list its Nigerian subsidiary on the Nigerian stock exchange. Using the following assumptions by the two different advisors, calculate the prospective costs of debt, equity, and the WACC for Mobi-SA. Using the following assumptions by the two different advisors, calculate the prospective costs of debt, equity, and the WACC for Mobi-SA:

Assumptions	Symbol	Standard Chartered Bank of South Africa	First Bank of Nigeria
Estimate of correlation between security and market	β	0.75	0.7
Estimate of standard deviation of Mobi-SA's returns	ρ_{jm}	20%	25%
Estimate of standard deviation of market's return	σ_j	15%	18%
Risk-free rate of interest	k_{rf}	10%	10%
Estimate of Mobi-SA's cost of debt in Nigerian market	k_d	15%	15%
Estimate of market return, forward-looking	k_m	11%	12%
Corporate tax	t	30%	30%
Proportion of debt	D/V	40%	50%
Proportion of equity	E/V	60%	50%

6. **Xiaomi's Cost of Capital.** Xiaomi has rapidly grown during the last five years to become one of the largest smartphone manufacturers. Having most of its sales in China, its average annual sales over the last five years amounted to around 100 billion Chinese yuan (CNY). Now that the company is planning on expanding into global markets outside China, it needs to carefully measure its weighted average cost of capital in order to make prudent decisions on new investment proposals.

Assuming a risk-free rate of 4.375%, an effective tax rate of 29%, and a market risk premium of 5%, what is the estimated weighted average cost of capital for its two competitors ChiFoSmart and ChinaFone? How can you estimate a comparable WACC for Xiaomi?

	ChiFoSmart	ChinaFone	Xiaomi
Company sales	CNY 10 billion	CNY 15 billion	CNY 100 billion
Company's beta	0.75	0.67	??
Credit rating	A	A	AA
Weighted average cost of debt	7%	6.625 %	6.5%
Debt to total capital	30%	38%	22%
International sales/ Sales	5%	15%	20%

7. **The Tombs.** You have joined your friends at the local watering hole, The Tombs, for your weekly debate on international finance. The topic this week is whether the cost of equity can ever be cheaper than the cost of debt. The group has chosen Brazil in the mid-1990s as the subject of the debate. One of the group members has torn a table of data out of a book (shown below), which is then the subject of the analysis.

Larry argues, "It's all about expected versus delivered. You can talk about what equity investors expect, but they often find that what is delivered for years at a time is so small—even sometimes negative—that in effect, the cost of equity is cheaper than the cost of debt."

Moe interrupts, "But you're missing the point. The cost of capital is what the investor requires in compensation for the risk taken going into the investment. If he doesn't end up getting it, and that was happening here, then he pulls his capital out and walks."

Curly is the theoretician. "Ladies, this is not about empirical results; it is about the fundamental concept of risk-adjusted returns. An investor in equities knows he will reap returns only after all compensation has been made to debt providers. He is therefore always subject to a higher level of risk to his return than debt instruments, and as the capital asset pricing model states, equity investors set their expected returns as a risk-adjusted factor over and above the returns to risk-free instruments."

Brazilian Economic Performance	1995	1996	1997	1998	1999
Inflation rate (IPC)	23.20%	10.00%	4.80%	1.00%	10.50%
Bank lending rate	53.10%	27.10%	24.70%	29.20%	30.70%
Exchange rate (reais/$)	0.972	1.039	1.117	1.207	1.700
Equity returns (São Paulo Bovespa)	16.0%	28.0%	30.2%	33.5%	151.9%

At this point, Larry and Moe simply stare at Curly—pause—and order more beer. Using the Brazilian data presented, comment on this week's debate at The Tombs.

Genedak-Hogan

Use the table below to answer Problems 8 through 10. Genedak-Hogan is an American conglomerate that is actively debating the impacts of international diversification of its operations on its capital structure and cost of capital. The firm is planning on reducing consolidated debt after diversification.

8. **Genedak-Hogan Cost of Equity.** Senior management at Genedak-Hogan are actively debating the implications of diversification on its cost of equity. All agree that the company's returns will be less correlated with the reference market return in the future, the financial advisors believe that the market will assess an additional 3.0% risk premium for "going international" to the basic CAPM cost of equity. Calculate Genedak-Hogan's cost of equity before and after international diversification of its operations, with and without the hypothetical additional risk premium, and comment on the discussion.

9. **Genedak-Hogan's WACC.** Calculate the weighted average cost of capital for Genedak-Hogan before and after international diversification.
   a. Did the reduction in debt costs reduce the firm's weighted average cost of capital? How would you describe the impact of international diversification on its costs of capital?
   b. Adding the hypothetical risk premium to the cost of equity introduced in Problem 8 (an added 3.0% to the cost of equity because of international diversification), what is the firm's WACC?

10. **Genedak-Hogan's WACC and Effective Tax Rate.** Many MNEs have greater ability to control and reduce their effective tax rates when expanding international operations. If Genedak-Hogan was able to reduce its consolidated effective tax rate from 35% to 32%, what would be the impact on its WACC?

Assumptions	Symbol	Before Diversification	After Diversification
Correlation between G-H and the market	ρ_{jm}	0.88	0.76
Standard deviation of G-H's returns	σ_j	28.0%	26.0%
Standard deviation of market's returns	σ_m	18.0%	18.0%
Risk-free rate of interest	k_{rf}	3.0%	3.0%
Additional equity risk premium for internationalization	RPM	0.0%	3.0%
Estimate of G-H's cost of debt in U.S. market	k_d	7.2%	7.0%
Market risk premium	$k_m - k_{rf}$	5.5%	5.5%
Corporate tax rate	t	35.0%	35.0%
Proportion of debt	D/V	38%	32%
Proportion of equity	E/V	62%	68%

Internet Exercises

1. **International Diversification via Mutual Funds.** All major mutual fund companies now offer a variety of internationally diversified mutual funds. The degree of international composition across funds, however, differs significantly. Use the Web sites listed, and others of interest, to
   a. Distinguish between international funds, global funds, worldwide funds, and overseas funds

   b. Determine how international funds have been performing, in U.S. dollar terms, relative to mutual funds offering purely domestic portfolios

Fidelity	www.fidelity.com/funds/
T. Rowe Price	www.troweprice.com/
Merrill Lynch	www.ml.com/
Kemper	www.kempercorporation.com/

2. **Novo Industri.** Novo Industri A/S merged with Nordisk Gentofte in 1989. Nordisk Gentofte was Novo's main European competitor. The combined

company, now called Novo Nordisk, has become the leading producer of insulin worldwide. Its main competitor is Eli Lilly of the United States. Using standard investor information, and the Web sites for Novo Nordisk and Eli Lilly, determine if, during the most recent five years, Novo Nordisk has maintained a cost of capital competitive with Eli Lilly. In particular, examine the P/E ratios, share prices, debt ratios, and betas. Try to calculate each firm's actual cost of capital.

| Novo Nordisk | www.novonordisk.com |
| Eli Lilly and Company | www.lilly.com |

| BigCharts.com | www.bigcharts.com |
| Yahoo! Finance | www.finance.yahoo.com |

3. **Cost of Capital Calculator.** Ibbotson and Associates, a unit of Morningstar, is one of the leading providers of quantitative estimates of the cost of capital across markets. Use the following Web site—specifically the Cost of Capital Center—to prepare an overview of the major theoretical approaches and numerical estimates for cross-border costs of capital by Ibbotson and Associates.

| Ibbotson and Associates | corporate.morningstar.com |

Raising Equity and Debt Globally

Do what you will, the capital is at hazard. All that can be required of a trustee to invest, is, that he shall conduct himself faithfully and exercise a sound discretion. He is to observe how men of prudence, discretion, and intelligence manage their own affairs, not in regard to speculation, but in regard to the permanent disposition of their funds, considering the probable income, as well as the probable safety of the capital to be invested.

—*Prudent Man Rule*, Justice Samuel Putnam, 1830.

LEARNING OBJECTIVES

- Design a strategy to source equity globally

- Analyze the motivations and goals of a firm cross-listing its shares on foreign equity markets

- Analyze the motivations and goals of a firm issuing new equity shares on foreign equity markets

- Understand the many barriers to effectively penetrating foreign equity markets through cross-listing and selling equity abroad

- Examine the various financial instruments that can be used to source equity in the global equity markets

- Extend the theory of optimal financial structure to the multinational enterprise (MNE)

- Analyze the factors that, in practice, determine the financial structure of foreign subsidiaries within the context of the MNE

- Evaluate the various internal and external sources of funds available for the financing of foreign subsidiaries

- Identify the relevant characteristics of different international debt instruments in financing both the MNE itself, and its various foreign affiliate components

Chapter 12 analyzed why gaining access to global capital markets should lower a firm's cost of capital, increase its access to capital, and improve the liquidity of its shares by overcoming market segmentation. A firm pursuing this lofty goal, particularly a firm from a segmented or emerging market, must first design a financial strategy that will attract international investors. This involves choosing among alternative paths to access global capital markets.

This chapter focuses on firms resident in less liquid, segmented, or emerging markets. They are the ones that need to tap liquid and unsegmented markets in order to attain the global cost and availability of capital. Firms resident in large and highly industrialized countries already have access to their own domestic, liquid, and unsegmented markets. Although they too source equity and debt abroad, it is unlikely to have as significant an impact on their cost and availability of capital. In fact, for these firms, sourcing funds abroad is often motivated solely by the need to fund large foreign acquisitions rather than to fund existing operations.

This chapter begins with the design of a financial strategy to source both equity and debt globally. It then analyzes the optimal financial structure for an MNE and its subsidiaries, one that minimizes its cost of capital. We then explore the alternative paths that a firm may follow in raising capital in global markets. The chapter concludes with the Mini-Case, *Petrobrás of Brazil and the Cost of Capital*, which examines how the international markets discriminate in their treatment of a multinational firm on the basis of its home market and its industry.

Designing a Strategy to Source Capital Globally

Designing a capital sourcing strategy requires management to agree upon a long-run financial objective and then choose among the various alternative paths to get there. Exhibit 13.1 is a visual presentation of alternative paths to the ultimate objective of attaining a global cost and availability of capital.

Normally, the choice of paths and implementation is aided by an early appointment of an investment bank as official advisor to the firm. Investment bankers are in touch with the

---

EXHIBIT 13.1 **Alternative Paths to Globalize the Cost and Availability of Capital**

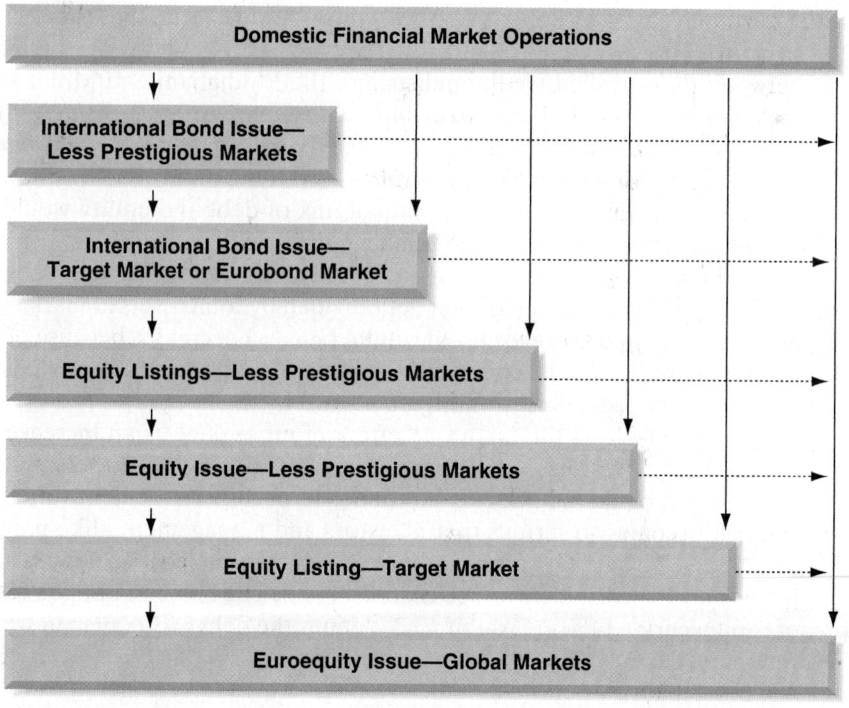

Source: Oxelhiem, Stonehill, Randøy, Vikkula, Dullum, and Modén, *Corporate Strategies in Internationalizing the Cost of Capital*, Copenhagen: Copenhagen Business School Press, 1998, p. 119. Reprinted with permission.

potential foreign investors and their current requirements. They can also help navigate the various institutional requirements and barriers that must be satisfied. Their services include advising if, when, and where a cross-listing should be initiated. They usually prepare the required prospectus if an equity or debt issue is desired, help to price the issue, and maintain an aftermarket to prevent the share price from falling below its initial price.

Most firms raise their initial capital in their own domestic market (see Exhibit 13.1). Next, they are tempted to skip all the intermediate steps and drop to the bottom line, a euroequity issue in global markets. This is the time when a good investment bank advisor will offer a "reality check." Most firms that have only raised capital in their domestic market are not sufficiently well known to attract foreign investors. Remember from Chapter 12 that Novo was advised by its investment bankers to start with a convertible eurobond issue and simultaneously cross-list their shares and their bonds in London. This was despite the fact that Novo had an outstanding track record of financial and business performance.

Exhibit 13.1 shows that most firms should start sourcing abroad with an international bond issue. It could be placed on a less prestigious foreign market. This could be followed by an international bond issue in a target market or in the eurobond market. The next step might be to cross-list and issue equity in one of the less prestigious markets in order to attract the attention of international investors. The next step could be to cross-list shares on a highly liquid prestigious foreign stock exchange such as London (LSE), NYSE, Euronext, or NASDAQ. The ultimate step would be to place a directed equity issue in a prestigious target market or a euroequity issue in global equity markets.

Optimal Financial Structure

After many years of debate, finance theorists now agree that there is an optimal financial structure for a firm, and practically, they agree on how it is determined. The great debate between the so-called traditionalists and the Modigliani and Miller school of thought has ended in compromise: *When taxes and bankruptcy costs are considered, a firm has an optimal financial structure determined by that particular mix of debt and equity that minimizes the firm's cost of capital for a given level of business risk.* If the business risk of new projects differs from the risk of existing projects, the optimal mix of debt and equity would change to recognize trade-offs between business and financial risks.

Exhibit 13.2 illustrates how the cost of capital varies with the amount of debt employed. As the debt ratio, defined as total debt divided by total assets at market values, increases, the after-tax weighted average cost of capital (k_{WACC}) decreases because of the heavier weight of low-cost debt $[k_d(1 - t)]$ compared to high-cost equity (k_e). The low cost of debt is, of course, due to the tax deductibility of interest shown by the term $(1 - t)$.

Partly offsetting the favorable effect of more debt, is an increase in the cost of equity (k_e), because investors perceive greater financial risk. Nevertheless, the after-tax weighted average cost of capital (k_{WACC}) continues to decline as the debt ratio increases, until financial risk becomes so serious that investors and management alike perceive a real danger of insolvency. This result causes a sharp increase in the cost of new debt and equity, thereby increasing the weighted average cost of capital. The low point on the resulting U-shaped cost of capital curve, 14% in Exhibit 13.2, defines the debt ratio range in which the cost of capital is minimized.

Most theorists believe that the low point is actually a rather broad flat area encompassing a wide range of debt ratios, 30% to 60% in Exhibit 13.2, where little difference exists in the cost of capital. They also generally agree that, at least in the United States, the range of the flat area and the location of a particular firm's debt ratio within that range are determined by

EXHIBIT 13.2   The Cost of Capital and Financial Structure

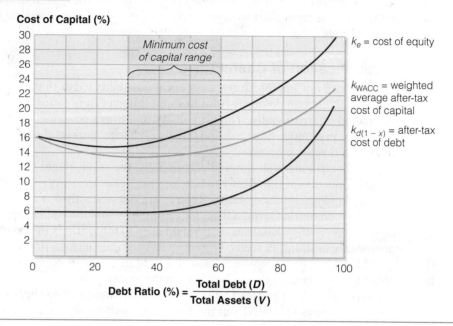

Cost of Capital (%)

Minimum cost of capital range

k_e = cost of equity

k_{WACC} = weighted average after-tax cost of capital

$k_{d(1-x)}$ = after-tax cost of debt

$$\text{Debt Ratio (\%)} = \frac{\text{Total Debt } (D)}{\text{Total Assets } (V)}$$

such variables as 1) the industry in which it competes; 2) volatility of its sales and operating income; and 3) the collateral value of its assets.

Optimal Financial Structure and the MNE

The domestic theory of optimal financial structures needs to be modified by four more variables in order to accommodate the case of the MNE. These variables are 1) availability of capital; 2) diversification of cash flows; 3) foreign exchange risk; and 4) expectations of international portfolio investors.[1]

Availability of Capital

Chapter 12 demonstrated that access to capital in global markets allows an MNE to lower its cost of equity and debt compared with most domestic firms. It also permits an MNE to maintain its desired debt ratio, even when significant amounts of new funds must be raised. In other words, a multinational firm's marginal cost of capital is constant for considerable ranges of its capital budget. This statement is not true for most small domestic firms because they do not have access to the national equity or debt markets. They must either rely on internally generated funds or borrow for the short and medium terms from commercial banks.

Multinational firms domiciled in countries that have illiquid capital markets are in almost the same situation as small domestic firms unless they have gained a global cost and availability of capital. They must rely on internally generated funds and bank borrowing. If they

---

[1]An excellent recent study on the practical dimensions of optimal capital structure can be found in "An Empirical Model of Optimal Capital Structure," Jules H. Van Binsbergen, John R. Graham, and Jie Yang, *Journal of Applied Corporate Finance*, Vol. 23, No. 4, Fall 2011, pp. 34–59.

need to raise significant amounts of new funds to finance growth opportunities, they may need to borrow more than would be optimal from the viewpoint of minimizing their cost of capital. This is equivalent to saying that their marginal cost of capital is increasing at higher budget levels.

Diversification of Cash Flows

As explained in Chapter 12, the theoretical possibility exists that multinational firms are in a better position than domestic firms to support higher debt ratios because their cash flows are diversified internationally. The probability of a firm's covering fixed charges under varying conditions in product, financial, and foreign exchange markets should increase if the variability of its cash flows is minimized.

By diversifying cash flows internationally, the MNE might be able to achieve the same kind of reduction in cash flow variability as portfolio investors receive from diversifying their security holdings internationally. Returns are not perfectly correlated between countries. In contrast, a domestic German firm, for example, would not enjoy the benefit of international cash flow diversification. Instead, it would need to rely entirely on its own net cash inflow from domestic operations. Perceived financial risk for the German firm would be greater than for a multinational firm because the variability of its German domestic cash flows could not be offset by positive cash flows elsewhere in the world.

As discussed in Chapter 12, the diversification argument has been challenged by empirical research findings that MNEs in the United States actually have lower debt ratios than their domestic counterparts. The agency costs of debt were higher for the MNEs, as were political risks, foreign exchange risks, and asymmetric information.

Foreign Exchange Risk and the Cost of Debt

When a firm issues foreign currency denominated debt, its effective cost equals the after-tax cost of repaying the principal and interest in terms of the firm's own currency. This amount includes the nominal cost of principal and interest in foreign currency terms, adjusted for any foreign exchange gains or losses.

For example, if a U.S.-based firm borrows SF1,500,000 for one year at 5.00% interest, and during the year the Swiss franc appreciates from an initial rate of SF1.5000/$ to SF1.4400/$, what is the dollar cost of this debt $(k_d^\$)$? The dollar proceeds of the initial borrowing are calculated at the current spot rate of SF1.5000/$:

$$\frac{SF1,500,000}{SF1.5000/\$} = \$1,000,000$$

At the end of one year the U.S.-based firm is responsible for repaying the SF1,500,000 principal plus 5.00% interest, or a total of SF1,575,000. This repayment, however, must be made at an ending spot rate of SF1.4400/$:

$$\frac{SF1,500,000 \times 1.05}{SF1.4400/\$} = \$1,093,750$$

The actual dollar cost of the loan's repayment is not the nominal 5.00% paid in Swiss franc interest, but 9.375%:

$$\left[\frac{\$1,093,750}{\$1,000,000}\right] - 1 = 0.09375 \approx 9.375\%$$

The dollar cost is higher than expected due to appreciation of the Swiss franc against the U.S. dollar. This total home-currency cost is actually the result of the combined percentage cost of debt and percentage change in the foreign currency's value. We can find the total cost of borrowing Swiss francs by a U.S.-dollar based firm, $k_d^\$$, by multiplying one plus the Swiss franc interest expense, k_d^{SF}, by one plus the percentage change in the SF/$ exchange rate, s:

$$k_d^\$ = [(1 + k_d^{SF}) \times (1 + s)] - 1$$

where $k_d^{SF} = 5.00\%$ and $s = 4.1667\%$. The percentage change in the value of the Swiss franc versus the U.S. dollar, when the home currency is the U.S. dollar, is

$$\frac{S_1 - S_2}{S_2} \times 100 = \frac{\text{SF1.5000/\$} - \text{SF1.4400/\$}}{\text{SF1.4400/\$}} \times 100 = +4.1667\%$$

The total expense, combining the nominal interest rate and the percentage change in the exchange rate, is

$$k_d^\$ = [(1 + .0500) \times (1 + .041667)] - 1 = .09375 \approx 9.375\%$$

The total percentage cost of capital is 9.375%, not simply the foreign currency interest payment of 5%. The after-tax cost of this Swiss franc denominated debt, when the U.S. income tax rate is 34%, is

$$k_d^\$(1 - t) = 9.375\% \times 0.66 = 6.1875\%$$

The firm would report the added 4.1667% cost of this debt in terms of U.S. dollars as a foreign exchange transaction loss, and it would be deductible for tax purposes.

Expectations of International Portfolio Investors

Chapter 12 highlighted the fact that the key to gaining a global cost and availability of capital is attracting and retaining international portfolio investors. Those investors' expectations for a firm's debt ratio and overall financial structures are based on global norms that have developed over the past 30 years. Because a large proportion of international portfolio investors are based in the most liquid and unsegmented capital markets, such as the United States and the United Kingdom, their expectations tend to predominate and override individual national norms. Therefore, regardless of other factors, if a firm wants to raise capital in global markets, it must adopt global norms that are close to the U.S. and U.K. norms. Debt ratios up to 60% appear to be acceptable. Higher debt ratios are more difficult to sell to international portfolio investors.

Raising Equity Globally

Once a multinational firm has established its financial strategy and considered its *desired* and *target capital structure*, it then proceeds to raise capital outside of its domestic market—both debt and equity—using a variety of capital raising paths and instruments.

Exhibit 13.3 describes three key critical elements to understanding the issues that any firm must confront when seeking to raise equity capital. Although the business press does not often make a clear distinction, there is a fundamental distinction between an *equity issuance* and an *equity listing*. A firm seeking to raise equity capital is ultimately in search of an *issuance*—the IPO or SPO described in Exhibit 13.3. This generates cash proceeds to be used for funding

---

EXHIBIT 13.3   **Equity Avenues, Activities, and Attributes**

- **Equity Issuance**

  - *Initial Public Offering* (IPO)—the initial sale of shares to the public of a private company. IPOs raise capital and typically use underwriters.

  - *Seasoned Public Offering* (SPO)—a subsequent sale of additional shares in the publicly traded company, raising additional equity capital.

  - *Euroequity*—the initial sale of shares in two or more markets and countries simultaneously.

  - *Directed Issue*—the sale of shares by a publicly traded company to a specific target investor or market, public or private, often in a different country.

- **Equity Listing**

  - Shares of a publicly traded firm are listed for purchase or sale on an exchange. An investment banking firm is typically retained to make a market in the shares.

  - *Cross-listing* is the listing of a company's shares on an exchange in a different country market. It is intended to expand the potential market for the firm's shares to a larger universe of investors.

  - *Depositary receipt* (DR)—a certificate of ownership in the shares of a company issued by a bank, representing a claim on underlying foreign securities. In the United States they are termed *American Depositary Receipts* (ADRs), and when sold globally, *Global Depositary Receipts* (GDRs).

- **Private Placement**

  - The sale of a security (equity or debt) to a private investor. The private investors are typically institutions such as pension funds, insurance companies, or high net-worth private entities.

  - *Rule 144A private placement sales* are sales of securities to *qualified institutional buyers* (QIBs) in the United States without SEC registration. QIBs are nonbank firms that own and invest in $100 million or more on a discretionary basis.

  - *Private Equity*—equity investments in firms by large limited partnerships, institutional investors, or wealthy private investors, with the intention of taking the subject firms private, revitalizing their businesses, and then selling them publicly or privately in one to five years.

---

and executing the business. But often issuances must be preceded by *listings*, in which the shares are traded on an exchange and, therefore, in a specific country market, gaining name recognition, visibility, and hopefully preparing the market for an issuance.

That said, an issuance need not be public. A firm, public or private, can place an issue with private investors, a *private placement*. (Note that *private placement* may refer to either equity or debt.) Private placements can take a variety of different forms, and the intent of investors may be passive (e.g., Rule 144A investors) or active (e.g., private equity, where the investor intends to control and change the firm).

Publicly traded companies, in addition to raising equity capital, are also in pursuit of greater market visibility and reaching ever-larger potential investor audiences. The expectation is that the growing investor audience will result in higher share prices over time—increasing the returns to owners. Privately held companies are more singular in their objective: to raise greater quantities of equity at the lowest possible cost—privately. As discussed in Chapter 4, ownership trends in the industrialized markets have tended toward more private ownership, while many multinational firms from emerging market countries have shown growing interest in going public.

Exhibit 13.4 provides and overview of the four major equity alternatives available to multinational firms today. A firm wishing to raise equity capital outside of its home market may take a *public pathway* or a *private* one. The *public pathway* includes a *directed public share issue* or a *euroequity issue*. Alternatively, and one that has been used with greater frequency over the past decade, is a *private pathway*—private placements, private equity, or a private share sale under strategic alliance.

EXHIBIT 13.4   Equity Alternatives in the Global Market

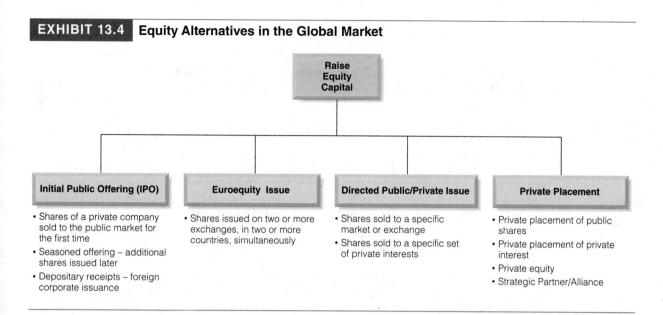

Initial Public Offering (IPO). A private firm initiates public ownership of the company through an *initial public offering,* or IPO. Most IPOs begin with the organization of an underwriting and syndication group comprised of investment banking service providers. This group then assists the company in preparing the regulatory filings and disclosures required, depending on the country and stock exchange the firm is using. The firm will, in the months preceding the IPO date, publish a *prospectus*. The prospectus will provide a description of the company's history, business, operating and financing results, associated business, financial or political risks, and the company's business plan for the future, all to aid prospective buyers in their assessment of the firm.

The initial issuance of shares by a company typically represents somewhere between 15% and 25% of the ownership in the firm (although a number in recent years have been as little as 6% to 8%). The company may follow the IPO with additional share sales called *seasoned offerings*, in which more of the firm's ownership is sold in the public market. The total shares or proportion of shares traded in the public market is often referred to as the *public float* or *free float.*

Once a firm has "gone public," it is open to a considerably higher level of public scrutiny. This scrutiny arises from the detailed public disclosures and financial filings it must make periodically as required by government security regulators and individual stock exchanges. This continuous disclosure is not trivial in either cost or competitive implications. Public firm financial disclosures can be seen as divulging a tremendous amount of information that customers, suppliers, partners, and competitors may use in their relationship with the firm. Private firms have a distinct competitive advantage in this arena.[2]

An added distinction about the publicly traded firm's shares is that they only raise capital for the firm upon issuance. Although the daily rise and fall of share prices drives the returns to the owners of those shares, that daily price movement does not change the capital of the company.

[2]A publicly traded firm like Walmart will produce hundreds of pages of operational details, financial results, and management discussion on a quarterly basis. That is in comparison to large private firms like Cargill or Koch, where finding a full single page of financial results would be an achievement.

Euroequity Issue. A *euroequity* or *euroequity issue* is an initial public offering on multiple exchanges in multiple countries at the same time. Almost all euroequity issues are underwritten by an international syndicate. The term "euro" in this context does not imply that the issuers or investors are located in Europe, nor does it mean the shares are denominated in the euros. It is a generic term for international securities issues originating and being sold anywhere in the world. The euroequity seeks to raise more capital in its issuance by reaching as many different investors as possible. Two examples of high-profile euroequity issues would be those of British Telecommunications and the famous Italian luxury goods producer, Gucci.

The largest and most spectacular issues have been made in conjunction with a wave of privatizations of state-owned enterprises (SOEs). The Thatcher government in the United Kingdom created the model when it privatized British Telecom in December 1984. That issue was so large that it was necessary and desirable to sell tranches to foreign investors in addition to the sale to domestic investors. (A *tranche* is an allocation of shares, typically to underwriters that are expected to sell to investors in their designated geographic markets.) The objective is both to raise the funds and to ensure post-issue worldwide liquidity.

Euroequity privatization issues have been particularly popular with international portfolio investors because most of the firms are very large, with excellent credit ratings and profitable quasi-government monopolies at the time of privatization. The British privatization model has been so successful that numerous others have followed like the Deutsche Telecom initial public offering of $13 billion in 1996.

State-owned enterprises (SOEs)—government-owned firms from emerging markets— have successfully implemented large-scale privatization programs with these foreign tranches. Telefonos de Mexico, the giant Mexican telephone company, completed a $2 billion euroequity issue in 1991 and has continued to have an extremely liquid listing on the NYSE.

One of the largest euroequity offerings by a firm resident in a an illiquid market was the 1993 sale of $3 billion in shares by YPF Sociedad Anónima, Argentina's state-owned oil company. About 75% of its shares were placed in tranches outside of Argentina, with 46% in the United States alone. Its underwriting syndicate represented a virtual "who's who" of the world's leading investment banks.

Directed Public Share Issues. A *directed public share issue* or *directed issue* is defined as one that is targeted at investors in a single country and underwritten in whole or in part by investment institutions from that country. The issue may or may not be denominated in the currency of the target market and is typically combined with a cross-listing on a stock exchange in the target market.[3]

A directed issue might be motivated by a need to fund acquisitions or major capital investments in a target foreign market. This is an especially important source of equity for firms that reside in smaller capital markets and that have outgrown that market.

Nycomed, a small but well-respected Norwegian pharmaceutical firm, was an example of this type of motivation for a directed issue combined with cross-listing. Its commercial strategy for growth was to leverage its sophisticated knowledge of certain market niches and technologies within the pharmaceutical field by acquiring other promising firms—primarily firms in Europe and the United Sates—that possessed relevant technologies, personnel, or market niches. The acquisitions were paid for partly with cash and partly with shares. The

---

[3]The share issue by Novo in 1981 (Chapter 12) was a good example of a successful directed share issue that both improved the liquidity of Novo's shares and lowered its cost of capital.

GLOBAL FINANCE IN PRACTICE   13.1

The Planned Directed Equity Issue of PA Resources of Sweden

One example of the use of directed public share issues was the 2005 issuance of PA Resources (PAR.ST), a Swedish oil and gas reserve acquisition and development firm. First listed on the Oslo, Norway, stock exchange in 2001, PAR announced in 2005 a potential private placement of up to 7 million shares that were specifically directed at Norwegian and international investors (non-U.S. investors). The proceeds of the issuance were expected to partially fund recent oil and gas reserve acquisitions made by the company in the North Sea and Tunisia.

The directed issue was reportedly heavily over-subscribed following the announcement. Like many directed issuances outside the United States the offer expressly stated that the securities would not be offered or sold in the U.S., as the issue had not and would not be registered in the U.S. under the U.S. Securities Act of 1933.

company funded its acquisition strategy by selling two directed issues abroad. In 1989 it cross-listed on the London Stock Exchange (LSE) and raised $100 million in equity from foreign investors. Nycomed followed its LSE listing and issuance with a cross-listing and issuance on the NYSE, raising another $75 million from U.S. investors.

Global Finance in Practice 13.1 offers another example of a directed issue, in this case, a publicly traded firm in Sweden and Norway issuing a euroequity to partially fund the development of a recent oil property acquisition.

Depositary Receipts

Depositary receipts (DRs) are negotiable certificates issued by a bank to represent the underlying shares of stock that are held in trust at a foreign custodian bank. *Global depositary receipts* (GDRs) refer to certificates traded outside of the United States, and *American depositary receipts* (ADRs) refer to certificates traded in the United States and denominated in U.S. dollars. For a company that is incorporated outside the United States and that wants to be listed on a U.S. stock exchange, the primary way of doing so is through an ADR program. For a company incorporated anywhere in the world that wants to be listed in any foreign market, this is done via a GDR program.

ADRs are sold, registered, and transferred in the U.S. in the same manner as any share of stock, with each ADR representing either a multiple or portion of the underlying foreign share. This multiple/portion allows ADRs to carry a price per share appropriate for the U.S. market (typically under $20 per share), even if the price of the foreign share is inappropriate when converted to U.S. dollars directly. A number of ADRs, like the ADR of Telefonos de Mexico (TelMex) of Mexico shown in Exhibit 13.5, have been some of the most active shares on U.S. exchanges for many years.

The first ADR program was created for a British company, Selfridges Provincial Stores Limited, a famous British retailer, in 1927. Created by J.P. Morgan, the shares were listed on the New York Curb Exchange, which in later years was transformed into the American Stock Exchange. As with many financial innovations, depositary receipts were created to defeat a regulatory restriction. In this case, the British government had prohibited British companies from registering their shares on foreign markets without British transfer agents. Depositary receipts, in essence, create a synthetic share abroad, and therefore do not require actual registration of shares outside Britain.

EXHIBIT 13.5   **TelMex's American Depositary Receipt** (sample)

ADR Mechanics

Exhibit 13.6 illustrates the issuance process of a DR program, in this case a U.S.-based investor purchasing shares in a publicly traded Brazilian company—an American depositary receipt or ADR program:

1. The U.S. investor instructs his broker to make a purchase of shares in the publicly traded Brazilian company.

2. The U.S. broker contacts a local broker in Brazil (either through the broker's international offices or directly), placing the order.

3. The Brazilian broker purchases the desired ordinary shares and delivers them to a custodian bank in Brazil.

4. The U.S. broker converts the U.S. dollars received from the investor into Brazilian *reais* to pay the Brazilian broker for the shares purchased.

5. On the same day that the shares are delivered to the Brazilian custodian bank, the custodian notifies the U.S. depositary bank of their deposit.

6. Upon notification, the U.S. depositary bank issues and delivers DRs for the Brazilian company shares to the U.S. broker.

7. The U.S. broker then delivers the DRs to the U.S. investor.

EXHIBIT 13.6	The Structural Execution of ADRs

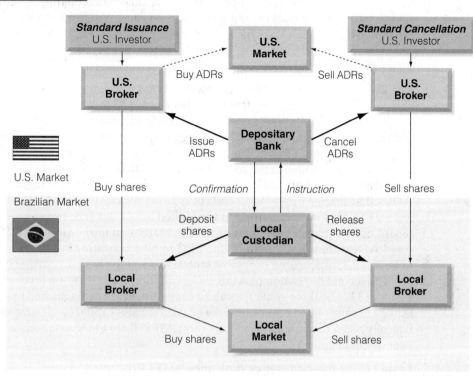

Source: Based on *Depository Receipts Reference Guide*, JPMorgan, 2005, p. 33.

The DRs are now held and tradable like any other common stock share in the United States. In addition to the process just described, it is possible for the U.S. broker to obtain the DRs for the U.S. investor by purchasing existing DRs, not requiring a new issuance. Exhibit 13.6 also describes the alternative process mechanics of a sale or cancellation of ADRs.

Once the ADRs are created, they are tradable in the U.S. market like any other U.S. security. ADRs can be sold to other U.S. investors by simply transferring them from the existing ADR holder (the seller) to another DR holder (the buyer). This is termed *intra-market trading*. This transaction would be settled in the same manner as any other U.S. transaction, with settlement in U.S. dollars on the third business day after the trade date and typically using the depository trust company (DTC). Intra-market trading accounts for nearly 95% of all DR trading today.

ADRs can be exchanged for the underlying foreign shares, or vice versa, so arbitrage keeps foreign and U.S. prices of any given share the same after adjusting for transfer costs. For example, investor demand in one market will cause a price rise there, which will cause an arbitrage rise in the price on the other market even when investors there are not as bullish on the stock.

ADRs convey certain technical advantages to U.S. shareholders. Dividends paid by a foreign firm are passed to its custodial bank and then to the bank that issued the ADR. The issuing bank exchanges the foreign currency dividends for U.S. dollars and sends the dollar dividend to the ADR holders. ADRs are in registered form, rather than in bearer form.[4] Transfer of ownership occurs in the United States in accordance with U.S. laws and procedures. Normally, trading costs are lower than when buying or selling the underlying shares in their home market, and settlement is faster. Withholding taxes is simpler because it is handled by the depositary bank.

ADR Program Structures

The previous section described the issuance of a DR (an ADR in this case) on a Brazilian company's shares resulting from the desire of a U.S.-based investor to buy shares in a Brazilian company. But DR programs can also be viewed from the perspective of the Brazilian company—as part of its financial strategy to reach investors in the United States.

ADR programs differ in whether they are *sponsored* and in their certification *level*. *Sponsored ADRs* are created at the request of a foreign firm wanting its shares listed or traded in the United States. The firm applies to the U.S. SEC and a U.S. bank for registration and issuance of ADRs. The foreign firm pays all costs of creating such sponsored ADRs. If a foreign firm does not seek to have its shares listed in the United States but U.S. investors are interested, a U.S. securities firm may initiate creation of the ADRs—an *unsponsored ADR* program. Unsponsored ADRs are still required by the SEC to obtain approval of the firm's whose shares are to be listed. Unsponsored programs represent a relatively small portion of all DR programs.

The second dimension of ADR differentiation is certification level, described in detail in Exhibit 13.7. The three general levels of commitment are distinguished by degree of disclosure, listing alternatives, whether they may be used to raise capital (issue new shares), and the time typically taken to implement the programs. (SEC Rule 144A programs are described in detail later in this chapter.)

Level I (*over-the-counter* or *pink sheets*) DR Programs. Level I programs are the easiest and fastest programs to execute. A Level I program allows the foreign securities to be purchased and held by U.S. investors without being registered with the SEC. It is the least costly approach but might have a minimal favorable impact on liquidity.

EXHIBIT 13.7   American Depositary Receipt (ADR) Programs by Level

Type	Description	Degree of Disclosure	Listing Alternatives	Ability to Raise Capital	Implementation Timetable
Level I	Over-the-Counter ADR Program	None: home country standards	Over-the-counter (OTC)	—	6 weeks
Level I GDR	Rule 144A/ Reg. S GDR Program	None	Not listed	Yes, available only to QIBs	3 weeks
Level II	U.S.-Listed ADR Program	Detailed Sarbanes Oxley	U.S. stock exchange listings	—	13 weeks
Level II GDR	Rule 144A/ Reg. S GDR Program	None	DIFX	None	2 weeks
Level III	U.S.-Listed ADR Program	Rigorous Sarbanes Oxley	U.S. stock exchange listings	Yes, public offering	14 weeks
Level III GDR	Rule 144A/ Reg. S GDR Program	EU Prospectus Directive and/or U.S. Rule 144A	London, Luxembourg, U.S. Portal	Yes, available to QIBs	2 weeks

---

[4]*Bearer form* is when there is no official registry of ownership—whomever holds it, owns it.

Level II DR Programs. Level II applies to firms that want to list existing shares on a U.S. stock exchange. They must meet the full registration requirements of the SEC and the rules of the specific exchange. This also means reconciling their financial accounts with those used under U.S. GAAP, raising the cost considerably.

Level III DR Programs. Level III applies to the sale of a new equity issued in the United States—raising equity capital. It requires full registration with the SEC and an elaborate stock prospectus. This is the most expensive alternative, but is the most fruitful for foreign firms wishing to raise capital in the world's largest capital markets and possibly generate greater returns for all shareholders.

DR Markets Today: Who, What, and Where

The rapid growth in emerging markets in recent years has been partly a result of the ability of companies from these countries to both list their shares and issue new shares on global equity markets. Their desire to access greater pools of affordable capital, as well as the desire for many of their owners to monetize existing value, has led to an influx of emerging market companies into the DR market.

The Who. The *Who* of global DR programs today is a mix of major multinationals from all over the world, but in recent years participation has shifted back toward industrial country companies. For example, in 2013 the largest issues came from established multinationals like BP, Vodafone, Royal Dutch Shell, and Nestlé, but also included Lukoil and Gazprom of Russia and Taiwan Semiconductor Manufacturing of Taiwan. The oil and gas sector was clearly the largest in both 2012 and 2013, but followed closely by pharmaceutical and telecommunications firms. It's also important to note that in recent years, as illustrated by Exhibit 13.8, the market has clearly been in decline.

EXHIBIT 13.8 **Equity Capital Raised through Depositary Receipts**

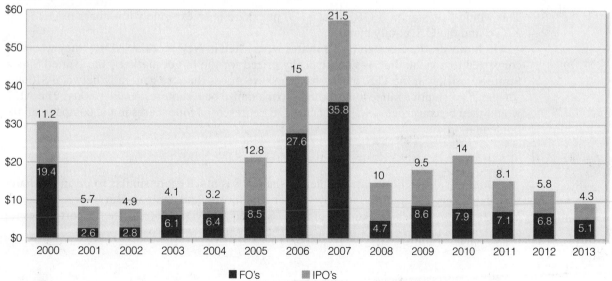

Source: "Depositary Receipts, Year in Review 2013," JPMorgan, p. 5. Data derived by JPMorgan from other depositary banks, Bloomberg, and stock exchanges, January 2014. Reprinted with permission.

The What. The *What* of the global DR market today is a fairly even split between *IPO* and *follow-on* offerings or FOs (additional offerings of equity shares post-IPO). It does appear that IPOs continue to make up the majority of DR equity-raising activity.

The Where. Given the dominance of emerging market companies in DR markets today, it is not surprising that the *Where* of the DR market is dominated by New York and London. By the end of 2013 there were more than 2,300 sponsored DR programs from more than 86 countries. Of those 2,300, just over half were U.S. programs (ADRs), with the remainder being GDR programs split between the London and Luxembourg stock exchanges.

Even more important than the number of programs participating in the DR markets is the capital that has been raised by companies via DR programs globally. Exhibit 13.8 distinguishes between equity capital raised through initial equity share offerings (IPOs) and seasoned offerings (follow-on). The DR market has periodically proved very fruitful as an avenue for raising capital. It is also obvious which years have been better for equity issuances—years like 2000 and 2006–2007.

Global Registered Shares (GRS)

A *global registered share* (GRS) is a share of equity that is traded across borders and markets without conversion, where one share on the home exchange equals one share on the foreign exchange. The identical share is listed on different stock exchanges, but listed in the currency of the exchange. GRSs can theoretically be traded "with the sun"—following markets as they open and close around the globe and around the clock. The shares are traded electronically, eliminating the specialized forms and depositaries required by share issuances like DRs.

The differences between GRSs and GDRs can be seen in the following example. Assume a German multinational has shares listed on the Frankfurt Stock Exchange, and those shares are currently trading at €4.00 per share. If the current spot rate is $1.20/€, those same shares would be listed on the NYSE at $4.80 per share.

$$€4.00 \times \$1.20/€ = \$4.80$$

This would be a standard GRS. But $4.80 per share is an extremely low share price for the NYSE and the U.S. equity market.

If, however, the German firm's shares were listed in New York as ADRs, they would be converted to a value that was strategically priced for the target market—the United States. Strategic pricing in the U.S. means having share prices that are generally between $10 and $20 per share, a price range long-thought to maximize buyer interest and liquidity. The ADR would then be constructed so that each ADR represented four shares in the company on the home market, or:

$$\$4.80 \times 4 = \$19.20 \text{ per share}$$

Does this distinction matter? Clearly the GRS is much more similar to ordinary shares than depositary receipts, and it allows easier comparison and analysis. But if target pricing is important in key markets like that of the U.S., then the ADR offers better opportunities for a foreign firm to gain greater presence and activity.[5]

---

[5]GRSs are not a new innovation, as they are identical to the structure used for cross-border trading of Canadian equities in the United States for many years. More than 70 Canadian firms are listed on the NYSE-Euronext. Of course, one could argue that has been facilitated by near-parity of the U.S. and Canadian dollar for years as well.

There are two fundamental arguments used by proponents of GRSs over ADRs, both based on pure forces of globalization:

1. Investors and markets alike will continue to grow in their desire for securities, which are increasingly identical across markets—taking on the characteristics of commodity-like securities, changing only by the currency of denomination of the local exchange.

2. Regulations governing security trading across country markets will continue to converge towards a common set of global principles, eliminating the need for securities customized for local market attributes or requirements.

Other potential distinctions include the possibility of retaining all voting rights (GRSs do by definition while some ADRs may not) and the general principle that ADRs are designed for one singular cultural and legal environment—the United States. All argument aside, at least to date, the GRS has not replaced the ADR or GDR.

Private Placement

Raising equity through *private placement* is increasingly common across the globe. Publicly traded and private firms alike raise private equity capital on occasion. A *private placement* is the sale of a security to a small set of qualified institutional buyers. The investors are traditionally insurance companies and investment companies. Since the securities are not registered for sale to the public, investors have typically followed a "buy and hold" policy. In the case of debt, terms are often custom designed on a negotiated basis. Private placement markets now exist in most countries.

SEC Rule 144A

In 1990, the SEC approved *Rule 144A*. It permits *qualified institutional buyers* (QIBs) to trade privately placed securities without the previous holding period restrictions and without requiring SEC registration.

A qualified institutional buyer (QIB) is an entity (except a bank or a savings and loan) that owns and invests on a discretionary basis $100 million in securities of non-affiliates. Banks and savings and loans must meet this test but also must have a minimum net worth of $25 million. The SEC has estimated that about 4,000 QIBs exist, mainly investment advisors, investment companies, insurance companies, pension funds, and charitable institutions. Simultaneously, the SEC modified its regulations to permit foreign issuers to tap the U.S. private placement market through an SEC Rule 144A issue, also without SEC registration. A trading system called *PORTAL* was established to support the distribution of primary issues and to create a liquid secondary market for these issues.

Since SEC registration has been identified as the main barrier to foreign firms wishing to raise funds in the United States, SEC Rule 144A placements are proving attractive to foreign issuers of both equity and debt securities. Atlas Copco, the Swedish multinational engineering firm, was the first foreign firm to take advantage of SEC Rule 144A. It raised $49 million in the United States through an ADR equity placement as part of its larger $214 million euroequity issue in 1990. Since then, several billion dollars have been raised each year by foreign issuers with private equity placements in the United States. However, it does not appear that such placements have a favorable effect on either liquidity or stock price.

Private Equity Funds

Private equity funds are usually limited partnerships of institutional and wealthy investors, such as college endowment funds, that raise capital in the most liquid capital markets. They are best known for buying control of publicly owned firms, taking them private, improving management, and then reselling them after one to three years. They are resold in a variety of ways including selling the firms to other firms, to other private equity funds, or by taking them public once again. The private equity funds themselves are frequently very large, but may also utilize a large amount of debt to fund their takeovers. These "alternatives" as they are called, demand fees of 2% of assets plus 20% of profits. Equity funds have had some highly visible successes.

Many mature family-owned firms resident in emerging markets are unlikely to qualify for a global cost and availability of capital even if they follow the strategy suggested in this chapter. Although they might be consistently profitable and growing, they are still too small, too invisible to foreign investors, lacking in managerial depth, and unable to fund the up-front costs of a globalization strategy. For these firms, private equity funds may be a solution.

Private equity funds differ from traditional venture capital funds. The latter usually operate mainly in highly developed countries. They typically invest in start-up firms with the goal of exiting the investment with an initial public offering (IPO) placed in those same highly liquid markets. Very little venture capital is available in emerging markets, partly because it would be difficult to exit with an IPO in an illiquid market. The same exiting problem faces the private equity funds, but they appear to have a longer time horizon. They invest in already mature and profitable companies. They are content with growing companies through better management and mergers with other firms.

Foreign Equity Listing and Issuance

According to the alternative equity pathways in the global market illustrated earlier in Exhibit 3.4, a firm needs to choose one or more stock market on which to cross-list its shares and sell new equity. Just where to go depends mainly on the firm's specific motives and the willingness of the host stock market to accept the firm. By cross-listing and selling its shares on a foreign exchange, a firm typically tries to accomplish one or more of the following objectives:

- Improve the liquidity of its existing shares and support a liquid secondary market for new equity issues in foreign markets

- Increase its share price by overcoming mispricing in a segmented and illiquid home capital market

- Increase the firm's visibility and political acceptance to its customers, suppliers, creditors, and host governments

- Establish a liquid secondary market for shares used to acquire other firms in the host market and to compensate local management and employees of foreign subsidiaries[7]

Improving Liquidity

Quite often foreign investors have acquired a firm's shares through normal brokerage channels, even though the shares are not listed in the investor's home market or are not traded in the investor's preferred currency. Cross-listing is a way to encourage such investors to

---

[7]A recent example of this trading expansion opportunity is Kosmos Energy. Following the company's IPO in the United States in May 2011 (NYSE: KOS), the company listed its shares on the Ghanaian Stock Exchange. Ghana was the country in which the oil company had made its major discoveries and generated nearly all of its income.

continue to hold and trade these shares, thus marginally improving secondary market liquidity. This is usually done through ADRs.

Firms domiciled in countries with small illiquid capital markets often outgrow those markets and are forced to raise new equity abroad. Listing on a stock exchange in the market in which these funds are to be raised is typically required by the underwriters to ensure post-issue liquidity in the shares.

The first section of this chapter suggested that firms start by cross-listing in a less liquid market, followed by an equity issue in that market (see Exhibit 13.1). In order to maximize liquidity, however, the firm ideally should cross-list and issue equity in a more liquid market and eventually offer a global equity issue.

In order to maximize liquidity, it is desirable to cross-list and/or sell equity in the most liquid markets. Stock markets have, however, been subject to two major forces in recent years, which are changing their very behavior and liquidity—*demutualization* and *diversification*.

Demutualization is the ongoing process by which the small controlling seat owners on a number of exchanges have been giving up their exclusive powers. As a result, the actual ownership of the exchanges has become increasingly public. Diversification represents the growing diversity of both products (derivatives, currencies, etc.) and foreign companies/shares being listed. This has increased the activities and profitability of many exchanges while simultaneously offering a more global mix for reduced cost and increased service.

Stock Exchanges. With respect to stock exchanges, New York and London are clearly the most liquid. The recent merger of the New York Stock Exchange (NYSE) and Euronext, which itself was a merger of stock exchanges in Amsterdam, Brussels, and Paris, has extended the NYSE's lead over both the NASDAQ (New York) and the London Stock Exchange (LSE). Tokyo has declined a bit over the past 20 years in terms of trading value globally, as many foreign firms chose to delist from the Tokyo exchange. Few foreign firms remain cross-listed now in Tokyo. Deutsche Börse (Germany) has a fairly liquid market for domestic shares but a much lower level of liquidity for trading foreign shares. On the other hand, it is an appropriate target market for firms resident in the European Union, especially those that have adopted the euro. It is also used as a supplementary cross-listing location for firms that are already cross-listed on the LSE, NYSE, or NASDAQ.

Why are New York and London so dominant? They offer what global financial firms are looking for: plenty of skilled people, ready access to capital, good infrastructure, attractive regulatory and tax environments, and low levels of corruption. Location and the use of English, increasingly acknowledged as the language of global finance, are also important factors.

Electronic Trading. Most exchanges have moved heavily into electronic trading in recent years. In fact, the U.S. stock market is now a network of 50 different venues connected by an electronic system of published quotes and sales prices. This shift to electronic trading has had broad-reaching effects. For example, the role of the *specialist* on the floor of the NYSE has been greatly reduced with a corresponding reduction in employment by specialist firms. Specialists are no longer responsible for ensuring an orderly movement for their stocks, but they are still important in making more liquid markets for the less-traded shares. The same fate has reduced the importance of market makers on the London Stock Exchange (LSE).

Electronic trading has allowed hedge funds and other high frequency traders to dominate the market. High-frequency traders now account for 60% of daily volumes. Conversely, volume controlled by the NYSE fell from 80% in 2005 to 25% in 2010. Trades are executed immediately by computer. Spreads between buy and sell orders are now in decimal points as low as a penny a share instead of an eighth of a point. Liquidity has greatly increased but so has the risk of unexpected swings in prices. For example, on May 6, 2010, the Dow Jones Average fell 9.2% at one point but eventually recovered by the end of the day. During that single day of trading, nineteen billion shares were bought and sold.

Promoting Shares and Share Prices

Although cross-listing and equity issuance can occur together, their impacts are separable and significant in and of themselves.

Cross-Listing. Does merely cross-listing on a foreign stock exchange have a favorable impact on share prices? It depends on the degree to which markets are segmented.

If a firm's home capital market is segmented, the firm could theoretically benefit by cross-listing in a foreign market if that market values the firm or its industry more than does the home market. This was certainly the situation experienced by Novo when it listed on the NYSE in 1981 (see Chapter 12). However, most capital markets are becoming more integrated with global markets. Even emerging markets are less segmented than they were just a few years ago.

Equity Issuance. It is well known that the combined impact of a new equity issue undertaken simultaneously with a cross-listing has a more favorable impact on stock price than cross-listing alone. This occurs because the new issue creates an instantly enlarged shareholder base. Marketing efforts by the underwriters prior to the issue engender higher levels of visibility. Post-issue efforts by the underwriters to support at least the initial offering price also reduce investor risk.

Increasing Visibility and Political Acceptance

MNEs list in markets where they have substantial physical operations. Commercial objectives are to enhance corporate image, advertise trademarks and products, get better local press coverage, and become more familiar with the local financial community in order to raise working capital locally.

Political objectives might include the need to meet local ownership requirements for a multinational firm's foreign joint venture. Local ownership of the parent firm's shares might provide a forum for publicizing the firm's activities and how they support the host country.

Establish Liquid Secondary Markets

The establishment of a local liquid market for the firm's equity may aid in financing acquisitions and in the creation of stock-based management compensation programs for subsidiaries.

Funding Growth by Acquisitions. Firms that follow a strategy of growth by acquisition are always looking for creative alternatives to cash for funding these acquisitions. Offering their shares as partial payment is considerably more attractive if those shares have a liquid secondary market. In that case, the target's shareholders have an easy way to convert their acquired shares to cash if they prefer cash to a share swap. However, a share swap is often attractive as a tax-free exchange.

Compensating Management and Employees. If an MNE wishes to use stock options and share purchase compensation plans as a component of the compensation scheme for local management and employees, local listing on a liquid secondary market would enhance the perceived value of such plans. It should reduce transaction and foreign exchange costs for the local beneficiaries.

Barriers to Cross-Listing and Selling Equity Abroad

Although a firm may decide to cross-list and/or sell equity abroad, certain barriers exist. The most serious barriers are the future commitment to providing full and transparent disclosure of operating results and balance sheets as well as a continuous program of investor relations.

The Commitment to Disclosure and Investor Relations. A decision to cross-list must be balanced against the implied increased commitment to full disclosure and a continuing investor relations program. For firms resident in the Anglo-American markets, listing abroad might not appear to be much of a barrier. For example, the SEC's disclosure rules for listing in the United States are so stringent and costly that any other market's rules are mere child's play. Reversing the logic, however, non-U.S. firms must consider disclosure requirements carefully before cross-listing in the United States. Not only are the disclosure requirements breathtaking, timely quarterly information is also required by U.S. regulators and investors. As a result, the foreign firm must maintain a costly continuous investor relations program for its U.S. shareholders, including frequent "road shows" and the time-consuming personal involvement of top management.

Disclosure Is a Double-Edged Sword. The U.S. school of thought presumes that the worldwide trend toward more comprehensive, more transparent, and more standardized financial disclosure of operating results and financial positions will have the desirable effect of lowering the cost of equity capital. As we observed in 2002 and 2008, lack of full and accurate disclosure and poor transparency contributed to the U.S. stock market decline as investors fled to safer securities such as U.S. government bonds. This action increased the equity cost of capital for all firms.

The opposing school of thought—the other edge of the sword—is that the U.S. level of required disclosure is an onerous, costly burden. It discourages many potential listers, and thereby narrows the choice of securities available to U.S. investors at reasonable transaction costs.

Raising Debt Globally

The international debt markets offer the borrower a variety of different maturities, repayment structures, and currencies of denomination. The markets and their many different instruments vary by source of funding, pricing structure, maturity, and subordination or linkage to other debt and equity instruments.

Exhibit 13.9 provides an overview of the three basic categories described in the following sections, along with their primary components as issued or traded in the international debt markets today. As shown in the exhibit, the three major sources of debt funding on the international markets are the international bank loans and syndicated credits, euronote market, and international bond market.

Bank Loans and Syndications

International Bank Loans. International bank loans have traditionally been sourced in the eurocurrency loan markets. Eurodollar bank loans are also called "eurodollar credits" or simply "eurocredits." The latter title is broader because it encompasses nondollar loans in the eurocurrency loan market. The key factor attracting both depositors and borrowers to the eurocurrency loan market is the narrow interest rate spread within that market. The difference between deposit and loan rates is often less than 1%.

EXHIBIT 13.9   International Debt Markets and Instruments

International Bank Loans and Syndicated Credits
(floating-rate, short- to medium-term)
→ International Bank Loans
→ Eurocredits
→ Syndicated Credits

Euronote Market
(floating-rate, short- to medium-term)
→ Euronotes and Euronote Facilities
→ Eurocommercial Paper (ECP)
→ Euro Medium-Term Notes (EMTNs)

International Bond Market
(fixed and floating-rate medium- to long-term)
→ Eurobond
• straight fixed-rate issue
• floating-rate note (FRN)
• equity-related issue
→ Foreign Bond

Eurocredits. *Eurocredits* are bank loans to MNEs, sovereign governments, international institutions, and banks denominated in eurocurrencies and extended by banks in countries other than the country in whose currency the loan is denominated. The basic borrowing interest rate for eurocredits has long been tied to the London Interbank Offered Rate (LIBOR), which is the deposit rate applicable to interbank loans within London. Eurocredits are lent for both short- and medium-term maturities, with maturities for six months or less regarded as routine. Most eurocredits are for a fixed term with no provision for early repayment.

Syndicated Credits. The syndication of loans has enabled banks to spread the risk of very large loans among a number of banks. Syndication is particularly important because many large MNEs need credit in excess of a single bank's loan limit. A *syndicated bank credit* is arranged by a lead bank on behalf of its client. Before finalizing the loan agreement, the lead bank seeks the participation of a group of banks, with each participant providing a portion of the total funds needed. The lead bank will work with the borrower to determine the amount of the total credit, the floating-rate base and spread over the base rate, maturity, and fee structure for managing the participating banks. The periodic expenses of the syndicated credit are composed of two elements:

1. Actual interest expense of the loan, normally stated as a spread in basis points over a variable-rate base such as LIBOR

2. Commitment fees paid on any unused portions of the credit—the spread paid over LIBOR by the borrower is considered the risk premium, reflecting the general business and financial risk applicable to the borrower's repayment capability

Euronote Market

The *euronote market* is the collective term used to describe short- to medium-term debt instruments sourced in the eurocurrency markets. Although a multitude of differentiated financial products exists, they can be divided into two major groups—underwritten facilities and nonunderwritten facilities. *Underwritten facilities* are used for the sale of euronotes in a number of different forms. *Nonunderwritten facilities* are used for the sale and distribution of euro-commercial paper (ECP) and euro medium-term notes (EMTNs).

Euronotes and Euronote Facilities.   A major development in international money markets was the establishment of underwriting facilities for the sale of short-term, negotiable, promissory notes — *euronotes*. Among the facilities for their issuance were *revolving underwriting facilities* (rufs), *note issuance facilities* (nifs), and *standby note issuance facilities* (snifs). These facilities were provided by international investment and commercial banks. The euronote was a substantially cheaper source of short-term funds than were syndicated loans because the securitized and underwritten form allowed the ready establishment of liquid secondary markets, allowing the notes to be placed directly with the investing public. The banks received substantial fees initially for their underwriting and placement services.

Eurocommercial Paper (ECP).   *Eurocommercial paper* (ECP), like commercial paper issued in domestic markets around the world, is a short-term debt obligation (nonunderwritten) of a corporation or bank. Maturities are typically one, three, and six months. The paper is sold normally at a discount or occasionally with a stated coupon. Although the market is capable of supporting issues in any major currency, over 90% of issues outstanding are denominated in U.S. dollars.

Euro Medium-Term Notes (EMTNs).   The *euro medium-term note (EMTN)* market effectively bridges the maturity gap between ECP and the longer-term and less flexible international bond. Although many of these notes were initially underwritten, most EMTNs are now nonunderwritten.

The rapid initial growth of the EMTN market followed directly on the heels of the same basic instrument that began in the U.S. domestic market when the U.S. SEC instituted *SEC Rule #415*, allowing companies to obtain *shelf registrations* for debt issues. Once such a registration was obtained, the corporation could issue notes on a continuous basis without the need to obtain new registrations for each additional issue. This, in turn, allowed a firm to sell short- and medium-term notes through a much cheaper and more flexible issuance facility than ordinary bonds.

The EMTN's basic characteristics are similar to those of a bond, with principal, maturity, coupon structures, and rates being comparable. The EMTN's typical maturities range from as little as nine months to a maximum of 10 years. Coupons are typically paid semiannually, and coupon rates are comparable to similar bond issues. The EMTN does, however, have three unique characteristics: 1) the EMTN is a facility, allowing continuous issuance over a period of time, unlike a bond issue that is essentially sold all at once; 2) because EMTNs are sold continuously, in order to make debt service (coupon redemption) manageable, coupons are paid on set calendar dates regardless of the date of issuance; 3) EMTNs are issued in relatively small denominations, from $2 million to $5 million, making medium-term debt acquisition much more flexible than the large minimums customarily needed in the international bond markets.

International Bond Market

The international bond market sports a rich array of innovative instruments created by imaginative investment bankers who are unfettered by the usual controls and regulations governing domestic capital markets. Indeed, the international bond market rivals the international banking market in terms of the quantity and cost of funds provided to international borrowers. All international bonds fall within two generic classifications, eurobonds and foreign bonds. The distinction between categories is based on whether the borrower is a domestic or a foreign resident, and whether the issue is denominated in the local currency or a foreign currency.

Eurobonds. A *Eurobond* is underwritten by an international syndicate of banks and other securities firms, and is sold exclusively in countries other than the country in whose currency the issue is denominated. For example, a bond issued by a firm resident in the United States, denominated in U.S. dollars, and sold to investors in Europe and Japan (but not to investors in the United States), is a eurobond.

Eurobonds are issued by MNEs, large domestic corporations, sovereign governments, governmental enterprises, and international institutions. They are offered simultaneously in a number of different national capital markets, but not in the capital market or to residents of the country in whose currency the bond is denominated. Almost all eurobonds are in bearer form with call provisions (the ability of the issuer to call the bond in prior to maturity) and sinking funds (required accumulations of funds by the firms to assure repayment of the obligation).

The syndicate that offers a new issue of eurobonds might be composed of underwriters from a number of countries, including European banks, foreign branches of U.S. banks, banks from offshore financial centers, investment and merchant banks, and nonbank securities firms. There are three types of eurobond issues:

- **The Straight Fixed-Rate Issue**. The *straight fixed-rate issue* is structured like most domestic bonds, with a fixed coupon, set maturity date, and full principal repayment upon final maturity. Coupons are normally paid annually, rather than semiannually, primarily because the bonds are bearer bonds and annual coupon redemption is more convenient for the holders.

- **The Floating-Rate Note**. The *floating-rate note (FRN)* normally pays a semiannual coupon that is determined using a variable-rate base. A typical coupon would be set at some fixed spread over LIBOR. This structure, like most variable-rate interest-bearing instruments, was designed to allow investors to shift more of the interest-rate risk of a financial investment to the borrower. Although many FRNs have fixed maturities, in recent years many issues are perpetuities, with no principal repayment, taking on the characteristics of equity.

- **The Equity-Related Issue**. The *equity-related international bond* resembles the straight fixed-rate issue in practically all price and payment characteristics, with the added feature that it is convertible to stock prior to maturity at a specified price per share (or alternatively, number of shares per bond). The borrower is able to issue debt with lower coupon payments due to the added value of the equity conversion feature.

Foreign Bonds. A *foreign bond* is underwritten by a syndicate composed of members from a single country, sold principally within that country, and denominated in the currency of that country. The issuer, however, is from another country. A bond issued by a firm resident in Sweden, denominated in U.S. dollars, and sold in the United States to U.S. investors by U.S. investment bankers, is a foreign bond. Foreign bonds have nicknames: foreign bonds sold in the United States are *Yankee bonds*; foreign bonds sold in Japan are *Samurai bonds*; and foreign bonds sold in the United Kingdom are *Bulldogs*.

Unique Characteristics of Eurobond Markets

Although the eurobond market evolved at about the same time as the eurodollar market, the two markets exist for different reasons, and each could exist independently of the other. The eurobond market owes its existence to several unique factors: the absence of regulatory interference, less stringent disclosure practices, favorable tax treatment, and ratings.

Absence of Regulatory Interference. National governments often impose tight controls on foreign issuers of securities denominated in the local currency and sold within their national boundaries. However, governments in general have less stringent limitations for securities denominated in foreign currencies and sold within their markets to holders of those foreign currencies. In effect, eurobond sales fall outside the regulatory domain of any single nation.

Less Stringent Disclosure.   Disclosure requirements in the eurobond market are much less stringent than those of the U.S. Securities and Exchange Commission (SEC) for sales within the United States. U.S. firms often find that the registration costs of a eurobond offering are less than those of a domestic issue and that less time is needed to bring a new issue to market. Non-U.S. firms often prefer eurodollar bonds over bonds sold within the United States because they do not wish to undergo the costs and disclosure needed to register with the SEC. However, the SEC has relaxed disclosure requirements for certain private placements (Rule #144A), which has improved the attractiveness of the U.S. domestic bond and equity markets.

Favorable Tax Treatment.   Eurobonds offer tax anonymity and flexibility. Interest paid on eurobonds is generally not subject to an income withholding tax. As one might expect, eurobond interest is not always reported to tax authorities. Eurobonds are usually issued in bearer form, meaning that the name and country of residence of the owner is not on the certificate. To receive interest, the bearer cuts an interest coupon from the bond and turns it in at a banking institution listed on the issue as a paying agent. European investors are accustomed to the privacy provided by bearer bonds and are very reluctant to purchase registered bonds, which require holders to reveal their names before they receive interest. It follows, then, that bearer bond status is often tied to tax avoidance.

Access to debt capital is obviously impacted by everything from the legal and tax environments to basic societal norms. Indeed, even religion plays a part in the use and availability of debt capital. *Global Finance in Practice 13.2* illustrates one area rarely seen by Westerners, *Islamic finance*.

GLOBAL FINANCE IN PRACTICE 13.2

Islamic Finance

Muslims, the followers of Islam, now make up roughly one-fourth of the world's population. The countries of the world that are predominantly Muslim create roughly 10% of global GDP and comprise a large share of the emerging marketplace. Islamic law speaks to many dimensions of the individual and organizational behaviors for its practitioners—including business. Islamic finance, the specific area of our interest, imposes a number of restrictions on Muslims, which have a dramatic impact on the funding and structure of Muslim businesses.

The Islamic form of finance is as old as the religion of Islam itself. The basis for all Islamic finance lies in the principles of the Sharia, or Islamic Law, which is taken from the Qur'an. Observance of these principles precipitates restrictions on business and finance practices as follows:

■ Making money from money is not permissible

■ Earning interest is prohibited

■ Profit and loss should be shared

■ Speculation (gambling) is prohibited

■ Investments should support only halal activities

For the conduct of business, the key to understanding the Sharia prohibition on earning interest is to understand that profitability from traditional Western investments arises from the returns associated with carrying risk. For example, a traditional Western bank may extend a loan to a business. It is agreed that the bank will receive its principal and interest in return regardless of the ultimate profitability of the business (the borrower). In fact, the debt is paid off before returns to equity occur. Similarly, an individual who deposits their money in a Western bank will receive an interest earning on their deposit regardless of the profitability of the bank and of the bank's associated investments.

Under Sharia law, however, an Islamic bank cannot pay interest to depositors. Therefore, the depositors in an Islamic bank are, in effect, shareholders (much like credit unions in the West), and the returns they receive are a function of the profitability of the bank's investments. Their returns cannot be fixed or guaranteed, because that would break the principle of profit and loss being shared.

Recently, however, a number of Islamic banking institutions have opened in Europe and North America. A Muslim now can enter into a sequence of purchases that allows him to purchase a home without departing from Islamic principles. The buyer selects the property, which is then purchased by an Islamic bank. The bank in turn resells the house to the prospective buyer at a higher price. The buyer is allowed to pay off the purchase over a series of years. Although the difference in purchase prices is, by Western thinking, implicit interest, this structure does conform to Sharia law. Unfortunately, in both the United States and the United Kingdom, the difference is not a tax deductible expense for the homeowner as interest would be.

Ratings. Rating agencies, such as Moody's and Standard and Poor's (S&P), provide ratings for selected international bonds for a fee. Moody's ratings for international bonds imply the same creditworthiness as for domestic bonds of U.S. issuers. Moody's limits its evaluation to the issuer's ability to obtain the necessary currency to repay the issue according to the original terms of the bond. The agency excludes any assessment of risk to the investor caused by changing exchange rates.

Moody's rates international bonds at request of the issuer. Based on supporting financial statements and other material obtained from the issuer, it makes a preliminary rating and then informs the issuer who has an opportunity to comment. After Moody's determines its final rating, the issuer may decide not to have the rating published. Consequently, a disproportionately large number of published international ratings fall into the highest categories, since issuers that receive a lower rating do not allow publication.

Purchasers of eurobonds do not rely only on bond-rating services or on detailed analyses of financial statements. The general reputation of the issuing corporation and its underwriters has been a major factor in obtaining favorable terms. For this reason, larger and better-known MNEs, state enterprises, and sovereign governments are able to obtain the lowest interest rates. Firms whose names are better known to the general public, possibly because they manufacture consumer goods, are often believed to have an advantage over equally qualified firms whose products are less widely known.

Summary Points

- Designing a capital sourcing strategy requires management to design a long-run financial strategy. The firm must then choose among the various alternative paths to achieve its goals, including where to cross-list its shares, and where to issue new equity, and in what form.

- The domestic theory of optimal financial structures needs to be modified by four variables in order to accommodate the case of the MNE: 1) the availability of capital; 2) diversification of cash flows; 3) foreign exchange risk; and 4) the expectations of international portfolio investors.

- A multinational firm's marginal cost of capital is constant for considerable ranges of its capital budget. This statement is not true for most small domestic firms because they do not have access to the national equity or debt markets.

- By diversifying cash flows internationally, the MNE may be able to achieve the same kind of reduction in cash flow variability that portfolio investors receive from diversifying their security holdings internationally.

- When a firm issues foreign currency-denominated debt, its effective cost equals the after-tax cost of repaying the principal and interest in terms of the firm's own currency. This amount includes the nominal cost of principal and interest in foreign currency terms, adjusted for any foreign exchange gains or losses.

- There is a variety of different equity pathways that firms may choose between when pursuing global sources of equity, including euroequity issues, direct foreign issuances, depositary receipt programs, and private placements.

- Depositary receipt programs, either American or Global, provide an extremely effective way for firms from outside of the established industrial country markets to improve the liquidity of their existing shares, or issue new shares.

- Private placement is a growing segment of the market, allowing firms from emerging markets to raise capital in the largest of capital markets with limited disclosure and cost.

- The international debt markets offer the borrower a variety of different maturities, repayment structures, and currencies of denomination. The markets and their many different instruments vary by source of funding, pricing structure, maturity, and subordination or linkage to other debt and equity instruments.

- The three major sources of debt funding on the international markets are international bank loans and syndicated credits, the euronote market, and the international bond market.

- Eurocurrency markets serve two valuable purposes: 1) eurocurrency deposits are an efficient and convenient money market device for holding excess corporate liquidity, and 2) the eurocurrency market is a major source of short-term bank loans to finance corporate working capital needs, including the financing of imports and exports.

MINI-CASE

Petrobrás of Brazil and the Cost of Capital[1]

The national oil company of Brazil, Petrobrás, suffered from an ailment common in emerging markets—a high and uncompetitive cost of capital. Despite being widely considered the global leader in deepwater technology (the ability to drill and develop oil and gas fields more than a mile below the ocean's surface), unless it could devise a strategy to lower its cost of capital, it would be unable to exploit its true organizational competitive advantage.

Many market analysts argued that the Brazilian company should follow the strategy employed by a number of Mexican companies and buy its way out of its dilemma. If Petrobrás were to acquire one of the many independent North American oil and gas companies, it might transform itself from being wholly "Brazilian" to partially "American" in the eyes of capital markets, and possibly lower its weighted average cost of capital (WACC) to between 6% and 8%.

Petróleo Brasileiro S.A. (Petrobrás) was an integrated oil and gas company founded in 1954 by the Brazilian government as the national oil company of Brazil. The company was listed publicly in São Paulo in 1997 and on the New York Stock Exchange (NYSE: PBR) in 2000. Despite the equity listings, the Brazilian government continued to be the controlling shareholder, with 33% of the total capital and 55% of the voting shares. As the national oil company of Brazil, the company's singular purpose was the reduction of Brazil's dependency on imported oil. A side effect of this focus, however, had been a lack of international diversification. Many of the company's critics argued that being both Brazilian and undiversified internationally resulted in an uncompetitive cost of capital.

Need for Diversification

Petrobrás in 2002 was the largest company in Brazil, and the largest publicly traded oil company in Latin America. It was not, however, international in its operations. This inherent lack of international diversification was apparent to international investors, who assigned the company the same country risk factors and premiums they did to all other Brazilian companies. The result was a cost of capital in 2002, as seen in Exhibit A, that was 6% higher than the other firms shown.

Petrobrás embarked on a globalization strategy, with several major transactions heading up the process. In December 2001, Repsol-YPF of Argentina and Petrobrás concluded an exchange of operating assets valued at $500 million. In the exchange, Petrobrás received 99% interest in the Eg3 S.A. service station chain, while Repsol-YPF gained a 30% stake in a refinery, a 10% stake in an offshore oil field, and a fuel resale right to 230 service stations in Brazil. The agreement included an eight-year guarantee against currency risks.

In October 2002, Petrobrás purchased Perez Companc (Pecom) of Argentina. Pecom had quickly come into play following the Argentine financial crisis in January 2002. Although Pecom had significant international reserves and production capability, the combined forces of a devalued Argentine peso, a largely dollar-denominated debt portfolio, and a multitude of Argentine government regulations that hindered its ability to hold and leverage hard currency resources, the company had moved quickly to find a buyer to refund its financial structure. Petrobrás took advantage of the opportunity. Pecom's ownership had been split between its original controlling family owners and their foundation, 58.6%, and public flotation of the remaining 41.4%.

[1]Copyright © 2008 Thunderbird School of Global Management. All rights reserved. This case was prepared by Professor Michael H. Moffett for the purpose of classroom discussion only and not to indicate either effective or ineffective management.

EXHIBIT A   Petrobrás' Uncompetitive Cost of Capital

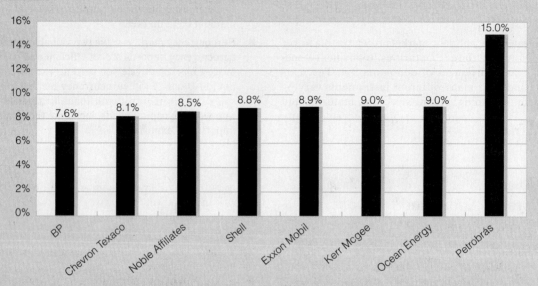

Source: MorganStanley Research, January 18, 2002, p. 5.

Petrobrás had purchased the controlling interest, the full 58.6% interest, outright from the family.

Over the next three years, Petrobrás focused on restructuring much of its debt (and the debt it had acquired via the Pecom acquisition) and investing in its own growth. But progress toward revitalizing its financial structure came slowly, and by 2005 there was renewed discussion of a new equity issuance to increase the firm's equity capital.[2] But at what cost? What was the company's cost of capital?

Country Risk

Exhibit A presented the cost of capital of a number of major oil and gas companies across the world, including Petrobrás in 2002. This comparison could occur only if all capital costs were calculated in a common currency, in this case, the U.S. dollar. The global oil and gas markets had long been considered "dollar-denominated," and any company operating in these markets, regardless of where it actually operated in the world, was considered to have the dollar as its functional currency. Once that company listed its shares in a U.S. equity market, the dollarization of its capital costs became even more accepted.

But what was the cost of capital—in dollar terms—for a Brazilian business? Brazil has a long history of bouts with high inflation, economic instability, and currency devaluations and depreciations (depending on the regime *de jure*).

One of the leading indicators of the global market's opinion of Brazilian country risk was the *sovereign spread*, the additional yield or cost of dollar funds that the Brazilian government had to pay on global markets over and above that which the U.S. Treasury paid to borrow dollar funds. As illustrated in Exhibit B, the Brazilian sovereign spread had been both high and volatile over the past decade.[3] The spread was sometimes as low as 400 basis points (4.0%), as in recent years, or as high as 2,400 basis points (24%), during the 2002 financial crisis in which the real was first devalued then floated. And that was merely the cost of debt for the government of Brazil. How was this sovereign spread reflected in the cost of debt and equity for a Brazilian company like Petrobrás?

One approach to the estimation of Petrobrás' cost of debt in U.S. dollar terms ($k_d^\$$) was to build it up: the government of Brazil's cost of dollar funds adjusted for a private corporate credit spread.

$$k_d^\$ = \begin{matrix} \text{U.S. Treasury} \\ \text{risk-free rate} \end{matrix} + \begin{matrix} \text{Brazilian} \\ \text{sovereign} \\ \text{spread} \end{matrix} + \begin{matrix} \text{Petrobrás} \\ \text{credit} \\ \text{spread} \end{matrix}$$

$$k_d^\$ = 4.000\% + 4.000\% + 1.000\% = 9.000\%$$

If the U.S. Treasury risk-free rate was estimated using the Treasury 10-year bond rate (yield), a base rate

[2]By 2005, the company's financial strategy was showing significant diversification. Total corporate funding was well-balanced: bonds, $4 billion; BNDES (bonds issued under the auspices of a Brazilian economic development agency), $3 billion; project finance, $5 billion; other, $4 billion.

[3]The measure of sovereign spread presented in Exhibit B is that calculated by JPMorgan in its Emerging Market Bond Index Plus (EMBI+) index. This is the most widely used measure of country risk by practitioners.

EXHIBIT B   The Brazilian Sovereign Spread

Basis Point Spread over United States

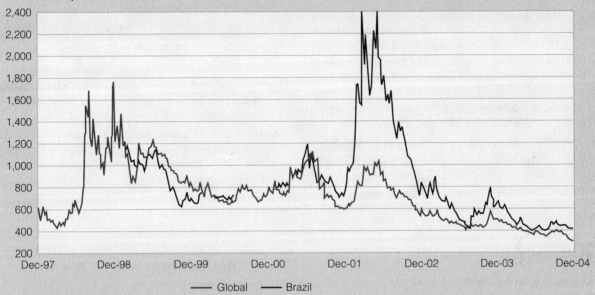

Source: JPMorgan's EMBI+ Spread, as quoted by Latin Focus, www.latin-focus.com/latinfocus/countries/ brazilbisprd.htm, August 2005.

in August 2005 could be 4.0%. The Brazilian sovereign spread, as seen in Exhibit B, appeared to be 400 basis points, or an additional 4.0%. Even if Petrobrás' credit spread was only 1.0%, the company's current cost of dollar debt would be 9%. This cost was clearly higher than the cost of debt for most of the world's oil majors who were probably paying only 5% on average for debt in late 2005.

Petrobrás' cost of equity would be similarly affected by the country risk-adjusted risk-free rate of interest. Using a simple expression of the Capital Asset Pricing Model (CAPM) to estimate the company's cost of equity capital in dollar terms ($k_e^\$$):

$$k_e^\$ = \text{risk-free rate}$$
$$+ (\beta_{\text{Petrobrás}} \times \text{market risk premium}) = 8.000\%$$
$$+ (1.10 \times 5.500\%) = 14.05\%$$

This calculation assumed the same risk-free rate as used in the cost of debt previously, with a beta (NYSE basis) of 1.10 and a market risk premium of 5.500%. Even with these relatively conservative assumptions (many would argue that the company's beta was actually higher or lower, and that the market risk premium was 6.0% or higher), the company's cost of equity was 14%.

Finally, the corporate weighted average cost of capital (WACC) could be calculated:

$$\text{WACC} = (\text{debt/capital} \times k_d^\$ \times (1 - \text{tax rate})) +$$
$$(\text{equity/capital} \times k_e^\$)$$

Assuming a long-term target capital structure of one-third debt and two-thirds equity and an effective corporate tax rate of 28% (after special tax concessions, surcharges, and incentives for the Brazilian oil and gas industry), Petrobrás' WACC was estimated at a little over 11.5%:

$$\text{WACC} = (0.333 \times 9.000\% \times 0.72) +$$
$$(0.667 \times 14.050\%) = 11.529\%$$

So, after all of the efforts to internationally diversify the firm and internationalize its cost of capital, why was Petrobrás' cost of capital still so much higher than its global counterparts? Not only was the company's weighted average cost of capital high compared to other major global players, this was the same high cost of capital used as the basic discount rate in evaluating many potential investments and acquisitions.

A number of the investment banking firms that covered Petrobrás noted that the company's share price had shown a very high correlation with the EMBI+ sovereign spread for Brazil (shown in Exhibit B), hovering around 0.84 for a number of years. Similarly, Petrobrás' share price was also historically correlated—inversely—with the Brazilian reais/U.S. dollar exchange rate. This correlation had averaged −0.88 over the 2000–2004 period. Finally, the question of whether Petrobrás was considered an oil company or a Brazilian company was also somewhat in question:

Petrobrás' stock performance appears more highly correlated to the Brazilian equity market and credit spreads based on historical trading patterns, suggesting that one's view on the direction of the broad Brazilian market is important in making an investment decision on the company. If the historical trend were to hold, an improvement in Brazilian risk perception should provide a fillip to Petrobrás' share price performance.

—"Petrobrás: A Diamond in the Rough,"
JPMorgan Latin American Equity Research,
June 18, 2004, pp. 26–27.

CASE QUESTIONS

1. Why do you think Petrobrás' cost of capital is so high? Are there better ways, or other ways, of calculating its weighted average cost of capital?

2. Does this method of using the sovereign spread also compensate for currency risk?

3. The final quote on "one's view on the direction of the broad Brazilian market" suggests that potential investors consider the relative attractiveness of Brazil in their investment decision. How does this perception show up in the calculation of the company's cost of capital?

4. Is the cost of capital really a relevant factor in the competitiveness and strategy of a company like Petrobrás? Does the corporate cost of capital really affect competitiveness?

Questions

1. **Sourcing Global Debt and Equity Markets.** What is the sequence of strategies used to source both equity and debt capital globally? Should a firm start by sourcing global debt or equity markets?

2. **Depositary Receipts—Definitions.** Define the following terms:
   a. ADRs
   b. GDRs
   c. Sponsored depositary receipts
   d. Unsponsored depositary receipts

3. **Depository Receipts (DRs).** What are the benefits of DRs to issuers and investors? What are the risks associated with delisting DRs?

4. **Cross-Listing.** What are the main benefits and disadvantages to firms that cross-list their shares on multiple stock markets?

5. **GDR and Domestic Share Prices.** Should there be a strong co-movement of GDR price with that of the underlying domestic share?

6. **Barriers to Cross-Listing.** What are the main barriers to cross-listing abroad?

7. **Alternative Instruments.** What are five alternative instruments that can be used to source equity in global markets?

8. **Directed Public Share Issue.**
   a. What is a "directed public share issue?"
   b. What are some of the motivations for directed public share issues?

9. **Euroequity Public Share Issue.** What is a "euroequity public share issue?"

10. **Private Placement under SEC Rule 144A.**
    a. What is SEC Rule 144A?

b. Why might a foreign firm choose to sell its equity in the United States under SEC Rule 144A?

11. **Private Equity Funds.**
    a. What is a private equity fund?
    b. How do private equity funds differ from traditional venture capital firms?
    c. How do private equity funds raise their own capital, and how does this action give them a competitive advantage over local banks and investment funds?

12. **Optimal Capital Structure Objective.** What, in simple wording, is the objective when seeking an optimal capital structure?

13. **Varying Debt Proportions.** As debt in a firm's capital structure is increased from no debt to a significant proportion of debt (say, 60%), what tends to happen to the cost of debt, the cost of equity, and the overall weighted average cost of capital?

14. **Availability of Capital.** How does the availability of capital influence the theory of optimal capital structure for a multinational enterprise?

15. **Marginal Cost.** Define "marginal" weighted average cost of capital.

16. **Diversified Cash Flows.** If a multinational firm is able to diversify its sources of cash inflow so that it receives those flows from several countries and in several currencies, do you think that diversification tends to increase or decrease its weighted average cost of capital?

17. **Ex-Post Cost of Borrowing.** Many firms in many countries borrow at nominal costs that later prove to be very different. For example, Deutsche Bank recently borrowed at a nominal cost of 9.59% per annum, but later that debt was selling to yield 7.24%. At the same time, the Kingdom of Thailand borrowed

at a nominal cost of 8.70% but later found the debt was sold in the market at a yield of 11.87%. What caused these changes, and what might management do to benefit (as Deutsche Bank did) rather than suffer (as the Kingdom of Thailand did)?

18. **Local Norms.** Should foreign subsidiaries of multinational firms conform to the capital structure norms of the host country or to the norms of their parent's country? Discuss.

19. **Argentina.** In January 2002, the government of Argentina broke away from its currency board system that had tied the peso to the U.S. dollar and devalued the peso from APs1.0000/$ to APs1.40000. This caused some Argentine firms with dollar-denominated debt to go bankrupt. Should a U.S. or European parent in good financial health "rescue" its Argentine subsidiary that would otherwise go bankrupt because of the inept nature of Argentine political and economic management in the four or five years prior to January 2002? Assume the parent has not entered into a formal agreement to guarantee the debt of its Argentine subsidiary.

20. **Internal Financing.** What is the difference between "internal" financing and "external" financing for a subsidiary? List three types of internal financing and three types of external financing available to a foreign subsidiary.

21. **Eurodollar and Euro Deposits.** What is the difference between eurodollar and euro? What is the reason for the international expansion of the eurodollar and euro markets during the last few decades?

22. **International Debt Instruments.** Bank borrowing has been the long-time manner by which corporations and governments borrowed funds for short periods of time. What then, is an advantage over bank borrowing of each of the following:
    a. Syndicated loans
    b. Euronotes
    c. Euro-commercial paper
    d. Euro medium-term notes
    e. International bonds

23. **Eurobond versus Foreign Bonds.** What is the difference between a "eurobond" and a "foreign bond" and why do two types of international bonds exist?

Problems

1. **JPMorgan: Petrobrás' WACC.** JPMorgan's Latin American Equity Research department produced the following WACC calculation for Petrobrás of Brazil versus Lukoil of Russia in their June 18, 2004, report. Evaluate the methodology and assumptions used in the calculation. Assume a 28% tax rate for both companies.

	Petrobrás	Lukoil
Risk-free rate	4.8%	4.8%
Sovereign risk	7.0%	3.0%
Equity risk premium	4.5%	5.7%
Market cost of equity	16.3%	13.5%
Beta (relevered)	0.87	1.04
Cost of debt	8.4%	6.8%
Debt/capital ratio	0.333	0.475
WACC	14.7%	12.3%

2. **UNIBANCO: Petrobrás' WACC.** UNIBANCO estimated the weighted average cost of capital for Petrobrás to be 13.2% in Brazilian reais in August of 2004. Evaluate the methodology and assumptions used in the calculation.

Risk-free rate	4.5%	Cost of debt (after-tax)	5.7%
Beta	0.99	Tax rate	34%
Market premium	6.0%	Debt/total capital	40%
Country risk premium	5.5%	WACC (R$)	13.2%
Cost of equity ($)	15.9%		

3. **Citigroup SmithBarney (Dollar): Petrobrás' WACC.** Citigroup regularly performs a U.S. dollar-based discount cash flow (DCF) valuation of Petrobrás in its coverage. That DCF analysis requires the use of a discount rate based on the company's weighted average cost of capital. Evaluate the methodology and assumptions used in the 2003 Actual and 2004 Estimates of Petrobrás' WACC below.

Capital Cost Components	July 28, 2005		March 8, 2005	
	2003A	2004E	2003A	2004E
Risk-free rate	9.400%	9.400%	9.000%	9.000%
Levered beta	1.07	1.09	1.08	1.10
Risk premium	5.500%	5.500%	5.500%	5.500%
Cost of equity	15.285%	15.395%	14.940%	15.050%
Cost of debt	8.400%	8.400%	9.000%	9.000%
Tax rate	28.500%	27.100%	28.500%	27.100%
Cost of debt, after-tax	6.006%	6.124%	6.435%	6.561%
Debt/capital ratio	32.700%	32.400%	32.700%	32.400%
Equity/capital ratio	67.300%	67.600%	67.300%	67.600%
WACC	12.20%	12.30%	12.10%	12.30%

4. **Citigroup SmithBarney (Reais).** In a report dated June 17, 2003, Citigroup SmithBarney calculated a WACC for Petrobrás denominated in Brazilian reais (R$). Evaluate the methodology and assumptions used in this cost of capital calculation.

Risk-free rate (Brazilian C-Bond)	9.90%
Petrobrás levered beta	1.40
Market risk premium	5.50%
Cost of equity	17.60%
Cost of debt	10.00%
Brazilian corporate tax rate	34.00%
Long-term debt ratio (% of capital)	50.60%
WACC (R$)	12.00%

5. **BBVA Investment Bank: Petrobrás' WACC.** BBVA utilized a rather innovative approach to dealing with both country and currency risk in their December 20, 2004, report on Petrobrás. Evaluate the methodology and assumptions used in this cost of capital calculation.

Cost of Capital Component	2003 Estimate	2004 Estimate
U.S. 10-year risk-free rate (in $)	4.10%	4.40%
Country risk premium (in $)	6.00%	4.00%
Petrobrás premium "adjustment"	1.00%	1.00%
Petrobrás risk-free rate (in $)	9.10%	7.40%
Market risk premium (in $)	6.00%	6.00%
Petrobrás beta (β)	0.80	0.80
Cost of equity (in $)	13.90%	12.20%
Projected 10-year currency devaluation	2.50%	2.50%
Cost of equity (in R$)	16.75%	14.44%
Petrobrás cost of debt after-tax (in R$)	5.50%	5.50%
Long-term equity ratio (% of capital)	69%	72%
Long-term debt ratio (% of capital)	31%	28%
WACC (in R$)	13.30%	12.00%

6. **Petrobrás' WACC Comparison.** The various estimates of the cost of capital for Petrobrás of Brazil appear to be very different, but are they? Organize your answers to Problems 1–5 into those whose costs of capital are in U.S. dollars versus Brazilian reais. Use the estimates for 2004 shown in Problem 5 as the basis of comparison.

7. **Al-Niger Co. (Nigeria).** Al-Niger Co., an oil firm headquartered in Abuja (Nigeria), borrows €10,000,000 for one year at an annual rate of interest of 8%.

a. What is the cost of this debt in Nigerian nairas (NGN) if the euro depreciates from NGN225/€ to NGN200/€ over the year?
b. What is the cost of this debt in Nigerian nairas (NGN) if the euro appreciates from NGN 225/€ to NGN250/€ over the year?

8. **McDougan Associates (USA).** McDougan Associates, a U.S.-based investment partnership, borrows €80,000,000 at a time when the exchange rate is $1.3460/€. The entire principal is to be repaid in three years, and interest is 6.250% per annum, paid annually in euros. The euro is expected to depreciate against the dollar at 3% per annum. What is the effective cost of this loan for McDougan?

9. **Sunrise Manufacturing, Inc.** Sunrise Manufacturing, Inc., a U.S. multinational company, has the following debt components in its consolidated capital section. Sunrise's finance staff estimates their cost of equity to be 20%. Current exchange rates are listed below. Income taxes are 30% around the world after allowing for credits. Calculate Sunrise's weighted average cost of capital. Are any assumptions implicit in your calculation?

Assumption	Value
Tax rate	30.00%
10-year euro bonds (€)	6,000,000
20-year yen bonds (¥)	750,000,000
Spot rate ($/€)	1.2400
Spot rate ($/£)	1.8600
Spot rate (¥/$)	109.00

10. **ChocTurk Co.** ChocTurk Co. is a Turkish chocolate manufacturer that exports its products to neighboring European nations. Since its clients are mostly European, ChocTurk Co. evaluates all business results and financial transactions in euros. It needs to borrow €5,000,000 or the foreign currency equivalent for four years. It decides to issue bonds, making one annual payment at the end of each year. The following are the alternatives:

a. Sell Japanese yen bonds at par yielding 2% per annum. The current exchange rate is ¥136/€, and the yen is expected to strengthen against the dollar by 3% per annum.
b. Sell bonds denominated in pounds sterling at par yielding 5% per annum. The current exchange rate is £0.7350/€, and the pound is expected to weaken against the euro by 4% per annum.
c. Sell euro bonds at par yielding 4% per annum.

Which course of action do you recommend ChocTurk Co. take and why?

Problem 12.

A-Malaysia (accounts in ringgits)		A-Mexico (accounts in pesos)	
Long-term debt	RM11,400,000	Long-term debt	Ps20,000,000
Shareholders' equity	RM15,200,000	Shareholders' equity	Ps60,000,000

Adamantine Architectonics (Nonconsolidated Balance Sheet—Selected Items Only)			
Investment in subsidiaries		Parent long-term debt	$12,000,000
In A-Malaysia	$4,000,000	Common stock	5,000,000
In A-Mexico	6,000,000	Retained earnings	20,000,000
Current exchange rates:			
Malaysia	RM3.80/$		
Mexico	Ps10/$		

11. **Petrol Ibérico.** Petrol Ibérico, a European gas company, is borrowing $650,000,000 via a syndicated eurocredit for six years at 80 basis points over LIBOR. LIBOR for the loan will be reset every six months. The funds will be provided by a syndicate of eight leading investment bankers, which will charge up-front fees totaling 1.2% of the principal amount. What is the effective interest cost for the first year if LIBOR is 4.00% for the first six months and 4.20% for the second six months.

12. **Adamantine Architectonics.** Adamantine Architectonics consists of a U.S. parent and wholly owned subsidiaries in Malaysia (A-Malaysia) and Mexico (A-Mexico). Selected portions of their nonconsolidated balance sheets, translated into U.S. dollars, are shown in the table at the top of this page. What are the debt and equity proportions in Adamantine's consolidated balance sheet?

13. **Inter-KSA (Saudi Arabia).** Inter-KSA is a Saudi Arabian airline company specializing in internal flights that needs €50,000,000 for one year to finance working capital. The airline firm has two alternatives for borrowing:
    a. Borrow €50,000,000 in Paris at 7% per annum.
    b. Borrow Saudi riyals SAR 225,000,000 in Saudi Arabia at 9% per annum and then exchange the riyals at the cross rate of 1 EUR = 4.5 SAR.

    At what ending exchange rate would Inter-KSA be indifferent between borrowing euros and borrowing Saudi riyals?

14. **Pantheon Capital, S.A.** If Pantheon Capital, S.A. is raising funds via a euro medium-term note with the following characteristics, how much in dollars will Pantheon receive for each $1,000 note sold?

    Coupon rate: 8.00% payable semiannually on June 30 and December 31

    Date of issuance: February 28, 2011

    Maturity: August 31, 2011

15. **British Bank.** A British bank plans to sell £5,000,000 of commercial paper in Frankfurt with a 90-day maturity and discounted to yield 4.6% per annum. What will be the immediate proceeds to the British bank?

Internet Exercises

1. **Global Equities.** Bloomberg provides extensive coverage of the global equity markets 24 hours a day. Using the Bloomberg site listed here, note differences in the performance indices on the same equity markets at the same point in time all around the world.

   Bloomberg   www.bloomberg.com/
   markets/stocks/world-indexes/

2. **JPMorgan and Bank of New York Mellon.** JPMorgan and Bank of New York Mellon provide up-to-the-minute performance of American Depositary Receipts (ADRs) in the U.S. marketplace. The site highlights the high-performing equities of the day.
   a. Prepare a briefing for senior management in your firm encouraging them to consider internationally diversifying the firm's liquid asset portfolio with ADRs.
   b. Identify whether the ADR program level (I, II, III, 144A) has any significance to which securities you believe the firm should consider.

   JPMorgan ADRs   www.adr.com
   Bank of New York Mellon www.adrbnymellon.com

3. **London Stock Exchange.** The London Stock Exchange (LSE) lists many different global depositary receipts among its active equities. Use the LSE's Internet site to track the performance of the largest GDRs active today.

   London Stock Exchange   www.londonstockexchange
   .com/traders-and-brokers/
   security-types/gdrs/gdrs.htm

Financial Structure of Foreign Subsidiaries

If we accept the theory that minimizing the cost of capital for a given level of business risk and capital budget is an objective that should be implemented from the perspective of the consolidated MNE, then the financial structure of each subsidiary is relevant only to the extent that it affects this overall goal. In other words, an individual subsidiary does not really have an independent cost of capital. Therefore, its financial structure should not be based on the objective of minimizing its cost of capital.

Financial structure norms for firms vary widely from one country to another but vary less for firms domiciled in the same country. This statement is the conclusion of a long line of empirical studies that have investigated the question of what factors drive financial structure. Most of these international studies concluded that country-specific environmental variables are key determinants of debt ratios. These variables include historical development, taxation, corporate governance, bank influence, existence of a viable corporate bond market, attitude toward risk, government regulation, availability of capital, and agency costs, to name a few.

Local Norms

Within the constraint of minimizing its consolidated worldwide cost of capital, should an MNE take differing country debt ratio norms into consideration when determining its desired debt ratio for foreign subsidiaries? For definition purposes the debt considered here should include only funds borrowed from sources outside the MNE. This debt would include local and foreign currency loans as well as eurocurrency loans.[11]

The main advantages of a finance structure for foreign subsidiaries that conforms to local debt norms are as follows:

- A localized financial structure reduces criticism of foreign subsidiaries that have been operating with too high a proportion of debt (judged by local standards), often resulting in the accusation that they are not contributing a fair share of risk capital to the host country.

- A localized financial structure helps management evaluate return on equity investment relative to local competitors in the same industry.

- In economies where interest rates are relatively high because of a scarcity of capital, the high cost of local funds reminds management that return on assets needs to exceed the local price of capital.

The main disadvantages of localized financial structures are as follows:

- An MNE is expected to have a comparative advantage over local firms in overcoming imperfections in national capital markets through better availability of capital and the ability to diversify risk.

[11]The reason for this definition is that parent loans to foreign subsidiaries are often regarded as equivalent to equity investment both by host countries and by investing firms. A parent loan is usually subordinated to other debt and does not create the same threat of insolvency as an external loan. Furthermore, the choice of debt or equity investment is often arbitrary and subject to negotiation between host country and parent firm.

- If each foreign subsidiary of an MNE localizes its financial structure, the resulting consolidated balance sheet might show a financial structure that does not conform to any particular country's norm.

- The debt ratio of a foreign subsidiary is only cosmetic, because lenders ultimately look to the parent and its consolidated worldwide cash flow as the source of repayment.

In our opinion, a compromise position is possible. Both multinational and domestic firms should try to minimize their overall weighted average cost of capital for a given level of business risk and capital budget, as finance theory suggests. However, if debt is available to a foreign subsidiary at equal cost to that which could be raised elsewhere, after adjusting for foreign exchange risk, then localizing the foreign subsidiary's financial structure should incur no cost penalty and would also enjoy the advantages listed above.

Financing the Foreign Subsidiary

In addition to choosing an appropriate financial structure for foreign subsidiaries, financial managers of multinational firms need to choose among alternative sources of funds—internal and external to the multinational—with which to finance foreign subsidiaries.

Ideally, the choice among the sources of funds should minimize the cost of external funds after adjusting for foreign exchange risk. The firm should choose internal sources in order to minimize worldwide taxes and political risk, while ensuring that managerial motivation in the

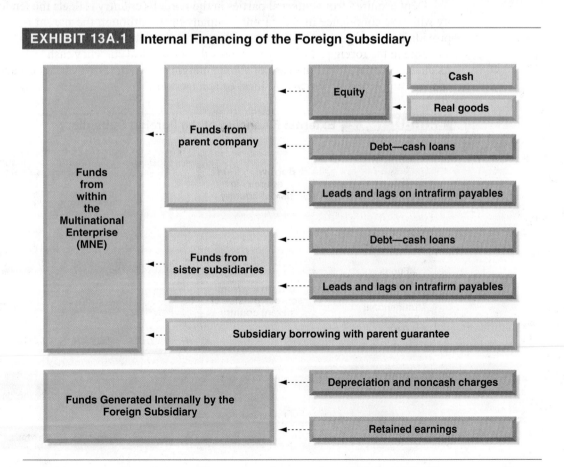

EXHIBIT 13A.1   **Internal Financing of the Foreign Subsidiary**

foreign subsidiaries is geared toward minimizing the firm's consolidated worldwide cost of capital, rather than the subsidiary's cost of capital.

Internal Sources of Funding

Exhibit 13A.1 provides an overview of the *internal* sources of financing for foreign subsidiaries. In general, although a minimum amount of equity capital from the parent company is required, multinationals often strive to minimize the amount of equity in foreign subsidiaries in order to limit risks of losing that capital. Equity investment can take the form of either cash or real goods (machinery, equipment, inventory, etc.).

While debt is the preferable form of subsidiary financing, access to local host country debt is limited in the early stages of a foreign subsidiary's life. Without a history of proven operational capability and debt service capability, the foreign subsidiary may need to acquire its debt from the parent company or from unrelated parties with a parental guarantee (after operations have been initiated). Once the operational and financial capabilities of the subsidiary have been established, it may then actually enjoy preferred access to debt locally.

External Sources of Funding

Exhibit 13A.2 provides an overview of the sources of foreign subsidiary financing *external* to the MNE. The sources are first decomposed into three categories: 1) debt from the parent's country; 2) debt from countries outside the parent's country; and 3) local equity.

Debt acquired from external parties in the parent's country reflects the lenders' familiarity with and confidence in the parent company itself, although the parent is in this case not providing explicit guarantees for the repayment of the debt. Local currency debt is particularly valuable to the foreign subsidiary that has substantial local currency cash inflows arising from its business activities. In the case of some emerging markets, however, local currency debt is in short supply for all borrowers, local or foreign.

EXHIBIT 13A.2   **External Financing of the Foreign Subsidiary**

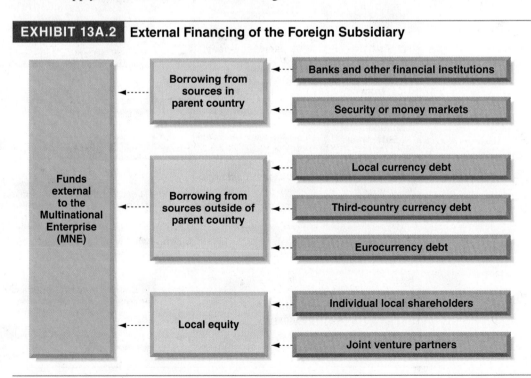

Multinational Tax Management

*Over and over again courts have said that there is noth-
ing sinister in so arranging one's affairs as to keep taxes
as low as possible. Everybody does so, rich and poor, and
all do right, for nobody owes any public duty to pay more
than the law demands: taxes are enforced extractions, not
voluntary contributions. To demand more in the name of
morals is mere cant.*

—Judge Learned Hand, Commissioner v. Newman,

159 F.2d 848 (CA-2, 1947).

LEARNING OBJECTIVES

- Identify the differences between tax systems employed by government around the globe

- Compare corporate income and withholding tax rates used across countries and the way tax treaties affect MNEs

- Explain how value-added taxes are levied by some countries today

- Explain the use of transfer pricing to manage corporate tax burdens

- Compare tax liabilities of domestic and foreign source income for U.S.-based firms

- Examine how U.S.-based multinationals manage their foreign tax credits and deficits to minimize global taxes

- Explain the use of transfer pricing to manage corporate tax burdens

Tax planning for multinational operations is an extremely complex but vitally important aspect of international business. To plan effectively, MNEs must understand not only the intricacies of their own operations worldwide, but also the different structures and interpretations of tax liabilities across countries. The primary objective of multinational tax planning is the minimization of the firm's worldwide tax burden. This objective, however, must not be pursued without full recognition that decision-making within the firm must always be based on the economic fundamentals of the firm's line of business, and not on convoluted policies undertaken purely for the reduction of tax liability. As evident from previous chapters, taxes have a major impact on corporate net income and cash flow through their influence on foreign investment decisions, financial structure, cost of capital, foreign exchange management, and financial control.

This chapter provides an overview of how taxes are applied to MNEs globally; how the United States taxes the global earnings of U.S.-based MNEs; and how U.S.-based multinationals manage their global tax liabilities. We do this in four parts. The first section acquaints the reader with the overall international tax environment. The second part examines transfer pricing. The third part describes how the United States taxes income of MNEs. Although we use U.S. taxes as illustrations, our intention is not to make this chapter or this book U.S.-centric; most U.S. practices have close parallels in other countries, modified to fit their specific national systems. The fourth part of the chapter examines the use of tax-haven subsidiaries and international offshore financial centers, and concludes with a Mini-Case on Google's current global tax strategy.

Tax Principles

The sections that follow explain the most important aspects of the international tax environments and specific features that affect MNEs. Before we explain the specifics of multinational taxation in practice, however, it is necessary to introduce two fundamental tax principles: tax morality and tax neutrality.

Tax Morality

The MNE faces not only a morass of foreign taxes, but also an ethical question. In many countries, taxpayers—corporate or individual—do not voluntarily comply with the tax laws. This is termed *tax morality*. Smaller domestic firms and individuals are the chief violators. The MNE must decide whether to follow a practice of full disclosure to tax authorities or adopt the philosophy of "when in Rome, do as the Romans do." Given the local prominence of most foreign subsidiaries and the political sensitivity of their position, most MNEs follow the full disclosure practice. Some firms, however, believe that their competitive position would be eroded if they did not avoid taxes to the same extent as their domestic competitors. There is obviously no prescriptive answer to the problem, since business ethics are partly a function of cultural heritage and historical development.

Some countries have imposed what seem to be arbitrary punitive tax penalties on MNEs for presumed violations of local tax laws. Property or wealth tax assessments are sometimes perceived by the foreign firm to be excessively large when compared with those levied on locally owned firms. The problem then is how to respond to tax penalties that are punitive or discriminatory.

Tax Neutrality

When a government decides to levy a tax, it must consider not only the potential revenue from the tax and how efficiently it can be collected, but also the effect the proposed tax can have on private economic behavior. For example, the U.S. government's policy on taxation of foreign-source income does not have as its sole objective the raising of revenue; rather it has multiple objectives, including the following:

- Neutralizing tax incentives that might favor (or disfavor) U.S. private investment in developed countries
- Providing an incentive for U.S. private investment in developing countries
- Improving the U.S. balance of payments by removing the advantages of artificial tax havens and encouraging repatriation of funds
- Raising revenue

The ideal tax should not only raise revenue efficiently but also have as few negative effects on economic behavior as possible. Some theorists argue that the ideal tax should be completely neutral in its effect on private decisions and completely equitable among taxpayers. This is *tax neutrality*. However, other theorists claim that national policy objectives such as balance of payments or investment in developing countries should be encouraged through an active tax incentive policy, as opposed to requiring taxes to be neutral and equitable. Most tax systems compromise between these two viewpoints.

One way to view neutrality is to require that the burden of taxation on each dollar, euro, pound, or yen of profit earned in home-country operations by an MNE be equal to the burden of taxation on each currency-equivalent of profit earned by the same firm in its foreign operations. This is called *domestic tax neutrality*. A second way to view neutrality is to require that the tax burden on each foreign subsidiary of the firm be equal to the tax burden on its competitors in the same country. This is called *foreign tax neutrality* The latter interpretation is often supported by MNEs because it focuses more on the competitiveness of the individual firm in individual country-markets.

The concept of *tax equity* is also difficult to define and measure. In theory, an equitable tax is one that imposes the same total tax burden on all taxpayers who are similarly situated and located in the same tax jurisdiction. In the case of foreign investment income, the U.S. Treasury argues that since the United States uses the nationality principle to claim tax jurisdiction, U.S.-owned foreign subsidiaries are in the same tax jurisdiction as U.S. domestic subsidiaries. Therefore, a dollar earned in foreign operations should be taxed at the same rate and paid at the same time as a dollar earned in domestic operations.

National Tax Environments

Despite the fundamental objectives of national tax authorities, it is widely agreed that taxes do affect economic decisions made by MNEs. Tax treaties between nations, and differential tax structures, rates, and practices all result in a less than level playing field for the MNEs competing on world markets. Different countries use different categorizations of income (e.g., distributed versus undistributed profits), use different tax rates, and have radically different tax regimes, all of which drive different global tax management strategies by multinational firms.

Nations structure their tax systems along two basic approaches: the *worldwide approach* or the *territorial approach*. Both approaches are attempts to determine which firms, foreign or domestic by incorporation, or which incomes, foreign or domestic in origin, are subject to the taxation of host-country tax authorities.

Worldwide Approach. The *worldwide approach*, also referred to as the *residential* or *national approach*, levies taxes on the income earned by firms that are incorporated in the host country, regardless of where the income was earned (domestically or abroad). An MNE earning income both at home and abroad would therefore find its worldwide income taxed by its host-country tax authorities.

For example, the United States taxes the income earned by firms based in the United States regardless of whether the income earned by the firm is domestically sourced or foreign sourced. In the United States, ordinary foreign-sourced income is taxed only as remitted to the parent firm. As with all questions of tax, however, numerous conditions and exceptions exist. The primary problem is that this does not address the income earned by foreign firms operating within the United States. Countries like the United States then apply the principle of territorial taxation to foreign firms within their legal jurisdiction, taxing all income earned by foreign firms in the United States.

Territorial Approach. The *territorial approach*, also termed the *source approach*, focuses on the income earned by firms within the legal jurisdiction of the host country, not on the country of firm incorporation. Countries like Germany, which follow the territorial approach, apply taxes equally to foreign or domestic firms on income earned within the country, but in principle not on income earned outside the country. The territorial approach, like the worldwide approach, results in a major gap in coverage if resident firms earn income outside the country, but are not taxed by the country in which the profits are earned. In this case, tax authorities extend tax coverage to income earned abroad if it is not currently covered by foreign tax jurisdictions. Once again, a mix of the two tax approaches is necessary for full coverage of income.

As illustrated by Exhibit 14.1, the U.S. is one of only five Organization for Economic Cooperation and Development (OECD) countries that utilizes a worldwide system. The predominance of territorial systems has grown rapidly, as more than half of these same OECD countries used worldwide systems only 10 years ago. In 2009 alone, both Japan and the United Kingdom switched from worldwide to territorial systems.

Tax Deferral. If the worldwide approach to international taxation were followed to the letter, it would end the tax-deferral privilege for many MNEs. Foreign subsidiaries of MNEs pay host-country corporate income taxes, but many parent countries defer claiming additional income taxes on that foreign-source income until it is remitted to the parent firm—this is called *tax deferral*. For example, U.S. corporate income taxes on some types of foreign-source income of U.S.-owned subsidiaries incorporated abroad are deferred until the earnings are remitted to the U.S. parent. However, the ability to defer corporate income taxes is highly restricted and has been the subject of many of the tax law changes in the past three decades.

The deferral privilege has been challenged a number of times in recent U.S. presidential elections. A number of different candidates have argued that tax deferrals create an incentive for outsourcing abroad—so-called offshoring—of certain manufacturing and service activities by U.S. firms. The added concern to the potential loss of American jobs was the potential reduction in tax collections in the United States, enlarging the already sizable U.S. government fiscal deficit.

Tax Treaties

A network of bilateral tax treaties, many of which are modeled after one proposed by the OECD, provides a means of reducing double taxation. Tax treaties normally define whether taxes are to be imposed on income earned in one country by the nationals of another, and if so, how. Tax treaties are bilateral, with the two signatories specifying what rates are applicable to which types of income between the two countries.

Individual bilateral tax jurisdictions as specified through tax treaties are particularly important for firms that are primarily exporting to another country rather than doing

EXHIBIT 14.1	**Tax Regimes of the OECD 30**				**Worldwide Taxation**
	Territorial Taxation				
Australia	France	Japan	Slovak Republic		Ireland
Austria	Germany	Luxembourg	Spain		Korea
Belgium	Greece	Netherlands	Sweden		Mexico
Canada	Hungary	New Zealand	Switzerland		Poland
Czech Republic	Iceland	Norway	Turkey		United States
Denmark	Italy	Portugal	United Kingdom		
Finland					

Source: "Special Report: The Importance of Tax Deferral and a Lower Corporate Tax Rate," Tax Foundation, February 2010, No. 174, p. 4.

business in that country via a "permanent establishment" (for example, a manufacturing plant). A firm that only exports would not want any of its other worldwide income taxed by the importing country. Tax treaties define what is a "permanent establishment" and what constitutes a limited presence for tax purposes. Tax treaties also typically result in reduced withholding tax rates between the two signatory countries, the negotiation of the treaty itself serving as a forum for opening and expanding business relationships between the two countries.

Tax Types

Taxes are classified as *direct taxes* if they are applied directly to income or *indirect taxes* if they are based on some other measurable performance characteristic of the firm. Exhibit 14.2 illustrates the wide range of corporate income tax rates across the world today.

Income Tax. Most governments rely on income taxes, both personal and corporate, for their primary revenue source. Corporate income tax rates differ widely globally, and take a variety of different forms. Some countries, for example, impose different corporate tax rates on distributed income (often lower) versus undistributed income (often higher), in an attempt to motivate companies to distribute greater portions of their income to their owners. As shown in Exhibit 14.2, corporate income taxes vary from 0% in a number of offshore tax havens like the Bahamas, Cayman Islands, Guernsey, Isle of Man, Panama, and Vanuatu; 10% in Paraguay and Qatar; 19% in Poland; to as high as 40% in the United States and 40.69% in Japan.

These differences reflect a rapidly changing global tax environment. Corporate income taxes have been falling rapidly and widely over the past decade, and as illustrated in Exhibit 14.3, the lower rates today are predominantly in the non-OECD countries. The highly industrialized world, for better or worse, has been reluctant to reduce corporate income tax rates as aggressively as many emerging market nations. Corporate income tax rates, like any burden on the profitability of commercial enterprise, has become a competitive element used by many countries to attempt to promote inward investment from abroad. In 2011, for the first time in the past 50 years, the global average corporate income tax rate fell below 23%.

Withholding Tax. Passive income (such as dividends, interest, and royalties) earned by a resident of one country within the tax jurisdiction of a second country, are normally subject to a withholding tax in the second country. The reason for the institution of withholding taxes is actually quite simple: governments recognize that most international investors will not file a tax return in each country in which they invest. The government, therefore, wishes to ensure that a minimum tax payment is received. As the term "withholding" implies, taxes are withheld by the corporation from the payment made to the investor, and the taxes withheld are then turned over to government authorities. Withholding taxes are a major subject of bilateral tax treaties and generally range between 0 and 25%.

Value-Added Tax. One type of tax that has achieved great prominence is the value-added tax. The *value-added tax* is a type of national sales tax collected at each stage of production or sale of consumption goods in proportion to the value added during that stage. In general, production goods such as plant and equipment have not been subject to the value-added tax. Certain necessities—such as medicines and other health-related expenses, education and religious activities, and the postal service—are usually exempt or taxed at lower rates.

The value-added tax has been adopted as the main source of revenue from indirect taxation by all members of the European Union, most other countries in Western Europe, a number of Latin American countries, Canada, and scattered other countries. A numerical example of a value-added tax computation is shown in Exhibit 14.4.

EXHIBIT 14.2 Corporate Income Tax Rates for Selected Countries

Country	Rate	Country	Rate	Country	Rate
Afghanistan	20%	Guatemala	31%	Paraguay	10%
Albania	10%	Guernsey	0%	Peru	30%
Angola	35%	Honduras	35%	Philippines	30%
Argentina	35%	Hong Kong	16.5%	Poland	19%
Armenia	20%	Hungary	19%	Portugal	25%
Aruba	28%	Iceland	20%	Qatar	10%
Australia	30%	India	33.22%	Romania	16%
Austria	25%	Indonesia	25%	Russia	20%
Bahamas	0%	Iran	25%	St. Maarten	34%
Bahrain	0%	Ireland	12.5%	Samoa	27%
Bangladesh	27.5%	Isle of Man	0%	Saudi Arabia	20%
Barbados	25%	Israel	24%	Serbia	10%
Belarus	24%	Italy	31.4%	Singapore	17%
Belgium	33.99%	Jamaica	33.33%	Slovak Republic	19%
Bermuda	0%	Japan	40.69%	Slovenia	20%
Bosnia and Herzegovina	10%	Jordan	14/24/30	South Africa	34.55%
Botswana	25%	Kazakhstan	20%	Spain	30%
Brazil	34%	Korea, Republic of	24.2%	Sri Lanka	35%
Bulgaria	10%	Kuwait	15%	Sudan	10/15/30/35
Canada	28.3%	Latvia	15%	Sweden	26.3%
Cayman Islands	0%	Libya	20%	Switzerland	11.6–24.4%
Chile	20%	Lithuania	15/5/0	Syria	28%
China	25%	Luxembourg	28.80%	Taiwan	17%
Colombia	33%	Macau	12%	Tanzania	30%
Costa Rica	30%	Macedonia	10%	Thailand	30%
Croatia	20%	Malaysia	25%	Tunisia	30%
Cyprus	10%	Malta	35%	Turkey	20%
Czech Republic	19%	Mauritius	15%	Ukraine	23%
Denmark	25%	Mexico	30%	United Arab Emirates	0/20/55
Dominican Republic	25%	Montenegro	9%	United Kingdom	28%
Ecuador	24%	Mozambique	32%	United States	40%
Egypt	20%	Netherlands	20/25	Uruguay	25%
Estonia	21%	New Zealand	28%	Vanuatu	0%
Fiji	28%	Nigeria	30%	Venezuela	34%
Finland	26%	Norway	28%	Vietnam	25%
France	33.33%	Oman	12%	Yemen	20%
Germany	29.37%	Pakistan	35%	Zambia	35%
Gibraltar	10%	Panama	0%	Zimbabwe	25.75%
Greece	24%	Papua New Guinea	30%		

Source: *KPMG's Corporate and Indirect Tax Rate Survey, 2011.* The Netherlands Antilles tax regime has been dismantled.

| EXHIBIT 14.3 | Worldwide Corporate Income Tax Rates, 2006–2011 |

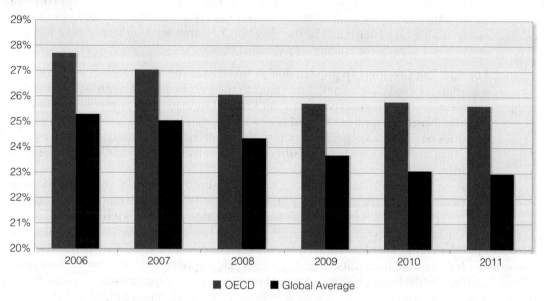

■ OECD   ■ Global Average

Source: KPMG Corporate and Indirect Tax Survey, 2011, p. 23.

Other National Taxes. There are other national taxes, which vary in importance from country to country. The turnover tax (tax on the purchase or sale of securities in some countries) and higher taxes on undistributed profits (a higher income tax rate on retained earnings of firms) are examples of other national taxes. Property and inheritance taxes, also termed

| EXHIBIT 14.4 | Value-Added Tax Applied to the Sale of a Wooden Fence Post |

This is an example of how a wooden fence post would be assessed for value-added taxes in the course of its production and subsequent sale. A value-added tax of 10% is assumed.

Step 1	The original tree owner sells to the lumber mill, for $0.20, that part of a tree that ultimately becomes the fence post. The grower has added $0.20 in value up to this point by planting and raising the tree. While collecting $0.20 from the lumber mill, the grower must set aside $0.02 to pay the value-added tax to the government.
Step 2	The lumber mill processes the tree into fence posts and sells each post for $0.40 to the lumber wholesaler. The lumber mill has added $0.20 in value ($0.40 less $0.20) through its processing activities. Therefore the lumber mill owner must set aside $0.02 to pay the mill's value-added tax to the government. In practice, the owner would probably calculate the mill's tax liability as 10% of $0.40, or $0.04, with a tax credit of $0.02 for the value-added tax already paid by the tree owner.
Steps 3 and 4	The lumber wholesaler and retailer also add value to the fence post through their selling and distribution activities. They are assessed $0.01 and $0.03 respectively, making the cumulative value-added tax collected by the government $0.08, or 10% of the final sales price.

Stage of Production	Sales Price	Value Added	Value-Added Tax at 10%	Cumulative Value-Added Tax
Tree owner	$0.20	$0.20	$0.02	$0.02
Lumber mill	$0.40	$0.20	$0.02	$0.04
Lumber wholesaler	$0.50	$0.10	$0.01	$0.05
Lumber retailer	$0.80	$0.30	$0.03	$0.08

transfer taxes, are imposed in a variety of ways to achieve intended social redistribution of income and wealth as much as to raise revenue. There are other "red-tape charges" for public services that are in reality user taxes. Sometimes foreign exchange purchases or sales are in effect hidden taxes inasmuch as the government earns revenue rather than just regulating imports and exports for balance of payments reasons.

Foreign Tax Credits. To prevent double taxation of the same income, most countries grant a foreign tax credit for income taxes paid to the host country. Countries differ on how they calculate the foreign tax credit and what kinds of limitations they place on the total amount claimed. Normally foreign tax credits are also available for withholding taxes paid to other countries on dividends, royalties, interest, and other income remitted to the parent. The value-added tax and other sales taxes are not eligible for a foreign tax credit but are typically deductible from pre-tax income as an expense.

A tax credit is a direct reduction of taxes that would otherwise be due and payable. It differs from a deductible expense, which is an expense used to reduce taxable income before the tax rate is applied. A $100 tax credit reduces taxes payable by the full $100, whereas a $100 deductible expense reduces taxable income by $100 and taxes payable by $100 $\times$ t where t is the tax rate. Tax credits are more valuable on a dollar-for-dollar basis than are deductible expenses.

If there were no credits for foreign taxes paid, sequential taxation by the host government and then by the home government would result in a very high cumulative tax rate. For example, assume the wholly owned foreign subsidiary of an MNE earns $10,000 before local income taxes and pays a dividend equal to all of its after-tax income. The host-country income tax rate is 30%, and the home country of the parent tax rate is 35%, assuming no withholding taxes. Total taxation with and without tax credits is shown in Exhibit 14.5.

If tax credits are not allowed, sequential levying of both a 30% host-country tax and then a 35% home-country tax on the income that remains results in an effective 54.5% tax as a percentage of the original before tax income, a cumulative rate that would make many MNEs uncompetitive with local firms. The effect of allowing tax credits is to limit total taxation on the original before-tax income to no more than the highest single rate among jurisdictions. In the case depicted in Exhibit 14.5, the effective overall tax rate of 35% with foreign tax credits is equivalent to the higher tax rate of the home country (and is the tax rate payable if the income had been earned at home).

The $500 of additional home-country tax under the tax credit system in Exhibit 14.5 is the amount needed to bring total taxation ($3,000 already paid plus the additional $500) up to but not beyond 35% of the original $10,000 of before-tax foreign income.

EXHIBIT 14.5   Foreign Tax Credits

	Without Foreign Tax Credits	With Foreign Tax Credits
Before-tax foreign income	$10,000	$10,000
Less foreign tax @ 30%	−3,000	−3,000
Available to parent and paid as dividend	$ 7,000	$ 7,000
Less additional parent-country tax at 35%	−2,450	
Less incremental tax (after credits)	——	−500
Profit after all taxes	$ 4,550	$ 6,500
Total taxes, both jurisdictions	$ 5,450	$ 3,500
Effective overall tax rate (total taxes paid ÷ foreign income)	54.5%	35.0%

The problem, however, is that if this company repatriates the profits of its foreign businesses to the parent company, it owes more taxes. Period. If it leaves those profits in that foreign country, it enjoys what is referred to as *deferral*—it is able to defer incurring additional parent-country taxes on the foreign-source income until it does repatriate those earnings. As shown in *Global Finance in Practice 14.1*, this has motivated some countries like the United States to try periodically to provide tax incentives for repatriating profits.

Transfer Pricing

The pricing of goods, services, and technology transferred to a foreign subsidiary from an affiliated company—*transfer pricing*—is the first and foremost method of transferring funds out of a foreign subsidiary. These costs enter directly into the cost of goods sold component

GLOBAL FINANCE IN PRACTICE 14.1

Offshore Profits and Dividend Repatriation

It is estimated that U.S.-based multinationals have one trillion dollars in un-repatriated profits offshore. Repatriating those profits, given the relatively higher effective corporate income tax rate in the U.S. compared to many other countries, would trigger significant additional tax charges in the U.S. In an effort to facilitate repatriation of those profits in 2004, the U.S. government passed the *Homeland Investment Act of 2004*. The Act provided a window of opportunity in 2005 in which profits could be repatriated with only an additional tax obligation of 5.25%.

The temporary tax law change clearly had the desired impact of stimulating the repatriation of profits, as illustrated in the exhibit. Dividend repatriations skyrocketed in 2005 to over $360 billion from $60 billion the previous year. After the temporary tax revision expired, repatriated dividends returned to trend.

The apparent political motivation for the original tax holiday was jobs creation in the United States by U.S. companies. However, evidence indicates that U.S. parent companies used the repatriated profits for a variety of purposes, such as returning money to shareholders via dividends and share repurchases, but not for creating new jobs. As discussions get underway regarding another tax holiday aimed at repatriating over one trillion dollars in corporate profits held offshore, these same debates are rising once again.

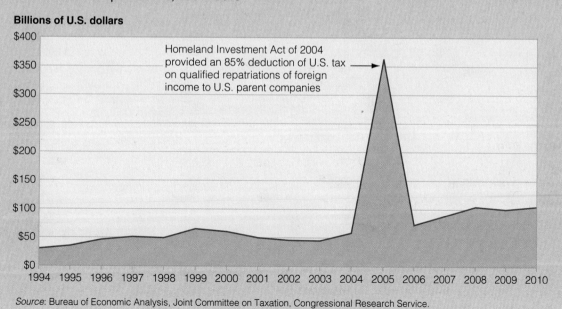

U.S. Dividend Repatriations, 1994–2010

Source: Bureau of Economic Analysis, Joint Committee on Taxation, Congressional Research Service.

of the subsidiary's income statement. This is a particularly sensitive problem for MNEs. Even purely domestic firms find it difficult to reach agreement on the best method for setting prices on transactions between related units. In the multinational case, managers must balance conflicting considerations. These include fund positioning and income taxes.

Fund Positioning Effect. A parent firm wishing to transfer funds out of a particular country can charge higher prices on goods sold to its subsidiary in that country—to the degree that government regulations allow. A foreign subsidiary can be financed by the reverse technique, a lowering of transfer prices. Payment by the subsidiary for imports from its parent or sister subsidiary transfers funds out of the subsidiary. A higher transfer price permits funds to be accumulated in the selling country. Transfer pricing may also be used to transfer funds between sister subsidiaries. Multiple sourcing of component parts on a worldwide basis allows the act of switching between suppliers from within the corporate family to function as a device to transfer funds.

Income Tax Effect

A major consideration in setting a transfer price is the income tax effect. Worldwide corporate profits may be influenced by setting transfer prices to minimize taxable income in a country with a high income tax rate and to maximize taxable income in a country with a low income tax rate. A parent wishing to reduce the taxable profits of a subsidiary in a high-tax environment may set transfer prices at a higher rate to increase the costs of the subsidiary, thereby reducing taxable income.

The income tax effect is illustrated in the hypothetical example presented in Exhibit 14.6. Trident Europe is operating in a relatively high-tax environment, assuming German corporate

EXHIBIT 14.6	**Effect of Low versus High Transfer Price on Trident Europe's Net Income** (thousands of U.S. dollars)		
	Trident U.S. (subsidiary)	Trident Europe (subsidiary)	Europe and USA Combined
Low-Markup Policy			
Sales	$1,400	$2,000	$2,000
Less cost of goods sold*	(1,000)	(1,400)	(1,000)
Gross profit	$ 400	$ 600	$1,000
Less operating expenses	(100)	(100)	(200)
Taxable income	$ 300	$ 500	$ 800
Less income taxes	35% (105)	45% (225)	(330)
Net income	$ 195	$ 275	$ 470
High-Markup Policy			
Sales	$1,700	$2,000	$2,000
Less cost of goods sold*	(1,000)	(1,700)	(1,000)
Gross profit	$ 700	$ 300	$1,000
Less operating expenses	(100)	(100)	(200)
Taxable income	$ 600	$ 200	$ 800
Less income taxes	35% (210)	45% (90)	(300)
Net income	$ 390	$ 110	$ 500

* Trident U.S.'s sales price becomes cost of goods sold for Trident Europe.

income taxes of 45%. Trident U.S. is in a significantly lower tax environment, assuming a U.S. corporate income tax rate of 35%, motivating Trident to charge Trident Europe a higher transfer price on goods produced in the United States and sold to Trident Europe.

If Trident Corporation adopts a high-markup policy by "selling" its merchandise at an intracompany sales price of $1,700,000, the same $800,000 of pre-tax consolidated income is allocated more heavily to low-tax Trident U.S. and less heavily to high-tax Trident Europe. (Note that it is Trident Corporation, the corporate parent that must adopt a transfer pricing policy that directly alters the profitability of each of the individual subsidiaries.) As a consequence, total taxes drop by $30,000 and consolidated net income increases by $30,000 to $500,000. All while total sales remain constant.

Trident would naturally prefer the high-markup policy for sales from the United States to Europe (Germany in this case). Needless to say, government tax authorities are aware of the potential income distortion from transfer price manipulation. A variety of regulations and court cases exist on the reasonableness of transfer prices, including fees and royalties as well as prices set for merchandise. If a government taxing authority does not accept a transfer price, taxable income will be deemed larger than was calculated by the firm, and taxes will be increased.

Section 482 of the U.S. Internal Revenue Code is typical of laws circumscribing freedom to set transfer prices. Under this authority, the IRS can reallocate gross income, deductions, credits, or allowances between related corporations in order to prevent tax evasion or to reflect more clearly a proper allocation of income. Under these guidelines, the burden of proof is on the taxpaying firm to show that the IRS has been arbitrary or unreasonable in reallocating income. This "guilty until proved innocent" approach means that MNEs must keep good documentation of the logic and costs behind their transfer prices. The "correct price" according to the guidelines is the one that reflects an arm's length price, that is, a sale of the same goods or service to a comparable unrelated customer.

IRS regulations provide three methods to establish arm's length prices: comparable uncontrolled prices, resale prices, and cost-plus calculations. All three of these methods are recommended for use in member countries by the Organization for Economic Cooperation and Development (OECD) Committee on Fiscal Affairs. In some cases, combinations of these three methods are used.

Managerial Incentives and Evaluation

When a firm is organized with decentralized profit centers, transfer pricing between centers can disrupt evaluation of managerial performance. This problem is not unique to MNEs; it is also a controversial issue in the "centralization versus decentralization" debate in domestic circles. In the domestic case, however, a modicum of coordination at the corporate level can alleviate some of the distortion that occurs when any profit center suboptimizes its profit for the corporate good. Also, in most domestic cases, the company can file a single (for that country) consolidated tax return, so the issue of cost allocation between affiliates is not critical from a tax-payment point of view.

In the multinational case, coordination is often hindered by longer and less-efficient channels of communication, the need to consider the unique variables that influence international pricing, and separate taxation. Even with the best of intent, a manager in one country finds it difficult to know what is best for the firm as a whole when buying at a negotiated price from related companies in another country. If corporate headquarters establishes transfer prices and sourcing alternatives, one of the main advantages of a decentralized profit center system disappears: local management loses the incentive to act for its own benefit.

To illustrate, refer to Exhibit 14.6, where an increase in the transfer price led to a worldwide income gain: Trident Corporation's income rose by $195,000 (from $195,000 to $390,000) while

Trident Europe's income fell by only $165,000 (from $275,000 to $110,000), for a net gain of $30,000. Should the managers of the European subsidiary lose their bonuses (or their jobs) because of their "sub-par" performance? Bonuses are usually determined by a company-wide formula based in part on the profitability of individual subsidiaries, but in this case, Trident Europe "sacrificed" for the greater good of the whole. Arbitrarily changing transfer prices can create measurement problems.

Transferring profit from high-tax Trident Europe to low-tax Trident Corporation in the United States changes the following for one or both companies:

- Import tariffs paid (importer only) and hence profit levels
- Measurements of foreign exchange exposure, such as the amount of net exposed assets, because of changes in amounts of cash and receivables
- Liquidity tests, such as the current ratio, receivables turnover, and inventory turnover
- Operating efficiency, as measured by the ratio of gross profit to either sales or to total assets
- Income tax payments
- Profitability, as measured by the ratio of net income to either sales or capital invested
- Dividend payout ratio, in that a constant dividend will show as a varied payout ratio as net income changes (alternatively, if the payout ratio is kept constant, the amount of dividend is changed by a change in transfer price)
- Internal growth rate, as measured by the ratio of retained earnings to existing ownership equity

Effect on Joint-Venture Partners

Joint ventures pose a special problem in transfer pricing, because serving the interest of local stockholders by maximizing local profit may be suboptimal from the overall viewpoint of the MNE. Often, the conflicting interests are irreconcilable. Indeed, the local joint venture partner could be viewed as a potential "Trojan horse" if they complain to local authorities about the MNE's transfer pricing policy.

Tax Management at Trident

Exhibit 14.7 summarizes the key tax management issue for Trident when remitting dividend income back to the United States from Trident Germany and Trident Brazil. Trident's dividend remittances from its two foreign subsidiaries create two different and offsetting tax credit positions.

- Because corporate income tax rates in Germany (40%) are higher than those in the United States (35%), dividends remitted to the U.S. parent result in excess foreign tax credits. Any applicable withholding taxes on dividends between Germany and the U.S. only increase the amount of the excess credit.
- Because corporate income tax rates in Brazil (25%) are lower than those in the United States (35%), dividends remitted to the U.S. parent result in deficit foreign tax credits. If there are withholding taxes applied to the dividends by Brazil on remittances to the United States, this will reduce the size of the deficit, but not eliminate it.

Trident's management would like to manage the two dividend remittances in order to match the deficits with the credits. The most straightforward method of doing this would be to adjust the amount of dividend distributed from each foreign subsidiary so that, after

EXHIBIT 14.7   Trident's Tax Management of Foreign-Source Income

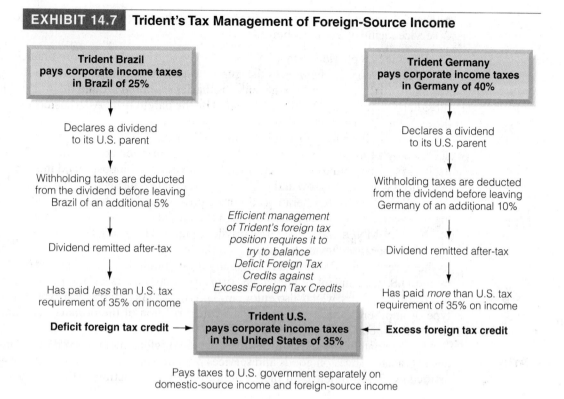

all applicable income and withholding taxes have been applied, Trident's excess foreign tax credits from Trident Germany exactly match the excess foreign tax deficits from Trident Brazil. There are a number of other methods of managing the global tax liabilities of Trident, so-called *repositioning of funds*, where firms strive to structure global operations to record their profits in a low-tax environment, as shown in the Mini-Case on Google at the end of this chapter.

Tax-Haven Subsidiaries and International Offshore Financial Centers

Many MNEs have foreign subsidiaries that act as tax havens for corporate funds awaiting reinvestment or repatriation. Tax-haven subsidiaries, categorically referred to as International Offshore Financial Centers, are partially a result of tax-deferral features on earned foreign income allowed by some of the parent countries. Tax-haven subsidiaries are typically established in a country that can meet the following requirements:

■ A low tax on foreign investment or sales income earned by resident corporations and a low dividend withholding tax on dividends paid to the parent firm.

■ A stable currency to permit easy conversion of funds into and out of the local currency. This requirement can be met by permitting and facilitating the use of eurocurrencies.

■ The facilities to support financial services; for example, good communications, professional qualified office workers, and reputable banking services.

■ A stable government that encourages the establishment of foreign-owned financial and service facilities within its borders.

Exhibit 14.8 provides a map of most of the world's major offshore financial centers. The typical tax-haven subsidiary owns the common stock of its related operating foreign subsidiaries. There might be several tax-haven subsidiaries scattered around the world. The tax-haven subsidiary's equity is typically 100% owned by the parent firm. All transfers of funds might go through the tax-haven subsidiaries, including dividends and equity financing. Thus, the parent country's tax on foreign-source income, which might normally be paid when a dividend is declared by a foreign subsidiary, could continue to be deferred until the tax-haven subsidiary itself pays a dividend to the parent firm. This event can be postponed indefinitely if foreign operations continue to grow and require new internal financing from the tax-haven subsidiary. Thus, MNEs are able to operate a corporate pool of funds for foreign operations without having to repatriate foreign earnings through the parent country's tax machine.

For U.S. MNEs, the tax-deferral privilege enjoyed by foreign subsidiaries (it is considered a privilege because they do not pay tax on the foreign income until they remit dividends back to the parent company) was not originally a tax loophole. On the contrary, it was granted by the U.S. government to allow U.S. firms to expand overseas and place them on par with foreign competitors, which also enjoy similar types of tax deferral and export subsidies of one type or another. Exhibit 14.9 provides a categorization of the primary activities of offshore financial centers.

Unfortunately, some U.S. firms distorted the original intent of tax deferral into tax avoidance. Transfer prices on goods and services bought from or sold to related subsidiaries were artificially rigged to leave all the income from the transaction in the tax-haven subsidiary.

EXHIBIT 14.8   International Offshore Financial Centers

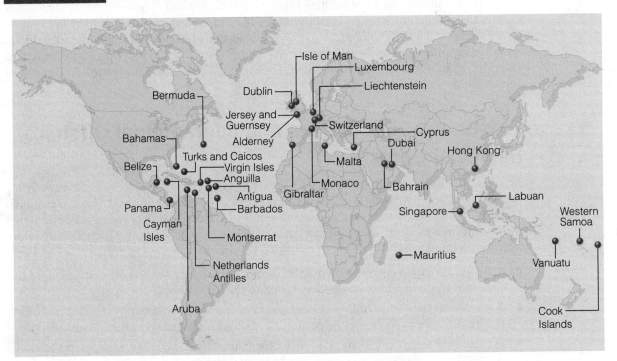

EXHIBIT 14.9	The Activities of Offshore Financial Centers

Offshore financial centers provide financial management services to foreign users in exchange for foreign exchange earnings. There are several comparative advantages for clients, including very low tax rates, minimal administrative formalities, and confidentiality and discretion. This environment allows wealthy international clients to minimize potential tax liability while protecting income and assets from political, fiscal, and legal risks. There are many vehicles through which offshore financial services can be provided. They include the following:

■ Offshore banking, which can handle foreign exchange operations for corporations or banks. These operations are not subject to capital, corporate, capital gains, dividend, or interest taxes or to exchange controls.

■ International business corporations, which are often tax-exempt, limited-liability companies used to operate businesses or raise capital through issuing shares, bonds, or other instruments.

■ Offshore insurance companies, which are established to minimize taxes and manage risk.

■ Asset management and protection, which allows individuals and corporations in countries with fragile banking systems or unstable political regimes to keep assets offshore to protect against the collapse of domestic currencies and banks.

■ Tax planning, which means multinationals may route transactions through offshore centers to minimize taxes through transfer pricing. Individuals can make use of favorable tax regimes offered by offshore centers through trusts and foundations.

The tax concessions and secrecy offered by offshore financial centers can be used for many legitimate purposes, but they have also been used for illegitimate ends, including money laundering and tax evasion.

This manipulation could be done by routing the legal title to the goods or services through the tax-haven subsidiary, even though physically the goods or services never entered the tax-haven country. Needless to say, tax authorities of both exporting and importing countries were dismayed by the lack of taxable income in such transactions.

One purpose of the U.S. Internal Revenue Act of 1962 was to eliminate the tax advantages of these "paper" foreign corporations without destroying the tax-deferral privilege for those foreign manufacturing and sales subsidiaries that were established for business and economic motives rather than tax motives. Although the tax motive has been removed, some firms have found these subsidiaries useful as finance control centers for foreign operations, as illustrated in this chapter's Mini-Case.

Summary Points

■ Nations typically structure their tax systems along one of two basic approaches: the worldwide approach or the territorial approach. Both approaches are attempts to determine which firms, foreign or domestic by incorporation, or which incomes, foreign or domestic in origin, are subject to the taxation of host-country tax authorities.

■ A network of bilateral tax treaties, many of which are modeled after one proposed by the Organization for Economic Cooperation and Development (OECD), provides a means of reducing double taxation.

■ Tax treaties normally define whether taxes are to be imposed on income earned in one country by the nationals of another, and if so, how. Tax treaties are bilateral, with the two signatories specifying what rates are applicable to which types of income between the two countries.

■ The value-added tax is a type of national sales tax collected at each stage of production or sale of goods purchased by consumers—consumption goods—in proportion to the value added during that stage.

■ Transfer pricing is the pricing of goods, services, and technology between related companies. High- or low-transfer prices have an effect on income taxes, fund positioning, managerial incentives and evaluation, and joint venture partners.

■ The United States differentiates foreign source income from domestic source income. Each is taxed separately, and tax deficits/credits in one category may not be used against deficits/credits in the other category. If a U.S.-based MNE receives income from a foreign country that imposes higher corporate income taxes than does the United States (or combined income and

- withholding tax), total creditable taxes will exceed U.S. taxes on that foreign income. The result is excess foreign tax credits.
- All firms wish to manage their tax liabilities globally so that they do not end up paying more on foreign-sourced income than they do on domestically sourced income.

- MNEs have foreign subsidiaries that act as tax havens for corporate funds awaiting reinvestment or repatriation. Tax havens are typically located in countries that have a low corporate tax rate, a stable currency, facilities to support financial services, and a stable government.

MINI-CASE

Google, Taxes, and "Do No Evil"[1]

It's called capitalism.

—Eric Schmidt, Chairman, Google, 2012.

Google, the dominant Internet search engine famous for encouraging all employees to *Do no evil* in the company code of conduct, has been the subject of much scrutiny over its global tax strategy in recent years. Google's overall tax rate, taxes paid in total globally on pre-tax earnings, has averaged roughly 22% in recent years. But Google generated $5.5 billion in revenue in the United Kingdom in 2012, paying only $55 million in taxes to the U.K. tax authorities. Combined with royalties paid from other countries

and other markets, Google Bermuda earned £8.8 billion in royalties in 2012—untaxed royalties. The company did not break the law, it simply structured its global operations to legally minimize its global tax liabilities.

Google's Bermuda Subsidiary

Google's offshore tax strategy, the *Double-Irish-Dutch Sandwich*, is based on repositioning the ownership of many of its patents, copyrights, and other intellectual property to a subsidiary in a low-tax environment like Ireland (see Exhibit A), and then establishing high transfer prices on various forms of services and overheads to other units, leaving most of the profits in the near-zero tax environment of Bermuda.

There is nothing illegal about Google's tax strategy. The company negotiated for years with the U.S. tax authority,

EXHIBIT A   Google's Global Tax Structure and the U.K.

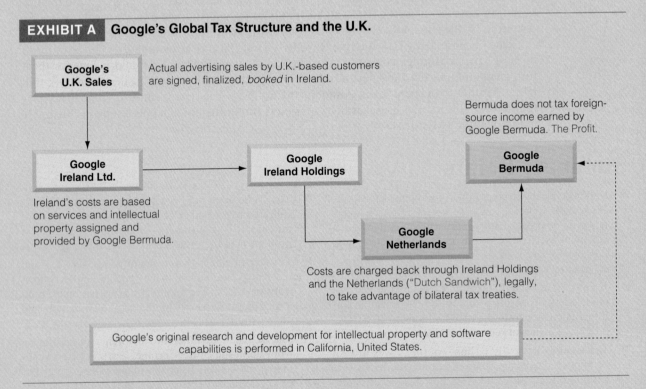

Google's U.K. Sales — Actual advertising sales by U.K.-based customers are signed, finalized, *booked* in Ireland.

Google Ireland Ltd. — Ireland's costs are based on services and intellectual property assigned and provided by Google Bermuda.

Google Ireland Holdings

Google Netherlands

Google Bermuda — Bermuda does not tax foreign-source income earned by Google Bermuda. The Profit.

Costs are charged back through Ireland Holdings and the Netherlands ("Dutch Sandwich"), legally, to take advantage of bilateral tax treaties.

Google's original research and development for intellectual property and software capabilities is performed in California, United States.

[1]Copyright © 2014 Thunderbird School of Global Management. All rights reserved. This case was prepared by Professor Michael H. Moffett for the purpose of classroom discussion only and not to indicate either effective or ineffective management.

the Internal Revenue Service (IRS), eventually gaining IRS consent in what is known as an *advanced pricing agreement*. The agreement, as yet undisclosed, established allowable transfer prices and practices between the various Google-owned units used to minimize global taxes.

The Other PE

But Google's tax structure and strategy is not a concern just to the U.S. tax authorities, as the Inland Revenue Service in the U.K. has also been frustrated by the magnitude of sales generated by the company resulting in such a low tax liability.

What is core to Google's structure shown in Exhibit A is known as *permanent establishment* (PE). Permanent establishment rules allow firms such as Google to fix a tax base in a low-tax country like Ireland, while generating lots of business in a country where tax rates are higher, like France. Companies in principle are taxed not on "where they do business," but on "where they finalize their business deals with customers"—the country or jurisdiction where the final contract is signed. In the case of Google, that means most sales throughout the European Union are finalized in Ireland.

And, of course, Google is not alone. It is estimated that 75% of the top 50 U.S. software, Internet, and computer hardware companies use similar PE structures that help them avoid taxes. Apple too has been the subject of intense scrutiny, as noted in Exhibit B.

Illegal, Unfair, Unethical, and Immoral

The debate that has raged in recent years about Google, Apple, and many other multinational companies is that they are generating massive profits around the world and often paying few corporate income taxes—anywhere to anyone. All the while many other multinationals continue to pay effective tax rates in the high 20s to low 30s (percentage of consolidated pre-tax income). Not a level playing field, and one that many traditional manufacturers, who cannot move their products and property digitally around the globe, feel is biased against them.

Most multinationals like Apple and Google are probably not doing anything illegal. They have simply learned all the rules very well, and are pursuing shareholder returns in as optimal a manner as possible. Whereas illegal activities are termed *tax evasion*, *tax avoidance* is used to describe extremely aggressive strategies and structures used by business to reduce taxes far below what most governments expected. This latter category would include the use of offshore tax havens. The question that remains is whether they are pursuing nonfinancial interests or responsibilities of the firm equitably or ethically.

CASE QUESTIONS

1. Corporate income taxes are payable on profits. How would you describe "profits" that result from the Google "Double-Irish-Dutch" tax strategy?

2. What are some possible changes to the tax code that would bring the tax liabilities payable by Google to onshore U.K.?

3. Do you believe that Google or other companies like Apple should pay more taxes? Would that make them better citizens yet make them bad business managers? What would you consider a better balance or compromise?

EXHIBIT B   Apple and Taxes

Apple does not use tax gimmicks. Apple does not move its intellectual property into offshore tax havens and use it to sell products back into the U.S. in order to avoid U.S. tax; it does not use revolving loans from foreign subsidiaries to fund its domestic operations; it does not hold money on a Caribbean island; and it does not have a bank account in the Cayman Islands. Apple has substantial foreign cash because it sells the majority of its products outside the U.S.

—Apple CEO Tim Cook, in testimony before the U.S. Senate Permanent Subcommittee on Investigations, 2013.

A U.S. Senate committee in a recent report characterized Apple's use of a Dublin, Ireland booking center as the hub of a complex tax strategy which enabled Apple to save $44 billion in "otherwise taxable offshore income." Apple uses non-tax resident subsidiaries in Ireland to receive the majority of its global non-U.S. income. It is also suspected that Apple negotiated a preferential tax agreement with Ireland to lower its effective tax rate on Irish-booked profits at an effective rate below 2%, significantly below the low 12.5% statutory tax rate. Effectively, in the end, Apple's international operations do not pay taxes of substance in any country.

Tensions rose even higher in April 2013 when Apple launched the largest single bond issuance in global history, some $17 billion. The funds were to be used to partially finance a $55 billion share buyback program. But by borrowing the funds in the U.S. market (where it will enjoy a tax deduction on the bond interest expenses of $308 million per year), and not repatriating the cash from its offshore hoard of roughly $130 billion, the company avoids an additional $9.2 billion in U.S. taxes.

Questions

1. **Tax Morality.**
   a. Discuss "tax morality" in regard to tax evasion and avoidance.
   b. What are the implications of MNEs' decisions to invest in low-tax nations? How can MNEs weigh their cost-cutting decisions against their corporate social responsibilities?

2. **Tax Neutrality.**
   a. Define the term "tax neutrality."
   b. What is the difference between domestic neutrality and foreign neutrality?
   c. What are a country's objectives when determining tax policy on foreign source income?

3. **Approaches to Taxing MNEs.** Different countries adopt diverse approaches to taxing income generated by MNEs. What are the main advantages of each of these tax approaches? Explain how these approaches impact the competitiveness of MNEs.

4. **Tax Incentives.** Answer the following questions:
   a. What tax incentives do nations offer MNEs?
   b. Mention the advantages and disadvantages of these tax incentives.

5. **Tax Treaties.** Answer the following questions:
   a. What is tax competition?
   b. What are the advantages and disadvantages of tax wars?
   c. How can tax treaties mitigate tax wars?

6. **Tax Types.** Taxes are classified based on whether they are applied directly to income, called direct taxes, or to some other measurable performance characteristic of the firm, called indirect taxes. Identify each of the following as a "direct tax," an "indirect tax," or something else:
   a. Corporate income tax paid by a Japanese subsidiary on its operating income
   b. Royalties paid to Saudi Arabia for oil extracted and shipped to world markets
   c. Interest received by a U.S. parent on bank deposits held in London
   d. Interest received by a U.S. parent on a loan to a subsidiary in Mexico
   e. Principal repayment received by U.S. parent from Belgium on a loan to a wholly owned subsidiary in Belgium
   f. Excise tax paid on cigarettes manufactured and sold within the United States
   g. Property taxes paid on the corporate headquarters building in Seattle
   h. A direct contribution to the International Committee of the Red Cross for refugee relief
   i. Deferred income tax, shown as a deduction on the U.S. parent's consolidated income tax
   j. Withholding taxes withheld by Germany on dividends paid to a United Kingdom parent corporation

7. **Foreign Tax Credit.** What is a foreign tax credit? Why do countries give credit for taxes paid on foreign source income?

8. **Value-Added Tax.** Answer the following questions:
   a. Compare sales tax to value-added tax.
   b. Sales taxes and VAT are a major source of fiscal revenue, reaping more proceeds in developed nations in comparison to emerging economies. What are the factors that make countries levy different levels of these taxes?

9. **Transfer Pricing Motivation.** What is a transfer price and can a government regulate it? What difficulties and motives does a parent multinational firm face in setting transfer prices?

10. **Sister Subsidiaries.** Subsidiary Alpha in Country Able faces a 40% income tax rate. Subsidiary Beta in Country Baker faces only a 20% income tax rate. Presently, each subsidiary imports from the other an amount of goods and services exactly equal in monetary value to what each exports to the other. This method of balancing intracompany trade was imposed by a management team keen to reduce all costs, including the costs (spread between bid and ask) of foreign exchange transactions. Both subsidiaries are profitable, and both could purchase all components domestically at approximately the same prices as they are paying to their foreign sister subsidiary. Does this seem like an optimal situation?

11. **Correct Transfer Pricing.** What is meant by "correct" or proper transfer pricing? How can local national authorities impose "correct" transfer pricing on MNEs? What is the main requisite for the implementation of proper transfer pricing?

12. **Tax Treaties.** How do tax treaties affect the operations and structure of MNEs?

13. **Tax-Haven Subsidiary.** Explain how a tax-haven subsidiary is sometimes used to alter tax deferral into tax avoidance.

Problems

1. **TexManchester's Foreign-Source Income.** TexManchester is a textile manufacturing firm based in Manchester, U.K. The firm distributes linen and clothing items in over 50 nations worldwide. The strategy team is in the process of constructing the firm's five-year strategy. They need to build a spreadsheet analyzing the subsidiary earnings/distribution in 2015 and in 2020 (including impending changes) as detailed in the table below.

Baseline Values	2015	2020 (exp)
a. Foreign corporate income tax rate	20%	45%
b. U.K. corporate income tax rate	21%	30%
c. Foreign dividend withholding tax rate	12%	0%
d. U.K. ownership in foreign firm	100%	70%
e. Dividend payout rate of foreign firm	100%	100%

a. Calculate the total tax payment, foreign and domestic combined, for TexManchester's income (given that taxable income is £3,400,000).
b. Calculate the effective tax rate paid by the U.K.-based parent company on its income.
c. Assuming that there were no withholding taxes on dividends, calculate the total tax payment and effective tax rate if the foreign corporate tax rate was 45%.
d. Calculate the total tax payment and effective tax rate if the income was earned by a branch of TexManchester.

2. **EcuAir (Ecuador).** MexAir is a Mexican-based airline firm with a wholly owned subsidiary in Ecuador. The subsidiary, EcuAir, has just completed a strategic planning report for its parent company, MexAir. The following table summarizes the estimates of expected earnings and payout rates for the years 2012–2015.

EcuAir (Ecuador) Income Items (millions MXN)	2012	2013	2014	2015
Earnings before interest and taxes (EBIT)	100,000	120,000	135,000	150,000
Less interest expenses	(8,500)	(10,000)	(13,000)	(15,00)
Earnings before taxes (EBT)	91,500	110,000	122,000	135,000

The current Ecuadorian corporate tax rate on this category of income is 20%. Ecuador imposes no withholding taxes on dividends remitted to Mexican investors (per the Mexican–Ecuadorian bilateral tax treaty). The Mexican corporate income tax rate is 25%. The parent company wants to repatriate 50% of net income as dividends annually.

a. What is the net income available for distribution by the Ecuadorian subsidiary for the years 2012–2015?
b. What is the amount of the dividend remittance expected to the Mexican parent each year?
c. After calculation of Mexican tax liabilities, what is the total dividend after tax (all Ecuadorian and Mexican taxes) expected each year?

d. What is the effective tax rate on this foreign-sourced income per year?

3. **Kraftstoff of Germany.** Kraftstoff is a German-based company that manufactures electronic fuel-injection carburetor assemblies for several large automobile companies in Germany, including Mercedes, BMW, and Opel. The firm, like many firms in Germany today, is revising its financial policies in line with the increasing degree of disclosure required by firms that wish to list their shares publicly in or out of Germany.

Kraftstoff's primary problem is that the German corporate income tax code applies a different income tax rate to income depending on whether it is retained (45%) or distributed to stockholders (30%).
a. If Kraftstoff planned to distribute 50% of its net income, what would be its total net income and total corporate tax bills?
b. If Kraftstoff was attempting to choose between a 40% and 60% payout rate to stockholders, what arguments and values would management use in order to convince stockholders which of the two payouts is in everyone's best interest?

Chinglish Dirk

Use the following company case to answer Problems 4–6. Chinglish Dirk Company (Hong Kong) exports razor blades to its wholly owned parent company, Torrington Edge (Great Britain). Hong Kong tax rates are 16% and British tax rates are 30%. Chinglish calculates its profit per container as follows (all values in British pounds).

Constructing Transfer (Sales) Price per Unit	Chinglish Dirk (British pounds)	Torrington Edge (British pounds)
Direct costs	£10,000	£16,100
Overhead	4,000	1,000
Total costs	£14,000	£17,100
Desired markup	2,100	2,565
Transfer price (sales price)	£16,100	£19,665
Income Statement		
Sales price	£16,100,000	£19,665,000
Less total costs	(14,000,000)	(17,100,000)
Taxable income	£2,100,000	£2,565,000
Less taxes	(336,000)	(769,500)
Profit, after-tax	£1,764,000	£1,795,500

4. **Chinglish Dirk (A).** Corporate management of Torrington Edge is considering repositioning profits within the multinational company. What happens to the profits of Chinglish Dirk and Torrington Edge, and the consolidated results of both, if the markup at

Chinglish was increased to 20% and the markup at Torrington was reduced to 10%? What is the impact of this repositioning on consolidated tax payments?

5. **Chinglish Dirk (B).** Encouraged by the results from the previous problem's analysis, corporate management of Torrington Edge wishes to continue to reposition profit in Hong Kong. It is, however, facing two constraints. First, the final sales price in Great Britain must be £20,000 or less to remain competitive. Secondly, the British tax authorities-in working with Torrington Edge's cost accounting staff-has established a maximum transfer price allowed (from Hong Kong) of £17,800. What combination of markups do you recommend for Torrington Edge to institute? What is the impact of this repositioning on consolidated profits on after-tax and total tax payments?

6. **Chinglish Dirk (C).** Not to leave any potential tax repositioning opportunities unexplored, Torrington Edge wants to combine the components of Problem 4 with a redistribution of overhead costs. If overhead costs could be reallocated between the two units, but still total £5,000 per unit and maintain a minimum of £1,750 per unit in Hong Kong, what is the impact of this repositioning on consolidated profits after-tax and total tax payments?

Internet Exercises

1. **Global Taxes.** Web sites like TaxWorld.org provide detailed insights into the conduct of business and the associated tax and accounting requirements of doing business in a variety of countries.

| International Tax Resources | www.taxworld.org/ OtherSites/International/ international.htm |

2. **International Taxpayer.** The United States Internal Revenue Service (IRS) provides detailed support and document requirements for international taxpayers. Use the IRS site to find the legal rules and regulations and definitions for international residents tax liabilities when earning income and profits in the United States.

| U.S. IRS Taxpayer | www.irs.gov/businesses/ small/international/ index.html |

3. **Official Government Tax Authorities.** Tax laws are constantly changing, and an MNE's tax planning and management processes must therefore include a continual updating of tax practices by country. Use the following government tax sites to address specific issues related to those countries:

| Hong Kong's ownership change to China | www.gov.hk/en/business/ taxes/profittax/ |
| Ireland's international financial services center | www.revenue.ie/ |

4. **Tax Practices for International Business.** Many of the major accounting firms provide online information and advisory services for international business activities as related to tax and accounting practices. Use the following Web sites to find current information on tax law changes and practices.

Ernst and Young	www.ey.com/tax/
Deloitte & Touche	www.deloitte.com/view/ en_US/us/Services/tax/ index.htm
KPMG	www.kpmg.com/
Price Waterhouse Coopers	www.pwc.com/us/en/tax-services/index.jhtml
Ernst & Young	www.eyi.com/

International Trade Finance

Financial statements are like fine perfume: to be sniffed but not swallowed. —Abraham Brilloff.

LEARNING OBJECTIVES

- Learn how international trade alters both the supply chain and general value chain of the domestic firm, thereby beginning the globalization process in the trade phase

- Identify the key elements of an import or export business transaction

- Discover how the three key documents in import/export—the letter of credit, the draft, and the bill of lading—combine to finance both the transaction and to manage its risks

- Identify what the documentation sequence is for a typical international trade transaction

- Learn how the various stages and their costs affect the ability of an exporter to enter a foreign market and potentially compete in both credit terms and pricing

- See what organizations and resources are available for exporters to aid in managing trade risk and financing

- Examine the various trade financing alternatives

The purpose of this chapter is to explain how international trade—exports and imports—is financed. The content is of direct practical relevance to both domestic firms—that simply import and export—and to multinational firms—that trade with related and unrelated entities.

The chapter begins by explaining the types of trade relationships that exist. Next, we explain the trade dilemma: exporters want to be paid before they export and importers do not want to pay until they receive the goods. The benefits of the current international trade protocols are then explained, followed by a section describing the elements of a trade transaction and the documents used to facilitate a trade's completion and financing. Next international trade risks are identified, namely, currency risk and noncompletion risk. This is followed by sections describing the key trade documents—including letter of credit, draft, and bill of lading—and summarizing the documentation of a typical trade transaction. Finally, various types of short-term receivables financing are compared and the use of forfaiting for longer term receivables is discussed. The Mini-Case at the end of the chapter, *Crosswell International and Brazil*, illustrates how an export requires the integration of management, marketing, and finance.

The Trade Relationship

As we saw in Chapter 1, the first significant global activity by a domestic firm is the importing and exporting of goods and services. The purpose of this chapter is to analyze the *international trade phase* for a domestic firm, which begins to import goods and services from foreign suppliers and to export to foreign buyers. In the case of Trident, this trade phase began with suppliers from Mexico and buyers from Canada.

Trade financing shares a number of common characteristics with the traditional value chain activities conducted by all firms. All companies must search out suppliers for the many goods and services required as inputs to their own goods production or service provision processes. Trident's Purchasing and Procurement Department must determine whether each potential supplier is capable of producing the product to required quality specifications and in a timely and reliable manner, and whether the supplier will work with Trident in the ongoing process of product and process improvement for continued competitiveness. All must be at an acceptable price and payment terms. As illustrated in Exhibit 15.1, this same series of issues applies to potential customers, as their continued business is equally critical to Trident's operations and success.

Understanding the nature of the relationship between the exporter and the importer is critical to understanding the methods for import-export financing utilized in industry. Exhibit 15.2 provides an overview of the three categories of import/export relationships: *unaffiliated unknown*, *unaffiliated known*, and *affiliated*.

- A foreign importer with which Trident has not previously conducted business would be considered *unaffiliated unknown*. In this case, the two parties would need to enter into a detailed sales contract, outlining the specific responsibilities and expectations of the business agreement. Trident would also need to seek out protection against the possibility that the importer would not make payment in full in a timely fashion.

- A foreign importer with which Trident has previously conducted business successfully would be considered *unaffiliated known*. In this case, the two parties may still enter into a detailed sales contract, but specific terms and shipments or provisions of services may be significantly looser in definition. Depending on the depth of the relationship, Trident may seek some third-party protection against noncompletion or conduct the business on an open account basis.

- A foreign importer which is a subsidiary business unit of Trident, such as Trident Brazil, would be an *affiliated* party (sometimes referred to as *intrafirm trade*). Because both

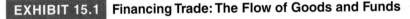

EXHIBIT 15.1   **Financing Trade: The Flow of Goods and Funds**

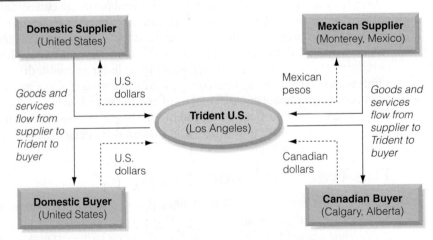

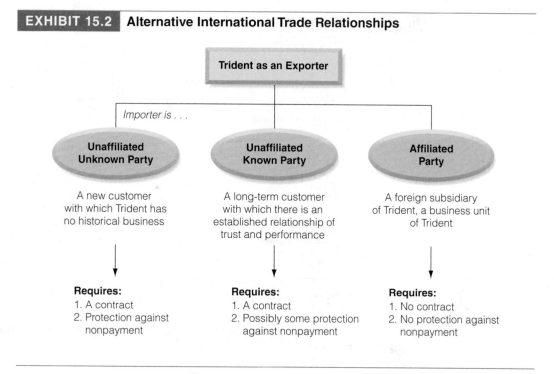

EXHIBIT 15.2   Alternative International Trade Relationships

Trident as an Exporter

Importer is . . .

Unaffiliated Unknown Party	Unaffiliated Known Party	Affiliated Party
A new customer with which Trident has no historical business	A long-term customer with which there is an established relationship of trust and performance	A foreign subsidiary of Trident, a business unit of Trident
Requires: 1. A contract 2. Protection against nonpayment	Requires: 1. A contract 2. Possibly some protection against nonpayment	Requires: 1. No contract 2. No protection against nonpayment

businesses are part of the same MNE, the most common practice would be to conduct the trade transaction without a contract or protection against nonpayment. This is not, however, always the case. In a variety of international business situations it may still be in Trident's best interest to detail the conditions for the business transaction, and to possibly protect against any political or country-based interruption to the completion of the trade transaction.

International trade must work around a fundamental dilemma. Imagine an importer and an exporter who would like to do business with one another. Because of the distance between the two, it is not possible to simultaneously hand over goods with one hand and accept payment with the other. The importer would prefer the arrangement at the top of Exhibit 15.3, while the exporter's preference is shown at the bottom.

The fundamental dilemma of being reluctant to trust a stranger in a foreign land is resolved by using a highly respected bank as intermediary. A greatly simplified view is described in Exhibit 15.4. In this simplified view, the importer obtains the bank's promise to pay on its behalf, knowing that the exporter will trust the bank. The bank's promise to pay is called a *letter of credit*. The exporter ships the merchandise to the importer's country. Title to the merchandise is given to the bank on a document called a *bill of lading*. The exporter asks the bank to pay for the goods, and the bank does so. The document requesting payment is called a *sight draft*. The bank, having paid for the goods, now passes title to the importer, whom the bank trusts. At that time or later, depending on their agreement, the importer reimburses the bank.

Financial managers of MNEs must understand these three basic documents, because their firms will often trade with unaffiliated parties, and also because the system of documentation

EXHIBIT 15.3   The Mechanics of Import and Export

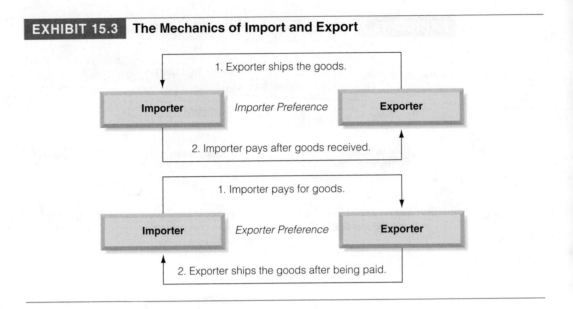

provides a source of short-term capital that can be drawn upon even when shipments are to sister subsidiaries.

Benefits of the System

The three key documents and their interaction will be discussed in detail later in this chapter. They constitute a system developed and modified over centuries to protect both importer and exporter from the risk of noncompletion and foreign exchange risk, as well as to provide a means of financing.

EXHIBIT 15.4   The Bank as the Import/Export Intermediary

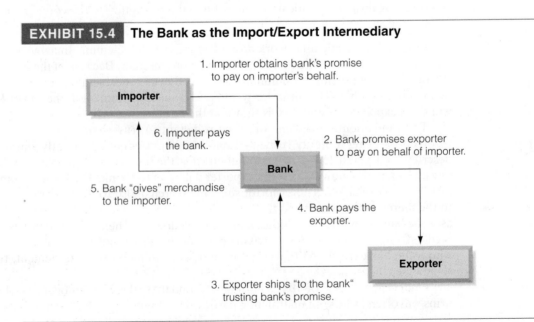

Protection against Risk of Noncompletion

As stated above, once importer and exporter agree on terms, the seller usually prefers to maintain legal title to the goods until paid, or at least until assured of payment. The buyer, however, will be reluctant to pay before receiving the goods, or at least before receiving title to them. Each wants assurance that the other party will complete its portion of the transaction. The letter of credit, bill of lading, and sight draft are part of a system carefully constructed to determine who bears the financial loss if one of the parties defaults at any time.

Protection against Foreign Exchange Risk

In international trade, foreign exchange risk arises from transaction exposure. If the transaction requires payment in the exporter's currency, the importer carries the foreign exchange risk. If the transaction calls for payment in the importer's currency, the exporter has the foreign exchange risk.

Transaction exposure can be hedged by the techniques described in Chapter 9, but in order to hedge, the exposed party must be certain that payment of a specified amount will be made on or near a particular date. The three key documents described in this chapter ensure both amount and time of payment and thus lay the groundwork for effective hedging.

The risk of noncompletion and foreign exchange risk are most important when the international trade is episodic, with no outstanding agreement for recurring shipments and no sustained relationship between buyer and seller. When the import/export relationship is of a recurring nature, as in the case of manufactured goods shipped weekly or monthly to a final assembly or retail outlet in another country, and when the relationship is between countries whose currencies are considered strong, the exporter may well bill the importer on open account after a normal credit check.

Financing the Trade

Most international trade involves a time lag during which funds are tied up while the merchandise is in transit. Once the risks of noncompletion and of exchange rate changes are disposed of, banks are willing to finance goods in transit. A bank can finance goods in transit, as well as goods held for sale, based on the key documents, without exposing itself to questions about the quality of merchandise or aspects of shipment.

Noncompletion Risks

In order to understand the risks associated with international trade transactions, it is helpful to understand the sequence of events in any such transaction. Exhibit 15.5 illustrates, in principle, the series of events associated with a single export transaction.

From a financial management perspective, the two primary risks associated with an international trade transaction are currency risk (discussed previously in Chapters 9 and 10) and *risk of noncompletion*. Exhibit 15.5 illustrates the traditional business problem of credit management: the exporter quotes a price, finalizes a contract, and ships the goods, losing physical control over the goods based on trust of the buyer or the promise of a bank to pay based on documents presented. The risk of default on the part of the importer—*risk of noncompletion*—is present as soon as the financing period begins, as depicted in Exhibit 15.5.

In many cases, the initial task of analyzing the creditworthiness of foreign customers is similar to procedures for analyzing domestic customers. If Trident has had no experience with a foreign customer but the customer is a large, well-known firm in its home country, Trident may simply ask for a bank credit report on that firm. Trident may also talk to other firms that have had dealings with the foreign customer. If these investigations show the foreign

EXHIBIT 15.5 **The Trade Transaction Timeline and Structure**

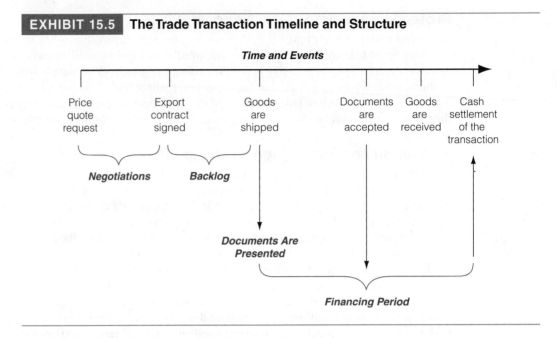

customer (and country) to be completely trustworthy, Trident would likely ship to them on open account, with a credit limit, just as they would for a domestic customer. This is the least costly method of handling exports because there are no heavy documentation or bank charges. However, before a regular trading relationship has been established with a new or unknown firm, Trident must face the possibility of nonpayment for its exports or noncompletion of its imports. The risk of nonpayment can be eliminated through the use of a letter of credit issued by a creditworthy bank.

Key Documents

The three key documents described in the following pages—the letter of credit, draft, and bill of lading—constitute a system developed and modified over centuries to protect both importer and exporter from the risk of noncompletion of the trade transaction as well as to provide a means of financing. These three key trade documents are part of a carefully constructed system to determine who bears the financial loss if one of the parties defaults at any time.

Letter of Credit (L/C)

A *letter of credit* (L/C) is a document issued by a bank at the request of an importer (the applicant/buyer) by which the bank promises to pay an exporter (the beneficiary of the letter) upon presentation of documents specified in the L/C. An L/C reduces the risk of noncompletion, because the bank agrees to pay against documents rather than actual merchandise. The relationship between the three parties can be seen in Exhibit 15.6.

A beneficiary (exporter) and an applicant (importer) agree on a transaction and the importer then applies to its local bank for the issuance of an L/C. The importer's bank issues an L/C and cuts a sales contract based on its assessment of the importer's creditworthiness, or the bank might require a cash deposit or other collateral from the importer in advance. The importer's bank will want to know the type of transaction, the amount of money involved, and what documents must accompany the draft that will be drawn against the L/C.

| EXHIBIT 15.6 | Parties to a Letter of Credit (L/C) |

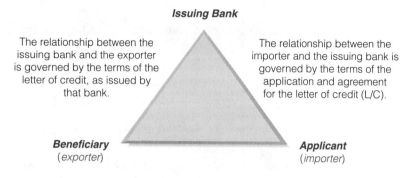

Issuing Bank

The relationship between the issuing bank and the exporter is governed by the terms of the letter of credit, as issued by that bank.

The relationship between the importer and the issuing bank is governed by the terms of the application and agreement for the letter of credit (L/C).

Beneficiary
(*exporter*)

Applicant
(*importer*)

The relationship between the importer and the exporter is governed by the sales contract.

If the importer's bank is satisfied with the credit standing of the applicant, it will issue an L/C guaranteeing to pay for the merchandise if shipped in accordance with the instructions and conditions contained in the L/C.

The essence of an L/C is the promise of the issuing bank to pay *against specified documents*, which must accompany any draft drawn against the credit. The L/C is not a guarantee of the underlying commercial transaction. Indeed, the L/C is a separate transaction from any sales or other contracts on which it might be based. To constitute a true L/C transaction, the following elements must be present with respect to the issuing bank:

1. The issuing bank must receive a fee or other valid business consideration for issuing the L/C.
2. The bank's L/C must contain a specified expiration date or a definite maturity.
3. The bank's commitment must have a stated maximum amount of money.
4. The bank's obligation to pay must arise only on the presentation of specific documents, and the bank must not be called on to determine disputed questions of fact or law.
5. The bank's customer must have an unqualified obligation to reimburse the bank on the same condition as the bank has paid.

Commercial letters of credit are also classified based on whether they are revocable and confirmed.

▪ **Irrevocable versus Revocable.** An *irrevocable L/C* obligates the issuing bank to honor drafts drawn in compliance with the credit and can be neither canceled nor modified without the consent of all parties, including in particular the beneficiary (exporter). A *revocable L/C* can be canceled or amended at any time before payment; it is intended to serve as a means of arranging payment but not as a guarantee of payment.

▪ **Confirmed versus Unconfirmed.** A *confirmed L/C* is issued by one bank and can be confirmed by another bank, in which case the confirming bank can honor drafts drawn in compliance with the L/C. An *unconfirmed L/C* is the obligation only of the issuing bank. An exporter is likely to want a foreign bank's L/C confirmed by a domestic bank when the exporter has doubts about the foreign bank's ability to pay. Such doubts can arise when the exporter is unsure of the financial standing of the foreign bank, or if political or economic conditions in the foreign country are unstable. The essence of an L/C is shown in Exhibit 15.7.

EXHIBIT 15.7   **Essence of a Letter of Credit (L/C)**

> **Bank of the East, Ltd.**
> [*Name of Issuing Bank*]
>
> Date: September 18, 2011
> L/C Number 123456
>
> Bank of the East, Ltd. hereby issues this irrevocable documentary Letter of Credit to Jones Company [*name of exporter*] for US$500,000, payable 90 days after sight by a draft drawn against Bank of the East, Ltd., in accordance with Letter of Credit number 123456.
>
> The draft is to be accompanied by the following documents:
>
> 1. Commercial invoice in triplicate
> 2. Packing list
> 3. Clean on board order bill of lading
> 4. Insurance documents, paid for by buyer
>
> At maturity Bank of the East, Ltd. will pay the face amount of the draft to the bearer of that draft.
>
> *Authorized Signature*

Most commercial letters of credit are *documentary*, meaning that certain documents must be included with drafts drawn under their terms. Required documents usually include a bill of lading (discussed in more detail later in the chapter), a commercial invoice, and any of the following: consular invoice, insurance certificate or policy, and packing list.

Advantages and Disadvantages of Letters of Credit. The primary advantage of an L/C is that it reduces risk—the exporter can sell against a bank's promise to pay rather than against the promise of a commercial firm. The exporter is also in a more secure position as to the availability of foreign exchange to pay for the sale, since banks are more likely to be aware of foreign exchange conditions and rules than is the importing firm itself. If the importing country should change its foreign exchange rules during the course of a transaction, the government is likely to allow already outstanding bank letters of credit to be honored for fear of throwing its own domestic banks into international disrepute. Of course, if the L/C is confirmed by a bank in the exporter's country, the exporter avoids any problem of blocked foreign exchange.

An exporter may find that an order backed by an irrevocable L/C will facilitate obtaining pre-export financing in the home country. If the exporter's reputation for delivery is good, a local bank may lend funds to process and prepare the merchandise for shipment. Once the merchandise is shipped in compliance with the terms and conditions of the L/C, payment for the business transaction is made and funds will be generated to repay the pre-export loan.

Another advantage of an L/C to the importer is that the importer need not pay out funds until the documents have arrived at a local port or airfield and unless all conditions stated in the credit have been fulfilled.

The main disadvantages of L/Cs are the fees charged by the importer's bank for issuing its L/C and the possibility that the L/C reduces the importer's borrowing line of credit with its bank. It may, in fact, be a competitive disadvantage for the exporter to demand automatically an L/C from an importer, especially if the importer has a good credit record and there is no concern regarding the economic or political conditions of the importer's country.

In balance, though, the value of the L/C has been well established since the beginning of commerce, as detailed in *Global Finance in Practice 15.1*.

Draft

A *draft*, sometimes called a *bill of exchange* (B/E), is the instrument normally used in international commerce to effect payment. A draft is simply an order written by an exporter (seller) instructing an importer (buyer) or its agent to pay a specified amount of money at a specified time. Thus, it is the exporter's formal demand for payment from the importer.

The person or business initiating the draft is known as the *maker* (also known as the *drawer* or *originator*). Normally, maker is the exporter who sells and ships the merchandise. The party to whom the draft is addressed is the *drawee*. The drawee is asked to *honor* the draft, that is, to pay the amount requested according to the stated terms. In commercial transactions, the drawee is either the buyer, in which case the draft is called a *trade draft*, or the buyer's bank, in which case the draft is called a *bank draft*. Bank drafts are usually drawn according to the terms of an L/C. A draft may be drawn as a bearer instrument, or it may designate a person to whom payment is to be made. This person, known as the *payee*, may be the drawer itself or it may be some other party such as the drawer's bank.

Negotiable Instruments. If properly drawn, drafts can become negotiable instruments. As such, they provide a convenient instrument for financing the international movement of the merchandise. To become a *negotiable instrument*, a draft must conform to the following requirements (Uniform Commercial Code, Section 3104(1)):

1. It must be in writing and signed by the maker or drawer.
2. It must contain an unconditional promise or order to pay a definite sum of money.
3. It must be payable on demand or at a fixed or determinable future date.
4. It must be payable to order or to bearer.

If a draft is drawn in conformity with the above requirements, a person receiving it with proper endorsements becomes a "holder in due course." This is a privileged legal status that enables the holder to receive payment despite any personal disagreements between drawee

---

GLOBAL FINANCE IN PRACTICE 15.1

Florence—The Birthplace of Trade Financing

Merchant banking for international trade largely began in a landlocked city, Florence, Italy. In the late 13th and early 14th century as commerce grew throughout Europe and the Mediterranean, banking began to develop in both Venice and Florence.

It was a time in which commerce was still in its infancy, with the Catholic Church prohibiting many aspects of commerce, including the loaning of money in return for interest—*usury*. Although usury has come to mean the illegal activity of charging excessive rates of interest, the term originally referred to charging interest of any kind. ·

The *florin* is a small gold coin first minted in Florence in 1252. Named after the city, the florin flourished as a means

of transacting trade across Europe in the following century. Merchants conducted their trade on a bench—a *banco*—which eventually gave rise to the term for the safe place in which to keep one's money.

But the coins were heavy, and if a merchant were traveling from one city or country to another to conduct trade, the weight was substantial, as was the chance of being robbed. So the merchants created the first financial derivative, a draft on the banco—a *letter of exchange*—which could be carried from one city to another and was recognized as a credit for florins on account at their home banco. Payment was guaranteed within three months. Of course, with the creation of banks came the first failures—*bankruptcies*.

From the very beginning, whether it was the loaning of money, the validity of a letter of exchange, or even the value of a currency, all were instruments or activities that involved risk, or *risque* in the Italian of the time.

and maker because of controversy over the underlying transaction. If the drawee dishonors the draft, payment must be made to any holder in due course by any prior endorser or by the maker. This clear definition of the rights of parties who hold a negotiable instrument as a holder in due course has contributed significantly to the widespread acceptance of various forms of drafts, including personal checks.

Types of Drafts. Drafts are of two types: *sight drafts* and *time drafts*. A *sight draft* is payable on presentation to the drawee; the drawee must pay at once or dishonor the draft. A *time draft*, also called a *usance draft*, allows a delay in payment. It is presented to the drawee, who accepts it by writing or stamping a notice of acceptance on its face. Once accepted, the time draft becomes a promise to pay by the accepting party (the buyer). When a time draft is drawn on and accepted by a bank, it becomes a *bankers' acceptance*; when drawn on and accepted by a business firm, it becomes a *trade acceptance*.

The time period of a draft is referred to as its *tenor*. To qualify as a negotiable instrument, and so be attractive to a holder in due course, a draft must be payable on a fixed or determinable future date. For example, "60 days after sight" is a fixed date, which is established precisely at the time the draft is accepted. However, payment "on arrival of goods" is not determinable since the date of arrival cannot be known in advance. Indeed, there is no assurance that the goods will arrive at all.

Bankers' Acceptances. When a draft is accepted by a bank, it becomes a bankers' acceptance. As such it is the unconditional promise of that bank to make payment on the draft when it matures. In quality, the bankers' acceptance is practically identical to a marketable bank certificate of deposit (CD). The holder of a bankers' acceptance need not wait until maturity to liquidate the investment, but may sell the acceptance in the money market, where constant trading in such instruments occurs. The amount of the discount depends entirely on the credit rating of the bank that signs the acceptance, or another bank that reconfirmed the bankers' acceptance, for a fee. The total cost or *all-in cost* of using a bankers' acceptance compared to other short-term financing instruments is analyzed later in this chapter.

Bill of Lading (B/L)

The third key document for financing international trade is the *bill of lading* (B/L). The bill of lading is issued to the exporter by a common carrier transporting the merchandise. It serves three purposes: as a receipt, a contract, and a document of title.

As a receipt, the bill of lading indicates that the carrier has received the merchandise described on the face of the document. The carrier is not responsible for ascertaining that the containers hold what is alleged to be their contents, so descriptions of merchandise on bills of lading are usually short and simple. If shipping charges are paid in advance, the bill of lading will usually be stamped "freight paid" or "freight prepaid." If merchandise is shipped collect—a less common procedure internationally than domestically—the carrier maintains a lien on the goods until freight is paid.

As a contract, the bill of lading indicates the obligation of the carrier to provide certain transportation in return for certain charges. Common carriers cannot disclaim responsibility for their negligence by inserting special clauses in a bill of lading. The bill of lading may specify alternative ports in the event that delivery cannot be made to the designated port, or it may specify that the goods will be returned to the exporter at the exporter's expense.

As a document of title, the bill of lading is used to obtain payment or a written promise of payment before the merchandise is released to the importer. The bill of lading can also function as collateral against which funds may be advanced to the exporter by its local bank prior to or during shipment and before final payment by the importer.

The bill of lading is typically made payable to the order of the exporter, who thus retains title to the goods after they have been handed to the carrier. Title to the merchandise remains with the exporter until payment is received, at which time the exporter endorses the bill of lading (which is negotiable) in blank (making it a bearer instrument) or to the party making the payment, usually a bank. The most common procedure would be for payment to be advanced against a documentary draft accompanied by the endorsed order bill of lading. After paying the draft, the exporter's bank forwards the documents through bank clearing channels to the bank of the importer. The importer's bank, in turn, releases the documents to the importer after payment (sight drafts); after acceptance (time drafts addressed to the importer and marked D/A); or after payment terms have been agreed upon (drafts drawn on the importer's bank under provisions of an L/C).

Documentation in a Typical Trade Transaction

Although a trade transaction could conceivably be handled in many ways, we shall now turn to a hypothetical example that illustrates the interaction of the various documents. Assume that Trident U.S. receives an order from a Canadian buyer. For Trident, this will be an export financed under an L/C requiring a bill of lading, with the exporter collecting via a time draft that was accepted by the Canadian buyer's bank. Such a transaction proceeds as follows, illustrated in Exhibit 15.8.

1. The Canadian buyer (the Importer in Exhibit 15.8) places an order with Trident (the Exporter in Exhibit 15.8), asking if Trident is willing to ship under an L/C.

2. Trident agrees to ship under an L/C and specifies relevant information such as prices and terms.

3. The Canadian buyer applies to its bank, Northland Bank (Bank Y in Exhibit 15.8), for an L/C to be issued in favor of Trident for the merchandise it wishes to buy.

4. Northland Bank issues the L/C in favor of Trident and sends it to Trident's bank, Southland Bank (Bank X in Exhibit 15.8).

5. Southland Bank advises Trident of the opening of an L/C in Trident's favor. Southland Bank may or may not confirm the L/C to add its own guarantee to the document.

6. Trident ships the goods to the Canadian buyer.

7. Trident prepares a time draft and presents it to its bank, Southland Bank. The draft is drawn (i.e., addressed to) Northland Bank in accordance with Northland Bank's L/C and accompanied by other documents as required, including the bill of lading. Trident endorses the bill of lading in blank (making it a bearer instrument) so that title to the goods goes with the holder of the documents—Southland Bank at this point in the transaction.

8. Southland Bank presents the draft and documents to Northland Bank for acceptance. Northland Bank accepts the draft by stamping and signing it (making it a bankers' acceptance), takes possession of the documents, and promises to pay the now-accepted draft at maturity—say, 60 days.

9. Northland Bank returns the accepted draft to Southland Bank. Alternatively, Southland Bank might ask Northland Bank to accept and discount the draft. Should this occur, Northland Bank would remit the cash less a discount fee rather than return the accepted draft to Southland Bank.

10. Southland Bank, having received back the accepted draft, now a bankers' acceptance, may choose between several alternatives. Southland Bank may sell the acceptance in the

---

EXHIBIT 15.8 **Steps in a Typical Trade Transaction**

1. Importer orders goods.

3. Importer arranges L/C with its bank.

2. Exporter agrees to fill order.

Exporter **Importer**

6. Exporter ships goods to importer.

11. Bank X pays exporter.

7. Exporter presents draft and documents to its bank, Bank X.

12. Bank Y obtains importer's note and releases shipment.

13. Importer pays its bank.

8. Bank X presents draft and documents to Bank Y.

Bank X **Bank Y**

5. Bank X advises exporter of L/C.

9. Bank Y accepts draft, promising to pay in 60 days, and returns accepted draft to Bank X.

4. Bank Y sends L/C to Bank X.

Public Investor

10. Bank X sells acceptance to investor.

14. Investor presents acceptance and is paid by Bank Y.

---

open market at a discount to an investor, typically a corporation or financial institution with excess cash it wants to invest for a short period of time. Southland Bank may also hold the acceptance in its own portfolio.

11. If Southland Bank discounted the acceptance with Northland Bank (mentioned in Step 9) or discounted it in the local money market, Southland Bank will transfer the proceeds less any fees and discount to Trident. Another possibility would be for Trident itself to take possession of the acceptance, hold it for 60 days, and present it for collection. Normally, however, exporters prefer to receive the discounted cash value of the acceptance at once rather than wait for the acceptance to mature and receive a slightly greater amount of cash at a later date.

12. Northland Bank notifies the Canadian buyer of the arrival of the documents. The Canadian buyer signs a note or makes some other agreed upon plan to pay Northland Bank for the merchandise in 60 days, Northland Bank releases the underlying documents so that the Canadian buyer can obtain physical possession of the shipment at once.

13. After 60 days, Northland Bank receives funds from the Canadian buyer to pay the maturing acceptance.

14. On the same day, the 60th day after acceptance, the holder of the matured acceptance presents it for payment and receives its face value. The holder may present it directly to Northland Bank, or return it to Southland Bank and have Southland Bank collect it through normal banking channels.

Although this is a typical transaction involving an L/C, few international trade transactions are probably ever truly typical. Business, and more specifically international business, requires flexibility and creativity by management at all times. The Mini-Case at the end of this chapter presents an application of the mechanics of a real business situation. The result is a classic challenge to management: When and on what basis should typical procedures be compromised in order to accomplish strategic goals?

Government Programs to Help Finance Exports

Governments of most export-oriented industrialized countries have special financial institutions that provide some form of subsidized credit to their own national exporters. These export finance institutions offer terms that are better than those generally available from the private sector. Thus, domestic taxpayers are subsidizing sales to foreign buyers in order to create employment and maintain a technological edge. The most important institutions usually offer export credit insurance and an export-import bank for export financing.

Export Credit Insurance

The exporter who insists on cash or an L/C payment for foreign shipments is likely to lose orders to competitors from other countries that provide more favorable credit terms. Better credit terms are often made possible by means of *export credit insurance*, which provides assurance to the exporter or the exporter's bank that, should the foreign customer default on payment, the insurance company will pay for a major portion of the loss. Because of the availability of export credit insurance, commercial banks are willing to provide medium- to long-term financing (five to seven years) for exports. Importers prefer that the exporter purchase export credit insurance to pay for nonperformance risk by the importer. In this way, the importer does not need to pay to have an L/C issued and does not reduce its credit line.

Competition between nations to increase exports by lengthening the period for which credit transactions can be insured may lead to a credit war and to unsound credit decisions. To prevent such an unhealthy development, a number of leading trading nations joined together in 1934 to create the Berne Union (officially, the Union d'Assureurs des Credits Internationaux) for the purpose of establishing a voluntary international understanding on export credit terms. The Berne Union recommends maximum credit terms for many items including, for example, heavy capital goods (five years), light capital goods (three years), and consumer durable goods (one year).

In the United States, export credit insurance is provided by the *Foreign Credit Insurance Association* (FCIA). This is an unincorporated association of private commercial insurance companies operating in cooperation with the Export-Import Bank (discussed in the next section). The FCIA provides policies protecting U.S. exporters against the risk of nonpayment by foreign debtors as a result of commercial and political risks. Losses due to commercial risk are those that result from the insolvency or protracted payment default of the buyer. Political losses arise from actions of governments beyond the control of buyer or seller.

Export-Import Bank and Export Financing

The *Export-Import Bank* (also called Eximbank) is another independent agency of the U.S. government, established in 1934 to stimulate and facilitate the foreign trade of the United States. Interestingly, the Eximbank was originally created primarily to facilitate exports to the Soviet Union. In 1945, the Eximbank was re-chartered "to aid in financing and to facilitate exports and imports and the exchange of commodities between the United States and any foreign country or the agencies or nationals thereof."

The Eximbank facilitates the financing of U.S. exports through various loan guarantee and insurance programs. The Eximbank guarantees repayment of medium-term (181 days to five years) and long-term (five years to ten years) export loans extended by U.S. banks to foreign borrowers. The Eximbank's medium- and long-term, direct-lending operation is based on participation with private sources of funds. Essentially, the Eximbank lends dollars to borrowers outside the United States for the purchase of U.S. goods and services. Proceeds of such loans are paid to U.S. suppliers. The loans themselves are repaid with interest in dollars to the Eximbank. The Eximbank requires private participation in these direct loans in order to: 1) ensure that it complements rather than competes with private sources of export financing; 2) spread its resources more broadly; and 3) ensure that private financial institutions will continue to provide export credit.

The Eximbank also guarantees lease transactions, finances the costs involved in the preparation by U.S. firms of engineering, planning, and feasibility studies for non-U.S. clients on large capital projects; and supplies counseling for exporters, banks, or others needing help in finding financing for U.S. goods.

Trade Financing Alternatives

In order to finance international trade receivables, firms use the same financing instruments that they use for domestic trade receivables, plus a few specialized instruments that are only available for financing international trade. Exhibit 15.9 identifies the main short-term financing instruments and their approximate costs.

Bankers' Acceptances

Bankers' acceptances, described earlier in this chapter, can be used to finance both domestic and international trade receivables. Exhibit 15.9 shows that bankers' acceptances earn a yield comparable to other money market instruments, especially marketable bank certificates of deposit. However, the all-in cost to a firm of creating and discounting a bankers' acceptance also depends upon the commission charged by the bank that accepts the firm's draft.

The first owner of the bankers' acceptance created from an international trade transaction will be the exporter, who receives the accepted draft back after the bank has stamped it "accepted." The exporter may hold the acceptance until maturity and then collect. On an

---

EXHIBIT 15.9 **Instruments for Financing Short-Term Domestic and International Trade Receivables**

Instrument	Cost or Yield for 3-Month Maturity
Bankers' acceptances *	1.14% yield annualized
Trade acceptances *	1.17% yield annualized
Factoring	Variable rate but much higher cost than bank credit lines
Securitization	Variable rate but competitive with bank credit lines
Bank credit lines	4.25% plus points (fewer points if covered by export credit insurance)
Commercial paper *	1.15% yield annualized

* These instruments compete with 3-month marketable bank time certificates of deposit that yield 1.17%.

acceptance of, say, $100,000 for three months the exporter would receive the face amount less the bank's acceptance commission of 1.5% per annum:

Face amount of the acceptance	$100,000
Less 1.5% per annum commission for three months	− 375 (.015 × 3/12 × $100,000)
Amount received by exporter in three months	$ 99,625

Alternatively, the exporter may "discount"—that is, sell at a reduced price—the acceptance to its bank in order to receive funds at once. The exporter will then receive the face amount of the acceptance less both the acceptance fee and the going market rate of discount for bankers' acceptances. If the discount rate were 1.14% per annum as shown in Exhibit 15.9, the exporter would receive the following:

Face amount of the acceptance	$100,000
Less 1.5% per annum commission for three months	− 375 (.015 × 3/12 × $100,000)
Less 1.14% per annum discount rate for three months	− 285 (.0114 × 3/12 × $100,000)
Amount received by exporter at once	$ 99,340

Therefore, the annualized all-in cost of financing this bankers' acceptance is as follows:

$$\frac{\text{Commission} + \text{Discount}}{\text{Proceeds}} \times \frac{360}{90} = \frac{\$375 + \$285}{\$99,340} \times \frac{360}{90} = 0.0266 \text{ or } 2.66\%$$

The discounting bank may hold the acceptance in its own portfolio, earning for itself the 1.14% per annum discount rate, or the acceptance may be resold in the acceptance market to portfolio investors. Investors buying bankers' acceptances provide the funds that finance the transaction.

Trade Acceptances

Trade acceptances are similar to bankers' acceptances except that the accepting entity is a commercial firm, like General Motors Acceptance Corporation (GMAC), rather than a bank. The cost of a trade acceptance depends on the credit rating of the accepting firm plus the commission it charges. Like bankers' acceptances, trade acceptances are sold at a discount to banks and other investors at a rate that is competitive with other money market instruments (see Exhibit 15.9).

Factoring

Specialized firms, known as factors, purchase receivables at a discount on either a non-recourse or recourse basis. Non-recourse means that the factor assumes the credit, political, and foreign exchange risk of the receivables it purchases. Recourse means that the factor can give back receivables that are not collectable. Since the factor must bear the cost and risk of assessing the creditworthiness of each receivable, the cost of factoring is usually quite high. It is more than borrowing at the prime rate plus points.

The all-in cost of factoring non-recourse receivables is similar in structure to acceptances. The factor charges a commission to cover the non-recourse risk, typically 1.5%–2.5%, plus interest deducted as a discount from the initial proceeds. On the other hand, the firm selling the non-recourse receivables avoids the cost of determining the creditworthiness of its customers. It also does not have to show debt borrowed to finance these receivables on its balance sheet. Furthermore, the firm avoids both foreign exchange and political risk on these non-recourse receivables. *Global Finance in Practice 15.2* provides an example of the costs.

Securitization

The *securitization* of export receivables for financing trade is an attractive supplement to bankers' acceptance financing and factoring. A firm can securitize its export receivables by selling them to a legal entity established to create marketable securities based on a package of individual export receivables. An advantage of this technique is to remove the export receivables from the exporter's balance sheet because they have been sold without recourse.

The receivables are normally sold at a discount. The size of the discount depends on four factors:

1. The historic collection risk of the exporter
2. The cost of credit insurance
3. The cost of securing the desirable cash flow stream to the investors
4. The size of the financing and services fees

Securitization is more cost effective if there is a large value of transactions with a known credit history and default probability. A large exporter could establish its own securitization entity. While the initial setup cost is high, the entity can be used on an ongoing basis. As an alternative, smaller exporters could use a common securitization entity provided by a financial institution, thereby saving the expensive setup costs.

Bank Credit Lines

A firm's bank credit line can typically be used to finance, up to a fixed upper limit, say 80%, of accounts receivable. Export receivables can be eligible for inclusion in bank credit line financing. However, credit information on foreign customers may be more difficult to collect and assess. If a firm covers its export receivables with export credit insurance, it can greatly reduce the credit risk of those receivables. This insurance enables the bank credit line to cover more export receivables and lower the interest rate for that coverage. Of course, any foreign exchange risk must be handled by the transaction exposure techniques described in Chapter 9.

The cost of using a bank credit line is usually the prime rate of interest plus points to reflect a particular firm's credit risk. As usual, 100 points is equal to 1%. In the United States,

---

GLOBAL FINANCE IN PRACTICE 15.2

Factoring in Practice

A U.S.-based manufacturer that may have suffered significant losses during first the global credit crisis and the following global recession is cash-short. Sales, profits, and cash flows, have fallen. The company is now struggling to service its high levels of debt. It does, however, have a number of new sales agreements. It is considering factoring one of its biggest new sales, a sale for $5 million to a Japanese company. The receivable is due in 90 days. After contacting a factoring agent, it is quoted the following numbers.

Face amount of receivable	$5,000,000
Non-recourse fee (1.5%)	−75,000
Factoring fee (2.5% per month × 3 months)	−375,000
Net proceeds on sale (received now)	$4,550,000

If the company wishes to factor its receivable it will net $4.55 million, 91% of the face amount. Although this may at first sight appear expensive, the firm would net the proceeds in cash up-front, not having to wait 90 days for payment. And it would not be responsible for collecting on the receivable. If the firm were able to "factor-in" the cost of factoring in the initial sale, all the better. Alternatively, it might offer a discount for cash paid in the first 10 days after shipment.

borrowers are also expected to maintain a compensating deposit balance at the lending institution. In Europe and many other places, lending is done on an overdraft basis. An overdraft agreement allows a firm to overdraw its bank account up to the limit of its credit line. Interest at prime plus points is based only on the amount of overdraft borrowed. In either case, the all-in cost of bank borrowing using a credit line is higher than acceptance financing as shown in Exhibit 15.9.

Commercial Paper

A firm can issue commercial paper—unsecured promissory notes—to fund its short-term financing needs, including both domestic and export receivables. However, it is only the large well-known firms with favorable credit ratings that have access to either the domestic or euro commercial paper market. As shown in Exhibit 15.9, commercial paper interest rates lie at the low end of the yield curve.

Forfaiting: Medium- and Long-Term Financing

Forfaiting is a specialized technique to eliminate the risk of nonpayment by importers in instances where the importing firm and/or its government is perceived by the exporter to be too risky for open account credit. The name of the technique comes from the French *à forfait*, a term that implies "to forfeit or surrender a right."

Role of the Forfaiter

The essence of forfaiting is the non-recourse sale by an exporter of bank-guaranteed promissory notes, bills of exchange, or similar documents received from an importer in another country. The exporter receives cash at the time of the transaction by selling the notes or bills at a discount from their face value to a specialized finance firm called a forfaiter. The forfaiter arranges the entire operation prior to the execution of the transaction. Although the exporting firm is responsible for the quality of delivered goods, it receives a clear and unconditional cash payment at the time of the transaction. All political and commercial risk of nonpayment by the importer is carried by the guaranteeing bank. Small exporters who trust their clients to pay find the forfaiting technique invaluable because it eases cash flow problems.

During the Soviet era, expertise in the technique was centered in German and Austrian banks, which used forfaiting to finance sales of capital equipment to eastern European, "Soviet Bloc," countries. British, Scandinavian, Italian, Spanish, and French exporters have now adopted the technique, but U.S. and Canadian exporters are reported to be slow to use forfaiting, possibly because they are suspicious of its simplicity and lack of complex documentation. Nevertheless, some American firms now specialize in the technique, and the Association of Forfaiters in the Americas (AFIA) has more than 20 members. Major export destinations financed via the forfaiting technique are Asia, Eastern Europe, the Middle East, and Latin America.

A Typical Forfaiting Transaction

A typical forfaiting transaction involves five parties, as shown in Exhibit 15.10. The steps in the process are as follows:

Step 1: Agreement. Importer and exporter agree on a series of imports to be paid for over a period of time, typically three to five years. However, periods up to 10 years or as short as 180 days have been financed by the technique. The normal minimum size for a transaction is

---

EXHIBIT 15.10 Typical Forfaiting Transaction

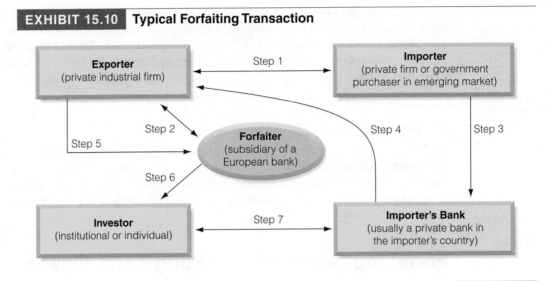

$100,000. The importer agrees to make periodic payments, often against progress on delivery or completion of a project.

Step 2: Commitment. The forfaiter promises to finance the transaction at a fixed discount rate, with payment to be made when the exporter delivers to the forfaiter the appropriate promissory notes or other specified paper. The agreed-upon discount rate is based on the cost of funds in the Euromarket, usually on LIBOR for the average life of the transaction, plus a margin over LIBOR to reflect the perceived risk in the deal. This risk premium is influenced by the size and tenor of the deal, country risk, and the quality of the guarantor institution. On a five-year deal, for example, with 10 semiannual payments, the rate used would be based on the 2.25-year LIBOR rate. This discount rate is normally added to the invoice value of the transaction so that the cost of financing is ultimately borne by the importer. The forfaiter charges an additional commitment fee of from 0.5% per annum to as high as 6.0% per annum from the date of its commitment to finance until receipt of the actual discount paper issued in accordance with the finance contract. This fee is also normally added to the invoice cost and passed on to the importer.

Step 3: *Aval* or Guarantee. The importer obligates itself to pay for its purchases by issuing a series of promissory notes, usually maturing every six or twelve months, against progress on delivery or completion of the project. These promissory notes are first delivered to the importer's bank where they are endorsed (that is, guaranteed) by that bank. In Europe, this unconditional guarantee is referred to as an *aval*, which translates into English as "backing." At this point, the importer's bank becomes the primary obligor in the eyes of all subsequent holders of the notes. The bank's aval or guarantee must be irrevocable, unconditional, divisible, and assignable. Because U.S. banks do not issue avals, U.S. transactions are guaranteed by a standby letter of credit (L/C), which is functionally similar to an aval but more cumbersome. For example, L/Cs can normally be transferred only once.

Step 4: Delivery of Notes. The now-endorsed promissory notes are delivered to the exporter.

Step 5: Discounting. The exporter endorses the notes "without recourse" and discounts them with the forfaiter, receiving the agreed-upon proceeds. Proceeds are usually received two days after the documents are presented. By endorsing the notes "without recourse," the exporter frees itself from any liability for future payment on the notes and thus receives the discounted proceeds without having to worry about any further payment difficulties.

Step 6: Investment. The forfaiting bank either holds the notes until full maturity as an investment or endorses and rediscounts them in the international money market. Such subsequent sale by the forfaiter is usually without recourse. The major rediscount markets are in London and Switzerland, plus New York for notes issued in conjunction with Latin American business.

Step 7: Maturity. At maturity, the investor holding the notes presents them for collection to the importer or to the importer's bank. The promise of the importer's bank is what gives the documents their value.

In effect, the forfaiter functions both as a money market firm (e.g., a lender of short-term financing) and a specialist in packaging financial deals involving country risk. As a money market firm, the forfaiter divides the discounted notes into appropriately sized packages and resells them to various investors having different maturity preferences. As a country risk specialist, the forfaiter assesses the risk that the notes will eventually be paid by the importer or the importer's bank and puts together a deal that satisfies the needs of both exporter and importer.

Success of the forfaiting technique springs from the belief that the aval or guarantee of a commercial bank can be depended on. Although commercial banks are the normal and preferred guarantors, guarantees by government banks or government ministries of finance are accepted in some cases. On occasion, large commercial enterprises have been accepted as debtors without a bank guarantee. An additional aspect of the technique is that the endorsing bank's aval is perceived to be an "off balance sheet" obligation—the debt is presumably not considered by others in assessing the financial structure of the commercial banks.

Summary Points

- International trade takes place between three categories of relationships: unaffiliated unknown parties, unaffiliated known parties, and affiliated parties.

- International trade transactions between affiliated parties typically do not require contractual arrangements or external financing. Trade transactions between unaffiliated parties typically require contracts and some type of external financing, such as that available through letters of credit.

- Over many years, established procedures have arisen to finance international trade. The basic procedure rests on the interrelationship between three key documents, the letter of credit (L/C), the bill of lading, and the draft.

- In the L/C, the bank substitutes its credit for that of the importer and promises to pay if certain documents are submitted to the bank. The exporter may now rely on the promise of the bank rather than on the promise of the importer.

- The exporter typically ships on a bill of lading, attaches the bill of lading to a draft ordering payment from the importer's bank, and presents these documents, plus any of a number of additional documents, through its own bank to the importer's bank.

- If the documents are in order, the importer's bank either pays the draft (a sight draft) or accepts the

draft (a time draft). In the latter case, the bank promises to pay in the future. At this step, the importer's bank acquires title to the merchandise through the bill of lading and releases the merchandise to the importer.

- If a sight draft is used, the exporter is paid at once. If a time draft is used, the exporter receives the accepted draft, now a bankers' acceptance, back from the bank. The exporter may hold the bankers' acceptance until maturity or sell it at a discount in the money market.

- The total costs of an exporter entering a foreign market include the transaction costs of the trade financing, the import and export duties and tariffs applied by exporting and importing nations, and the costs of foreign market penetration, which include distribution expenses, inventory costs, and transportation expenses.

- Export credit insurance provides assurance to exporters (or exporters' banks) that should the foreign customer default on payment, the insurance company will pay for a major portion of the loss.

- Trade financing uses the same financing instruments as in domestic receivables financing, plus some specialized instruments that are only available for financing international trade. A popular instrument for short-term financing is a bankers' acceptance. Its all-in cost is comparable to other money market instruments, such as marketable bank certificates of deposit.

- Other short-term financing instruments with a domestic counterpart are trade acceptances, factoring, securitization, bank credit lines (usually covered by export credit insurance), and commercial paper.

- Forfaiting is an international trade technique that can provide medium- and long-term financing.

MINI-CASE

Crosswell International and Brazil[1]

Crosswell International is a U.S.-based manufacturer and distributor of health care products, including children's diapers. Crosswell has been approached by Leonardo Sousa, the president of Material Hospitalar, a distributor of health care products throughout Brazil. Sousa is interested in distributing Crosswell's major diaper product, *Precious Diapers*, but only if an acceptable arrangement regarding pricing and payment terms can be reached.

Exporting to Brazil

Crosswell's manager for export operations, Geoff Mathieux, followed up the preliminary discussions by putting together an estimate of export costs and pricing for discussion purposes with Sousa. Crosswell needs to know all of the costs and pricing assumptions for the entire supply and value chain as it reaches the consumer. Mathieux believes it critical that any arrangement that Crosswell enters into results in a price to consumers in the Brazilian marketplace that is both fair to all parties involved and competitive, given the market niche Crosswell hopes to penetrate. This first cut on pricing *Precious Diapers* into Brazil is presented in Exhibit A.

Crosswell proposes to sell the basic diaper line to the Brazilian distributor for $34.00 per case, FAS (free alongside ship) Miami docks. This means that the seller, Crosswell, agrees to cover all costs associated with getting the diapers to the Miami docks. The costs of loading the diapers aboard ship, of the actual shipping (freight), and of the associated documents is $4.32 per case. The running subtotal, $38.32 per case, is termed CFR (cost and freight). Finally, the insurance expenses related to the potential loss of the goods while in transit to final port of destination, export insurance, are $0.86 per case. The total CIF (cost, insurance, and freight) is $39.18 per case, or 97.95 Brazilian real per case, assuming an exchange rate of 2.50 Brazilian real (R$) per U.S. dollar ($). In summary, the CIF cost of R$97.95 is the price charged by the exporter to the importer on arrival in Brazil, and is calculated as follows:

$$CIF = FAS + Freight + Export\ Insurance$$
$$= (\$34.00 + \$4.32 + \$0.86) \times R\$2.50/\$ = R\$97.95.$$

The actual cost to the distributor in getting the diapers through the port and customs warehouses must also be calculated in terms of what Leonardo Sousa's costs are in reality. The various fees and taxes detailed in Exhibit A raise the fully landed cost of the *Precious Diapers* to R$107.63 per case. The distributor would now bear storage and inventory costs totaling R$8.33 per case, which would bring the costs to R$115.96. The distributor then adds a margin for distribution services of 20% (R$23.19), raising the price as sold to the final retailer to R$139.15 per case.

Finally, the retailer (a supermarket or other retailer of consumer health care products) would include its expenses, taxes, and markup to reach the final shelf price to the customer of R$245.48 per case. This final retail price estimate now allows both Crosswell and Material Hospitalar to evaluate the price competitiveness of the *Precious Ultra-Thin Diaper* in the Brazilian marketplace, and provides a basis for further negotiations between the two parties.

The *Precious Ultra-Thin Diaper* will be shipped via container. Each container will hold 968 cases of diapers. The costs and prices in Exhibit A are calculated on a per case basis, although some costs and fees are assessed by container.

Mathieux provides the export price quotation shown in Exhibit A, an outline of a potential representation agreement (for Sousa to represent Crosswell's product lines in the Brazilian marketplace), and payment and credit terms to Leonardo Sousa. Crosswell's payment and credit terms are that Sousa either pay in full in cash in advance, or with a confirmed irrevocable documentary L/C with a time draft specifying a tenor of 60 days.

Crosswell also requests from Sousa financial statements, banking references, foreign commercial references, descriptions of regional sales forces, and sales forecasts for the *Precious Diaper* line. These last requests by Crosswell are very important for Crosswell to be able to assess Material Hospitalar's ability to be a dependable, creditworthy, and capable long-term partner and representative of the firm in the

[1]Copyright © 1996, Thunderbird School of Global Management. All rights reserved. This case was prepared by Doug Mathieux and Geoff Mathieux under the direction of Professors Michael H. Moffett and James L. Mills for the purpose of classroom discussion, and not to indicate either effective or ineffective management.

EXHIBIT A   Export Pricing for the *Precious Diaper* Line to Brazil

The *Precious Ultra-Thin Diaper* will be shipped via container. Each container will hold 968 cases of diapers. The costs and prices below are calculated on a per case basis, although some costs and fees are assessed by container.

Exports Costs and Pricing to Brazil	Per Case	Rates and Calculation
FAS price per case, Miami	$34.00	
Freight, loading, and documentation	4.32	$4,180 per container/968 = $4.32
CFR price per case, Brazilian port (Santos)	$38.32	
Export insurance	0.86	2.25% of CIF
CIF to Brazilian port	$39.18	
CIF to Brazilian port, in Brazilian *real*	R$97.95	2.50 Real/US$ × $39.18
Brazilian Importation Costs		
Import duties	1.96	2.00% of CIF
Merchant marine renovation fee	2.70	25.00% of freight
Port storage fees	1.27	1.30% of CIF
Port handling fees	0.01	R$12 per container
Additional handling fees	0.26	20.00% of storage and handling
Customs brokerage fees	1.96	2.00% of CIF
Import license fee	0.05	R$50 per container
Local transportation charges	1.47	1.50% of CIF
Total cost to distributor in real	R$107.63	
Distributor's Costs and Pricing		
Storage cost	1.47	1.50% of CIF × months
Cost of financing diaper inventory	6.86	7.00% of CIF × months
Distributor's margin	23.19	20.00% of Price + storage + financing
Price to retailer in real	R$139.15	
Brazilian Retailer Costs & Pricing		
Industrial product tax (IPT)	20.87	15.00% of price to retailer
Mercantile circulation services tax (MCS)	28.80	18.00% of price + IPT
Retailer costs and markup	56.65	30.00% of price + IPT + MCS
Price to consumer in real	R$245.48	

Diaper Prices to Consumers	Diapers per Case	Price per Diaper
Small size	352	R$ 0.70
Medium size	256	R$ 0.96
Large size	192	R$ 1.28

Brazilian marketplace. The discussions that follow focus on finding acceptable common ground between the two parties and working to increase the competitiveness of the *Precious Diaper* in the Brazilian marketplace.

Crosswell's Proposal

The proposed sale by Crosswell to Material Hospitalar, at least in the initial shipment, is for 10 containers of 968 cases of diapers at $39.18 per case, CIF Brazil, payable in U.S. dollars. This is a total invoice amount of $379,262.40. Payment terms are that a confirmed L/C will be required of Material Hospitalar on a U.S. bank. The payment will be based on a time draft of 60 days, presentation to the bank for acceptance with other documents on the date of shipment. Both the exporter and the exporter's bank will expect payment from the importer or importer's bank 60 days from this date of shipment.

What Should Crosswell Expect? Assuming Material Hospitalar acquires the L/C and it is confirmed by Crosswell's bank in the United States, Crosswell will ship the goods after the initial agreement, say 15 days, as illustrated in Exhibit B.

Simultaneous with the shipment, when Crosswell has lost physical control over the goods, Crosswell will present the bill of lading (acquired at the time of shipment) with the other needed documents to its bank requesting payment. Because the export is under a confirmed L/C, assuming all documents are in order, Crosswell's bank will give Crosswell two choices:

1. Wait the full time period of the time draft of 60 days and receive the entire payment in full ($379,262.40).

2. Receive the discounted value of this amount today. The discounted amount, assuming U.S. dollar interest rate of 6.00% per annum (1.00% per 60 days):

$$\frac{\$379,262.40}{(1 + 0.01)} = \frac{\$379,262.40}{1.01} = \$375,507.33$$

Because the invoice is denominated in U.S. dollars, Crosswell need not worry about currency value changes (currency risk). And because its bank has confirmed the L/C, it is protected against changes or deteriorations in Material Hospitalar's ability to pay on the future date.

What Should Material Hospitalar Expect? Material Hospitalar will receive the goods on or before day 60. It will then move the goods through its distribution system to retailers. Depending on the payment terms between Material Hospitalar and its buyers (retailers), it could either receive cash or terms for payment for the goods. Because Material Hospitalar purchased the goods via the 60-day time draft and an L/C from its Brazilian bank, total payment of $379,262.40 is due on day 90 (shipment and presentation of documents was on day 30 + 60-day time draft) to the Brazilian bank. Material Hospitalar, because it is a Brazilian-based company and has agreed to make payment in U.S. dollars (foreign currency), carries the currency risk of the transaction.

Crosswell/Material Hospitalar's Concern
The concern the two companies hold, however, is that the total price to the consumer in Brazil, R$245.48 per case, or R$0.70/diaper (small size), is too high. The major competitors in the Brazilian market for premium quality diapers, Kenko do Brasil (Japan), Johnson and Johnson (U.S.), and Procter and Gamble (U.S.), are cheaper (see Exhibit C).

EXHIBIT B　Export Payment Terms on Crosswell's Export to Brazil

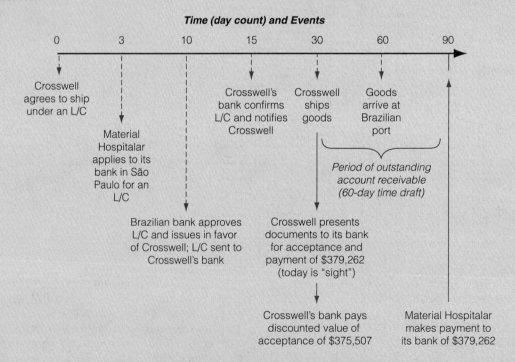

EXHIBIT C	Competitive Diaper Prices in the Brazilian Market (in Brazilian real)			
		Price per Diaper by Size		
Company (Country)	**Brand**	**Small**	**Medium**	**Large**
Kenko (Japan)	Monica Plus	0.68	0.85	1.18
Procter and Gamble (USA)	Pampers Uni	0.65	0.80	1.08
Johnson and Johnson (USA)	Sempre Seca Plus	0.65	0.80	1.08
Crosswell (USA)	Precious	0.70	0.96	1.40

The competitors all manufacture in-country, thus avoiding the series of import duties and tariffs, which have added significantly to Crosswell's landed prices in the Brazilian marketplace.

MINI-CASE QUESTIONS

1. How are pricing, currency of denomination, and financing interrelated in the value-chain for Crosswell's penetration of the Brazilian market? Can you summarize them using Exhibit B?

2. How important is Sousa to the value-chain of Crosswell? What worries might Crosswell have regarding Sousa's ability to fulfill his obligations?

3. If Crosswell is to penetrate the market, some way of reducing its prices will be required. What do you suggest?

Questions

1. **Unaffiliated Buyers.** Why might different documentation be used for an export to a non-affiliated foreign buyer who is a new customer as compared to an export to a non-affiliated foreign buyer to whom the exporter has been selling for many years?

2. **Affiliated Buyers.** For what reason might an exporter use standard international trade documentation (letter of credit, draft, order bill of lading) on an intrafirm export to its parent or sister subsidiary?

3. **Intra-firm Trade.** Why has the volume of intra-firm trade surged in the past two decades? What are the main advantages and disadvantages of intra-firm trade?

4. **Documents.** Explain the difference between a letter of credit (L/C) and a draft. How are they linked?

5. **Risks.** What is the major difference between "currency risk" and "risk of noncompletion?" How are these risks handled in a typical international trade transaction?

6. **Letter of Credit.** Identify each party to a letter of credit (L/C) and indicate its responsibility.

7. **Letters of Credit.** What is the difference between confirmed and unconfirmed letters of credit?

8. **Documenting an Export of Hard Drives.** List the steps involved in the export of computer hard disk drives from Penang, Malaysia, to San Jose, California, using an unconfirmed letter of credit authorizing payment on sight.

9. **Documenting an Export of Lumber from Portland to Yokohama.** List the steps involved in the export of lumber from Portland, Oregon, to Yokohama, Japan, using a confirmed letter of credit, payment to be made in 120 days.

10. **Governmental Trade Promotion Measures.** As part of an overall export-promotion strategy, various governments have followed measures to enhance their exports and international trade mainly through providing export credit insurance and by extending financing to exporters. Explain the economic effectiveness of these measures and their impact on societal welfare.

Problems

1. **Nikken Microsystems (A).** Assume Nikken Microsystems has sold Internet servers to Telecom España for €700,000. Payment is due in three months and will be made with a trade acceptance from Telecom España

Acceptance. The acceptance fee is 1.0% per annum of the face amount of the note. This acceptance will be sold at a 4% per annum discount. What is the annualized percentage all-in cost in euros of this method of trade financing?

2. **Nikken Microsystems (B).** Assume that Nikken Microsystems prefers to receive U.S. dollars rather than euros for the trade transaction described in Problem 1. It is considering two alternatives: 1) sell the acceptance for euros at once and convert the euros immediately to U.S. dollars at the spot rate of exchange of $1.00/€ or 2) hold the euro acceptance until maturity but at the start sell the expected euro proceeds forward for dollars at the 3-month forward rate of $1.02/€.
   a. What are the U.S. dollar net proceeds received at once from the discounted trade acceptance in alternative 1?
   b. What are the U.S. dollar net proceeds received in three months in alternative 2?
   c. What is the break-even investment rate that would equalize the net U.S. dollar proceeds from both alternatives?
   d. Which alternative should Nikken Microsystems choose?

3. **Timmico Co. (A).** Timmico Co. is a South Korean automobile company that exports cars and lorries to Saudi Arabia and invoices its customers in euros. SaudiAutoImp Co. has purchased €15,000,000 of merchandise from Timmico Co., with payment due in 244 days. The payment will be made with a bankers' acceptance issued by Korea Exchange Bank at a fee of 3.625% per annum. Timmico Co. has a weighted average cost of capital of 12%. If Timmico Co. holds this acceptance to maturity, what is its annualized percentage all-in cost?

4. **Timmico Co. (B).** Assuming the facts in Problem 3, Saudi Investment Bank is now willing to buy Timmico Co.'s bankers' acceptance for a discount of 7.5% per annum. What would be Timmico Co.'s annualized percentage all-in cost of financing its €15,000,000 receivable?

5. **Alliasha-Toshiba.** Alliasha-Toshiba buys its laptops from Toshiba-France, and sells them to French customers. One of its customers is Pret-a-Print, a printing service firm that buys laptops from Alliasha-Toshiba at wholesale price. Final payment is due to Alliasha-Toshiba in three months. Pret-a-Print bought €175,000 worth of laptops from Alliasha-Toshiba, with a cash down payment of €35,000 and the balance due in 3 months without any interest charged as a sales incentive. Alliasha-Toshiba will have the Pret-a-Print receivable accepted by Alliance Acceptance for a

3.5% fee and then sell it at a 5% per annum discount to BNP Paribas.
   a. What is the annualized percentage all-in cost to Alliasha-Toshiba?
   b. What are Alliasha-Toshiba's net cash proceeds, including the cash down payment?

6. **Forfaiting at Umaru Oil (Nigeria).** Umaru Oil of Nigeria has purchased $1,000,000 of oil drilling equipment from Gunslinger Drilling of Houston, Texas. Umaru Oil must pay for this purchase over the next five years at a rate of $200,000 per year due on March 1 of each year.

   Bank of Zurich, a Swiss forfaiter, has agreed to buy the five notes of $200,000 each at a discount. The discount rate would be approximately 8% per annum based on the expected 3-year LIBOR rate plus 200 basis points, paid by Umaru Oil. Bank of Zurich would also charge Umaru Oil an additional commitment fee of 2% per annum from the date of its commitment to finance until receipt of the actual discounted notes issued in accordance with the financing contract. The $200,000 promissory notes will come due on March 1 in successive years.

   The promissory notes issued by Umaru Oil will be endorsed by their bank, Lagos City Bank, for a 1% fee and delivered to Gunslinger Drilling. At this point, Gunslinger Drilling will endorse the notes without recourse and discount them with the forfaiter, Bank of Zurich, receiving the full $200,000 principal amount. Bank of Zurich will sell the notes by rediscounting them to investors in the international money market without recourse. At maturity, the investors holding the notes will present them for collection at Lagos City Bank. If Lagos City Bank defaults on payment, the investors will collect on the notes from Bank of Zurich.

   a. What is the annualized percentage all-in cost to Umaru Oil of financing the first $200,000 note due March 1, 2011?
   b. What might motivate Umaru Oil to use this relatively expensive alternative for financing?

7. **Sunny Coast Enterprises (A).** Sunny Coast Enterprises has sold a combination of films and DVDs to Hong Kong Media Incorporated for US$100,000, with payment due in six months. Sunny Coast Enterprises has the following alternatives for financing this receivable: 1) Use its bank credit line. Interest would be at the prime rate of 5% plus 150 basis points per annum. Sunny Coast Enterprises would need to maintain a compensating balance of 20% of the loan's face amount. No interest will be paid on the compensating

balance by the bank. 2) Use its bank credit line but purchase export credit insurance for a 1% fee. Because of the reduced risk, the bank interest rate would be reduced to 5% per annum without any points.

a. What are the annualized percentage all-in costs of each alternative?

b. What are the advantages and disadvantages of each alternative?

c. Which alternative would you recommend?

8. **Sunny Coast Enterprises (B).** Sunny Coast Enterprises has been approached by a factor that offers to purchase the Hong Kong Media Imports receivable at a 16% per annum discount plus a 2% charge for a non-recourse clause.

a. What is the annualized percentage all-in cost of this factoring alternative?

b. What are the advantages and disadvantages of the factoring alternative compared to the alternatives in Problem 7?

9. **ThaiTenSport.** ThaiTenSport (Bangkok) is considering bidding to sell £2,000,000 of tennis rackets to CairoPro Club, a newly founded Egyptian tennis club. Payment would be due in six months. Since ThaiTenSport cannot find good credit information on CairoPro Club, ThaiTenSport wants to protect its credit risk. It is considering the following financing solution.

CairoPro's Egyptian bank in Cairo issues a letter of credit on behalf of CairoPro and agrees to accept ThaiTenSport's draft for £2,000,000, due in six months. The acceptance fee would cost ThaiTenSport £5,000 and reduce CairoPro's available credit line by £2,000,000. The bankers' acceptance note of £2,000,000 would be sold at a 3.75% per annum discount in the money market. What is the annualized percentage all-in-cost to ThaiTenSport of this bankers' acceptance financing?

10. **ThaiTenSport (B).** ThaiTenSport could also buy export credit insurance from Export-Import Bank of Thailand for 2% premium. It finances the £2,000,000 receivable from CairoPro from its credit line at 5% per annum interest. No compensating bank balance would be required.

a. What is ThaiTenSport's annualized percentage all-in cost of financing?

b. What are CairoPro's costs?

c. What are the advantages and disadvantages of this alternative compared to the bankers' acceptance financing in Problem 9? Which alternative would you recommend?

11. **VenezaCot Co.** VenezaCot Co. of Caracas, Venezuela, has received an order for 50,000 cotton towels from JapoImp Co. of Tokyo, Japan. The towels will be exported to Japan under the terms of a letter of credit issued by a Japanese bank on behalf of JapoImp Co. The letter of credit specifies that the face value of the shipment, ¥8,000,000, will be paid 60 days later after the Japanese bank accepts a draft drawn by VenezaCot Co. in accordance with the terms of the letter of credit.

The current discount rate on a two-month bankers' acceptance is 7.5% per annum, and VenezaCot Co. estimates its weighted average cost of capital to be 28% per annum. The commission for selling a bankers' acceptance in the discount market is 2.5% of the face amount.

How much cash will VenezaCot Co. receive from the sale if it holds the acceptance until maturity? Do you recommend that VenezaCot Co. hold the acceptance until maturity or discount it at once in the Japanese bankers' acceptance market?

12. **Swishing Shoe Company.** Swishing Shoe Company of Durham, North Carolina, has received an order for 50,000 cartons of athletic shoes from Southampton Footware, Ltd., of England, payment to be in British pounds sterling. The shoes will be shipped to Southampton Footware under the terms of a letter of credit issued by a London bank on behalf of Southampton Footware. The letter of credit specifies that the face value of the shipment, £400,000, will be paid 120 days after the London bank accepts a draft drawn by Southampton Footware in accordance with the terms of the letter of credit.

The current discount rate in London on 120-day bankers' acceptances is 12% per annum, and Southampton Footware estimates its weighted average cost of capital to be 18% per annum. The commission for selling a bankers' acceptance in the discount market is 2.0% of the face amount.

a. Would Swishing Shoe Company gain by holding the acceptance to maturity, as compared to discounting the bankers' acceptance at once?

b. Does Swishing Shoe Company incur any other risks in this transaction?

13. **Going Abroad.** Assume that Great Britain charges an import duty of 10% on shoes imported into the United Kingdom. Swishing Shoe Company, in Problem 12, discovers that it can manufacture shoes in Ireland and import them into Britain free of any import duty. What factors should Swishing consider in deciding to continue to export shoes from North Carolina versus manufacture them in Ireland?

Internet Exercises

1. **Letter of Credit Services.** Commercial banks worldwide provide a variety of services to aid in the financing of foreign trade. Contact any of the many major multinational banks (a few are listed below) and determine what types of letter of credit services and other trade financing services they are able to provide.

Bank of America	www.bankamerica.com
Barclays	www.barclays.com
Deutsche Bank	www.deutschebank.com
Union Bank of Switzerland	www.unionbank.com
Swiss Bank Corporation	www.swissbank.com

2. **The Balanced World.** The Balance World Web site is the equivalent of a social networking site for those interested in discussing a multitude of financial issues in greater depth and breadth. There is no limit to breadth of topics in finance and financial management that are posted and discussed.

The Balanced World	www.thebalancedworld.com/

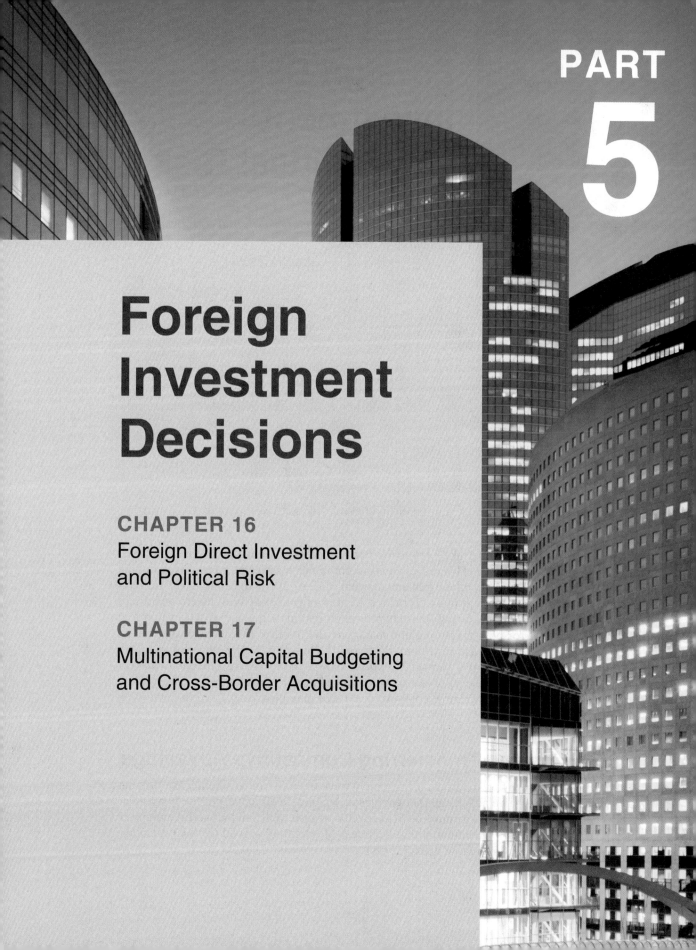

Foreign Investment Decisions

CHAPTER 16

Foreign Direct Investment and Political Risk

"People don't want a quarter-inch drill. They want a quarter-inch hole."

— Theodore Levitt, Harvard Business School.

LEARNING OBJECTIVES

■ Demonstrate how key competitive advantages support a strategy to originate and sustain direct foreign investment

■ Show how the OLI Paradigm provides a theoretical foundation for the globalization process

■ Identify factors and forces that must be considered in the determination of where multinational enterprises invest

■ Illustrate the managerial and competitive dimensions of the alternative methods for foreign investment

■ Learn how to define and classify foreign investment risks

■ Analyze firm-specific, country-specific, and global-specific risks

The strategic decision to undertake *foreign direct investment* (FDI), and thus become an MNE, starts with a self-evaluation. This self-evaluation combines a series of questions including the nature of the firm's competitive advantage, what business form and commensurate risks the firm should use and accept upon entry, and what political risks—both macro and micro in context—the firm will be facing. This chapter explores this sequence of self-evaluation, as well as methods for both measuring and managing the political risks confronting MNEs today in both the established industrial markets and the most promising emerging markets. The Mini-Case at the end of this chapter, *Corporate Competition from the Emerging Markets*, highlights the growing complexity of emerging market competitiveness in the global economy and how many of tomorrow's most competitive MNEs may be arising from the emerging markets themselves.

Sustaining and Transferring Competitive Advantage

In deciding whether to invest abroad, management must first determine whether the firm has a sustainable competitive advantage that enables it to compete effectively in the home market. The competitive advantage must be firm-specific, transferable, and powerful enough to compensate the firm for the potential disadvantages of operating abroad (foreign exchange risks, political risks, and increased agency costs).

Based on observations of firms that have successfully invested abroad, we can conclude that some of the competitive advantages enjoyed by MNEs are 1) economies of scale and scope arising from their large size; 2) managerial and marketing expertise; 3) advanced technology owing to their heavy emphasis on research; 4) financial strength; 5) differentiated products; and sometimes 6) competitiveness of their home markets.

Economies of Scale and Scope

Economies of scale and scope can be developed in production, marketing, finance, research and development, transportation, and purchasing. All of these areas have significant competitive advantages of being large, whether size is due to international or domestic operations. Production economies can come from the use of large-scale automated plant and equipment or from an ability to rationalize production through global specialization.

For example, some automobile manufacturers, such as Ford, rationalize manufacturing by producing engines in one country, transmissions in another, and bodies in another and assembling still elsewhere, with the location often being dictated by comparative advantage. Marketing economies occur when firms are large enough to use the most efficient advertising media to create global brand identification, as well as to establish global distribution, warehousing, and servicing systems. Financial economies derive from access to the full range of financial instruments and sources of funds, such as the euroequity and eurobond markets. In-house research and development programs are typically restricted to large firms because of the minimum-size threshold for establishing a laboratory and scientific staff. Transportation economies accrue to firms that can ship in carload or shipload lots. Purchasing economies come from quantity discounts and market power.

Managerial and Marketing Expertise

Managerial expertise includes skill in managing large industrial organizations from both a human and a technical viewpoint. It also encompasses knowledge of modern analytical techniques and their application in functional areas of business. Managerial expertise can be developed through prior experience in foreign markets. In most empirical studies, multinational firms have been observed to export to a market before establishing a production facility there. Likewise, they have prior experience sourcing raw materials and human capital in other foreign countries either through imports, licensing, or FDI. In this manner, the MNEs can partially overcome the supposed superior local knowledge of host-country firms.

Advanced Technology

Advanced technology includes both scientific and engineering skills. It is not limited to MNEs, but firms in the most industrialized countries have had an advantage in terms of access to continuing new technology spin-offs from the military and space programs. Empirical studies have supported the importance of technology as a characteristic of MNEs.

Financial Strength

Companies demonstrate financial strength by achieving and maintaining a global cost and availability of capital. This is a critical competitive cost variable that enables them to fund FDI and other foreign activities. MNEs that are resident in liquid and unsegmented capital markets are normally blessed with this attribute. However, MNEs that are resident in small industrial or emerging market countries can still follow a proactive strategy of seeking foreign portfolio and corporate investors.

Small- and medium-size firms often lack the characteristics that attract foreign (and maybe domestic) investors. They are too small or unattractive to achieve a global cost of capital. This limits their ability to fund FDI, and their higher marginal cost of capital reduces the number of foreign projects that can generate the higher required rate of return.

Differentiated Products

Firms create their own firm-specific advantages by producing and marketing differentiated products. Such products originate from research-based innovations or heavy marketing expenditures to gain brand identification. Furthermore, the research and marketing process continues to produce a steady stream of new differentiated products. It is difficult and costly for competitors to copy such products, and they always face a time lag if they try. Having developed differentiated products for the domestic home market, the firm may decide to market them worldwide, a decision consistent with the desire to maximize return on heavy research and marketing expenditures.

Competitiveness of the Home Market

A strongly competitive home market can sharpen a firm's competitive advantage relative to firms located in less competitive home markets. This phenomenon is known as the "competitive advantage of nations," a concept originated by Michael Porter of Harvard, and summarized in Exhibit 16.1.[1]

A firm's success in competing in a particular industry depends partly on the availability of factors of production (land, labor, capital, and technology) appropriate for that industry. Countries that are either naturally endowed with the appropriate factors or able to create them will probably spawn firms that are both competitive at home and potentially so abroad. For example, a well-educated workforce in the home market creates a competitive advantage for firms in certain high-tech industries. Firms facing sophisticated and demanding customers in the home market are able to hone their marketing, production, and quality control skills. Japan is such a market.

EXHIBIT 16.1   **The Competitive Advantage of Nations**

A firm's competitiveness can be significantly strengthened based on its having competed in a highly competitive home market. Home country competitive advantage must be based on at least one of four critical components.

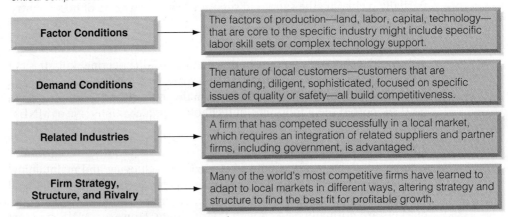

Factor Conditions	The factors of production—land, labor, capital, technology—that are core to the specific industry might include specific labor skill sets or complex technology support.
Demand Conditions	The nature of local customers—customers that are demanding, diligent, sophisticated, focused on specific issues of quality or safety—all build competitiveness.
Related Industries	A firm that has competed successfully in a local market, which requires an integration of related suppliers and partner firms, including government, is advantaged.
Firm Strategy, Structure, and Rivalry	Many of the world's most competitive firms have learned to adapt to local markets in different ways, altering strategy and structure to find the best fit for profitable growth.

Source: Based on concepts described by Michael Porter in "The Competitive Advantage of Nations," *Harvard Business Review*, March–April 1990.

---

[1] Michael Porter, *The Competitive Advantage of Nations*, London: Macmillan Press, 1990.

Firms in industries that are surrounded by a critical mass of related industries and suppliers will be more competitive because of this supporting cast. For example, electronic firms located in centers of excellence, such as in the San Francisco Bay area, are surrounded by efficient, creative suppliers who enjoy access to educational institutions at the forefront of knowledge.

A competitive home market forces firms to fine-tune their operational and control strategies for their specific industry and country environment. Japanese firms learned how to organize to implement their famous just-in-time inventory control system. One key was to use numerous subcontractors and suppliers that were encouraged to locate near the final assembly plants.

In some cases, host-country markets have not been large or competitive, but MNEs located there have nevertheless developed global niche markets served by foreign subsidiaries. Global competition in oligopolistic industries substitutes for domestic competition. For example, a number of MNEs resident in Scandinavia, Switzerland, and the Netherlands fall into this category. They include Novo Nordisk (Denmark), Norske Hydro (Norway), Nokia (Finland), L.M. Ericsson (Sweden), Astra (Sweden), ABB (Sweden/Switzerland), Roche Holding (Switzerland), Royal Dutch Shell (the Netherlands), Unilever (the Netherlands), and Philips (the Netherlands).

Emerging market countries have also spawned aspiring global MNEs in niche markets even though they lack competitive home-country markets. Some of these are traditional exporters in natural resource fields such as oil, agriculture, and minerals, but they are in transition to becoming MNEs. They typically start with foreign sales subsidiaries, joint ventures, and strategic alliances. Examples are Petrobrás (Brazil), YPF (Argentina), and Cemex (Mexico). Another category is firms that have been recently privatized in the telecommunications industry. Examples are Telefonos de Mexico and Telebrás (Brazil). Still others started as electronic component manufacturers but are making the transition to manufacturing abroad. Examples are Samsung Electronics (Korea) and Acer Computer (Taiwan).

The OLI Paradigm and Internationalization

The *OLI Paradigm* (Buckley and Casson, 1976; Dunning, 1977) is an attempt to create an overall framework to explain why MNEs choose FDI rather than serve foreign markets through alternative modes such as licensing, joint ventures, strategic alliances, management contracts, and exporting.[2]

The OLI Paradigm states first that a firm must first have some competitive advantage in its home market—"O" for ownership advantages—that can be transferred abroad if the firm is to be successful in foreign direct investment. Second, the firm must be attracted by specific characteristics of the foreign market—"L" for location advantages—that will allow it to exploit its competitive advantages in that market. Third, the firm will maintain its competitive position by attempting to control the entire value chain in its industry—"I" for internationalization advantages. This leads it to foreign direct investment rather than licensing or outsourcing.

Ownership Advantages

As described earlier, a firm must have competitive advantages in its home market. These must be firm-specific, not easily copied, and in a form that allows them to be transferred to foreign subsidiaries. For example, economies of scale and financial strength are not necessarily

[2]Peter J. Buckley and Mark Casson, *The Future of the Multinational Enterprise*, London: McMillan, 1976; and John H. Dunning, "Trade Location of Economic Activity and the MNE: A Search for an Eclectic Approach," in *The International Allocation of Economic Activity*, Bertil Ohlin, Per-Ove Hesselborn, and Per Magnus Wijkman, eds., New York: Holmes and Meier, 1977, pp. 395–418.

firm-specific because they can be achieved by many other firms. Certain kinds of technology can be purchased, licensed, or copied. Even differentiated products can lose their advantage to slightly altered versions, given enough marketing effort and the right price.

Location Advantages

These factors are typically market imperfections or genuine comparative advantages that attract FDI to particular locations. These factors might include a low-cost but productive labor force, unique sources of raw materials, a large domestic market, defensive investments to counter other competitors, or centers of technological excellence.

Internationalization Advantages

According to the theory, the key ingredient for maintaining a firm-specific competitive advantage is possession of proprietary information and control of the human capital that can generate new information through expertise in research. Needless to say, once again, large research-intensive firms are most likely to fit this description.

Minimizing transactions costs is the key factor in determining the success of an internationalization strategy. Wholly owned FDI reduces the agency costs that arise from asymmetric information, lack of trust, and the need to monitor foreign partners, suppliers, and financial institutions. Self-financing eliminates the need to observe specific debt covenants on foreign subsidiaries that are financed locally or by joint venture partners. If a multinational firm has a low global cost and high availability of capital, why share it with joint venture partners, distributors, licensees, and local banks, all of which probably have a higher cost of capital?

The Financial Strategy

Financial strategies are directly related to the OLI Paradigm in explaining FDI, as shown in Exhibit 16.2. Proactive financial strategies can be formulated in advance by the MNE's financial managers. These include strategies necessary to gain an advantage from lower global cost and greater availability of capital. Other proactive financial strategies are negotiating financial subsidies and/or reduced taxation to increase free cash flows, reducing financial agency costs through FDI, and reducing operating and transaction exposure through FDI.

Reactive financial strategies, as illustrated in Exhibit 16.2, depend on discovering market imperfections. For example, the MNE can exploit misaligned exchange rates and stock prices. It also needs to react to capital controls that prevent the free movement of funds and react to opportunities to minimize worldwide taxation.

Deciding Where to Invest

The decision about where to invest abroad for the first time is not the same as the decision about where to reinvest abroad. This decision is influenced by behavioral factors. A firm learns from its first few investments abroad and what it learns influences subsequent investments.

In theory, a firm should identify its competitive advantages. Then it should search worldwide for market imperfections and comparative advantage until it finds a country where it expects to enjoy a competitive advantage large enough to generate a risk-adjusted return above the firm's *hurdle rate*, the minimum acceptable rate of return on new investments.

In practice, firms have been observed to follow a sequential search pattern as described in the behavioral theory of the firm. Human rationality is bounded by one's ability to gather and process all the information that would be needed to make a perfectly rational decision

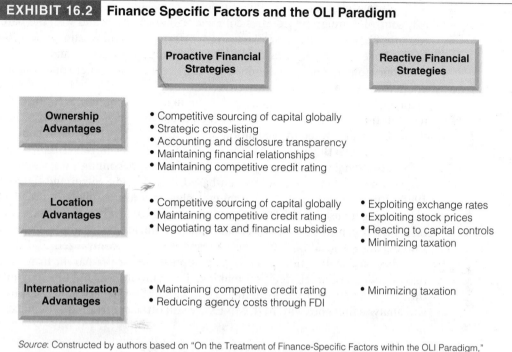

EXHIBIT 16.2 | **Finance Specific Factors and the OLI Paradigm**

Proactive Financial Strategies

Reactive Financial Strategies

Ownership Advantages
- Competitive sourcing of capital globally
- Strategic cross-listing
- Accounting and disclosure transparency
- Maintaining financial relationships
- Maintaining competitive credit rating

Location Advantages
- Competitive sourcing of capital globally
- Maintaining competitive credit rating
- Negotiating tax and financial subsidies

- Exploiting exchange rates
- Exploiting stock prices
- Reacting to capital controls
- Minimizing taxation

Internationalization Advantages
- Maintaining competitive credit rating
- Reducing agency costs through FDI

- Minimizing taxation

Source: Constructed by authors based on "On the Treatment of Finance-Specific Factors within the OLI Paradigm," by Lars Oxelheim, Arthur Stonehill, and Trond Randøy, *International Business Review* 10, 2001, pp. 381–398.

based on all the facts. This observation lies behind two behavioral theories of FDI described next—the behavioral approach and the international network theory.

The Behavioral Approach to FDI

The behavioral approach to analyzing the FDI decision is typified by the so-called Swedish School of economists.[3] The Swedish School has rather successfully explained not just the initial decision to invest abroad but also later decisions to reinvest elsewhere and to change the structure of a firm's international involvement over time. Based on the internationalization process of a sample of Swedish MNEs, the economists observed that these firms tended to invest first in countries that were not too far distant in psychic terms. Close psychic distance defined countries with a cultural, legal, and institutional environment similar to Sweden's, such as Norway, Denmark, Finland, Germany, and the United Kingdom. The initial investments were modest in size to minimize the risk of an uncertain foreign environment. As the Swedish firms learned from their initial investments, they became willing to take greater risks with respect to both the psychic distance of the countries and the size of the investments.

MNEs in a Network Perspective

As the Swedish MNEs grew and matured, so did the nature of their international involvement, what is often termed the *network perspective*. Today, each MNE is perceived as being a member of an international network, with nodes based in each of the foreign subsidiaries, as well as the

[3]Johansen, John, and F. Wiedersheim-Paul, "The Internationalization of the Firm: Four Swedish Case Studies," *Journal of Management Studies*, Vol. 12, No. 3, 1975; and John Johansen and Jan Erik Vahlne, "The Internationalization of the Firm: A Model of Knowledge Development and Increasing Foreign Market Commitments," *Journal of International Business Studies*, Vol. 8, No. 1, 1977.

parent firm itself. Centralized (hierarchical) control has given way to decentralized (heterarchical) control. Foreign subsidiaries compete with each other and with the parent for expanded resource commitments, thus influencing the strategy and reinvestment decisions. Many of these MNEs have become political coalitions with competing internal and external networks. Each subsidiary (and the parent) is embedded in its host country's network of suppliers and customers. It is also a member of a worldwide network based on its industry. Finally, it is a member of an organizational network under the nominal control of the parent firm. Complicating matters still further is the possibility that the parent itself may have evolved into a transnational firm, one that is owned by a coalition of investors located in different countries.[4]

Asea Brown Boveri (ABB) is an example of a Swedish-Swiss firm that has passed through the international evolutionary process all the way to becoming a transnational firm. ABB was formed through a merger of Sweden-based ASEA and Switzerland-based Brown Boveri in 1991. Both firms were already dominant players internationally in the electrotechnical and engineering industries. ABB has literally hundreds of foreign subsidiaries, which are managed on a very decentralized basis. ABB's "flat" organization structure and transnational ownership encourage local initiative, quick response, and decentralized FDI decisions. Although overall strategic direction is the legal responsibility of the parent firm, foreign subsidiaries play a major role in all decision-making. Their input in turn is strongly influenced by their own membership in their local and worldwide industry networks. Despite all the planning and analysis that goes with FDI, MNEs are still often confronted with unexpected challenges.

Modes of Foreign Investment

The globalization process includes a sequence of decisions regarding where production is to occur, who is to own or control intellectual property, and who is to own the actual production facilities. Exhibit 16.3 provides a roadmap to explain this FDI sequence.

Exporting versus Production Abroad

There are several advantages to limiting a firm's activities to exports. Exporting has none of the unique risks facing FDI, joint ventures, strategic alliances, and licensing. Political risks are minimal. Agency costs, such as monitoring and evaluating foreign units, are avoided. The amount of front-end investment is typically lower than in other modes of foreign involvement. Foreign exchange risks remain, however. The fact that a significant share of exports (and imports) is executed between MNEs and their foreign subsidiaries and affiliates further reduces the risk of exports compared to other modes of involvement.

There are also disadvantages of limiting a firm's activities to exports. A firm is not able to internalize and exploit the results of its research and development as effectively as if it invested directly. The firm also risks losing markets to imitators and global competitors that might be more cost efficient in production abroad and distribution. As these firms capture foreign markets, they might become so strong that they can export into the domestic exporter's own market. Remember that defensive FDI is often motivated by the need to prevent this kind of predatory behavior as well as to preempt foreign markets before competitors can get started.

Licensing and Management Contracts

Licensing is a popular method for domestic firms to profit from foreign markets without the need to commit sizable funds. Since the foreign producer is typically wholly owned locally, political risk is minimized. In recent years, a number of host countries have demanded that

[4]Forsgren, Mats, *Managing the Internationalization Process: The Swedish Case*, London: Routledge, 1989.

EXHIBIT 16.3   **The FDI Sequence: Foreign Presence and Investment**

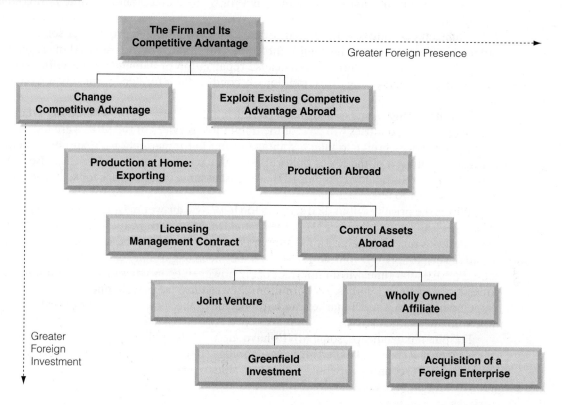

Source: Adapted from Gunter Dufey and R. Mirus, "Foreign Direct Investment: Theory and Strategic Considerations," unpublished, University of Michigan, 1985. Reprinted with permission from the authors. All rights reserved.

MNEs sell their services in pieces ("unbundled form") rather than only through FDI. Such countries would like their local firms to purchase managerial expertise and knowledge of product and factor markets through management contracts, and purchase technology through licensing agreements.

The main disadvantage of licensing is that license fees are likely to be lower than FDI profits, although the return on the marginal investment might be higher. Other disadvantages include the following:

- Possible loss of quality control
- Establishment of a potential competitor in third-country markets
- Possible improvement of the technology by the local licensee, which then enters the firm's home market
- Possible loss of opportunity to enter the licensee's market with FDI later
- Risk that technology will be stolen
- High agency costs

MNEs have not typically used licensing of independent firms. On the contrary, most licensing arrangements have been with their own foreign subsidiaries or joint ventures. License fees are a way to spread the corporate research and development cost among all operating units and a means of repatriating profits in a form more acceptable to some host countries than dividends.

Management contracts are similar to licensing insofar as they provide for some cash flow from a foreign source without significant foreign investment or exposure. Management contracts probably lessen political risk because repatriation of managers is easy. International consulting and engineering firms traditionally conduct their foreign business based on a management contract.

Whether licensing and management contracts are cost effective compared to FDI depends on the price host countries will pay for the unbundled services. If the price were high enough, many firms would prefer to take advantage of market imperfections in an unbundled way, particularly in view of the lower political, foreign exchange, and business risks. Because we observe MNEs continuing to prefer FDI, we must assume that the price for selling unbundled services is still too low.

Why is the price of unbundled services too low? The answer may lie in the synergy created when services are bundled as FDI in the first place. Managerial expertise is often dependent on a delicate mix of organizational support factors that cannot be transferred abroad efficiently. Technology is a continuous process, but licensing usually captures only the technology at a particular time. Most important of all, however, economies of scale cannot be sold or transferred in small bundles. By definition, they require large-scale operations. A relatively large operation in a small market can hardly achieve the same economies of scale as a large operation in a large market.

Despite the handicaps, some MNEs have successfully sold unbundled services. An example is sales of managerial expertise and technology to the OPEC countries. In this case, however, the OPEC countries are both willing and able to pay a price high enough to approach the returns on FDI (bundled services) while receiving only the lesser benefits of the unbundled services.

Joint Venture versus Wholly Owned Subsidiary

A *joint venture* (JV) is defined here as shared ownership in a foreign business. A foreign business unit that is partially owned by the parent company is typically termed a foreign affiliate. A foreign business unit that is 50% or more owned (and therefore controlled) by the parent company is typically designated a foreign subsidiary. A JV would therefore typically be described as a foreign affiliate, but not a foreign subsidiary.

A joint venture between an MNE and a host-country partner is a viable strategy if, and only if, the MNE finds the right partner. Some of the obvious advantages of having a compatible local partner are as follows:

- The local partner understands the customs, mores, and institutions of the local environment. An MNE might need years to acquire such knowledge on its own with a 100%-owned greenfield subsidiary. (Greenfield investments are started with a clean slate, having no prior history of development.)

- The local partner can provide competent management, not just at the top but also at the middle levels of management.

- If the host country requires that foreign firms share ownership with local firms or investors, 100% foreign ownership is not a realistic alternative to a joint venture.

- The local partner's contacts and reputation enhance access to the host-country's capital markets.

- The local partner may possess technology that is appropriate for the local environment or perhaps can be used worldwide.

- The public image of a firm that is partially locally owned may improve its sales possibilities if the purpose of the investment is to serve the local market.

Despite this impressive list of advantages, joint ventures are not as common as 100%-owned foreign subsidiaries because MNEs fear interference by the local partner in certain critical decision areas. Indeed, what is optimal from the viewpoint of the local venture may be suboptimal for the multinational operation as a whole. The most important potential conflicts or difficulties are these:

- Political risk is increased rather than reduced if the wrong partner is chosen. The local partner must be credible and ethical or the venture is worse off for being a joint venture.

- Local and foreign partners may have divergent views about the need for cash dividends, or about the desirability of growth financed from retained earnings versus new financing.

- Transfer pricing on products or components bought from or sold to related companies creates a potential for conflict of interest.

- Control of financing is another problem area. An MNE cannot justify its use of cheap or available funds raised in one country to finance joint venture operations in another country.

- Ability of a firm to rationalize production on a worldwide basis can be jeopardized if such rationalization would act to the disadvantage of local joint venture partners.

- Financial disclosure of local results might be necessary with locally traded shares, whereas if the firm is wholly owned from abroad such disclosure is not needed. Disclosure gives nondisclosing competitors an advantage in setting strategy.

Valuation of equity shares is difficult. How much should the local partner pay for its share? What is the value of contributed technology, or of contributed land in a country where all land is state owned? It is highly unlikely that foreign and host-country partners have similar opportunity costs of capital, expectations about the required rate of return, or similar perceptions of appropriate premiums for business, foreign exchange, and political risks. Insofar as the venture is a component of the portfolio of each investor, its contribution to portfolio return and variance may be quite different for each.

Strategic Alliances

The term strategic alliance conveys different meanings to different observers. In one form of cross-border strategic alliance, two firms exchange a share of ownership with one another. A strategic alliance can be a takeover defense if the prime purpose is for a firm to place some of its stock in stable and friendly hands. If that is all that occurs, it is just another form of portfolio investment.

In a more comprehensive strategic alliance, in addition to exchanging stock, the partners establish a separate joint venture to develop and manufacture a product or service. Numerous examples of such strategic alliances can be found in the automotive, electronics, telecommunications, and aircraft industries. Such alliances are particularly suited to high-tech industries where the cost of research and development is high and timely introduction of improvements is important.

A third level of cooperation might include joint marketing and servicing agreements in which each partner represents the other in certain markets. Some observers believe such arrangements begin to resemble the cartels prevalent in the 1920s and 1930s. Because they reduce competition, cartels have been banned by international agreements and many national laws.

Predicting Political Risk

How can multinational firms anticipate political risks such as government regulations that, from the firm's perspective, are discriminatory or wealth depriving? First, the firm must be able to define and classify the political risks it may face.

Defining and Classifying Political Risk

In order for an MNE to identify, measure, and manage its political risks, it needs to define and classify these risks. At the macro level, firms attempt to assess a host country's political stability and attitude toward foreign investors. At the micro level, firms analyze whether their firm-specific activities are likely to conflict with host-country goals as evidenced by existing regulations. The most difficult task, however, is to anticipate changes in host-country goal priorities, new regulations to implement reordered priorities, and the likely impact of such changes on the firm's operations.

Exhibit 16.4 further classifies the political risks facing MNEs as being firm-specific, country-specific, or global-specific.

- Firm-specific risks, also known as micro risks, are those that affect the MNE at the project or corporate level. Governance risk due to goal conflict between an MNE and its host government is the main political firm-specific risk.

- Country-specific risks, also known as macro risks, are those that affect the MNE at the project or corporate level but originate at the country level. The two main political risk categories at the country level are transfer risk and cultural and institutional risks. Cultural and institutional risks spring from ownership structure, human resource norms, religious heritage, nepotism and corruption, intellectual property rights, and protectionism.

EXHIBIT 16.4   **Classification of Political Risks**

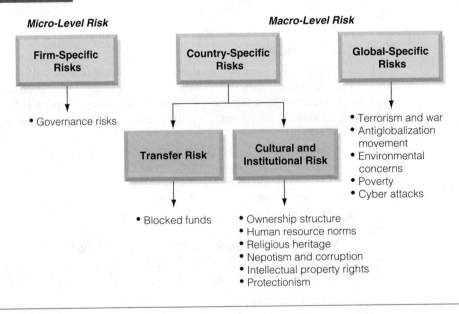

■ Global-specific risks are those that affect the MNE at the project or corporate level but originate at the global level. Examples are terrorism, the antiglobalization movement, environmental concerns, poverty, and cyber attacks.

This method of classification differs sharply from the traditional method that classifies risks according to the disciplines of economics, finance, political science, sociology, and law. We prefer our classification system because it is easier to relate the identified political risks to existing and recommended strategies to manage these risks.

Predicting Firm-Specific Risk (Micro Risk)

From the viewpoint of a multinational firm, assessing the political stability of a host country is only the first step in predicting firm-specific risk, since the real objective is to anticipate the effect of political changes on activities of a specific firm. Indeed, different foreign firms operating within the same country may have very different degrees of vulnerability to changes in host-country policy or regulations. One does not expect a Kentucky Fried Chicken franchise to experience the same risk as a Ford manufacturing plant.

The need for firm-specific analyses of political risk has led to a demand for "tailor-made" studies undertaken in-house by professional political risk analysts. This demand is heightened by the observation that outside professional risk analysts rarely even agree on the degree of macro-political risk that exists in any set of countries.

In-house political risk analysts relate the macro risk attributes of specific countries to the particular characteristics and vulnerabilities of their client firms. Mineral extractive firms, manufacturing firms, multinational banks, private insurance carriers, and worldwide hotel chains are all exposed in fundamentally different ways to politically inspired restrictions. Even with the best possible firm-specific analysis, MNEs cannot be sure that the political or economic situation will not change. Thus, it is necessary to plan protective steps in advance to minimize the risk of damage from unanticipated changes.

Predicting Country-Specific Risk (Macro Risk)

Macro political risk analysis is still an emerging field of study. Political scientists in academia, industry, and government study country risk for the benefit of multinational firms, government foreign policy decision-makers, and defense planners.

Political risk studies usually include an analysis of the historical stability of the country in question, evidence of present turmoil or dissatisfaction, indications of economic stability, and trends in cultural and religious activities. Data are usually assembled by reading local newspapers, monitoring radio and television broadcasts, reading publications from diplomatic sources, tapping the knowledge of outstanding expert consultants, contacting other business-people who have had recent experience in the host country, and finally conducting on-site visits.

Despite this impressive list of activities, the prediction track record of business firms, the diplomatic service, and the military has been spotty at best. When one analyzes trends, whether in politics or economics, the tendency is to predict an extension of the same trends into the future. It is a rare forecaster who is able to predict a cataclysmic change in direction. Who predicted the overthrow of Ferdinand Marcos in the Philippines? Indeed, who predicted the collapse of communism in the Soviet Union and the Eastern European satellites? Who predicted the fall of President Suharto in Indonesia in 1998? As illustrated by *Global Finance in Practice 16.1*, the 2011 public protests in Egypt serve as one corporate reminder of risk and the reaction of markets to perceived vulnerability.

Despite the difficulty of predicting country risk, the MNE must still attempt to do so in order to prepare itself for the unknown. A number of institutional services provide updated country risk ratings on a regular basis.

GLOBAL FINANCE IN PRACTICE 16.1

Apache Takes a Hit from Egyptian Protests

The January and February 2011 protests in Egypt took billions of dollars of value away from Apache Corporation (NYSE: APA). The U.S.-based oil exploration and production company has significant holdings and operations in Egypt, and the political turmoil that engulfed the country in early 2011 caused the investment public to start dumping Apache's shares. Although actual oil and gas production was not disrupted during this period, Apache did evacuate all expatriate workers from Egypt. Egypt made up roughly 30% of Apache's revenue in 2011, 26% of total production, and 13% of its estimated proved reserves of oil and gas.

Apache Corporation's Share Price (NYSE: APA)

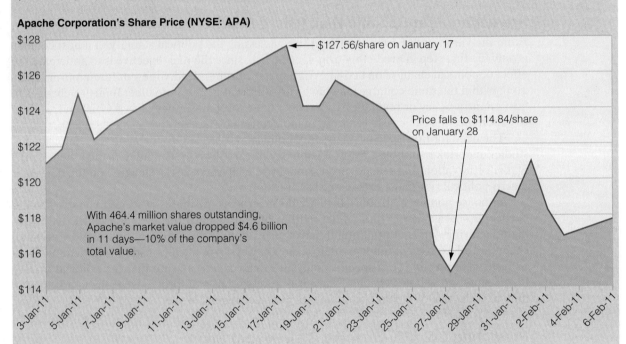

$127.56/share on January 17

Price falls to $114.84/share on January 28

With 464.4 million shares outstanding, Apache's market value dropped $4.6 billion in 11 days—10% of the company's total value.

Predicting Global-Specific Risk (Macro Risk)

Predicting global-specific risk is even more difficult than the other two types of political risk. Nobody predicted the surprise attacks on the World Trade Center and the Pentagon in the United States on September 11, 2001. On the other hand, the aftermath of this attack, that is, the war on global terrorism, increased U.S. homeland security, and the destruction of part of the terrorist network in Afghanistan was predictable. Nevertheless, we have come to expect future surprise terrorist attacks. U.S.-based MNEs are particularly exposed not only to Al-Qaeda but also to other unpredictable interest groups willing to use terror or mob action to promote such diverse causes as antiglobalization, environmental protection, and even anarchy. Since there is a great need to predict terrorism, we can expect to see a number of new indices, similar to country-specific indices, but devoted to ranking different types of terrorist threats, their locations, and potential targets.

Firm-Specific Political Risk: Governance Risk

The firm-specific political risks that confront MNEs include foreign exchange risks and governance risks. The various business and foreign exchange risks were detailed in Chapters 9 and 10. We focus our discussion here on governance risks.

Governance risk is measured by the MNE's ability to exercise effective control over its operations within a country's legal and political environment. For an MNE, however, governance is a subject similar in structure to consolidated profitability—it must be addressed for the individual business unit and subsidiary, as well as for the MNE as a whole.

The most important type of governance risk for the MNE on the subsidiary level arises from a goal conflict between bona fide objectives of host governments and the private firms operating within their spheres of influence. Governments are normally responsive to a constituency consisting of their citizens. Firms are responsive to a constituency consisting of their owners and other stakeholders. The valid needs of these two separate sets of constituents need not be the same, but governments set the rules. Consequently, governments impose constraints on the activities of private firms as part of their normal administrative and legislative functioning.

Historically, conflicts between objectives of MNEs and host governments have arisen over such issues as the firm's impact on economic development, perceived infringement on national sovereignty, foreign control of key industries, sharing or nonsharing of ownership and control with local interests, impact on a host-country's balance of payments, influence on the foreign exchange value of its currency, control over export markets, use of domestic versus foreign executives and workers, and exploitation of national resources. Attitudes about conflicts are often colored by views about free enterprise versus state socialism, the degree of nationalism or internationalism present, or the place of religious views in determining appropriate economic and financial behavior.

The best approach to goal conflict management is to anticipate problems and negotiate understandings ahead of time. Different cultures apply different ethics to the question of honoring prior "contracts," especially when they were negotiated with a previous administration. Nevertheless, prenegotiation of all conceivable areas of conflict provides a better basis for a successful future for both parties than does overlooking the possibility that divergent objectives will evolve over time. Prenegotiation often includes negotiating investment agreements, buying investment insurance and guarantees, and designing risk-reducing operating strategies to be used after the foreign investment decision has been made.

Investment Agreements

An *investment agreement* spells out specific rights and responsibilities of both the foreign firm and the host government. The presence of MNEs is as often sought by development-seeking host governments, just as a particular foreign location may be sought by an MNE. All parties have alternatives and so bargaining is appropriate.

An investment agreement should spell out policies on financial and managerial issues, including the following:

- The basis on which fund flows, such as dividends, management fees, royalties, patent fees, and loan repayments, may be remitted
- The basis for setting transfer prices
- The right to export to third-country markets
- Obligations to build, or fund, social and economic overhead projects, such as schools, hospitals, and retirement systems
- Methods of taxation, including the rate, the type of taxation, and means by which the rate base is determined
- Access to host-country capital markets, particularly for long-term borrowing
- Permission for 100% foreign ownership versus required local ownership (joint venture) participation

- Price controls, if any, applicable to sales in the host-country markets
- Requirements for local sourcing versus import of raw materials and components
- Permission to use expatriate managerial and technical personnel, and to bring them and their personal possessions into the country free of exorbitant charges or import duties
- Provision for arbitration of disputes
- Provision for planned divestment, should such be required, indicating how the going concern will be valued and to whom it will be sold

Investment Insurance and Guarantees: OPIC

MNEs can sometimes transfer political risk to a host-country public agency through an investment insurance and guarantee program. Many developed countries have such programs to protect investments by their nationals in developing countries.

The U.S. investment insurance and guarantee program is managed by the government-owned *Overseas Private Investment Corporation* (OPIC). An OPIC's purpose is to mobilize and facilitate the participation of U.S. private capital and skills in the economic and social progress of less-developed friendly countries and areas, thereby complementing the developmental assistance of the United States. An OPIC offers insurance coverage for four separate types of political risk, which have their own specific definitions for insurance purposes:

1. Inconvertibility is the risk that the investor will not be able to convert profits, royalties, fees, or other income, as well as the original capital invested, into dollars.
2. Expropriation is the risk that the host government takes a specific step that for one year prevents the investor or the foreign subsidiary from exercising effective control over use of the property.
3. War, revolution, insurrection, and civil strife coverage applies primarily to the damage of physical property of the insured, although in some cases inability of a foreign subsidiary to repay a loan because of a war may be covered.
4. Business income coverage provides compensation for loss of business income resulting from events of political violence that directly cause damage to the assets of a foreign enterprise.

Operating Strategies after the FDI Decision

Although an investment agreement creates obligations on the part of both foreign investor and host government, conditions change and agreements are often revised in the light of such changes. The changed conditions may be economic, or they may be the result of political changes within the host government. The firm that sticks rigidly to the legal interpretation of its original agreement may well find that the host government first applies pressure in areas not covered by the agreement and then possibly reinterprets the agreement to conform to the political reality of that country. Most MNEs, in their own self-interest, follow a policy of adapting to changing host-country priorities whenever possible. The essence of such adaptation is anticipating host-country priorities and ensuring that the activities of the firm are of continued value to the host country. Such an approach assumes the host government acts rationally in seeking its country's self-interest and is based on the idea that the firm should initiate reductions in goal conflict. Future bargaining position can be enhanced by careful consideration of policies in production, logistics, marketing, finance, organization, and personnel.

Local Sourcing

Host governments may require foreign firms to purchase raw material and components locally as a way to maximize value-added benefits and to increase local employment. From the viewpoint of the foreign firm trying to adapt to host-country goals, local sourcing reduces political risk, albeit at a trade-off with other factors. Local strikes or other turmoil may shut down the operation and such issues as quality control, high local prices because of lack of economies of scale, and unreliable delivery schedules become important. Often, through local sourcing, the MNE lowers political risk only by increasing its financial and commercial risk.

Facility Location

Production facilities may be located to minimize risk. The natural location of different stages of production may be resource-oriented, footloose, or market-oriented. Oil, for instance, is drilled in and around the Persian Gulf, Russia, Venezuela, and Indonesia. No choice exists for where this activity takes place. Refining is footloose; a refining facility can be moved easily to another location or country. Whenever possible, oil companies have built refineries in politically safe countries, such as Western Europe, or small islands (such as Singapore or Curaçao), even though costs might be reduced by refining nearer the oil fields. They have traded reduced political risk and financial exposure for higher transportation and refining costs.

Control

Control—of transportation, technology, markets, brands and trademarks—is key to the management of a multitude of political risks.

Transportation. Control of transportation has been an important means to reduce political risk. Oil pipelines that cross national frontiers, oil tankers, ore carriers, refrigerated ships, and railroads have all been controlled at times to influence the bargaining power of both nations and companies.

Technology. Control of key patents and processes is a viable way to reduce political risk. If a host country cannot operate a plant because it does not have technicians capable of running the process, or of keeping up with changing technology, abrogation of an investment agreement with a foreign firm is unlikely. Control of technology works best when the foreign firm is steadily improving its technology.

Markets. Control of markets is a common strategy to enhance a firm's bargaining position. As effective as the OPEC cartel was in raising the price received for crude oil by its member countries in the 1970s, marketing was still controlled by the international oil companies. OPEC's need for the oil companies limited the degree to which its members could dictate terms. In more recent years, OPEC members have established some marketing outlets of their own, such as Kuwait's extensive chain of Q8 gas stations in Europe.

Control of export markets for manufactured goods is also a source of leverage in dealings between MNEs and host governments. The MNE would prefer to serve world markets from sources of its own choosing, basing the decision on considerations of production cost, transportation, tariff barriers, political risk exposure, and competition. The selling pattern that maximizes long-run profits from the viewpoint of the worldwide firm rarely maximizes exports, or value added, from the perspective of the host countries. Some will argue that if the same plants were owned by local nationals and were not part of a worldwide integrated system, more goods would be exported by the host country. The contrary argument is that self-contained local firms might never obtain foreign market share because they lack economies of scale on the production side and are unable to market in foreign countries.

Brand Name and Trademark. Control of a brand name or trademark can have an effect almost identical to that of controlling technology. It gives the MNE a monopoly on something that may or may not have substantive value but quite likely represents value in the eyes of consumers. Ability to market under a world brand name is valuable for local firms and thus represents an important bargaining attribute for maintaining an investment position.

Thin Equity Base

Foreign subsidiaries can be financed with a thin equity base and a large proportion of local debt. If the debt is borrowed from locally owned banks, host-government actions that weaken the financial viability of the firm also endanger local creditors.

Multiple-Source Borrowing

If the firm must finance with foreign source debt, it may borrow from banks in a number of countries rather than just from host-country banks. If, for example, debt is owed to banks in Tokyo, Frankfurt, London, and New York, nationals in a number of foreign countries have a vested interest in keeping the borrowing subsidiary financially strong. If the multinational is U.S.-owned, a fallout between the United States and the host government is less likely to cause the local government to move against the firm if it also owes funds to these other countries.

Country-Specific Risk: Transfer Risk

Country-specific risks affect all firms, domestic and foreign, that are resident in a host country. Exhibit 16.5 presents a taxonomy of most of the contemporary political risks that emanate from a specific country location. The main country-specific political risks are transfer risk, cultural risk, and institutional risk. This section focuses on transfer risk.

Blocked Funds

Transfer risk is the risk of limitations on the MNE's ability to transfer funds into and out of a host country without restrictions. When a government runs short of foreign exchange and cannot obtain additional funds through borrowing or attracting new foreign investment, it usually limits transfers of foreign exchange out of the country, a restriction known as blocked funds. In theory, such limitations do not discriminate against foreign-owned firms because they apply to everyone; in practice, though, foreign firms have more at stake because of their foreign ownership. Depending on the size of a foreign exchange shortage, the host government might simply require approval of all transfers of funds abroad, thus reserving the right to set a priority on the use of scarce foreign exchange in favor of necessities rather than luxuries. In very severe cases, the government might make its currency nonconvertible into other currencies, thereby fully blocking transfers of funds abroad. In between these positions are policies that restrict the size and timing of dividends, debt amortization, royalties, and service fees. MNEs can react to the potential for blocked funds at three stages:

1. Prior to investing, a firm can analyze the effect of blocked funds on expected return on investment, the desired local financial structure, and optimal links with subsidiaries.
2. During operations, a firm can attempt to move funds through a variety of repositioning techniques.
3. Funds that cannot be moved must be reinvested in the local country in a manner that avoids deterioration in their real value because of inflation or exchange depreciation.

EXHIBIT 16.5	Management Strategies for Country-Specific Risks

Transfer Risk

Cultural and Institutional Risk

Blocked Funds

- Preinvestment strategy to anticipate blocked funds
- Fronting loans
- Creating unrelated exports
- Obtaining special dispensation
- Forced reinvestment

Ownership Structure

- Joint venture

Religious Heritage

- Understand and respect host country religious heritage

Nepotism and Corruption

- Disclose bribery policy to both employees and clients
- Retain a local legal advisor

Human Resource Norms

- Local management and staffing

Intellectual Property

- Legal action in host country courts
- Support worldwide treaty to protect intellectual property rights

Protectionism

- Support government actions to create regional markets

Preinvestment Strategy to Anticipate Blocked Funds

Management can consider blocked funds in their capital budgeting analysis. Temporary blockage of funds normally reduces the expected net present value and internal rate of return on a proposed investment. Whether the investment should nevertheless be undertaken depends on whether the expected rate of return, even with blocked funds, exceeds the required rate of return on investments of the same risk class. Preinvestment analysis also includes the potential to minimize the effect of blocked funds by financing with local borrowing instead of parent equity, swap agreements, and other techniques to reduce local currency exposure and thus the need to repatriate funds. Sourcing and sales links with subsidiaries can be predetermined to maximize the potential for moving blocked funds.

Moving Blocked Funds

What can a multinational firm do to transfer funds out of countries having exchange or remittance restrictions? At least six popular strategies are used:

1. Providing alternative conduits for repatriating funds
2. Transferring pricing goods and services between related units of the MNE
3. Leading and lagging payments
4. Signing fronting loans
5. Creating unrelated exports
6. Obtaining special dispensation

Fronting Loans. A *fronting loan* is a parent-to-subsidiary loan channeled through a financial intermediary, usually a large international bank. Fronting loans differ from "parallel" or "back-to-back" loans, discussed in Chapter 10. The latter are offsetting loans between commercial businesses arranged outside the banking system. Fronting loans are sometimes referred to as link financing.

In a direct intracompany loan, a parent or sister subsidiary loans directly to the borrowing subsidiary, and later, the borrowing subsidiary repays the principal and interest. In a fronting loan, by contrast, the "lending" parent or subsidiary deposits funds in, say, a London bank, and that bank loans the same amount to the borrowing subsidiary in the host country. From the London bank's point of view, the loan is risk-free, because the bank has 100% collateral in the form of the parent's deposit. In effect, the bank "fronts" for the parent—hence the name. Interest paid by the borrowing subsidiary to the bank is usually slightly higher than the rate paid by the bank to the parent, allowing the bank a margin for expenses and profit.

The bank chosen for the fronting loan is usually in a neutral country, away from both the lender's and the borrower's legal jurisdiction. Use of fronting loans increases the chances for repayment should political turmoil occur between the home and host countries. Government authorities are more likely to allow a local subsidiary to repay a loan to a large international bank in a neutral country than to allow the same subsidiary to repay a loan directly to its parent. To stop payment to the international bank would hurt the international credit image of the country, whereas to stop payment to the parent corporation would have minimal impact on that image and might even provide some domestic political advantage.

Creating Unrelated Exports. Another approach to blocked funds, which benefits both the subsidiary and host country, is the creation of unrelated exports. Because the main reason for stringent exchange controls is usually a host country's persistent inability to earn hard currencies, anything an MNE can do to create new exports from the host country helps the situation and provides a potential means to transfer funds out. Some new exports can often be created from present productive capacity with little or no additional investment, especially if they are in product lines related to existing operations. Other new exports may require reinvestment or new funds, although if the funds reinvested consist of those already blocked, little is lost in the way of opportunity costs.

Special Dispensation. If all else fails and the multinational firm is investing in an industry that is important to the economic development of the host country, the firm may bargain for special dispensation to repatriate some portion of the funds that otherwise would be blocked. Firms in "desirable" industries such as telecommunications, semiconductor manufacturing, instrumentation, pharmaceuticals, or other research and high-tech industries may receive preference over firms in mature industries. The amount of preference received depends on bargaining among the informed parties, the government and the business firm, either of which is free to back away from the proposed investment if unsatisfied with the terms.

Self-Fulfilling Prophecies. In seeking "escape routes" for blocked funds—or for that matter in trying to position funds through any of the techniques discussed in this chapter—the MNE may increase political risk and cause a change from partial blockage to full blockage. The possibility of such a self-fulfilling cycle exists any time a firm takes action that, no matter how legal, thwarts the underlying intent of politically motivated controls. In the statehouses of the world, as in the editorial offices of the local press and TV, MNEs and their subsidiaries are always potential scapegoats.

Forced Reinvestment. If funds are indeed blocked from transfer into foreign exchange, they are by definition "reinvested." Under such a situation, the firm must find local opportunities that will maximize the rate of return for a given acceptable level of risk.

If blockage is expected to be temporary, the most obvious alternative is to invest in local money market instruments. Unfortunately, in many countries, such instruments are not available in sufficient quantity or with adequate liquidity. In some cases, government Treasury bills, bank deposits, and other short-term instruments have yields that are kept artificially low relative to local rates of inflation or probable changes in exchange rates. Thus, the firm often loses real value during the period of blockage.

If short- or intermediate-term portfolio investments, such as bonds, bank time deposits, or direct loans to other companies, are not possible, investment in additional production facilities may be the only alternative. Often, this investment is what the host country is seeking by its exchange controls, even if the existence of exchange controls is by itself counterproductive to the idea of additional foreign investment. Examples of forced direct reinvestment can be cited for Peru, where an airline invested in hotels and in maintenance facilities for other airlines; for Turkey, where a fish canning company constructed a plant to manufacture cans needed for packing the catch; and for Argentina, where an automobile company integrated vertically by acquiring a transmission manufacturing plant previously owned by a supplier.

If investment opportunities in additional production facilities are not available, funds may simply be used to acquire other assets expected to increase in value with local inflation. Typical purchases might be land, office buildings, or commodities that are exported to global markets. Even inventory stockpiling might be a reasonable investment, given the low opportunity cost of the blocked funds.

Country-Specific Risk: Cultural and Institutional Risk

When investing in some of the emerging markets, MNEs that are resident in the most industrialized countries face serious risks because of cultural and institutional differences. Many such differences include the following:

- Differences in allowable ownership structures
- Differences in human resource norms
- Differences in religious heritage
- Nepotism and corruption in the host country
- Protection of intellectual property rights
- Protectionism
- Legal liabilities

Ownership Structure

Historically, many countries have required that MNEs share ownership of their foreign subsidiaries with local firms or citizens. Thus, joint ventures were the only way an MNE could operate in some host countries. Prominent countries that used to require majority local ownership were Japan, Mexico, China, India, and Korea. This requirement has been eliminated or modified in more recent years by these countries and most others. However, firms in certain industries are still either excluded from ownership completely or must accept being a minority owner. These industries are typically related to national defense, agriculture, banking, or other sectors that are deemed critical for the host nation.

Human Resource Norms

MNEs are often required by host countries to employ a certain proportion of host-country citizens rather than staffing mainly with foreign expatriates. It is often very difficult to fire local employees due to host-country labor laws and union contracts. This lack of flexibility to downsize in response to business cycles affects both MNEs and their local competitors. It also qualifies as a country-specific risk. Cultural differences can also inhibit an MNE's staffing policies. For example, it is somewhat difficult for a woman manager to be accepted by local employees and managers in many Middle Eastern countries. The most extreme example of discrimination against women has been highlighted in Afghanistan when the Taliban were in power. Since the Taliban's downfall in late 2001, several women have been suggested for important government roles in Afghanistan, and it is expected that over time the private sector in Afghanistan will also begin to reintegrate women into the workforce.

Religious Heritage

MNEs in some cases may encounter host country environments in which the political attitudes, and therefore business attitudes, of the state are intertwined with religious beliefs that conflict with MNE business practices. Despite religious differences, however, MNEs have operated successfully in emerging markets, especially in extractive and natural resource industries, such as oil, natural gas, minerals, and forest products. The main MNE strategy is to understand and respect the host country's religious traditions.

Nepotism and Corruption

MNEs must deal with endemic nepotism and corruption in a number of important foreign investment locations. Indonesia was famous for nepotism and corruption under the now-deposed Suharto government. Nigeria, Kenya, Uganda, and a number of other African countries have a history of nepotism and corruption after they threw out their colonial governments after World War II. China and Russia have recently launched well-publicized crackdowns on those evils.

Bribery is not limited to emerging markets. It is also a problem in even the most industrialized countries, including the United States and Japan. In fact, the United States has an antibribery law that would imprison any U.S. business executive found guilty of bribing a foreign government official. This law was passed in reaction to an attempt by a U.S. aircraft manufacturer's attempt to bribe a senior Japanese government official.

MNEs are caught in a dilemma. Should they employ bribery if their local competitors use this strategy? The nearly universal response is, absolutely not. Most MNEs have a set of principles and practices that they follow in the execution of their business globally. These principles and ethics are universal, and not situation specific. Regardless of what competitors may or may not do, the individual MNE must follow its own set of principles—even if it means losing the business.

Intellectual Property Rights

Rogue businesses in some host countries have historically infringed on the intellectual property rights of both MNEs and individuals. Intellectual property rights grant the exclusive use of patented technology and copyrighted creative materials. Examples of patented technology are unique manufactured products, processing techniques, and prescription pharmaceutical drugs. Examples of copyrighted creative materials are software programs, educational materials (textbooks), and entertainment products (e.g., music, film, art).

MNEs and individuals need to protect their intellectual property rights through the legal process. However, in some countries, courts have historically not done a fair job of protecting intellectual property rights of anyone, much less of foreign MNEs. In those countries, the legal process is costly and subject to bribery.

The agreement on Trade-Related Aspects of Intellectual Property Rights (TRIPS) to protect intellectual property rights has been ratified by most major countries. It remains to be seen whether host governments are strong enough to enforce their official efforts to stamp out intellectual piracy. Complicating this task is the thin line that exists between the real item being protected and generic versions of the same item.

Protectionism

Protectionism is defined as the attempt by a national government to protect certain of its designated industries from foreign competition through such methods as tariffs or other import restrictions. Protected industries are usually related to defense, agriculture, and "infant" industries.

Defense. Even though the U.S. is a vocal proponent of open markets, a foreign firm proposing to buy a U.S. critical defense supplier would not be welcome. The same attitude exists in many other countries, such as France, which has always wished to maintain an independent defense capability.

Agriculture. Agriculture is another sensitive industry. No MNE would be foolish enough as to attempt to buy agricultural properties, such as rice operations, in Japan. Japan has worked diligently to maintain an independent ability to feed its own population. Agriculture is the typical "Mother Earth" industry that most countries want to protect for their own citizens.

Infant Industries. The traditional protectionist argument is that newly emerging "infant" industries need protection from foreign competition until they are firmly established. The infant industry argument is usually directed at limiting imports but not necessarily MNEs. In fact, most host countries encourage MNEs to establish operations in new industries that do not presently exist in the host country. Sometimes the host country offers foreign MNEs "infant industry" status for a limited number of years. This status could lead to tax subsidies, construction of infrastructure, employee training, and other aids to help the MNE get started. Host countries are especially interested in attracting MNEs that promise to export, either to their own foreign subsidiaries elsewhere or to unrelated parties.

Tariff and Non-Tariff Barriers. The traditional methods for countries to implement protectionist barriers were through tariff and non-tariff regulations. A multitude of international negotiations and treaties have greatly reduced the general level of tariffs over the past decades. However, many non-tariff barriers remain. These non-tariff barriers restrict imports by something other than a financial cost and are often difficult to identify because they are promulgated as health, safety, or sanitation requirements.

Strategies to Manage Protectionism. MNEs have only a very limited ability to overcome host country protectionism. However, MNEs do enthusiastically support efforts to reduce protectionism by joining in regional markets. The best examples of regional markets are the European Union (EU), the North American Free Trade Association (NAFTA), and the Latin American Free Trade Association (MERCOSUR). Among the objectives of regional markets are elimination of internal trade barriers, such as tariffs and non-tariff barriers, as well as the free movement of citizens for employment purposes.

Legal Liabilities

Despite good intentions, MNEs are often confronted with unexpected legal liabilities. Global Finance in Practice 16.2 illustrates why Hospira, a U.S.-based pharmaceutical manufacturer, decided to cancel an FDI project in Italy as a result of potential legal and associated financial liabilities.

Global-Specific Risk

Global-specific risks faced by MNEs have come to the forefront in recent years. Exhibit 16.6 summarizes some of these risks, and strategies that can be used to manage them. The most visible recent risk was, of course, the attack by terrorists on the twin towers of the World Trade

GLOBAL FINANCE IN PRACTICE 16.2

Drugs, Public Policy, and the Death Penalty in 2011

Foreign direct investment can be a very tricky thing. Just ask Hospira, a U.S.-based pharmaceutical manufacturer. Hospira, of Lake Forest, Illinois (U.S.), stopped manufacturing of Pentothal (sodium thiopental) in North Carolina in the United States in mid-2009. It intended to shift all production to Italy. Hospira's press release read as follows:

Hospira Statement Regarding Pentothal™ (Sodium Thiopental) Market Exit

LAKE FOREST, Ill., Jan. 21, 2011—Hospira announced today it will exit the sodium thiopental market and no longer attempt to resume production of its product, Pentothal™.

Hospira had intended to produce Pentothal at its Italian plant. In the last month, we've had ongoing dialogue with the Italian authorities concerning the use of Pentothal in capital punishment procedures in the United States—a use Hospira has never condoned. Italy's intent is that we control the product all the way to the ultimate end user to prevent use in capital punishment. These discussions and internal deliberation, as well as conversations with wholesalers—the primary distributors of the product to customers—led us to believe we could not prevent the drug from being diverted to departments of corrections for use in capital punishment procedures.

Based on this understanding, we cannot take the risk that we will be held liable by the Italian authorities if the product is diverted for use in capital punishment. Exposing our employees or facilities to liability is not a risk we are prepared to take.

Given the issues surrounding the product, including the government's requirements and challenges bringing the drug back to market, Hospira has decided to exit the market. We regret that issues outside of our control forced Hospira's decision to exit the market, and that our many hospital customers who use the drug for its well-established medical benefits will not be able to obtain the product from Hospira.

Source: Hospira.com. Reprinted with permission.

The news was met with dismay by the medical industry. Pentothal, at one time a widely used anesthetic, is today only used in a variety of special cases. The drug is preferred in specific cases because it does not cause blood pressure to drop severely, including the care of the elderly, patients with heart disease, or expecting mothers requiring emerging C-sections in which the possibility of low blood pressure is threatening. Second-best solutions would now have to be good enough.

Center in New York on September 11, 2001. Many MNEs had major operations in the World Trade Center and suffered heavy casualties among their employees. In addition to terrorism, other global-specific risks include the antiglobalization movement, environmental concerns, poverty in emerging markets, and cyber attacks on computer information systems.

Terrorism and War

Although the World Trade Center attack and its aftermath, the war in Afghanistan, have affected nearly everyone worldwide, many other acts of terrorism have been committed in recent years. More terrorist acts are expected to occur in the future. Particularly exposed are the foreign subsidiaries of MNEs and their employees. As mentioned earlier, foreign subsidiaries are especially exposed to war, ethnic strife, and terrorism because they are symbols of their respective parent countries.

Crisis Planning. No MNE has the tools to avert terrorism. Hedging, diversification, insurance, and the like are not suited to the task. Therefore, MNEs must depend on governments to fight terrorism and protect their foreign subsidiaries (and now even the parent firm). In return, governments expect financial, material, and verbal support from MNEs to support antiterrorist legislation and proactive initiatives to destroy terrorist cells wherever they exist.

MNEs can be subject to damage by being in harm's way. Nearly every year one or more host countries experience some form of ethnic strife, outright war with other countries, or terrorism. It seems that foreign MNEs are often singled out as symbols of "oppression" because they represent their parent country, especially if it is the United States.

EXHIBIT 16.6	Management Strategies for Global-Specific Risks

Terrorism and War
- Support government efforts to fight terrorism and war
- Crisis planning
- Cross-border supply chain integration

Antiglobalization
- Support government efforts to reduce trade barriers
- Recognize that MNEs are the targets

Environmental Concerns
- Show sensitivity to environmental concerns
- Support government efforts to maintain a level playing field for pollution controls

Poverty
- Provide stable, relatively well-paying jobs
- Establish the strictest of occupational safety standards

Cyber Attacks
- No effective strategy except Internet security efforts
- Support government anticyber attack efforts

*MNE movement toward multiple primary objectives:
Profitability, Sustainable Development, Corporate Social Responsibility*

Cross-Border Supply Chain Integration. The drive to increase efficiency in manufacturing has driven many MNEs to adopt just-in-time (JIT) near-zero inventory systems. Focusing on so-called inventory velocity, the speed at which inventory moves through a manufacturing process, arriving only as needed and not before, has allowed these MNEs to generate increasing profits and cash flows with less capital being bottled-up in the production cycle itself. This finely tuned supply chain system, however, is subject to significant political risk if the supply chain itself extends across borders.

Supply Chain Interruptions. Consider the cases of Dell Computer, Ford Motor Company, Dairy Queen, Apple Computer, Herman Miller, and The Limited in the days following the terrorist attacks of September 11, 2001. An immediate result of the attacks of the morning of September 11 was the grounding of all aircraft into or out of the United States. Similarly, the land (Mexico and Canada) and sea borders of the United States were also shut down and not reopened for several days in some specific sites. Ford Motor Company shut down five of its manufacturing plants in the days following September 11 because of inadequate inventories of critical automotive inputs supplied from Canada. Dairy Queen experienced such significant delays in key confectionary ingredients that many of its stores were also temporarily closed.

Dell Computer, with one of the most highly acclaimed and admired virtually integrated supply chains, depends on computer parts and subassembly suppliers and manufacturers in both Mexico and Canada to fulfill its everyday assembly and sales needs. In recent years, Dell has carried less than three full days sales of total inventory—by cost of goods value. Suppliers are integrated electronically with Dell's order fulfillment system, and deliver required components and subassemblies as sales demands require. But with the closure of borders and grounding of air freight, the company was literally brought to a near standstill because of its supply chain's reliance on the ability to treat business units and suppliers in different countries as if they were all part of a single seamless political unit. Unfortunately, that proved not to be the case with this particular unpredictable catastrophic terrorist event.

As a result of these newly learned lessons, many MNEs are now evaluating the degree of exposure their own supply chains possess in regard to cross-border stoppages or other cross-border political events. These companies are not, however, about to abandon JIT. It is estimated that many U.S. companies alone have saved more than $1 billion a year in inventory carrying costs by using JIT methods over the past decade. This substantial benefit is now being weighed against the costs and risks associated with the post-September 11 supply chain interruptions.

To avoid suffering a similar fate in the future, manufacturers, retailers, and suppliers are now employing a range of tactics:

- **Inventory Management.** Manufacturers and assemblers are now considering carrying more buffer inventory in order to hedge against supply and production-line disruptions. Retailers, meanwhile, should think about the timing and frequency of their replenishment. Rather than stocking up across the board, companies are focusing on the most critical parts to the product or service, and those components, which are uniquely available from international sources.

- **Sourcing.** Manufacturers are now being more selective about where the critical inputs to their products come from. Although sourcing strategies will have to vary by location (those involving Mexico for example will differ dramatically from Canada), firms are attempting to work more closely with existing suppliers to minimize cross-border exposures and reduce the potential costs with future stoppages.

- **Transportation.** Retailers and manufacturers alike are reassessing their cross-border shipping arrangements. Although the mode of transportation employed is a function of value, volume, and weight, many firms are now reassessing whether higher costs for faster shipment balance out the more tenuous delivery under airline stoppages from labor, terrorist, or even bankruptcy disruptions in the future.

Antiglobalization Movement

During the past decade, there has been a growing negative reaction by some groups to reduced trade barriers and efforts to create regional markets, particularly to NAFTA and the European Union. NAFTA has been vigorously opposed by those sectors of the labor movement that could lose jobs to Mexico. Opposition within the European Union centers on loss of cultural identity, dilution of individual national control as new members are admitted, overcentralization of power in a large bureaucracy in Brussels, and most recently, the disappearance of individual national currencies in mid-2002, when the euro became the only currency in 12 of the 15 member nations.

The antiglobalization movement has become more visible following riots in Seattle during the 2001 annual meeting of the World Trade Organization. However, antiglobalization forces were not solely responsible for these riots, or for subsequent riots in Quebec and Prague in 2001. Other disaffected groups, such as environmentalists and even anarchists, joined in to make their causes more visible.

MNEs do not have the tools to combat antiglobalism. Indeed they are blamed for fostering the problem in the first place. Once again, MNEs must rely on governments and crisis planning to manage these risks.

Environmental Concerns

MNEs have been accused of "exporting" their environmental problems to other countries. The accusation is that MNEs, frustrated by pollution controls in their home country, have relocated these activities to countries with weaker pollution controls. Another accusation is that MNEs contribute to the problem of global warming. However, that accusation applies to all firms in all countries. It is based on the manufacturing methods employed by specific industries and on consumers' desire for certain products, such as large automobiles and sport utility vehicles that are not fuel efficient.

Once again, solving environmental problems is dependent on governments passing legislation and implementing pollution control standards. In 2001, a treaty attempting to reduce global warming was ratified by most nations, with the notable exception of the United States. However, the United States has promised to combat global warming using its own strategies. The United States objected to provisions in the worldwide treaty that allowed emerging nations to follow less restrictive standards, while the economic burden would fall on the most industrialized countries, particularly the United States.

Poverty

MNEs have located foreign subsidiaries in countries plagued by extremely uneven income distribution. At one end of the spectrum is an elite class of well-educated, well-connected, and productive persons. At the other end is a very large class of persons living at or below the poverty level. They lack education, social and economic infrastructure, and political power.

MNEs might be contributing to this disparity by employing the elite class to manage their operations. On the other hand, MNEs are creating relatively stable and well-paying jobs for those who would be otherwise unemployed and living below the poverty level. Despite being accused of supporting "sweat shop" conditions, MNEs usually compare favorably to their local competitors.

Cyber Attacks

The rapid growth of the Internet has fostered a whole new generation of scam artists and cranks that disrupt the usefulness of the World Wide Web. This is both a domestic and an international problem. MNEs can face costly cyber attacks by disaffected persons with a grudge because of their visibility and the complexity of their internal information systems.

At this time, we know of no uniquely international strategies that MNEs can use to combat cyber attacks. MNEs are using the same strategies to manage foreign cyber attacks as they use for domestic attacks. Once again, they must rely on governments to control cyber attacks.

Summary Points

- In order to invest abroad a firm must have a sustainable competitive advantage in the home market. This must be strong enough and transferable enough to overcome the disadvantages of operating abroad.

- Competitive advantages stem from economies of scale and scope arising from large size; managerial and marketing expertise; superior technology; financial strength; differentiated products; and competitiveness of the home market.

- The OLI Paradigm is an attempt to create an overall framework to explain why MNEs choose FDI rather than serve foreign markets through alternative modes, such as licensing, joint ventures, strategic alliances, management contracts, and exporting.

- Finance-specific strategies are directly related to the OLI Paradigm, including both proactive and reactive financial strategies.

- The decision about where to invest is influenced by economic and behavioral factors, as well as the stage of a firm's historical development.

- The most internationalized firms can be viewed from a network perspective. The parent firm and each of the foreign subsidiaries are members of networks. The networks are composed of relationships within a worldwide industry, within the host countries with suppliers and customers, and within the multinational firm itself.

- Exporting avoids political risk but not foreign exchange risk. It requires the least up-front investment but it might eventually lose markets to imitators and global competitors that might be more cost efficient in production abroad and distribution.

- Alternative (to wholly owned foreign subsidiaries) modes of foreign involvement exist. They include joint venture, strategic alliances, licensing, management contracts, and traditional exporting.

- The success of a joint venture depends primarily on the right choice of a partner. For this reason and a number of issues related to possible conflicts in decision-making between a joint venture and a multinational parent, the 100%-owned foreign subsidiary approach is more common.

- Political risks can be defined by classifying them on three levels: firm-specific, country-specific, or global-specific. Firm-specific risks, also known as micro risks, affect the MNE at the project or corporate level. Country-specific risks, also known as macro risks, affect the MNE at the project or corporate level but originate at the country level. Global-specific risks affect the MNE at the project or corporate level but originate at the global level.

- The main tools used to manage goal conflict are to negotiate an investment agreement; to purchase investment insurance and guarantees; and to modify operating strategies in production, logistics, marketing, finance, organization, and personnel.

- The main country-specific risks are transfer risk, known as blocked funds, and certain cultural and institutional risks.

- Cultural and institutional risks emanate from host-country policies with respect to ownership structure, human resource norms, religious heritage, nepotism and corruption, intellectual property rights, protectionism, and legal liabilities.

- Managing cultural and institutional risks requires the MNE to understand the differences, take legal actions in host-country courts, support worldwide treaties to protect intellectual property rights, and support government efforts to create regional markets.

- The main global-specific risks are currently caused by terrorism and war, the antiglobalization movement, environmental concerns, poverty, and cyber attacks.

- In order to manage global-specific risks, MNEs should adopt a crisis plan to protect its employees and property. However, the main reliance remains on governments to protect its citizens and firms from these global-specific threats.

MINI-CASE

Corporate Competition from the Emerging Markets

BCG [Boston Consulting Group] argues that this is because they have managed to resolve three trade-offs that are usually associated with corporate growth: of volume against margin; rapid expansion against low leverage (debt); and growth against dividends. On average the challengers have increased their sales three times faster than their established global peers since 2005. Yet they have also reduced their debt-to-equity ratio by three percentage points and achieved a higher ratio of dividends to share price in every year but one.

— "Nipping at Their Heels: Firms from the Developing World Are Rapidly Catching Up with Their Old-World Competitors," *The Economist*, January 22, 2011, p. 80.

Leadership in all companies, public and private, new and old, start-ups and maturing, have all heard the same threat in recent years: the emerging market competitors are coming. Despite the threat, there have been other forces at work that would prevent their advancing—or advancing too fast: the ability to raise sufficient capital at a reasonable cost; the ability to reach the larger and more profitable markets; the competition in markets that value name recognition and brand identity; and global reach. But a number of market prognosticators—the gurus and consultants—are now contending that these new competitors are already here.

One such analysis was recently published by BCG, the Boston Consulting Group.[1] BCG labels these firms the global challengers, companies based in rapidly developing economies that are "shaking up" the established economic order. Their list of 100 global companies, most of which are from Brazil (13), Russia (6), India (20), and China (33) (the so-called BRICs), and Mexico (7), are all innovative and aggressive, but have also proven to be financially fit.

The value created by these firms for their shareholders is very convincing. The total shareholder return (TSR) for the global challengers between 2005 and 2009 was 22%; the same TSR for their global peers, public companies in comparable business lines from the industrialized economies, was a mere 5%. These firms have, according to BCG, been able to achieve these results by resolving three classic trade-offs confronting emerging players. These strategic trade-offs turn out to be uniquely financial in character.

The Three Trade-Offs

The three trade-offs could also be characterized as three financial dimensions of competitiveness—the market, the financing, and the offered return.

[1]"Companies on the Move, Rising Stars from Rapidly Developing Economies Are Reshaping Global Industries," Boston Consulting Group, January 2011.

Trade-Off #1: Volume versus Margin. Traditional business thinking assumes that large-scale, large-market sales, like that of Walmart, requires incredibly low prices, which in turn impose low margin returns to the scale competitors. Higher margin products and services are usually reserved for specialty market segments, which may be much more expensive to service, but are found justifiable by the higher prices and higher margins they offer. BCG argues that the global challengers have been able to have both volume and margin, relying on exceptionally low direct costs of materials and labor, combined with the latest in technology and execution found in the developed country markets.

Trade-Off #2: Rapid Expansion versus Low Leverage. One of the key advantages always held by the world's largest companies is their preferred access to capital. The advantages afforded companies in large market economies—capitalist economies—is access to plentiful and affordable capital. Companies arising from the emerging markets have often been held back in their expansion efforts, not having the capital to exercise their ambitions. Only after gaining access to the world's largest capital markets, providers of both debt and equity, can these firms pose a serious threat beyond their immediate country market or region. In the past, access meant higher levels of debt and the associated risks and burdens of higher leverage.

But the global challengers have again fought off the trade-off, finding ways to increase both equity and debt in proportion, and therefore to grow without taking on a riskier financial structure. The obvious solution has been to gain increasing access to affordable equity, often in London and New York.

Trade-Off #3: Growth versus Dividends. Financial theory has always emphasized the critical distinctions between what opportunities and threats growth firms and value firms offer investors. Growth firms are typically smaller firms, start-ups, companies with unique business models based on new technologies or services. They have enormous upside potential, but need more time, more experience, more breadth, and most importantly, more capital. Investors in these companies know the risks are high, and as a result, accept those risks in focusing on prospective returns from capital gains, not dividend distributions. Investors also know that these firms, often very small firms, will show large share price movements quickly with commensurate business developments. For that, the firm needs to be nimble, quick, and not laden with debt.

Value companies—a polite term for mature or older, larger, well-established global competitors—are of a size in which new business developments, new markets, or new technologies, are rarely large enough to move share prices significantly and quickly. Investors in these companies, according to agency theory, do not "trust management" to take sufficient risks to generate returns. Therefore, they prefer the firm to bear some artificial financial burdens to assure diligence. Those financial burdens are typically higher levels of debt and growing distributions of profit as dividends. Both elements serve as financial disciplines, requiring management to maintain watchfulness over costs and cash flows to service debt, and generate sufficient profitability over time to supply dividends.

The global challengers have arguably thwarted this trade-off as well, paying dividends at growing rates and similar dividend yields to more mature firms with stronger and sustained cash flows. This may actually be the easiest of the three to accomplish given their already substantial sizes and strong profitability.

Continuing Questions

Many still have doubts. If these global challengers can defeat these traditional financial trade-offs, can they overcome the corporate strategic challenges that so many firms from so many markets flailed against before them? As the Economist notes, "All this is impressive, but it seems implausible that these trade-offs have been 'resolved.' "[2]

Many emerging market analysts and rapidly developing economy analysts argue that these firms not only *understand emerging markets*, but also they have *demonstrated sustained innovation* and *remained financially healthy*. Others argue that these three factors are likely to be more simultaneous than causal. It is clear, however, that most of these new global players are arising from large underdeveloped and underserved markets—markets that are providing large bases for their rapid development.

One strategy being rapidly deployed by many of these firms is the use of strategic partnerships, joint ventures, or share swap agreements.[3] In each of these forms, the companies are gaining a competitive reach, a global partner, and access to technology and markets without major growth on their part.

Despite the use of these partnerships, this does not directly address the continuing debate as to whether firms can grow as successfully into different businesses in different markets—diversified global conglomerates. Although a strategy employed in the past, it is one not followed frequently today.

CASE QUESTIONS

1. How are the three trade-offs interconnected according to financial principles?

2. Do you believe these firms have truly resolved or conquered these trade-offs, or have they benefitted from some other competitive advantages at this stage of their development?

[2]"Nipping at Their Heels: Firms from the Developing World Are Rapidly Catching Up with Their Old-World Competitors," *The Economist*, January 22, 2011, p. 80.
[3]"Big Emerging Market Mergers Create Global Competitors," Gordon Platt, *Global Finance*, July/August 2009.

Questions

1. **Evolving into Multinationalism.** As a firm evolves from purely domestic into a true multinational enterprise, it must consider 1) its competitive advantages, 2) its production location, 3) the type of control it wants to have over any foreign operations, and 4) how much monetary capital to invest abroad. Explain how each of these considerations is important to the success of foreign operations.

2. **Market Imperfections.** MNEs strive to take advantage of market imperfections in national markets for products, factors of production, and financial assets. Large international firms are better able to exploit such imperfections. What are their main competitive advantages?

3. **Competitive Advantage.** When firms decide to invest in foreign countries, their decision is based on the competitive advantage of the firm as well as those of the host country. What are some of competitive advantages enjoyed by both the firms and host nations?

4. **Economies of Scale and Scope.** Explain briefly how economies of scale and scope can be developed in production, marketing, finance, research and development, transportation, and purchasing.

5. **Competitiveness of the Home Market.** A strongly competitive home market can sharpen a firm's competitive advantage relative to firms located in less competitive markets. Explain what is meant by the "competitive advantage of nations."

6. **OLI Paradigm.** The OLI paradigm attempts to explain why MNEs choose FDI to alternative modes of foreign market entry. Explain how the financial strategies of MNEs from emerging markets are directly related to the OLI Paradigm.

7. **Financial Links to OLI.** Financial strategies are directly related to the OLI Paradigm.
    a. Explain how proactive financial strategies are related to OLI.
    b. Explain how reactive financial strategies are related to OLI.

8. **Where to Invest.** The decision about where to invest abroad is influenced by behavioral factors.
    a. Explain the behavioral approach to FDI.
    b. Explain the international network theory explanation of FDI.

9. **Exporting versus Producing Abroad.** What are the advantages and disadvantages of limiting a firm's activities to exporting compared to producing abroad?

10. **Licensing and Management Contracts versus Producing Abroad.** What are the advantages and disadvantages of licensing and management contracts compared to producing abroad?

11. **MNE Entry in a Foreign Market.** What is the optimal entry mode into a foreign market for MNEs that require tight control over technological know-how? Explain.

12. **Greenfield Investment versus Acquisition.** What are the advantages and disadvantages of serving a foreign market through a greenfield foreign direct investment compared to an acquisition of a local firm in the target market?

13. **Strategic Alliance.** What are the main advantages and disadvantages that parties should consider before forming strategic alliances?

14. **Governance Risk.** Explain the methods by which MNEs can tackle issues of governance as they expand into new nations.

15. **Investment Agreement.** An investment agreement spells out specific rights and responsibilities of both the foreign firm and the host government. What are the main financial policies that should be included in an investment agreement?

16. **Investment Insurance and Guarantees: OPIC.** Answer the following questions:
    a. What is OPIC?
    b. What types of political risks can OPIC insure against?

17. **Operating Strategies after the FDI Decision.** The following operating strategies, among others, are expected to reduce damage from political risk. Explain each and how it reduces damage.
    a. Local sourcing
    b. Facility location
    c. Control of technology
    d. Thin equity base
    e. Multiple-source borrowing

18. **Micro and Macro Political Risks.** What are the various micro and macro political risks that MNEs have to assess before deciding to invest in a foreign country?

19. **Blocked Funds.** Why do MNEs operate in countries that impose transfer restrictions and how can they manage impending transfer risks?

20. **Sovereign Credit Risk.** Is sovereign credit risk an example of a micro or macro risk? How can it impact MNEs?

21. **Strategies to Manage Cultural and Institutional Risks.** Explain the strategies that an MNE can use to manage each of the cultural and institutional risks that you identified in Question 20, except protectionism.

22. **Protectionism Defined.** Respond to the following:
    a. Define protectionism and identify the industries that are typically protected.
    b. Explain the "infant industry" argument for protectionism.

23. **Managing Protectionism.** Answer the following questions:
    a. What are the traditional methods for countries to implement protectionism?
    b. What are some typical non-tariff barriers to trade?
    c. How can MNEs overcome host country protectionism?

24. **Global-Specific Risks.** What are the main types of political risks that are global in origin?

25. **Managing Global-Specific Risks.** What are the main strategies used by MNEs to manage the global-specific risks you have identified in Question 24?

26. **Reputation Risk.** MNEs are forbidden to engage in unethical transactions by the local anti-bribery, anti-child-labor, and anti-corruption laws of the countries in which they operate as well as those of their home country. With the rise in global ethical concerns, the MNE can develop reputational risks if it outsources some of its operations to corruption-prone suppliers. Discuss how MNEs can limit these risks.

Internet Exercises

1. **Global Corruption Report.** Transparency International (TI) is considered by many to be the leading nongovernmental anticorruption organization in the world today. Recently, it has introduced its own annual survey analyzing current developments, identifying ongoing challenges, and offering potential solutions to individuals and organizations. One dimension of this analysis is the Bribe Payers Index. Visit TI's Web site to view the latest edition of the Bribe Payers Index.

Corruption Index	www.transparency.org/policy_research/surveys_indices/cpi
Bribe Payers Index	www.transparency.org/policy_research/surveys_indices/bpi

2. **Sovereign Credit Ratings Criteria.** The evaluation of credit risk and all other relevant risks associated with the multitude of borrowers on world debt markets requires a structured approach to international risk assessment. Use Standard and Poor's criteria, described in depth on their Web page, to differentiate the various risks (local currency risk, default risk, currency risk, transfer risk, etc.) contained in major sovereign ratings worldwide. (You may need to complete a free login for this site.)

Standard and Poor's	www.standardandpoors.com/ratings/sovereigns/ratings-list/en/

3. **Milken Capital Access Index.** The Milken Institute's Capital Access Index (CAI) is one of the most recent informational indices that aids in the evaluation of how accessible world capital markets are to MNEs and governments of many emerging market countries. According to the CAI, which countries have seen the largest deterioration in their access to capital in the last two years?

Milken Institute	www.milken-inst.org/

4. **Overseas Private Investment Corporation.** The Overseas Private Investment Corporation (OPIC) provides long-term political risk insurance and limited recourse project financing aid to U.S.-based firms investing abroad. Using the organization's Web page, answer the following questions:
    a. Exactly what types of risk will OPIC insure against?
    b. What financial limits and restrictions are there on this insurance protection?
    c. How should a project be structured to aid in its approval for OPIC coverage?

Overseas Private Investment Corp.	www.opic.gov/

5. **Political Risk and Emerging Markets.** Check the World Bank's political risk insurance blog for current issues and topics in emerging markets.

Political Insurance Blog	blogs.worldbank.org/miga/category/tags/political-risk-insurance

CHAPTER 17

Multinational Capital Budgeting and Cross-Border Acquisitions

Whales only get harpooned when they come to the surface, and turtles can only move forward when they stick their neck out, but investors face risk no matter what they do. —Charles A. Jaffe.

LEARNING OBJECTIVES

- Extend the domestic capital budgeting analysis to evaluate a greenfield foreign project
- Distinguish between the project viewpoint and the parent viewpoint when analyzing a potential foreign investment
- Adjust the capital budgeting analysis of a foreign project for risk
- Introduce the use of real option analysis as a complement to discounted cash flow analysis
- Examine the use of project finance to fund and evaluate large global projects
- Introduce the principles of cross-border mergers and acquisitions

This chapter describes in detail the issues and principles related to the investment in real productive assets in foreign countries, generally referred to as *multinational capital budgeting*. The chapter first describes the complexities of budgeting for a foreign project. Second, we describe the insights gained by valuing a project from both the *project's viewpoint* and the *parent's viewpoint* using an illustrative case involving a hypothetical investment by Cemex of Mexico in Indonesia. This illustrative case also explores both *real option analysis*. Next, the use of *project financing* today is discussed, and the final section describes the stages involved in affecting cross-border acquisitions. The chapter concludes with the Mini-Case, *Elan and Royalty Pharma*, about a hostile takeover (acquisition) attempt that played-out in the summer of 2013.

Although the original decision to undertake an investment in a particular foreign country may be determined by a mix of strategic, behavioral, and economic factors, the specific project should be justified—as should all reinvestment decisions—by traditional financial analysis. For example, a production efficiency opportunity may exist for a U.S. firm to invest abroad, but the type of plant, mix of labor and capital, kinds of equipment, method of financing, and other project variables must be analyzed within the traditional financial framework of discounted cash flows. The firm must also consider the impact of the proposed foreign project on consolidated net earnings, cash flows from subsidiaries in other countries, and on the market value of the parent firm.

Multinational capital budgeting for a foreign project uses the same theoretical framework as domestic capital budgeting—with a few very important differences. The basic steps are as follows:

- Identify the initial capital invested or put at risk.
- Estimate cash flows to be derived from the project over time, including an estimate of the terminal or salvage value of the investment.
- Identify the appropriate discount rate for determining the present value of the expected cash flows.
- Apply traditional capital budgeting decision criteria such as net present value (NPV) and internal rate of return (IRR) to determine the acceptability of or priority ranking of potential projects.

Complexities of Budgeting for a Foreign Project

Capital budgeting for a foreign project is considerably more complex than the domestic case. Several factors contribute to this greater complexity:

- Parent cash flows must be distinguished from project cash flows. Each of these two types of flows contributes to a different view of value.
- Parent cash flows often depend on the form of financing. Thus, we cannot clearly separate cash flows from financing decisions, as we can in domestic capital budgeting.
- Additional cash flows generated by a new investment in one foreign subsidiary may be in part or in whole taken away from another subsidiary, with the net result that the project is favorable from a single subsidiary's point of view but contributes nothing to worldwide cash flows.
- The parent must explicitly recognize remittance of funds because of differing tax systems, legal and political constraints on the movement of funds, local business norms, and differences in the way financial markets and institutions function.
- An array of nonfinancial payments can generate cash flows from subsidiaries to the parent, including payment of license fees and payments for imports from the parent.
- Managers must anticipate differing rates of national inflation because of their potential to cause changes in competitive position, and thus changes in cash flows over a period of time.
- Managers must keep the possibility of unanticipated foreign exchange rate changes in mind because of possible direct effects on the value of local cash flows, as well as indirect effects on the competitive position of the foreign subsidiary.
- Use of segmented national capital markets may create an opportunity for financial gains or may lead to additional financial costs.
- Use of host-government subsidized loans complicates both capital structure and the parent's ability to determine an appropriate weighted average cost of capital for discounting purposes.
- Managers must evaluate political risk because political events can drastically reduce the value or availability of expected cash flows.
- Terminal value is more difficult to estimate because potential purchasers from the host, parent, or third countries, or from the private or public sector, may have widely divergent perspectives on the value to them of acquiring the project.

Since the same theoretical capital budgeting framework is used to choose among competing foreign and domestic projects, it is critical that we have a common standard. Thus, all foreign complexities must be quantified as modifications to either expected cash flow or the rate of discount. Although in practice many firms make such modifications arbitrarily, readily available information, theoretical deduction, or just plain common sense can be used to make less arbitrary and more reasonable choices.

Project versus Parent Valuation

A strong theoretical argument exists in favor of analyzing any foreign project from the viewpoint of the parent. Cash flows to the parent are ultimately the basis for dividends to stockholders, reinvestment elsewhere in the world, repayment of corporate-wide debt, and other purposes that affect the firm's many interest groups. However, since most of a project's cash flows to its parent or sister subsidiaries are financial cash flows rather than operating cash flows, the parent viewpoint usually violates a cardinal concept of capital budgeting, namely, that financial cash flows should not be mixed with operating cash flows. Often the difference is not important because the two are almost identical, but in some instances a sharp divergence in these cash flows will exist. For example, funds that are permanently blocked from repatriation, or "forcibly reinvested," are not available for dividends to the stockholders or for repayment of parent corporate debt. Therefore, shareholders will not perceive the blocked earnings as contributing to the value of the firm, and creditors will not count on them in calculating interest coverage ratios and other evidence of ability to service debt.

Evaluation of a project from the local viewpoint serves some useful purposes, but it should be subordinated to evaluation from the parent's viewpoint. In evaluating a foreign project's performance relative to the potential of a competing project in the same host country, we must pay attention to the project's local return. Almost any project should at least be able to earn a cash return equal to the yield available on host government bonds with a maturity equal to the project's economic life, if a free market exists for such bonds. Host-government bonds ordinarily reflect the local risk-free rate of return, including a premium equal to the expected rate of inflation. If a project cannot earn more than such a bond yield, the parent firm should buy host government bonds rather than invest in a riskier project—or, better yet, invest somewhere else!

Multinational firms should invest only if they can earn a risk-adjusted return greater than locally based competitors can earn on the same project. If they are unable to earn superior returns on foreign projects, their stockholders would be better off buying shares in local firms, where possible, and letting those companies carry out the local projects. Apart from these theoretical arguments, surveys over the past 35 years show that in practice multinational firms continue to evaluate foreign investments from both the parent and project viewpoint.

The attention paid to project returns in various surveys probably reflects emphasis on maximizing reported consolidated net earnings per share as a corporate financial goal. As long as foreign earnings are not blocked, they can be consolidated with the earnings of both the remaining subsidiaries and the parent. As mentioned previously, U.S. firms must consolidate foreign subsidiaries that are over 50% owned. If a firm is owned between 20% and 49% by a parent, it is called an *affiliate*. *Affiliates* are consolidated with the parent owner on a pro rata basis. Subsidiaries less than 20% owned are normally carried as unconsolidated investments. Even in the case of temporarily blocked funds, some of the most mature MNEs do not necessarily eliminate a project from financial consideration. They take a very long-run view of world business opportunities.

If reinvestment opportunities in the country where funds are blocked are at least equal to the parent firm's required rate of return (after adjusting for anticipated exchange rate changes), temporary blockage of transfer may have little practical effect on the capital budgeting outcome, because future project cash flows will be increased by the returns on forced reinvestment. Since large multinationals hold a portfolio of domestic and foreign projects, corporate liquidity is not impaired if a few projects have blocked funds; alternate sources of funds are available to meet all planned uses of funds. Furthermore, a long-run historical perspective on blocked funds does indeed lend support to the belief that funds are almost never permanently blocked. However, waiting for the release of such funds can be frustrating, and sometimes the blocked funds lose value while blocked because of inflation or unexpected exchange rate deterioration, even though they have been reinvested in the host country to protect at least part of their value in real terms.

In conclusion, most firms appear to evaluate foreign projects from both parent and project viewpoints. The parent's viewpoint gives results closer to the traditional meaning of net present value in capital budgeting. Project valuation provides a closer approximation of the effect on consolidated earnings per share, which all surveys indicate is of major concern to practicing managers. To illustrate the foreign complexities of multinational capital budgeting, we analyze a hypothetical market-seeking foreign direct investment by Cemex in Indonesia.

Illustrative Case: Cemex Enters Indonesia[1]

Cementos Mexicanos, Cemex, is considering the construction of a cement manufacturing facility on the Indonesian island of Sumatra. The project, Semen Indonesia (the Indonesian word for "cement" is *semen*), would be a wholly owned greenfield investment with a total installed capacity of 20 million metric tonnes per year (mmt/y). Although that is large by Asian production standards, Cemex believes that its latest cement manufacturing technology would be most efficiently utilized with a production facility of this scale.

Cemex has three driving reasons for the project: 1) the firm wishes to initiate a productive presence of its own in Southeast Asia, a relatively new market for Cemex; 2) the long-term prospects for Asian infrastructure development and growth appear very good over the longer term; and 3) there are positive prospects for Indonesia to act as a produce-for-export site as a result of the depreciation of the Indonesian rupiah (Rp) in recent years.

Cemex, the world's third-largest cement manufacturer, is an MNE headquartered in an emerging market but competing in a global arena. The firm competes in the global marketplace for both market share and capital. The international cement market, like markets in other commodities such as oil, is a dollar-based market. For this reason, and for comparisons against its major competitors in both Germany and Switzerland, Cemex considers the U.S. dollar its functional currency.

Cemex's shares are listed in both Mexico City and New York (OTC: CMXSY). The firm has successfully raised capital—both debt and equity—outside Mexico in U.S. dollars. Its investor base is increasingly global, with the U.S. share turnover rising rapidly as a percentage of total trading. As a result, its cost and availability of capital are internationalized and dominated by U.S. dollar investors. Ultimately, the Semen Indonesia project will be evaluated—in both cash flows and capital cost—in U.S. dollars.

Overview

A roadmap of the complete multinational capital budgeting analysis for Cemex in Indonesia is illustrated in Exhibit 17.1. Starting at the top left, the parent company invests U.S. dollar denominated capital, which flows clockwise through the creation and operation of an Indonesian subsidiary, which then generates cash flows that are eventually returned in a variety of forms to the parent company—in U.S. dollars. The first step is to construct a set of pro forma

---

[1]Cemex is a real company. However, the greenfield investment described here is hypothetical.

EXHIBIT 17.1   A Roadmap to the Construction of Semen Indonesia's Capital Budget

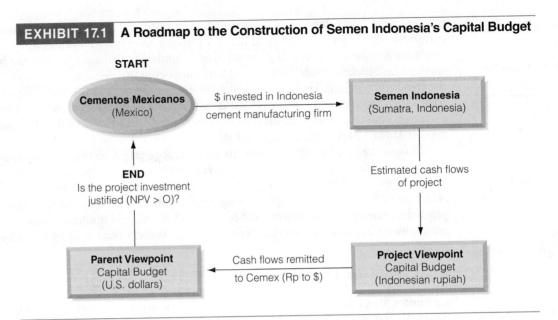

financial statements for Semen Indonesia, all in Indonesian rupiah (Rp). The next step is to create two capital budgets, the *project viewpoint* and *parent viewpoint*.

Semen Indonesia will take only one year to build the plant, with actual operations commencing in year 1. The Indonesian government has only recently deregulated the heavier industries to allow foreign ownership.

The following analysis is conducted assuming that purchasing power parity (PPP) holds for the Rp/$ exchange rate for the life of the Indonesian project. This is a standard financial assumption made by Cemex for its foreign investments.

If we assume an initial spot rate of Rp10,000/$, and Indonesian and U.S. inflation rates of 30% and 3% per annum, respectively, for the life of the project, forecasted spot exchange rates follow the usual PPP calculation. For example, the forecasted exchange rate for year 1 of the project would be as follows:

$$\text{Spot rate (year 1)} = \text{Rp10,000/\$} \times \frac{1 + .30}{1 + .03} = \text{Rp12,621/\$}$$

The financial statements shown in Exhibits 17.2 through 17.5 are based on these assumptions.

Capital Investment. Although the cost of building new cement manufacturing capacity anywhere in the industrial countries is now estimated at roughly $150/tonne of installed capacity, Cemex believed that it could build a state-of-the-art production and shipment facility in Sumatra at roughly $110/tonne (see Exhibit 17.2). Assuming a 20 million metric ton per year (mmt/y) capacity, and a year 0 average exchange rate of Rp10,000/$, this cost will constitute an investment of Rp22 trillion ($2.2 billion). This figure includes an investment of Rp17.6 trillion in plant and equipment, giving rise to an annual depreciation charge of Rp1.76 trillion if we assume a 10-year straight-line depreciation schedule. The relatively short depreciation schedule is one of the policies of the Indonesian tax authorities meant to attract foreign investment.

Financing. This massive investment would be financed with 50% equity—all from Cemex—and 50% debt—75% from Cemex and 25% from a bank consortium arranged by the

EXHIBIT 17.2	Investment and Financing of the Semen Indonesia Project

(all values in 000s unless otherwise noted)

Investment		Financing	
Average exchange rate, Rp/$	10,000	Equity	11,000,000,000
Cost of installed capacity ($/tonne)	$110	Debt:	11,000,000,000
Installed capacity	20,000	Rupiah debt	2,750,000,000
Investment in $	$2,200,000	$ debt in rupiah	8,250,000,000
Investment in rupiah	22,000,000,000	Total	22,000,000,000
Percentage of investment in plant & equip	80%		
Plant and equipment (000s Rp)	17,600,000,000	Note: $ debt principal	$825,000
Depreciation of capital equipment (years)	10.00		
Annual depreciation (millions)	(1,760,000)		
Costs of Capital: Cemex			
Risk-free rate	6.000%	Cemex beta	1.50
Credit premium	2.000%	Equity risk premium	7.000%
Cost of debt	8.000%	Cost of equity	16.500%
Corporate income tax rate	35.000%	Percent equity	60.0%
Cost of debt after-tax	5.200%	**WACC**	**11.980%**
Percent debt	40.0%		
Cost of Capital: Semen Indonesia			
Risk-free rate	33.000%	Semen Indonesia beta	1.000
Credit premium	2.000%	Equity risk premium	6.000%
Cost of rupiah debt	35.000%	Cost of equity	40.000%
Indonesia corporate income tax rate	30.000%	Percent equity	50.0%
Cost of $ debt, after-tax	5.200%	**WACC**	**33.257%**
Cost of $ debt, (rupiah equivalent)	38.835%		
Cost of $ debt, after-tax (rupiah eq)	27.184%		
Percent debt	50.0%		

The cost of the $ loan is stated in rupiah terms assuming purchasing power parity and U.S. dollar and Indonesian inflation rates of 3% and 30% per annum, respectively, throughout the subject period.

Semen Indonesia (Rp)	Amount	Financing Proportion	Cost	After-Tax Cost	Component Cost
Rupiah loan	2,750,000,000	12.5%	35.000%	24.500%	3.063%
Cemex loan	8,250,000,000	37.5%	38.835%	27.184%	10.194%
Total debt	11,000,000,000	50.0%			
Equity	11,000,000,000	50.0%	40.000%	40.000%	20.000%
Total financing	22,000,000,000	100.0%		**WACC**	**33.257%**

Indonesian government. Cemex's own U.S. dollar-based weighted average cost of capital (WACC) was currently estimated at 11.98%. The WACC for the project itself on a local Indonesian level in rupiah terms was estimated at 33.257%. The details of this calculation are discussed later in this chapter.

The cost of the U.S. dollar-denominated loan is stated in rupiah terms assuming purchasing power parity and U.S. dollar and Indonesian inflation rates of 3% and 30% per annum, respectively, throughout the subject period.

The explicit debt structures, including repayment schedules, are presented in Exhibit 17.3. The loan arranged by the Indonesian government, part of the government's economic development incentive program, is an eight-year loan, in rupiah, at 35% annual interest, fully amortizing. The interest payments are fully deductible against corporate tax liabilities.

The majority of the debt, however, is being provided by the parent company, Cemex. After raising the capital from its financing subsidiary, Cemex will relend the capital to Semen Indonesia. The loan is denominated in U.S. dollars, five years maturity, with an annual interest rate of 10%. Because the debt will have to be repaid from the rupiah earnings of the Indonesian enterprise, the pro forma financial statements are constructed so that the expected costs of servicing the dollar debt are included in the firm's pro forma income statement. The dollar loan, if the rupiah follows the purchasing power parity forecast, will have an effective interest expense in rupiah terms of 38.835% before taxes. We find this rate by determining the internal rate of return of repaying the dollar loan in full in rupiah (see Exhibit 17.3).

The loan by Cemex to the Indonesian subsidiary is denominated in U.S. dollars. Therefore, the loan will have to be repaid in U.S. dollars, not rupiah. At the time of the loan agreement, the spot exchange rate is Rp10,000/$. This is the assumption used in calculating the "scheduled" repaying of principal and interest in rupiah. The rupiah, however, is expected to depreciate in line with purchasing power parity. As it is repaid, the "actual" exchange rate will therefore give rise to a foreign exchange loss as it takes more and more rupiah to acquire U.S. dollars for debt service, both principal and interest. The foreign exchange losses on this debt service will be recognized on the Indonesian income statement.

Revenues. Given the current existing cement manufacturing in Indonesia, and its currently depressed state as a result of the Asian crisis, all sales are based on export. The 20 mmt/y facility is expected to operate at only 40% capacity (producing 8 million metric tonnes). Cement produced will be sold in the export market at $58/tonne (delivered). Note also that, at least for the conservative baseline analysis, we assume no increase in the price received over time.

Costs. The cash costs of cement manufacturing (labor, materials, power, etc.) are estimated at Rp115,000 per tonne for 1999, rising at about the rate of inflation, 30% per year. Additional production costs of Rp20,000 per tonne for year 1 are also assumed to rise at the rate of inflation. As a result of all production being exported, loading costs of $2.00/tonne and shipping of $10.00/tonne must also be included. Note that these costs are originally stated in U.S. dollars, and for the purposes of Semen Indonesia's income statement, they must be converted to rupiah terms. This is the case because both shiploading and shipping costs are international services governed by contracts denominated in dollars. As a result, they are expected to rise over time only at the U.S. dollar rate of inflation (3%).

Semen Indonesia's pro forma income statement is illustrated in Exhibit 17.4. This is the typical financial statement measurement of the profitability of any business, whether domestic or international. The baseline analysis assumes a capacity utilization rate of only 40% (year 1), 50% (year 2), and 60% in the following years. Management believes this is necessary since existing in-country cement manufacturers are averaging only 40% of capacity at this time.

Tax credits resulting from current period losses are carried forward toward next year's tax liabilities. Dividends are not distributed in the first year of operations as a result of losses, and are distributed at a 50% rate in years 2000–2003.

Additional expenses in the pro forma financial analysis include license fees paid by the subsidiary to the parent company of 2.0% of sales, and general and administrative expenses

EXHIBIT 17.3	Semen Indonesia's Debt Service Schedules and Foreign Exchange Gains/Losses

Spot rate (Rp/$)	10,000	12,621	15,930	20,106	25,376	32,028
Project Year	0	1	2	3	4	5
Indonesian loan @ 35% for 8 years (millions of rupiah)						
Loan principal	2,750,000					
Interest payment		(962,500)	(928,921)	(883,590)	(822,393)	(739,777)
Principal payment		(95,939)	(129,518)	(174,849)	(236,046)	(318,662)
Total payment		(1,058,439)	(1,058,439)	(1,058,439)	(1,058,439)	(1,058,439)
Cemex loan @ 10% for 5 years (millions of U.S. dollars)						
Loan principal	825					
Interest payment		($82.50)	($68.99)	($54.12)	($37.77)	($19.78)
Principal payment		($135.13)	($148.65)	($163.51)	($179.86)	($197.85)
Total payment		($217.63)	($217.63)	($217.63)	($217.63)	($217.63)
Cemex loan converted to Rp at scheduled and current spot rates (millions of Rp):						
Scheduled at Rp10,000/$:						
Interest payment		(825,000)	(689,867)	(541,221)	(377,710)	(197,848)
Principal payment		(1,351,329)	(1,486,462)	(1,635,108)	(1,798,619)	(1,978,481)
Total payment		(2,176,329)	(2,176,329)	(2,176,329)	(2,176,329)	(2,176,329)
Actual (at current spot rate):						
Interest payment		(1,041,262)	(1,098,949)	(1,088,160)	(958,480)	(633,669)
Principal payment		(1,705,561)	(2,367,915)	(3,287,494)	(4,564,190)	(6,336,691)
Total payment		(2,746,823)	(3,466,864)	(4,375,654)	(5,522,670)	(6,970,360)
Cash flows in Rp on Cemex loan (millions of Rp):						
Total actual cash flows	8,250,000	(2,746,823)	(3,466,864)	(4,375,654)	(5,522,670)	(6,970,360)
IRR of cash flows	**38.835%**					
Foreign exchange gains (losses) on Cemex loan (millions of Rp):						
Foreign exchange gains (losses) on interest		(216,262)	(409,082)	(546,940)	(580,770)	(435,821)
Foreign exchange gains (losses) on principal		(354,232)	(881,453)	(1,652,385)	(2,765,571)	(4,358,210)
Total foreign exchange losses on debt		(570,494)	(1,290,535)	(2,199,325)	(3,346,341)	(4,794,031)

The loan by Cemex to the Indonesian subsidiary is denominated in U.S. dollars. Therefore, the loan will have to be repaid in U.S. dollars, not rupiah. At the time of the loan agreement, the spot exchange rate is Rp10,000/$. This is the assumption used in calculating the "scheduled" repaying of principal and interest in rupiah. The rupiah, however, is expected to depreciate in line with purchasing power parity. As it is repaid, the "actual" exchange rate will therefore give rise to a foreign exchange loss as it takes more and more rupiah to acquire U.S. dollars for debt service, both principal and interest. The foreign exchange losses on this debt service will be recognized on the Indonesian income statement.

for Indonesian operations of 8.0% per year (and growing an additional 1% per year). Foreign exchange gains and losses are those related to the servicing of the U.S. dollar-denominated debt provided by the parent and are drawn from the bottom of Exhibit 17.3. In summary, the subsidiary operation is expected to begin turning an accounting profit in its fourth year of operations (2000), with profits rising as capacity utilization increases over time.

EXHIBIT 17.4	Semen Indonesia's Pro Forma Income Statement (millions of rupiah)				
Exchange rate (Rp/$)	10,000	12,621	15,930	20,106	25,376	32,028
Project Year	0	1	2	3	4	5
Sales volume		8.00	10.00	12.00	12.00	12.00
Sales price ($)		58.00	58.00	58.00	58.00	58.00
Sales price (Rp)		732,039	923,933	1,166,128	1,471,813	1,857,627
Total revenue		5,856,311	9,239,325	13,993,541	17,661,751	22,291,530
Less cash costs		(920,000)	(1,495,000)	(2,332,200)	(3,031,860)	(3,941,418)
Less other production costs		(160,000)	(260,000)	(405,600)	(527,280)	(685,464)
Less loading costs		(201,942)	(328,155)	(511,922)	(665,499)	(865,149)
Less shipping costs		(1,009,709)	(1,640,777)	(2,559,612)	(3,327,495)	(4,325,744)
Total production costs		(2,291,650)	(3,723,932)	(5,809,334)	(7,552,134)	(9,817,774)
Gross profit		3,564,660	5,515,393	8,184,207	10,109,617	12,473,756
Gross margin		*60.9%*	*59.7%*	*58.5%*	*57.2%*	*56.0%*
Less license fees		(117,126)	(184,787)	(279,871)	(353,235)	(445,831)
Less general and administrative		(468,505)	(831,539)	(1,399,354)	(1,942,793)	(2,674,984)
EBITDA		2,979,029	4,499,067	6,504,982	7,813,589	9,352,941
Less depreciation and amortization		(1,760,000)	(1,760,000)	(1,760,000)	(1,760,000)	(1,760,000)
EBIT		1,219,029	2,739,067	4,744,982	6,053,589	7,592,941
Less interest on Cemex debt		(825,000)	(689,867)	(541,221)	(377,710)	(197,848)
Foreign exchange losses on debt		(570,494)	(1,290,535)	(2,199,325)	(3,346,341)	(4,794,031)
Less interest on local debt		(962,500)	(928,921)	(883,590)	(822,393)	(739,777)
EBT		(1,138,965)	(170,256)	1,120,846	1,507,145	1,861,285
Less income taxes (30%)		—	—	—	(395,631)	(558,386)
Net income		(1,138,965)	(170,256)	1,120,846	1,111,514	1,302,900
Net income (millions of $)		(90)	(11)	56	44	41
Return on sales		*−19.4%*	*−1.8%*	*8.0%*	*6.3%*	*5.8%*
Dividends distributed		—	—	560,423	555,757	651,450
Retained		(1,138,965)	(170,256)	560,423	555,757	651,450

EBITDA = earnings before interest, taxes, depreciation, and amortization. EBIT = earnings before interest and taxes; EBT = earnings before taxes.

Tax credits resulting from current period losses are carried forward toward next year's tax liabilities. Dividends are not distributed in the first year of operations as a result of losses, and are distributed at a 50% rate in years 2000–2003.

All calculations are exact, but may appear not to add due to reported decimal places. The tax payment for year 3 is zero, and year 4 is less than 30%, as a result of tax loss carry-forwards from previous years.

Project Viewpoint Capital Budget

The capital budget for the Semen Indonesia project from a project viewpoint is shown in Exhibit 17.5. We find the net cash flow—or *free cash flow* as it is often labeled—by summing EBITDA (earnings before interest, taxes, depreciation, and amortization), recalculated taxes, changes in net working capital (the sum of the net additions to receivables, inventories, and payables necessary to support sales growth), and capital investment.

Note that EBIT, not EBT, is used in the capital budget, which contains both depreciation and interest expense. Depreciation and amortization are noncash expenses of the firm and therefore contribute positive cash flow. Because the capital budget creates cash flows that will

EXHIBIT 17.5	Semen Indonesia Capital Budget: Project Viewpoint (millions of rupiah)					
Exchange rate (Rp/$)	10,000	12,621	15,930	20,106	25,376	32,028
Project Year	0	1	2	3	4	5
EBIT		1,219,029	2,739,067	4,744,982	6,053,589	7,592,941
Less recalculated taxes @ 30%		(365,709)	(821,720)	(1,423,495)	(1,816,077)	(2,277,882)
Add back depreciation		1,760,000	1,760,000	1,760,000	1,760,000	1,760,000
Net operating cash flow		2,613,320	3,677,347	5,081,487	5,997,512	7,075,059
Less changes to NWC		(240,670)	(139,028)	(195,379)	(150,748)	(190,265)
Initial investment	(22,000,000)					
Terminal value						21,274,102
Free cash flow (FCF)	(22,000,000)	2,372,650	3,538,319	4,886,109	5,846,764	28,158,896
NPV @ 33.257%	(7,606,313)					
IRR	19.1%					

NWC = net working capital. NPV = net present value. Discount rate is Semen Indonesia's WACC of 33.257%. IRR = internal rate of return, the rate of discount yielding an NPV of exactly zero. Values in exhibit are exact and are rounded to the nearest million.

be discounted to present value with a discount rate, and the discount rate includes the cost of debt-interest—we do not wish to subtract interest twice. Therefore, taxes are recalculated on the basis of EBITDA.[2] The firm's cost of capital used in discounting also includes the deductibility of debt interest in its calculation.

The initial investment of Rp22 trillion is the total capital invested to support these earnings. Although receivables average 50 to 55 days sales outstanding (DSO) and inventories average 65 to 70 DSO, payables and trade credit are also relatively long at 114 DSO in the Indonesian cement industry. Semen Indonesia expects to add approximately 15 net DSO to its investment with sales growth. The remaining elements to complete the project viewpoint's capital budget are the terminal value (discussed below) and the discount rate of 33.257% (the firm's weighted average cost of capital).

Terminal Value. The *terminal value* (TV) of the project represents the continuing value of the cement manufacturing facility in the years after year 5, the last year of the detailed pro forma financial analysis shown in Exhibit 17.5. This value, like all asset values according to financial theory, is the present value of all future free cash flows that the asset is expected to yield. We calculate the TV as the present value of a perpetual *net operating cash flow* (NOCF) generated in the fifth year by Semen Indonesia, the growth rate assumed for that net operating cash flow (g), and the firm's weighted average cost of capital (k_{wacc}):

$$\text{Terminal Value} = \frac{\text{NOCF}_5 (1 + g)}{k_{wacc} - g} = \frac{7,075,059 (1 + 0)}{.33257 - 0} = \text{Rp21,274,102}$$

or Rp21,274,102 trillion. The assumption that g = 0, that is, that net operating cash flows will not grow past year 5 is probably not true, but it is a prudent assumption for Cemex to make when estimating future cash flows. The results of the capital budget from the project viewpoint indicate a negative net present value (NPV) and an internal rate of return (IRR) of

[2]This highlights the distinction between an income statement and a capital budget. The project's income statement shows losses the first two years of operations as a result of interest expenses and forecast foreign exchange losses, so it is not expected to pay taxes. But the capital budget, constructed on the basis of EBITDA, before these financing and foreign exchange expenses, calculates a positive tax payment.

only 19.1% compared to the 33.257% cost of capital. These are the returns the project would yield to a local or Indonesian investor in Indonesian rupiah. The project, from this viewpoint, is not acceptable.

Repatriating Cash Flows to Cemex

Exhibit 17.6 now collects all incremental earnings to Cemex from the prospective investment project in Indonesia. As described in the section preceding the case, "Project versus Parent Valuation," a foreign investor's assessment of a project's returns depends on the actual cash

EXHIBIT 17.6	Semen Indonesia's Remittance of Income to Parent Company (millions of rupiah and $)					
Exchange rate (Rp/$)	10,000	12,621	15,930	20,106	25,376	32,028
Project Year	0	1	2	3	4	5
Dividend Remittance						
Dividends paid (Rp)	—	—	—	560,423	555,757	651,450
Less Indonesian withholding taxes	—	—	—	(84,063)	(83,364)	(97,717)
Net dividend remitted (Rp)	—	—	—	476,360	472,393	553,732
Net dividend remitted ($)	—	—	—	23.69	18.62	17.29
License Fees Remittance						
License fees remitted (Rp)		117,126	184,787	279,871	353,235	445,831
Less Indonesian withholding taxes		(5,856)	(9,239)	(13,994)	(17,662)	(22,292)
Net license fees remitted (Rp)		111,270	175,547	265,877	335,573	423,539
Net license fees remitted ($)		8.82	11.02	13.22	13.22	13.22
Debt Service Remittance						
Promised interest paid ($)		82.50	68.99	54.12	37.77	19.78
Less Indonesian withholding tax @ 10%		(8.25)	(6.90)	(5.41)	(3.78)	(1.98)
Net interest remitted ($)		74.25	62.09	48.71	33.99	17.81
Principal payments remitted ($)		135.13	148.65	163.51	179.86	197.85
Total principal and interest remitted		$209.38	$210.73	$212.22	$213.86	$215.65
Capital Budget: Parent Viewpoint (millions of U.S. dollars)						
Dividends		—	—	23.7	18.6	17.3
License fees		8.8	11.0	13.2	13.2	13.2
Debt service		209.4	210.7	212.2	213.9	215.7
Total earnings		218.2	221.8	249.1	245.7	246.2
Initial investment	(1,925.0)					
Terminal value						664.2
Net cash flows	(1,925.0)	218.2	221.8	249.1	245.7	910.4
NPV @ 17.98%	**(903.9)**					
IRR	**−1.12%**					

NPV calculated using a company-determined discount rate of WACC + foreign investment premium, or 11.98% + 6.00% = 17.98%.

flows that are returned to it in its own currency. For Cemex, this means that the investment must be analyzed in terms of U.S. dollar cash inflows and outflows associated with the investment over the life of the project, after-tax, discounted at its appropriate cost of capital.

The *parent viewpoint capital budget* is constructed in two steps:

1. First, we isolate the individual cash flows, adjusted for any withholding taxes imposed by the Indonesian government and converted to U.S. dollars. (Statutory withholding taxes on international transfers are set by bilateral tax treaties, but individual firms may negotiate lower rates with governmental tax authorities. In the case of Semen Indonesia, dividends will be charged a 15% withholding tax, 10% on interest payments, and 5% license fees.) Mexico does not tax repatriated earnings since they have already been taxed in Indonesia. (The United States does levy a contingent tax on repatriated earnings of foreign source income, as discussed in Chapter 14.)

2. The second step, the actual *parent viewpoint capital budget*, combines these U.S. dollar after-tax cash flows with the initial investment to determine the net present value of the proposed Semen Indonesia subsidiary in the eyes (and pocketbook) of Cemex. This is illustrated in Exhibit 17.6, which shows all incremental earnings to Cemex from the prospective investment project. A specific peculiarity of this parent viewpoint capital budget is that only the capital invested into the project by Cemex itself, $1,925 million, is included in the initial investment (the $1,100 million in equity and the $825 million loan). The Indonesian debt of Rp 2.75 billion ($275 million) is not included in the Cemex parent viewpoint capital budget.

Parent Viewpoint Capital Budget

Finally, all cash flow estimates are now constructed to form the parent viewpoint's capital budget, detailed in the bottom of Exhibit 17.6. The cash flows generated by Semen Indonesia from its Indonesian operations, dividends, license fees, debt service, and terminal value are now valued in U.S. dollar terms after-tax.

In order to evaluate the project's cash flows that are returned to the parent company, Cemex must discount these at the corporate cost of capital. Remembering that Cemex considers its functional currency to be the U.S. dollar, it calculates its cost of capital in U.S. dollars. As described in Chapter 12, the customary weighted average cost of capital formula is as follows:

$$k_{\text{wacc}} = k_e \frac{E}{V} + k_d (1 - t) \frac{D}{V},$$

k_e = risk-adjusted cost of equity

k_d = before-tax cost of debt

t = marginal tax rate

E = market value of the firm's equity

D = market value of the firm's debt

V = total market value of the firm's securities $(E + D)$

Cemex's cost of equity is calculated using the capital asset pricing model (CAPM):

$$k_e = k_{rf} + (k_m - k_{rf}) \beta_{\text{Cemex}} = 6.00\% + (13.00\% - 6.00\%)1.5 = 16.50\%$$

k_e = risk-adjusted cost of equity

k_{rf} = risk-free rate of interest (U.S. Treasury intermediate bond yield)

k_m = expected rate of return in U.S. equity markets (large stock)

β_{Cemex} = measure of Cemex's individual risk relative to the market

The calculation assumes the current risk-free rate is 6.00%, the expected return on U.S. equities is 13.00%, and Cemex's beta is 1.5. The result is a cost of equity—required rate of return on equity investment in Cemex—of 16.50%.

The investment will be funded internally by the parent company, roughly in the same debt/equity proportions as the consolidated firm, 40% debt (D/V) and 60% equity (E/V). The current cost of debt for Cemex is 8.00%, and the effective tax rate is 35%. The cost of equity, when combined with the other components, results in a weighted average cost of capital for Cemex of

$$k_{wacc} = k_e \frac{E}{V} + k_d (1 - t) \frac{D}{V} = (16.50\%)(.60) + (8.00\%)(1 - .35)(.40) = 11.98\%$$

Cemex customarily uses this weighted average cost of capital of 11.98% to discount prospective investment cash flows for project ranking purposes. The Indonesian investment poses a variety of risks, however, which the typical domestic investment does not.

If Cemex were undertaking an investment of the same relative degree of risk as the firm itself, a simple discount rate of 11.980% might be adequate. Cemex, however, generally requires new investments to yield an additional 3% over the cost of capital for domestic investments, and 6% more for international projects (these are company-required spreads, and will differ dramatically across companies). The discount rate for Semen Indonesia's cash flows repatriated to Cemex will therefore be discounted at 11.98% + 6.00%, or 17.98%. The project's baseline analysis indicates a negative NPV with an IRR of −1.12%, which means that it is an unacceptable investment from the parent's viewpoint.

Most corporations require that new investments more than cover the cost of the capital employed in their undertaking. It is therefore not unusual for the firm to require a hurdle rate of 3% to 6% above its cost of capital in order to identify potential investments that will literally add value to stockholder wealth. An NPV of zero means the investment is "acceptable," but NPV values that exceed zero are literally the present value of wealth that is expected to be added to the value of the firm and its shareholders. For foreign projects, as discussed previously, we must adjust for agency costs and foreign exchange risks and costs.

Sensitivity Analysis: Project Viewpoint

So far, the project investigation team has used a set of "most likely" assumptions to forecast rates of return. It is now time to subject the most likely outcome to sensitivity analyses. The same probabilistic techniques are available to test the sensitivity of results to political and foreign exchange risks as are used to test sensitivity to business and financial risks. Many decision makers feel more uncomfortable about the necessity to guess probabilities for unfamiliar political and foreign exchange events than they do about guessing their own more familiar business or financial risks. Therefore, it is more common to test sensitivity to political and foreign exchange risk by simulating what would happen to net present value and earnings under a variety of "what if" scenarios.

Political Risk. *What if Indonesia imposes controls on the payment of dividends or license fees to Cemex?* The impact of blocked funds on the rate of return from Cemex's perspective would depend on when the blockage occurs, what reinvestment opportunities exist for the blocked funds in Indonesia, and when the blocked funds would eventually be released to Cemex. We could simulate various scenarios for blocked funds and rerun the cash flow analysis in Exhibit 17.6 to estimate the effect on Cemex's rate of return.

What if Indonesia should expropriate Semen Indonesia? The effect of expropriation would depend on the following factors:

1. When the expropriation occurs, in terms of number of years after the business began operation

2. How much compensation the Indonesian government will pay, and how long after expropriation the payment will be made

3. How much debt is still outstanding to Indonesian lenders, and whether the parent, Cemex, will have to pay this debt because of its parental guarantee

4. The tax consequences of the expropriation

5. Whether the future cash flows are forgone

Many expropriations eventually result in some form of compensation to the former owners. This compensation can come from a negotiated settlement with the host government or from payment of political risk insurance by the parent government. Negotiating a settlement takes time, and the eventual compensation is sometimes paid in installments over a further period of time. Thus, the present value of the compensation is often much lower than its nominal value. Furthermore, most settlements are based on book value of the firm at the time of expropriation rather than the firm's market value.

The tax consequences of expropriation would depend on the timing and amount of capital loss recognized by Mexico. This loss would usually be based on the uncompensated book value of the Indonesian investment. The problem is that there is often some doubt as to when a write-off is appropriate for tax purposes, particularly if negotiations for a settlement drag on. In some ways, a nice clear expropriation without hope of compensation, such as occurred in Cuba in the early 1960s, is preferred to a slow "bleeding death" in protracted negotiations. The former leads to an earlier use of the tax shield and a one-shot write-off against earnings, whereas the latter tends to depress earnings for years, as legal and other costs continue and no tax shelter is achieved.

Foreign Exchange Risk. The project investigation team assumed that the Indonesian rupiah would depreciate versus the U.S. dollar at the purchasing power parity "rate" (approximately 20.767% per year in the baseline analysis). *What if the rate of rupiah depreciation were greater?* Although this event would make the assumed cash flows to Cemex worth less in dollars, operating exposure analysis would be necessary to determine whether the cheaper rupiah made Semen Indonesia more competitive. For example, since Semen Indonesia's exports to Taiwan are denominated in U.S. dollars, a weakening of the rupiah versus the dollar could result in greater rupiah earnings from those export sales. This serves to somewhat offset the imported components that Semen Indonesia purchases from the parent company that are also denominated in U.S. dollars. Semen Indonesia is representative of firms today that have both cash inflows and outflows denominated in foreign currencies, providing a partial natural hedge against currency movements.

What if the rupiah should appreciate against the dollar? The same kind of economic exposure analysis is needed. In this particular case, we might guess that the effect would be positive on both local sales in Indonesia and the value in dollars of dividends and license fees paid to Cemex by Semen Indonesia. Note, however, that an appreciation of the rupiah might lead to more competition within Indonesia from firms in other countries with now lower cost structures, lessening Semen Indonesia's sales.

Other Sensitivity Variables. The project rate of return to Cemex would also be sensitive to a change in the assumed terminal value, the capacity utilization rate, the size of the license fee paid by Semen Indonesia, the size of the initial project cost, the amount of working capital financed locally, and the tax rates in Indonesia and Mexico. Since some of these variables are within control of Cemex, it is still possible that the Semen Indonesia project could be improved in its value to the firm and become acceptable.

Sensitivity Analysis: Parent Viewpoint Measurement

When a foreign project is analyzed from the parent's point of view, the additional risk that stems from its "foreign" location can be measured in at least two ways, *adjusting the discount rates* or *adjusting the cash flows*.

Adjusting Discount Rates. The first method is to treat all foreign risk as a single problem, by adjusting the discount rate applicable to foreign projects relative to the rate used for domestic projects to reflect the greater foreign exchange risk, political risk, agency costs, asymmetric information, and other uncertainties perceived in foreign operations. However, adjusting the discount rate applied to a foreign project's cash flow to reflect these uncertainties does not penalize net present value in proportion either to the actual amount at risk or to possible variations in the nature of that risk over time. Combining all risks into a single discount rate may thus cause us to discard much information about the uncertainties of the future.

In the case of foreign exchange risk, changes in exchange rates have a potential effect on future cash flows because of operating exposure. The direction of the effect, however, can either decrease or increase net cash inflows, depending on where the products are sold and where inputs are sourced. To increase the discount rate applicable to a foreign project on the assumption that the foreign currency might depreciate more than expected, is to ignore the possible favorable effect of a foreign currency depreciation on the project's competitive position. Increased sales volume might more than offset a lower value of the local currency. Such an increase in the discount rate also ignores the possibility that the foreign currency may appreciate (two-sided risk).

Adjusting Cash Flows. In the second method, we incorporate foreign risks in adjustments to forecasted cash flows of the project. The discount rate for the foreign project is risk-adjusted only for overall business and financial risk, in the same manner as for domestic projects. Simulation-based assessment utilizes scenario development to estimate cash flows to the parent arising from the project over time under different alternative economic futures.

Certainty regarding the quantity and timing of cash flows in a prospective foreign investment is, to quote Shakespeare, "the stuff that dreams are made of." Due to the complexity of economic forces at work in major investment projects, it is paramount that the analyst understand the subjectivity of the forecast cash flows. Humility in analysis is a valuable trait.

Shortcomings of Each. In many cases, however, neither adjusting the discount rate nor adjusting cash flows is optimal. For example, political uncertainties are a threat to the entire investment, not just the annual cash flows. Potential loss depends partly on the terminal value of the unrecovered parent investment, which will vary depending on how the project was financed, whether political risk insurance was obtained, and what investment horizon is contemplated. Furthermore, if the political climate were expected to be unfavorable in the near future, any investment would probably be unacceptable. Political uncertainty usually relates to possible adverse events that might occur in the more distant future, but that cannot be foreseen at the present. Adjusting the discount rate for political risk thus penalizes early cash flows too heavily while not penalizing distant cash flows enough.

Repercussions to the Investor. Apart from anticipated political and foreign exchange risks, MNEs sometimes worry that taking on foreign projects may increase the firm's overall cost of capital because of investors' perceptions of foreign risk. This worry seemed reasonable if a firm had significant investments in Iraq, Iran, Russia, Serbia, or Afghanistan in recent years. However, the argument loses persuasiveness when applied to diversified foreign investments with a heavy balance in the industrial countries of Canada, Western Europe, Australia, Latin America, and Asia where, in fact, the bulk of FDI is located. These countries have a reputation for treating foreign investments by consistent standards, and empirical evidence confirms that a foreign presence in these countries may not increase the cost of capital. In fact, some studies indicate that required returns on foreign projects may even be lower than those for domestic projects.

MNE Practices. Surveys of MNEs over the past 35 years have shown that about half of them adjust the discount rate and half adjust the cash flows. One recent survey indicated a rising use of adjusting discount rates over adjusting cash flows. However, the survey also indicated an increasing use of multifactor methods—discount rate adjustment, cash flow adjustment, real options analysis, and qualitative criteria—in evaluating foreign investments.[3]

Portfolio Risk Measurement

The field of finance has distinguished two different definitions of risk: 1) the risk of the individual security (standard deviation of expected return) and 2) the risk of the individual security as a component of a portfolio (*beta*). A foreign investment undertaken in order to enter a local or regional market—market seeking—will have returns that are more or less correlated with those of the local market. A portfolio-based assessment of the investment's prospects would then seem appropriate. A foreign investment undertaken for *resource-seeking* or *production-seeking* purposes may have returns related to those of the parent company or units located somewhere else in the world and have little to do with local markets. Cemex's proposed investment in Semen Indonesia is both *market-seeking* and *production-seeking* (for export). The decision about which approach is to be used by the MNE in evaluating prospective foreign investments may be the single most important analytical decision it makes. An investment's acceptability may change dramatically across criteria.

For comparisons within the local host country, we should overlook a project's actual financing or parent-influenced debt capacity, since these would probably be different for local investors than they are for a multinational owner. In addition, the risks of the project to local investors might differ from those perceived by a foreign multinational owner because of the opportunities an MNE has to take advantage of market imperfections. Moreover, the local project may be only one out of an internationally diversified portfolio of projects for the multinational owner; if undertaken by local investors it might have to stand alone without international diversification. Since diversification reduces risk, the MNE can require a lower rate of return than is required by local investors.

Thus, the discount rate used locally must be a hypothetical rate based on a judgment as to what independent local investors would probably demand were they to own the business. Consequently, application of the local discount rate to local cash flows provides only a rough measure of the value of the project as a stand-alone local venture, rather than an absolute valuation.

Real Option Analysis

The discounted cash flow (DCF) approach used in the valuation of Semen Indonesia—and capital budgeting and valuation in general—has long had its critics. Investments that have long lives, cash flow returns in later years, or higher levels of risk than those typical of the

[3]Tom Keck, Eric Levengood, and Al Longield, "Using Discounted Cash Flow Analysis in an International Setting: A Survey of Issues in Modeling the Cost of Capital," *Journal of Applied Corporate Finance*, Vol. 11, No. 3, Fall 1998, pp. 82–99.

firm's current business activities are often rejected by traditional DCF financial analysis. More importantly, when MNEs evaluate competitive projects, traditional discounted cash flow analysis is typically unable to capture the strategic options that an individual investment option may offer. This has led to the development of real option analysis. Real option analysis is the application of option theory to capital budgeting decisions.

Real options present a different way of thinking about investment values. At its core, it is a cross between decision-tree analysis and pure option-based valuation. It is particularly useful when analyzing investment projects that will follow very different value paths at decision points in time where management decisions are made regarding project pursuit. This wide range of potential outcomes is at the heart of real option theory. These wide ranges of value are volatilities, the basic element of option pricing theory described previously.

Real option valuation also allows us to analyze a number of managerial decisions, which in practice characterize many major capital investment projects:

- The option to defer
- The option to abandon
- The option to alter capacity
- The option to start up or shut down (switching)

Real option analysis treats cash flows in terms of future value in a positive sense, whereas DCF treats future cash flows negatively (on a discounted basis). Real option analysis is a particularly powerful device when addressing potential investment projects with extremely long life spans or investments that do not commence until future dates. Real option analysis acknowledges the way information is gathered over time to support decision-making. Management learns from both active (searching it out) and passive (observing market conditions) knowledge-gathering and then uses this knowledge to make better decisions.

Project Financing

One of the hottest topics in international finance today is *project finance*, which refers to the arrangement of financing for long-term capital projects, large in scale, long in life, and generally high in risk. This is a very general definition, however, because there are many different forms and structures that fall under this generic heading.

Project finance is not new. Examples of project finance go back centuries, and include many famous early international businesses such as the Dutch East India Company and the British East India Company. These entrepreneurial importers financed their trade ventures to Asia on a voyage-by-voyage basis, with each voyage's financing being like venture capital—investors would be repaid when the shipper returned and the fruits of the Asian marketplace were sold at the docks to Mediterranean and European merchants. If all went well, the individual shareholders of the voyage were paid in full.

Project finance is used widely today in the development of large-scale infrastructure projects in China, India, and many other emerging markets. Although each individual project has unique characteristics, most are highly leveraged transactions, with debt making up more than 60% of the total financing. Equity is a small component of project financing for two reasons: first, the simple scale of the investment project often precludes a single investor or even a collection of private investors from being able to fund it; second, many of these projects involve subjects traditionally funded by governments—such as electrical power generation, dam building, highway construction, energy exploration, production, and distribution.

This level of debt, however, places an enormous burden on cash flow for debt service. Therefore, project financing usually requires a number of additional levels of risk reduction. The lenders involved in these investments must feel secure that they will be repaid; bankers are not by nature entrepreneurs, and do not enjoy entrepreneurial returns from project finance. Project finance has a number of basic properties that are critical to its success.

Separability of the Project from Its Investors

The project is established as an individual legal entity, separate from the legal and financial responsibilities of its individual investors. This not only serves to protect the assets of equity investors, but also it provides a controlled platform upon which creditors can evaluate the risks associated with the singular project, the ability of the project's cash flows to service debt, and to rest assured that the debt service payments will be automatically allocated by and from the project itself (and not from a decision by management within an MNE).

Long-Lived and Capital-Intensive Singular Projects

Not only must the individual project be separable and large in proportion to the financial resources of its owners, but also its business line must be singular in its construction, operation, and size (capacity). The size is set at inception, and is seldom, if ever, changed over the project's life.

Cash Flow Predictability from Third Party Commitments

An oil field or electric power plant produces a homogeneous commodity product that can produce predictable cash flows if third party commitments to take and pay can be established. In addition to revenue predictability, nonfinancial costs of production need to be controlled over time, usually through long-term supplier contracts with price adjustment clauses based on inflation. The predictability of net cash inflows to long-term contracts eliminates much of the individual project's business risk, allowing the financial structure to be heavily debt-financed and still be safe from financial distress.

The predictability of the project's revenue stream is essential in securing project financing. Typical contract provisions that are intended to assure adequate cash flow normally include the following clauses: quantity and quality of the project's output; a pricing formula that enhances the predictability of adequate margin to cover operating costs and debt service payments; a clear statement of the circumstances that permit significant changes in the contract, such as *force majeure* or adverse business conditions.

Finite Projects with Finite Lives

Even with a longer-term investment, it is critical that the project have a definite ending point at which all debt and equity has been repaid. Because the project is a stand-alone investment in which its cash flows go directly to the servicing of its capital structure and not to reinvestment for growth or other investment alternatives, investors of all kinds need assurances that the project's returns will be attained in a finite period. There is no capital appreciation, only cash flow.

Examples of project finance include some of the largest individual investments undertaken in the past three decades, such as British Petroleum's financing of its interest in the North Sea, and the Trans-Alaska Pipeline. The Trans-Alaska Pipeline was a joint venture between Standard Oil of Ohio, Atlantic Richfield, Exxon, British Petroleum, Mobil Oil, Philips Petroleum, Union Oil, and Amerada Hess. Each of these projects was at or above $1 billion, and represented capital expenditures that no single firm would or could attempt to finance. Yet, through a joint venture arrangement, the higher than normal risk absorbed by the capital employed could be managed.

Cross-Border Mergers and Acquisitions

The drivers of M&A activity, summarized in Exhibit 17.7, are both macro in scope—the global competitive environment—and micro in scope—the variety of industry and firm-level forces and actions driving individual firm value. The primary forces of change in the global competitive environment—technological change, regulatory change, and capital market change—create new business opportunities for MNEs, which they pursue aggressively.

But the global competitive environment is really just the playing field, the ground upon which the individual players compete. MNEs undertake cross-border mergers and acquisitions for a variety of reasons. As shown in Exhibit 17.7, the drivers are strategic responses by MNEs to defend and enhance their global competitiveness.

As opposed to greenfield investment, a cross-border acquisition has a number of significant advantages. First and foremost, it is quicker. Greenfield investment frequently requires extended periods of physical construction and organizational development. By acquiring an existing firm, the MNE shortens the time required to gain a presence and facilitate competitive entry into the market. Second, acquisition may be a cost-effective way of gaining competitive advantages, such as technology, brand names valued in the target market, and logistical and distribution advantages, while simultaneously eliminating a local competitor. Third, specific to cross-border acquisitions, international economic, political, and foreign exchange conditions may result in market imperfections, allowing target firms to be undervalued.

Cross-border acquisitions are not, however, without their pitfalls. As with all acquisitions—domestic or cross-border—there are problems of paying too much or suffering excessive financing costs. Melding corporate cultures can be traumatic. Managing the post-acquisition process is frequently characterized by downsizing to gain economies of scale and scope in overhead functions. This results in nonproductive impacts on the firm as individuals attempt to save their own jobs. Internationally, additional difficulties arise from host governments intervening in pricing, financing, employment guarantees, market segmentation, and general nationalism and favoritism. In fact, the ability to successfully

---

EXHIBIT 17.7   **Driving Forces behind Cross Border Mergers and Acquisitions**

Changes in the Global Business Environment

- Changes in technology
- Changes in regulation
- Changes in capital markets

Create business opportunities for select firms to both enhance and defend their competitive positions in global markets

- Gaining access to strategic proprietary assets
- Gaining market power and dominance
- Achieving synergies in local/global operations and across different industries
- Becoming larger, and then reaping the benefits of size in competition and negotiation
- Diversifying and spreading their risks wider
- Exploiting financial opportunities they may possess and others desire

complete cross-border acquisitions may itself be a test of competency of the MNE when entering emerging markets.

The Cross-Border Acquisition Process

Although the field of finance has sometimes viewed acquisition as mainly an issue of valuation, it is a much more complex and rich process than simply determining what price to pay. As depicted in Exhibit 17.8, the process begins with the strategic drivers discussed in the previous section.

The process of acquiring an enterprise anywhere in the world has three common elements: 1) identification and valuation of the target, 2) execution of the acquisition offer and purchase—the *tender*, and 3) management of the post-acquisition transition.

Stage 1: Identification and Valuation. Identification of potential acquisition targets requires a well-defined corporate strategy and focus.

The identification of the target market typically precedes the identification of the target firm. Entering a highly developed market offers the widest choice of publicly traded firms with relatively well-defined markets and publicly disclosed financial and operational data. In this case, the tender offer is made publicly, although target company management may openly recommend that its shareholders reject the offer. If enough shareholders take the offer, the acquiring company may gain sufficient ownership influence or control to change management. During this rather confrontational process, it is up to the board of the target company to continue to take actions consistent with protecting the rights of shareholders. The board may need to provide rather strong oversight of management during this process to ensure that the acts of management are consistent with protecting and building shareholder value.

Once identification has been completed, the process of valuing the target begins. A variety of valuation techniques are widely used in global business today, each with its own merits. In addition to the fundamental methodologies of discounted cash flow (DCF) and multiples (earnings and cash flows), there are also industry-specific measures that focus on the most

---

EXHIBIT 17.8   The Cross-Border Acquisition Process

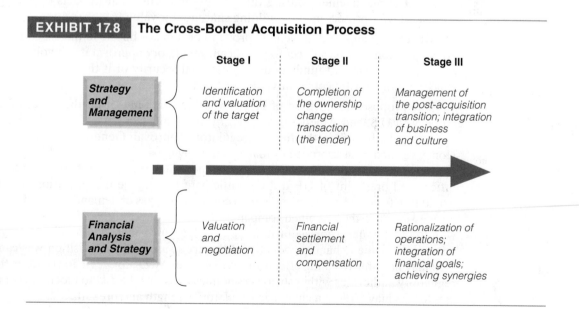

significant elements of value in business lines. The completion of various alternative valuations for the target firm aids not only in gaining a more complete picture of what price must be paid to complete the transaction, but also in determining whether the price is attractive.

Stage 2: Execution of the Acquisition. Once an acquisition target has been identified and valued, the process of gaining approval from management and ownership of the target, getting approvals from government regulatory bodies, and finally determining method of compensation—the complete *execution* of the acquisition strategy—can be time-consuming and complex.

Gaining the approval of the target company has been the highlight of some of the most famous acquisitions in business history. The critical distinction here is whether the acquisition is supported or not by the target company's management.

Although there is probably no "typical transaction," many acquisitions flow relatively smoothly through a friendly process. The acquiring firm will approach the management of the target company and attempt to convince them of the business logic of the acquisition. (Gaining their support is sometimes difficult, but assuring target company management that it will not be replaced is often quite convincing!) If the target's management is supportive, management may then recommend to stockholders that they accept the offer of the acquiring company. One problem that occasionally surfaces at this stage is that influential shareholders may object to the offer, either in principle or based on price, and may therefore feel that management is not taking appropriate steps to protect and build their shareholder value.

The process takes on a very different dynamic when the acquisition is not supported by the target company management—the so-called hostile takeover. The acquiring company may choose to pursue the acquisition without the target's support, and instead go directly to the target shareholders. In this case, the tender offer is made publicly, although target company management may openly recommend that its shareholders reject the offer. If enough shareholders take the offer, the acquiring company may gain sufficient ownership influence or control to change management. During this rather confrontational process, it is up to the board of the target company to continue to take actions consistent with protecting the rights of shareholders. As in Stage 1, the board may need to provide rather strong oversight of management during this process to ensure that the acts of management are consistent with protecting and building shareholder value.

Regulatory approval alone may prove to be a major hurdle in the execution of the deal. An acquisition may be subject to significant regulatory approval if it involves a company in an industry considered fundamental to national security or if there is concern over major concentration and anticompetitive results from consolidation.

The proposed acquisition of Honeywell International (itself the result of a merger of Honeywell U.S. and Allied-Signal U.S.) by General Electric (U.S.) in 2001 was something of a watershed event in the field of regulatory approval. General Electric's acquisition of Honeywell had been approved by management, ownership, and U.S. regulatory bodies when it then sought approval within the European Union. Jack Welch, the charismatic chief executive officer and president of GE did not anticipate the degree of opposition that the merger would face from EU authorities. After a continuing series of demands by the EU that specific businesses within the combined companies be sold off to reduce anticompetitive effects, Welch withdrew the request for acquisition approval, arguing that the liquidations would destroy most of the value-enhancing benefits of the acquisition. The acquisition was canceled. This case may have far-reaching effects on cross-border M&A for years to come, as the power of regulatory authorities within strong economic zones like the EU to block the combination of two MNEs may foretell a change in regulatory strength and breadth.

The last act within this second stage of cross-border acquisition, *compensation settlement*, is the payment to shareholders of the target company. Shareholders of the target company are typically paid either in shares of the acquiring company or in cash. If a share exchange occurs, the exchange is generally defined by some ratio of acquiring company shares to target company shares (say, two shares of acquirer in exchange for three shares of target), and the stockholder is typically not taxed—the shares of ownership are simply replaced by other shares in a nontaxable transaction.

If cash is paid to the target company shareholder, it is the same as if the shareholder sold the shares on the open market, resulting in a capital gain or loss (a gain, it is hoped, in the case of an acquisition) with tax liabilities. Because of the tax ramifications, shareholders are typically more receptive to share exchanges so that they may choose whether and when tax liabilities will arise.

A variety of factors go into the determination of the type of settlement. The availability of cash, the size of the acquisition, the friendliness of the takeover, and the relative valuations of both acquiring firm and target firm affect the decision. One of the most destructive forces that sometimes arises at this stage is regulatory delay and its impact on the share prices of the two firms. If regulatory body approval drags out over time, the possibility of a drop in share price increases and can change the attractiveness of the share swap.

Stage 3: Post-Acquisition Management. Although the headlines and flash of investment banking activities are typically focused on the valuation and bidding process in an acquisition transaction, post-transaction management is probably the most critical of the three stages in determining an acquisition's success or failure. An acquiring firm can pay too little or too much, but if the post transaction is not managed effectively, the entire return on the investment is squandered. Post-acquisition management is the stage in which the motivations for the transaction must be realized—motivations such as more effective management, synergies arising from the new combination, or the injection of capital at a cost and availability previously out of the reach of the acquisition target, must be effectively implemented after the transaction. The biggest problem, however, is nearly always melding corporate cultures.

The clash of corporate cultures and personalities pose both the biggest risk and the biggest potential gain from cross-border mergers and acquisitions. Although not readily measurable as are price/earnings ratios or share price premiums, in the end, the value is either gained or lost in the hearts and minds of the stakeholders.

Currency Risks in Cross-Border Acquisitions

The pursuit and execution of a cross-border acquisition poses a number of challenging foreign currency risks and exposures for an MNE. As illustrated by Exhibit 17.9, the nature of the currency exposure related to any specific cross-border acquisition evolves as the bidding and negotiating process itself evolves across the bidding, financing, transaction (settlement), and operating stages.

The assorted risks, both in the timing and information related to the various stages of a cross-border acquisition, make the management of the currency exposures difficult. As illustrated in Exhibit 17.9, the uncertainty related to the multitude of stages declines over time as stages are completed and contracts and agreements reached.

The initial bid, if denominated in a foreign currency, creates a *contingent foreign currency exposure* for the bidder. This contingent exposure grows in certainty of occurrence over

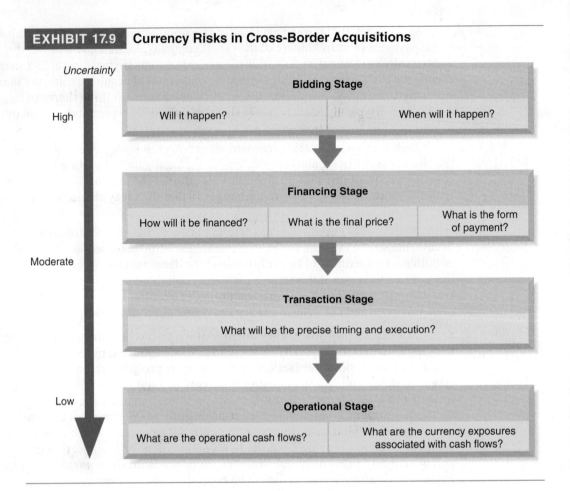

EXHIBIT 17.9 Currency Risks in Cross-Border Acquisitions

Uncertainty

High

Moderate

Low

Bidding Stage

Will it happen? | When will it happen?

Financing Stage

How will it be financed? | What is the final price? | What is the form of payment?

Transaction Stage

What will be the precise timing and execution?

Operational Stage

What are the operational cash flows? | What are the currency exposures associated with cash flows?

time as negotiations continue, regulatory requests and approvals are gained, and competitive bidders emerge. Although a variety of hedging strategies might be employed, the use of a purchased currency call option is the simplest. The option's notional principal would be for the estimated purchase price, but the maturity, for the sake of conservatism, might possibly be significantly longer than probably needed to allow for extended bidding, regulatory, and negotiation delays.

Once the bidder has successfully won the acquisition, the exposure evolves from a *contingent exposure* to a *transaction exposure*. Although a variety of uncertainties remain as to the exact timing of the transaction settlement, the certainty over the occurrence of the currency exposure is largely eliminated. Some combination of forward contracts and purchased currency options may then be used to manage the currency risks associated with the completion of the cross-border acquisition.

Once consummated, the currency risks and exposures of the cross-border acquisition, now a property and foreign subsidiary of the MNE, changes from being a transaction-based cash flow exposure to the MNE to part of its multinational structure and therefore part of its operating exposure from that time forward. Time, as is always the case involving currency exposure management in multinational business, is the greatest enemy to the MNE. As illustrated by *Global Finance in Practice 17.1*, however, things do not always work out for the worst.

GLOBAL FINANCE IN PRACTICE 17.1

Statoil of Norway's Acquisition of Esso of Sweden

Statoil's acquisition of Svenska Esso (Exxon's wholly owned subsidiary operating in Sweden) in 1986 was one of the more uniquely challenging cross-border acquisitions ever completed. First, Statoil was the national oil company of Norway, and therefore a government-owned and operated business bidding for a private company in another country. Second, if completed, the acquisition's financing as proposed would increase the financial obligations of Svenska Esso (debt levels and therefore debt service), reducing the company's tax liabilities to Sweden for many years to come. The proposed cross-border transaction was characterized as a value transfer from the Swedish government to the Norwegian government.

As a result of the extended period of bidding, negotiation, and regulatory approvals, the currency risk of the transaction was both large and extensive. Statoil, being a Norwegian oil company, was a Norwegian kroner (NOK)-based company with the U.S. dollar as its functional currency as a result of the global oil industry being dollar-denominated. Svenska Esso, although Swedish by incorporation, was the wholly owned subsidiary of a U.S.-based MNE, Exxon, and the final bid and cash settlement on the sale was therefore U.S. dollar-denominated.

On March 26, 1985, Statoil and Exxon agreed upon the sale of Svenska Esso for $260 million, or NOK2.47 billion at the current exchange rate of NOK9.50/$. (This was by all modern standards the weakest the Norwegian krone had ever been against the dollar, and many currency analysts believed the dollar to be significantly overvalued at the time.) The sale could not be consummated without the approval of the Swedish government. That approval process—eventually requiring the approval of Swedish Prime Minister Olaf Palme—took nine months. Because Statoil considered the U.S. dollar as its true operating currency, it chose not to hedge the purchase price currency exposure. At the time of settlement the krone had appreciated to NOK7.65/$, for a final acquisition cost in Norwegian kroner of NOK1.989 billion. Statoil saved nearly 20% on the purchase price, NOK0.481 billion, as a result of not hedging the exposure.

Summary Points

- Parent cash flows must be distinguished from project cash flows. Each of these two types of flows contributes to a different view of value.

- Parent cash flows often depend on the form of financing. Thus, cash flows cannot be clearly separated from financing decisions, as is done in domestic capital budgeting.

- Remittance of funds to the parent must be explicitly recognized because of differing tax systems, legal and political constraints on the movement of funds, local business norms, and differences in how financial markets and institutions function.

- Cash flows from subsidiaries to parent can be generated by an array of nonfinancial payments, including payment of license fees and payments for imports from the parent.

- Differing rates of national inflation must be anticipated because of their importance in causing changes in competitive position, and thus in cash flows over a period of time.

- When a foreign project is analyzed from the project's point of view, risk analysis focuses on the use of sensitivities, as well as consideration of foreign exchange and political risks associated with the project's execution over time.

- When a foreign project is analyzed from the parent's point of view, the additional risk that stems from its "foreign" location can be measured in at least two ways, adjusting the discount rates or adjusting the cash flows.

- Real option analysis is a different way of thinking about investment values. At its core, it is a cross between decision-tree analysis and pure option-based valuation. It allows us to evaluate the option to defer, the option to abandon, the option to alter size or capacity, and the option to start up or shut down a project.

- Project finance is used widely today in the development of large-scale infrastructure projects in many emerging markets. Although each individual project has unique characteristics, most are highly leveraged transactions, with debt making up more than 60% of the total financing.

- Equity is a small component of project financing for two reasons: first, the simple scale of the investment project often precludes a single investor or even a collection of private investors from being able to fund it; second, many of these projects involve subjects traditionally funded by governments—such as electrical power generation, dam building, highway construction, energy exploration, production, and distribution.

- The process of acquiring an enterprise anywhere in the world has three common elements: 1) identification and valuation of the target; 2) completion of the ownership change transaction (the tender); and 3) the management of the post-acquisition transition.

- The settlement stage of a cross-border merger or acquisition requires gaining the approval and cooperation of management, shareholders, and eventually regulatory authorities.

- Cross-border mergers, acquisitions, and strategic alliances, all face similar challenges: They must value the target enterprise on the basis of its projected performance in its market. This process of enterprise valuation combines elements of strategy, management, and finance.

MINI-CASE

Elan and Royalty Pharma[1]

We lived a long time with Elan (ELN). We always appreciated its science and scientists, and, at times, we hated its former management, or whoever caused it to turn from ascending towards becoming a citadel of sciences, especially neurosciences, into an almost bankrupt firm with less everything valuable in it than what was necessary for its survival. What saved it at the time was the emergence of Tysabri, for multiple sclerosis, which we knew it was second to none in treatment of relapsing remitting multiple sclerosis. We were certain that this drug, like Aaron's cane, would swallow up all magicians' staffs.

— "Biogen Idec Pays Elan $3.25 Billion for Tysabri: Do We Leave, Or Stay?," *Seeking Alpha*, February 6, 2013.

Elan's shareholders (Elan Corporation, NYSE: ELN) were faced with a difficult choice. Elan's management had made four proposals to shareholders in an attempt to defend itself against a hostile takeover from Royalty Pharma (U.S.), a privately held company. If shareholders voted in favor of any of the four initiatives, it would kill Royalty Pharma's offer. That would allow Elan to stay independent and remain under the control of a management team that had not sparked confidence in recent years. All votes had to be filed by midnight June 16, 2013.

The Players

Elan Corporation was a global biopharmaceutical company headquartered in Dublin, Ireland. Elan focused on the discovery, development and marketing of therapeutic products in neurology including Alzheimer's disease and Parkinson's disease and autoimmune diseases such as multiple sclerosis and Crohn's disease. But over time the company had spun-out, sold-off, or closed most of its business activities. By the spring of 2013, Elan was a company of only two assets: a large pile of cash and a perpetual royalty stream on a leading therapeutic for multiple sclerosis called Tysabri, which it had co-developed with Biogen.

The solution to Elan's problem was the sale of its interest in Tysabri to its partner Biogen. In February 2013 Elan sold its 50% rights in Tysabri to Biogen in return for $3.29 billion in cash and a perpetual royalty stream on Tysabri. Whereas previously Elan earned returns on only its 50% share of Tysabri, the royalty agreement was based on 100% of the asset. The royalty was a step-up rate structure on worldwide sales of 12% in year 1, 18% all subsequent years, plus 25% on all global sales above $2 billion.

The ink had barely dried on Elan's sale agreement in February 2013 when it was approached by a private U.S. firm, Royalty Pharma, about the possible purchase of Elan for $11 per share. Elan acknowledged the proposal publicly, and stated it would consider the proposal along with other strategic options.

Royalty Pharma (RP) is a privately held company (owned by private equity interests) that acquires royalty interests in marketed or late-stage pharmaceutical products. Its business allows the owners of these intellectual products to monetize their interests in order to pursue additional business development opportunities. RP accepts the risk that the price they paid for the asset interest will actually accrue over time. RP owns royalty rights; it does not operate or market.

In March 2013, possibly tired of waiting, RP issued a statement directly to Elan shareholders to encourage them to vote for the proposed acquisition of Elan for $11 per share. At that time, Elan issued a response to RP's statement that characterized the Royalty Pharma proposal as "conditional and opportunistic."

Elan's Defense

Elan's leadership was now under considerable pressure by shareholders to explain why shareholders should *not* tender their shares to Royalty Pharma. In May, Elan began to detail a collection of initiatives to redefine the company. Going forward, Elan described a series of four complex strategic initiatives that it would pursue to grow and diversify the firm beyond its current two-asset portfolio.

[1]Copyright © 2014 Thunderbird School of Global Management. All rights reserved. This case was prepared by Professor Michael H. Moffett for the purpose of classroom discussion only.

Because the company was currently in the offer period of a proposed acquisition, Irish securities laws required that all four of Elan's proposals be approved by shareholders. But from the beginning that appeared difficult given public perception that the initiatives were purely defensive.

Royalty Pharma responded publicly with a letter to Elan's stockholders questioning whether Elan's leadership was really acting in the best interests of the shareholders. It then increased its tender offer to $12.50/share plus a *Contingent Value Right* (CVR). The CVR was a conditional element where all shareholders would receive an additional amount per share in the future—up to an additional $2.50 per share—if Tysabri's future sales reached specific milestone targets. Royalty Pharma's CVR offer required Tysabri sales to hit $2.6 billion by 2015 and $3.1 billion by 2017. Royalty Pharma also made it very clear that if shareholders were to approve any of the Elan's four management proposals, the acquisition offer would lapse.

The Value Debate

Elan, as of May 2013, consisted of $1.787 billion in cash, the Tysabri royalty stream, a few remaining prospective pipeline products, and between $100 and $200 million in annual expenses associated with its management. Elan's management team wanted to use its cash and its annual royalty earnings to build a new business. Royalty Pharma

just wanted to buy Elan, take the cash and royalty stream assets, and shut Elan down.

The valuation debate on Elan revolved around the value of the Tysabri royalty stream. That meant predicting what actual sales were likely to be in the coming decade. Exhibit A presents Royalty Pharma's synopsis of the sales debate, noting that Elan's claims on value have been selectively high, while Royal Pharma has based its latest offer on the Street Consensus numbers.

Predicting royalty earnings on biotechnology products is not all that different than predicting the sales of any product. Pricing, competition, regulation, government policy, changing demographics and conditions—all could change future global sales. That said, there were several more distinct factors of concern.

First, Tysabri was scheduled to go off-patent in 2020 (original patent filing was in 2000). The Street Consensus forecast, the one advocated by Royalty Pharma, predicted Tysabri global sales to peak in that year at $2.74 billion. Sales would slide, but continue, in the following years. Second, competitive products were already entering the market. In the spring, Biogen had finally received FDA approval on an oral treatment for relapsing-remitting forms of multiple sclerosis. It was only one of several new treatments coming to the market. Royalty Pharma had pointed to declining new patient adds over the past two quarters as evidence

---

EXHIBIT A **Forecasts of Tysabri's Worldwide Sales**

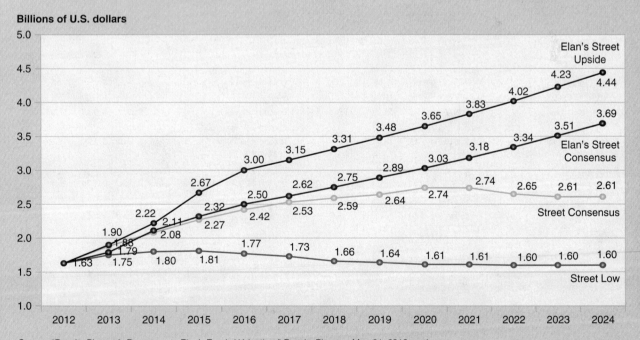

Source: "Royalty Pharma's Response to Elan's Tysabri Valuation," Royalty Pharma, May 31, 2013, p. 4.

EXHIBIT B   Valuing Elan: Prospective Royalties on Tysabri Plus Cash

Millions of U.S. dollars	Rates	Actual 2012	2013	2014	2015	2016	2017	2018	2019	2020	2021	2022	2023	2024
Worldwide Sales		1,631	1,884	2,082	2,266	2,418	2,530	2,591	2,643	2,742	2,744	2,653	2,609	2,611
year-over-year growth			15.5%	10.5%	8.8%	6.7%	4.6%	2.4%	2.0%	3.7%	0.1%	−3.3%	−1.7%	0.1%
Royalties to Elan:														
$0 to $2 billion in sales	18%		151	360	360	360	360	360	360	360	360	360	360	360
Greater than $2 bn	25%			21	67	105	133	148	161	186	186	163	152	153
Total Royalties			151	381	427	465	493	508	521	546	546	523	512	513
Expenses			(75)	(77)	(78)	(80)	(81)	(83)	(84)	(86)	(88)	(90)	(91)	(93)
Pre-tax Income			76	304	349	385	412	425	437	460	458	433	421	420
Less Taxes	1%	12.5%	(1)	(3)	(3)	(4)	(4)	(53)	(55)	(57)	(57)	(54)	(53)	(52)
Net Income			75	300	345	381	407	372	382	402	401	379	369	367
WACC			7.5%	7.5%	7.5%	7.5%	7.5%	7.5%	7.5%	10.0%	10.0%	10.0%	10.0%	10.0%
Discount Factor			1.0000	0.9302	0.8653	0.8050	0.7488	0.6966	0.6480	0.5132	0.4665	0.4241	0.3855	0.3505
PV of Net Income			75	280	299	306	305	259	248	206	187	161	142	129
Perpetuity value	−2%													2,999
Discount Factor														0.3505
PV of Perpetuity														1,051
NPV (cumulative PV)		$3,647												
Shares outstanding (millions)		518												
Value per share		$ 7.04												
Cash		1,787												
Cash value per share		$ 3.45												
Elan, total value per share		$10.49												

(2%) Perpetuity Growth Rate		Total	Per Share	% of Total
Discounted value 2013–2020		$1,977	$ 3.82	54.2%
Discounted value 2021–2024		$ 619	$ 1.19	17.0%
Perpetuity value beyond 2024	−2%	$1,051	$ 2.03	28.8%
Total Tysabri Value		$3,647	$ 7.04	100.0%
Cash		$1,787	$ 3.45	
Total Elan Value		$5,434	$10.49	

(4%) Perpetuity Growth Rate		Total	Per Share	% of Total
Discounted value 2013–2020		$1,977	$ 3.82	56.8%
Discounted value 2021–2024		$ 619	$ 1.19	17.8%
Perpetuity value beyond 2024	−4%	$ 883	$ 1.70	25.4%
Total Tysabri Value		$3,479	$ 6.72	100.0%
Cash		$1,787	$ 3.45	
Total Elan Value		$5,266	$10.17	

Notes: Valuation based on that presented in "Royalty Pharma's Response to Elan's Tysabri Valuation," May 29, 2013, p. 12. Royalties paid for the first 12 months, approximately 2013 in length, are at 12%. Perpetuity value (terminal value) assumes net revenues "grow" at −2% per annum indefinitely and are discounted at 10%. Assumes same 518 million shares outstanding as Elan stated on May 29, 2013. Elan's tax loss carry-forwards reduce the effective tax rate to 1% through 2017; beginning in 2018 the royalty stream is subject to Irish taxation at 12.5%. Royalty Pharma believes that the WACC should rise from 7.50% to 10.0% beginning in 2020 when Tysabri goes off-patent.

that aggressive future sales forecasts for Tysabri may be unrealistic—already.

For these and other reasons Royalty Pharma had argued that a conservative sales forecast was critically important for investors to use when deciding whether or not to go with management or Royalty Pharma's offer. Royalty Pharma's valuation, presented in Exhibit B, used this sales forecast for its baseline analysis. Royalty Pharma's valuation of Elan was based on the following critical assumptions:

- Tysabri's worldwide sales, the top-line of the valuation, were based on the Street Consensus.

- Elan's operating expenses would remain relatively flat, rising at 1% to 2% per year, from $75 million in 2013.

- Elan's net operating losses and Irish incorporation would reduce effective taxes to 1% per year through 2017, rising to Ireland's still relatively low corporate tax rate of 12.5% per year afterward.

- The discount rate would be 7.5% per year up until going off-patent in 2017, rising to 10% after that.

- Perpetuity value (terminal value) would be based on year 2024's income, discounted at 12%, and assuming an annual growth rate of either −2% or −4% as Tysabri's sales slide into the future.

- Outstanding shares were 518 million shares as of May 29, 2013, according to Elan's most recent communications.

- Elan's cash total was $1.787 billion, according to Elan's most recent communications.

The result was a base valuation of $10.49 or $10.17 per share, depending on the terminal value decline assumption. As typical of most valuations, the top-line—total sales—was the single largest driver for all future projected cash flows. The shares outstanding assumption, 518 million shares, reflected the results of a large share repurchase program which Elan had pursued right up to mid-May of 2013. Note that Royalty Pharma expressly decomposed its total valuation into three pieces: 1) the under patent period, 2) the post-patent period, and 3) the perpetuity value.

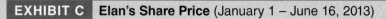

EXHIBIT C   **Elan's Share Price** (January 1 – June 16, 2013)

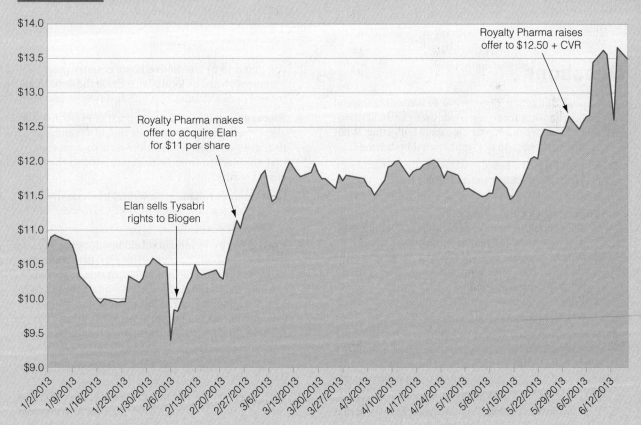

In Royalty Pharma's opinion, the post-patent period represented a significantly higher risk period for actual Tysabri sales.

Market Valuation. Despite the debate over Elan's value, as a publicly traded company, the market made its opinion known every single trading day. On the day prior to receiving the first indication of interest from Royalty Pharma, Elan was trading at $11 per share. (In the days that follow, the market is factoring in what it thinks the effective offer price is from a suitor like Royalty Pharma and the probability of the acquisition occurring.) Elan's share price history for 2013 is shown in Exhibit C.

Elan's management had made their case to shareholders. The collection of initiatives that Elan's leadership wished to pursue had to be approved, however, by shareholders. The Extraordinary General Meeting (EGM) of shareholders would be held on Monday, June 17th. At that meeting the results of the shareholder vote (all votes were due by the previous Friday) would be announced.

In the days leading up to the EGM, the battle had become very public, and in the words of one journalist, "quite chippy." In a *Financial Times* editorial, one former Elan board member, Jack Schuler, wrote "I have no confidence that Kelly Martin [Elan's CEO] or the other Elan board members will act in the interests of shareholders. I hope the Elan shareholders realise that their only option is to sell the company to the highest bidder." Elan's current non-executive chairman then responded: "I note that Elan's share price has trebled since Mr. Schuler's departure. The board and management team remain wholly focused on continued value creation and will continue to act in the best interests of our shareholders."

Shareholders had to decide—quickly.

CASE QUESTIONS

1. Using the sales forecasts for Tysabri presented in Exhibit A, and using the discounted cash flow model presented in Exhibit B, what do you think Elan is worth?

2. What other considerations do you think should be included in the valuation of Elan?

3. What would be your recommendation to shareholders—to approve management's proposals killing RP's offer—or say "no" to the proposals, probably prompting the acceptance of RP's offer?

Questions

1. **Capital Budgeting Theoretical Framework.** Capital budgeting for a foreign project uses the same theoretical framework as domestic capital budgeting. What are the basic steps in domestic capital budgeting?

2. **Foreign Complexities.** Capital budgeting for a foreign project is considerably more complex than the domestic case. What are the factors that add complexity?

3. **Project versus Parent Valuation.**
   a. Why should a foreign project be evaluated both from a project and parent viewpoint?
   b. Which viewpoint, project or parent, gives results closer to the traditional meaning of net present value in capital budgeting?
   c. Which viewpoint gives results closer to the effect on consolidated earnings per share?

4. **Which Cash Flows?** Capital projects provide both operating cash flows and financial cash flows. Why are operating cash flows preferred for domestic capital budgeting but financial cash flows given major consideration in international projects?

5. **Risk-Adjusted Return.** Should the anticipated internal rate of return (IRR) for a proposed foreign project be compared to a) alternative home country proposals, b) returns earned by local companies in the same industry and/or risk class, or c) both? Justify your answer.

6. **Blocked Cash Flows.** In the context of evaluating foreign investment proposals, how should a multinational firm evaluate cash flows in the host foreign country that are blocked from being repatriated to the firm's home country?

7. **Host Country Inflation.** How does host country inflation impact the operations of MNEs? How can MNEs mitigate these effects?

8. **Cost of Equity.** A foreign subsidiary does not have an independent cost of capital. However, in order to estimate the discount rate for a comparable host-country firm, the analyst should try to calculate a hypothetical cost of capital. As part of this process, the analyst can estimate the subsidiary's proxy cost of equity by using the traditional equation: Define each variable in this equation and explain how the variable might be different for a proxy host country firm compared to the parent MNE.

9. **Viewpoints.** What are the differences in the cash flows used in a project point of view analysis and a parent point of view analysis?

10. **Foreign Exchange, Expropriation, and Political Risks.** What are the main differences between foreign exchange, expropriation, and political risks?

11. **Cross-Border Mergers and Acquisitions.** Explain why cross-border mergers and acquisitions are difficult to implement.

12. **Investment Analysis.** Compare and contrast NPV, APV, and real option analysis, explaining how each of these analysis techniques affect investment decisions.

Problems

1. **Branded Co. (Italy).** Branded Co. (Italy) is considering investing Venezuelan bolivar VEF20,000,000 in Venezuela to build a wholly owned high fashion plant to export globally. After five years, the subsidiary, BrandVen, will be sold to Venezuelan investors for VEF40,000,000. A pro forma income statement for the Venezuelan operation predicts the generation of VEF3,500,000 of annual cash flow, and is listed below.

Sales revenue	15,000,000
Less cash operating expenses	(7,000,000)
Gross income	8,000,000
Less depreciation expenses	(500,000)
Earnings before interest and taxes	7,500,000
Less Venezuelan taxes at 35%	(2,625,000)
Net income	4,875,000
Add back depreciation	500,000
Annual cash flow	5,375,000

The initial investment will be made on December 31, 2014, and cash flows will occur on December 31 of each succeeding year. Annual cash dividends to BrandVen from Venezuela will equal 75% of accounting income.

The Italian corporate tax rate is 20% and the Venezuelan corporate tax rate is 35%. Since the Venezuelan tax rate is greater than the Italian tax rate, annual dividends paid to Branded Co. will not be subject to additional taxes in Italy. There are no capital gains taxes on the final sale. Branded Co. uses a weighted average cost of capital of 18% on domestic investments, but will add 8 percentage points for the Venezuelan investment because of perceived greater risk. Branded Co. forecasts the Venezuelan bolivar/euro exchange rate for December 31 for the next six years as listed below.

	VEF/€		VEF/€
2014	7	2017	7.5
2015	7.1	2018	7.6
2016	7.25	2019	7.75

What is the net present value and internal rate of return on this investment?

2. **Emancipation Co.** Emancipation Co., South Africa, expects to receive cash dividends from an Irish joint venture over the coming three years. The first dividend, to be paid on December 31, 2015, is expected to be €1,000,000. The dividend is then expected to grow 15% per year over the following two years. The current exchange rate (December 31, 2014) is ZAR 13/€. Emancipation Co.'s weighted average cost of capital is 17.5%.
   a. What is the present value of the expected euro dividend stream if the euro is expected to appreciate 6% per annum against the South African rand (ZAR)?
   b. What is the present value of the expected dividend stream if the euro were to depreciate 5% per annum against the rand?

3. **YummyYummies (Bangladesh).** ArtemisPrivEqui, a Greek-based private equity firm, is trying to determine what it should pay for YummyYummies, a food processing firm in Bangladesh. ArtemisPrivEqui estimates that YummyYummies will generate a free cash flow of 80 million Bangladeshi taka (BDT) next year (2016), and that this free cash flow will continue to grow at a constant rate of 10.0% per annum indefinitely.

A private equity firm like ArtemisPrivEqui, however, is not interested in owning a company for long, and plans to sell the Bangladeshi firm at the end of three years for approximately 10 times YummyYummies's free cash flow in that year. The current spot exchange rate is BDT78/€, but the Bangladeshi inflation rate is expected to remain at a relatively high rate of 12% per annum compared to the Greek euro inflation rate of only 2.0% per annum. ArtemisPrivEqui expects to earn at least a 15% annual rate of return on international investments like YummyYummies.
   a. What is YummyYummies's worth if the Bangladeshi taka were to remain fixed over the three-year investment period?
   b. What is YummyYummies's worth if the Bangladeshi taka were to change in value over time according to purchasing power parity?

4. **Finisterra, S.A.** Finisterra, S.A., located in the state of Baja California, Mexico, manufactures frozen Mexican food that enjoys a large following in the U.S. states of California and Arizona. In order to be closer to its

Problem 5.

Carloco in Cairo (after tax)	2015	2016	2017	2018	2019	2020
Net EGP cash flow	(15,000)	10,000	8,200	9,000	9,500	10,000
Euro cash outflows	—	(150)	(200)	(200)	(200)	—
Carloco in Amman (after tax)						
Net JOD cash flow	(5,000)	4,000	4,500	5,000	5,500	6,000
Euro cash outflows	—	(100)	(150)	(200)	(300)	—

U.S. market, Finisterra is considering moving some of its manufacturing operations to southern California. Operations in California would begin in year 1 and have the following attributes.

Assumptions	Value
Sales price per unit, year 1 ($)	$ 5.00
Sales price increase, per year	3.00%
Initial sales volume, year 1, units	1,000,000
Sales volume increase, per year	10.00%
Production costs per unit, year 1	$ 4.00
Production cost per unit increase, per year	4.00%
General and administrative expenses per year	$100,000
Depreciation expenses per year	$ 80,000
Finisterra's WACC (pesos)	16.00%
Terminal value discount rate	20.00%

The operations in California will pay 80% of its accounting profit to Finisterra as an annual cash dividend. Mexican taxes are calculated on grossed up dividends from foreign countries, with a credit for host-country taxes already paid. What is the maximum U.S. dollar price Finisterra should offer in year 1 for the investment?

5. **Carloco Carpets Co.** Carloco Carpets Co., Germany, manufactures high-grade dyes for textiles. Until now, manufacturing was being subcontracted to other companies, but for quality control reasons Carloco has decided to manufacture its own products in the Middle East. Analysis has narrowed the choice to two possibilities, Cairo, Egypt, and Amman, Jordan. At the moment, only the following summary of expected, after tax, cash flows is available. Although most operating outflows would be in Egyptian pounds or Jordanian dinars, some additional euro cash outflows would be necessary, as shown in the table at the top of this page.

The Egyptian pound (EGP) currently trades at EGP8.40/€ and the Jordanian dinar (JOD) trades at JOD0.78/€. Carloco expects the Egyptian pound to appreciate 5.0% per year against the euro, and the Jordanian dinar to depreciate 3.0% per year against the euro. If the weighted average cost of capital for Carloco Carpets Co. is 22.0%, which project looks more promising?

6. **ScotchOrganic Co.** Privately owned ScotchOrganic Co. is considering investing in Romania to cut down on transportation costs to Eastern European markets. The original investment in Romanian leu (RON) would amount to RON62,500,000 or £10,000,000 at the current cross rate of RON6.25/£, all in fixed assets, which will be depreciated over 10 years by the straight-line method. An additional RON25,000,000 will be needed for working capital.

For capital budgeting purposes, ScotchOrganic Co. assumes a sale as a going concern at the end of the third year at a price, after all taxes, equal to the net book value of fixed assets alone (not including working capital). All free cash flow will be repatriated to Scotland as soon as possible. In evaluating the venture, the British pound forecasts are shown in the table below.

Problem 6.

Assumptions	0	1	2	3
Original investment Romanian leu (RON)	62,500,000			
Spot exchange rate (RON/£)	6.25	6.20	6.15	6.10
Unit demand		150,000	175,000	200,000
Unit sales price		£3.00	£3.50	£3.75
Fixed cash operating expenses		£250,000	£275,000	£300,000
Depreciation		£ 150,000	£ 150,000	£ 150,000
Investment in working capital (RON)	25,000,000			

Variable manufacturing costs are expected to be 75% of sales. No additional funds need be invested in pounds during the period under consideration. Romania imposes no restrictions on repatriation of any funds of any sort. The Romanian corporate tax rate is 20% and the Scottish rate is 25%. Both countries allow a tax credit for taxes paid in other countries. ScotchOrganic Co. uses 15% as its weighted average cost of capital, and its objective is to maximize present value. Is the investment attractive to ScotchOrganic Co.?

Hermosa Beach Components (U.S.)

Use the following information and assumptions to answer Problems 7–10.

Hermosa Beach Components, Inc., of California exports 24,000 sets of low-density light bulbs per year to Argentina under an import license that expires in five years. In Argentina, the bulbs are sold for the Argentine peso equivalent of $60 per set. Direct manufacturing costs in the United States and shipping together amount to $40 per set. The market for this type of bulb in Argentina is stable, neither growing nor shrinking, and Hermosa holds the major portion of the market.

The Argentine government has invited Hermosa to open a manufacturing plant so imported bulbs can be replaced by local production. If Hermosa makes the investment, it will operate the plant for five years and then sell the building and equipment to Argentine investors at net book value at the time of sale plus the value of any net working capital. (Net working capital is the amount of current assets less any portion financed by local debt.) Hermosa will be allowed to repatriate all net income and depreciation funds to the United States each year. Hermosa traditionally evaluates all foreign investments in U.S. dollar terms.

- **Investment.**   Hermosa's anticipated cash outlay in U.S. dollars in 2012 would be as follows:

Building and equipment	$1,000,000
Net working capital	1,000,000
Total investment	$2,000,000

All investment outlays will be made in 2012, and all operating cash flows will occur at the end of years 2013 through 2017.

- **Depreciation and Investment Recovery.**   Building and equipment will be depreciated over five years on a straight-line basis. At the end of the fifth year, the

$1,000,000 of net working capital may also be repatriated to the United States, as may the remaining net book value of the plant.

- **Sales Price of Bulbs.**   Locally manufactured bulbs will be sold for the Argentine peso equivalent of $60 per set.

- **Operating Expenses per Set of Bulbs.**   Material purchases are as follows:

Materials purchased in Argentina (U.S. dollar equivalent)	$20 per set
Materials imported from Hermosa Beach-USA	10 per set
Total variable costs	$30 per set

- **Transfer Prices.**   The $10 transfer price per set for raw material sold by the parent consists of $5 of direct and indirect costs incurred in the United States on their manufacture, creating $5 of pre-tax profit to Hermosa Beach.

- **Taxes.**   The corporate income tax rate is 40% in both Argentina and the United States (combined federal and state/province). There are no capital gains taxes on the future sale of the Argentine subsidiary, either in Argentina or the United States.

- **Discount Rate.**   Hermosa Components uses a 15% discount rate to evaluate all domestic and foreign projects.

7. **Hermosa Components: Baseline Analysis.** Evaluate the proposed investment in Argentina by Hermosa Components (U.S.). Hermosa's management wishes the baseline analysis to be performed in U.S. dollars (and implicitly also assumes the exchange rate remains fixed throughout the life of the project). Create a project viewpoint capital budget and a parent viewpoint capital budget. What do you conclude from your analysis?

8. **Hermosa Components: Revenue Growth Scenario.** As a result of their analysis in Problem 7, Hermosa wishes to explore the implications of being able to grow sales volume by 4% per year. Argentine inflation is expected to average 5% per year, so sales price and material cost increases of 7% and 6% per year, respectively, are thought reasonable. Although material costs in Argentina are expected to rise, U.S.-based costs are not expected to change over the five-year period. Evaluate this scenario for both the project and parent viewpoints. Is the project under this revenue growth scenario acceptable?

9. **Hermosa Components: Revenue Growth and Sales Price Scenario.** In addition to the assumptions employed in Problem 8, Hermosa now wishes

to evaluate the prospect of being able to sell the Argentine subsidiary at the end of year 5 at a multiple of the business' earnings in that year. Hermosa believes that a multiple of six is a conservative estimate of the market value of the firm at that time. Evaluate the project and parent viewpoint capital budgets.

10. **Hermosa Components: Revenue Growth, Sales Price, and Currency Risk Scenario.** Melinda Deane, a new analyst at Hermosa and a recent MBA graduate, believes that it is a fundamental error to evaluate the Argentine project's prospective earnings and cash flows in dollars, rather than first estimating their Argentine peso (Ps) value and then converting cash flow returns to the United States in dollars. She believes the correct method is to use the end-of-year spot rate in 2012 of Ps3.50/$ and assume it will change in relation to purchasing power. (She is assuming U.S. inflation to be 1% per annum and Argentine inflation to be 5% per annum.) She also believes that Hermosa should use a risk-adjusted discount rate in Argentina which reflects Argentine capital costs (20% is her estimate) and a risk-adjusted discount rate for the parent viewpoint capital budget (18%) on the assumption that international projects in a risky currency environment should require a higher expected return than other lower-risk projects. How do these assumptions and changes alter Hermosa's perspective on the proposed investment?

Internet Exercises

1. **Capital Projects and the EBRD.** The European Bank for Reconstruction and Development (EBRD) was established to foster market-oriented business development in the former Soviet Bloc. Use the EBRD Web site to determine which projects and companies EBRD is currently undertaking.

   European Bank for Reconstruction
   and Development   www.ebrd.com

2. **Emerging Markets: China.** Long-term investment projects such as electrical power generation require a thorough understanding of all attributes of doing business in that country. China is currently the focus of investment and market penetration strategies of multinational firms worldwide. Using the Web (you might start with the Web sites listed below), build a database on doing business in China, and prepare an update of many of the factors discussed in this chapter.

   Ministry of Foreign Trade and
   Economic Cooperation, PRC   english.mofcom.gov.cn/

   China Investment Trust
   and Investment Corporation   www.citic.com/wps/portal/
                                 enlimited

   ChinaNet Investment Pages   www.chinanet-online.com

3. **BeyondBrics: The *Financial Times'* Emerging Market Hub.** Check the FT's blog on emerging markets for the latest debates and guest editorials.

   Financial Times Blog on
   Emerging Markets   blogs.ft.com/beyond-brics/

Answers to Selected End-of-Chapter Problems

Chapter 1: Multinational Financial Management: Opportunities and Challenges

6. a. €7.21
   b. France = 35.6%, Switzerland = 6.2%, U.K. = 48.3%, Denmark = 9.9%
   c. 64.4%
9. Appreciation case: 9.7%
   Depreciation case: −12.9%

Chapter 2: The International Monetary System

6. 12.1982
7. 14.15% depreciation
9. If 20%, 6.76; if 30%, 6.24

Chapter 3: The Balance of Payments

	2000	2001	2002	2003	2004	2005	2006	2007	2008	2009	2010	2011	2012
1.	−4,813	1,786	−5,431	−15,369	−18,031	−13,372	−9,596	−17,784	−4,915	−4,439	17,479	28,762	−5,212
2.	289	−259	−201	−433	−678	542	869	588	−3,098	−1,351	−4,345	−9,142	−11,717
3.	−4,524	1,527	−5,632	−15,802	−18,709	−12,830	−8,727	−17,196	−8,013	−5,790	13,134	19,620	−16,929
4.	−15,103	−8,721	−17,385	−30,674	−40,066	−41,032	−41,504	−58,031	−47,786	−44,999	−37,177	−33,635	−57,036

Chapter 4: Financial Goals and Corporate Governance

1. a. 11.905%
   b. 32.083%
   c. Dividend yield = 7.083%; capital gains = 25%; total shareholder return = 32.083%
2. a. 64.23%
   b. 4.19%
   c. 71.12%

Chapter 5: The Foreign Exchange Market

1. a. 4.72
   b. 21,243
10. a. Profit of 26,143.79
    b. Loss of (26,086.96)

Chapter 6: International Parity Conditions

4. a. 1.0941

    b. 1.1155, and 948.19

7. A CIA profit potential of –0.042% tells Takeshi
    he should borrow Japanese yen and invest in the
    higher yielding currency, the U.S. dollar, to earn a
    CIA profit of 55,000.

Chapter 7: Foreign Currency Derivatives and Swaps

1. a. ($49,080.00)

    b. $38,920.00

    c. ($9,080.00)

4. a. Sallie should buy a call on Singapore dollars

    b. $0.65046

    c. Gross profit = $0.05000   Net profit = $0.04954

    d. Gross profit = $0.15000   Net profit = $0.14954

Chapter 8: Foreign Exchange Rate Determination

1. 134.56

6. a. 5

    b. 237.7%

8. –2.71%

Chapter 9: Transaction Exposure

2. Foreign exchange loss of $921,400,000

10. Do nothing: Could be anything

    Forward: $216,049.38

    Money market: $212,190.81

    Forward is preferable choice if bank allows an
    expanded line

Chapter 10: Translation Exposure

1. a. Translation loss is ($2,400,000)

    b. Loss is accumulated on the consolidated balance
        sheet, and does not pass through the consolidated
        income if the subsidiary is foreign currency
        functional

5. Net exposure = €480,000; Translation = £ 349,116

Chapter 11: Operating Exposure

3. Case 1: Same yuan price: £360,000,000

    Case 2: Same pound price: £648,000,000 (better)

7. $8,900,601

Chapter 12: The Global Cost and Availability of Capital

1. a. 6.550%

    b. 5.950%

8. Before diversification: 10.529%

    After diversification: 12.038%

Chapter 13: Raising Equity and Debt Globally

1. Petrobras: 14.674%

    Lukoil: 12.286%

2. 13.23%

Chapter 14: Multinational Tax Management

1. Case 1: 29.6%; Case 2: 45%

    Case 2: 45.0%

4. Change in consolidated tax payments of –11.17%

Chapter 15: International Trade Finance

3. 15.716%

5. a. 8.685%

    b. €172,025

Chapter 16: Foreign Direct Investment and Political Risk

No quantitative problems in this chapter.

Chapter 17: Multinational Capital Budgeting and Cross-Border Acquisitions

1. NPV of investment (project viewpoint): 6,758,769

    NPV of investment (parent viewpoint): 77,539

4. Ps 28,442771 or $3,555,346

Glossary

Absolute advantage. The ability of an individual party or country to produce more of a product or service with the same inputs as another party. It is therefore possible for a country to have no absolute advantage in any international trade activity. *See also* Comparative advantage.

Absolute purchasing power parity. The theory that the exact rate of exchange between two currencies is found by equalizing the purchasing power of the two currencies.

Accounting exposure. Another name for translation exposure. *See* Translation exposure.

ADR. *See* American Depositary Receipt.

Affiliate. *See* Foreign affiliate.

Affiliated. In business, a close association between two companies. Usually implies a partial but not controlling equity or ownership position by one in the other.

Agency theory. The costs and risks of aligning interests between shareholders of the firm and their agents, management, in the conduct of firm business and strategy. Also referred to as the *agency problem* or *agency issue.*

All-in cost. The total cost, including interest rate and fees, associated with a loan or debt obligation.

American Depositary Receipt (ADR). A certificate of ownership, issued by a U.S. bank, representing a claim on underlying foreign securities. ADRs may be traded in lieu of trading in the actual underlying shares.

American option. An option that can be exercised at any time up to and including the expiration date.

American terms. Foreign exchange quotations for the U.S. dollar, expressed as the number of U.S. dollars per unit of non-U.S. currency.

Anchor currency. *See* Reserve currency.

Anticipated exposure. A foreign exchange exposure that is believed by management to have a very high likelihood of occurring, but is not yet contractual, and is therefore not yet certain.

Appreciation. In the context of exchange rate changes, a rise in the foreign exchange value of a currency that is pegged to other currencies or to gold. Also called revaluation.

Arbitrage. A trading strategy based on the purchase of a commodity, including foreign exchange, in one market at one price while simultaneously selling it in another market at a more advantageous price, in order to obtain a risk-free profit on the price differential.

Arbitrageur. An individual or company that practices arbitrage.

Arm's-length price. The price at which a willing buyer and a willing unrelated seller freely agree to carry out a transaction. In effect, a free market price. Applied by tax authorities in judging the appropriateness of transfer prices between related companies.

Ask. The price at which a dealer is willing to sell foreign exchange, securities or commodities. Also called offer price.

Asset market approach. A strategy that determines whether foreigners are willing to hold claims in monetary form, depending on an extensive set of investment considerations or drivers.

At-the-money (ATM). An option whose exercise price is the same as the spot price of the underlying currency.

Aval. An endorsement by a third party, acting as guarantor, for the full amount of a debt. The third party (guarantor) commits to cover the payment of the amount of the credit title and its interest in the event the original debtor does not fulfill his or her obligation.

Backlog exposure. The period of time between contract initiation and fulfillment through delivery of services or shipping of goods.

Back-to-back loan. A loan in which two companies in separate countries borrow each other's currency for a specific period of time and repay the other's currency at an agreed maturity. Sometimes the two loans are channeled through an intermediate bank. Back-to-back financing is also called link financing.

Balance of payments (BOP). A financial statement summarizing the flow of goods, services, and investment funds between residents of a given country and residents of the rest of the world.

Balance on goods and services. A sub-balance within the Current Account of a nation's balance of payments, indicating the net position in the export and import of both goods manufacturing and services trade.

Balance of trade (BOT). An entry in the balance of payments measuring the difference between the monetary value of merchandise exports and merchandise imports.

Balance sheet hedge. An accounting strategy that requires an equal amount of exposed foreign currency assets and liabilities on a firm's consolidated balance sheet.

483

Bank draft. A check for payment drawing upon a bank's own account; a check whose payment is guaranteed by a bank.

Bank for International Settlements (BIS). A bank in Basel, Switzerland, that functions as a bank for European central banks.

Bank rate. The interest rate at which central banks for various countries lend to their own monetary institutions.

Bankers' acceptance. An unconditional promise by a bank to make payment on a draft when it matures. This comes in the form of the bank's endorsement (acceptance) of a draft drawn against that bank in accordance with the terms of a letter of credit issued by the bank.

Barter. International trade conducted by the direct exchange of physical goods, rather than by separate purchases and sales at prices and exchange rates set by a free market.

Basic balance. In a country's balance of payments, the net of exports and imports of goods and services, unilateral transfers, and long-term capital flows.

Basis point. One one-hundredth of one percentage point, often used in quotations of spreads between interest rates or to describe changes in yields in securities.

Basis risk. A type of interest rate risk in which the interest rate base is mismatched.

Bearer bond. Corporate or governmental debt in bond form that is not registered to any owner. Possession of the bond implies ownership, and interest is obtained by clipping a coupon attached to the bond. The advantage of the bearer form is easy transfer at the time of a sale, easy use as collateral for a debt, and what some cynics call taxpayer anonymity, meaning that governments find it hard to trace interest payments in order to collect income taxes. Bearer bonds are common in Europe, but are seldom issued any more in the United States. The alternate form to a bearer bond is a registered bond.

Beta. Second letter of the Greek alphabet, used as a statistical measure of risk in the Capital Asset Pricing Model. Beta is the covariance between returns on a given asset and returns on the market portfolio, divided by the variance of returns on the market portfolio.

Bid. The price that a dealer is willing to pay to purchase foreign exchange or a security.

Bid-ask spread. The difference between a bid and an ask quotation.

Big Bang. The October 1986 liberalization of the London capital markets.

Bill of exchange (B/E). A written order requesting one party (such as an importer) to pay a specified amount of money at a specified time to the writer of the bill. Also called a draft. *See* Sight draft.

Bill of lading (B/L). A contract between a common carrier and a shipper to transport goods to a named destination. The bill of lading is also a receipt for the goods. Bills of lading are usually negotiable, meaning they are made to the order of a particular party and can be endorsed to transfer title to another party.

Black market. An illegal foreign exchange market.

Blocked funds. Funds in one country's currency that may not be exchanged freely for foreign currencies because of exchange controls.

Border tax adjustments. The fiscal practice, under the General Agreement on Tariffs and Trade, by which imported goods are subject to some or all of the tax charged in the importing country and re-exported goods are exempt from some or all of the tax charged in the exporting country.

Branch. A foreign operation not incorporated in the host country, in contrast to a subsidiary.

Bretton Woods Conference. An international conference in 1944 that established the international monetary system—the *Bretton Woods Agreement*—that was in effect from 1945 to 1971. The conference was held in Bretton Woods, New Hampshire, United States.

BRIC. A frequently used acronym for the four largest emerging market countries–Brazil, Russia, India, and China.

Bridge financing. Short-term financing from a bank, used while a borrower obtains medium- or long-term fixed-rate financing from capital markets.

Bulldog. British pound-denominated bond issued within the United Kingdom by a foreign borrower.

Cable. The U.S. dollar per British pound cross rate.

CAD. Cash against documents. International trade term.

Call. An option with the right, but not the obligation, to buy foreign exchange or another financial contract at a specified price within a specified time. *See* Option.

Capex. Capital expenditures.

Capital account. A section of the balance of payments accounts. Under the revised format of the International Monetary Fund, the capital account measures capital transfers and the acquisition and disposal of nonproduced, nonfinancial assets. Under traditional definitions, still used by many countries, the capital account measures public and private international lending and investment. Most of the traditional definition of the capital account is now incorporated into IMF statements as the financial account.

Capital Asset Pricing Model (CAPM). A theoretical model that relates the return on an asset to its risk, where risk is the contribution of the asset to the volatility of a portfolio. Risk and return are presumed to be determined in competitive and efficient financial markets.

Capital budgeting. The analytical approach used to determine whether investment in long-lived assets or projects is viable.

Capital control. Restrictions, requirements, taxes or prohibitions on the movements of capital across borders as imposed and enforced by governments.

Capital flight. Movement of funds out of a country because of political risk.

Capital markets. The financial markets of various countries in which various types of long-term debt and/or ownership securities, or claims on those securities, are purchased and sold.

Capital mobility. The degree to which private capital moves freely from country to country in search of the most promising investment opportunities.

Carry trade. The strategy of borrowing in a low interest rate currency to fund investing in higher yielding currencies. Also termed *currency carry trade*, the strategy is speculative in that currency risk is present and not managed or hedged.

Cash budgeting. Planning for future receipts and disbursements of cash.

Cash flow return on investment (CFROI). A measure of corporate performance in which the numerator equals profit from continuing operations less cash taxes and depreciation. This is divided by cash investment, which is taken to mean the replacement cost of capital employed.

Caveat emptor. Latin for "buyer beware."

Certificate of Deposit (CD). A negotiable receipt issued by a bank for funds deposited for a certain period of time. CDs can be purchased or sold prior to their maturity in a secondary market, making them an interest-earning marketable security.

CFR. Cost and freight charges included.

CIF (cost, insurance, and freight). *See* Cost, insurance, and freight.

CKD. Completely knocked down. International trade term for components shipped into a country for assembly there. Often used in the automobile industry.

Clearinghouse. An institution through which financial obligations are cleared by the process of settling the obligations of various members.

Clearinghouse Interbank Payments System (CHIPS). A New York-based computerized clearing system used by banks to settle interbank foreign exchange obligations (mostly U.S. dollars) between members.

Collar option. The simultaneous purchase of a put option and sale of a call option, or vice versa, resulting in a form of hybrid option.

COMECON. Acronym for Council for Mutual Economic Assistance. An association of the former Soviet Union and Eastern European governments formed to facilitate international trade among European Communist countries. COMECON ceased to exist after the breakup of the Soviet Union.

Commercial risk. In banking, the likelihood that a foreign debtor will be unable to repay its debts because of business events, as distinct from political ones.

Common market. An association through treaty of two or more countries that agree to remove all trade barriers between themselves. The best known is the European Common Market, now called the European Union.

Comparative advantage. A theory that everyone gains if each nation specializes in the production of those goods that it produces relatively most efficiently and imports those goods that other countries produce relatively most efficiently. The theory supports free trade arguments.

Competitive exposure. *See* Operating exposure.

Concession agreement. An understanding or contract between a foreign corporation and a host government defining the rules under which the corporation may operate in that country.

Consolidated financial statement. A corporate financial statement in which accounts of a parent company and its subsidiaries are added together to produce a statement which reports the status of the worldwide enterprise as if it were a single corporation. Internal obligations are eliminated in consolidated statements.

Consolidation. In the context of accounting for multinational corporations, the process of preparing a single reporting currency financial statement, which combines financial statements of subsidiaries that are in fact measured in different currencies.

Contagion. The spread of a crisis in one country to its neighboring countries and other countries with similar characteristics—at least in the eyes of cross-border investors.

Contingent foreign currency exposure. The final determination of the exposure is contingent upon another firm's decision, such as a decision to invest or the winning of a business or construction bid.

Contingent Value Right (CVR). A right given to shareholders of an acquired company (or company facing acquisition) that promises them to receive additional cash or shares if a specified event occurs. CVRs are similar to options because they carry an expiration date related to the time in which the contingent event must occur.

Continuous Linked Settlements (CLS). A U.S. financial institution that provides foreign exchange settlement services to members.

Contractual hedge. A foreign currency hedging agreement or contract, typically using a financial derivative such as a forward contract or foreign currency option.

Controlled foreign corporation (CFC). A foreign corporation in which U.S. shareholders own more than 50% of the combined voting power or total value. Under U.S. tax law, U.S. shareholders may be liable for taxes on undistributed earnings of the controlled foreign corporation.

Convertible bond. A bond or other fixed-income security that may be exchanged for a number of shares of common stock.

Convertible currency. A currency that can be exchanged freely for any other currency without government restrictions.

Corporate governance. The relationship among stakeholders used to determine and control the strategic direction and performance of an organization.

Corporate wealth maximization. The corporate goal of maximizing the total wealth of the corporation rather than just the shareholders' wealth. Wealth is defined to include not just financial wealth but also the technical, marketing, and human resources of the corporation.

Correspondent bank. A bank that holds deposits for and provides services to another bank, located in another geographic area, on a reciprocal basis.

Cost and freight (CFR). Price, as quoted by an exporter, that includes the cost of transportation to the named port of destination.

Cost, insurance, and freight (CIF). Exporter's quoted price including the cost of packaging, freight or carriage, insurance premium, and other charges paid in respect of the goods from the time of loading in the country of export to their arrival at the named port of destination or place of transshipment.

Cost of capital. The cost, expressed as a percentage and on a weighted average basis, of raising equity and debt at current market rates. More commonly referred to as the *weighted average cost of capital*, or WACC.

Cost of carry. The financing costs, primarily interest expense, of funding an asset such as inventory.

Cost of cover. The cost of hedging.

Counterparty. The opposite party in a double transaction, which involves an exchange of financial instruments or obligations now and a reversal of that same transaction at an agreed-upon later date.

Counterparty risk. The potential exposure any individual firm bears that the second party to any financial contract may be unable to fulfill its obligations under the contract's specifications.

Countertrade. A type of international trade in which parties exchange goods directly rather than for money; a type of barter.

Countervailing duty. An import duty charged to offset an export subsidy by another country.

Country risk. In banking, the likelihood that unexpected events within a host country will influence a client's or a government's ability to repay a loan. Country risk is often divided into sovereign (political) risk and foreign exchange (currency) risk.

Country-specific-risks. Political risks that affect the MNE at the country level, such as transfer risk (blocked funds) and cultural and institutional risks.

Covered interest arbitrage (CIA). The process whereby an investor earns a risk-free profit by (1) borrowing funds in one currency, (2) exchanging those funds in the spot market for a foreign currency, (3) investing the foreign currency at interest rates in a foreign country, (4) selling forward, at the time of original investment, the investment proceeds to be received at maturity, (5) using the proceeds of the forward sale to repay the original loan, and (6) sustaining a remaining profit balance.

Covered transaction. A foreign currency exposure which has been hedged or "covered."

Covering. A transaction in the forward foreign exchange market or money market that protects the value of future cash flows. Covering is another term for hedging. *See* Hedge.

Crawling peg. A foreign exchange rate system in which the exchange rate is adjusted very frequently to reflect prevailing rate of inflation.

Credit enhancement. A process of restructuring or recombining assets of different risk profiles in order to obtain a higher credit rating for the combined product.

Credit risk. The possibility that a borrower's credit worth, at the time of renewing a credit, is reclassified by the lender.

Crisis planning. The process of educating management and other employees about how to react to various scenarios of violence or other disruptive events.

Cross-border acquisition. A purchase in which one firm acquires another firm located in a different country.

Cross-currency interest rate swap. *See* Currency swap.

Cross-currency swap. *See* Currency swap.

Cross-listing. The listing of shares of common stock on two or more stock exchanges.

Cross rate. An exchange rate between two currencies derived by dividing each currency's exchange rate with a third currency. Colloquially, it is often used to refer to a specific currency pair such as the euro/yen cross rate, as the yen/dollar and dollar/euro are the more common currency quotations.

Cryptocurrency. A currency created and exchanged using the secure information processes and principles of cryptography. One of the first and most well-known cryptocurrencies is Bitcoin.

Cumulative translation adjustment (CTA) account. An entry in a translated balance sheet in which gains and/or losses from translation have been accumulated over a period of years.

Currency basket. The value of a portfolio of specific amounts of individual currencies, used as the basis for setting the market value of another currency. Also called currency cocktail.

Currency board. A currency board exists when a country's central bank commits to back its money supply entirely with foreign reserves at all times.

Currency swap. A transaction in which two counterparties exchange specific amounts of two different currencies at the outset, and then repay over time according to an agreed-upon contract that reflects interest payments and possibly amortization of principal. In a currency swap, the cash flows are similar to those in a spot and forward foreign exchange transaction. *See also* Swap.

Currency switching. Where a firm uses foreign exchange received in the course of business to settle obligations to a third party, often located in a third country.

Current account. In the balance of payments, the net flow of goods, services, and unilateral transfers (such as gifts) between a country and all foreign countries.

Current rate method. A method of translating the financial statements of foreign subsidiaries into the parent's reporting currency. All assets and liabilities are translated at the current exchange rate.

Current/noncurrent method. A method of translating the financial statements of foreign subsidiaries into the parent's reporting currency. All current assets and current liabilities are translated at the current rate, and all noncurrent accounts at their historical rates.

D/A. Documents against acceptance. International trade term.

D/P. Documents against payment. International trade term.

D/S. Days after sight. International trade term.

Deductible expense. A business expense which is recognized by tax officials as deductible toward the firm's income tax liabilities.

Deemed-paid tax. That portion of taxes paid to a foreign government that is allowed as a credit (reduction) in taxes due to a home government.

Delta. The change in an option's price divided by the change in the price of the underlying instrument. Hedging strategies are based on delta ratios.

Demand deposit. A bank deposit that can be withdrawn or transferred at any time without notice, in contrast to a time deposit where (theoretically) the bank may require a waiting period before the deposit can be withdrawn. Demand deposits may or may not earn interest. A time deposit is the opposite of a demand deposit.

Depositary receipt (DR). *See* American Depositary Receipt.

Depreciation. A market-driven change in the value of a currency that results in reduced value or purchasing power.

Derivative. An asset that derives all changes in value on a separate underlying asset.

Devaluation. The action of a government or central bank authority to drop the spot foreign exchange value of a currency that is pegged to another currency or to gold.

Dim Sum Bond Market. The market for Chinese renminbi (yuan) denominated securities as issued in Hong Kong.

Direct intervention. The purchase or the sale of a country's home currency by its own fiscal or monetary authority in order to influence the value of the domestic currency.

Direct quote. The price of a unit of foreign exchange expressed in the home country's currency. The term has meaning only when the home country is specified.

Direct tax. A tax paid directly to the government by the person on whom it is imposed.

Directed public share issue. An issue that is targeted at investors in a single country and underwritten in whole or in part by investment institutions from that country.

Dirty float. A system of floating (i.e., market-determined) exchange rates in which the government intervenes from time to time to influence the foreign exchange value of its currency.

Discount. In the foreign exchange market, the amount by which a currency is cheaper for future delivery than for spot (immediate) delivery. The opposite of discount is premium.

Dividend yield. The current period dividend distribution as a percentage of the beginning of period share price.

Dollarization. The use of the U.S. dollar as the official currency of a country.

Domestic International Sales Corporation (DISC). Under the U.S. tax code, a type of subsidiary formed to reduce taxes on exported U.S.-produced goods. It has been ruled illegal by the World Trade Organization.

Draft. An unconditional written order requesting one party (such as an importer) to pay a specified amount of money at a specified time to the order of the writer of the draft. Also called a bill of exchange. Personal checks are one type of draft.

Dragon bond. A U.S. dollar-denominated bond sold in the so-called Dragon economies of Asia, such as Hong Kong, Taiwan, and Singapore.

Dual-currency basket. The use of an index or *basket* composed of two other foreign currencies to benchmark or manage a country's own currency value.

Dumping. The practice of offering goods for sale in a foreign market at a price that is lower than that of the same product in the home market or a third country. As used in GATT, a special case of differential pricing.

Economic exposure. Another name for operating exposure. *See* Operating exposure.

Economic Value Added (EVA). A widely used measure of corporate financial performance. It is calculated as the difference between net operating profits after tax for the business and the cost of capital invested (both debt and equity). EVA is a registered trademark of Stern Stewart & Company.

Edge Act and Agreement Corporation. Subsidiary of a U.S. bank incorporated under federal law to engage in various international banking and financing operations, including equity participations that are not allowed to regular domestic banks. The Edge Act subsidiary may be located in a state other than that of the parent bank.

Effective exchange rate. An index measuring the change in value of a foreign currency determined by calculating a weighted average of bilateral exchange rates. The weighting reflects the importance of each foreign country's trade with the home country.

Effective tax rate. Actual taxes paid as a percentage of actual income before tax.

Efficient market. A market in which all relevant information is already reflected in market prices. The term is most frequently applied to foreign exchange markets and securities markets.

EOM. End of month. International trade term.

Equity issuance. The issuance to the public market of shares of ownership in a publicly traded company.

Equity listing. The listing of a company's shares on a public stock exchange.

Equity risk premium. The average annual return of the market expected by investors over and above riskless debt.

Euro. A single new currency unit adopted by the 11 participating members of the European Union's European Monetary System in January 1999, replacing their individual currencies. The euro's use has expanded with EU expansion since 1999, totalling 18 participating countries as of 2014.

Eurobank. A bank, or bank department, that bids for time deposits and makes loans in currencies other than that of the country where the bank is located.

Eurobond. A bond originally offered outside the country in whose currency it is denominated. For example, a dollar-denominated bond originally offered for sale to investors outside the United States.

Eurocommercial paper (ECP). Short-term notes (30, 60, 90, 120, 180, 270, and 360 days) sold in international money markets.

Eurocredit. Bank loans to MNEs, sovereign governments, international institutions, and banks denominated in eurocurrencies and extended by banks in countries other than the country in whose currency the loan is denominated.

Eurocurrency. A currency deposited in a bank located in a country other than the country issuing the currency.

Eurodollar. A U.S. dollar deposited in a bank outside the United States. A eurodollar is a type of eurocurrency.

Euroequity. A new equity issue that is underwritten and distributed in multiple foreign equity markets, sometimes simultaneously with distribution in the domestic market.

Euronote. Short- to medium-term debt instruments sold in the eurocurrency market.

European Central Bank (ECB). Conducts monetary policy of the European Monetary Union. Its goal is to safeguard the stability of the euro and minimize inflation.

European Currency Unit (ECU). A composite currency created by the European Monetary System prior to the euro, which was designed to function as a reserve currency numeraire. The ECU was used as the numeraire for denominating a number of financial instruments and obligations.

European Economic Community (EEC). The European common market originally composed of Austria, Belgium, Denmark, Finland, France, Germany, Greece, Ireland, Italy, Luxembourg, the Netherlands, Portugal, Spain, and the United Kingdom. Officially renamed the European Union (EU) January 1, 1994. It has continued to expand its membership over time.

European Free Trade Association (EFTA). European countries not part of the European Union but having no internal tariffs.

European Monetary System (EMS). A system of exchange rate and monetary system linkages first established in 1979 between fifteen European countries. The EMS laid the groundwork for the eventual creation of the euro. The EMS has continued to expand its membership over time.

European option. An option that can be exercised only on the day on which it expires.

European terms. Foreign exchange quotations for the U.S. dollar, expressed as the number of non-U.S. currency units per U.S. dollar.

European Union (EU). The official name of the former European Economic Community (EEC) as of January 1, 1994.

Eurozone. The countries that officially use the euro as their currency.

Ex dock. Followed by the name of a port of import. International trade term in which seller agrees to pay for the costs (shipping, insurance, customs duties, etc.) of placing the goods on the dock at the named port.

Exchange rate. The price of a unit of one country's currency expressed in terms of the currency of some other country.

Exchange Rate Mechanism (ERM). The means by which members of the EMS formerly maintained their currency exchange rates within an agreed-upon range with respect to the other member currencies.

Exchange rate pass-through. The degree to which the prices of imported and exported goods change as a result of exchange rate changes.

Exercise price. Same as the *strike price*; the agreed upon rate of exchange within an option contract to buy or sell the underlying asset.

Export credit insurance. Provides assurance to the exporter or the exporter's bank that, should the foreign customer default on payment, the insurance company will pay for a major portion of the loss. *See also* Foreign Credit Insurance Association (FCIA).

Export-Import Bank (Eximbank). A U.S. government agency created to finance and otherwise facilitate imports and exports.

Exposed asset. An asset whose value is subject to change as a result of the translation of its value from local currency financial statements to home currency financial statements as a result of financial statement consolidation. The change in value typically results from moving from historical to current exchange rates for translation and remeasurement.

Expropriation. Official government seizure of private property, recognized by international law as the right of any sovereign state provided expropriated owners are given prompt compensation and fair market value in convertible currencies.

Factoring. Specialized firms, known as factors, purchase receivables at a discount on either a non-recourse or recourse basis.

FAF. Fly away free. International trade term.

Fair value. The estimated true market value of an item or asset.

FAQ. Free at quay. International trade term.

FAS (free alongside ship). An international trade term in which the seller's quoted price for goods includes all costs of delivery of the goods alongside a vessel at the port of embarkation.

FASB 8. A regulation of the Financial Accounting Standards Board requiring U.S. companies to translate foreign affiliate financial statements by the temporal method. FASB 8 was in effect from 1975 to 1981. It is still used under specific circumstances.

FASB 52. A regulation of the Financial Accounting Standards Board requiring U.S. companies to translate foreign subsidiary financial statements by the current rate (closing rate) method. FASB 52 became effective in 1981.

FI. Free in. International trade term meaning that all expenses for loading into the hold of a vessel apply to the account of the consignee.

Fiat currency. Money or currency which derives its value from government regulation or proclamation. Unlike commodity money or *specie*, its value is not tied or based on a precious metal or other physical commodity.

Financial account. A section of the balance of payments accounts. Under the revised format of the International Monetary Fund, the financial account measures long-term financial flows including direct foreign investment, portfolio investments, and other long-term movements. Under the traditional definition, which is still used by many countries, items in the financial account were included in the capital account.

Financial derivative. A financial instrument, such as a futures contract or option, whose value is derived from an underlying asset like a stock or currency.

Financial engineering. Those basic building blocks, such as spot positions, forwards, and options, used to construct positions that provide the user with desired risk and return characteristics.

Financing cash flow. Cash flows originating from financing activities of the firm, including interest payments and dividend distributions.

Firm-specific risks. Political risks that affect the MNE at the project or corporate level. Governance risk due to goal conflict between an MNE and its host government is the main political firm-specific risk.

First in, first out (FIFO). An inventory valuation approach in which the cost of the earliest inventory purchases is charged against current sales. The opposite is LIFO, or last in, first out.

Fisher Effect. A theory that nominal interest rates in two or more countries should be equal to the required real rate of return to investors plus compensation for the expected amount of inflation in each country.

Fixed exchange rates. Foreign exchange rates tied to the currency of a major country (such as the United States), to gold, or to a basket of currencies such as Special Drawing Rights.

Flexible exchange rates. The opposite of fixed exchange rates. The foreign exchange rate is adjusted periodically by the country's monetary authorities in accordance with their judgment and/or an external set of economic indicators.

Floating exchange rates. Foreign exchange rates determined by demand and supply in an open market that is presumably free of government interference.

Floating-rate note (FRN). Medium-term securities with interest rates pegged to LIBOR and adjusted quarterly or semiannually.

FOB. Free on board. International trade term in which exporter's quoted price includes the cost of loading goods into transport vessels at a named point.

Follow-on offering (FO). Additional offerings of equity shares post-IPO.

Forced delistings. The requirement by a stock exchange for a publicly traded share on that exchange to be delisted from active trading, typically from failure to maintain a minimum level of market capitalization.

Foreign affiliate. A foreign business unit that is less than 50% owned by the parent company.

Foreign bond. A bond issued by a foreign corporation or government for sale in the domestic capital market of another country, and denominated in the currency of that country.

Foreign Corrupt Practices Act of 1977. A U.S. law that punishes companies and their executives if they pay bribes or make other improper payments to foreigners.

Foreign Credit Insurance Association (FCIA). An unincorporated association of private commercial insurance companies, in cooperation with the Export-Import Bank of the United States, that provides export credit insurance to U.S. firms.

Foreign currency intervention. Any activity or policy initiative by a government or central bank with the intent of changing a currency value on the open market. They may include *direct intervention*, where the central bank may buy or sell its own currency, or *indirect intervention*, in which it may change interest rates in order to change the attractiveness of domestic currency obligations in the eyes of foreign investors.

Foreign currency option. A financial contract or derivative which guarantees the holder the right to buy or sell a specific amount of foreign currency at a specific rate by a stated expiration or maturity date.

Foreign currency translation. The process of restating foreign currency accounts of subsidiaries into the reporting currency of the parent company in order to prepare a consolidated financial statement.

Foreign direct investment (FDI). Purchase of physical assets, such as plant and equipment, in a foreign country, to be managed by the parent corporation. FDI is distinguished from foreign portfolio investment.

Foreign exchange broker. An individual or firm that arranges foreign exchange transactions between two parties, but is not itself a principal in the trade. Foreign exchange brokers earn a commission for their efforts.

Foreign exchange dealer (or trader). An individual or firm that buys foreign exchange from one party (at a bid price), and then sells it (at an ask price) to another party. The dealer is a principal in two transactions and profits via the spread between the bid and ask prices.

Foreign exchange intervention. The active entry into the foreign exchange market by buying and selling a currency by an official authority in order to manage or fix the currency's value relative to other traded currencies.

Foreign exchange rate. The price of one country's currency in terms of another currency, or in terms of a commodity such as gold or silver. Also termed *foreign currency exchange rate*. *See also* Exchange rate.

Foreign exchange risk. The likelihood that an unexpected change in exchange rates will alter the home currency value of foreign currency cash payments expected from a foreign source. Also, the likelihood that an unexpected change in exchange rates will alter the amount of home currency needed to repay a debt denominated in a foreign currency.

Foreign sales corporation (FSC). Under U.S. tax code, a type of foreign corporation that provides tax-exempt or tax-deferred income for U.S. persons or corporations having export-oriented activities.

Foreign tax credit. The amount by which a domestic firm may reduce (credit) domestic income taxes for income tax payments to a foreign government.

Foreign tax neutrality. The principle that tax obligations or tax burdens are the same on taxable earnings, regardless of where the earnings were generated, in domestic or foreign markets.

Forfaiting (forfeiting). A technique for arranging non-recourse medium-term export financing, used most frequently to finance imports into Eastern Europe. A third party, usually a specialized financial institution, guaranteeing the financing.

Forward-ATM. The strike rate or exercise price of a foreign exchange derivative set equivalent to the forward exchange rate.

Forward contract. An agreement to exchange currencies of different countries at a specified future date and at a specified forward rate.

Forward differential. The difference between spot and forward rates, expressed as an annual percentage.

Forward discount. *See* Forward differential.

Forward exchange rate or Forward rate. An exchange rate quoted for settlement at some future date. The rate used in a forward transaction.

Forward premium. *See* Forward differential.

Forward rate agreement (FRA). An interbank-traded contract to buy or sell interest rate payments on a notional principal.

Forward transaction. An agreed-upon foreign exchange transaction to be settled at a specified future date, often one, two, or three months after the transaction date.

Free cash flow. Operating cash flow less capital expenditures (capex).

Free float. The portion of publicly traded shares of a corporation that are held by public investors as opposed to locked-in stock held by promoters (underwriters), company officers, controlling-interest investors, or government.

Free-trade zone. An area within a country into which foreign goods may be brought duty free, often for purposes of additional manufacture, inventory storage, or packaging. Such goods are subject to duty only when they leave the duty-free zone to enter other parts of the country.

Freely floating exchange rates. Exchange rates determined in a free market without government interference, in contrast to dirty float.

Fronting loan. A parent-to-subsidiary loan that is channeled through a financial intermediary such as a large international bank in order to reduce political risk. Presumably government authorities are less likely to prevent a foreign subsidiary repaying an established bank than repaying the subsidiary's corporate parent.

Functional currency. In the context of translating financial statements, the currency of the primary economic environment in which a foreign subsidiary operates and in which it generates cash flows.

Futures, or futures contracts. Exchange-traded agreements calling for future delivery of a standard amount of any good, e.g., foreign exchange, at a fixed time, place, and price.

Gamma. A measure of the sensitivity of an option's delta ratio to small unit changes in the price of the underlying security.

Gap risk. A type of interest rate risk in which the timing of maturities is mismatched.

General Agreement on Tariffs and Trade (GATT). A framework of rules for nations to manage their trade policies, negotiate lower international tariff barriers, and settle trade disputes.

Generally Accepted Accounting Principles (GAAP). Approved accounting principles for U.S. firms, defined by the Financial Accounting Standards Board (FASB).

Global depositary receipt (GDR). Similar to American Depositary Receipts (ADRs), it is a bank certificate issued in multiple countries for shares in a foreign company. Actual company shares are held by a foreign branch of an international bank. The shares are traded as domestic shares, but are offered for sale globally by sponsoring banks.

Global registered shares (GRS). Similar to ordinary shares, global registered shares have the added benefit of being tradable on equity exchanges around the globe in a variety of currencies.

Global reserve currency. *See* Reserve currency.

Global-specific risks. Political risks that originate at the global level, such as terrorism, the antiglobalization movement, environmental concerns, poverty, and cyber attacks.

Gold standard or Gold-exchange standard. A monetary system in which currencies are defined in terms of their gold content, and payment imbalances between countries are settled in gold.

Greenfield investment. An initial investment in a new foreign subsidiary with no predecessor operation in that location. This is in contrast to a new subsidiary created by the purchase of an already existing operation. An investment which starts, conceptually if not literally, with an undeveloped "green field."

Gross up. *See* Deemed-paid tax.

Haircut. The percentage of the market value of a financial asset recognized as the collateral value or redeemed value of the asset.

Hard currency. A freely convertible currency that is not expected to depreciate in value in the foreseeable future.

Hedge accounting. An accounting procedure that specifies that gains and losses on hedging instruments be recognized in earnings at the same time that the effects of changes in the value of the items being hedged are recognized.

Hedging. Purchasing a contract (including forward foreign exchange) or tangible good that will rise in value and offset a drop in value of another contract or tangible good. Hedges are undertaken to reduce risk by protecting an owner from loss.

Historical exchange rate. In accounting, the exchange rate in effect when an asset or liability was acquired.

Holder. The owner of.

Home currency. The currency of a company's incorporation; the currency for financial reporting purposes.

Hot money. Money that moves internationally from one currency and/or country to another in response to interest rate differences, and moves away immediately when the interest advantage disappears.

Hurdle rate. The required rate of return by a firm on a potential new investment in order to approve accepting the investment. The rate is typically based on the company's current cost of capital, including debt and equity. In some cases the firm will require some premium or additional margin on certain investments above and beyond its cost of capital in the calculation of the hurdle rate (e.g., cost of capital + premium = hurdle rate).

Hybrid foreign currency options. Purchase of a put option and the simultaneous sale of a call (or vice versa) so that the overall cost is less than the cost of a straight option.

Hyperinflation countries. Countries with a very high rate of inflation. Under United States FASB 52, these are defined as countries where the cumulative three-year inflation amounts to 100% or more.

IMM. *See* International Monetary Market.

Impossible trinity. An ideal currency would have exchange rate stability, full financial integration, and monetary independence.

In-house bank. An internal bank established within an MNE if its needs are either too large or too sophisticated for local banks. The in-house bank is not a separate corporation but performs a set of functions by the existing treasury department. Acting as an independent entity, the in-house bank transacts with various internal business units of the firm on an arm's length basis.

In-the-money (ITM). Circumstance in which an option is profitable, excluding the cost of the premium, if exercised immediately.

Indication. A quotation, typically in the form of a bid rate and ask rate, for a currency or other financial asset.

Indirect intervention. Actions taken by central banks or other monetary authorities to influence the supply and demand for a country's own currency. The most common form of indirect intervention is the alteration of interest rates.

Indirect quote. The price of a unit of a home country's currency expressed in terms of a foreign country's currency.

Initial public offering (IPO). The initial sale of shares of ownership of a company to the general public. The issuing firm raises capital for the conduct of its business and return to its original owners through the IPO.

Integrated foreign entity. An entity that operates as an extension of the parent company, with cash flows and general business lines that are highly interrelated with those of the parent.

Intellectual property rights. Legislation that grants the exclusive use of patented technology and copyrighted creative materials. A worldwide treaty to protect intellectual property rights has been ratified by most major countries, including most recently by China.

Interest rate futures. *See* Futures, or futures contracts.

Interest rate parity (IRP). A theory that the differences in national interest rates for securities of similar risk and maturity should be equal to but opposite in sign (positive or negative) to the forward exchange rate discount or premium for the foreign currency.

Interest rate risk. The risk to the organization arising from interest-bearing debt obligations, either fixed or floating rate obligations. It is typically used to refer to the changing interest rates which a company may incur by borrowing at floating rates of interest.

Interest rate swap. A transaction in which two counterparties exchange interest payment streams of different character (such as floating vs. fixed), based on an underlying notional principal amount.

Internal bank. The use of an internal unit of the corporation to act as a bank for exchanges of capital, currencies, or obligations between various units of the company.

Internal rate of return (IRR). A capital budgeting approach in which a discount rate is found that matches the present value of expected future cash inflows with the present value of outflows.

Internalization. A theory that the key ingredient for maintaining a firm-specific competitive advantage in international competition is the possession of proprietary information and control of human capital that can generate new information through expertise in research, management, marketing, or technology.

International Bank for Reconstruction and Development (IBRD or World Bank). International development bank owned by member nations that makes development loans to member countries.

International Banking Facility (IBF). A department within a U.S. bank that may accept foreign deposits and make loans to foreign borrowers as if it were a foreign subsidiary. IBFs are free of U.S. reserve requirements, deposit insurance, and interest rate regulations.

International CAPM (ICAPM). A strategy in which the primary distinction in the estimation of the cost of equity for an individual firm using an internationalized version of the domestic capital asset pricing model is the definition of the "market" and a recalculation of the firm's beta for that market.

International Fisher effect. A theory that the spot exchange rate should change by an amount equal to the difference in interest rates between two countries.

International Monetary Fund (IMF). An international organization created in 1944 to promote exchange rate stability and provide temporary financing for countries experiencing balance of payments difficulties.

International Monetary Market (IMM). A branch of the Chicago Mercantile Exchange that specializes in trading currency and financial futures contracts.

International monetary system. The structure within which foreign exchange rates are determined, international trade and capital flows are accommodated, and balance of payments adjustments made.

International Swaps and Derivatives Association (ISDA). A New York City trade association for over the country (OTC) derivatives. The ISDA maintains the documentation used in most of the financial services trading of financial derivatives used globally.

Intrafirm trade. Trade in goods and services between incorporated units of the same multinational business or enterprise.

Intrinsic value. The financial gain if an option is exercised immediately.

Investment agreement. An agreement that spells out specific rights and responsibilities of both the investing foreign firm and the host government.

Investment grade. A credit rating, typically assigned by Moody's, Standard & Poors, or Fitch, symbolizing the assured ability of a borrower to repay in a timely manner regardless of business or market conditions. Denoted as BBB- (or equivalent by credit rating agency) or higher.

Islamic finance. Banking or financing activity that is consistent with the principles of *sharia* and Islamic economics.

J-curve. The adjustment path of a country's trade balance following a devaluation or significant depreciation of the country's currency. The path first worsens as a result of existing contracts before improving as a result of more competitive pricing conditions.

Joint venture (JV). A business venture that is owned by two or more entities, often from different countries.

Jumbo loans. Loans of $1 billion or more.

Kangaroo bonds. Australian dollar-denominated bonds issued within Australia by a foreign borrower.

Lag. In the context of leads and lags, payment of a financial obligation later than is expected or required.

Lambda. A measure of the sensitivity of an option premium to a unit change in volatility.

Last in, first out (LIFO). An inventory valuation approach in which the cost of the latest inventory purchases is charged against current sales. The opposite is FIFO, or first in, first out.

Law of one price. The concept that if an identical product or service can be sold in two different markets, and no restrictions exist on the sale or transportation costs of moving the product between markets, the product's price should be the same in both markets.

Lead. In the context of *leads and lags*, the payment of a financial obligation earlier than is expected or required.

Legal tender. A medium of payment allowed by law or recognized by a legal system to be valid for meeting a financial obligation.

Lender-of-last-resort. The body or institution within an economy which is ultimately capable of preserving the financial survival or viability of individual institutions. Typically the country's central bank.

Letter of credit (L/C). An instrument issued by a bank, in which the bank promises to pay a beneficiary upon presentation of documents specified in the letter.

Link financing. *See* Back-to-back loan or Fronting loan.

Liquid. The ability to exchange an asset for cash at or near its fair market value.

Location-specific advantage. Market imperfections or genuine comparative advantages that attract foreign direct investment to particular locations.

London Interbank Offered Rate (LIBOR). The deposit rate applicable to interbank loans in London. LIBOR is used as the reference rate for many international interest rate transactions.

Long position. A position in which foreign currency assets exceed foreign currency liabilities. The opposite of a long position is a short position.

Maastricht Treaty. A treaty among the 12 European Union countries that specified a plan and timetable for the introduction of a single European currency, to be called the euro.

Macro risk. *See* Country-specific risk.

Macroeconomic uncertainty. Operating exposure's sensitivity to key macroeconomic variables, such as exchange rates, interest rates, and inflation rates.

Managed float. A country allows its currency to trade within a given band of exchange rates.

Margin. A deposit made as security for a financial transaction otherwise financed on credit.

Mark-to-market. The condition in which the value of a futures contract is assigned to market value daily, and all changes in value are paid in cash daily. The value of the contract is revalued using the closing price for the day. The amount to be paid is called the variation margin.

Market capitalization. The total market value of a publicly traded company, calculated as the total number of shares outstanding multiplied by the market-determined price per share.

Market liquidity. The degree to which a firm can issue a new security without depressing the existing market price, as well as the degree to which a change in price of its securities elicits a substantial order flow.

Market segmentation. The divergence within a national market of required rates of return. If all capital markets are fully integrated, securities of comparable expected return and risk should have the same required rate of return in each national market after adjusting for foreign exchange risk and political risk.

Matching currency cash flows. The strategy of offsetting anticipated continuous long exposure to a particular currency by acquiring debt denominated in that currency.

Merchant bank. A bank that specializes in helping corporations and governments finance by any of a variety of market and/or traditional techniques. European merchant banks are sometimes differentiated from clearing banks, which tend to focus on bank deposits and clearing balances for the majority of the population.

Micro risk. *See* Firm-specific risk.

Monetary assets or liabilities. Assets in the form of cash or claims to cash (such as accounts receivable), or liabilities payable in cash. Monetary assets minus monetary liabilities are called net monetary assets.

Monetary/nonmonetary method. A method of translating the financial statements of foreign subsidiaries into the parent's reporting currency. All monetary accounts are translated at the current rate, and all nonmonetary accounts are translated at their historical rates. Sometimes called temporal method in the United States.

Money laundering. The process of depositing or inserting illegally generated money or cash into the financial system.

Money market hedge. The use of foreign currency borrowing to reduce transaction or accounting foreign exchange exposure.

Money markets. The financial markets in various countries in which various types of short-term debt instruments, including bank loans, are purchased and sold.

Moral hazard. When an individual or organization takes on more risk than it would normally as a result of the existence or support of a secondary insuring or protecting authority or organization.

Mortgage Backed Security (MBS or MBO). A derivative security composed of residential or commercial real estate mortgages.

Most-favored-nation (MFN) treatment. The application by a country of import duties on the same, or most favored, basis to all countries accorded such treatment. Any tariff reduction granted in a bilateral negotiation will be extended to all other nations granted most-favored-nation status.

Multilateral netting. The process of netting intracompany payments in order to reduce the size and frequency of cash and currency exchanges.

Multinational enterprise (MNE). A firm that has operating subsidiaries, branches, or affiliates located in foreign countries.

Natural hedge. The use or existence of an offsetting or matching cash flow from firm operating activities to hedge a currency exposure.

Negotiable instrument. A written draft or promissory note, signed by the maker or drawer, that contains an unconditional promise or order to pay a definite sum of money on demand or at a determinable future date, and is payable to order or to bearer. A holder of a negotiable instrument is entitled to payment despite any personal disagreements between the drawee and maker.

Nepotism. The practice of showing favor to relatives over other qualified persons in conferring such benefits as the awarding of contracts, granting of special prices, promotions to various ranks, etc.

Net international investment position (NIIP). The net difference between a country's external financial assets and liabilities as defined by nationality of ownership. A country's external debt includes both its government debt and private debt, and similarly its public and privately held legal residents.

Net present value. A capital budgeting approach in which the present value of expected future cash inflows is subtracted from the present value of outflows.

Net working capital (NWC). Accounts receivable plus inventories less accounts payable.

Netting. The mutual offsetting of sums due between two or more business entities.

Nominal exchange rate. The actual foreign exchange quotation, in contrast to *real exchange rate*, which is adjusted for changes in purchasing power.

Nondeliverable forward (NDF). A forward or futures contract on currencies, settled on the basis of the differential between the contracted forward rate and occurring spot rate, but settled in the currency of the traders. For example, a forward contract on the Chinese yuan that is settled in dollars, not yuan.

Nontariff barrier. Trade restrictive practices other than custom tariffs, such as import quotas, voluntary restrictions, variable levies, and special health regulations.

North American Free Trade Agreement (NAFTA). A treaty allowing free trade and investment between Canada, the United States, and Mexico.

Note issuance facility (nif). An agreement by which a syndicate of banks indicates a willingness to accept short-term notes from borrowers and resell those notes in the eurocurrency markets. The discount rate is often tied to LIBOR.

Notional principal. The size of a derivative contract, in total currency value, as used in futures contracts, forward contracts, option contracts, or swap agreements.

NPV. *See* Net present value.

NSF. Not-sufficient funds. Term used by a bank when a draft or check is drawn on an account not having a sufficient credit balance.

O/A. Open account. Arrangement in which the importer (or other buyer) pays for the goods only after the goods are received and inspected. The importer is billed directly after shipment, and payment is not tied to any promissory notes or similar documents.

Offer. The price at which a trader is willing to sell foreign exchange, securities, or commodities. Also called ask.

Official reserves account. Total reserves held by official monetary authorities within the country, such as gold, SDRs, and major currencies.

Offshore finance subsidiary. A foreign financial subsidiary owned by a corporation in another country. Offshore finance subsidiaries are usually located in tax-free or low-tax jurisdictions to enable the parent multinational firm to finance international operations without being subject to home country taxes or regulations.

OLI paradigm. An attempt to create an overall framework to explain why MNEs choose foreign direct investment rather than serve foreign markets through alternative modes such as licensing, joint ventures, strategic alliances, management contracts, and exporting.

On the run. International banks of the highest credit quality that are willing to exchange obligations, on the interbank market, on a no-name basis.

Open account. A sale where goods are shipped and delivered before payment is due or made. Payment is typically made anywhere between 30 and 90 days later, depending on industry and national practices.

Operating cash flows. The primary cash flows generated by a business from the conduct of trade, typically composed of earnings, depreciation and amortization, and changes in net working capital.

Operating exposure. The potential for a change in expected cash flows, and thus in value, of a foreign subsidiary as a result of an unexpected change in exchange rates. Also called economic exposure.

Option. A financial derivative contract providing rights to exchange but not obligations. In foreign exchange, a contract giving the purchaser the right, but not the obligation, to buy or sell a given amount of foreign exchange at a fixed price per unit for a specified time period. Options to buy are calls and options to sell are puts.

Order bill of lading. A shipping document through which possession and title to the shipment reside with the owner of the bill.

Organization of Petroleum Exporting Countries (OPEC). An alliance of most major crude oil producing countries, formed for the purpose of allocating and controlling production quotas so as to influence the price of crude oil in world markets.

Originate-to-Distribute (OTD). A common practice in the U.S. real estate market during the 2001–2007 real estate boom in which a real estate lender, or originator, makes loans expressly for the purpose of immediate resale.

Out-of-the-money (OTM). An option that would not be profitable, excluding the cost of the premium, if exercised immediately.

Outright forward. *See* Forward rate.

Outright forward transaction. *See* Forward transaction.

Outright quotation. The full price, in one currency, of a unit of another currency. *See* Points quotation.

Outsourcing. *See* Supply chain management.

Overseas Private Investment Corporation (OPIC). A U.S. government-owned insurance company that insures U.S. corporations against various political risks.

Overshooting. A behavior in financial markets in which a major market adjustment in price changes "overshoots" or surpasses the likely value it will settle at after a longer adjustment period. A market movement akin to an "overreaction."

Over-the-counter (OTC) market. A market for share of stock, options (including foreign currency options), or other financial contracts conducted via electronic connections between dealers. The over-the-counter market has no physical location or address, and is thus differentiated from organized exchanges that have a physical location where trading takes place.

Overvalued currency. A currency with a current foreign exchange value (i.e., current price in the foreign exchange market) greater than the worth of that currency. Because "worth" is a subjective concept, overvaluation is a matter of opinion. If the euro has a current market value of $1.20 (i.e., the current exchange rate is $1.20/€) at a time when its "true" value as derived from purchasing power parity or some other method is deemed to be $1.10, the euro is overvalued. The opposite of overvalued is undervalued.

Owner-specific advantage. A firm must have competitive advantages in its home market. These must be firm-specific, not easily copied, and in a form that allows them to be transferred to foreign subsidiaries.

Panda Bond. The issuance of a yuan-denominated bond in the Chinese market by a foreign borrower.

Parallel loan. Another name for a back-to-back loan, in which two companies in separate countries borrow each other's currency for a specific period of time, and repay the other's currency at an agreed maturity.

Parallel market. An unofficial foreign exchange market tolerated by a government but not officially sanctioned. The exact boundary between a parallel market and a black market is not very clear, but official tolerance of what would otherwise be a black market leads to use of the term parallel market.

Parity conditions. In the context of international finance, a set of basic economic relationships that provide for equilibrium between spot and forward foreign exchange rates, interest rates, and inflation rates.

Participating forward. A complex option position which combines a bought put and a sold call option at the same strike price to create a net zero position. Also called zero-cost option and forward participation agreement.

Pass-through or Pass-through period. The time it takes for an exchange rate change to be reflected in market prices of products or services.

Phi. The expected change in an option premium caused by a small change in the foreign interest rate (interest rate for the foreign currency).

Plain vanilla swap. An interest rate swap agreement exchange fixed interest payments for floating interest payments, all in the same currency.

Points. The smallest units of price change quoted, given a conventional number of digits in which a quotation is stated.

Points quotation. A forward quotation expressed only as the number of decimal points (usually four decimal points) by which it differs from the spot quotation.

Political risk. The possibility that political events in a particular country will influence the economic well-being of firms in that country. *See also* Sovereign risk.

Portfolio investment. Purchase of foreign stocks and bonds, in contrast to foreign direct investment.

Possessions corporation. A U.S. corporation, the subsidiary of another U.S. corporation located in a U.S. possession such as Puerto Rico, that for tax purposes is treated as if it were a foreign corporation.

Premium. In a foreign exchange market, the amount by which a currency is more expensive for future delivery than for spot (immediate) delivery. The opposite of premium is discount.

Price elasticity of demand. From economic theory, the percentage change in the quantity demanded as a result of a one percent change in the product price.

Principal agent problem. *See* Agency problem.

Private equity. Assets that are composed of equity shares in companies that are not publicly traded.

Private placement. The sale of a security issue to a small set of qualified institutional buyers.

Profit warning. The public announcement by a publicly traded company that current period earnings will fall significantly either from a previously reported period or investor expectations.

Project financing. Arrangement of financing for long-term capital projects, large in scale, long in life, and generally high in risk.

Prospectus. A document disclosing the prospective risks and returns associated with the proposed public sale of a security. The prospectus commonly includes material information such as a description of the company's business, financial statements, biographies of officers and directors, detailed information about their

compensation, any litigation that is pending, a list of material properties and any other material information.

Protectionism. A political attitude or policy intended to inhibit or prohibit the import of foreign goods and services. The opposite of free trade policies.

Psychic distance. Firms tend to invest first in countries with a similar cultural, legal, and institutional environment.

Public debt. The debt obligation of a governmental body or sovereign authority.

Purchasing power parity (PPP). A theory that the price of internationally traded commodities should be the same in every country, and hence the exchange rate between the two currencies should be the ratio of prices in the two countries.

Put. An option to sell foreign exchange or financial contracts. *See* Option.

Qualified institutional buyer (QIB). An entity (except a bank or a savings and loan) that owns and invests on a discretionary basis a minimum of $100 million in securities of non-affiliates.

Quota. A limit, mandatory or voluntary, set on the import of a product.

Quotation. In foreign exchange trading, the pair of prices (bid and ask) at which a dealer is willing to buy or sell foreign exchange.

Range forward. A complex option position that combines the purchase of a put option and the sale of a call option with strike prices equidistant from the forward rate. Also called *flexible forward, cylinder option, option fence, mini-max,* and *zero-cost tunnel.*

Real exchange rate. An index of foreign exchange adjusted for relative price-level changes from a base point in time, typically a month or a year. Sometimes referred to as real effective exchange rate, it is used to measure purchasing-power-adjusted changes in exchange rates.

Real option analysis. The application of option theory to capital budgeting decisions.

Reference rate. The rate of interest used in a standardized quotation, loan agreement, or financial derivative valuation.

Registered bond. Corporate or governmental debt in a bond form in which the owner's name appears on the bond and in the issuer's records, and interest payments are made to the owner.

Reinvoicing center. A central financial subsidiary used by a multinational firm to reduce transaction exposure by having all home country exports billed in the home currency and then reinvoiced to each operating subsidiary in that subsidiary's local currency.

Relative price of bonds approach. *See* Portfolio approach.

Relative purchasing power parity. A theory that if the spot exchange rate between two countries starts in equilibrium, any change in the differential rate of inflation between them tends to be offset over the long run by an equal but opposite change in the spot exchange rate.

Renminbi (RMB). The alternative official name (the yuan, CNY) of the currency of the People's Republic of China.

Reporting currency. In the context of translating financial statements, the currency in which a parent firm prepares its own financial statements. Usually this is the parent's home currency.

Repositioning of funds. The movement of funds from one currency or country to another. An MNE faces a variety of political, tax, foreign exchange, and liquidity constraints that limit its ability to move funds easily and without cost.

Representative office. A representative office established by a bank in a foreign country to help clients doing business in that country. It also functions as a geographically convenient location from which to visit correspondent banks in its region rather than sending bankers from the parent bank at greater financial and physical cost.

Repricing risk. The risk of changes in interest rates charged or earned at the time a financial contract's rate is reset.

Reserve currency. A currency used by a government or central banking authority as a resource asset or currency to be used in market interventions to alter the market value of the domestic currency.

Residential approach. The levy of taxes against the worldwide income earned by a business by home country tax authorities regardless of where or in which country the income was earned.

Restricted stock. Stock shares given to management that are not tradable or transferable before a specified future date (when they vest) or other specified conditions.

Revaluation. A rise in the foreign exchange value of a currency that is pegged to other currencies or to gold. Also called appreciation.

Rho. The expected change in an option premium caused by a small change in the domestic interest rate (interest rate for the home currency).

Risk. The likelihood that an actual outcome will differ from an expected outcome. The actual outcome could be better or worse than expected (two-sided risk), although in common practice risk is more often used only in the context of an adverse outcome (one-sided risk). Risk can exist for any number of uncertain future situations, including future spot rates or the results of political events.

Rules of the Game. The basis of exchange rate determination under the international gold standard during most of the 19th and early 20th centuries. All countries agreed informally to follow the rule of buying and selling their currency at a fixed and predetermined price against gold.

Risk-sharing. A contractual arrangement in which the buyer and seller agree to share or split currency movement impacts on payments between them.

Roll-over risk. The risk of refinancing debt (renewing), such as the re-issue of a short term debt obligation like commercial paper.

Samurai bond. Yen-denominated bond issued within Japan by a foreign borrower.

Sarbanes-Oxley Act. An act passed in 2002 to regulate corporate governance in the United States.

SEC Rule 144A. Permits qualified institutional buyers to trade privately placed securities without requiring SEC registration.

SEC Rule 415. Security and Exchange Commission rules which allows shelf registration of security offerings to the public without a separate prospectus for each act of offering. A single prospectus is used for multiple future offerings.

Section 482. The set of U.S. Treasury regulations governing transfer prices.

Securitization. The replacement of nonmarketable loans (such as direct bank loans) with negotiable securities (such as publicly traded marketable notes and bonds), so that the risk can be spread widely among many investors, each of whom can add or subtract the amount of risk carried by buying or selling the marketable security.

Seignorage. The net revenues or proceeds garnered by a government from the printing of its money.

Self-sustaining foreign entity. One that operates in the local economic environment independent of the parent company.

Selling short (shorting). The sale of an asset which the seller does not (yet) own. The premise is that the seller believes he will be able to purchase the asset for contract fulfillment at a lower price before sale contract expiration.

Shared services. A charge to compensate the parent for costs incurred in the general management of international operations and for other corporate services provided to foreign subsidiaries that must be recovered by the parent firm.

Shareholder wealth maximization (SWM). The corporate goal of maximizing the total value of the shareholders' investment in the company.

Sharpe measure (SHP). Calculates the average return over and above the risk-free rate of return per unit of portfolio risk. It uses the standard deviation of a portfolio's total return as the measure of risk.

Shelf registrations. *See* SEC Rule 415.

Shogun bonds. Foreign currency-denominated bonds issued within Japan by Japanese corporations.

Short position. *See* Long position.

SIBOR. Singapore interbank offered rate.

Sight draft. A bill of exchange (B/E) that is due on demand; i.e., when presented to the bank. *See also* Bill of exchange.

SIMEX. Singapore International Monetary Exchange.

Society for Worldwide Interbank Financial Telecommunications (SWIFT). A dedicated computer network providing funds transfer messages between member banks around the world.

Soft currency. A currency expected to drop in value relative to other currencies. Free trading in a currency deemed soft is often restricted by the monetary authorities of the issuing country.

Sovereign debt. The debt obligation or a sovereign or governmental authority or body.

Sovereign risk. The risk that a host government may unilaterally repudiate its foreign obligations or may prevent local firms from honoring their foreign obligations. Sovereign risk is often regarded as a subset of political risk.

Sovereign spread. The credit spread paid by a sovereign borrower on a major foreign currency denominated debt obligation. For example, the credit spread paid by the Venezuelan government to borrow U.S. dollars over and above a similar maturity issuance by the U.S. Treasury.

Special Drawing Right (SDR). An international reserve asset, defined by the International Monetary Fund as the value of a weighted basket of five currencies.

Special-purpose vehicle (SPV) or special-purpose entity (SPE). An off-balance sheet legal entity, typically a partnership, set up for a very special business purpose that will isolate or limit the partner's financial risks associated with risks associated with the SPV's activities or assets. Similar in function to an SIV.

Speculation. An attempt to make a profit by trading on expectations about future prices.

Speculative grade. A credit quality that is below BBB, below investment grade. The designation implies a possibility of borrower default in the event of unfavorable economic or business conditions.

Spot rate. The price at which foreign exchange can be purchased (its bid) or sold (its ask) in a spot transaction. *See* Spot transaction.

Spot transaction. A foreign exchange transaction to be settled (paid for) on the second following business day.

Spread. The difference between the bid (buying) quote and the ask (selling) quote.

Stakeholder capitalism model (SCM). Another name for corporate wealth maximization.

State-owned enterprise (SOE). Any organization or business which is owned (in-whole or in-part) and controlled by government, typically created to conduct commercial business activities.

Statutory tax rate. The legally imposed tax rate.

Strategic alliance. A formal relationship, short of a merger or acquisition, between two companies, formed for the purpose of gaining synergies because in some aspect the two companies complement each other.

Strike price. The agreed upon rate of exchange within an option contract.

Stripped bonds. Bonds issued by investment bankers against coupons or the maturity (corpus) portion of original bearer bonds, where the original bonds are held in trust by the investment banker. Whereas the original bonds will have coupons promising interest at each interest date (say June and December for each of the next twenty years), a given stripped bond will represent a claim against all interest payments from the entire original issue due on a particular interest date. A stripped bond is in effect a zero coupon bond manufactured by the investment banker.

Subpart F. A type of foreign income, as defined in the U.S. tax code, which under certain conditions is taxed immediately in the United States even though it has not been repatriated to the United States. It is income of a type that is otherwise easily shifted offshore to avoid current taxation.

Subprime (subprime mortgage). Subprime borrowers have a higher perceived risk of default, normally as a result of credit history elements which may include bankruptcy, loan delinquency, default, or simply a borrower with limited experience or history of debt. They are nearly exclusively floating-rate structures, and carry significantly higher interest rate spreads over the floating bases like LIBOR.

Subsidiary. A foreign operation incorporated in the host country and owned 50% or more by a parent corporation. Foreign operations that are not incorporated are called branches.

Supply chain management. A strategy that focuses on cost reduction through imports from less costly foreign locations with lower wages.

Sushi bonds. Eurodollar or other non-yen-denominated bonds issued by a Japanese corporation for sale to Japanese investors.

Swap. This term is used in many contexts. In general it is the simultaneous purchase and sale of foreign exchange or securities, with the purchase executed at once and the sale back to the same party carried out at an agreed-upon price to be completed at a specified future date. Swaps include interest rate swaps, currency swaps, and credit swaps.

Swap rate. A forward foreign exchange quotation expressed in terms of the number of points by which the forward rate differs from the spot rate.

SWIFT. *See* Society for Worldwide Interbank Financial Telecommunications.

Syndicated loan. A large loan made by a group of banks to a large multinational firm or government. Syndicated loans allow the participating banks to maintain diversification by not lending too much to a single borrower.

Synthetic forward. A complex option position which combines the purchase of a put option and the sale of a call option, or vice versa, both at the forward rate. Theoretically, the combined position should have a net-zero premium.

Systematic risk. In portfolio theory, the risk of the market itself, i.e., risk that cannot be diversified away.

T/A. Trade acceptance. International trade term.

Tariff. A duty or tax on imports that can be levied as a percentage of cost or as a specific amount per unit of import.

Tax deferral. Foreign subsidiaries of MNEs pay host country corporate income taxes, but many parent countries, including the United States, defer claiming additional taxes on that foreign source income until it is remitted to the parent firm.

Tax exposure. The potential for tax liability on a given income stream or on the value of an asset. Usually used in the context of a multinational firm being able to minimize its tax liabilities by locating some portion of operations in a country where the tax liability is minimized.

Tax haven. A country with either no or very low tax rates that uses its tax structure to attract foreign investment or international financial dealings.

Tax morality. The consideration of conduct by an MNE to decide whether to follow a practice of full disclosure to local tax authorities or adopt the philosophy, "When in Rome, do as the Romans do."

Tax neutrality. In domestic tax, the requirement that the burden of taxation on earnings in home country operations by an MNE be equal to the burden of taxation on each currency equivalent of profit earned by the same firm in its foreign operations. Foreign tax neutrality requires that the tax burden on each foreign subsidiary of the firm be equal to the tax burden on its competitors in the same country.

Tax on undistributed profits. A different income tax applied to retained earnings from that applied to distributed earnings (dividends).

Tax treaties. A network of bilateral treaties that provide a means of reducing double taxation.

Technical analysis. The focus on price and volume data to determine past trends that are expected to continue into the future. Analysts believe that future exchange rates are based on the current exchange rate.

TED Spread. Treasury Eurodollar Spread. The difference, in basis points, between the 3-month interest rate swap index or the 3-month LIBOR interest rate, and the 90-day U.S. Treasury bill rate. It is sometimes used as an indicator of credit crisis or fear over bank credit quality.

Temporal method. In the United States, term for a codification of a translation method essentially similar to the monetary/nonmonetary method.

Tender. To offer for sale or purchase.

Tenor. The length of time of a contract or debt obligation; loan repayment period.

Tequila effect. Term used to describe how the Mexican peso crisis of December 1994 quickly spread to other Latin American currency and equity markets through the contagion effect.

Terminal value (TV). The continuing value of a project or investment beyond the period shown in detail. It represents the present value at a future point in time of all future cash flows assuming a stable perpetual growth rate.

Terms of trade. The weighted average exchange ratio between a nation's export prices and its import prices, used to measure gains from trade. Gains from trade refers to increases in total consumption resulting from production specialization and international trade.

Territorial approach (territorial taxation). Taxation of income earned by firms within the legal jurisdiction of the host country, not on the country of the firm's incorporation.

Theta. The expected change in an option premium caused by a small change in the time to expiration.

Time draft. A draft that allows a delay in payment. It is presented to the drawee, who accepts it by writing a notice of acceptance on its face. Once accepted, the time draft becomes a promise to pay by the accepting party. *See also* Bankers' acceptance.

Total Shareholder Return (TSR). A measure of corporate performance based on the sum of share price appreciation and current dividends.

Tranche. An allocation of shares, typically to underwriters that are expected to sell to investors in their designated geographic markets.

Transaction exposure. The potential for a change in the value of outstanding financial obligations entered into prior to a change in exchange rates but not due to be settled until after the exchange rates change.

Transfer pricing. The setting of prices to be charged by one unit (such as a foreign subsidiary) of a multi-unit corporation to another unit (such as the parent corporation) for goods or services sold between such related units.

Translation exposure. The potential for an accounting-derived change in owners' equity resulting from exchange rate changes and the need to restate financial statements of foreign subsidiaries in the single currency of the parent corporation. *See also* Accounting exposure.

Transnational firm. A company owned by a coalition of investors located in different countries.

Transparency. The degree to which an investor can discern the true activities and value drivers of a company from the disclosures and financial results reported.

Treynor measure (TRN). A calculation of the average return over and above the risk-free rate of return per unit of portfolio risk. It uses the portfolio's beta as the measure of risk.

Triangular arbitrage. An arbitrage activity of exchanging currency A for currency B for currency C back to currency A to exploit slight disequilibrium in exchange rates.

Triffin Dilemma (or Triffin Paradox). The potential conflict in objectives which may arise between domestic monetary policy and currency policy when a country's currency is used as a reserve currency.

Trilemma of international finance. The difficult but required choice which a government must make between three conflicting international financial system goals: 1) a fixed exchange rate; 2) independent monetary policy; and 3) free mobility of capital.

Turnover tax. A tax based on turnover or sales, and is similar in structure to a VAT, in which taxes may be assessed on intermediate stages of a good's production.

Unaffiliated. An independent third-party.

Unbiased predictor. A theory that spot prices at some future date will be equal to today's forward rates.

Unbundling. Dividing cash flows from a subsidiary to a parent into their many separate components, such as royalties, lease payments, dividends, etc., so as to increase the likelihood that some fund flows will be allowed during economically difficult times.

Uncovered interest arbitrage (UIA). The process by which investors borrow in countries and currencies exhibiting relatively low interest rates and convert the proceeds into currencies that offer much higher interest rates. The transaction is "uncovered" because the investor does not sell the higher yielding currency proceeds forward.

Undervalued currency. The status of currency with a current foreign exchange value (i.e., current price in the foreign exchange market) below the worth of that currency. Because "worth" is a subjective concept, undervaluation is a matter of opinion. If the euro has a current market value of $1.20 (i.e., the current exchange rate is $1.20/€) at a time when its "true" value as derived from purchasing power parity or some other method is deemed to be $1.30, the euro is undervalued. The opposite of undervalued is overvalued.

Unsystematic risk. In a portfolio, the amount of risk that can be eliminated by diversification.

Value date. The date when value is given (i.e., funds are deposited) for foreign exchange transactions between banks.

Value-added tax. A type of national sales tax collected at each stage of production or sale of consumption goods, and levied in proportion to the value added during that stage.

Value today. A spot foreign exchange transaction in which delivery and payment are made on the same day as the contract. Normal delivery is two business days after the contract.

Value tomorrow. A spot foreign exchange transaction in which delivery and payment are made on the next business day after the contract. Normal delivery is two business days after the contract.

Volatility. In connection with options, the standard deviation of daily spot price movement.

Weighted average cost of capital (WACC). The sum of the proportionally weighted costs of different sources of capital, used as the minimum acceptable target return on new investments.

Wire transfer. Electronic transfer of funds.

Working capital management. The management of the net working capital requirements (A/R plus inventories less A/P) of the firm.

World Bank. *See* International Bank for Reconstruction and Development.

Worldwide approach (to taxes). The principle that taxes are levied on the income earned by firms that are incorporated in a host country, regardless of where the income was earned.

Writer. Seller.

Yankee bond. Dollar-denominated bond issued within the United States by a foreign borrower.

Yield to maturity. The rate of interest (discount) that equates future cash flows of a bond, both interest and principal, with the present market price. Yield to maturity is thus the time-adjusted rate of return earned by a bond investor.

Yuan (CNY). The official currency of the People's Republic of China, also termed the renminbi.

Zero coupon bond. A bond that pays no periodic interest, but returns a given amount of principal at a stated maturity date. Zero coupon bonds are sold at a discount from the maturity amount to provide the holder a compound rate of return for the holding period.

Index

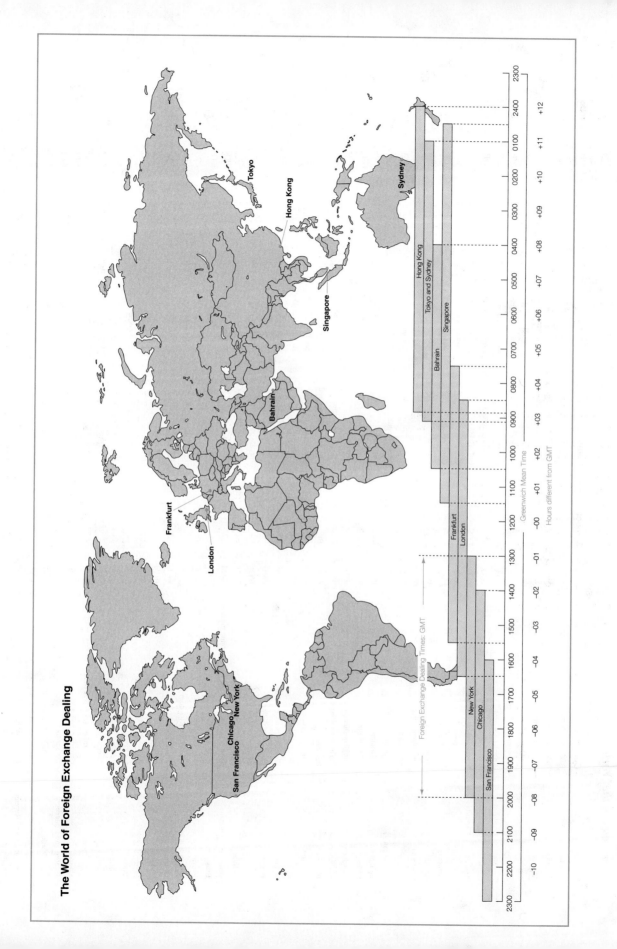

The World of Foreign Exchange Dealing

Currencies of the World

Country	Currency	ISO-4217 Code	Symbol
Afghanistan	Afghan afghani	AFN	
Albania	Albanian lek	ALL	
Algeria	Algerian dinar	DZD	
American Samoa	*see* United States		
Andorra	*see* Spain and France		
Angola	Angolan kwanza	AOA	
Anguilla	East Caribbean dollar	XCD	EC$
Antigua and Barbuda	East Caribbean dollar	XCD	EC$
Argentina	Argentine peso	ARS	
Armenia	Armenian dram	AMD	
Aruba	Aruban florin	AWG	ƒ
Australia	Australian dollar	AUD	$
Austria	European euro	EUR	€
Azerbaijan	Azerbaijani manat	AZN	
Bahamas	Bahamian dollar	BSD	B$
Bahrain	Bahraini dinar	BHD	
Bangladesh	Bangladeshi taka	BDT	
Barbados	Barbadian dollar	BBD	Bds$
Belarus	Belarusian ruble	BYR	Br
Belgium	European euro	EUR	€
Belize	Belize dollar	BZD	BZ$
Benin	West African CFA franc	XOF	CFA
Bermuda	Bermudian dollar	BMD	BD$
Bhutan	Bhutanese ngultrum	BTN	Nu.
Bolivia	Bolivian boliviano	BOB	Bs.
Bosnia-Herzegovina	Bosnia and Herzegovina konvertibilna marka	BAM	KM
Botswana	Botswana pula	BWP	P
Brazil	Brazilian real	BRL	R$
British Indian Ocean Territory	*see* United Kingdom		
Brunei	Brunei dollar	BND	B$
Bulgaria	Bulgarian lev	BGN	
Burkina Faso	West African CFA franc	XOF	CFA
Burma	*see* Myanmar		
Burundi	Burundi franc	BIF	FBu
Cambodia	Cambodian riel	KHR	
Cameroon	Central African CFA franc	XAF	CFA
Canada	Canadian dollar	CAD	$
Canton and Enderbury Islands	*see* Kiribati		
Cape Verde	Cape Verdean escudo	CVE	Esc
Cayman Islands	Cayman Islands dollar	KYD	KY$
Central African Republic	Central African CFA franc	XAF	CFA
Chad	Central African CFA franc	XAF	CFA
Chile	Chilean peso	CLP	$

Country	Currency	ISO-4217 Code	Symbol
China	Chinese renminbi	CNY	¥
Christmas Island	*see* Australia		
Cocos (Keeling) Islands	*see* Australia		
Colombia	Colombian peso	COP	Col$
Comoros	Comorian franc	KMF	
Congo	Central African CFA franc	XAF	CFA
Congo, Democratic Republic	Congolese franc	CDF	F
Cook Islands	*see* New Zealand		
Costa Rica	Costa Rican colon	CRC	₡
Côte d'Ivoire	West African CFA franc	XOF	CFA
Croatia	Croatian kuna	HRK	kn
Cuba	Cuban peso	CUC	$
Cyprus	European euro	EUR	€
Czech Republic	Czech koruna	CZK	Kč
Denmark	Danish krone	DKK	Kr
Djibouti	Djiboutian franc	DJF	Fdj
Dominica	East Caribbean dollar	XCD	EC$
Dominican Republic	Dominican peso	DOP	RD$
Dronning Maud Land	*see* Norway		
East Timor	*see* Timor-Leste		
Ecuador	uses the U.S. Dollar		
Egypt	Egyptian pound	EGP	£
El Salvador	uses the U.S. Dollar		
Equatorial Guinea	Central African CFA franc	GQE	CFA
Eritrea	Eritrean nakfa	ERN	Nfa
Estonia	Estonian kroon	EEK	KR
Ethiopia	Ethiopian birr	ETB	Br
Faeroe Islands (Føroyar)	*see* Denmark		
Falkland Islands	Falkland Islands pound	FKP	£
Fiji	Fiji dollar	FJD	FJ$
Finland	European euro	EUR	€
France	European euro	EUR	€
French Guiana	*see* France		
French Polynesia	CFP franc	XPF	F
Gabon	Central African CFA franc	XAF	CFA
Gambia	Gambian dalasi	GMD	D
Georgia	Georgian lari	GEL	
Germany	European euro	EUR	€
Ghana	Ghanaian cedi	GHS	
Gibraltar	Gibraltar pound	GIP	£
Great Britain	*see* United Kingdom		
Greece	European euro	EUR	€
Greenland	*see* Denmark		

Country	Currency	ISO-4217 Code	Symbol
Grenada	East Caribbean dollar	XCD	EC$
Guadeloupe	*see* France		
Guam	*see* United States		
Guatemala	Guatemalan quetzal	GTQ	Q
Guernsey	*see* United Kingdom		
Guinea-Bissau	West African CFA franc	XOF	CFA
Guinea	Guinean franc	GNF	FG
Guyana	Guyanese dollar	GYD	GY$
Haiti	Haitian gourde	HTG	G
Heard and McDonald Islands	*see* Australia		
Honduras	Honduran lempira	HNL	L
Hong Kong	Hong Kong dollar	HKD	HK$
Hungary	Hungarian forint	HUF	Ft
Iceland	Icelandic króna	ISK	kr
India	Indian rupee	INR	₹
Indonesia	Indonesian rupiah	IDR	Rp
International Monetary Fund	Special Drawing Rights	XDR	SDR
Iran	Iranian rial	IRR	
Iraq	Iraqi dinar	IQD	
Ireland	European euro	EUR	€
Isle of Man	*see* United Kingdom		
Israel	Israeli new sheqel	ILS	
Italy	European euro	EUR	€
Ivory Coast	*see* Côte d'Ivoire		
Jamaica	Jamaican dollar	JMD	J$
Japan	Japanese yen	JPY	¥
Jersey	*see* United Kingdom		
Johnston Island	*see* United States		
Jordan	Jordanian dinar	JOD	
Kampuchea	*see* Cambodia		
Kazakhstan	Kazakhstani tenge	KZT	T
Kenya	Kenyan shilling	KES	KSh
Kiribati	*see* Australia		
Korea, North	North Korean won	KPW	W
Korea, South	South Korean won	KRW	W
Kuwait	Kuwaiti dinar	KWD	
Kyrgyzstan	Kyrgyzstani som	KGS	
Laos	Lao kip	LAK	KN
Latvia	Latvian lats	LVL	Ls
Lebanon	Lebanese lira	LBP	
Lesotho	Lesotho loti	LSL	M
Liberia	Liberian dollar	LRD	L$
Libya	Libyan dinar	LYD	LD

Country	Currency	ISO-4217 Code	Symbol
Liechtenstein	uses the Swiss Franc		
Lithuania	Lithuanian litas	LTL	Lt
Luxembourg	European euro	EUR	€
Macau	Macanese pataca	MOP	P
Macedonia (Former Yug. Rep.)	Macedonian denar	MKD	
Madagascar	Malagasy ariary	MGA	FMG
Malawi	Malawian kwacha	MWK	MK
Malaysia	Malaysian ringgit	MYR	RM
Maldives	Maldivian rufiyaa	MVR	Rf
Mali	West African CFA franc	XOF	CFA
Malta	European Euro	EUR	€
Martinique	*see* France		
Mauritania	Mauritanian ouguiya	MRO	UM
Mauritius	Mauritian rupee	MUR	Rs
Mayotte	*see* France		
Micronesia	*see* United States		
Midway Islands	*see* United States		
Mexico	Mexican peso	MXN	$
Moldova	Moldovan leu	MDL	
Monaco	*see* France		
Mongolia	Mongolian tugrik	MNT	₮
Montenegro	*see* Italy		
Montserrat	East Caribbean dollar	XCD	EC$
Morocco	Moroccan dirham	MAD	
Mozambique	Mozambican metical	MZM	MTn
Myanmar	Myanma kyat	MMK	K
Nauru	*see* Australia		
Namibia	Namibian dollar	NAD	N$
Nepal	Nepalese rupee	NPR	NRs
Netherlands Antilles	Netherlands Antillean gulden	ANG	NAf
Netherlands	European euro	EUR	€
New Caledonia	CFP franc	XPF	F
New Zealand	New Zealand dollar	NZD	NZ$
Nicaragua	Nicaraguan córdoba	NIO	C$
Niger	West African CFA franc	XOF	CFA
Nigeria	Nigerian naira	NGN	₦
Niue	*see* New Zealand		
Norfolk Island	*see* Australia		
Northern Mariana Islands	*see* United States		
Norway	Norwegian krone	NOK	kr
Oman	Omani rial	OMR	
Pakistan	Pakistani rupee	PKR	Rs.
Palau	*see* United States		

Currencies of the World (continued)

Country	Currency	ISO-4217 Code	Symbol
Panama	Panamanian balboa	PAB	B/
Panama Canal Zone	see United States		
Papua New Guinea	Papua New Guinean kina	PGK	K
Paraguay	Paraguayan guarani	PYG	
Peru	Peruvian nuevo sol	PEN	S/.
Philippines	Philippine peso	PHP	₱
Pitcairn Island	see New Zealand		
Poland	Polish zloty	PLN	
Portugal	European euro	EUR	€
Puerto Rico	see United States		
Qatar	Qatari riyal	QAR	QR
Reunion	see France		
Romania	Romanian leu	RON	L
Russia	Russian ruble	RUB	R
Rwanda	Rwandan franc	RWF	RF
Samoa (Western)	see Western Samoa		
Samoa (America)	see United States		
San Marino	see Italy		
São Tomé and Príncipe	São Tomé and Príncipe dobra	STD	Db
Saudi Arabia	Saudi riyal	SAR	SR
Sénégal	West African CFA franc	XOF	CFA
Serbia	Serbian dinar	RSD	din.
Seychelles	Seychellois rupee	SCR	SR
Sierra Leone	Sierra Leonean leone	SLL	Le
Singapore	Singapore dollar	SGD	S$
Slovakia	European Euro	EUR	€
Slovenia	European euro	EUR	€
Solomon Islands	Solomon Islands dollar	SBD	SI$
Somalia	Somali shilling	SOS	Sh.
South Africa	South African rand	ZAR	R
Spain	European euro	EUR	€
Sri Lanka	Sri Lankan rupee	LKR	Rs
St. Helena	Saint Helena pound	SHP	£
St. Kitts and Nevis	East Caribbean dollar	XCD	EC$
St. Lucia	East Caribbean dollar	XCD	EC$
St. Vincent and the Grenadines	East Caribbean dollar	XCD	EC$
Sudan	Sudanese pound	SDG	
Suriname	Surinamese dollar	SRD	$
Svalbard and Jan Mayen Islands	see Norway		

Country	Currency	ISO-4217 Code	Symbol
Swaziland	Swazi lilangeni	SZL	E
Sweden	Swedish krona	SEK	kr
Switzerland	Swiss franc	CHF	Fr.
Syria	Syrian pound	SYP	
Tahiti	see French Polynesia		
Taiwan	New Taiwan dollar	TWD	NT$
Tajikistan	Tajikistani somoni	TJS	
Tanzania	Tanzanian shilling	TZS	
Thailand	Thai baht	THB	฿
Timor-Leste	uses the U.S. dollar		
Togo	West African CFA franc	XOF	CFA
Trinidad and Tobago	Trinidad and Tobago dollar	TTD	TT$
Tunisia	Tunisian dinar	TND	DT
Turkey	Turkish new lira	TRY	YTL
Turkmenistan	Turkmen manat	TMM	m
Turks and Caicos Islands	see United States		
Tuvalu	see Australia		
Uganda	Ugandan shilling	UGX	USh
Ukraine	Ukrainian hryvnia	UAH	
United Arab Emirates	UAE dirham	AED	
United Kingdom	British pound	GBP	£
United States of America	United States dollar	USD	US$
Upper Volta	see Burkina Faso		
Uruguay	Uruguayan peso	UYU	$U
Uzbekistan	Uzbekistani som	UZS	
Vanuatu	Vanuatu vatu	VUV	VT
Vatican	see Italy		
Venezuela	Venezuelan bolivar	VEB	Bs
Vietnam	Vietnamese dong	VND	đ
Virgin Islands	see United States		
Wake Island	see United States		
Wallis and Futuna Islands	CFP franc	XPF	F
Western Sahara	see Spain, Mauritania, and Morocco		
Western Samoa	Samoan tala	WST	WS$
Yemen	Yemeni rial	YER	
Zaïre	see Congo, Democratic Republic		
Zambia	Zambian kwacha	ZMK	ZK
Zimbabwe	Zimbabwean dollar	ZWD	Z$

© 2011 by Werner Antweiler, University of British Columbia. All rights reserved. The Pacific Exchange Rate Service is located in Vancouver, Canada. A continuously updated version of this table can be found on the Web at http://pacific.commerce.ubc.ca/xr/currency_table.html. This Web site was accessed in May 2011 to create the table shown here.